Social Constructionism

Social Constructionism: Sources and Stirrings in Theory and Practice offers an introduction to the different theorists and schools of thought that have contributed to the development of contemporary social constructionist ideas, charting a course through the ideas that underpin the discipline. From the *New Science* of Vico in the eighteenth century, through to Marxist writers, ethnomethodologists and Wittgenstein, ideas as to how socio-cultural processes provide the resources that make us human are traced to the present day. Despite constructionists often being criticized as 'relativists', 'activists' and 'anti-establishment' and for making no concrete contributions, their ideas are now being adopted by practically oriented disciplines such as management consultancy, advertising, therapy, education and nursing. Andy Lock and Tom Strong aim to provoke a wider grasp of an alternative history and tradition that has developed alongside the one emphasized in traditional histories of the social sciences.

ANDY LOCK is Professor of Psychology in the School of Psychology at Massey University, New Zealand.

TOM STRONG is Professor of Applied Psychology in the Faculty of Education at the University of Calgary, Canada.

Social Constructionism
Sources and Stirrings in Theory and Practice

Andy Lock
Massey University

Tom Strong
University of Calgary

CAMBRIDGE
UNIVERSITY PRESS

CAMBRIDGE UNIVERSITY PRESS

Cambridge, New York, Melbourne, Madrid, Cape Town, Singapore,
São Paulo, Delhi, Tokyo, Mexico City

Cambridge University Press
The Edinburgh Building, Cambridge CB2 8RU, UK

Published in the United States of America by Cambridge University Press, New York

www.cambridge.org
Information on this title: www.cambridge.org/9780521708357

First published 2010
Reprinted 2011

Printed in the United Kingdom at the University Press, Cambridge

A catalogue record for this publication is available from the British Library

Library of Congress Cataloguing in Publication data
Lock, Andrew.
  Social constructionism : sources and stirrings in theory and practice / Andy Lock, Tom Strong.
    p.   cm.
  ISBN 978-0-521-88199-9 (hardback)
  1. Social constructionism.   2. Sociology.   I. Strong, Thomas.   II. Title.
  HM1093.L63   2010
  302–dc22
  2009049664

ISBN 978-0-521-88199-9 Hardback
ISBN 978-0-521-70835-7 Paperback

To Angus Macdonald who got me into this helping business, showing me how important it was to be irreverent while being helpful. And to John Shotter for inspiration, and for his intellectual leadership and good people sense.   (Tom Strong)

For Tracy Riley and John Shotter   (Andy Lock)

Contents

Preface

'Social constructionism' comes in a number of guises, but none seems to sit well with mainstream behavioural scientists. In the current climate, what is taught in undergraduate, graduate and professional courses is becoming more and more determined by the requirements of those professional societies that 'accredit' or 'approve' courses. By these routes, people can become, for example, 'registered' or 'chartered' psychologists, titles reserved for the identification of those who have received a 'proper' training in the discipline. It is also becoming increasingly common that people who attain these titles are required to 'keep at it', and demonstrate they remain up to date with the current discipline. They do this by undertaking various forms of 'professional development', particularly by participating in approved courses or attending approved conferences, lectures, seminars, and the like. It is quite possible to gain and retain this recognition without ever coming across any of the work, writers and ideas that we are concerned with in this book: in fact, it is generally the case. In our view, this is a rather odd situation.

Its oddity is well put by the philosopher Thomas Nagel. He pointed out thirty-five years ago (1974: 435–6) that 'the subjective character of experience … is not captured by any of the familiar, recently devised reductive analyses of the mental, for all of them are logically compatible with its absence … If the analysis leaves something out, the problem will be falsely posed.' And the situation is much the same today: not only is the fact that humans have experiences ignored in the formulation of mainstream behavioural science theories, but so, too, for most of the time, is the fact that those experiences have an intersubjective aspect, and that without this the characteristic human activity of speaking with each other in ways that make various degrees of sense would not be possible. The oddity is, on this analysis, that what constitutes an approved education is clearly wrong-headed, because the problems of the discipline have been 'falsely posed'.

What might one do, having come to this realization? There are many options that have been taken up by people who would, to different degrees, feel that there was something amiss in the mainstream of the behavioural sciences. One is critique; another is rejection – either passive or active; another is polemic; yet another … There are many options. And many of these options appear, to us, only to increase the polarization between the camps. That is not our purpose here. Our concern is to see psychology going about its business as an academic and practical discipline more adequately than it currently does. In pursuit of this, we have marshalled many of the sources in which people, past and present, have set out the ideas that are called on when issues of language, meaning, subjectivity, intersubjectivity, how conversations work, and so on, become a focus of inquiry. The material we present here is what we refer to in our title as the 'sources'. No set of ideas exists in a vacuum, and that is true of those that underwrite many current varieties of work that loosely comprise the various 'social constructionist' stances that are being taken. At the same time, these sources contain many under-utilized ideas that, we believe, provide a richer picture of the human skills that need to be better investigated and understood through psychology's efforts.

We use the word 'stirrings' to denote a different intention. These sources have been variously elaborated and used for different purposes, not just around the behavioural sciences, but in the social sciences more generally. They have 'stirred things up', a lot of things, and yet it is very difficult, we have found, when reading about particular emerging schools of thought, to gain a fuller idea their parentage, and what is new in them. In addition, our reading of these sources has served to stir us up. There are, inevitably, two voices here, and at least the vestiges of our arguments over our draft chapters will be apparent. But that is good, for that is the nature of human reality: it is located and constructed within the conduct of conversation. This book is intended in that spirit.

Acknowledgements

Andy Lock

My part in this book has its roots in two pivotal events in my life. The first was being assigned John Shotter as my undergraduate tutor back in the 1960s. At that time I was much more into those facets of the western cultural revolution my generation grew up in than the demands of the academy I had the qualifications to attend, and thereby keep myself out of what I took to be the potentially mind-numbing alternatives such as becoming a bank teller, a clerk, or a bulldozer operator. I started university studying zoology, botany and chemistry, but quickly dropped chemistry when I discovered I could get away with two hours a week as a subsidiary psychology student rather than the eight hours a week that chemistry required. I slowly drifted to psychology because the zoology I was being presented with was the science of living things once they were dead – the departmental motto could well have been: 'If it moves, kill it and cut it up.' Psychology gave me the opportunity to concentrate on what living things did in their lives, and my honours thesis, 'The socioecology of sand martin, *Riparia riparia*, breeding behaviour', came out of this move. But John's tutorials opened my world to totally new ideas. For a long time, John completely baffled even as he fascinated me. He responded to any question I asked with either 'Well …', or 'Actually …', and then continued for ten or more minutes saying things that I supposed were of relevance to what I had asked, but quite how I couldn't figure out.

My response was to write down the names of people he mentioned, and once he had mentioned somebody five times, I would spend a morning in the library looking them up: Vygotsky, George Herbert Mead, T. S. Eliot, Kurt Vonnegut, Samuel Beckett; these were among the first group. My ignorance at the time is revealed by the fact that it was a shock for me to discover that only one of these people could traditionally be regarded as a psychologist. But that shock did enable me to pose my first ever sensible question to John in a tutorial: 'So what's this all about then?' His answer was: 'Well, that's what we have to try and find out.' And through working for a Ph.D. on mother–infant interaction, writing and editing some books on how language and communication were socially constructed, pursuing an interest in what it was like to be a human living in a different culture, I found myself, in 1994, still well ensconced in my ivory tower, at the tail-end of editing a book on the evolutionary origins of human activities.

That is when the second pivotal event occurred: I met Michael White and David Epston in Adelaide.

Michael was giving a keynote address at a conference on postmodernism and psychology organized by John Kaye, as was John Shotter himself. Since by then John and I had been part of the British academic diaspora in reaction to the Thatcherite transformation going on at home, it seemed like a good opportunity to catch up with him. The rest was just serendipity. I went along to Michael's lecture because it was a keynote. He talked about the ways in which selves were constructed out of the social practices and discourses that were in their cultures, and I could comfortably nod along with this. He then really shook me up, by shifting to how he and his 'brother' David were using these ideas in their therapeutic practice, and with new discourses, to help people who were variously troubled to find ways to reconstruct themselves, so as to be able to deal with their situations in more preferable ways. I went along to a workshop that he and David led, and that experience produced a realization that maybe, for the first time in my life, some of my ivory tower baggage, accumulated over the preceding twenty-five years, might possibly have some purchase on the real world, and be of use. Later, in conversation, David asked if I was that Lock who had written about indigenous psychologies back in the 1980s, because he had read it and quite liked it. In that case, maybe I really did know something that could be useful. At the same time, the event made me doubly aware of the continuing depths of my ignorance. I wasn't a practitioner. Their ways of talking were foreign to mine, which was loaded with an objective, expert stance, rather than their participant, ethical stance. Maybe, too, there was a vast amount of what I had read that I had never understood in the same way that they had. I am still not a practitioner. I have, through the privilege of writing some papers over the years with David and his colleagues, been taught by a master at how better to use language carefully, though I have a long, long way to go before I get out of my ingrained, enlightenment habits. And in this book with Tom I have been made to re-engage with those areas of ignorance that have been an ongoing part of being me since John first made me conscious of them.

This book originated in a collaborative course that Tom and I, along with Ken and Mary Gergen, teach online, and with contributions to our seminars from John Shotter and Rom Harré, as a part of the Discursive Therapies programme at Massey University. I am grateful to them, and to our other partners in the programme (see our home page at http://therapy.massey.ac.nz) for the supportive environment that they sustain. Ken and Mary, John and Rom have been particularly generous in providing us with materials, clarifications to our questions, and encouragement over the years. The students with whom we have explored these ideas over the past five years deserve a great deal of praise and sympathy for helping us clarify our understandings, and for adding the richness of their experiences as new perspectives for us to pursue. Thanks are also due to my colleagues here at Massey, particularly my last two School chairs, Ian Evans and Mandy Morgan, who have provided a protective atmosphere in which it has been possible to read and think – an opportunity that seems to be getting harder to find in present-day universities. Tom's student, Melissa Gray, provided us with some invaluable assistance in marshalling our references; and Helen Page at Massey brought her skills to bear on bringing together the final manuscript from the ravages Tom and I inflicted on it through the different word-processors and operating systems our computers imposed on our drafts as they went to and fro through e-mail. We are also grateful for the efforts of Janet Tyrrell for her diligence and suggestions as copy editor as the manuscript moved towards production.

My biggest debt, of course, is to those closest to me. My wife, Tracy Riley, has stoically endured many late evening monologues on many arcane topics with a rare equanimity, and put up with continuing moments of my 'being there, but not being there'. I am most grateful for your support. And Hannah, Duncan, Joe and Shelby: thanks guys for putting up with a distracted Dad.

Tom Strong

For me, this book began about twelve years ago in cyberspace, between breaks in seeing clients as I shuttled from town to town, practising as a consulting psychologist out of hospital consulting rooms across north-western British Columbia. I was part of a time warp, it seemed, when innovative and exciting new ideas about practice (narrative, solution-focused, collaborative) had gripped the imaginations and conversations of many practitioners. The excitement died down, as did the energizing conferences, notices for new 'postmodern' books, and introduction of new practices. By the end of the 1990s a resumption of the scientist-practitioner narrative was in high gear as the *DSM-IV-TR* and evidence-based practices (largely CBT) assumed dominance in training, research and service delivery. But, in the mid to late 1990s I began a series of online dialogues with people from all over the world about this postmodern – later to be known to me as social constructionist – 'revolution' in thinking and practice. Thus began my largely online collaboration with Andy on the other side of the world.

Like me, Andy had become an occasional contributor to listservs such as the marriage and family therapy listserv, a Bakhtin discussion group and Lois Shawver's later postmodern therapies listserv. Andy had marshalled a very interesting group of thinkers together on his 'virtual faculty' at Massey, a number of whom are included in this book. In 1998 I left my gorgeous and friendly little town of Smithers, a marriage and that full-time, continually-in-transit, private practice. I resumed academic life and became further embedded in dialogues and thinking behind the social constructionist revolution in thought and practice I wanted to be more informed about. My view then was that there were different constructionist practices described by writers such as Michael White and Steve deShazer, but the ideas from which these practices were derived were *rich* and scarcely accessible to the average practitioner. Andy was well connected, and as I moved into academic life he asked me to join him in a very innovative 'discursive therapies' programme offered by Massey University in New Zealand. Andy would be the researcher/theorist and I'd be the practitioner/theorist on a course where we shared the ideas of thinkers as diverse as Vico, Garfinkel, Wittgenstein and Bateson. My theory at the time was 'thin' and largely restricted to what I gleaned from the therapist-authors of the time. So, working with Andy meant filling my head with less than light reading. From our course materials, we thought: why not write a book? Thus, a new, but largely pleasurable ordeal developed as we went far beyond our original course materials to writing the book you are now reading.

Looking back, I have a lot of people to thank, and a lot of dialogues under way that were not part of my life when I first connected with Andy and these ideas. No single practitioner influenced my thinking and practice more than did Michael White, who embodied many of the values that guide me today: social justice, creativity and a deep respect for people's dignity and untapped resourcefulness. Of Harlene Anderson, David Epston, Jaakko Seikkula and Steve deShazer, similar things could be said. They took complicated ideas and translated them into collaborative and generative practices that are strikingly different from those in the scripts used in dominant forms of helping practice today. But, take a further step back and one finds incredible, path-breaking scholars providing the conceptual undergirding for these new practices: John Shotter, Ken Gergen and Rom Harré. Most remarkable about their influential writings were their abilities to critique dominant ideas and practices while synthetically drawing from audacious thinkers who strayed from the usual narrative that continues to inform mainstream helping practice. These people have been my practical and intellectual inspiration.

I picked up an extra family out of this collaboration, over my four trips to New Zealand these last few years: Tracy, Hannah, Duncan, Shelby and Joe (Andy's Lock–Riley clan), and by extension colleagues at Massey University. The University of Calgary has become a good home base for me to work from, with particular acknowledgement to Vicki Schwean. I also appreciate the support shown me while at the University of Northern British Columbia. I am very thankful for ongoing dialogues with Jerry Gale, Lynn Hoffman, Lois Holzman, Chris Kinman, Sheila McNamee, David Pare, Peter Rober, Sally St George, Nick Todd, Karl Tomm, Allan Wade and Dan Wulff. I have been particularly blessed to have worked with some great students who kept me thinking and reading: Robbie Busch, Shari Couture, Allison Foskett, Margaret Fuller, Greg Godard, Tom Hope, Dawn Johnston, Ottar Ness, Nathan Pyle, Olga Sutherland and Don Zeman, among others. On a more personal note, I want to thank those most supportive to me this last few years, particularly when I was going through some challenging times: my parents (Irv and Irene Strong), Heather Strong, Angus Macdonald, Phil Pine, Doug McDonald, and my new-found Cuban friends. Finally, to my daughter, Arista, I look forward to keeping our conversations developing in ways we both gain from.

1   Introduction

> … problems are solved, not by giving new information, but by arranging what
> we have always known.   (Wittgenstein, 1953, aphorism 109)

There have been curious rumblings of late in the social sciences and the helping
professions that draw from them. Increasing numbers of academics have called
into question the notion that the social sciences could do for the helping professions
what the natural sciences have done for engineering or biomedicine. Even the language used for articulating such notions has become suspect, as communications
theorists and linguistic philosophers have turned our most fundamental social
reality – being in conversation with each other – into a matter of critical reflection.
At the same time, larger cultural issues have come to the fore. Where are women
and minority culture people represented in the so-called universal knowledge of
'man' to be applied in helping others? The very foundations of what seemed a
secure knowledge base have been under assault. New helping practices, and ways
of thinking about them, have been emerging that look positively anarchic compared to orderly helping protocols and received social scientific knowledge about
humans, and humans in interaction. The ideals of enlightenment science, applied
to human endeavours and concerns, if you go along with the critics, come up short
in delivering the equivalents of the kinds of understandings and practices that get
bridges built, or people on the moon. Worse, social scientists have been accused
of 'othering' people in ways that reduce them to what cybernetician Heinz von
Foerster terms 'trivial machines' (e.g., 2003). When extended to the thinking and
conversational practices of helping professionals, these traditional assumptions
about humans and what it means to engage them often translate clients into pro-
viders of needed information and passive recipients of professional understandings and directives. This approach to helping practice, and to the social sciences
that support it, continues to flourish. But, a sizeable minority of therapists, educators, human relations experts, organizational development professionals and
others have begun to engage clients in new ways, as 'new' ideas about humans
and change have emerged.

Therapeutic talk or discourse has traditionally been seen as secondary to the
actual business of therapy – a necessary conduit for exchanging information
between therapist and client, but seldom more. Therapy primarily developed, as
have most applied sciences (such as medicine and engineering), by mapping particular experiential domains in ways responsive to human intervention. The role

that discourse plays in such mapping and intervening endeavours – whether by scientists or lay folk – has only recently been recognized as a focus for analysis and intervention. This recognition serves to remind us that the phenomena of our experience cannot objectively announce their meanings and implications to us. Talk is not a neutral 'tool' used to get 'the real work' done: talk is where the real work of therapy happens (Friedman, 1993; Maranhão, 1986).

At the same time, there has been a clear increase over the past few decades in the number of people in academic psychology adopting what we can loosely term 'qualitative methods' in their investigations, using these to elucidate how humans conduct their everyday affairs. Yet such investigators are very much second-class citizens within the pecking order of their discipline, which defines itself as a science, firmly committed to the formulation of research questions that can be empirically pursued by quantitative measurements in a hypothetico-deductive framework of experimentation at the individual level, or through quantifiable survey and questionnaire methods across groups of individuals at the social level. Science is good – look what it has done for human living conditions – and consequently any work outside the dominant paradigm cannot be as good. Yet there is a contradiction at the root of this preferential valuing of the experimental approach over any other, for it is a judgement that cannot be decided by performing an experiment. Worse, a contradiction would remain even if this judgement were capable of being decided in this way: unless those conducting an experiment are able to tell what, through their actions, they are responsible for finding and what would have happened anyway, then experiments would not be a viable method of finding out anything. A sense of responsibility as to the outcomes of one's actions is fundamental to conducting experiments, and successful scientists gain their reputations on that basis (otherwise why would scientists cite research by author and date?).

In addition, there has been a growing sense over the past fifty years that simplistic and determinist accounts of human activity are just that. In a changing world there has arisen a more pressing concern with issues of rights, relationships and seemingly arbitrary changes in how lives and perceptions are transformed over time. Such changes clearly do not occur as a result of biological processes, but as a result of the differing ways that meanings are constructed and reconstructed through peoples' histories in interacting with each other: how people experience the world and make sense of it is primarily the product of socio-cultural processes. Further, these processes have their human roots in history rather than biology. It is more the case that 'knowledge and social action go together' in development (Burr, 2003: 5), rather than that knowledge is separate from action and somehow informs it. And further, there has been the recognition that there is a political component to social science in general and psychology in particular – that 'facts' are not neutral and out there waiting to be discovered, so as to guarantee one overarching account of 'this is the way things are'. Instead, such 'facts' are constructed in fields of activities, and worked up into ideologies that benefit some people while disempowering others.

These issues as to the political status of facts and the ideologies they enable are of crucial importance in a world undergoing globalization. Many different indigenous groups have identified an oppressive aspect to the colonial use of the behavioural sciences when they have been variously imposed upon them. Their own values have been disrespected, because they were held to be based on superstitions, and not on science. Worse might follow in the future as the developed economies of the west play out their new roles in interacting with those of the developing countries rooted in very different indigenous traditions. A new imperialism is potentially very dangerous here. Cultural clashes at the level of not understanding each other's mundane behaviours are potentially explosive. A pivotal event in western–Asian relations occurred in February 1972. President Richard Nixon of the USA was making a state visit to China, at a time when the Vietnamese war was in progress. At the state banquet in Nixon's honour, the Chinese premier selected morsels from the communal dish for Nixon with his own chopsticks. By this action, Premier Chou extended to Nixon a great honour, for to make this action signalled that Nixon was 'one of the family'. From Nixon's cultural perspective, the act was an insult: 'I am quite capable of making my own choices, and your personal chopsticks are contaminated: please, at least, use the public utensils, but don't presume to make choices for me.' The misunderstanding was, fortunately, resolved successfully, but the potential for affront is clear. The potential for worse consequences is heightened if the principles of western, empirical facts about the social psychology of human nature are imposed on people emerging from very different cultural backgrounds.

This same point applies within, not just between, cultures. Western cultures have a range of helping professions that have particular codes of practice. Typically, such practices have developed as applications of a knowledge base that is seen as foundational. For example, in education, theories of learning are hypothesized and then evaluated for their practical applications. The key has been that practitioners can point to such a body of knowledge to warrant the continued use of such practices. One such foundational assumption has been that human and social problems can be 'correctly' identified and then correspondingly addressed with interventions derived from such knowledge. The scare quotes around 'correctly' underscore how theory-driven and tautological this whole approach to explaining and addressing problems can be. None of this is news to practitioners. In recent decades, new practices tied to new theories (for which there is empirical support) have proliferated. Psychotherapy illustrates this well with its over 400 recognized approaches. Which one of these should we nail our colours to? They cannot all be correct, can they? On this point Lynn Hoffman (2002), a prominent figure in the history of family therapy, offers a radical insight: that we have reached a social constructionist era in therapy (e.g., Strong and Paré, 2004; Gubrium and Holstein, 2007), where instead of continuing to develop and adhere to particular models of practice we should set them aside for useful and ethically sound ideas.

The worries we have just raised are generally regarded by those who practise a scientific behavioural science as those of 'the looney fringe', people who have been mistakenly lured into various sets of unreliable ideas – such as post-structuralism or postmodernism. But the points we have raised above are rooted in a deeper history, nowhere more intensely concentrated than in a methodological debate in Germany in the mid-1800s: the *Methodenstreit* (literally, 'strife over methods'). Initially confined to the field of economics, it became spread out across the entire gamut of the social sciences. The debate was centred on exactly the issues we have been noting above: can the human sciences be pursued with the same methods that are used in the natural sciences? The debate revolved around the issues we recognize today: 'understanding' (which is sought in the human sciences) versus 'explanation' (which is sought in the natural sciences). It is not a debate that has been fully resolved, partly because in everyday culture we, as English speakers, do not clearly distinguish these two terms.

Consider the following statements:

David is depressed because he has just lost his job.
David is depressed because of an imbalance in the chemistry of his brain.

In everyday parlance, both of these statements offer us some kind of explanation as to why David is depressed, but, at the same time, we would feel that both offer us a way of understanding why he is in that state. Yet, these are very different kinds of statements. The first tells us about David's situation as a person immersed in experiences of his world that mean certain things for him; the second tells us about how particular chemicals alter his mood. What has never been properly resolved, even today, is how David's experiences may have been structured in such a way that losing his job might lead to a chemical imbalances that alter his mood; while the same event in another's life might lead to a different set of chemicals being released that result in his becoming euphoric; or in yet another have no discernible effect whatsoever. And why no resolution?

Any answer here is necessarily multi-faceted and imprecise. Experience, or subjectivity, is at the root of things. In our historically inherited ways of looking at the world, experiences are subjective, difficult to investigate, and since they come with wide variations of mood, difficult to do much about if we, or others, report them as problematic. People's reactions to situations require normative evaluations: is it more normal for David to be depressed at losing his job; his colleague to be ecstatic; or a third person not to apparently give a damn? Having made a judgement that David's or the others' experiences of their situations need to be changed (and on what grounds can that decision be made?), what can be done about it that might have any reasonable chance of success? Could he perhaps be talked out of it? But if it is the case that David's state can be diagnosed, against objective criteria, as suffering from depression, this then leads us to an objectively revealed remedy: change the imbalance of his chemicals with the appropriate drug. The pragmatic and economic payoff is a no-brainer.

Taking this second route as the preferred one has a good hundred years of history behind it in the behavioural sciences. Behaviourism supplanted mentalistic views, and thus got rid of the problematic issues associated with retaining any reference to experience and subjectivity in accounts of behaviour. Behaviour became something that was objectively observed, and thus amenable to quantification and predictive control. And there is no denying that this is a very effective tactic for constructing ways of predicting and controlling rat and pigeon behaviour. Then, as concerns grew in the 1950s in psychology as to whether it was completely satisfactory to explain behaviour without any recourse to 'intervening variables' operating inside an organism to mediate the link between a stimulus and response, the climate of the day borrowed ideas from the high technology of the day, and came up with a psychology of information processing, which is still a major component of the academic discipline today.

There can be no denying the apparent successes of a cognitivist account of memory, perception, social judgement, and so on. But, and it is a big but, the very characteristics that define being a human being – that we are blessed with conscious experience – are, because of the nexus of historical chance we have alluded to above, not even entertained in this view of 'how things are'. It follows, then, that when a psychological paradigm is adopted for practical purposes to help sort out characteristically human problems, the people and institutions being addressed are considered in a highly impoverished way, and the effort involved not only fails to deliver on its promises, but often actually alienates those it seeks to help. As Patrick McGoohan, Number 6 in the cult 1960s British TV series, *The Prisoner*, continually railed: 'I am not a number, I am a free man.'

When we began writing this book, we had what we thought were two fairly straightforward aims. One was to outline some of the sources that have recently come together in the social sciences to rehabilitate the fact that people – and presumably other animals – actually do have a meaningful experience of the world. This rehabilitation was one we thought we could pin a simple label to: 'Social Constructionism'. This is the claim that we are not just individually encapsulated information processors, but are inherently social beings who go through a remarkable process of becoming enculturated adults and experience the world in all its glories and disappointments: simply put, we are humans who are constructed through our inherent immersion in a shared experiential world with other people. In addition, we were convinced that 'what is really going on' in human affairs, and in the ways we come to be part of them, carry them on, and pass them on to our children, was a much more mysterious – and challenging – process to get a handle on than the dominant paradigms ever considered. We wanted to bring out the other side of the *Methodenstreit* debate that seems to have dropped out of view: that psychology needs to be about how people make sense of and influence each other in the great project of constructing and conserving the ways our inter-subjective experiences constitute our lives as we live them.

Our second aim was to convey a flavour of how these hidden currents of thought can be picked up, and are being picked up, in the practices of brave and innovative practitioners who share, often intuitively, some of the worries we have as to how the practical application of psychology is being more and more constrained, in counter-productive ways, by the headlong prescription of so-called expert knowledge as the only legitimate way to be able to call oneself a professional. If we are not autonomous, encapsulated, information processors, then what are the consequences of the alternative view of who we might be, as socially constructed beings, for how any informed interventions might be carried out? These two aims remain the organizing principles inherent in our narrative here. But many more strands, tangents and pointers to future dialogues have emerged in the process of our collaborative writing. This book is both longer than it was intended to be, and shorter than it needs to be. It has been composed by two people coming together from shared sensibilities to undertake a project that seemed like a straightforward, 'good idea' at the time. In writing together, we have come to be more aware that what we separately took to cohere in our backgrounds, and what we thought we shared, was more of a chimera than a fact. But at the same time, through our arguments, we have come to a different feeling of shared sensibilities, and a different appreciation of the practice of what we want to call 'socially constructing ways of going on', in keeping a conversation productive, and in re-igniting age-old debates as a contribution to an ongoing conversational sustenance of cultural life.

With respect to our title – 'Social constructionism: sources and stirrings' – the 'sources' component will be fairly clear: we have aimed to present some core ideas that have developed in often unrelated efforts that we find useful to our own efforts of elucidating 'what's going on, and how can it be assisted to keep going on in more respectful ways'. On 'stirrings', our conversations about our sources have certainly stirred us up in the course of combining our ideas into what we hope has some coherence as a narrative. We have felt pressured, on a number of occasions, to strive for at least a semblance of coherence, because that is something readers of books expect. But, at the same time, we have not been seeking an authoritative coherence that we could then, as experts, hold out as a party line that must be obeyed. Social constructionism appears to us, at this point, to be very much a work in progress. It is here that we have found our two initial aims were not as simple as we first suspected: social constructionism has more sources and resources than we expected, and quite often those who might think of themselves as social constructionists appear to be unaware of them. Thus our intention is more to stir up ideas for you, as the reader, to interact with, and evaluate as to how they might, or might not, be taken up in your own work.

What is social constructionism?

There is no one school of social constructionism. Rather, it is a broad church. There are, though, some expansive tenets that hold it together. First, it is concerned with meaning and understanding as the central feature of human activities. With respect to meaning, the focus is on how it is that a symbolically based language does what it does, which is to provide a very different quality of social experience for two people who speak the same language as compared to two people who are speaking different languages. We have an immediate grasp of what is being said in the former case; we just hear noise in the latter case. Our grasp may be partial and unclear, and there is thus a need to continue a conversation back and forth, until what is being said becomes clearer, and we can say, 'OK, now I understand.' Over developmental time, new skills in interrogating symbols to reach understandings become possible: we might talk through an argument to ourselves in private, or wrestle with the assembly instructions for some piece of knock-together furniture. But these private activities retain a conversational structure. Second, then, is the view that meaning and understanding have their beginnings in social interaction, in shared agreements as to what these symbolic forms are to be taken to be.

Third, ways of meaning-making, being inherently embedded in socio-cultural processes, are specific to particular times and places. Thus, the meanings of particular events, and our ways of understanding them, vary over different situations. These variations can be trivial: people wish to present themselves as fashionably dressed, for example, and clearly what is regarded as fashionable varies within cultures over time (compare how people are dressed in photographs in 1900 and in 2000) and across space (how the President of the United States dresses as compared to the King of Saudi Arabia). On the other hand, they can be much more substantive. Hepworth (1999), for example, has pointed out how western ways of making sense of self-starvation have changed quite markedly over historical time: medieval women who adopted this practice were regarded as saints who were shedding their attachment to worldly pleasures and sustaining themselves on heavenly rather than physical nourishment. These women did not relate to their experience through the modern discourse of 'anorexia'. Similarly, the Delphic Oracle was revered for hearing the voices of Gods, rather than positioned as 'schizophrenic'. Such Oracles were revered as 'blessed' rather than marginalized as 'ill'. The different discourses in which their experiences were available to be constituted and made sense of place both of these historical examples in very different relations to very different problems from their modern counterparts.

Fourth, and following from this, most social constructionists have an uneasy relationship with 'essentialism': that is, with the idea that one of the major goals of psychology is to uncover the essential characteristics of people. If people fashion who they are within their varying socio-cultural traditions, then they are instrumental in creating the discourses they use to define themselves. Thus, people are self-defining and socially constructed participants in their shared lives. There are no pre-defined entities within them that objective methods can seek to delineate but, rather, our ways of making sense to each other are constructed to yield quite different ways of being selves. This is similar to saying that there is no inherent model inside a piece of clay that a potter works to reveal, as this time a cup, this time a plate, this time a vase: the actions of the potter work with the physical properties of the clay to create the resulting forms. In this sense, social constructionists are interested in delineating the processes that operate in the socio-cultural conduct of action to produce the discourses within which people construe themselves. This is not to deny that humans have certain propensities, of course, but it is to claim that many of these propensities are rather amorphous, like clay, to begin with. We do appear, for instance, to have a special interest in human faces from very early on in our lives, and this interest is intrinsic to the establishment and growth of our relationships with others. But those relationships come to be structured and conducted in very different ways, and place very different moral demands upon people, across time and space.

As a result of this anti-essentialist sentiment, social constructionism has an uncomfortable relationship with ideas about realism, and hence with science, and is often characterized, pejoratively, for being relativistic. The arguments that have been conducted around this conceptual nexus of terms has, in our view, largely generated more heat than light, and we are not saying much about the issues at this point. They will, however, inevitably rear their heads as we go on, as they did for us in marshalling our material. We will move to what we took as an unlikely position when we first started. One of the trends over the past fifty years or so has been the movement in some quarters from an enlightenment concern to uncover *the* truth about the world to a post-enlightenment suspicion of such a (or any) metanarrative. The shift is, in many senses, one from a world of investigation dominated by questions of epistemology – what is the best way to uncover the nature of this world we live in? – to questions of ontology – what sorts of worlds can we live in, and by what criteria can we decide how one might be preferable to another? This nexus of concern has led to the critical comment by the socio-biologist Richard Dawkins (1995: 31–2): 'Show me a cultural relativist at 30,000 feet and I'll show you a hypocrite.' Now, we could develop our own critique here as to why this throwaway line totally misses the point, but in fact we find ourselves ending up wanting to rewrite it: 'Show us a social constructionist at 30,000 feet and we'll show you a genuine scientist.' There is, though, a lot of ground to cover before getting to that position. This is an unexpected outcome for us, especially as it runs counter to what is the fifth, and perhaps final, point of agreement among social constructionists.

This fifth point is the adoption of a critical perspective to the topics at hand, that is, a concern with revealing the operations of the social world, and the political apportioning of power that is often accomplished unawares, so as to change these operations and replace them with something that is more just (this being opposed to traditional theorizing which seeks only to explain and understand these processes). This sense of 'critical' gets its modern impetus from Marx in the eleventh of his 'Theses on Feuerbach': 'Philosophers have only interpreted the world in certain ways; the point is to change it.' This is not meant to equate social constructionism with Marxism, but the shared sensibility is clear, as in this position statement by Ken Gergen (1994a: 53):

> The [social constructionist] is little likely to ask about the truth, validity, or objectivity of a given account, what predictions follow from a theory, how well a statement reflects the true intentions or emotions of a speaker, or how an utterance is made possible by cognitive processing. Rather, for the [social constructionist], samples of language are integers within patterns of

relationship. They are not maps or mirrors of other domains – referential worlds or interior impulses – but outgrowths of specific modes of life, rituals of exchange, relations of control and domination, and so on. The chief questions to be asked of generalised truth claims are thus, how do they function, in which rituals are they essential, what activities are facilitated and what impeded, who is harmed and who gains by such claims?

We do not dissent from this. But we have come to feel that there is more that a social constructionist stance can offer to the social sciences than just political critique in the pursuit of greater social justice. Our provisional view is that there is more to social reality than language: that there is a pre-linguistic domain to human social experience – more precisely a pre-predicative intersubjectivity – that provides the possibility for discursive life (as Gergen indicates above – language is an outgrowth of 'something'). It is in this context that we see stirring in the sources of social constructionism we discuss here a major potential within the social sciences: a preliminary, just now becoming graspable, sense of the very fabric within which human lives are constituted. We have our lives in what Schutz (Chapter 3 below) terms 'the lifeworld', and because we live 'in it' it is something very difficult to notice, and hence to investigate by the methods we have inherited from a very different tradition of objective methods. The sensibilities that inform social constructionism provide, we strongly suspect, the necessary perspectives to reveal and clarify a new foundation for inquiring into, and understanding, human 'nature' (which is both a paradoxical and exciting aspect of contemporary constructionism).

Others, of course, approach social constructionism differently. Danziger (1997b), for example, has suggested that social constructionist thought has two strands. He saw a 'dark' and largely Continental strand that draws heavily on the works of Foucault and subsequent post-structural and postmodern thought, with a concern for issues of power, the articulation of subjectivity, the relativity of knowledge, and the exercise of these with respect to gender, subjectivity and colonialist discourses, for example. Then there is a 'light', and predominantly Anglo-American strand that is rooted in more traditional and pragmatic concerns that stem from the dominant empirical tradition, while rejecting much of the Cartesian baggage that tradition brings with it: How does everyday life work? How is discourse done? Why are traditional accounts drawn from a psychology based on experimental procedures and statistical analyses of the relations between dependent and independent variables lacking in their descriptions and explanations of 'what's going on'? If we are anywhere, we are very much on the 'light side' of this divide. But while we largely present 'light-side' constructionist thinkers, our constructionism focuses on recognizing multiple possibilities for meaning and transformative action where some convention or taken-for-granted understanding or habit has held sway.

We approach this book from the perspective that there is a discernible and important counter-narrative one can trace back from contemporary social constructionism. While these ideas have received enough attention to endure in libraries and in obscure corners of the social sciences and humanities, they typically have shown up in piecemeal fashion (if at all) in the thinking of today's social constructionists. Deciding on what would go into our story was a challenge. How does one place the eighteenth-century ideas of Vico in the same narrative as those of Merleau-Ponty; or consider philology alongside performative notions of discourse? We see a convergence of thought in contemporary social constructionism as it is variously practised. What animates our story of constructionism is a very different view of being human than the one associated with current psychology or neuroscience. The sources of social constructionism we will relate show humans engaged in constructing and living by their own constructions. But, importantly, people are not talking heads, and so we trace phenomenological notions of embodied cognition through to their corporeal and social implications that are coming to be termed 'situated cognition'. Related to this strand in our narrative is another that sees meaning as performed, or reflexive – quite a different conception of human communication and judgement from one that sees them as comprised of information transmission, reception and processing.

An extension of this strand is one some associate with macro differences in how humans relate to physical reality and each other – in Foucault's notion of discourses or Wittgenstein's language games. A further strand arises from our interest in social practice where we turn to the micro, and look at what is brought to and transpires in and from dialogic interactions. Finally, running behind what we review is a correspondingly and dramatically different view of human science. Our aim is to share our sense of these different strands, or sources, of social constructionist thought and practice as we narrate our way through contributions made by thinkers for whom a modern approach to human science was coming up short. We think there is much in their strands of thought to inspire, confound, integrate, critique and adapt in ways you can re-author from our story.

In writing this 'counter-narrative' our aim has been to reach two primary groups of readers: those seeking an overview of thinkers and ideas informing the breadth of contemporary social constructionist thought; and practitioners (therapists, educators, organizational development consultants, etc.) seeking more solid footing in the challenging conceptual quicksand of social constructionism. To this end, we have adopted a chronological and thematic narrative, emphasizing links between ideas and the people and historico-cultural contexts within which such ideas make sense. Metaphorically speaking, we present a story of tributaries of thought, each having practical applications, with all converging on a common stream of thought and related practice. For us, modern psychology missed a chance to relate to everyday, human experience when it veered away from meaning and how it is socially (and variously) constructed, sustained, modified and negotiated. The lives, ideas and applications we relate thus show a focus on humans as social beings making sense of their experience by using what humans before and around them constructed and kept as meaningful.

There are, perforce, other stories and characters with which we could have peopled our plot. Where, might one ask, are postcolonial (Said, Bhabha) and feminist thinkers (Butler, Kristeva), or postmodern (Lyotard, Baudrillard) thinkers? Why doesn't the hugely influential Derrida or the Frankfurt critical theory school get more detailed mention? What about the recent explosion of construction-ist research practices that focus on entirely new practices of meaning-making (Denzin and Lincoln, 2005; Holstein and Gubrium, 2008)? We recognize that our omissions invite criticism, even concern, for what has been left out. Some of these omissions relate to our focus on what we see as sources of social construc-tionism. In this regard, our focus has been historical, on figures who stood out as highly original thinkers (e.g. Vico, Mead, Wittgenstein) generating ideas that inform contemporary social constructionist thinking and practice. Another factor was that we are constructing a particular kind of counter-narrative here, one that draws on embodied and situated understandings and practices. We also had to stop writing somewhere, and we still went over our original page allotment. But, we recognize there are others who deserve attention in a book like this.

While it might sound grandiose, we think the social constructionist story, given the extent to which mainstream social science has come to inform practices and thought in so many spheres of human life, is Copernican in its implications. We do not dispute the idea that people have brains, but these brains are more linked to bodies and other people than psychologists usually indicate. The differences are not subtle when comparing social constructionist practice with other forms of social practice. So, throughout the book we will raise practical implications we see associated with the thinkers and ideas we bring up. We are not 'anti-scientific' in the least, but we do see a different kind of social science implicit in the ideas and practices we review. With this in mind we will also make occasional digres-sions into the history and sociology of science, as part of articulating the different science (i.e., from mainstream psychology) we see implicated in these ideas. In specific terms, then, each chapter will present readers with a stream of construc-tionist thought, and the thinkers and cultural contexts from which each stream emerged.

2   Giambattista Vico

Darwin has interested us in the history of Nature's Technology, i.e., in the formation of the organs of plants and animals, which organs serve as instruments of production for sustaining life. Does not the history of the productive organs of man, of organs that are the material basis of all social organisation, deserve equal attention? And would not such a history be easier to compile, since, as Vico says, human history differs from natural history in this, that we have made the former, but not the latter?   (Karl Marx, *Capital*, 1930/1867 vol. I, p. 372 n. 3)

Vico's science genuinely was new, both in his theory and in his practice; and the novelty remains even now, because he has only been partially understood, and understood usually in a tame, domesticated sense, which disguises his subversive meanings.   (Stuart Hampshire, *Joyce and Vico: The Middle Way*, *New York Review of Books*, 18 October 1973)

The poetic mind can make assertions that are nonsense for the rational mind.   (Verene, 1981: 77)

The world of civil society has certainly been made by men, and ... its principles are therefore to be recovered within the modifications of our own human mind.   (Vico, 1948[1744]: 331)

Contemporary social constructionism has deep historical roots that predate the modern era. The history of those premodern roots is beyond the focus of our efforts here. Instead we begin with a very original thinker who had grown disenchanted with the 'poverty' he associated with the ascending modern scientific conception of humans and their meaningful interaction. Writing three centuries ago, Vico articulated some important (yet largely ignored) challenges to this modern view, while advancing an approach to human science strikingly different from that of his time. For constructionist practitioners, Vico's thinking may initially seem remote, but we trust that you will find many interesting resonances and provocations.

Giovanni Battista, or Giambattista, Vico was born in Naples on 23 June 1668, and died there on 23 January 1744. He was, on the one hand, an historian who saw human history as a cyclical process, beginning in barbarism, spawning an heroic age which gradually moves towards democratic civilization, only to decline back into barbarism as a result of conquest, corruption or decay. Vico was the forerunner of the historical view know as historicism, more fully developed in the eighteenth century by Herder, and in the nineteenth century by Hegel and Marx: the claim that history is the key to any understanding of human 'nature'. On the other hand, he also developed a distinct philosophical position.

His most important work is regarded as his continually revised *Scienza Nuova* (*The New Science*, 1725, 1730, 1744). In this work, he confronted Cartesian and rationalistic conceptions of the mind and mentality, and constructed a philosophy grounded in language, rhetoric and law. In his *Scienza Nuova*, and other writings, Vico challenged Descartes' prioritizing the deduction of 'certain knowledge' in a logical fashion from basic premises as an adequate basis for a human science. More than that, however, he also challenged the notion, put forward by philosophers such as Hobbes and Spinoza, that there was a universal and constant human 'nature'. Vico, by contrast, put the view that human beings are historical beings and that the human mind is continually reconstructed into new forms over time.

Vico's work is difficult to approach. First, as one commentator has noted, Vico's *New Science* 'is a book so full of ideas that it almost bursts at the seams' (Burke, 1985: 32). Second, it is a chaotic book. It is a demonstration of his position almost more than an exposition of it: 'As a poetic encyclopedia, it is a model for what humans can make. More precisely, the New Science is written in the mixed mode of brief philosophical essays, poetic fragments, maxims, fables, and sentences. Its aim is to give a representation of the modifications of the human mind' (Mazzotta, 1998: 112). (This is perhaps why James Joyce styled the 'structure' of his novel *Finnegans Wake* after *The New Science*, and makes many allusions to Vico therein.) *The New Science* is, in style, a forerunner of Wittgenstein's *Philosophical Investigations* in that it is a collection of numbered paragraphs. Third, much of what Vico says is just plain daft and exaggerated from a modern perspective, and many of his 'arguments' are thus unconvincing, all of which detracts – along with the chaotic exuberance of dancing amongst ideas – from the remarkably prescient points that his work contains. We need to remember that Vico wrote around 300 years ago, and draws on concepts that are formulated in ways that *may* have made sense in his day, but which are somewhat unfamiliar to us now when we read them in a different place and time. This is especially frustrating given, for example, the explanatory work he does through his concept of 'providence'. Historically, providence has a 'Divine' connotation, Vico claiming that God is in contact with humans, and can – and does – intervene in historical affairs. How might the Divine be applied in current-day analyses of human affairs? In addition, there are many 'obscurities and ambiguities in what Vico has to say about providence' (Pompa, 1975: 51), such that quite what he intends is difficult to establish (see Pompa, ibid.: ch. 5 for a considered discussion) – let alone render it faithfully in modern terms. What we offer here, then, is an interpretation of Vico's ideas, more an attempt to get at his drift than his course, for we can find in his work the stirrings of many of the ideas that we will be discussing later in this book.[1]

---

[1] Berlin (1976: 4) notes that 'One can readily understand that in the case of a thinker so rich and so confused, and above all so genuinely seminal – the forerunner of so many of the boldest ideas of later, more celebrated thinkers [e.g., Michelet, Dilthey, Croce, Collingwood (and less certainly Herder and Hegel)] – there is a permanent temptation to read too much into him, especially to

Vico is the first genius in our field of interest. Here is Sir Isaiah Berlin's assessment of him:

> Vico's claim to originality will stand scrutiny from any point of vantage. His theories of the nature and development of the human mind, of culture, society and human history, are audacious and profound. He developed a novel theory of knowledge which in the hands of others played a decisive role. He distinguished for the first time a central type of human knowledge, which had been misunderstood or neglected by previous thinkers. He was a bold innovator in the realms of natural law and jurisprudence, aesthetics and the philosophy of mathematics. Indeed his conception of mathematical reasoning was so revolutionary that full justice could scarcely have been done to it until the transformation effected by the logicians of the twentieth century, and it has not been fully recognised for what it is even now. More than this, Vico virtually invented a new field of social knowledge, which embraces social anthropology, the comparative and historical studies of philology, linguistics, jurisprudence, literature, mythology, in effect the history of civilization in the broadest sense.   (1976: 3–4)

Vico lived a miserable life: in intellectual isolation with the knowledge he was making new discoveries of major importance; in abject poverty; crippled all his life by a childhood fall; with an elder son who became a criminal; and with a daughter sick from birth. Yet he relates in his autobiography that his conviction that he was the first to open new avenues of inquiry made him 'happy and serene'.

For our purposes, Vico foreshadows much that we find central to our particular concerns. First, he attacked Descartes' view that certainty could only be attained by rational methods applied to quantifiable data. The prevailing climate was that history cannot be quantified. Thus, it is not susceptible to logical or mathematical description, and therefore, for rationalists, it cannot be a certain science. As Descartes notes 'a man needs Greek or Latin no more than Low-Breton, to know the history of the Roman Empire' (1979 [1908]: 503). Thus, Descartes concludes, however much one might study history to establish the events of the Roman empire, the best that could be hoped for would provide us with no more knowledge than might have been possessed by Cicero's servant girl. Who could deny that mathematically codified knowledge was the highest human achievement, allowing increasingly infallible predictions? Vico was the man. Vico became convinced that the notion of timeless truths stated in universal mathematical symbols – that anyone, anywhere, anytime, could grasp because of the universality of human nature – was illusory. He thus provides a glimpse of a central anti-Cartesian tenet of social constructionism, and also presages some of the concerns with relativism that arise within it (as well as indicating a line that resolves it – see below).

---

sense intimations, perceive embryonic forms and prefigured contours of notions dear to the interpreter.' We plead guilty here, but are not ashamed of it. And as Berlin goes on: 'There is, as in the case of all authentic thinkers, no substitute for reading the original. This is no easy labour, but … the reward is great. Few intellectual pleasures are comparable to the discovery of a thinker of the first water' (ibid.).

Second, in arguing that any form of knowledge, including that established via logic or mathematics, can only be shown to be true by considering its historical genesis, Vico foreshadows many of the concerns of Marxist theorists, who have elaborated much of the groundwork for the socio-historical ideas that we will consider later (see Chapter 5 below). Indeed, there is little difference between Vico's claim that 'the order of ideas must follow the order of institutions' (1948: 238) and those of Marx and Engels. Third, his convictions led him to the view that whatever science might achieve, there was a sense in which 'we could know more about our own and other men's experiences – in which we acted as participants, indeed as authors, and not as mere observers – than we could ever know about non-human nature which we could only observe from the outside' (Berlin, 1976: 12). This leads us on not merely to contemporary forms of qualitative research, but to specific varieties of approach, such as the ethnomethodology of Harold Garfinkel, and the dramaturgical sociology of Erving Goffman (see Chapter 10 below).

Fourth, Vico places an understanding of others as central to humanity. He first distinguishes a form of knowledge – which he terms *per causas* – that a creator, divine or human, has as an 'insider's' knowledge of his or her actions, a knowledge that is very different from that one can have of objects and processes in the world one did not make. This is not a knowledge of disembodied facts, but an understanding 'from within':

> I know what it is to look like a tree, but I cannot know what it is to be a tree. But I do know what it is like to be a mind, because I possess one, and create with it ... Men 'create' in doing or knowing or desiring; in this they are active ... Because, by action, they 'create', or mentally live through the creations of others, they have a more direct and intimate acquaintance with action than with the natural data that they merely observe outside themselves.   (Berlin, 1976: 25–6)

History thus becomes something that can be understood by humans, for humans have made it, and by the use of their imagination (and rationality) have an opportunity to enter into and grasp the creations, institutions and knowledges that have been constructed by humans over time. But to do this requires an act of imagination. Vico accepts that he and his fellows are creatures born to a tradition of rational thought. This, he conjectures, however, is not a universal truth of all humans true for all times, and our rational tradition must itself have been constructed out of some other precursor. Consequently, we have a great difficulty in stepping outside of our own tradition to grasp what another mode of life might be like. It is not that we want to understand others by standing outside of them and studying them as objective objects, as we would tend to do in our current traditions of social science. Rather, we need to imagine our way into their stance towards the world, which he takes to be pre-rational and, having got there, work out the ways in which rationality could have been constructed. This is not a simple task. In attempting it, Vico faced issues that we will find recurring in the work of subsequent writers in this book: can we uncover an original mentality? What Vico attempted was to imagine himself *into* what it might be like to relate to the world prior to having access to the resources of a rational tradition, and from that point of origin offer an account of how the mind then made itself, recreated itself, as something that operates rationally: what is a 'pre-rational mentality' like? Asking this question Vico foreshadows Wittgenstein's concerns with the bases of 'language games' (see Chapter 8 below). And, for Vico, what follows from gaining an understanding of this pre-rational mentality is an act of subversion, a blow against the primacy of reason in the generation of knowledge.

Let us take a very arcane example of his subversive ideas. Language, in the Enlightenment, was the tool of reason. Once mastered, language was able to be used for rational purposes. Other uses of language, such as poetry, were, from this standpoint, thus secondary and derivative. Literary devices, such as synecdoche and metaphor, can be employed deliberately by rationally skilled speakers. Synecdoche is the trick of denoting a whole by the name of one of its parts. Thus in Latin, a sword is often referred to by the word that names its point. Naming a sword in this way is therefore a secondary function of language, because it implies that one must know the meaning of 'sword' and 'point' beforehand. Not so, says Vico (1948: 407): the primary reality of a sword for someone who wields or attempts to avoid it in battle *is* its point. The rationalists have it backward: objects and activities are directly known poetically in the first instance, in direct relation to human interests, fears and activities. The subsequently derived technique of using words rationally is secondary to this: the poetic use of language is the primary human reality.

In the course of offering his constructionist account of the growth of rationality, Vico moves to a fifth idea that will recur in our story (see, for example, Mead, Chapter 7 below): that 'the mind *itself* is an artifact constructed by social and linguistic practices' (Luft, 2003: 146): 'Minds are formed by the character of language, not language by the minds of those who speak it' (Vico, 1965: I. 1.95). His interest in words again sets Vico as a precursor of many notions more recently established in Wittgenstein's later writings: that words need not only refer or describe, but can themselves be acts, or intrinsic to action. Thus, he was 'the first to grasp the seminal and revolutionary truth that linguistic forms are one of the keys to the minds of those who use words, and indeed to the entire mental, social and cultural life of societies' (Berlin, 1976: 51).

A sixth point on which Vico anticipates contemporary concerns is that his work was an act of consciousness-raising.

> **Axiom LXIII; 236** The human mind is naturally inclined by the senses to see itself essentially in the body, and only with great difficulty does it come to understand itself by means of reflection.

There are a number of ideas condensed and anticipated here. 'Seeing the mind in the body' is to see people as active, pursuing life unreflectively in the exercise of their 'common sense', the form of life through which they are constructed:

> **Axiom XII; 142** Common sense is judgement without reflection, shared by an entire class, and entire people, an entire nation, or the entire human race.

'Seeing the mind in the unreflexive body' anticipates the work of Merleau-Ponty (Chapter 3 below), and his point that 'bodily experience forces us to acknowledge an imposition of meaning which is not the work of a universal constituting consciousness' (Merleau-Ponty, 1962: 147). Again, and we will be picking this up when we look at Mead's writings on the development of a 'perspective theory of meaning' (Chapter 7 below), despite the constitution of the mind through language; despite the variation of forms of life across geographical and historical contexts; despite this:

> **Axiom XXII; 161** There must in the nature of human institutions be a mental language common to all nations, which uniformly grasps the substance of things feasible in human social life and expresses it with as many diverse modifications as these same things may have diverse aspects.

Vico's human science departs from Descartes' idealized approach to accounting for humans and experience (that both can be objectively explained in lawful and universal ways). Such an approach depicts human experience as being like a knowable and tinkerable-with machine. But this approach comes with huge costs, leaving out the human qualities and origins of what we can know, including what we can know of our own experience and those of others. Vico, like many of the thinkers we will consider in this book, turned away from such idealizations. His was a messier, closer to the ground view of humans meaningfully engaged with each other, in different traditions and institutions of life. Accounting for such engagements, what people did and used within them, what they accomplished from them, and how these could be profitably reflected upon were the focus of some of Vico's scientific efforts.

Constructionist practitioners might recognize a familiar fork in the road. Descartes, Bacon and others had pursued a science that could wrest pronouncements of truth away from corrupt religious officials. This approach and its outcomes, idealized though it may have been, brought with it useful technological breakthroughs. But its premises overlooked important aspects of being human and living life within diverse traditions of meaning and action. In place of universal laws, Vico was suggesting varied understandings grounded in human interactions.

The essentials of Vico's ideas

Sir Isaiah Berlin (1976: xvi–xix) acutely distils seven theses that outline what he takes to be Vico's 'time-defying notions'. We draw heavily here on that summary.[2]

---

[2] As does Shotter (1981: see Chapter 16 below) in his own interpretation of Vico's importance to contemporary social concerns and practices.

1. Human nature is not fixed. As people act on the world, they not only transform it, they transform their relationship to it through their changing interests and needs, and in consequence, they change themselves and restructure their needs. There is no human essence that remains identical through this process of change.

2. Those who make things can understand their constructions in ways that mere observers of what is created cannot. Thus humans cannot understand nature in the same way that they can understand their own history, for they did not make nature, while they did construct their history through their actions. This claim is generally referred to as Vico's '*verum ipsum factum*' principle: that people can only get to the 'truth' of those things that they have created (*verum ipsum factum*), hence they cannot establish the truth about things they have not made – such as nature, which only God can understand since he made it.

> If *verum* is made by us, how can it reflect or describe in a demonstrable, irrefutable way the world outside itself? The answer, according to Vico, is that no matter what Cartesians may claim for physics, it cannot. Once one attempts to make one's own constructions (in this case, of thought) conform with things outside themselves and independent of them – with reality, say – then one can no longer guarantee them as *verum*, for the matter is no longer wholly within one's own control – reality must have its say too. Thus at best, Vico claims, one can only speak of *certum*, not logical truths but truths of ordinary observation and perception, the certainties in terms of which we live our daily lives.   (Shotter, 1981: 270)

3. People's knowledge of the external world thus differs in principle from the knowledge they can have of the worlds they have themselves created by imposing rules on their creations. Thus the Cartesian perspective must be in error when it tries to impose the reflective, detached, classificatory systems it derives from observation of the natural world upon human action.

4. Each of these worlds – cultures – that humans have established is characterized by distinct, pervasive patterns, such that there is a coherent style reflected among the thought, language, arts, social institutions, ways of life and action, across each culture. But this coherence is always under challenge, and as these challenges are variously elaborated, cultures change and assume different 'characters'. These changes occur in an order that is intelligible to those who possess sufficient self-awareness to marshal an understanding of the processes of change, which are neither fortuitous nor causal in nature, but flow from 'elements in, and forms of, life, explicable solely in terms of human goal-directed activity' (Berlin, 1976: xviii).

5. 'That people's creations – laws, institutions, religions, rituals, works of art, language, songs, rules of conduct and the like – are not artificial products created to please, or to exalt, or teach wisdom, nor weapons deliberately invented to manipulate or dominate people, or promote social stability or security, but are natural forms of self-expression, of communication with other human beings or with God' (Shotter, 1981: 268). Consequently, the way to understand

other people and their worlds is by 'trying to enter their minds, by finding out where they were at, by learning the rules and significance of their methods of expression – their myths, their songs, their dances, the form and idioms of their language, their marriage and funeral rites' (Berlin, 1976: xviii).

6. It is thus the case that, in understanding people, what they do and produce, must be approached by taking account of the terms and practices that are relevant to their location in their worlds, and not in terms of any universal standards and timeless principles.

7. Consequently, in addition to the traditional forms of knowledge – deductive (*a priori*), and empirical (*a posteriori*) – a new form of knowledge must be added: that of the reconstructive imagination. This 'involves "entering into" (*entrare*), working one's way into a means of expression not one's own; working back from the purpose and use of expressions to the larger mode of reality motivating them and in which they play their part, then back again from the whole to a more detailed rendering of the parts in terms of which it is actualized – this is, of course, the now familiar two-way trajectory of what Dilthey called the "hermeneutical circle"' (Shotter, 1981: 268).

Overall, in Sir Isiah Berlin's estimation, 'every one of these notions is a major advance in thought, any one of which by itself is sufficient to make the fortune of a philosopher' (1976: xix).

Jacobitti (1989, emphasis added) provides a similar assessment of these insights of Vico:

> Vico, observing Descartes and the French in hot pursuit of universal 'certainty,' observed wryly that 'in good Latin certum means particularized or, as the schools say, individuated' – and can, therefore, hardly lead to the universal (1948: 321). Indeed, Descartes' cogito had not found grounding or solved the problem of skepticism; *he had only deepened the abyss and led modernity off on a three hundred year expedition of tail chasing.* The skeptic, said Vico, had not doubted that he thought or that he existed. He was 'certain' of these things. What he doubted was whether his 'certainty' was knowledge (*sapientia*) or mere consciousness (*conscientia*). The Cogito, in short, simply proved that Descartes thought he existed. So what?

Indeed. The current intellectual landscape would be quite different had it had a Viconian rather than Cartesian heritage. We note here just three ways in which it might be different.

1. Vico, origins and communication

Our notions of language, where it might have come from, and how it develops, have become legitimate fields of scientific inquiry. From Vico's perspective, an empirical-scientific analysis of the relevant data will not really help us understand these problems, because language is something people make. Hence, to understand these questions of origins, we need to be looking for an answer that makes the beginnings of our human worlds true for us, and 'we must do this rather than merely formulate conceptual truths about the human world. If the human world is grasped in this conceptual fashion, we will know no more about it than we do of an object in physical science. Since physics does not create the object it knows, that object can never become fully intelligible' (Verene, 1981: 101).

Vico offers ways in which we might approach questions of the origins of language that are remarkably congruent with the current scientific literature, even while differently arrived at. One of the key concepts in his thinking about people is that they possess a '*sensus communis*', a shared sense that emerges when at least two people agree, prior to establishing their agreement in language, to treat some aspect of their shared world as something significant on which they can agree, so that they can coordinate their actions towards it. We might loosely term this 'intersubjectivity', a feeling that, when we look at each other, I am at some level cognizant that not only can I see you but you can see me, and when you look at an object and I follow your gaze to that place, I also appreciate that we are both looking at the same thing. How might this 'common sense' provide a grounding for language?

A Viconian fable

My dog hides under the bed during thunderstorms (Vico makes a lot of our reactions to thunder), and when fireworks are being set off. And while under the bed, my dog whimpers, an expression of his fear. Let us put another scared dog under there with him, whimpering away as well. Both dogs are making a noise which is motivated by their individual fear. However, if we add to these dogs (1) the ability to appreciate that their whimpering is not just indicative of their own fears, but also indicates what they are afraid of, and (2) the ability to understand that the other dog is whimpering because of the same thing, then we have the first stirrings of a canine (and hence human) common sense in Vico's scheme of things.

This first form of shared thought is viscerally located: thunder is felt, not just heard; fear is felt in oneself while seen in another. Mentation, to begin with, included the body as an integral part of itself, and 'the human mind is naturally inclined by the senses to see itself externally in the body, and only with great difficulty does it come to understand itself by means of reflection' (Vico, 1948: 236). The fear of both these dogs is occasioned by thunder and signified by their whimpering, but the source of their fear is outside of them. What else can make a dog feel fear? Big dogs that growl at them in the tones of little thunder. So what is this big thunder if not the growling of a very big dog? A big dog that both of them under the bed can share a grasp of, because they are exercising their natural powers of making sense of their world – what Vico calls the *universale fantastico*. The mind cannot, yet, reflect on itself, and so projects itself on to the world, in which thunder is apprehended as the growling of a very large, unseen dog.

Similarly, for Vico, the response of the first humans to thunder is to create a distinction between the seen and the unseen, in this case between the earth and the sky, within which the unseen body of Jove is located. The sky is God/Jove.

And thus, where previously we could only feel fright at the moment of a thunderclap, we now have a memory fixated upon the sky: the sky is an object from which fear might come again, an object created by our being able to identify our whimpering as indicative of the association of fear with the sky. The sky takes on a value through our agreed reference and orientation to it, but a reference that is imbued with our bodily feelings. And this, says Vico, provides us with our first framework for making sense of what we do, for if we are caught outdoors in a thunderstorm our joint actions will be to keep our heads down, and skulk off looking for shelter: actions that we jointly understand because we have participated in the construction of our own shared value for this state of affairs: we can know the shared truth of our actions because we have made it. Bodies are thus reunited with understandings, and 'knowledge' is re-socialized, rather than both kept separate in the Cartesian dissociation of body and mind.

2. The idea of construction

In the age of gods, the origins of human thought stem from the fear which created the gods: 'Thus it was fear which created the gods on earth ... not fear which some men created in others, but fear which the same men created in themselves' (Vico, 1948: 382). But subsequently

> XLIII: 196 Every gentile nation had its Hercules, who was the son of Jove.
> XLIII: 197 This axiom gives the beginnings of the heroism of the first peoples, born of the false belief that the heroes were of divine birth.

There is a movement from the age of gods to the age of heroes, from formulations of the world in terms of directly experienced forces of nature to a giving of human form to them. And in the heroic age, thought is dominated by a *universale fabulum*, not rationality. The fables and heroic tales of these times, what he calls the *generi fantastico*, are not tales of real events distilled into a particular genre:

> For Vico, fables are not embellishments of actual events or historical figures. There is not present epistemologically for the poetic or mythic mind: (1) an empirical or historical order of events which the mind (2) subsequently renders into fabulous form. Events themselves are given form through fables ... The fable, which depends upon the mind's power of *fantasia*, is the means by which the world first takes on a shape for the human.   (Verene, 1981: 71–2)

This is an incredibly modern point: that shared ways of understanding construct the form of what it is that is being understood. We will pick this point up again later, particularly with respect to Foucault (see Chapter 12 below). Finally, here, we find Vico also presaging recent insights as to the relation between social relations and discursive resources:

> In the development of human culture the formation of human experience in terms of imaginative universals gives way to the intelligible universal. For Vico, this process does not occur simply by modifying the imaginative

universal to provide the intelligible universal in thought. The process involves the alteration of social forms of life, specifically the movement from the ages of heroes to that of men. In Vico's work thought and society can be seen as co-determinative structures, wherein a certain type of thought is inconceivable without a certain social structure, and vice versa.   (Verene, 1981: 72–3)

3. Providence and the unintended consequences of joint action

How does co-determination work in human affairs? This is a question that much occupied Vico, given his realization that it is difficult to understand how people could make human institutions when no one individual could have had a grasp of the knowledge necessary to do this. It could be that institutions are founded in the exercise of reason – as is often attempted today by planners of various sorts. But the reality is that this is not the historical case: nobody designed capitalism, for example. Vico offers an answer as to how things come to be as they are, but it is difficult to follow. Why? Because his answer is 'divine providence'. This is a difficult idea to get one's head around in the twenty-first century. This answer also appears to point to a major contradiction in Vico's thinking. The problem is this. He claims in one of his numbered points, 'It is true that men themselves made this world of nations', and consequently history can be understood (the *verum ipsum factum* principle), *and* 'the world of civil society has certainly been made by men' (1948: 331) 'by choice' (ibid.: 1108), and thus can be understood. So why, then, does he claim, in Axiom VII, 132, that a force outside of human affairs is responsible, one which, being outside our making, we cannot understand: 'there is a divine providence ... For out of the passions of men each bent on his private advantage, for the sake of which they would live like beasts in the wilderness, it has made the civil institutions by which they may live in human society' (and see Pompa, 1975: ch. 5 for more details)? Part of the problem here, we suggest, is a contextual one. In more recent parlance, Vico appears to be pointing to a characteristic of social change that would be described as 'emergent', for example 'the arising of novel and coherent structures, patterns and properties during the process of self-organization in complex systems' (Goldstein, 1999: 49).

The structures of social groups are not planned, but emerge as a consequence of the 'unplanned' actions of individuals that create institutions. Institutions make demands on people, position them in certain ways, and constitute norms they must abide by. This does not happen by some extrinsic, transcendent power, but from the consequences of the developing set of social relations between people: institutions, naturally, generate constraints upon individuals; and institutions are 'unwittingly' constructed. We will encounter this point again, especially in relation to Shotter's elaboration of the properties of 'joint action' (see Chapter 16 below):

> although the making of a social structure is not to be explained by a motive or purpose proper to an individual as such, neither is it to be explained by

> reference to some superhuman agency; it is, we shall say, a product of *joint action*, a human product of human intelligence – not fate, nor chance, 'that which did all this was mind, for men did it with intelligence'. The making of a 'moral world' is something naturally provided for in the structure (the intentional structure) of joint action; providence – 'divine providence' – is such that a social order arises naturally in a human society.   (Shotter, 1981: 273)

At root, then, the problematic formulation of 'providence' dissolves when issues of time, place and culture are thought through. Vico stands as one of the first social constructionists.

Vico in practice

By now you are probably ready to accept Vico as a visionary and audacious thinker, but what relevance could his ideas possibly have for practising psychotherapy? Human intellectual history in the west seemed, by Vico's time, to have veered almost entirely in the direction Descartes established for detached rationality, while turning its back on the history that preceded it. With that shift in direction came a loss of curiosity for the very different questions that intrigued Vico. How did humans develop languages to enable them to think and communicate? What part do humans play in the understandings they know as 'common sense'? And what role do time and context-bound interpretations play in motivating humans to live as they do? Such questions are quite at odds with the pristine, dehistoricized, rationality championed by Descartes because they re-insert human beings back into how they came to know what they know. By flipping Descartes' assertion, 'I think therefore I am', into a question – 'how can you think *that*?' – Vico pointed to the role that humanly constructed language plays in what passes for knowledge. Just as geometry was constructed, not discovered, by humans, so too are the many other systems of thought created and drawn from by humans through their use of language. 'Common sense', for Vico, refers to humanly constructed understandings reinforced by our sense of moral accountability to those with whom we uphold that 'common' sense. Vico, in other words, asks us to turn a linguistic and social mirror on ourselves as we consider what we or our clients 'know'.

Vico offers us a first opportunity to link philosophical considerations to therapeutic practice. Like most philosophers, Vico's meaning can seem almost Rorschach-like, open to whatever we project on to his words, especially given the very different times and circumstances in which he wrote. While it can help to see Vico's core concepts reduced to the earlier mentioned seven theses Sir Isaiah Berlin derived from his work, it can also be rewarding to tackle Vico's prose directly (bearing in mind that it has been translated into contemporary terms). So, for a moment, let us try unpacking one of Vico's aphorisms in his section on poetic wisdom:

> Irony could clearly arise only in an age capable of reflection, because it consists of a falsehood which reflection disguises in a mask of truth. From this emerges

> an important principle of human institutions, which confirms the origin of
> poetry discovered in my Science. Since the pagan world's earliest people were as
> simple as children, who are by nature truthful, they could invent nothing false in
> their early myths. These myths must therefore have been *true narratives*, as we
> have defined them.   (Vico, 1948: 408)

This complex aphorism points to a pet theme of Vico: the linguistic nature of
human institutions, and how, through such institutions, humans create their own
truths (the *verum ipsum factum* principle). A few words hang together in a thematic cluster about truth and falsehood, such as irony, myths and mask. I (Tom)
confess to initially hitting a conceptual wall in the first sentence over 'mask of
truth' – I went back to Descartes' singular notion of apodictic, objective truth
and not Vico's view that truth was to be found *within* human institutions, plural.
Vico later seems to toy with his readers. Early people, like children, see their
institutional truths as necessarily *true*. Where, developmentally, do you suppose
Vico placed the Cartesians, for prescribing their notion of truth as universal?
And, what is he getting at in raising 'irony' and 'reflection' in his first sentence?
By now, this aphorism can start to read like a Vico jab in the ribs to reflect on
the embeddedness of truth in particular human stories and institutions. How do
we come to take things as singularly true, when variations on truth pertinent to
human institutions as diverse as cultures, disciplines or even families abound?
Where Descartes saw an over-arching, absolute truth, Vico saw many embedded
in humanly created and historicized social relations.

The Canadian songwriter Jane Siberry wrote: 'I was sure until they asked me.'
Vico asks us to reflect on our forms of knowing, because, like geometry, they are
ours. In what ways have we taken up Descartes' dictum and detached ourselves
from how we have come to make our experience intelligible through 'our' (and
our predecessors') use of language? Surely the phenomena of the world did not
present themselves to humans so-named, or what are we to make of the world's
different linguistic traditions where the same phenomena go by different names?
Has one language got things right, while others are wrong? Even within English,
how can a word like 'bad' mean 'GOOD!' to some, while the opposite to others?
This barrage of questions helps set up a further example for us to study before we
bear down on the therapeutic significance of this line of thought.

The founder of ethnomethodology, Harold Garfinkel (see Chapter 10 below),
turned in his later career to studying science as an institution, in the manner
we have been describing here. An example of his studies occurred in observing
the practices and language used by astronomers in 'discovering a pulsar'. In the
course of his transcribed observations, he noted how, using the instruments, scientific conventions, specific discourse and 'institutional memory' of astronomy as
a discipline, the astronomers 'discovered' a new pulsar. If you bristle at this example because there is something 'there' where the telescope found 'it', note that
Vico and most discursive thinkers are not claiming there is nothing 'there': rather,
they are suggesting that a phenomenon's meaning – even our means of discerning 'it' – are human constructions. Remember, Vico said 'let fully understanding

nature be God's business; our task, as humans, is to understand how we, through our institutions, create versions of truth'. Garfinkel's pulsar example shows how humans extend their institutions as they name and assign meaning to realms of experience. That such meanings should be treated as singular and objectively true makes about as much sense as saying that trees should be only seen as 'harvestable biomass' because that is how one human institution (the forestry industry) sees things.

Vico asks us to embrace the complexities of human meanings and related- ness and not buy fully into Descartes' seemingly elegant extra-human ration- ality. Descartes prescribed one humanly constructed model of rationality as *the* model by which knowing 'should' be known. Vico looked around and saw many models, historically and culturally developed. In this sense, Vico was asking us to engage with the world as it was, not on the basis of some Cartesian ideal of how it should be. Run history's movie up to the present, a time many consider an extension of the modern project Descartes helped to further, and most people seem caught in between Descartes' worldview and that of Vico. Truth, singular, is rife in the language brought to us by clients, and in the many circles of psychology that embrace a Cartesian view of psychology and person- hood. At the same time, the diversity of human existence has never been more evident; people have never had so many culturally or institutionally developed truths to draw from. Part of the inspiration for the discursive turn in therapy has come from this latter awareness: we can become constrained, unaware, by truths particular to the cultural institutions in which we participate. But, we can also go beyond them, by drawing on useful other truths that do work for us in our circumstances. However, occidental humans do have a tendency to idealize singular truths, and will go to incredible lengths to bend physical and social reality to make such truths fit.

In sitting down with clients, we are presented with versions of how things are. If we are Cartesian in our listening, we attend to distortions in what we are told, reminded that our task is to help clients adapt to the world 'as it is' (i.e., accord- ing to our more accurate view). Vico, however, asks us to listen for the 'common sense' in what we are told as usually rooted in institutional ways of thinking particular to cultural groups. Here Vico takes a different road from contemporary constructivists, such as George Kelly (e.g., 1955), who look upon meaning and knowing as individual projects, and thus idiosyncratic. 'Common sense' can be seen as discursive in so far as it is a shared way people have come to participate in, talk about, and thus understand aspects of life they share in common. But common sense carries a different connotation in the modern world where it is seen as a measure of our perceptual accuracy – our words mirroring or map- ping reality with varying degrees of correctness. As therapists we are faced with choices in how to listen to clients. The DSM-IV-TR is as much a human construc- tion as is geometry, and we can funnel our therapeutic conversations down such institutional channels. But we can think further about the institutional forms of understanding we bring to our interactions with clients and the extent to which we engage with clients from them; and how we might hold clients to talking solely on our institutional terms.

Vico's view of understanding was, however, not fixed to static forms of common sense endemic to these diverse human institutions. He saw our varied use of language as fluid and constructive, not merely descriptive or representative. But this should not be interpreted as implying that we can construct anything with our use of language – we still have our conversational others with whom we negotiate our understandings or we end up alienated or in conflict. Language use, for Vico, is also a culture's or relationship's resource for sustaining its particular moral order: the authority or legitimacy of any understanding is acquired in such negotiations, and in its continued use in discussions beyond them. Given that a child possesses fewer linguistic resources to do such negotiating, not surprisingly our earliest and time-worn understandings are our most resilient. Add to this that these understandings are often sustained in ongoing patterns of everyday discourse and – not surprisingly – reflecting upon these understandings as human constructions can seem disorienting. These are the understandings we have learned to take for granted. A therapeutic question arises here: are there not other understandings (conversational resources) available to us from human institutions that differ from those in which we acquired our original sense of 'what is true'? Vico saw it as possible for humans to live by radically different codes of values and meaning, because his understanding of history, and his cross-cultural experiences in Naples, pointed to such plural possibilities.

An important point we can take from Vico is becoming aware that any taken-for-granted 'common sense', or any narrative that strikes us as true, is but one of many possible ways of putting together how experience is or ought to be. Inviting reflection on the origins or 'locations' of meaning (later philosophers will describe this as 'deconstruction'), a therapeutic move developed to make 'conversational space' for other possible meanings, is a theme we will revisit as we go forward. Reflecting on the origins or locations of our meanings begs the question of whether there could be more useful alternatives. These meanings could persist in a way social therapists Fred Newman and Lois Holzman describe as 'fossilised or fetishised'. And it is important not lose sight of how we bring our own forms of (institutional) common sense to how we listen and respond to clients. What results from therapeutic conversations need not be an arm wrestle over whose common sense should dominate: what is needed are useful understandings that might develop out of the generative back and forth of therapy talk.

Coda

For our purposes, Vico has a number of claims to fame. First, there is his realization that humans have not developed their ability to employ reason, either as part of an attempt to understand themselves or their relation to the world, by the exercise of reason. Rather, reason, as a skill, develops over time, as a product of historical processes resulting from the exercise of other abilities, such as their desires and needs – the exercise of their will – through the free association of ideas that spark the imagination, and via the transformations that doing this engenders in society. In addition, we have Vico's insight that we know our world not because our souls or minds have structures that reflect it, but because we first created it; and further, that this creation is not an act of isolated individuals, but the product of humans' interactions with each other within the social institutions they spontaneously create among themselves. This is a central tenet animating contemporary constructionist thought.

Second, he points to how the outcomes of human interactions, and hence the developmental movers that enable rationality to be constructed, are themselves very often not what those involved in these interactions intended to happen. Institutions have come out of human history that are 'superior to that which men have proposed to themselves' (1948: 343).

> Men mean to gratify their bestial lust and abandon their offspring, and they inaugurate the chastity of marriage from which the families arise …
> The reigning order of nobles means to abuse their lordly freedom over the plebeians, and they are obliged to submit to the laws which establish popular liberty …   (1948: 1108)

Vico captures these unintended outcomes in an opaque way, characterizing his New Science as 'a rational civil theology of divine providence', because he is pointing to the demonstrable state of human affairs: how, 'without human discernment or counsel and often against the designs of men, Providence has ordered this great city of the human race' (1948: 342). As we noted above, we would likely frame this notion of 'providence' differently today. But this idea of change as it is constructed between people in their interactions, a process whose outcomes cannot be held to be the responsibility of any individual, is again a central issue in contemporary constructionist thinking.

Third, Vico's imaginative reconstruction of the vicissitudes of human experience through history leads him to a formulation of the relation between the universal and the local that still resonates through contemporary concerns. Vico's position is set out in two paragraphs in *The New Science*:

> 141: Human choice, by its nature most uncertain, is made certain and determined by the common sense of men with respect to human needs or utilities …
> 142: Common sense is judgement without reflection, shared by an entire class, an entire people, and entire nation, or the entire human race.

McMullin (1980: 85) puts this gloss on these axioms:

> Men act according to need and utility. The particular needs and utilities change. But not to act according to perceived need and utility would make one something other than man. Though human nature alters as institutions alter, there is nonetheless an invariant that binds the human race into one. All men exercise a prereflective judgement in respect to personal need and utility.

This notion of 'prereflective judgement' is one we will encounter again in the contexts of a number of different frameworks, ranging from the phenomenologists (see Chapter 3) through the ethnomethodologists (Chapter 10), through Wittgenstein (Chapter 8), to the current writings of Harré and Shotter (Chapters 15 and 16).

3 Phenomenology

Ah, not to be cut off,
not through the slightest partition
shut out from the law of the stars
The inner – what is it?
if not intensified sky
hurled through with birds and deep
with the winds of homecoming.
(Rainer Maria Rilke, 1995: 191)

Phenomenology, as we will consider it, begins with the work of Edmund Husserl in the first three decades of the twentieth century.[1] Its descendants include existential phenomenology, associated with Husserl's pupil, Heidegger – whose opacity makes Husserl look almost a paragon of clarity in comparison – and existentialism itself. Within the broad existential tradition the work of the French philosopher Maurice Merleau-Ponty has become recognized as important to present-day constructionist concerns in the broad sense. One of its other descendants, the social phenomenology of Alfred Schutz, has been a direct influence upon ethnomethodology, and thence discourse analysis in the broad sense. In addition, Schutz's legacy is centrally important in one of the founding documents of contemporary social constructionism, Berger and Luckmann's (1966) volume *The Social Construction of Reality* (Luckmann being a co-author with Schutz of *The Structures of the Life-World* (1973–89). Schutz grasped the principles of phenomenology sufficiently well to have been offered the position of Husserl's assistant in the 1920s (an offer he turned down). He notes that:

> In certain quarters the phenomenologist is held to be a kind of crystal gazer, a metaphysician or ontologist in the deprecatory sense of the words, at any rate a fellow who spurns all the empirical facts … Others, who are better informed, feel that phenomenology may have a certain significance for the social sciences, but they regard the phenomenologists as an esoteric group whose language is not understandable to an outsider … And in regard to Husserl's phenomenology there are also several special difficulties. The published part of his philosophy, characterised by a condensed presentation and highly technical language, is of a rather fragmentary character.   (1945: 77)

---

[1] Though the term had come into western philosophy earlier, in 1807, with Hegel's work *Phenomenology of Mind*, and gained more of its twentieth-century connotation from the work of Franz Brentano (whom Husserl studied under) in his *Psychology from an Empirical Standpoint* (1874).

In addition to being fragmentary, his published work constitutes only the tip of the iceberg: he left over 45,000 pages of manuscript – written in shorthand – that are only slowly reaching the light of day. Here, we are going to be very selective in peeking at Husserl, our interest being as much in how others (particularly Schutz and Merleau-Ponty – who actually described his reading of Husserl as 'an almost voluptuous experience' (quoted by Rojcewicz and Schuwer, 1989: xvi)) have been inspired by the phenomenological project, and contributed to a social perspective on the construction of meanings in the lived world of everyday life that is our focus.

For practitioners, our excursion into phenomenology can seem disorienting. An odd thing about social science is that it is usually practised from a third-person perspective which, of course, is not the way most of us relate to experience. Husserl sought directness and transcendence – the essence – in accounting for experience. Approaching experience in such a manner can lead to thinking that there must be a correct way of perceiving and articulating an experience's essence. That was Husserl's original target but he ended up somewhere much different. Phenomenologists seek to account for experience in all its richness, but experience does not articulate itself – humans do, via their varied languages and discourses. Therein lies a challenge for both phenomenologists and constructionist practitioners: how can one talk about or know an experience save through the languages we have acquired in interaction with others? Parking that question for now, let us approach helping as being partly a phenomenological challenge requiring rich and apt (from the client's standpoint) descriptions.

Early Husserl

Husserl was an admirer of Descartes' method of doubt, as he states in his 1931 volume *Cartesian Meditations*, but his argument was that Descartes made a fundamental error in not pursuing his doubts far enough. In Husserl's view, Descartes had consequently failed to realize that thinking, and the thinking subject, were themselves in need of a grounding (as, in point of fact, was the act of doubting). That is, there had to be something (i.e., phenomena) that could be thought about, prior to a thinking 'I', that could be doubted. Husserl's move was to argue that knowledge is constructed through having experience, in the sense of being conscious. Consequently, it is wrong to focus on knowledge per se so as to obtain an understanding of the relationships between observation, evidence and conclusions: certainty can only be attained by focusing on something that is prior to having knowledge. That 'something', in Husserl's view, was the fact of his own conscious experience, which could be interrogated to elucidate the founding conditions for the possibility of knowledge. Phenomenology is, then, focused on consciousness, and Husserl's work aimed to develop an appropriate methodology for studying consciousness 'from the inside'.

A number of points follow from Husserl's move. First, rather than aiming to resolve the then fundamental problems of philosophy – particularly putting mind and body back together – Husserl effectively regarded these as pseudo-problems generated by Descartes' failure to push his doubts further – problems which only existed because Descartes thought as he did. Second, then, we get an intimation as to why phenomenology has an appeal in the intellectual history of current social constructionists. The fundamental problems bequeathed to us by Cartesian thinking are only fundamental problems within the world constructed by Cartesian discourse. Husserl's move was to 'start again'; let us not begin with any discourse at all. Let us make the move that he came to call 'bracketing', or, following the Greek etymology, let us make an *epoché*, a suspension of all belief, a putting aside of all presuppositions as to what the 'nature of reality' might be. What we have left, in Husserl's view, is a pre-predicative form of experience, a primordial acceptance of a world as 'being there', which we do not have to be able to say anything about to guarantee its existence and properties. His point is that prior to being able to think, to ask questions about the *reality* of experience (and how it might be distinguished from hallucination), the fact that there *is experience* is unquestionable.

We might describe this experience as a naïve, primordial belief that one is in a world. But it is not a belief in the usual sense of the word, because beliefs imply predicates (and this presupposes subjects as distinct things that predicates can be entailed to: 'I believe that …'). For Husserl, experience is an all-in-one package, in which the knower and the known, the believer and the believed in, are undifferentiated, seamlessly united in the generation of 'experience as it is lived in'. An example is useful to clarify this. As I (Andy) am writing this, my cat has a litter of kittens that are at the 'mad' stage of kittenhood. One of them has figured out how to get on my desk by climbing up a number of bits of furniture. It is not brilliantly skilled at this, but can do it. Once it is here, though, it can't figure out a way down. It gets to the edge of the desk and appears to appreciate that it is a long way down; it won't jump, and so annoys me instead by getting distracted by piles of paper, pencils, keyboards, etc. In a sense, the kitten's actions are performed as if it knew about solid objects, depth, that it is too far to jump, etc. But Husserl would be saying 'No, it doesn't *know* any of these *facts*: it is a pre-predicative experience "it" is involved in.' Kitten-ness *in relation* to the world is what is being unreflectively lived in. There is no separation between the kitten and its world: both are fused in the experience being generated, with no awareness of separation on the kitten's part between it and the world: just a phenomenal experience not differentiated and apportioned between kitten and the world.

Indo-European languages are poorly constructed to talk about this kind of undifferentiated phenomenal consciousness in which subject and object, experience and experienced, are fused together. The problem goes way back. Thus, in formulating his *Sunyavada* (otherwise termed '*Madhyamika*', or the middle way) – a dialectic for the refutation of metaphysical propositions by demonstrating their relativity – the Buddhist scholar Nagarjuna (*c.* AD 200) was forced by his language to point to the 'void' (*sunya*, hence *Sunyavada* – Doctrine of the Void) thus:

> It cannot be called 'void' or 'not-void'
> Or both or neither;
> But in order to point it out
> It is called 'the Void'.   (*Madhyamika Shastra*, xv: 3)

So also here: a kitten's subjectivity does not exist for a kitten, and so there is no kitten to be distinguished from its experience, or to have 'its' experience. But in order to point this out, we are forced to talk about 'kittens' as if 'they' 'have' 'experiences'. Phenomenologically speaking, we might say that the kitten is one of many ways in which nature has constructed a way of experiencing itself, and it is that experience that is to be the focus of our studies.

It is this territory that Husserl took on. Thus, he had to invent a way of describing what he was trying to point out so as to delineate its topography; and consequently, his language does not make for easy reading. Husserl's difficulty is rather tragic. His writing is turgid, his technical vocabulary makes him often seem impenetrable and his critics largely ignored him for it. Perhaps somewhat bitterly at the end of his career, he observed that he

> who for decades did not speculate about a new Atlantis but instead actually journeyed in the trackless wilderness of a new continent and undertook the virgin cultivation of some of its areas will not allow himself to be deterred in any way by the rejection of geographers who judge his reports according to their habitual ways of experiencing and thinking and thereby excuse themselves from the pain of undertaking travels in the new land.   (1913: 422)

From his first study, *Philosophie der Arithmetik*, (1891, not translated into English), Husserl gradually became convinced that all 'objective' truths must be grounded in the living acts of human awareness. To study this grounding called for a new philosophical method able to describe how consciousness constitutes meaning from pre-reflective acts of perception. He began outlining this method in *The Logical Investigations* (1900), describing it as 'phenomenological' since it sought to elucidate the origins of knowledge by examining how the world first appears (Greek, *phaino*) in consciousness: the *phaino*mena of consciousness are the source of truth. The intent of phenomenology is to lead us back to 'the things in themselves' as we apprehend them prior to 'objectifying' them via conceptual judgement. The intention is to apprehend how the world is an experience that we live before it becomes an object which we know in any reflective manner. As a consequence of this, the Cartesian fundamental category of 'substance' is replaced by that of 'relation'. It is not the case, in Husserl's view, that a relation exists between two substances – for example, mind and world – that have a given, independent existence. Rather, the mind and the world are a relation – an indivisible locus of a phenomenon – that only subsequently, by the reflective exercise of logic, can be constructed as two separate entities.

It is in this experience-as-lived that Husserl introduces his method, the *epoché*: suspend belief in everything except that which is the primordial experience (and which itself needs to be, painstakingly, elucidated). Having made this *epoché*, Husserl's view is that philosophy can begin again with a description of consciousness that is free from the assumptions of all the historical, common-sense baggage we normally bring to the task of making sense of things. And:

> What is assumed at this point? Not the spatio-temporal world; none of the scientific theories which are used to interpret the world; no independent or continuous existence; no other human beings; not one's own bodily existence or empirically conditioned ego; not the ideal science of pure logic; or any of the idealizations of theoretical knowledge; in short nothing is assumed, and as a beginning there is only the self-validating cognitive experience itself.   (Farber, 1967: 43)

But at the same time, neither are such bracketed phenomena to be doubted, for this would be to introduce a (negative) presupposition. What phenomenology seeks to do is to put all questions aside and turn to the thus revealed 'contents' of consciousness – which are termed the 'phenomena' – and then to get a handle on these phenomena, and how they might have any meaning and relate to other phenomena. There are two points in Husserl's 'getting a handle' on these topics so as to reformulate philosophy that we will briefly dwell on.

Consciousness and intentionality

The intentional nature of consciousness had been previously stated by Brentano as the characteristic that distinguished mental from non-mental phenomena: consciousness is always consciousness of *something*. Husserl placed this notion at the centre of phenomenology: intentionality being an activity inherent in consciousness that defines and reveals the meaning of an object of consciousness. The significance that Husserl saw in this was that as consciousness is always directed toward 'an object', there is a unity between the mind and that of which it is conscious, and not a duality (any distinction drawn between subject and object is a culturally constructed one, not the reality of the situation). There is thus no Cartesian problem of having to construct any convoluted proofs for the reality of physical objects. Husserl is asking about something quite different: what is the meaning of these phenomena which are constituted in the relation between consciousness and the things it is necessarily conscious of as a condition of its own existence. There is no subject–object dichotomy at the root of consciousness; rather there is a relation in which meaning arises. Phenomenology is the systematic investigation of these contents of consciousness.

In his investigation of these contents, Husserl moved in directions that were controversial even among his own converts. Husserl's reaction to these criticisms was to move explicitly to a consideration of the 'lived-world', the *Lebenswelt*. This, and the foundations of the phenomenological method established in his early period, mark the point of departure for Schutz's work.

The *Lebenswelt*

Emerging criticisms of Husserl's approach in the 1920s were that, first, he was taking a very individual perspective of 'solitary' consciousness as his field of inquiry, and that, second, he was becoming increasingly concerned with the 'essential' contents of that consciousness, thus pointing attention away from the phenomena composing lived reality and towards abstract theorizations. Husserl's antidote to this was to move, in his later philosophy, beyond the boundaries of individual consciousness to consider the world of everyday experience, and thus 'intersubjectivity' as well as 'subjectivity'. For example:

> Transcendental intersubjectivity is the concretely autonomous absolute existing basis [*Seinsboden*] out of which everything transcendent (and, with it, every-thing that belongs to the real world) obtains its existential sense as that of something which only in a relative and therewith in-complete sense is an existing thing, namely as being an intentional unity which in truth exists from out of transcendental bestowal of sense, of harmonious confirmation, and from an habituality of lasting conviction that belongs to it by essential necessity.   (Husserl, 1927/1981: 31)

According to Husserl, intersubjective experience is fundamental to construct-ing: ourselves as objective subjects; others as experiencing subjects; and the entire objective spatio-temporal world that we conduct our unreflective social interactions within. Husserl's phenomenology attempts to reconstruct the bases on which these achievements are constituted. Here he places a great deal of explanatory work on the notion of 'empathy'. Empathy, at first sight, appears to entail our consciously attributing intentional activity to others, such that we can put ourselves in their shoes (see also Dilthey, Chapter 4). To study how we do this, Husserl brackets these beliefs to isolate out their basis, what justifies our ever believing such things. And it is important to do this, because only in this way can we uncover the rational structures that underlie our intersubjective experience.

It is this shift of emphasis to the 'world of daily life' (the *Lebenswelt*) that constitutes the springboard for Schutz's work:

> the world is from the outset not the private world of the individual, but an intersubjective world, common to all of us, in which we have not a theoretical but an eminently practical interest. The world of everyday life is the scene and also the object of our actions and interactions … we work and operate not only within but upon the world.   (Schutz, 1945: 533)

Social activity thus comes to replace solitary, individual contemplation as the grounding of our knowledge and thinking, and the 'phenomenological method' is that which enables us to elucidate the character of this pre-theoretical 'givenness' that we have our 'being' in. These maxims were the starting point for the work of Alfred Schutz. We pick up on Schutz's work here, before returning to the ways in which Husserl, in his later writings, developed his approach to the *Lebenswelt* into a much wider critique of the foundations of science.

Most of us have at least flirted with the notion that we can understand things 'as they are'. This makes Husserl's inquiry particularly instructive. In a sense, he took the 'things themselves' line of thought as far as he could as an individualist project. To what extent can we bracket ourselves from cultural and historical experience to know things as they 'really' are? Or is this how one gets hopelessly solipsistic (self-fulfilling and self-limiting), even narcissistic? There is a longstanding humanist ideal about getting to the essence of experience that often guides people's self-help efforts. Husserl's rigorous inquiry ran aground here, on the idea that one can independently arrive at understandings essential to understanding and addressing the human condition. But there is a seduction that runs deep in western discourse that says that one must get to the bottom of things, as if this could happen independently of the cultural means (e.g., language) used to make sense of those things.

Let us throw out some challenging questions at this point: (1) If one cannot know things 'as they are' in any absolute sense, where does the notion of 'assessment' fit in your thinking about being helpful? (2) What might a client's rich phenomenological account of experience offer them that everyday talk about such experiences cannot? (3) Where does this leave helping practice with respect to the many theories about 'how things are' found in social science? (4) If experience is always mediated by our cultural ways of making sense and acting, how does one judge what makes for a good account of experience?

Alfred Schutz

Alfred Schutz was born in Vienna in 1899. He served in the Austro-Hungarian army during the First World War, and then studied law and social science in Vienna. He worked in financial positions in the banking sector, and emigrated to the USA in 1938, arriving there in 1939. He joined what was to become the Graduate Faculty of the New School for Social Research, and concurrently with his academic position resumed a full-time career in the financial sector. He died in 1959.

Drawing from the phenomenology of Husserl, Schutz's standpoint was firmly located within the conscious experience of the individual, since the individual human is the spatio-temporal point at which conscious experience is to be found. His overall standpoint shares a deal in common with that of George Herbert Mead (see Chapter 7), as Schutz himself acknowledged. That is, both of them were concerned with making sense of peoples' actions from an 'insider's perspective'. The view was that individuals have particular perspectives upon the world that make sense of their experiences very much as 'their experiences'. The paramount questions were: 'How is this done?' 'What is it that enables people to make sense of their worlds?' 'How does this sense-making process operate, and what is it composed of?' We will approach Schutz's answers under three headings: the first deals with how a 'life-world' is constructed; the second with the nature of 'action' in the 'life-world'; and the third with Schutz's more socially oriented views as to how to analyse relationships between the separate subjectivities that interact with each other to make up social groups.

Acting in the life-world: cognition

A person's everyday actions call on a 'stock of knowledge' that has been consti-tuted in and by previous experiences and actions. Meanings, to use Husserl's term, have *sedimented* into us as reliably usable ways of making and sharing sense. We may think of this stock of knowledge as existing at different levels. There is a rela-tively small kernel of it that is clear, distinct or internally consistent. Around this kernel are graduated zones of varying vagueness, obscurity and ambiguity:

> zones of things just taken for granted, blind beliefs, bare suppositions, mere guesswork, zones in which it will merely do to 'put one's trust'. And finally, there are regions of our complete ignorance.   (Schutz, 1953: 6)

But this knowledge has no given structure and is in continual flux, so that at any given moment its characteristics are reformulated as they are called upon by the demands of any particular 'Now'. This notion clearly distinguishes Schutz's approach from the traditional cognitive conceptions of contemporary mainstream psychology – which is only to be expected, since the two approaches begin from very different standpoints. That is, contemporary cognitive psychology assumes that our minds contain knowledge that has been structured by our experience, and we 'refer' to this knowledge when we deal with the world. Schutz's concep-tion is much more active and organic: it is more like a 'grasp' that informs action rather than an abstract representation of reality – a 'knowing how' as opposed to a 'knowing that'.

In addition, the world also has an element of what Schutz terms 'cognitive prestructurisation' to it, in that while each individual constructs his or her own 'world' out of his or her own experience of it, this is done with the help of build-ing blocks and methods that pre-exist any particular individual. Consequently, one of Schutz's goals is to analyse the interplay between an individual's efforts at making sense of the world and the already given prestructurization of the world as it is given in experience itself. Not surprisingly, he considers 'the typifying medium par excellence by which socially derived knowledge is transmitted is the vocabulary and syntax of everyday language' (Schutz, 1953: 9). Schutz points out that language is much more than those linguistic elements that can be looked up in dictionaries, or formalizations of syntactic rules, important though these are. These formal characteristics, along with bits of slang, transient connotations and the like, might be translatable into another language, but a native grasp of a language is only accessible to members of the in-group. This is something that is

> not teachable and cannot be learned in the same way as, for example, the vocabulary. In order to command a language freely as a scheme of expression, one must have written a love letter in it; one has to know how to

> pray and curse in it and how to say things with every shade appropriate to the
> addressee and the situation. Only members of the in-group have the scheme
> of expression as a genuine one in hand and command it freely within their
> thinking as usual.   (Schutz, 1953: 10)

Thus, 'to know a language' means *to know how to use it.*

Schutz makes this point concrete by considering the problems confronted by a 'stranger', 'the man who has to place in question nearly everything that seems to be unquestionable to the members of the approached group' (1944: 502). The historical situation of the culture of the new group may be accessible to the stranger, but it is not a part of his or her biography. The stranger is a person without history in his or her new land, reliant on their own 'home base' orientation. This orientation does not work in their new situation, but in addition brings with it its own model of what this new society 'ought to be like' – an outsider's model that is often counter-productive while proving inadequate. Again, what one knows as an outsider is a subject of one's *thought*: what are now needed are the recipes for *action*: a major mismatch.

There is no easy solution to this mismatch. First:

> He who wants to use a map successfully has first of all to know his standpoint
> in two respects: its location on the ground and its representation on the map ...
> This means that only members of the in-group, having a definite status in the
> hierarchy and also being aware of it, can use its cultural pattern as a natural
> and trustworthy scheme of orientation.   (Schutz, 1944: 504)

Second, it is only for members of the in-group that cultural patterns and recipes coincide as schemes of interpretation as well as expression. For the stranger they can at best be 'at hand, but not in hand' (ibid.). This, Schutz notes by analogy to learning another language, is 'the difference between the passive understanding of a language and its active mastering as a means for realizing one's own acts and thoughts' (ibid.).

There is a motivational aspect underlying everyday action. In any situation, what is attended to, communicated and understood is only a fraction of what could be noticed, acted on, etc. What, then, is it that makes some things relevant and others not? On occasion some factors of the situation can 'impose' themselves and their relevance on the actor, a kind of tunnel vision that arises when one is focused on a particular task to the extent that one can be blind to apparently non-relevant factors. On other occasions the actor may focus on different factors, and these assume a kind of 'volitional' relevance. In his later work, Schutz distinguished, in addition to imposed and volitional relevancies, another three forms: motivational, thematic and interpretational (1966b).

Motivational relevance comes from the actor's interests at a particular time in a specific situation, and alerts the actor to the particular elements of the situation which serve to define it in the light of the actor's interests at hand. Motivational relevance can be imposed – things have to be paid attention to so as to deal with them – or volitional, and thus definitive of the situation at hand in terms of the actor's plans and intentions. If this is not the case, then these motivations must be suspended, and the situation becomes problematic. The actor has to turn from a potential actor to a potential problem solver. This requires defining the problem, and this requires a shift from action to investigation.

In these situations, Schutz talks of *thematic motivation*. The actor, instead of proceeding with his or her plans, must concentrate on investigating the situation: problem solving takes priority over the original project. *Interpretational relevance* is an extension of this. A frustrating problem needs to be set in a wider context to appreciate its possible parameters (as grasped within the actor's horizon). If the problem is 'simple' from the present position, its resolution can occur quickly, and action can be resumed. If it is difficult, then further reflection will be needed before action can be continued. The 'simplicity' of the problem is, however, not something that can be objectively defined. In certain circumstances, the actor can be positioned in the 'Now' in such a way that an almost obvious solution can escape his or her grasp.

The final topic Schutz considers concerning the way in which our worlds are made practically manageable is that of *typification* (see also Wittgenstein, Chapter 8, and Garfinkel, Chapter 10, for their related discussions of 'normativity'). The world does not present us with a problem of working out what every new encounter might be. Consciousness structures itself around a set of similarities that are evoked when we come across something 'new'. Every encounter with the world is 'informed' by previous ones, and thus 'the factual world of our experience … is experienced from the outset as a typical one' (1950: 388). Now while this whole issue is very much the stock in trade of traditional cognitive psychology, the phenomenolgical approach does not seek to reduce this phenomenon to some theoretical explanation, but to recognize its existence within conscious experience. What we find is that 'what has been experienced in the actual perception of one object is apperceptively [i.e., spontaneously] transferred to any other similar object, perceived merely as to its type' (ibid.: 389). Similarly, such typifications enter into the organization of our social lives:

> What the sociologist calls 'system,' 'role,' 'status,' 'role expectation,'
> 'situation,' and 'institutionalization,' is experienced by the individual actor
> on the social scene in entirely different terms. To him, all the factors denoted
> by these concepts are elements of a network of typifications – typifications
> of human individuals, of their course-of-action patterns, of their motives and
> goals, or of the sociocultural products which originated in their actions …
> [Typifications] function as both a scheme of interpretation and as a scheme
> of orientation for each member of the in-group and constitute therewith a
> universe of discourse among them.   (Schutz, 1959: 79)

Typifications play a role in planning. Appealing to Husserl, Schutz distinguished two types of anticipatory typifications: those he terms 'and so forth and so on', and the 'I can do it again' type (see also Wittgenstein, Chapter 8):

> The former idealization implies the assumption, valid until counter-evidence
> appears, that what has been proved to be adequate knowledge so far will also
> in the future stand the test. The later idealization implies the assumption, valid

until counter-evidence appears, that, in similar circumstances, I may bring about by my action a state of affairs similar to that I succeeded in producing by a previous similar action. In other words, these idealizations imply the assumption that the basic structure of the world as I know it, and therewith the type and style of my experiencing it and of my acting within it, will remain unchanged – unchanged, that is, until further notice.   (1959: 80)

There is a lot to consider here as we relate Schutz's notions of relevance, motivation and typifications to professional helping. Thinking itself is associated with particular personal and social relevances far beyond merely processing information or factoids. Much of this relates to shared and personal ways of being and valorizing aspects of experience. These often go unreflected-upon in shaping thought and action. This can become a useful focus of helping dialogue, given that encounters with others who do not share the same notions of relevance or motivation can relate to these notions as novel and possibly worth reflecting upon. The same goes with typifications, which can be seen as routinized understandings emanating from 'provinces of relevance' that may not be shared. Cross-cultural experiences, even those with members of other families or institutions, can bring out this sense of how one can act from very different senses of what is typical and relevant. Where help is sometimes needed is when typifications and relevances from one context do not fare well in another context. Family therapist Carl Whittaker jokingly spoke of something along these lines in suggesting (we paraphrase) that marriage was where 'two scapegoats from their families of origin get sent out to replicate their families and learn they have to come up with a family of their own' (Whittaker and Bumberry, 1988). At issue, is how to recognize when typifications and relevances might need modification given new social circumstances where they are not shared. And this takes us on to consider our second theme from Schutz: the nature of action in the life-world.

Acting in the life-world: action and work

What of the active, as opposed to cognitive, components of everyday life? Schutz distinguishes two active forms of *conduct* (any 'subjectively meaningful experience emanating from our spontaneous life' (1945: 536)) – 'action' and 'work'. *Action* is any form of conduct that has been 'devised in advance'. Actions can be purely 'thought', as in trying to solve a problem. Those actions that lead to the body doing something upon the world he terms *working*: 'action in the outer world, based upon a project and characterised by the intention to bring about the projected state of affairs by bodily movements' (ibid.).

Why do people perform actions and work? They have motives, says Schutz, and these can be distinguished as two varieties: 'in-order-to motives' and 'because motives'. This is a distinction not clearly made in everyday English, which allows 'in-order-to' motives to be expressed as 'because' motives (but not the other way round). 'In-order-to motives' are behind those actions performed from goal-directed motives, and which thus project action into the future. 'Because motives' are anchored in the past, and are translated into the present as 'reasons' for action. In-order-to motives inform action as it is being conducted, and are directly perceived as part of the on-going experience of acting. In this sense, then, they are subjective. They are 'the attitude of the actor living in the process of his ongoing activity' (1945: 537). By contrast, 'because' motives are not available to consciousness while it is involved in action, but only in retrospect or prospect, reflectively (cf. Mead's distinction between the 'I' and 'me', Chapter 7). A 'because' motive is, in this sense, 'not subjective'.

An action can be 'conscious' or 'unconscious'. Schutz uses these terms by defining 'conscious' in a specific way, so that everything that is not conscious is 'unconscious' by default: 'Our actions are conscious if we have previously mapped them out "in the future perfect tense" … We have a picture in our mind of what we are going to do' (1967: 63). In one sense, since conscious actions are based on plans, they could be termed 'rational'. However, given the fluctuating nature of everyday knowledge, Schutz prefers to refer to action as 'reasonable' rather than 'rational', in that we are hardly ever likely to be in possession of knowledge of all the actually or potentially relevant factors that need to be taken into account.

None of this, of course, exhausts Schutz's account of the process of acting in the life-world. Plans may be broken down into smaller projects. Plans determine interests, which focus attention, and reconfigure at-hand knowledge. Then there is the choosing among plans and projects, the choosing between objects, doubts, questions, interests, and so on: here, Schutz agrees with Dewey: 'choice is not the emergence of preference out of indifference. It is the emergence of a unified preference out of competing preferences' (Dewey, 1922: 190).

Where is this getting us? Let us forget about all the precise distinctions and terms Schutz is introducing here, and try and tease out his general frame of reference. His argument is that people do not have one structured set of knowledge that they refer to in different circumstances so as to tell themselves 'what to do next'. Nor is he describing our situation as one in which we have lots of different stocks of knowledge that we call upon in different circumstances. He is following Husserl's point that we are in an active relation to the world, and that our traditional notion of knowledge as a 'thing' is inappropriate if applied as an explanation of how we go on. Our actions are not shaped by perceiving the environment, interpreting it by reference to some set of knowledge, and then formulating a response. Quite so, Schutz claims. Rather, a better model is to think of our actions in the way we could think about how a wind-shaped tree has generated its shape as it grows. As a tree pushes out its twigs, it doesn't test the wind and refer the data back to some genetic blueprint, and then react with growth at particular points rather than others. It is trying to grow everywhere, and the site at which its form is established is *the very point of connection* where its active growth processes interface with the pressure of the wind as its growth pushes against the force that the immediately experienced environment is pushing back at it.

If we take this analogy a little further, we get to another issue Schutz is pointing at. As a tree grows, the results of its growth influence the environment as it affects other points in its growth. Windswept trees have a sloping profile, with the lowest growth being on the windward side, and since this growth provides some protection from the force of the wind for growth going on behind it, leeward twigs have an easier job in growing taller. What goes on at the interface of the tree's growth and the environment plays a role in structuring its overall form.

This, then, we trust, captures some of what Schutz is trying to articulate about how we, in the course of living in the world, front up to our everyday world. First, at any point in time, our conscious interface with the world 'goes on' as an ever-changing, active event. This 'going on' is conducted not by any reference to a coded past – a stock of knowledge – but with respect to a momentary tension. This tension exists between how the past has currently shaped the surrounding points at this interface, and the strivings that our consciousness is spontaneously aiming towards in the situation it thus finds itself. Second, what Schutz has effectively done here is to reorient phenomenology away from its concern with *being*, and towards articulating a grasp of *becoming*. The importance of this shift will become apparent when we look at how it is taken up, from a different motivational source, in the work of John Shotter (Chapter 16).

There is a dynamism to social living we must learn to live with, which is what Schutz is getting at here. A North American colloquialism for this suggests that one must 'roll with' how things develop socially. This is where an individualist view that does not take into account the social possibilities associated with planned actions can lead to conflict. In this sense, our projects, our understandings, our motivations even, encompass typifications of the 'otherness' of our social relations, enough so that these are often factored into our thinking in advance (see Billig in Chapter 13). We are not only responsive to what others do in response to us, our typifications of social life feature in how we think and act.

It is in this sense that I (Tom) have come sometimes to see my work as a therapist as 'resistance-informed', that any ideas or actions proposed to clients need to be customized according to the social sense they evoke from clients. There can often be a sense in suggesting actions or ideas to others that these are being too easily dismissed. Instead, such 'resistance' can be seen as important to revising earlier suggestions or moving on. This is not to suggest that the typifications clients cite or respond from as the basis for such 'resistance' cannot themselves be reflected upon. But this can result in professional impositions of meaning or action when otherwise the ideas or actions under discussion might be further specified (i.e., customized) using client responses evoked by the professional.

Acting in the life-world: sociality

> Knowledge of another's mind is possible only through the intermediary of events occurring on or produced by another's body ... His body, like all other material objects, is given to my original perception ... His psychological life,

> however, is not given to me in originary presence but only in copresence; it is not presented, but appresented.[2] By the mere continuous visual presence of the other's body and its movements, a system of appresentations, of well ordered indications of his psychological life and his experiences is constituted.   (Schutz, 1942: 338)

We already have the intimation that consciousness is shot through with sociality. 'Intersubjectivity' is one of the fundamental problems for phenomenology. Just how does an individually located experience of the world connect up with other individually located points of awareness and thereby concoct a socially distributed 'common sense'? This is not a problem unique to phenomenology. It is one of the really hard questions of all philosophy, generally referred to as the question of 'other minds'. Husserl spent a lot of time and effort in trying to resolve this. How do we know that other people 'really' exist? How do we get to solve the issue of solipsism?

Schutz regarded Husserl's efforts as dead ends, and rethought the issue. His solution is quite pragmatic, yet also probably 'true'. His claim was that intersubjectivity should be regarded as 'a fundamental ontological category of human existence' (1957: 82), and thus a precondition of any human experience, something that is accepted as unquestionably given with the appearance of other individuals as physically available to consciousness. Here is what Schutz has to say:

> If we retain the natural attitude as [humans] amongst other [humans], the existence of others is no more questionable to us than the existence of an outer world. We are simply born into a world of others, and as long as we stick to the natural attitude we have no doubt that intelligent fellow-[humans] do exist. Only if radical solipsists or behaviorists demand proof of this fact does it turn out that the existence of intelligent fellow-[humans] is a 'soft datum' and incapable of verification (Russell). But in their natural attitude even those thinkers do not doubt this 'soft datum'. *Otherwise they could not meet others in congresses where it is reciprocally proved that the intelligence of the other is a questionable fact.* As long as humans are not concocted like homunculi in retorts but are born and brought up by mothers, the sphere of the 'We' will be naively presupposed ... [Humans] take for granted the bodily existence of fellow [humans], their conscious life, the possibility of intercommunication, and the historical givenness of social organization and culture, just as [they] take for granted the world of nature into which [they] were] born.   (1942: 337–8; emphasis added).

This 'We' has a 'vivid presence' – a 'Nowness' rather than a 'Just nowness' (*modus preterito*): 'the other's speech and our listening are experienced as a vivid simultaneity' (ibid.: 342), although this experience of the other's stream of consciousness does not have to be language-based, but would be there in playing tennis, playing music with them or making love, for example. This differs from our experience of our selves, since selves can only be grasped at in the 'Just now', at least slightly after the fact of our acting. Schutz terms this vivid simultaneity of another's stream

---

[2] That is, the spontaneous interpretation of sensory perception in terms of past experiences or accumulated 'knowledge' of the perceived object. In this case, the 'knowledge' is probably innately given, as recent studies of human infancy have concluded.

of consciousness the *general thesis of the alter ego's existence:* the alter ego 'is that stream of consciousness whose activities I can seize in their presence by my own simultaneous activities' (ibid.: 343).

The central point from Schutz is that our bodies are *direct expressions* of ourselves – our inner lives – to each other, as a given of our human experience of the world. We are not solitary, doubting, reflective individuals shut off from the inner lives of others (though, with language, we might construct an image of ourselves as like that): we have a given, active grasp of each other's consciousness that informs our own, right from the start.

We are now at a key point shared by many of our thinkers and highly relevant to helping dialogue. Specifically, the primary social reality we have with each other is not words, but the varied responses that show how we are being received by each other. While we do not take up Derrida's ideas much in this book, this is where he was concerned about logocentrism, our excessive faith in semantics, overriding the myriad other ways we understand and respond to each other (Derrida, 1976). Intersubjectivity, in the way Schutz relates it, is not like sharing thought clouds of similar cognition so much as it is about attuning or coordinating our varied ways of being responsive to each other. In the language of professional helping we are talking about rapport, which can be seen as coming to share responsively not only words but a host of non-verbal features of responsive communications used to indicate shared relevance and meaning.

In modern life we do have communication technologies that take us out of the 'natural' realm of direct face-to-face interaction. Prior to this, however, we only started and finished our real-time social interactions by means of our feet: we could only walk in and out of interaction. Feet have long been superseded by writing, the telephone and the web: but real-time, face-to-face interaction is the originating form of meeting and interacting. Situations in which we are observers of interaction have also changed, but here the basic issues of being an observer as opposed to an interactant have not changed so dramatically. Schutz does not deal explicitly with these media influences upon our relationships. He does, however, outline a continuum in our relationships, between those with whom we have entered into 'We' relationships, and have thus had direct experience of as a 'thou', and our *contemporaries* with whom we have what he terms 'They' relationships, in which 'my knowledge of my contemporaries is … inferential and discursive' (1967: 184).

> When I board a train, for instance, I orient myself to the fact that the engineer in charge can be trusted to get me to my destination. My relationship to him is a They-relationship at this time, merely because my ideal type 'railroad engineer' means by definition 'one who gets passengers like myself to their destination.' It is therefore characteristic of my social relationships with my contemporaries that the orientation by means of ideal types is mutual. Corresponding to my ideal type 'engineer' there is the engineer's ideal type 'passenger.' Taking up mutual They orientations, we think of each other as 'one of them.'
>
> I am not therefore apprehended by my partner in the They-relationship as a real living person. From this it follows that I can expect from him only a typical understanding of my behavior.   (1967: 202–3)

Later, we will find an elaboration of this point by Rom Harré (Chapter 15) in his discussion of the notion of 'positioning'. But here, note how Schutz's observation can illuminate the relationship a therapist might enter into with his or her client: is it to be a 'we' or a 'they' one? And what different ethics arise from this decision? These questions began to emerge in Husserl's later work, in which he came to confront concerns as to what it was in western thought that allowed an absolutist adoption of a 'they' perspective over a 'we' perspective in the ideology of Nazi Germany. The questions are similarly to be found in the contemporaneous works of the Bakhtin circle in Stalinist Russia.

The later Husserl: towards Heidegger, existentialism and Maurice Merleau-Ponty

In the 1930s Husserl's concerns were pushed in new directions by his reflections on the rise of fascism in Germany, and his response is remarkably Viconian (though there is little to suggest he knew Vico's work). Prior to this time, Husserl had been motivated by the question of the founding conditions of rational certainty in individual consciousness. With what he saw as the breakdown of rationality in European life, and its replacement by the forces of irrationality, he sensed a need for an historical investigation of the origin, elaboration and conservation of rational culture. His ideas were outlined in lectures in Vienna and Prague between 1935 and 1937, and in a book in 1936, *The Crisis of European Sciences and Transcendental Phenomenology*, which did not become available in English until 1970. Husserl's thinking at this point, while coming out of his earlier work, was something he regarded as a quite new. His French translator, Walter Biemel, notes a letter from Husserl to a friend at this time: 'Precisely now that I have arrived at the beginning and that all is ended for me, I know that it is necessary to begin everything over again from the beginning' (2000: 153).

Husserl's concern was with the importance given to the 'ideal of reason' throughout western thought: why has a concern with an abstraction come to so dominate western worldviews? This 'ideal', for Husserl, was not something, he came to realize, that should be conceived as a final, complete system of knowledge, but rather as an adequate foundation for the rationalization of reason, which he saw as the foundation of civilized life. What he was striving for was a methodology by which future generations could cumulatively build knowledge to guide civilized life (see also Habermas, Chapter 4, on discourse ethics). He saw this 'ideal of reason' as peculiar to western civilization, having its beginnings in the seventh and sixth centuries BC with Plato and Aristotle. What they achieved, in his view, was the first break with practical reason and the creation of a detached observer, a new perspective in and on life.

Husserl considered that, prior to this development, the people of Greece had, like everyone else, lived in a 'pre-theoretical world' (an *Umwelt* or *Lebenswelt*), a pre-reflective world that is simply given to us by virtue of our being human beings, and in which values and meanings are, almost unconsciously, directed practically, towards the environmental world. This different, pre-literate, pre-reflective world has been pointed out by Jaynes in his interpretation of the activities of the Greek heroes as portrayed by Homer in the *Odyssey* and the *Iliad*:

> there is in general no consciousness in the Illiad ... There is ... no concept of will or word for it, the concept developing ominously late in Greek thought. Thus Illiadic men have no will of their own and certainly no notion of free will ... there is no subjective consciousness, no mind, soul or will in Illiadic men.   (1976: 39, 71)

These are controversial claims, and yet there is a strong sense throughout the Heroic literature of this and other times and places – through the *Rig Veda* to the late medieval Irish Bulls stories and sagas – of warriors who were not often, if ever, to be found reflecting on their actions, but just 'doing them'. The French historian Marc Bloch catches the tenor in his summary of these people of this period as sharing

> an emotionalism of a civilization in which moral or social convention did not yet require well-bred people to repress their tears or their raptures. The despairs, the rages, the impulsive acts, the sudden revulsions of feeling present great difficulties to historians, who are instinctively disposed to reconstruct the past in terms of the rational.   (1961b: 73)

These were people living in a pre-theoretical world of action, not reflection.

This pre-theoretical world, according to Husserl, was open to change, although those changes were merely local adjustments in the practical relationship people had with it. But, with the creation of the theoretical, detached attitude, the *Lebenswelt* is reduced to a world of appearances, and true knowledge of reality comes to be regarded as belonging to things which do not change: idealized essences that are universally true for all humans at all times. Limited opinions (*doxa*) are the knowledge of the *Lebenswelt*, and this is now marginalized by true knowledge (*episteme*). However, his view was that the ancient Greek philosophers were fully aware that *episteme* was only an idealization of the *Lebenswelt*, that its ground was the practical world.

> Had this ideal been faithfully followed in Western history, a theoretical knowledge tied to its roots in the practical world of human existence would have resulted. Theoretical knowledge would then have contributed to man's understanding of himself in his practical world. And that, Husserl points out, was precisely what was intended when the Renaissance assumed the ideal of classical antiquity. But this ideal, instead of being realized, underwent an internal decomposition.   (Rabil, 1967: 55)

This is difficult stuff, but worth following. Husserl begins his analysis with Euclidean geometry, which he sees as the first great revolution in western history. Geometry went beyond the relativity of the *Lebenswelt* by abstracting an object from the world and elaborating a set of axioms from which conclusions relating to the *Lebenswelt* could be deduced. It was Galileo whom Husserl saw as, firstly, beginning a second revolution while, secondly, destroying the ideal on which it was based.

> [Galileo's] perversion was due to the fact that as time passed the realization that geometry was based on an idealization of nature *produced by the human mind* was forgotten, and it came to be regarded as something true *in itself*, having no relation at all to the men who created it.   (Rabil, 1967: 55)

The result of this is that the thinking mind and the object it was thinking about became separated from each other.

> Galileo completed this revolutionary change by mathematizing all of nature, relegating the *Lebenswelt* so completely to the status of subjective appearance that the relation of knowledge to men who live in the *Lebenswelt* became a problem.   (ibid.: 56)

Descartes then took the next step. Recognizing that if nature were universally rendered by mathematics, then the psychical needed to be separated from the physical, since the mathematical nature of the world had been revealed by the rational powers of consciousness. Hence, the psychical world can only be restored to its place in the scheme of things by regarding the 'I' as a psychological reality that is left when mathematized nature has been subtracted from consciousness as a separate entity in its own right. Which, Husserl argues, is wrong-headed. Instead, what Descartes should have done was to bracket the self away with the world, and then regard both of them as constituted in the consciousness that was left. If he had carried his scepticism that far, then he would have transcended both subjectivism and objectivism by revealing each of these, to him and his way of thinking, independent components of the world, as just 'ideas' about an invented conception of reality – instead of turning our attention away from the nature of the only reality we have. If he had done so, Descartes would, in Husserl's view, have saved western philosophy from going down blind alleys for the next 300 years of its history.

Husserl's intention in this analysis was to show that the sickness he perceived in the modern European mind stemmed from new doubts which had arisen because philosophy itself had become perverted. This sickness required a catharsis, and this could only come by adopting the cure of transcendental phenomenology (which may be good philosophy, but appears rather naïve politics in the Germany of the Third Reich). What was needed, he claimed, was to restore our experience of the *Lebenswelt* prior to its scientific idealization, the *Lebenswelt* being

> the general context or horizon for all experience. In this sense it is the pregiven world. 'Pregiven' here should not be taken to mean that the *Lebenswelt* is the world of nature and natural objects alone. For it encompasses as well the cultural accomplishments of men, including the sciences, and therefore refers as much to intersubjective as to natural existence. Viewed in this perspective, science is a cultural accomplishment within the *Lebenswelt*. It does not point to some reality behind the *Lebenswelt* but is based rather on the abstraction of certain features within it … Science, therefore, emerges as a partial theme within the more universal *Lebenswelt*.   (Rabil, 1967: 58)

And thus we find Husserl giving an early articulation to the limitations of science as an appropriate method for dealing with human problems: it can only be, in this view, a partial theme, one that does not point to the hidden vicissitudes behind human reality in and of itself.

By now, you should understand our concerns about a Cartesian account of being individuals and being social, and all things in between. At the heart of the concern is an idealization (to use Schutz here) of human life as ultimately and predictably knowable. Such a view sees all spheres of life, for being knowable, as potentially amenable to human engineering. The problem with applying this view to human beings comes, as Bruno Latour provocatively wrote, when the 'objects' object (1996). A human science differs from the natural sciences in being conducted by humans (scientists) making sense of other humans who, in turn, are making sense of the scientists. To paraphrase cybernetician Heinz von Foerster (1984), we are not 'trivial machines' to be simply figured out, and then manipulated accordingly by knowledgeable others. In addition, and this is a criticism that can also be made of Husserl, this idealization ignores the fact that humans are embodied actors, not disembodied minds: for Husserl, the body remains 'a thing "inserted" between the rest of the material world and the "subjective" sphere' (Rojcewicz and Schuwer, 1989: 161). It is the role of the body in a phenomenological perspective that is the focus of the work of the French philosopher Merleau-Ponty.

Maurice Merleau-Ponty: phenomenology and the body

[Philosophy] reserves for itself what remains when the sciences have said all they can say, when one comes to it with the question: And we, living men on whom all this converges, what have we to do with this world?   (Merleau-Ponty, *L'Express*, 9 October 1954: 3)

The first philosophical act would appear to be a return to the world of actual experience which is prior to the objective world.   (1962: 57)

Maurice Merleau-Ponty was born in 1908 in Rochefort, France. He attended the École Normale Supérieure during the late 1920s, and began work as a schoolteacher, while continuing his studies in philosophy and psychology. The results of these studies were published in two books while he was serving in the infantry during World War II: *La Structure du comportement* (1942: English edition *The Structure of Behavior*, 1963); and *Phénoménologie de la perception* (1945: English edition *Phenomenology of Perception*, 1962). At the end of the war he was appointed Professor of Philosophy at the University of Lyon. He moved to Paris in 1949 as Professor of Philosophy specializing in child psychology. In 1952 he became one of the youngest people to be appointed to the Collège de France, taking up the Chair in Philosophy that had been held earlier in the century by Henri Bergson. He died in 1961. Current interest in his work rests on his treatment of the body within a phenomenological perspective.

The body has been peculiarly neglected in western thought, having a marginal position in most western philosophy, which in most of its various guises has been almost exclusively cerebral. Western philosophy has overlooked the mundane: that very few of us spend our time in detached contemplation of the world, but most of our time 'doing things', which involve bodily actions. Unfortunately, western languages make it difficult to talk about what is involved here other than in a dualistic way, since the body is generally talked of as a 'possession'. I talk about 'my body' on a lot of occasions; type with 'my' fingers; 'my' feet are killing me (although, perversely, 'I' get fat, not it). Merleau-Ponty's main aim is to reinstate the body as a body-subject, and clarify the nature of things from that phenomenological position. All of which does not make for an easy read.

For Merleau-Ponty, an object 'is an object only insofar as it can be moved away from me ... Its presence is such that it entails a possible absence. Now the permanence of my body is entirely different in kind' (1962: 90). In addition, my body acts quite unconsciously for me. I don't need to check that I still have two legs in order to stand up, since I am 'with' my body (although if one of them has gone to sleep while I have been sitting, then I might fall over). We will not explore all aspects of Merleau-Ponty's ideas here, nor seek to distinguish them precisely from those of his contemporary philosophical colleagues, such as Gabriel Marcel or Jean-Paul Sartre. Rather, we will concentrate on outlining his general notions of the body and where it should fit into constructionist thought.

The body

> Quality, light, colour, depth, which are there before us, are there only
> because they awaken an echo in our body and because the body welcomes
> them.   (Merleau-Ponty, 1964a: 164)

It is not sufficient, according to Merleau-Ponty, to pursue the phenomenological project of reuniting the subject that sees the world with the world that is seen, and then work out how reflection acts to give us a conception that the two can be constructed as separate phenomena, a perception that western philosophy has then reified as the 'truth' about 'the way things really are'. It is a start, but it leaves out our bodies. The trouble with our own bodies is that they are ambiguous. On the one hand, they are objects in our world, since we see them from our spatially located consciousness as 'outside' consciousness: 'my visual body includes a large gap at the level of my head; though, curiously, while 'my body is constantly perceived ... it remains marginal to all my perceptions' (Merleau-Ponty, 1964a: 94, 90). On the other hand, we cannot ever 'get rid' of our bodies: we cannot leave them behind when we walk out of a room, and we can never walk around them and see them from behind.

We also have the situation, which he analyses at length, that the body has the peculiar property of being able to be subject and object to itself. I can actively touch my one hand with the other, and one then feels itself as 'touching', and the other feels 'touched'. And:

> when I press my two hands together, it is not a matter of two sensations felt together as one perceives two objects placed side by side, but an ambiguous set-up in which both hands can alternate the role of 'touching' and being 'touched'.   (1962: 93)

This alternation is similar to the picture that Wittgenstein refers to, that one moment is a rabbit, and another a duck, but never the two simultaneously. Thus, Merleau-Ponty comes to view the body as the bedrock of consciousness, from which the separation of the mind and the body has been created as a conceptual abstraction. Consciousness is not primarily a matter of 'I think that', but of 'I can' (ibid.: 137). And the knowledge of 'I can' is not of a cerebral, abstracted nature, but of a concrete variety: 'it is knowledge in the hands, which is forthcoming only when bodily effort is made, and cannot be formulated in detachment from that effort' (ibid.: 144). It is not that we 'stand outside' our bodies and direct them; we are at one with them, moving with them as the situation demands.

This 'knowing' becomes apparent in driving a car, where, with time, the car becomes absorbed into our body's schemas, and we 'become it' – something we become conscious off only when we drive someone else's car, and it does not quite seem 'to fit, to feel quite right, to be habitual, yet'. The car becomes an 'area of sensitivity' that increases 'the scope and radius of the touch' (ibid.: 143). Intelligence is embodied, and this is revealed when we consider the practical mastery of a skill. With our bodies, we may have some general intentions for them to execute, but these become actual in their specific form only in respect of the specific contexts of situations as they develop around us. His argument is that:

> For the player in action the football field is not an 'object' … It is pervaded with lines of force (the 'yard lines'; those which demarcate the penalty area) and articulated in sectors (for example, 'the openings' between the adversaries) which call for a certain mode of action and which initiate and guide the action as if the player were unaware of it. The field itself is not given to him, but present as the immanent term of his practical intentions; the player becomes one with it and feels the direction of the goal, for example, just as immediately as the vertical and horizontal planes of his own body.   (1963: 168)

We might also think of the situation where we reach out to pick up a stone from the ground, only to discover the 'stone' is actually a frog. We have been acting through and with our bodies with expectations built into our mode of acting that are directed to an inanimate contact, to be shocked that we were in 'wrong mode'. Had we 'known' it was a frog, our body-subject would have adopted a very different approach: 'in order that we may be able to move our body towards an object, the object must first exist for it' (1962: 139). Hence, Merleau-Ponty's claim is that we *are* our bodies, and that our lived experience in this body denies a fundamental duality between subject and object, mind and body, etc. (ibid.: xii).

Because of this changed conception of 'knowledge-as-inherent-in-bodily-action' Merleau-Ponty also comes to conclusions that sound remarkably

Wittgensteinian (Chapter 8). Action is direct, and we move spontaneously in accord with our bodies. Consequently, in the specific case of gesturing to a friend to come nearer (as an example of all acts in the world), he considers there is no need to entertain there being a preceding thought which motivates our action, because action requires no interpretation or mental representation (ibid.: 111). We are unable to discern an interior state that comes before the expression of that state: 'I am not in front of my body, I am in it or rather I am it … If we can speak of interpretation in relation to the perception of one's own body, we shall have to say that it interprets itself' (ibid.: 150).

The body appears as if it has an intelligence of its own and, in a sense, it does, in that a great deal of what we do is unavailable to consciousness. The body is a kind of pathway between perception and action, a conduit through which the two inter-relate, and consequently merge into each other as the origin from which our later thoughts and understandings are constructed. There is a criss-crossing, an 'interpenetration' of subject and object in the actions of the body, and it is this recognition that is a prime mover in Merleau-Ponty's phenomenological critique of dualism. The world is not 'set over' from our consciousness: the world and consciousness meet in our bodies. And our bodies give to our perception an inherently social character, because in perception:

> I know unquestionably that that man over there sees, that my sensible world is also his, because I am present at his seeing, it is visible in his eyes' 'grasp of the scene'.   (1964b: 169)

There is never a 'moment of perception', in Merleau-Ponty's view, followed by another 'moment', which requires the subject to build up an interpretation of the world. Perception is allied with action and has a unity over time. We 'see' an object remaining stable as we move our heads and reveal different aspects of it, different perspectives, but it stays as the same object. Similarly through touch: we feel different surfaces and edges of a cube, but the cube remains a solid integration of itself as we feel it. We do not every moment have to stop and think, 'is this the same object as I was holding a moment ago?' But what happens when we feel a plastic, malleable object? It presents itself to us as having an enduring quality that maintains itself over transformations of shape. And remember, we also see what we touch, and smell it too. Thus, we build up through bodily experience a tacit grasp of the properties of things in the world that prime our bodies with an anticipation as to 'what to do with them' when we encounter them at a distance.

It is as though our experience is distilled into the perceptual object, and it has characters of its own that endure beyond us. While those characters come from our history of directly dealing with them, we 'lose sight' of this history. The origin of this knowledge is 'sedimented' into the object. Perception is synthetic across time, which is what enables us to benefit from past experience and form habits, and this sustains a kind of movement beyond that which is immediately presented to us in perception, and towards a distillation of past discoveries into the object itself: in knowing what this object is we know what to do with it next. 'Objectification' is a natural consequence of continuous perception. Consequently, the tendency towards 'scientific explanation' is quite natural: 'science was merely following uncritically the ideal of knowledge set up by the perceived thing' (1962: 56).

Our bodies are both expressive of and the site of our feelings. We do not connect to the world as passive observers who just think about it: we experience it with a number of senses, and bodily act upon it. We are not apart from the world, but transducers of it, intertwined with it: we experience it. There are not neutral objects detached from ourselves, but objects that have meanings mediated by our relationship with them, as having a practical or emotional or sensual meaning: meaning is something we 'live through', not reflect on. Our subjectivity is not that of a detached self that contemplates the world, but is 'through and through compounded of relationships with the world' (ibid.: xiv). And Merleau-Ponty casts this relationship in a specific way: 'the whole of nature is … our interlocutor in a sort of dialogue' (ibid.: 273). It provides a set of opportunities for us to take up or put down. It has an historical existence before us that has shaped many of the pre-reflective ways that we will react to it, and in the act of responding to it we give a shape to the world. And because we-as-our-bodies are a part of nature, then, almost paradoxically, 'inside and outside are inseparable. The world is wholly inside and I am wholly outside myself' (ibid.: 407).

Here we find an experiential base for meaning in perception: to understand meanings is not, at root, to know what words mean, but to know what things mean – in relation to our own perspective: in what he terms 'the ante-predicative life of consciousness' (ibid.: xvi). 'The word captures a certain style of the perceived world, it extracts and expresses an aspect, an "emotional essence"' (ibid.: 187). Consequently, 'There remains the problem of the passage from the perceptual meaning to the language meaning, from behaviour to thematization' (1968: 176). When something is 'captured' in language, it takes on a meaning that is of a different order to its existence in perceptual experience. Words have so much 'sedimented' into them because of their own history and the way in which they are learned in concert with already proficient others. Cultural meanings constructed in social practices reconstruct the meanings that result from the perspectives posited by Mead and von Uexküll (Chapter 7) as 'natural': hence the processes by which this occurs are a central component of the constructionist enterprise.

If we do not give 'the mental' the kind of privilege it is given in dualist or 'cognitive' thinking, then there are consequences for the nature of our subjectivity:

> If I try to study love or hate purely from inner observation, I will find very little to describe: a few pangs, a few heart throbs – in short, trite agitations which do not reveal the essence of love or hate … We must reject the prejudice which makes 'inner realities' out of love, hate or anger, leaving them accessible to one single witness: the person who feels them. Anger, shame, hate and love are not psychic facts hidden at the bottom of another's consciousness: they are types of behavior or styles of conduct which are visible from the outside.   (1964a: 52–3)

Thus, the notion of the body-subject requires a recognition of the public face of emotion. Hence, in other cultures, where an emotion might be expressed in markedly different ways compared to our own culture

> this difference of behaviour corresponds to a difference in the emotions themselves. It is not only the gesture that is contingent in relation to the body's organization, it is the manner itself in which we meet the situation and live it … Feelings and passional conduct are invented like words.   (1962: 189)

Merleau-Ponty's nuanced account of being human is highly sensory, if not sensual at times. Most psychology avoids such accounts, often truncating experience into cognitive components that come before and after some felt sense in our bodies. But with Merleau-Ponty human experience comes as an inseparable whole that simultaneously includes thinking, feeling and acting. In some cases, this sense of the wholeness of experience can be problematically lost, something that feeling really heard by others, or by turning focused attention to our bodies, can help to restore. There has been an increased emphasis lately in different forms of professional helping on bringing 'mindfulness' (e.g., Kabat-Zinn, 1990), a full-bodied sense of experiencing, based on eastern meditative practices, to people's different engagements with life. It is in our embodied interactions with others and experience that we benefit from a sort of dialogue with our circumstances. Feminist Rosalyn Diprose extends this thinking to human relatedness ('I live my body outside of myself through the mirror space of the other's body') (2002: 89). Turning to language, what becomes important are rich vocabularies that best articulate the bodily sense of what we might try to relate to ourselves and others.

4 Hermeneutics

> In ordinary experience we're all in the position of a dog in a library,
> surrounded by a world of meaning in plain sight that we don't even know
> is there.   (Frye, 1964: 79)

Mention the word 'meaning' and this can evoke agreement or contention, scientific or religious authority, timeless or ephemeral understanding, oneness with or distortion of shareable experience, a sense of correctly drawing from common knowledge or from one's idiosyncratic notions – and so on. To hermeneutic scholars meaning has 'meant' all these things and more. From the ancient Greeks onwards, meaning has been central to philosophy, spirituality, education, law, literature and psychology. In everyday life, reflecting on meaning seems unnecessary as long as our meanings work for us. Why, then, is there such a fuss about meaning? Questions and comments like the following can help orient us to the ongoing hermeneutic project of meaning:

When people say meaning depends on context, what are they talking about?
In what ways are sensing, understanding, articulating and explaining an experience related, and different?
What did spiritual leader X actually mean so many centuries ago?
Why and how are cultures A and B, despite different languages and traditions, able to understand, appreciate and cooperate with each other?
Surely there must be a language for describing things as they really are – or is there?

Hermeneutic scholars mostly look upon meaning as diversely practised ways of interpreting and understanding experience. Etymologically, hermeneutics borrows from the name of the ancient Greek god *Hermes* who served as interpreter for the gods. This spiritual tradition associated with the word is important to the project of hermeneutics, and speaks to a broader notion of meaning than is often associated with contemporary cognitive science's focus on 'information'. Indeed, the project of many early hermeneutic scholars was to 'recover' the spirit and intent of words, art and other symbols to the author, speaker or artist at the time they were first written, uttered or created. In the words of Hubert Dreyfus (1991), recent hermeneutic scholars, such as Heidegger, are 'plural realists' for how they 'locate' meaning in time, place and communicative interactions. Collectively and cumulatively, these hermeneutic projects have really stretched our notions of meaning and how experience can be understood and shared. One view of these projects is that they all aimed to help those served by hermeneutics to take on the views and meanings of others. But hermeneutic tensions continue to play out as religious literalists argue over true prescriptive meanings, as judges and legal scholars grapple with how to understand and word laws for later reference, and as speakers attempt to forge understandings and collective actions despite cultural differences.

Seen one way, a hermeneutic approach to practice suggests an interpretive endeavour where shared understandings are arrived at and transformation of meaning occurs. In this respect, Paul Ricoeur (1973) saw psychodynamic approaches to helping as quintessentially hermeneutic. We would not want to imply, however, that a hermeneutic approach to practice necessarily sees a practitioner supplying the understandings and transformative meaning *for* clients. Instead, our selective review of hermeneutic scholarship aims at providing some ways of conceptualizing understanding and meaning transformation as these might relate to professional helping.

In this chapter we will trace the hermeneutic project across centuries, bringing our considerations up to contemporary reflections on meaning and social interactions pertaining to meaning. To do this we will start from early hermeneutic efforts to get the meanings of myths and scripture 'correct', through efforts by Schleiermacher and Dilthey to develop hermeneutics as a human science of meaning, to Heidegger's phenomenological focus on being or ontology, to Gadamer's focus on interpretation as a dialogic activity, and we will end up with hermeneutic tensions brought out in the writings of Ricoeur, Habermas and Levinas. Our aim is to provide an overview of how hermeneutic questions about meaning relate to social practice.

Early hermeneutics

> Understanding has always the particular as its object.   (Wilhelm Dilthey, as cited in Bauman, 1978: 38)

Imagine warming up around a fire, feasting on the woolly mammoth you and your fellow cave-dwellers just brought down while different stories about the hunt and what was learned from it are being told. Then imagine being at another fire over in the next valley a couple of years later, roasting another mammoth, with a different group of cave-dwellers. At this latter fire you recount past successful hunts and relate the story of the earlier hunt. But, as you are doing this, a cousin who had been with you in the first hunt, says, 'No that isn't quite how it happened or what it meant for us.' Fast-forward a few millennia and you are in a heated discussion in Athens about a passage from Homer's *Odyssey* and the practical lessons on life it should be teaching. Finally, jump ahead to the time of the Spanish Inquisition when scholars in Protestant and Catholic universities were trying to establish the intended meanings behind what was written in the Bible. What each of these circumstances points out is a potential problem in sharing meaning. In the first case, one is faced with historical and perhaps perspectival accounts that don't line up. The second case shows speakers grappling with the pedagogical significance of a story, while the third tries to get at authors' meanings in some religious sense. Depending on your view of meaning you might have a question as to what the *real* meaning was in each case. You might also wonder how people holding different meanings or understandings come to relate them in ways that can be shared – or at least do not create holy wars. You might grapple with an even more basic question: should it matter that people mean differently?

Early hermeneutic scholars struggled with these kinds of questions and how they could answer them. How does one decide the meaning of an event, piece of art, utterance or written text? While we might have different interpretations, often what is needed are meanings we can hold in common – as part of our 'common sense'. Arriving at such common meaning can be complicated. One way to get there, of course, is to hand over such decisions to experts or other authority figures. Leaders saying 'X means Y', and that this should be so for others, works fine up to a point. But suppose experts or authorities disagree on the meaning of something central to how we get along? Suppose one wants to speak for what an author 'really meant' in writing a particular poem or piece of prose. An issue comes up here in trying to share a meaning – whether the one intended by an author, or one to be interpreted as authoritative by experts.

The early Greek and Roman hermeneutic scholars took on challenges not unlike those taken up by today's legal scholars. How should meanings that affect us all be decided? They and later hermeneutic scholars turned to particular methods to arrive at 'correct' meaning – a position Gadamer (1988) attacked with vigour in his magnum opus, *Truth and Method*. Methods for meaning could take all kinds of forms: group consensus, justifications by experts that others could judge, even traditions associated with correct story-telling. But somehow they needed to be shared, or at least accepted without contest. By Aristotle's time one finds prescriptions for poetry and rhetoric, suggesting how language use should feature in meaning. One challenge, and a tension throughout hermeneutic scholarship, was to try to replicate meaning for experiences (mimesis). A second is related to doing this in ways that made reference to contemporary meanings and circumstances inescapable. Homer wrote in a different era from that of Aristotle, and this made trying to present Homer's meaning as it was understood in his era a challenge for those reading later. This underscores a hermeneutic realization: meaning is contextualized and historicized, so trying to understand writings or sayings from one era or context, using those of a different context or era, creates problems. One cannot understand publishing in pre-Gutenberg Europe as one would understand publishing today.

Hermeneutic scholarship really took off in Germany in the eighteenth and nineteenth centuries as scholars attempted to make a human science out of meaning – a science quite different from that of the natural sciences. While many contributed to developing this 'science of meaning', it was Schleiermacher and

Dilthey who methodologically moved the hermeneutic project forward. What distinguished their science from the science of Descartes and Newton was their focus on 'spirit', history and culture in their approach to humanizing meaning. For Schleiermacher, the hermeneutic challenge was to interpret meaning in concert with the spirit and mind of an author when she or he was creating a text. This involved identifying with an author's intentions and concerns at the time of writing, and these identifications extended to the cultural circumstances or Zeitgeist at work in inspiring the author. Schleiermacher's *psychological* concern was with misunderstanding, getting an author's meaning wrong. This necessitated finding ways that would bring the hermeneutic scholar close to an author's original meaning-making efforts. So he advocated using the psychological understandings of his day (to fashion a kind of contextualized psychobiography of the author) while considering a text according to the grammatical structures used in articulating it. Try to imagine yourself inhabiting Shakespeare's psyche while examining the grammars used in Romeo and Juliet – to get his meaning – and you have a sense of Schleiermacher's methodological recommendations (that is, put yourself 'into the shoes or actions' of the person you want to understand) to avoid misunderstanding.

Dilthey later turned away from this sort of psychologizing, but where he did extend Schleiermacher's efforts was in considering meaning as reflecting the totality of a context which 'determined' its articulation. Rather than trying to put oneself in an author's shoes or soul, he related texts to the cultural contexts in which they were produced. In Bauman's (1978: 32) words, Dilthey was 'the great codifier of the 19th century hermeneutic', a practitioner of 'technical hermeneutics' (Grondin, 2003) who developed a systematic means of examining historical reasoning and creative processes for their spiritual significance. *Geisteswissenschaften* was the human science Dilthey intended, a means to correctly interpret canonical texts associated with particular eras according to 'laws of cultural being' (like laws of physics) operative in any era. Objects of understanding (texts, art) were, for Dilthey, expressions of *Spirit* (as related to Zeitgeists) that arise in order to creatively keep Spirit alive where past meaning has been insufficient or where strangeness compels new meaning. In other words, meaning comes from the ongoing objectification of Spirit as realized in an author's text when addressing meaningful challenges. Dilthey's science comes with making historically evident how Spirit was at work in authors producing texts. If you are inferring a sense of historic-cultural-spiritual determinism here, this fits with Dilthey's human science, or *Geisteswissenschaften*, his ambitious project which ultimately failed. There is no way, of course, to infer causal laws out of indeterminate historical processes or circumstances.

Tied to Dilthey's project were his efforts to link objects of understanding to a kind of collective mode of articulation and cultural conduct. His method used three 'etiological' (Bauman, 1978) categories: putting oneself in somebody else's place (that is, not shoes), while copying and reliving the circumstances and experience the author had in producing a text. The end result (an ideal for Dilthey) was to render a scientific understanding of the spirit and meaning of an author's text. By twenty-first-century standards this sounds downright flaky, but Dilthey's project highlights an enduring feature associated with hermeneutics: that meanings must be understood – at least in part – as historicized or shaped by the contexts and eras out of which they arose. This is not to suggest that authors' words are *determined* by their time and place, but it does suggest that their meanings are best understood and appreciated as engagements in life particular to a time and place.

The first great phase of hermeneutics came with trying to get more specific about relating meaning to human efforts in creating it in different places and times. To do this, hermeneutic scholars tried to connect with the motivations of authors, in the contexts in which they wrote. What initially seemed at stake were understandings of important texts and stories of their time (examples: the great myths of Greece, the scriptures at the time of the Inquisition). Early hermeneutic scholars aimed to capture both the ideas and animating spirit behind them in the works of important authors. These early hermeneutic scholars, however, abandoned the idea that literal or exactly the same understandings across eras and cultural contexts were possible. Instead, what one needed to do was to bridge chasms of meaning across different eras and contexts. Meanings for experience differ according to the linguistic resources and Zeitgeists of the eras from which people articulated them. To expect to use today's understandings to appreciate or 'get right' yesterday's understandings, and what was behind them spiritually, is a foolhardy prejudice. At a minimum the early hermeneutic scholars were suggesting a dialogue was needed to bridge one's present understandings with those of the past and elsewhere.

Martin Heidegger

> Our being amidst the things with which we concern ourselves most closely in the 'world' … guides the everyday way in which Dasein is interpreted, and covers up ontically Dasein's authentic being.   (Heidegger, 1969: 359)

In our consideration of meaning and hermeneutics, Heidegger's contribution can at first seem an anomaly. A devoted student of Edmund Husserl (see Chapter 3), Heidegger took his mentor's preoccupation with pre-predicative (wordless) experience a huge step forwards and a huge step backwards. Where Husserl sought a transcendental understanding of first-hand experience, Heidegger tried to answer an even more basic question: what makes understanding our ways of being in the world possible? Using Husserl's phenomenological tools and perspective, Heidegger examined the most taken-for-granted aspects of human engagements with social and physical reality. Heidegger's efforts were ontological, as opposed to epistemological. He concerned himself, not with theorizing about understanding, but with looking beyond this to our ways of living life without thought and reflection. Heidegger's approach was phenomenological in the sense that it points to our experience as participatory, even mundane to the point of escaping notice – not the pristine conceptual stuff pursued by most philosophers, including Husserl and Dilthey.

Heidegger is considered one of the twentieth century's most original and influential philosophers, and his *Being and Time* (1969, originally published in 1927) is a timeless classic. It also is one of the most challenging philosophical reads for its very foreign way of regarding experience, and articulating it, as in this zen-koan-like example from page 104:

> The modes of conspicuousness, obtrusiveness and obstinacy all have the function of bringing to the fore the characteristic of occurrentness in what is available.

Still, many important thinkers of the twentieth century – Gadamer, Foucault, Sartre, Derrida, Habermas, to name a few – regard Heidegger as a key influence on their writing. Heidegger was also a very controversial figure for aligning himself with Nazism as it was on the rise in Germany. Perhaps most remarkable about Heidegger's early work was the way he took the universalist project of Husserl's phenomenology to a conclusion that was both ontological and 'relativist'. By considering how people engaged in life in the ways they do, he was forced to confront how they do life differently, yet still successfully, in varied contexts. The most basic realities of participating in life largely go unquestioned – yet people 'do' life so differently across contexts. Most important is their attunement to how life is conducted unproblematically in these contexts, but not through understanding it in some conceptual, theory-testing way. 'Being' for Heidegger is a verb that points to our embeddedness in human activity. We are not born into a world that we theorize before we act within it, we join others already engaged in life. It is only when these engagements become problematic that we need to think about and come up with a language to account for them. Otherwise, our most basic activities occur without needing to break them down into a series of judgements, followed by deliberate actions. One way to regard Heidegger's work is to see context as fundamental to how people understand and act differently.

There is a richness and depth to *Being and Time* that has a bearing on many things we could consider (for example, how our moods are a reflection of our attuned ways of participating in our life contexts; how most coping is successfully mindless, 'authentic being'). To put the importance of his work in some perspective, Amazon lists for sale almost 1,500 books on or by Heidegger. Thus, we have had to be selective, bypassing aspects of Heidegger's work that have inspired volumes of writing, to narrow our focus to his more general contribution to the historical project of hermeneutics, as it informs our larger story here of social constructionism. Heidegger was regarded as a *hermeneutic phenomenologist* for straddling these two very different streams of thinking, and our considerations here will focus largely on his ontological sense of being as it is practised differently across contexts. We will also focus on his view that understanding emerges as a response to breakdowns in being, breakdowns requiring us to use culturally accessible tools or resources (language being one) to address. We hope we will be forgiven for giving an important thinker short shrift, by selectively linking mere portions of his scholarship to the much bigger, historical project of hermeneutics.

Being

> To be or not to be – *that* is the question.   (William Shakespeare, *Hamlet*)

By inquiring into the nature of being – our primordial engagement with life – Heidegger virtually inverted the phenomenological inquiries of his mentor, Husserl. Both, however, made a radical departure from the metaphysical and scientific attempts to explain reality that preceded them. Most philosophers and scientists had attempted a theory of how life works, offering general details to support their theories. With Kant this kind of theorizing reached a pinnacle: we develop cognitive maps for experience and rely on these thereafter to make our way about. This view of understanding, still rampant in today's cognitive theorizing, suggests a kind of conceptual filter for experience based on our maps and theories for experience. Otherwise, how could it be that reality is so differently regarded and engaged with by people of different cultures and eras?

The starting place for both Husserl and Heidegger – experience before it becomes understandable in specific culturally mediated and symbolized ways – was the same. But Husserl saw this as pointing to a oneness or commonality of consciousness humans might share (though he later came to realize they couldn't). The stuff of first-hand experience prompted Husserl's rallying cry: 'to the things themselves', as if one could know 'things' without using language or other cultural symbols to articulate or describe what one 'knows'. Heidegger, using Husserl's methods, explored the issue differently, asking how people create, understand and participate in the life contexts they constitute. How are our most fundamental ways of being possible, he asked? If human contexts are humanly made, humanly understood, and humanly engaged in – and thus serve as our contexts of being – how do we get by in these contexts?

One should get a visceral and participatory sense from Heidegger's phenomenological inquiry as his work takes us into a general level of description about being human that we typically take for granted. His is a philosophy of mundane everydayness. Intellectually, *Being and Time* is a colossal piece of phenomenology for taking readers into seldom-if-ever-considered descriptions of life in its micro- and macro-aspects. His key term *Dasein* focuses specifically on existence or living life at its most basic. Rather than stripping people from their cultural ways of being to posit transcendental experience, as Husserl did, Heidegger examined common elements in what it means to take up these ways of being, things we do successfully without thought or reflection. This isn't a pernicious mindlessness he was writing about: most human activities in life gain their elegance or automaticity through actions attuned to social and physical reality. It is only when this is not the case that we are confronted with a need to understand or act in some new way. Then, 'being' requires accessible (ready-to-hand was Heidegger's phrase) tools or resources appropriate to addressing the challenge, so that life can resume in ways that we do not need to consider unproven or suspect when using them. Heidegger's is a philosophy of human engagement with life, focusing on what we use and do to make that engagement work for us in ways we can successfully take for granted.

While it might seem trite and obvious, 'being' is how history (the 'time' of *Being and Time*) is made in selective ways for individuals and cultures – it informs what people use and do in their engagements with life and what results from those engagements. Heidegger, in his descriptive writing, placed readers in the midst of such engagements – much like joining workers as they work – for how this revealed being as participatory and a feature of acting in shared, responsive ways. Most philosophers aim for a kind of Cartesian detachment, from which they can articulate explanations of human endeavours in language presumably superior to that used by those engaged in such endeavours. Heidegger saw his phenomenological challenge (and Wittgenstein took a similar path in his later career) as basing his descriptions in the everyday practicalities and understandings of people engaging with life and each other. Life is a shared project, one requiring shared ways of being, and disruptions to such shared ways of being create instabilities in personal and social life. Therefore, his notion of 'authenticity', for example, relates more to identifications we draw from and are held to in our historical commitments to a communally shared life than it does to any personal project (Guignon, 2004). Our ontological task in becoming authentic, in Heideggerian terms, involves becoming more committed and attuned to the traditions and affordances accessible within our experience. But such commitments are also consequential, calling upon people either to extend their shared histories, or to reflect upon and address problematic engagements anew with the cultural tools and resources at hand.

Understanding, 'tools' and meaning

> Only if we are capable of dwelling, then can we build.   (Heidegger, 1971b: 160)

Understanding can be seen in two very different ways in Heidegger's writing. For the most part we engage in life without thinking about our engagements because our actions occur in unproblematic ways that don't require reflection. Understanding in this sense is about attunement with our contexts of being, including each other. But a different kind of understanding is required when problems arise in our engagements with life and others. It is then that we need to step back from how we have been engaged, to find tools and resources for addressing what has been problematic. There can be a kind of building (or repairing) the boat at sea feel to all of this, in that we use what is available or improvisable to meet life's challenges. The rest of the time we sail along just fine. But each time we meet a challenge we extend what we understand and use as knowledge. One case in point relates to our understandings of self. It is in novel or problematic interactions with reality that we are called upon to revise our understandings of self and environment. It is in such novel or problematic situations that new possibilities for being can be disclosed to us. These require our use of interpretive and other resources.

The idea of seeing language as a tool or resource for understanding – how we "bething" things, or talk so as to show them (Heidegger, 1971a) – fits well with Heidegger's view that we are engaged in life in ways that require us to be able to act within it resourcefully. It is in this manner that culture affords us different symbolic resources, like language, to help us make sense of problems and novelties, and to find ways to address them. Put another way, language is understandable to us when we find practical uses for it in our engagements with life. Alfred Schutz (1970) (see Chapter 3 above) saw language as helping us move from indicating things in our experience to typifying them. Once we have made use of language, and are able to incorporate it into our activities in ways that support our engagements, then we can typically use language without having to give it much thought. This notion, of not giving much thought to language use, is consistent with Heidegger's depiction of tools as 'ready-to-hand'. Carpenters engaged in building things, for example, reach for what is ready-to-hand in ways that also don't require much thought – that is, unless they need a tool that is not ready-to-hand to tackle some difficult job. Fortunately, the history behind our participation in life contexts has usually helped to create language that we need to bring to bear in facing problems and novel experiences. Seen educationally, language acquisition is a matter of having new words and concepts accessible to meet the challenges of our engagements with developing facets of life.

Where Piaget spoke of increasingly differentiating our understanding of life over time, Heidegger sees this as occurring according to what our engagements with life necessitate and make possible. Should we continue to live within ways of living that are unproblematically familiar, there will be no need to expand our vocabularies or linguistic tools (see also Elias, Chapter 11). But, problems in using the tools we have already acquired point to what Heidegger refers to as disclosures of possibility that require new tools (cf. Spinosa, Flores and Dreyfus, 1997). Once we have found such linguistic tools to help us face these disclosures of possibility we have expanded our understandings, competencies and ways of being. Doing this optimally enables us to attune to such life contexts and engagements. But problems can develop when we fall out of tune with a context of 'being'. In this respect, Heidegger gets psychological, suggesting that anxiety and other distressing moods reflect problematic engagements with life, engagements which we have failed to address with appropriate tools and actions.

Thus, meaning and understanding can be regarded in two primary ways when reading Heidegger: first, as shown by the linguistic and other interpretive tools we successfully bring to engaging life; and second, when new resources are called for when past interpretive efforts come up short for us. In the case of the former, people acquire, through addressing experiences with new possibilities, capacities to expand and deploy their stock of cultural-linguistic resources to address and inform their everyday familiar ways of being. We see this in the seeming ease and spontaneity of people using a range of words in effortless conversation. Where our words do not work, though, we are called upon to access new ones, or use the old ones in new ways. None of this occurs in a detached way, but as immediate responses to being engaged in life. And, as resources or tools, the language used need only get the job done – it need not be done in some universally correct manner. This is not to say that our engagements in life do not call for familiar uses of language or specific words, but to stick with the tool analogy, sometimes a screwdriver can be used as a pry-bar, should it get the job done. In short, meaning or understanding, for Heidegger, occur in ways that either are or are not an issue in our ways of being. Fortunately, the cultural worlds of possibility we participate in have already visited some of the inevitable life challenges that face us, and developed the linguistic and other tools we could find useful. But, somewhat like later Wittgenstein, Heidegger saw understanding as a problem requiring apt words that, once used in familiar ways, can serve us in going on where we might otherwise face problems and novelties. In this respect, Heidegger later saw the poetic use of language as something that distinguishes humans in how they address life problems: 'For man is man only because he is granted the promise of language, because he is needful to language, that he may speak it' (1971a: 90).

Later in Heidegger's career (1971a) he came to see language as a 'house of being', and that we dwelt in language for our social interactions. But it is important to note that there is a difference between understanding which usefully guides our engagements with the totality of our experience, and explanation which enables us to make a partial linguistic account of that totality. Said differently, an explanation of an experience falls short of the fullness of understanding what it means to be in that experience. As this relates to self-understanding (versus self-explaining), the self is seen as usually unreflectively taking part in experience, rather than moving about in it in self-conscious ways. This kind of attunement involves a one-ness with experience without a subject (i.e., self) / object (other person, thing, context, etc.) duality. Others have referred to this as a 'style' adopted in relating to experience and others (Spinosa et al., 1997). This may also convey an almost spiritual and ecological sense of one-ness which some have equated with Heidegger's notion of being (e.g. Zimmerman, 1993). But it also underscores the point we have been making all along, that disruptions to that one-ness necessitate more conscious, tool-using efforts to bring back a sense of attunement.

Heidegger in hermeneutic context

This tour through Heidegger has been deliberately brief and has focused almost entirely on how meaning and understanding relate to his notion of being. Heidegger, like Wittgenstein, merits volumes of attention for his rich and almost counter-intuitive contributions to the hermeneutic project. A key feature in Heidegger's consideration of being is how being is practised and understood differently in different contexts. In this sense, the ontological sense of being engaged non-reflectively in a context works fine until we are confronted with other ways of being as practised and understood in other contexts. It is in this regard that Heidegger and Gadamer speak of 'horizons of understanding'. The world to a person embedded within one context has a horizon that precludes other ways of understanding. People engaged in particular cultural spaces, with no contact with culturally different others, do not have to question their understandings and actions – they do what being calls from them, using the common sense they share with others. But, cross-cultural encounters have ways of pointing out how one contextual way of being and understanding may not be shared, and how trying to understand and act as if one did can create problems for coexisting and understanding with those from other contexts and (thus) different ways of being.

Let's back up to an important point about understanding and being: when we are attuned with our contexts we do this unreflectively – we do not have to think about how or if our language, thoughts or actions work for us. But, cross-cultural experience creates problems in this regard as this joke points out:

> A man in a foreign country approaches a rickshaw driver and asks, 'Excuse me, can you tell me where I can find a good restaurant?'
>
> The rickshaw driver, not knowing what was said, shrugs his shoulders to indicate he has not understood.
>
> The man then says: 'EXCUSE ME, CAN YOU TELL ME WHERE I CAN FIND A GOOD RESTAURANT!!'

The problem of understanding posed by the cross-cultural experience is one of not amplifying one's horizon of understanding, or the culture-specific ways of being associated with it, as the man in the joke above. Heidegger himself can be quite difficult to understand. His prose is near-impenetrable for the uninitiated, so those seeking a more accessible exposure are advised to consult Dreyfus' (1991) review of Division 1 of *Being and Time*, or check the many compendia about Heidegger, such as Guignon's (1993) edited volume. Heidegger's notion of horizons of understanding can, if one is not open to difference, operate as pre-understandings, the cultural or social equivalent to what some might call a closed mind. Heidegger did not spend much time thinking outside the horizons of his cultural box, so to speak, yet he does take us into familiarities of our lives that escape our notice because our ways of being are so seamlessly interwoven with them. What matters to Heidegger is that we delve deeper into them, further into what the history of our being can offer to acquire a rich language and other tools to enable us to live more deliberately and resourcefully. His calls to go historically and culturally deeper into Germanic ways of being sat well with Nazi cultural imperialism in the decade after *Being and Time* was published. Unsurprisingly, then, the notion of different horizons of understanding comes to figure hugely as an ethical issue in Gadamer's (1988) later and more dialogic form of hermeneutics. Levinas (e.g., 1998), in an even stronger direct response to Heidegger, was famously known for his maxim that relationships must come before ontology.

Hans-Georg Gadamer

> If we want to do justice to man's finite, historical mode of being, it is necessary to fundamentally rehabilitate the concept of prejudice and acknowledge the fact that there are legitimate prejudices.   (Gadamer, 1988: 277)

> Reality does not happen 'behind the back of language'; it happens rather behind the backs of those who live in the opinion that they have understood 'the world' (or can no longer understand it); that is, reality happens precisely within language.   (Gadamer, 1976: 35)

> Reaching an understanding in conversation presupposes that both parties are ready for it and are trying to recognize the full value of what is alien and opposed to them.   (Gadamer, 1988: 387

In some ways the history of the hermeneutic project can be seen as a continuing dialogue between thinkers of different eras and contexts. Each phase in its development responded to whatever seemed inadequate or objectionable with the previous phase or developer's ideas. Heidegger had taken hermeneutics in a direction quite different from where Dilthey had been heading, bringing into his considerations the phenomenological ideas and approach of Husserl. But where that brought him to was a view of meaning and social life profoundly different from the universalist aims of Husserl and much of modern psychology. Heidegger instead saw being as deeply contextualized in the life we successfully engage in without reflection. It is an insight that becomes obvious when one travels in foreign cultures, only to distressingly find that the most basic of our actions and understandings often do not work there. However, Heidegger's analyses can also lead to a sense that his hermeneutic circle (that one understands new experience by making reference to what is within one's contextual horizons) is ultimately a vicious circle. If Heidegger's hermeneutic and ontological challenge was for us to reflect deeper on our history and the contemporary social practices arising from it, he seemed to skip over the implications that follow when people interact from different life contexts, or backgrounds. Twentieth-century Germany not only strongly identified with its history, Nazis in particular saw in that history the grounds for their cultural superiority and a rationale for dominating the rest of the world. Thus, while Heidegger moved hermeneutics forward by phenomenologically examining peoples' engagements with life at its most basic, he also furnished a view of being ill-equipped to help people face the world's cultural diversity.

Gadamer was Heidegger's student around the time Heidegger was preparing *Being and Time* and only recently died in 2002 at the age of 102. Unlike Heidegger, he managed to sidestep overt affiliations with the Nazis and may even have seen his career suffer for this in its early stages (Grondin, 2003). A lifelong scholar, Gadamer brought a different perspective to considering the implications of Heidegger's ontologizing; he grew interested in what happened in dialogues between people from different backgrounds. He also advocated a more humble, yet more encompassing, sense of the importance of language to people's horizons of understanding and communicating. Late into his life he was game for some generative academic sparring with contemporaries such as Jurgen Habermas and Jacques Derrida. Ultimately, his ideas have been hugely influential on the development of a dialogical perspective on human interaction and social practice, particularly as this relates to developing shared meanings and overcoming differences in meaning. His was an ethical view that offers useful conceptual resources for responding to the increased cross-cultural interactions of today's media-linked, jet-setting world.

We will look at several aspects of Gadamer's philosophical hermeneutics, a term which he and others associate with the nature of human understanding. Much of our selective attention will focus on his classic book, *Truth and Method*, and his view that a requirement of understanding is for people to acknowledge and relax their prejudices so as to make room for the prejudices and views of others. This view follows from his notion that we understand and try to communicate from 'effective histories', histories that make evident some understandings while precluding others. Gadamer also had a lot to say about language and art as necessarily incomplete mediums for conveying inescapably prejudiced understanding. This, along with his concerns about our histories and prejudices, leads to his focus on dialogic interactions and a view that meaning arises *between* speakers from different backgrounds. While Gadamer did not write many books, his list of publications spans some 300 pages (Grondin, 2003) and there are many books written about Gadamer, or informed by him.

Rehabilitating prejudices

> Our question ... is how hermeneutics, once freed from the ontological obstructions of the scientific concept of objectivity, can do justice to the historicity of understanding.   (Gadamer, 1988: 265)

Prejudice is a word that can evoke strong reactions. Most of us do not want to be seen as prejudiced, yet Gadamer wrote that we must accept our prejudices in order to be able to move beyond them in our interactions with others who have different prejudices. This is the part of his philosophical hermeneutics which is most indebted to Heidegger. For Heidegger, understanding occurred in largely taken-for-granted ways that reflected our history and current participation in culturally shared ways of being, and is where his idea of 'horizons of understanding' comes from. It is also a direct challenge to the modern scientific notion that one could develop understandings that were universal and untainted by our subjectivities or cultural experience – the path Husserl unsuccessfully went down with his phenomenology. Horizons of understanding are bound up in our history and ways of being in such a way that they can offer no such panoramic or transcendental view. At best, our understandings are constrained to what our horizon of understanding makes evident – to what our histories enable us to understand. This view makes sense when different cultures and the people of them can afford to understand and act as if theirs is the only way of being. But, history shows this has never been the case, and in fact wars have resulted as cultures, religions and even academics tried to foist their realities on others. The colonial experience, slavery and totalitarian states are all products of some people dominating others to exploit or eliminate such differences. The word 'prejudice' comes culturally and historically freighted, evoking such painful experiences. Yet, Gadamer tried rehabilitating the word.

Heidegger's ontological view (remember: epistemologies refer to ways we claim to know what we know, while ontology refers to the default understanding of reality we live by) suggested that our most basic ways of being are grounded in understandings and actions we generally do not reflect upon. Thus, we are culturally blind to what is inside our horizons of understanding and action (cf. Vico, Chapter 1). Prejudice, in this sense, is inescapable when one engages with people of other backgrounds – regardless of intention, we find ourselves bringing our horizons, and their corresponding understandings and actions, with us to these encounters. This is why it often takes interacting with others in a foreign context to point out and challenge assumptions, attitudes and actions we would otherwise take for granted. We (Tom and Andy) run into this when visiting each other's countries, chuckling about why cars are driven on the 'wrong' side of the road. But things have not been so funny when one cultural group or speaker holds another to their ways of being, their horizons of understanding. This is where problems arise, as Gadamer wrote:

> The hermeneutical problem only emerges clearly when there is no powerful tradition to absorb one's own attitude into itself and when one is aware of confronting an alien tradition to which he has never belonged or one he no longer unquestioningly accepts.   (Gadamer, 1976: 46)

There is a lot to unpack here, so let us begin with the frequently used hermeneutical term 'tradition'. For Gadamer, this word highlights what he refers to as 'effective history'. This could be contrasted with an ahistorical view of being which suggests that our ways of understanding and acting owe nothing to the past. Gadamer was not so much saying that history determines what we say, do or understand; for him tradition shapes and provides the context for making sense of any understanding or action. Traditions are what individuals *extend* through their interactions with others. Participating in a tradition means understanding and doing things in ways consistent with it, but not merely rehashing what has come before. Attitudes also come along with our traditional ways of being and feature in how we carry forward those ways into our interactions with those from other traditions. Thus, traditions do not refer to conceptual understandings alone; they are qualitatively different ways of being as well. When traditions are merely extended our attitudes are carried forward and remain intact, and serve us in making sense of experiences. Even when one is confronted with experiences that are inconsistent with a tradition, the first impulse is typically to understand according to the accustomed terms and affective qualities one brings to such a new experience. From a narrative perspective, this is like fitting new developments into already storied understandings, making anomalies fit prior plotlines, something we will spend more time with when we turn to Paul Ricoeur. Returning to our quote above, however, Gadamer indicated that problems emerge when we lack a tradition that can help us do this. Elsewhere, such problems have been referred to as 'incommensurabilities' (Bernstein, 1983), or 'differends' (Lyotard, 1988), to denote what in effect are parallel and incompatible realities. Interactions with 'alien traditions' sometimes force us to confront differences we cannot understand or agree with. It is the last part of the quote above, however, that speaks to how new understandings come out of encounters with unfamiliarities.

There is a kind of innocence people can develop when they are exclusively attuned to a particular cultural reality, as if it was the only way of being. But encounters with people of different cultures disrupt that, highlighting how the experience they have been able to take for granted no longer can be taken for granted because others, in effect, point this out to us with their different ways of being. Melvin Pollner (1975) has gone so far as to write of such differences of experience as creating 'reality disjunctures'. It is what happens in and after these encounters between people of different cultures that concerns Gadamer, for this is where our prejudices are jarred into 'instabilities' that can seemingly require 'conversion experiences' or grounds for mourning (Spinosa et al., 1997). Psychologists might see this as a form of Festinger's (1957) 'cognitive dissonance' but that would miss the participatory and hermeneutic view of people *engaged* in different ways of being consistent with their different horizons of understanding and being. The point here is that more than conceptual understanding is involved – encounters between different parties cause not only disruptions of understanding but also problems in relatedness. This points to where our later considerations of ethics need to become a focus.

For now, however, it is more useful to think of people embedded in two foreign horizons of understanding and acting coming into contact – for what arises from that contact? To think of the people inside these horizons practising 'prejudice' is a different way of understanding the word from how it is used in everyday discourse. Gadamer is talking about how people often unwittingly act from contextualized meanings ('fore-meanings' he called them) and actions they are unaware of – and how these can remain as blind prejudices until contact with others points them out in ways we can change. Insisting that there is one objectively knowable horizon (read: our own) is a recipe for conversational disaster, and it overlooks the fundamental point we and Gadamer borrowed from Heidegger: that we are human in differently contextualized ways and this presents challenges when we interact with others not sharing our horizons. Gadamer-scholar Georgia Warnke (1987: 158) makes a nice point for summarizing what we have been saying so far: 'One learns that one's own historical horizon is part of an endlessly articulated and shifting universe of horizons and that to try to fix this universe in a final, immutable form or hierarchy is to miss the point.'

Language

> Language is the fundamental mode of operation of our being-in-the-world
> and the all-embracing form of the constitution of the world.   (Gadamer,
> 1976: 3)

Heidegger (1971a) related to words as tools and to language as something we
'dwell' in. Somewhat similarly, Gadamer regarded language as the medium
through which we understand experience, and are able to communicate our
understandings of experience to others. But Gadamer's concern was that, even
though language is how we understand reality, it is also necessarily partial and
that forgetting this creates problems. In his words,

> Experience has a definite immediacy which eludes every opinion about its
> meaning. Everything that is experienced is experienced by oneself, and part
> of its meaning is that it belongs to the unity of this self and thus contains an
> unmistakable and irreplaceable relation to the whole of this one life. Thus,
> essential to an experience is that it cannot be exhausted in what can be said
> of it or grasped as its meaning.   (1988: 67)

You might read a sense from this passage that Gadamer also sees the language we
use as having an integrity particular to the histories or contexts from which we
gain our meanings. At the same time, however, he is not equating such integrity
with a sense that the meanings capture things in total for an experience. Thus,
one person's account of experience need not be another's. But this also points out
where problems can arise.

Stepping back a bit, Gadamer sees a need for finding the 'right' word, and it
is in this sense that he shares Heidegger's later fascination with language as a
poetic resource. Indeed, Heidegger's 1936 lectures on 'The origin of the work
of art' (in Heidegger, 1971b) were an important influence. For Heidegger, art
and poetry were the means by which new realms of meaning or possibilities
(disclosive spaces) are opened up, and the spirit of new meaning is brought to
light – artists and poets help us to see and feel what we could not before their
art was created. Thus, when it comes to meaning, not just any old word will
do: what is needed is a 'word that really belongs to the thing – so that in it the
thing comes into language' (Gadamer, 1988: 417). It is in this sense that articulating experience in words or art takes on a spiritual dimension (a dimension
that hermeneutic scholars had plumbed since antiquity). For Gadamer, putting
language to new experiences is far from a benign task of creating information: it is a way for people to signify how they relate to experiences and objects
in meaningful, shareable ways. Diane Ackerman (1999: 4) wrote something
similar: 'Language is a play with words until they can impersonate physical
objects and abstract ideas.' It is this ability for our use of language to impersonate and animate reality, and for us to be unaware or forgetful of that, that
interested Gadamer. Language, staying with Heidegger, is our tool for such
acts of impersonation and when it works well it is no stand-in for reality; it is
the reality we understand. This poses a combination of existential challenges

for humans. We want a solidly grounded descriptive language to use in making our way about. But we also need a language we unproblematically share with others, particularly when getting about involves them. And, because circumstances change, we need a language that we can revise without losing our sense of being grounded. Things do not name themselves; humans name them in ways that make them things, and it can be a little vertigo-inducing to disrupt or call into question the word–reality hook-up that language makes possible. This is where traditions and relationships play such an important part in Gadamer's writing. Using language in familiarly shared ways socially grounds our understandings, warding off anarchy while mapping 'our' experiences in socially reliable ways (Steiner, 1975). The hubris, or mistake, that concerns Gadamer comes with thinking our language is correct, when others use language – successfully for them – differently.

When writing this chapter, Tom was taking beginner's Spanish classes in anticipation of a month-long trip to Cuba, where most of the conversation would be in Spanish. In Heidegger's sense he was about to dwell in a different house of language, but one where he felt ill-equipped to take part. Knowing some words, like 'el bano' (the bathroom) would presumably make huge differences in everyday life. Each new word seemed to open new social possibilities, while also making the Spanish 'house' more 'dwellable', or shareable. The words and grammatical phrases learned would, it was hoped, produce results similar to their English equivalents. In going to Cuba, Tom would be joining conversations rooted in traditions different from his, traditions that would be manifest in particular words and ways of saying them. Thus, learning Spanish was a case of learning not only what things mean in Spanish (i.e., a translation of their meaning from English), but in picking up nuances and aspects of meaning for Cubans that no dictionary could foretell. What would be real in their conversations was not yet Tom's reality.

While hermeneutic scholars see history as 'sedimenting' particular understandings through repeated use, Gadamer also felt language needed to be fluid and evolving. Thus, understanding language involves more than authoritatively taking up a culture's words and concepts from a dictionary to guide one's communications. The very notion that words can pre-map evolving circumstances, make them knowable in advance, troubled Gadamer. He instead saw new developments as meaningful 'events in a tradition', events which created a tension between articulations of the past being brought to bear on the present. This focus on 'events' relates to notions of how meaning is performed in ways that go beyond what was already known or articulated. As Gadamer (1988: 356) put it, 'every experience worthy of the name thwarts an expectation', and so we cannot expect our prior meanings necessarily to suffice, as new experiences call for apt and still-shareable language. It was this view of language, and recognizing the cultural myopia that can come from sticking to one's own tradition when trying to interact with those of other traditions, that brought Gadamer to his dialogical and ethical views.

Dialogue: understanding as collaboratively articulating the 'in-between'

> the fusion of horizons that takes place in understanding is actually the
> achievement of language.   (Gadamer, 1988: 378)

Gadamer recognized from early hermeneutic scholars that attempting to understand the historical meanings of authors involved a kind of dialogue with readers. Readers had to recognize that authors often wrote during different historico-cultural contexts, so trying to understand the author's meaning required more than translating their words from their own historico-cultural situatedness. An author's personal and culturally shared history, along with vocabularies nuanced and particularized to such histories, are what authors bring to, and bring out in, their writing. Someone reading the newspaper about Marconi's first radio transmission would not be able to understand blogs about global warming on today's internet. The same applies, but in a different way, when we reverse direction. Today's bloggers have little sense of the eventfulness of that first radio transmission, despite their blogging owing something to that event. The point we are building to had been reasonably established by eighteenth- and nineteenth-century hermeneutic scholars, but with Gadamer it takes on even greater significance, particularly in looking at dialogue.

For Gadamer, dialogue was how such differences in the situatedness of people's understandings could be worked out. Heidegger's prescription for turning inward and embracing cultural traditions (Gadamer's 'prejudices') could translate to intolerance or worse as the Nazi experience had shown. From Aristotle onwards, systematic differences in understanding had been talked about in terms of architectonics. By analogy, one could consider meaning in the way geologists refer to the world's tectonic plates which move about, causing earthquakes, mountain ranges or large rifts between plates. Staying with the analogy, if I bring my history to our dialogue and you bring yours, at best we can bump up against each other's meanings and experience conflict, dominance or alienation. 'Fusing horizons', the core phrase Gadamer associated with arriving at a shared understanding, sounds confusing if one stays with an architectonic view. Missing in such a view of differences in meaning is how such differences can be interpolated between people in ways they can work out. They find ways to succeed with this more often than they let their differences in understanding lead to fighting or staying distant from each other. Gadamer explored where language fits into understanding, as when people try to understand each other from different interpretive backgrounds.

At its most basic, Gadamer saw understanding as agreement (Grondin, 2003), a perspective he shared with the later Wittgenstein (1953). But such agreements necessitate ways of communicating that can take people beyond, or outside, the familiarities of their interpretive histories. This is not just a matter of agreeing to disagree, it also involves being open to being changed through communicating with others who have different ideas and values from those we bring to such communications. To do this requires different conversations or meaningful exchanges from those which ground us in the conversations in which we feel most 'at home'. We take part in many such conversations, and our horizons shift to accommodate understandings and ways of being different from ours, ways that we come to accept. But, it is in conversations where differences are alien or as-yet unaccepted (perhaps morally so) that our ways of understanding and conversing are most challenged. Good conversations change us, as Gadamer wrote:

> To reach an understanding in a dialogue is not merely a matter of putting oneself forward and successfully asserting one's point of view, but being transformed into a communion in which we do not remain what we were.   (1988: 378)

However, such conversations also require that we enter into them in ways that have us open to recognize the value in what we are being told, and that such openness be the place and means by which we transcend our former understandings. At a minimum, our horizons can expand to include different ways of understanding and valuing experience. At other times we might be swayed by others, or develop some hybrid understanding or appreciation that results from the exchange.

Gadamer saw the spirit of how dialogue occurred as important and he sometimes wrote that dialogue needed a spirit of 'play'. If no person can claim total meaning, and if we relax our commitments to prior developed meanings we use in attempting to understand and interact with a person or experience, then new possibilities can emerge. Quoting Gadamer again, 'play fulfils its purpose only if the player loses himself in play' (1988: 102). Play can permit things to happen 'in-between' people as their game (or their relationship in playing it), not the positions of the individuals involved, takes precedence. It is often in this spirit that artists collaborate, or that people attempt conversations in ways that dispense with prior, unsuccessful ways of communicating. It is in 'play' that speakers can 'occasion' unanticipated meanings as products of their interplay. This can happen in such activities as 'brainstorming' or 'think tanks' where different rules for communicating apply. To play in this sense, however, also involves seeing words as tools for collaboration and creativity, for 'achievements in language', as in the quote beginning this section. Like anything, dialogue can be fetishized in ways that can create a seeming panacea. Sometimes we do not want to agree with another's point of view, or engage openly with others we feel might harm us. But Gadamer's ethical challenge comes with how we engage differences in communication, how we open ourselves to possibilities for new meaning and personal change through dialogue.

Ethics and rationality

> Understanding becomes a special task only when natural life, this joint meaning of the meant where both intend a common *subject matter*, is disturbed.   (Gadamer, 1988: 180; italics in the original)

Central to Gadamer's hermeneutics is an idea that is both simple and complicated: new meaning is possible if we are open to being changed by interactions with others whose meanings are unfamiliar, or even challenging, to us. Ethics is what makes benefiting from the 'in-between' of unfamiliar (perhaps unwanted) dialogues possible, in relationships of reciprocal influence. For Heidegger, what creates our sense of attunement and oneness, culturally and relationally, are the familiarities we unproblematically share with others. Gadamer's ethics point to where this way of being can come up short for us. It is in our interactions with others who *don't* share our views and familiarities that we are jarred out of the understandings and ways of being we take for granted. These interactions afford opportunities aplenty for conflict, disengagement or efforts at domination. But they also offer opportunities to recognize and transcend the situatedness of our understandings and ways of being in encounters with differently situated others (Kogler, 1996). Gadamer's ethics – his 'true locus of hermeneutics' (1988: 295) – comes with how we engage others in the 'in-between' of such dialogic encounters.

Gadamer offers no method here, a point emphasized in the title of *Truth and Method* and repeated throughout the book. People have to be willing to suspend their methods (or ways of being) and prior knowledge to enter into and profit from meaningful dialogues. Fusing horizons is a dialogic process calling upon speakers to make conceptual and emotional room for, to be able to agree with, the validity of the understandings and actions of others. It means learning to live with the tensions involved in accepting and working through cultural and relational differences. Gadamer borrowed Aristotle's notion of phronesis (practical wisdom) to highlight the pragmatics needed for a view of rationality that goes beyond merely extending what is already known. Gadamer was a believer that dialogue, our openness to be transformed by our interactions with others, was our way of moving forward together with others in ways that would expand our knowledge. This is a view later taken up differently by Jurgen Habermas (1985), for whom the furthering of civilization depends on discourse ethics that enable rationality to develop optimally. Emmanuel Levinas (e.g., 1998) forgoes dialogue in the sense Gadamer intended (that is, reciprocal relatedness) for an ethical position of placing others and any knowledge claims before our personal interests. Gadamer's dialogic ethics were summed up as follows by his biographer, Jean Grondin (2003: 329):

> If the basic insight of hermeneutics is that the other may well be right, that our will to dominion must come to a halt before the other, then perhaps the destructive tendencies of the Industrial Revolution might be held in check.

Gadamer's hermeneutic horizon

Gadamer's hermeneutics took Heidegger's phenomenological hermeneutics, and the historically focused hermeneutics of Dilthey and Schleiermacher, in a direction useful for making sense of contemporary experiences of cultural diversity and media-facilitated cross-cultural experiences. For Gadamer, understanding involved participating in a tradition, a shared way of being and understanding that occurred in the languages of our conversations with others. In this sense, his hermeneutics focuses both on our embedded interactions with others and on the possibilities of transcending that embeddedness through conversations that could yield new traditions – in new languages and shared ways of being. Some have turned to the linguistic ideas of Gadamer and other philosophers (such as Foucault, Wittgenstein) to make the pragmatic claim that change is enabled by the vocabularies we use for articulating our circumstances and preferences (Rorty, 1979). For others (Bouma-Prediger, 1989; Martin and Sugarman, 1999) this focus overlooks a feature of hermeneutics that is key: the historicized and culturally grounded ways of being people bring to encounters where change might be needed. Change is not as simple as wordsmithing our way through (or linguistically flitting about) difficulties, because any new articulations are not ours alone. Nor can such articulations simply replace the tradition-anchored language and ways of being in which we are already interactionally embedded. A focus on language's role in understanding alone, in other words, overlooks the participatory (relationally responsive) and historically grounded nature of our shared use of language. Gadamer's view is that such changes involve changes in our relatedness, and in who we are as a result of those changes in relatedness as well. Thus, Gadamer saw dialogue as much more than a conceptual transmission and reception of information. People's emotions, spirits, and sense of relatedness are also involved. New meanings, to be viable, must take root in our ground of being.

Gadamer's fusion of horizons as a means to new understanding can sound quite imprecise, if not mystical. His interests are with the kinds of interactions between people that make such changes or fusions in meaning possible. He offers no prescriptions save for comments that we should enter into meaningful dialogues with a willingness to be moved by, and open to, ideas, values and ways of being foreign to ours. But, as hermeneutically inspired philosopher Charles Taylor (1989) has pointed out, we bring different 'moral topographies', different ways of understanding ourselves and others to such encounters – so much can seem at stake. As peace talks, difficult negotiations and immigration discussions in the national media demonstrate, constructive and forward-moving dialogue is very challenging. So, too, are efforts to resolve conflicts closer to our home and work. The interpretive work of fusing horizons involves more than passively receiving others' meanings and their implications; it requires reconciling different traditions and people's embeddedness in life contexts. Gadamer's message about meaning, dialogue and relational change is thus an open-ended challenge to be open and flexible in our interactions with 'others', if we are to find ways to co-exist and expand our understandings and ways of being.

Paul Ricoeur

> Hermeneutics is concerned with the permanent spirit of language … not as some decorative excess or effusion of subjectivity, but as the creative capacity of language to open up new worlds.   (In Kearney, 2004: 85)

Paul Ricoeur's hermeneutics takes up now-familiar themes (language, historicism, poetics, ethics), but his is a creative hermeneutics involving 'detours of meaning' (Kearney, 2004). Language and symbols are the means by which people interpretively refract prior understandings, possibly changed many times over by use since their origins, into creatively derived meanings brought to present circumstances as they interact with history and each other. The kind of ontological determinism one might associate with Heidegger's notion of 'being' oversimplified, for Ricoeur, the diverse understandings people encounter and have to derive sense from in life. For him, meaning is detoured through different symbolic and linguistic resources afforded us by history and culture. Language is a creative and resource-rich medium people can use to metaphorically and narratively synthesize experience and imagination into new meanings. Thus, Ricoeur saw in language poetic possibilities for creative transformation. Horizons of understanding have a decidedly more subjective, less culturally structured (than Heidegger or Gadamer) focus in his prodigious writing, which continued right up to his recent death in 2005.

Ricoeur's hermeneutics developed partly out of a view that human life requires reconciling dialectical tensions by reflectively and creatively using language. With Heidegger and Gadamer he saw words and symbols as inescapably partial takes on experiences that fit into historicized horizons of understanding. But, consistent with how Ricoeur wrote, he saw efforts to convey meaning as involving a subjective process of drawing from varied 'at-hand' linguistic resources to respond to any circumstance. This is a more poetic view of meaning than Heidegger's, which seemed almost structurally determined by history and cultural circumstance. In this sense Ricoeur is considered a post-structuralist hermeneutic scholar. His post-structuralist hermeneutics were partly derived from his early critical ('hermeneutics of suspicion') examination of Marxist and Freudian ideas as systems of understanding concerned with correcting 'false consciousness'. If such systems could be adapted to explain all facets of life, and yet still conflict in their explanations, where does that leave one when trying to understand facets of life using prior systems of structures of understanding? A post-structuralist upshot from Ricoeur's hermeneutics of suspicion comes with recognizing that critique can have no ontological foundation from which it can be undertaken. When one critiques one system of thought from a different system of thought (for example, Marxists criticizing capitalists, or vice versa), the implication is that all systems of thought can be critiqued as such. Marxism or capitalism could be seen as ways of explaining and critiquing other systems since, to the Marxist or capitalist, theirs is the foundational or correct system of thought. Ricoeur saw systems of thought as always partial and potentially combinable in synthetic ways to produce new understandings. His hermeneutics were based on 'suspicion' (doubts about any understanding as complete) and 'affirmation' (about still needing to have adequate understandings even if they could never be complete).

Ricoeur saw hermeneutics as a process of trying to understand through the detours taken by earlier thinkers who tried to understand any phenomenon. This particularly comes out when reading Ricoeur's erudite efforts to explicate a topic ('in its symbolic fullness', Kearney, 2004: 46) by showing the many 'detours' he takes, using understandings from literature, contemporary social science and so on. The detours can be seen as necessary to Ricoeur's comprehensiveness. In this way, he brings out past efforts to address a topic, pointing out their inadequacies and their merits, and where others later took these efforts, while moving on exhaustively to other inquiries and their results that might help shed light on a given topic. Our job as readers is to join Ricoeur in making sense of these varied inquiries and understandings – and the tensions between them – to pull together our own understanding. In some ways his detours are not just into partial understandings offered by prior authors but also refer to how such understandings elicit new responses from them. People in conversation can often have their words elicit such detours from a conversational partner who hears something that evokes a quite unanticipatable response from them. In this sense, Ricoeur's detours are not just through ideas that stray from a conventional linear narrative: they are also related to where such ideas detoured or took him in his own thinking as he attempted to fashion his own understandings of a concern. For Ricoeur, coherence of meaning is something each of us addresses as a subjective and poetic challenge – we narrate satisfying or adequate understandings using a variety of linguistic resources refracted through the historically derived meanings of others. He offers no final criterion or method for doing this. Meaning, put differently, involves pulling together others' ideas, along with ideas sparked by the thinking of others, into understandings one can affirm and feel confident in acting on.

Ricoeur's central focus, throughout his career, related to Aristotelian, big-picture questions, such as 'Who am I?' and 'How should I live?' Given that such questions have been answered in diverse ways, his efforts were less focused on deriving an authoritative answer, than in making evident these diverse ways and their subsequent historical emanations for how they could be brought to bear on any topic. Language and ideas, therefore, are resources for reflecting upon and attempting to answer such questions in subjectively and culturally satisfying ways. Ricoeur put legs on language, so to speak, borrowing from speech act theory and the later Wittgenstein to explore the reflexive and creative aspects of language use. His 1973 essay, 'The model of the text: Meaningful action considered as text', was influential in showing language use as potentially transformative – a theme he would devote much of his later career to examining. But Ricoeur was also clear that narrating answers to his broad questions was not an ahistorical exercise in deriving abstract knowledge. Our poetic challenge involves mediating understandings in using rival conceptual resources from the past to meet requirements of our present and future circumstances.

A hermeneutics of imagination also features in Ricoeur's writing, with poetics central to imagining and feeling inspired by experience anew. He saw language as an inherently creative resource and means for transcending former understandings with new 'plots' as well as 'texts'. Narratives (Ricoeur, 1984, vols. 1 and 2, 1985) are our means of articulating meaning in relation to our experiences of time. In this sense, we do more than describe; we narrate, articulating our experiences in particular ways that convey a sense of their meaning beyond simple information – using 'as-if' qualities we linguistically bestow upon them. Tied up with such narrating is how any narrative 'hangs together', its plot and where that plot seems poised to take us. But, consistent with his view that meaning is about detours and encounters with opportunities for new meaning, Ricoeur sees narration as the means by which we bring our available linguistic resources to imagining, then acting on, our narratives in ways open to new possibilities. This extends to our self-narratives (Ricoeur, 1992), which are fashioned with the linguistic resources of others, and in encounters with them that shape our understandings of self. Said differently, we understand ourselves through and in response to their words and ideas about us. This brings up numerous ethical concerns.

Ricoeur's ethics come out of a recognition that our poetic and narrative projects are shot through and through with sociality. The conversations and interactions from which we acquire our linguistic resources are social, and it will be in later versions of these conversations that our use of such resources will play out relationally (and politically). While our efforts to create meaning are subjective, their implications are social and thus factored into our imagining and narrating. We thus have responsibilities in how we make use of narrative resources to narrate the past in the present, while being faithful to narrated experiences of the past, as in the example of the Holocaust (Ricoeur, 1996). Ricoeur's ethics, in other words, go back to the connections people have with their linguistic resources and narratives – and each other. It is, however, our shared abilities to articulate and emplot new stories for a shared future that offer political and relational hope. His hermeneutics was one of making use of the varied linguistic and symbolic resources at hand (and he had quite a grasp of these) to address concerns of the present.

For practitioners, Ricoeur's approach suggests bringing a hermeneutics of suspicion (to test the adequacy or fit of ideas and language) together with a hermeneutics of affirmation (to arrive at understandings worth affirming and acting on). In this manner, helping conversations would be those focused on deriving the best ideas and understandings useful in addressing matters of personal or relational concern. The notion of 'best' itself is one that is worked out in discussions that critically reflect on understandings en route to developing ideas clients deem as best fitting them.

We have barely touched down on Ricoeur's work, for he is a thinker who has sometimes been described as an intellectual superstar. Ricoeur's influence has been widespread and enormous in a variety of disciplines, and he held both a Chair of Philosophy at the Sorbonne and a Chair of Theology at the University of Chicago. The author of many books and over 500 articles and chapters, his was a prolific life of reflecting on living meaningfully, through the vast linguistic resources that he brought to bear on any problem of meaning he addressed. His writings invite us to do the same.

Jürgen Habermas

The linguistic mediation of our relations to the world explains why the objectivity of the world that we presuppose in acting and speaking refers back to a communicative intersubjectivity among interlocutors. A fact about some object must be *stated* and, if necessary, *justified* before others who can object to my assertion. The particular demand for interpretation arises because even when we use language descriptively, we cannot disregard its world-disclosive character.   (Habermas, 2005: 93)

Jürgen Habermas is still very much active with his evolving view of hermeneutics. As someone who came from the Critical School of philosophy (as also Adorno, Horkheimer), his interests have largely focused on furthering the development of justice, rational discourse and shared knowledge. Coming of age at the time of the Nuremberg trials and Heidegger's postwar refusal to acknowledge his romanticizing of Nazi life, Habermas's career was motivated by a desire to improve the justness and rationality made possible by cultural discourse. Habermas's view is that democratic discourse can – in its larger machinations – provide a shared rationality and collective way of being: one that reflects the best a society can come up with in collectively going forward. His hermeneutics are therefore focused on how people can be critically intersubjective in ways that help to articulate an optimal and rational discourse, a discourse that will need to adapt continuously to new circumstances, and revise itself to be the best a culture can have at any time. Thus, Habermas's objectivity is accomplished through practices of communication that are consciously aiming for a rationality arrived at – in macro – through critical consensus via his 'dialogical principle of universalization'. Habermas shares views with his fellow hermeneutic scholars and social constructionists that objectivity, in the idealized sense of correct thing–word correspondence, is impossible. Instead, he sees understanding, critique, and action as occurring in normative ways – collectively repeatable ways he sees optimized in a form of discourse (universalized) ethics that embraces rational argumentation without presuming a foundational ontology. Democratic argument, for Habermas, can develop norms of ethical communication that permit optimal understandings and ways of relating. The Nazi experience clearly showed where critique and alternatives of understanding were stifled. Habermas's alternative reads as an idealization one might associate with the unrealized promises of Greek democracy, while at the same time offering some specifics for furthering his alternative.

The focal writing of Habermas's (1985) later career was his two-volume *Theory of Communicative Action*, which adopted insights from critical theory, speech act theory, the later Wittgenstein and hermeneutics. There he writes of a view of society that sees people socialized into ways of communicating with and appreciating others that broaden their abilities to entertain and critique different points of view. The development of these capacities is useful in furthering the potentials of communal and cultural discourse. How we communicate influences what results from our communications, and he sees this as a required egalitarian feature to aim for.

Habermas's discourse ethics adopt a 'discourse principle' such that any rule of action or choice is justified, and thus valid, only if all those affected by the rule or choice could accept it in a reasonable discourse. You would not be alone in seeing idealism in what Habermas was proposing.

As with other hermeneutic positions we have reviewed here, Habermas sees a kind of cultural-historical situatedness still at work in people creating his optimal discourse, though his ethics are only possible in a thoroughly democratized society. What is at stake is what he has referred to as the legitimation (Habermas, 1975) of what passes for understanding and action in contemporary society. He sees such a process of legitimation as necessarily occurring in and from democratic discourse. His optimal discourse and ethics are ongoing challenges that require collective critical reflection, debate and deliberative excellence. In this sense, discourse would be collaboratively constructed, evaluated, used and modified in ways appropriate to the culture it is meant to serve. This is not to arrive at some final version of how things should be. His writing suggests cultural prescriptions for such a discourse ethics, and the rational discourse he sees following from them, to occur. But, in some respects we have versions of this already occurring in less than ideal form. To use an example, legal discourse (our system of laws and judgements) develops out of a presumably optimally structured circumstance in which communication and argumentation can be used in addressing criminality and the need for further laws. This is an example of where we both idealize our legal system for what we hope it can provide, while living with and addressing its imperfections through on-going democratic debate. The system in total is a set of understandings and practices which we arguably enact and supplement through constant critical reflection. Transplanting this example to other spheres of life, however, helps to underscore further where Habermas's discourse ethics read as an idealization, even if it is an appealing idealization. People do not have equal voices, and the confidence to use them, that seem essential for such a discourse ethics to be truly shared. Still, if communal, cultural or even global discourse is incapable of creating and maintaining adequately (if not optimally) shared ways of being, then 'irrational' forms of dominance typically follow. Habermas has more faith in the shared potentials of discourse than most of us may, but his hermeneutic views are based in the big and small picture politics of our lives. His proposals are meant to turn us back to our communications with each other to come up with the best understandings and actions to live by. Having lived through one disastrous, totalitarian regime, Habermas is clear this is an on-going challenge since 'nothing entitles us to expect we have the final word' (2005: 202).

From a practical standpoint, the notion that people can optimize their communications and deliberations into a local version of discourse ethics is intriguing. Habermas has focused on a democratic ideal that resonates strongly for many. Looking at or developing useful norms for optimal communicative interaction might be an interesting exercise. But the next step – living by those norms – is no small challenge. For this reason, Habermas can be seen as offering ideas useful in sustaining cultural conversations for advancing understanding and action, but not so much to the smaller-scale conversations in spheres of shared social interaction.

Emmanuel Levinas

> ethics – precedes the understanding of being and survives ontology.
> (Emmanuel Levinas, as cited in Critchley, 1999: 74)

Emmanuel Levinas, a Jewish Lithuanian who studied with Husserl and Heidegger, and later endured imprisonment (he was spared the concentration camps for being captured as a French soldier) by the Nazis, took a very different position from those of his teachers. If Husserl's project had been to articulate the fundamentals of existence, and Heidegger's to contextualize them, Levinas's emphasis was to invert all of this and turn to relationships, our face-to-face contact with each other, as his primary focus. His writing is distinctly non-ontological, for a philosopher, and he had grave concerns about what can follow from our use of such language. Technically, his was not a hermeneutic philosophy, but his concerns about meaning and how it trumps what occurs in our relationships, and his views on language being unable to totalize, fit with our developing theme on discourse ethics. Where Gadamer and Ricoeur pointed to a dialogic quality in their ethical approach, Levinas proceeded from a very different maxim: that we place the needs and understandings of others before our own. He devoted his later philosophy to articulating this position.

Levinas adapted Husserl's phenomenology (his dissertation was the first French book published on Husserl in 1930), and Heidegger's view of our thrownness into the social worlds we participate in, to examine intersubjectivity, and its product – discourse. This ordering of examinations is important to his philosophy since he starts from what comes out of relationships, in discourse, before turning to what discourse explains. This move honours the hermeneutic and Husserlian insight that 'the things themselves' are constituted in a discourse which comes *after* humans have been in relationship. Language, in other words, is a human construction that constructs things in particular ways, and not some extra-human way of articulating things as they 'really' are. Consequently, problems can arise when people use language, and the understandings made possible by it, as if these understandings were requirements for others who spoke of things differently. Humberto Maturana and his colleagues (Mendez, Coddou and Maturana, 1988: 170) caught some of Levinas's concern about language when used to assert ontological claims: 'A claim to objective knowledge is an absolute demand for obedience.' When the ontological claims of people are asserted or argued over, conflict or efforts at dominance are typically not far behind. Neither Heidegger nor Husserl looked at relationships as anything but the given ground for our ways of being. Levinas's study was on intersubjectivity itself, what it means, in his view, to live with and for each other.

Ethics, for Levinas, begin in our face-to-face encounters, in our proximal relationships with each other that are beyond understanding in any total way. Anything less reduces (or potentially 'totalizes') our responsiveness to the full and intended meanings of our conversational partners. Thus, there are, for Levinas, infinite possibilities when we unconditionally open ourselves to the immediacies of this otherness that others show us. And it is the immediacy of what we may or may not experience and open ourselves to in our relationships that is Levinas's ethical concern, a concern that takes on spiritual dimensions in his writing. Most people are comfortable with the notion that spiritual experience transcends our ability to capture it fully in language, and Levinas brings that appreciation for language's shortcomings when trying to avoid linguistically totalizing 'others'. Language is incapable of capturing the immediacy of relatedness, or the fullness of who someone can be, so linguistic 'capture' is his concern. Since conversation is primary to relational life, his concern is a variation on de Saussure's ' "saying" and the "said" ' (*langue et parole*), where the said can overtake the saying in relating to others. This, for Levinas, is where our past descriptions and understandings ('traces') can become limiting prescriptions for how we relate to others, and expect them to be for us.

One thing we can take from Levinas's writing is his concern for how language can bind us to particular descriptions and perceptions of others and experiences. At worst, our descriptions can position us to relate from narrow meanings that limit the abilities of others to 'be otherwise'. Levinas reminds us that discourse and meaning are human creations and should therefore not be placed before or in between humans as the basis for relating. Proximity will trump authentic relatedness every time, if we let past (linguistic) understandings obscure and limit the immediate reality we share when relating to others. Jacques Derrida (1991) shared some of Levinas's concerns about language, in particular the capacity for linguistic descriptions to reduce understanding through its use. But, he was also concerned that Levinas saw relationships solely in terms of responsibilities for others. This creates a paradox: Levinas could be seen as having bound Derrida and us, as his others, to *his* prescription. Moving on, Levinas offers a more radical ethics than those served up by Gadamer, Ricoeur or Habermas – despite their shared focus on language, communications and human relatedness.

Our hermeneutic project retraced

It is only the experience of incomprehension which makes us, in a flash, aware of the task of understanding.   (Bauman, 1978: 195)

Once we relinquish a sense that our words and symbols *are* the things we ask them to represent to ourselves and others, then we are in a place where we can acknowledge our role in the meanings we live by. This realization bumped hermeneutic scholars out of the 'natural attitude' so central to Husserl's phenomenologizing, and into a realm where we are forced to look at what is involved in understanding.

These efforts in trying to come to terms with the understandings and meanings of others span some very interesting projects, as we have shown. Each of these efforts seemed to launch a new direction, as if it was a response to some historical dialogue, or a new iteration of history's hermeneutic circle. A few things are useful to pull out from reviewing these efforts.

First, there can be no underlying, objectively verifiable, reality that can be put into a final and total language all *can* or *must* agree with. Instead, time and place have something to do with why we understand differently, and can mean different things when we communicate. Second, the same is the case for language and how we infuse it with our spirit or attitudes as we articulate our experience, and share it with each other. We can use language to understand experiences in a variety of ways, provided we acknowledge, as we must, that our particular default understanding is not the only one possible, and we are open to other articulations of understanding. Finally, hermeneutics shows us the dangers of trying to understand and act with different 'others' should we mindlessly embrace and act as if there is only one cultural reality – our own.

Beyond this, there is a lot more we can take from hermeneutics, through its different developments. With Heidegger, it becomes obvious that Husserl's project of getting at transcendental, 'pre-predicative' experience could at best be a methodological advance. Rather than trying to account for 'things themselves', Heidegger's phenomenology suggested an important step was to consider what we take for granted, and to ask how we are even able to identify and make use of things in ways central to everyday life in the first place. Such identifications and use, he showed, was a product of our using linguistic and other tools to make distinctions that become constitutive of our ways of being. But being precedes us, and we are thrown into what people already understand and do, and have to take up our part in their ways of being. At our best, we use what our experiences with others have helped us recognize as being at hand, to engage life and others with elegance, spontaneity and attunement to shared experience. It is only when our inadequacies in doing this come up that we require new tools that open up or possibly disclose new ways of being. New technologies disclose new realities, as the internet has shown us. New language forms and new ways of talking can open up new possibilities for being. But what anchors us in any movement forward are the histories and cultural situatedness we bring to trying to address problems, while learning from possibilities that arise in overcoming them. Heidegger's contribution to hermeneutics in a sense provided a new conceptual foundation: historicized ways of being that ground us in mundane everyday life, until we are jarred into realizing there could be more to life than what we were accustomed to. This is why new understandings or suggestions simply do not make initial sense to people used to thinking and doing things other ways.

With Gadamer, the shortcomings of Heidegger's notion of thrownness, our embeddedness in horizons of understanding, become more evident. While hermeneutics was always about trying to understand others as they wanted to be understood, Heidegger took a phenomenological angle on the problem, showing the extent of the challenge. Horizons of understanding were modes of social engagement as much as they were different ways of seeing and naming reality. Given the differences of understanding and engagement found within such horizons, Dreyfus (1991) saw differently practised social realities. Gadamer took up the implicit challenges arising from Heidegger's 'being'. He turned to language, exploring the linguistic possibilities of dialogue to create understandings where differences would otherwise be barriers to shared ways of being together. For shared understandings to occur, however, people have to be willing to open themselves to what is unfamiliar, to let it be something they could be affected by, or agree to. They have to be open to reconfigure their former horizons and ways of being, and not just add to them. In Gadamer we find historically and culturally grounded persons having to reconcile their accustomed ways of understanding and being with those they have yet to come to terms with. Ricoeur's meaning-maker is even more complicated. He or she has the subjective task of using the linguistic and symbolic tools that indirectly became accessible (that is, as concepts, words and ideas that are used in different ways by people over time) to them to narrate their ways forward in their personal and shared lives. The ways we transcend the limitations of current understanding is with resources that help us narrate new ways forward in the lives we share with others.

From Gadamer onward, hermeneutics entails recognizing that meaning-making is a social and cultural process begging an ethics of cross-cultural and interpersonal communication. Some of this can sound like traditional notions of transference and countertransference, as practitioners and clients would invariably influence each other if their conversations were truly dialogic in the sense Gadamer intended. Gadamer and Ricoeur turned to the immediacies of dialogue to advocate that we position ourselves to hear and be moved by others. Habermas takes the more ambitious and abstract position, advising that we use our cultural institutions to create a 'discourse ethics' that makes possible deliberative excellence, where we can generate and evaluate our best understandings and practices for facing life's evolving challenges. While this sounds big-picture Utopian, it is an optimistic view consistent with participatory democracies and what they are capable of creating as shared understandings and ways of being. Finally, Levinas asks us to reflect on the primacy of our relatedness to others and how language can blunt our responsiveness to, and responsibilities for, each other.

Accompanying the view of hermeneutics we have been relating are profound implications for those who turn to modern science for a single correct description of reality that is amenable to human intervention. The whole project of science itself can be seen in hermeneutic terms, as situated ways of understanding, evaluating and acting. Thomas Kuhn (1962) suggested as much in describing science as having paradigms of inquiry. Objectivity itself, as historians of science Lorraine Daston and Peter Galison (2007) point out, is grounded in what they call 'epistemic virtues' – values and ways of conducting science particular to eras and scientific disciplines. If science were to offer the meta-language making life ultimately knowable, looking upon science in these hermeneutic ways presents the problems that Habermas raised about legitimating meanings. Science does not offer us descriptions of experiences outside of our cultural horizons of understanding and being. Rather, it is an historically and culturally grounded project that requires agreement like any other human and cultural endeavour to move forward. We cannot bracket ourselves out of our historical groundedness in the way Baron von Munchausen thought he could lift himself out of his circumstances – by his pigtail. We are stuck with the languages and traditions afforded us by contemporary science, but this doesn't reduce the cultural importance and usefulness of science, as R. J. Bernstein (1983: 203) indicated:

> Science is nothing more nor less than a very effective vocabulary for coping, one which is likely to win out over philosophy or any other cultural discipline when it comes to matters of prediction or following relatively clear patterns of argumentation. The point is not to get trapped into thinking that science is the only vocabulary available to us, or that it limits the possibility of inventing new vocabularies, or that philosophy or any other cultural discipline ought to be able to beat science at its own game.

For Ricoeur, there are many linguistic resources we can use in addressing our concerns and aspirations. The same goes for our understandings of personal experience and identity. The descriptions we construct for our making sense of any experience are *linguistic* descriptions, and words are how we relate ourselves to the qualitative aspects of those experiences as much as their physical or other properties. As Charles Taylor (1985) suggests, man (*sic*) is a self-interpreting animal; one who brings language and the qualities of experience into particular emotional and attitudinal alignments. Language is what helps us articulate our feelings and moods, and it thus plays a role in constituting how such aspects of our experience qualitatively stand for us. This is a point also raised in the later Wittgenstein (1953): that different uses of language constitute qualitatively different forms of life. Taylor, more recently (2007), has turned his attention to what a hermeneutic perspective offers to making sense of and addressing the complexities that follow from living in culturally and religiously diverse societies. The inference we draw here is that our resourceful use of language in ethically responsive dialogues with others is what helps us to collectively engage with and address differences in problems, aspirations and unfamiliar experiences.

Our historical overview brings us to several conclusions. First, hermeneutics reminds us that taken-for-granted understandings and actions historically ground us when engaging others and interacting with physical reality. The familiar is something we can usually afford to overlook, but not so the unfamiliar, and thus there will always be a tension between what we know and what unanticipated experience calls from us. Second, language offers creative resources we can use in making sense of and transforming experiences that stymie us. This means, however, that we must make a break from what is familiar, to try on or be receptive to what has been alien to us. This requires an ethic of openness to the unfamiliar, and a willingness to talk or work out differences so that they become shareable familiarities that can guide us into the future. Finally, a hermeneutic view of understanding suggests that any knowledge claim will always be partial, and related to some historical tradition, however rigorous, complete or encompassing that tradition may be. While we can look at processes for generating well-tested and agreed-upon knowledge – in such realms as science, justice or politics – the notion that any meaning can ultimately rule out plausible or useful others should be suspect.

5 Marxism and language

> The 'mind' is from the outset afflicted with the curse of being burdened with
> matter, which here makes its appearance in the form of agitated layers of air,
> sounds, in short, language. Language is as old as consciousness, language
> is practical, real consciousness that exists for other men as well, and only
> therefore does it exist for me; language, like consciousness, only arises from
> the need, the necessity, of intercourse with other men ... Consciousness is,
> therefore, from the very beginning a social product.   (Marx and Engels,
> 1845b/1976: 43–4)

> Individual consciousness is not the architect of the ideological superstructure, but
> only a tenant lodging in the social edifice of ideological signs.   (Voloshinov,
> 1986: 39)

The potentials of dialogue, and what follows from constraining such potentials,
possibly got its most thorough treatment by Marxist idealists. This can initially
seem odd to those who fast track from Marxist ideas to the repressive regimes of
Stalin or Mao. But on closer examination one finds affinities between Marx's ideas
and concerns and social constructionist ideas and practices. In particular, Marx
was concerned with what people produced socially, and how they could become
estranged from the products of their social interactions. Over-determined forms of
language-use and restricted communications between people offer striking examples of Marx's concerns. In today's post-Soviet age any consideration of Marx seems
dismissible, largely because of the failed cultural experiments where adaptations of
his thinking were used. In pre-Stalinist Russia, however, Marxist ideas animated
wide-ranging discussions pertaining to seemingly attainable new human and social
potentials. The 'Bakhtin Circle' hosted many such discussions, when there was 'an
energy in the air', as recalled by the Russian psychologist Alexander Luria:

> I began my career in the first years of the great Russian Revolution. This
> single, momentous event decisively influenced my life and that of everyone I
> knew ... From the outset it was apparent that I would have little opportunity
> to pursue the kind of well ordered, systematic education that serves as
> the cornerstone for most scientific careers. In its place life offered me the
> fantastically stimulating atmosphere of an active, rapidly changing society.
> My entire generation was infused with the energy of revolutionary change,
> the liberating energy people feel when they are part of a society that is able to
> make tremendous progress in a very short time.   (Luria, 1979: 17)

The exciting possibilities about dialogue and language-use discussed by members of the 'Bakhtin Circle' ran headlong into a brutal Stalinist monologue. Our

interests here in considering the ideas of the Bakhtin Circle relate to revisiting those exciting possibilities, and their generative potentials for helping dialogues.

We will primarily focus on the central figure in this circle, Mikhail Bakhtin, while occasionally referring to ideas from some of his Circle colleagues (Voloshinov, Medvedev, and Leont'ev). In particular, we will consider their views on the social and dialogic nature of language as it is performed: the view that, 'language lives only in the dialogic interaction of those who make use of it' (Bakhtin, 1984: 183).

The thinking of the Bakhtin Circle can be challenging to understand, because their approach goes against the grain of two assumptions that are nowadays part of the mental baggage that weigh our mainstream thinking down. First, the cognitive assumption that people have internal mental representations and rule systems that handle the task of speaking for them. Second, with respect to language, our intellectual landscape is shot through with a distinction made by de Saussure (1966/1916) between *langue* and *parole* that has been passed down to us via Chomsky's (1959) recast of this as *competence* and *performance*. For these theorists, actual utterances are rather messy actualizations of some underlying ideal form or generative plan of language that has been mastered by an individual as a way of encoding and decoding meanings that are stored in some mental lexicon. Whereas Chomsky's focus was on 'ideal speaker/listener interacting within a homogeneous speech community' (1965: 3), the Bakhtin Circle focused on actual performances by people in dialogue, despite the messiness of such communication.

This focus on participation in actual as opposed to idealized dialogue is important to where we will be heading in this chapter. It is an entirely different matter to be responsive in the immediacies of dialogue with a conversational partner, than to consider participation in such dialogues in an abstract third-party manner. It is in this sense that the Bakhtin Circle invited us into considering an 'insider's' view of dialogue, and their view was not unlike that of a lens which permits both microscopic and macroscopic views of dialogue. Such an alternation between views is important to their considerations of the forms of communication, and what can be possible within them. Returning briefly to Marx, it can help to remember that one of his paramount concerns was with how forms of social organization optimize or constrict the possibilities between people. It is in this respect that the Bakhtin Circle turned their critical eye toward forms of communication (particularly 'formalized' forms) that constrain people's possibilities for thought and action, while it considered the ideals of unfettered dialogue. But let us first contrast the Bakhtin Circle's Marxist critiques and lofty idealism with contemporary thinking.

The dominant view in today's psycholinguistics is that words have meanings that are learned and then stored in some kind of mental dictionary. Certain contextual features that are handled by pragmatic knowledge, similarly stored away and called on to somehow interpret for us what is actually going on, can modify these meanings. Syntactic rules enable us to put word meanings to different uses, such as passive and interrogative structures. Our 'minds' operate with this collection of definitions and rules, formulate what we want to say, convey this formulation through our nervous systems as commands to our vocalizing apparatus (which then makes the appropriate noise), and, in detailed theories, send simultaneous messages to our facial and postural muscles so as to put the appropriate non-verbal accompaniments to our intended message in place. Once we have made these noises they are propagated as sound waves to the ears and eyes of our addressees, conveyed via their nerves to those dictionary and other systems to be worked over so as to reveal their sense. Hence, by this account, our meanings, words and ways of talking are largely implicit, given what occurs via genetic coding and develops inside our skin.

The Bakhtin Circle instead turned to how meaningful communication develops and is made possible within our social interactions. They took this stance, following some insights of Marx and Engels, put forward in *The German Ideology* (1845), as to how dominant ideas come to hold sway in different forms of society. Every society has ways of judging actions, and classing some as legitimate and some as illegitimate. This 'legitimation' context is important, because that is what Marx and Engels were focusing on. Their argument can be stated as follows.

People have ways of greeting each other, for example. How greeting is done happens every time two people meet. In a small group of people, at the outset of human social life, individual acts of meeting are just that: encounters between differing temperaments. We might think here along the lines of Mead's dog-fight (see Chapter 7): the top dog will get different-style meetings from the bottom dog. But, to every meeting, each party brings a sense of 'outside observer', which informs how greetings should be done. Eventually, a style will emerge, and a set of justifications as to how greetings should be handled. In feudalism, honour and loyalty will be brought into being and articulated in those terms. In early modern times, freedom and equality will, perhaps, become the bedrock that underwrites the style of greeting, and be formalized and codified as 'the way things should be done'. By repeatedly using a shared language to describe and evaluate 'how things are', people come to share a common background or context from which to relate meaningfully and qualitatively to 'how things are'.

We are now at a notion Bakhtin and his circle referred to as 'formal communications' (Bakhtin and Medvedev, 1978), 'speech genres' (Bakhtin, 1981), or ideological discourses (Volosinov, 1973). These are recognizable ways in which our communications have become culturally structured or systematized into particular understandings and social conventions for communicating them. Greetings in rugby are usually undertaken differently from those occurring at City Hall. Of course, there can be considerable differences in how tightly prescribed any form of communication might be. But typically, people talking with each other over time come to adopt what John Shotter (1993a) refers to as 'conversational realities' (see Chapter 16 below), familiarities in their meanings and how they speak to each other. A challenge of course is to keep dialogue from being overtaken by such conventions in conversing and meaning. That would leave speakers facing the Marxist concern of becoming estranged from the meanings and ways of talking derived from their social efforts. Throughout the Bakhtin Circle's writings one finds a creative tension between formalized talk (de Saussure's *langue*) and the improvisable and generative qualities (*parole*) of dialogue. This is evident in the following quote from Bakhtin:

> an utterance is never just a reflection or an expression of something already existing outside it that is given and final. It always creates something that never existed before, something absolutely new and unrepeatable, and, moreover, it always has some relation to value (the true, the good, the beautiful, and so forth). But something created is always created out of something given (language, an observed phenomenon of reality, an experienced feeling, the speaking subject himself, something finalized in his world view, and so forth). What is given is completely transformed in what is created.   (Bakhtin, 1986: 119–20)

His colleague, Volosinov, wrote along the same lines: 'The immediate social situation and the broader social milieu wholly determine – and determine from within, so to speak – the structure of an utterance' (1973: 86). The Bakhtin Circle's view of meaning is thus one focused on what happens in communication between people; people – in immediate relationship, and people drawing from broader, formalized communications used by others in their cultural surround. It is in such 'between' relations that speakers and listeners restructure formalized meanings, thus reformulating them, giving them their own unique and immediate significance as to 'what it was we talked about'. This restructuring extends to *how* meanings are sent between conversational partners: in expressive interactions involving words, and a gamut of visual and aural expressions, of face, body posture, intonation, volume, and so on – on the fly, as it were – through which conversational meaning is created. Thus, their view is that 'language lives only in the dialogic interaction of those who make use of it' (Bakhtin, 1984: 183), and hence, as Volosinov (1986: 2) put it, 'the processes that basically define the content of the psyche occur not inside but outside the individual organism, although they involve its participation'. These words echo a consistent theme in this book – through Mead, Bateson, Wittgenstein, Vygotsky and others – that mind and meaning can be seen as socially realized and activated.

Of course, these preliminary ideas we have been relating from the Bakhtin Circle suggest a very different stance for helping practice from a view that meaning is already fixed in mental and actual dictionaries, such that communication involves transmissions and receptions based on what is in those dictionaries. It is in the immediacy of dialogues that the already spoken and conventional is given new life and a chance for new potentials in meaning and social possibility. Let us now shift to focus more specifically on Bakhtin and members of his circle, and some of their key ideas.

Mikhail Bakhtin

> To be means to communicate dialogically. When dialogue ends, everything ends. Thus dialogue, by its very essence, cannot and must not come to an end.   (Bakhtin, 1984: 252)

> There is no alibi for being.   (Bakhtin, as cited in Morson and Emerson, 1990: 31)

> The word cannot be assigned to a single speaker. The author (speaker) has his own inalienable right to the word, but the listener also has his rights, and those whose voices are heard in the word before the author comes upon it have their rights (after all, there are no words that belong to no one).   (Bakhtin, 1986: 121–2)

1920s Russia was a very different place intellectually from Stalin's or today's Russia. The ideas of Marx and Lenin were, for many intellectuals of that time, not only ways of creating a society that could more fairly replace Czarist Russia, they also suggested new potentials for considering human behaviour and accomplishments. From this intellectual backdrop, Mikhail Bakhtin and his circle of colleagues created a radically different view of how humans co-exist meaningfully. Bakhtin's views were largely inaccessible to western thinkers until the 1980s, when the postmodern revolution was gaining momentum.

Having lived under monopolistic rule – Russia had been held to the monologues of its monarchs – Bakhtin and his colleagues proposed a very different alternative: dialogic coexistence. Dialogue – where differences are welcomed and not homogenized into a single way of talking or understanding – were, for them, the glue for coexisting. But such views did not go over well once Stalin took firm hold of the Soviet Union in the late 1920s. Not long thereafter, Bakhtin was sent off to the Siberian Gulag, Volosinov was dead from tuberculosis by 1936, and Medvedev was arrested and disappeared in 1938. While the Bakhtin Circle flourished in the 1920s, they were a creative fount of ideas on the possibilities of dialogue, and on problems with formal or monologic understandings. Their thoughts on dialogue go way further than that, as will become apparent.

It is important to see a double-edge at work in Bakhtin's writing. While exploring the possibilities of dialogic communications and meaning, he and his colleagues also wrote penetrating critiques of 'formalized' meaning (Bakhtin and Medvedev, 1978; Gardiner, 1992). Formalized meanings were those which attempted to convey unquestionable authority, or passed for a presumed ('We-like') convergence of opinion. Bakhtin also tried to look at meaning and communications as they occurred across time, seeing centripetal (converging inwardly) and centrifugal (diverging outwardly) socio-dynamic processes at work, much like cultural oscillations between conservative and more liberal times. In Bakhtin's view, life is poorer for people living by singular truths and ways of being. His prototypes for this complexity were not from philosophy, psychology or sociology – they were from great works of literature, such as those by Dostoevsky or Rabelais. Bakhtin's ideas on meaning helped to set the stage for 'textual' thinkers such as Julia Kristeva, Jacques Derrida and Paul Ricoeur. There is a veritable trove of rich ideas in Bakhtin's writing and he has rightly become one of the most influential thinkers associated with 'postmodern' thought. Our tour through Bakhtin's ideas will focus primarily on his views on meaning and dialogue, weaving between his critical and his more generative ideas on both.

Meaning: heteroglossia and chronotopes

> For the word is not a material thing but rather the eternally mobile, eternally
> fickle medium of dialogic interaction. It never gravitates toward a single
> consciousness or a single voice. The life of the word is contained in its
> transfer from one mouth to another, from one context to another context,
> from one social collective to another, from one generation to another
> generation. In this process the word does not forget its own path and cannot
> completely free itself from the power of these concrete contexts into which
> it has entered.   (Bakhtin, 1984: 202)

Through his studies of literature, Bakhtin arrived at a complex view of meaning.
His view seems hermeneutic to a point (meaning is linked to authors' intentions
in time and cultural location), but it went far beyond, to consider what happens to
any words or texts as people make their meaningful claims on them. The idea that
meaning could be seen as the determinable property of people or cultures was of
great concern to Bakhtin. Finalized words or ultimate meanings meant the death
of dialogue, the silencing of other ways experience could be understood and communicated. This view put Bakhtin at odds with not only Stalinist Russia, but with
a modern era which looked upon finalized meaning as a crowning achievement of
hard-won scientific effort. Meaning, for Bakhtin, cannot be pinned down in such
a way. Instead, what he saw as more important was meaning as it played out in
the back and forth of dialogue. While we will focus on his ideas about dialogue in
greater detail later, here we will look upon meaning as a kind of 'answerability'
involving people in various forms of dialogue.

Trying to finalize meaning in an absolute sense, or as a consensual compromise, invariably deadened meaning for Bakhtin. It is in trying to refine and supplement meanings, through dialogue, that people's words and ideas come alive
for them. Meaning, in this sense, does not derive from an object or experience to
be articulated according to pre-specified dictionary meanings for words, but can
be better appreciated as an activity involving how words and symbols are used
between people. Such words or symbols are kept alive through how they refract
the meanings and uses of past speakers in responses (as an impulse) that engage
and influence others. Bakhtin was more interested in the processes and shifting
outcomes of dialogue than any of its products; for him, there could be no final
resting place for the word (Bakhtin, 1981).

Bakhtin found a prototype for his views in the early dialogues of Socrates,
as these were recorded by Plato (Baktin, 1984; Zappen, 2004). Plato's writing
itself evolved in ways that reflected increasingly more unitary and authoritative meaning (such as his later *Republic*), but the early Socratic dialogues
stand out as exemplars of speakers engaged in putting their best words to a
problem, and refining their thinking as they did so. Early Socrates engaged
his interlocutors in robust dialogues about different issues, looking upon dialogue as a means of adding to and clarifying understandings without arriving
at some final 'true' meaning. If this kind of 'dialogism' (Holquist, 1990) seems
unrealistic, that was partly Bakhtin's point. The words and symbols people use

in communicating take on more meanings as they are used across time, place and particular dialogues – or, in Bakhtin's view, such words and symbols can become 'corpses'.

Bakhtin was insistent that meaning needed to be understood in terms of the shifting times, places and purposes for its specific use. It was in this regard he wrote of chronotopes and heteroglossia as part of how he considered meaning as a 'once occurrent event of being' (Bakhtin, 1981). In a big-picture way, chronotopes refer to the contextualized timing of any meaning; pointing not only to the era in which an author (such as Rabelais) might have written, but also to the different, later circumstances when readers interpret the author's writing. It is in this sense that discourse analysts sometimes write of contexts in which utterances are 'occasioned'. Seen hermeneutically, Bakhtin is referring to how meaning needs to be understood as 'located', coming from some background of speech and intelligibility. But this would only capture part of how Bakhtin saw the complexities of meaning. Meaning was also about the addressability or answerability (Bakhtin, 1990) of people in communication with each other – how they respond to previous utterances while anticipating the responses they seek in how others might respond to them. It is in this respect that meaning, for Bakhtin, has to be seen in terms of its occurrence at a particular time and place.

Bakhtin's ideas get more challenging when we turn to his notion of heteroglossia. Heteroglossia refers to a plurality of possible meanings associated with the use of a word or symbol. Here Bakhtin gets quintessentially dialogic, writing things like the 'meaning of a word is only half mine', or 'words come to us with the tastes of others' uses'. What he is getting at is the idea that words and symbols take on particular lives of their own, in how people use them in the present. This also relates to how words acquire a personal and cultural freight prior to their use as well. When Gadamer (1988), for example, sought to 'rehabilitate' the word 'prejudice', it is clear that such a word comes with a legacy of prior uses that colours how it might be interpreted by others. This notion of considering how others might receive our words is partly related to heteroglossia, in that any speaker is positioned between the meanings for words used by prior speakers (including the conventional or formalized meanings of any word) and the intended recipient making sense of these words. The resultant meaning cannot be seen as either a statically defined utterance (as in a dictionary definition) or a meaning conforming solely to the intentions of a speaker (words mean what *I* intend them to mean). That would be like suggesting you are reading these words exactly how we mean them *now*, or how Wikipedia might have them defined. No, for Bakhtin, words come with meanings associated with our cultural situatedness and our personal autobiographies. But he does not stop there, going on to claim that meaning is an event occurring *between* people. We cannot control how others will understand us. Instead, speakers and listeners 'people' words according to the different intentions and contexts of understanding they bring to using and understanding them. Heteroglossia refers to such differences in understanding and trying be understood; and translated literally from Russian, it means 'different-speech-ness'.

For Bakhtin, heteroglossia refers to an aspect of meaning that escapes individual control. With all the various ways a particular word might be used or understood, one cannot control what others do with our intended meanings. Instead, meaning-making occurs as a dynamic and uncertain encounter. I have to live with how you make sense of me. At best, quizzical or unaccepting responses to us are a call for clarification or rewording, in the hopes you will better understand us, but we cannot control your understanding or inward acceptance of what we say. This puts a particular emphasis on the ethicality of our everyday use of words and symbols (Morson and Emerson, 1990), an ethics that arises in loyalties to past users of such words and symbols, and to our readers and conversational partners who will try to understand 'our' words and symbols. But, Bakhtin went even further, suggesting that a heteroglossic and dialogized word ultimately may not be shared, or even understood in singular terms. An example may help clarify things.

Consider the word 'married'. Think of the various ways this word can be understood. Then consider its potential uses and the range of historical and cultural meanings which could serve as backdrop in making sense of the term. Now, think of it being used in a conversation between two strangers on a plane: 'Are you married?' What might be packed into such a word for either speaker, if one answers that she is engaged while the other mentions a separation? While not all words are as filled with Rorschach-like projective potential, a heteroglossic appreciation for meaning should hopefully be getting clearer. We bring different histories to any word or symbol and then are faced with a challenge in how our use of them will play out when communicating with others. For the speakers on the plane, 'married' can mean lots of things, including the possibility that one of them sees a sexual opportunity worth inquiring about. The meanings in play are understandings needing to get worked out and these still might remain plural for them.

Meaning, for Bakhtin, also takes on a spiritual dimension in so far as it points to what he termed the unfinalizability of meaning in human relationships. We need to be openly responsive to meaning as it develops through our encounters in life, without insisting on the last word. Here is Bakhtin capturing a number of the dimensions we have been bringing to his word, heteroglossia:

> But no living word relates to its object in a singular way: between the word and its object, between the word and the speaking subject, there exists an elastic environment of other, alien words about the same object ... It is precisely in the process of living interaction with this specific environment that the word may be individualized and given stylistic shape.   (Bakhtin, as cited in Morson and Emerson, 1990: 51)

We will return to Bakhtin's notion of meaning later, but first we will examine his concepts of dialogue and polyphony, since these have direct bearing on how he regarded meaning.

Dialogue and polyphony

> Truth is not born nor is it to be found inside the head of an individual person, it is born between people collectively searching for truth, in the process of their dialogic interaction.   (Bakhtin, 1984: 110)

By now, it should be clear that Bakhtin saw meaning arising from dialogic interactions, and he cautioned against efforts to abstract meaning beyond, and outside of, dialogue. But the word 'dialogue' itself takes on dimensions in Bakhtin's writing that are seldom encountered elsewhere. It can help to start by contrasting dialogue with its opposite: monologue. Monologues are non-responsive and singular ways of conveying meaning. Imagine people talking past each other, ignoring each other, or trying to impose their understandings on each other. Then, contrast such scenarios with a good conversation where you felt heard, and in the course of your talking and listening were transported to ideas and shared experiences beyond those that you and your conversational partner could have come up with alone. Most dialogues occur somewhere in between the first set of scenarios and the second one.

Arguably, we are conversing with you now, as you respond in ways particular to your background and sense of possibility for what we are relating. Remember, Bakhtin took his notions of dialogue in part from authors who 'spoke' to him years after putting their words to the page. Our point is that dialogue refers to a mode of engagement between people who are responsive to each other's communications. Rigid monologues are impervious to that kind of responsiveness. Open dialogues, by contrast, see people open to and shaping each other's lives. Books and art, as well as face-to-face communications, present such opportunities for 'dialogue'. Some of this comes down to how such forms of communication occur, and what the nature of such communications permit.

Taking one giant step back, Bakhtin saw the potentials for dialogue alternating between two large tendencies: a centripetal tendency toward singular meanings and forms of communication, and a centrifugal tendency where meanings and ways of communicating proliferate. As mentioned earlier, politics plays out in such a manner over time, but so too do people in terms of how they relate to each other. In this regard, times of struggle more likely bring a narrow range of communications and meaning. But alongside these tendencies is a related notion of Bakhtin's (1984) in *Problems of Dostoevsky's Poetics*. 'Polyphony' refers to the multi-voiced nature of meaning and relating. When we were discussing heteroglossia we touched on some aspects related to polyphony, including the notion that words are accessible to us, but that this accessibility comes with other claims made on those words by other speakers, current and past. Polyphony, like heteroglossia, is another term that points to the complexity of meaning and conversation. Where some, like R. D. Laing, wrote of multiple selves, Bakhtin saw things quite differently, writing instead about multiple voices and dialogues, in responsive conversations we carry on in various ways (including our inner dialogues 'with them').

Polyphony refers to the simultaneous experience of engaging with multiple voices in (real or imagined) dialogue without merging them. Democracies are the epitome of polyphony in this regard, in that particular actions and meanings can result from them, yet ask individuals about such actions (e.g., laws) and varied understandings and ways of relating to them pour forth. At an individual level, when people speak of being torn or ambivalent over an issue, their pull to different dialogues, each with different meanings and kinds of responsiveness, can be at work in a polyphonic manner. Dostoevsky was a master at bringing these kinds of polyphonic tensions out in the experiences and dialogues of his characters. Polyphony in this regard means accepting such tensions and differences, and even though outcomes might favour one action or meaning, the tensions and differences do not necessarily abate. Polyphonic dialogue, in this sense, isn't necessarily warm and fuzzy: a promoter of mutuality it may not be. Bakhtin was referring to voices in a way that might sound schizophrenic, but what he wrote actually relates more to our loyalties or responsiveness to people with whom we have been, or could be, in dialogue. Imagine, with Bakhtin, that we bring to any conversation a polyphony of dialogues we are or have been engaged in, and that these influence our efforts to understand or be understood – and any simple notions about meaning must be jettisoned. It was from this sense of Bakhtin that Morson and Emerson wrote, 'too much is expected of the word' (1990: 80).

Dialogue is clearly a challenging, yet potentially rewarding, opportunity for Bakhtin. But all around him he saw actions and tendencies in the opposite direction; for example, a tendency toward 'authoritative discourses'. Authoritative discourse, in the sense referred to here, is a way to talk about TRUTH, while holding others to that way of talking. This could arise in ways of communicating expertise, religious authority, political sovereignty or academic knowledge. In centripetal times, people often turn to such authoritative discourses and their spokespersons for guidance and understanding, turning their backs on the apparent anarchy implied by polyphonic dialogues. What mattered to Bakhtin was how people acquired and acted from 'inwardly persuasive' discourses. Dialogue, in this sense, is a means to acquire such inwardly persuasive discourses, and to talk past the already spoken and unpersuasive meanings that could be associated with authoritative discourse. If you are anticipating Bakhtin's passage to Siberia coming up as a result here, that is understandable, since Marxist discourse went from a polyphony of sorts in Lenin's time to a repressive monologue in Stalin's. Bakhtin's point was with the meanings people still derived for themselves despite the Stalinist monologue – with how polyphony could still happen inwardly for them even if it could not occur in public political discourse.

Alongside his penchant for the ethical and creative immediacies of dialogue, Bakhtin was concerned with the more systematized ways people communicate. His book *Speech Genres* (1986) and his writing on formalized discourse (e.g., Bakhtin and Medvedev, 1978) take up themes more examined by Volosinov. Bakhtin's aim in this aspect of his writing was to help us break out of deterministic 'prisons' of language to develop linguistic ecosystems more reflective of our preferences and circumstances (Clark and Holquist, 1984). Tied to this are the affective qualities, or 'accents' that speakers using particular ways of communicating adopt in relating to phenomena. Seen as modes of address, these speech genres or discourses are ways we not only describe experience but, additionally, our choice of words and the emotional tone used in conveying them articulate qualitative relationships taken with respect to experience. This is easily recognized when one compares a botanist's language for nature to that of a hiker, though such genres can either be kept distinct or melded. Genres in this sense are prepackaged ways of understanding and communicating. In this respect they resemble Foucault's cultural discourses (see Chapter 12) or Wittgenstein's language games (see Chapter 8). While Bakhtin would not have borrowed from either of these thinkers, one finds a shared resonance in comments about genres being like the 'drive belts between the history of society [and] the history of language' (1986: 65).

One issue here is to see understanding and qualitative experience as bound up in genres we may fail to recognize: 'Many people who have an excellent command of language often feel quite helpless in certain spheres of communication precisely because they do not have a practical command of the generic forms used in the given spheres' (Bakhtin, 1986: 80). But Bakhtin saw such genres as 'codes', warning that a code is only a technical means of transmitting information; it does not have cognitive, creative significance. A code is a deliberately established, *killed context* (Bakhtin, as cited in Morson and Emerson, 1991: 290). The image that develops here is one of genres being emotionally laden, partial takes on experience that can become restrictive and self-referential if speakers do not recognize them and adjust their communications to make possible a wider range of articulations. Every genre, in this respect, also has what Bakhtin called a 'loophole' – a point we will pick up on later.

A further concept Bakhtin brings out in his doctoral dissertation, *Rabelais and his World*, is 'carnival' (1993a). Carnival, as he refers to it, is a time when social conventions and the cultural hierarchies they are embedded in are temporarily suspended. This affords an opportunity to flout conventional understandings and practices and engage in creative ways impossible under normal social circumstances. At the level of the individual, this is like disrupting one's mindset so that new possibilities can be (literally) entertained. Seen culturally, carnival offers a means to juxtapose the serious rigidities of social convention with humour, playfulness, irreverence, grotesqueness and 'out-of-character' behaviour. Carnival, in this sense, is a chance to see what could happen when things are other than normal. Drawing from Rabelais, Bakhtin (1993a: 10) wrote:

> one might say that carnival celebrated temporary liberation from the established order; it marked the suspension of all hierarchical rank, privileges, norms, and prohibitions. Carnival was the true feast of time, the feast of becoming, change, and renewal. It was hostile to all that was immortalized and completed.

It will perhaps not be surprising that Bakhtin's dissertation was poorly received by postwar Stalinists, who did not pass Bakhtin's dissertation, or receptively consider its cultural implications. But, as with Bakhtin's examination of Dostoevsky's prose for dialogic possibilities, Rabelais' writing afforded a rich polyphonic view of meaningful possibilities. Carnival, as a cultural and communications concept, points to a need (and a not uncommon cultural practice – think of Mardi Gras) – for stepping out of the ordinary conventions of everyday life, and temporarily live, relate and think otherwise. This would be an extreme version of Bakhtin's centrifugal tendencies, but it also points to what might result should we suspend social 'reality' as we normally live it.

Throughout Bakhtin's writing is his focus on the creative and ethical possibilities for creating new meanings. In this regard, sometimes meanings might need to be contested if too centripetal, if too stuck in ossified or authoritative discourses that constrain ways of understanding and communicating with each other. Or, meaning might need to be reined in if seen as too centrifugal, where dialogues of misunderstanding and social anarchy feature. We typically oscillate between these possibilities, and what matters is where our communications and understandings fit on a continuum between centripetal and centrifugal tendencies. Might we need to bring a bit more creative dialogue or carnivalesque relating to a circumstance where meaning and communicating seem overdetermined? Might we, conversely, sometimes need to rein in our discourse, so as to firm up meanings and relations into something more reliably familiar? There can be costs to being (or becoming) too ensconced on either side of this personal or cultural pendulum. In Bakhtin's circumstances, however, more dialogue made a lot of sense.

Peopling language in dialogue and creative understanding

> An object is ready-made, the linguistic means for its depiction are ready-made, the artist himself is ready-made, and his world-view is ready-made. And here with ready-made means, in light of a ready-made world-view, the ready-made poet reflects a ready-made object. But, in fact the object is created in the process of creativity, as are the poet himself, his world-view, and his means of expression.   (Bakhtin, as cited in Morson and Emerson, 1990: 171)

Given his focus on the ethical and creative potentials of dialogue, derived from authors of great works of fiction, it is not surprising to see the extent to which Bakhtin focused on the 'authorship' of people in dialogue. Correspondingly, his focus was also on how people could use their dialogic communications, their words and intonations, to 'creatively understand' each other. While Bakhtin, like his colleague Volosinov, saw understandings and ways of talking somewhat pre-packaged ideologically and conceptually in speech genres and discourses, his concern was with talking beyond the constraints of speech genres (1986). Thus, we get a view from Bakhtin of dialogue straddling the 'already there' of discourse and the responsive immediacies of face-to-face dialogue with others who may speak a different discourse. People in dialogue were no mere recyclers of discourse: for Bakhtin, they faced ethical and creative challenges in articulating understandings and meanings that reflected them personally and relationally. It was in this sense that he wrote of there being no alibi in life. Language, and how we use and communicate it, is our primary way of creating the best relationships and ways of living available to us. Thus, Bakhtin's focus on authorship can be seen as an appeal to more fully develop our capacities for authoring a preferred way of life.

Two places where he emphasized such authorship possibilities were in his view of 'double-voicing' or 'peopling' already-used language in ways reflecting one's purposes and circumstances; and, in addition, 'creatively understanding' each other through how we use language in responsive communications. In both cases he was railing against a view of language and communications that implied we were stuck with either as they were already occurring. While we may not all communicate with the capacities of Dostoevsky or Rabelais, we always have the capacity to supplement the meanings and ways of talking already in use. Implicit in Bakhtin's writing is a view that we can in agentive ways use language to improve our lives. 'Double-voicing' refers to our ability to fit language to our purposes, circumstances and moods. 'Passive-voicing' points out the opposite, that we use words in the manner others did before us. While others may have acquainted us with a word and their meaning, tone and context for its use, we are not bound to their articulation. In a Heideggerian sense (see Chapter 4), this would be like suggesting we cannot use a tool, such as a screwdriver, to pry things apart, because a screwdriver has only one purpose. For Bakhtin (1984), we need to 'people' words with our intentions, give words our voicing where others might have voiced them differently. This is Bakhtin's pitch for using language creatively, to go beyond a view that words are prescribed by the people who used them for their purposes before us. That would make us their ventriloquist dummies. But it was also in this sense that Bakhtin wrote of 'renting' words from prior speakers. We cannot do anything we want with their words either. There is the matter of how such words acquire their familiarity in everyday discourse such that others can recognize and accept our particular uses of them. But that does not stop people from using a word like 'bad' to serve different purposes – as in, 'You're "baaad!", Andy Lock.'

Self, creative understanding, and authorship

Bakhtin's view of 'self' is that of a person born into dialogues in which she or he learns to respond and contribute. As his biographers Clark and Holquist (1984: 64) wrote:

> the self, conceived by Bakhtin, is not a presence wherein is lodged the ultimate guarantor of unified meaning. The Bakhtinian self is never whole, since it can only exist dialogically. It is not a substance or essence in its own right but exists in a tensile relationship with all that is other and, most importantly, with other selves.

Analogous to the notion that words are linked to prior and anticipated speakers who have claims on their meaning, Bakhtin's self is configured similarly, in dialogic responsiveness to prior and anticipated partners in dialogue. This is not the same as saying they determine what we think, say and do. But the 'tensile relationship' Clark and Holquist refer to speaks to that element of our relatedness factored into our thoughts and responses to each other. For Charles Taylor (1989), we are embedded in webs of dialogue that shape who we are. What we are building to here is to suggest a more complex form of authorship than is often considered and which helps further illustrate what Bakhtin was about when he suggested our words in dialogues were only half ours. Most social science accounts of dialogue have a third-party feel to them, yet being engaged in dialogue is a very different matter. Bakhtin reinserts the self into a responsiveness to others that shapes but does not determine us. Monologues are the opposite to this kind of relatedness. Therefore our challenge comes with 'peopling' language through how we actively voice our feelings and intentions, and in choosing and accenting the words we use in responsive dialogues with others.

'Creative understanding' requires an orientation to hearing and using language that is not bound to the conventions of particular understandings or speech genres. For Bakhtin, any word or genre has a 'loophole' that leaves open 'the possibility of altering the ultimate, final meaning of one's words' (1984: 233). But our varying positions in responsive dialogues mean that we cannot unilaterally change our conversational partners' words; we face a challenge in arriving at new meaning through dialogue. Here is where 'creative understanding' has an element of negotiation that cuts in two directions: to prior meanings and to the meanings our conversational partners will derive from what we say. Bakhtin relates to one half of this challenge in writing,

> when we select words in the process of constructing an utterance, we by no means always take them from the system of language in their neutral, dictionary form. We usually take them from other utterances, and mainly from utterances that are kindred to ours in genre, that is, in theme, composition or style.   (1986: 87)

The other half comes with the challenge of how our utterances will be received and responded to. 'The word, the living word, inseparably linked with dialogic communion, by its very nature wants to be heard and answered' (Bakhtin, 1984: 300). Hence, we typically package what we say or write in order to stay in dialogue with our partners – to use words to call forth from our partners particular responses or understandings. Billig (1996) suggested that even our thinking, or inner dialogue, may be similarly structured. This would imply that our thoughts develop much as they would in actual conversation; the difference being that instead of actual conversational partners influencing what we say, anticipated or imagined partners step in and take this role. In this respect, we might internalize speech genres that then shape the processes and outcomes of our thinking. Fortunately, actual dialogue offers loopholes out of the potential circularities of thought raised by Billig, and 'loopholes' suggest possibilities for 'creative understanding'.

From a Bakhtinian perspective, it can help to see an understanding as something shown in the responses our words elicit from conversational partners. This puts an onus on how we complete each other's utterances in dialogue through what we say and show back to each other. 'Creative understanding' can be seen as an improvised step outside of our accustomed speech genres ('conversational scripts') to collaboratively explore meaningful possibilities afforded by any loophole. Of course, recognizing a loophole comes first, but this should not be hard, given the number of places in dialogue that words come up short for how we want to understand and be understood. Creative understanding can also arise through invitations to conversational partners to join in what Gadamer (1988) referred to as 'playing' beyond the conventions of language – going 'outside' the meanings and ways of talking that had been guiding the conversation up to the point where 'creative understanding' seemed a useful departure.

At a minimum, our use of words 're-accentuates' their meanings, as we put them to work in new circumstances, for new purposes. This is where Bakhtin clearly departs from most linguists, who see the meanings of words as already fixed in dictionary, or seemingly culturally mandated, meanings (Zappen, 2004). Such is a language where meaning is designated by the words alone. Our voicing or accentuating words in dialogues is what gives any words their affective tone, but also their sense of significance as we intend to be understood by others, and how they may relate to us and our words. John Shotter (see Chapter 16) refers to this 'tonal' dimension of relational responsiveness as follows: 'it is in the tone of one's utterances that one establishes the nature of one's momentary relationship with those around one, whether one is expecting their love and affirmation, or criticism and attack' (1995a: 63). 'Creative understanding', in this way, can also be seen as a means of departing from a particular mode of relating to an experience or to one another. In Bakhtin's sense, such ways of relating would be presupposed not only by the semantic content of words, but by the affective tone underscoring any words used in understanding or communicating an experience. Needed, in this sense then, are new genres, new creative ways of understanding that do not bind people to particular descriptions and ways of talking, given their accompanying affective tones.

In Bakhtin's view, understanding or authorship follows from language that is already dialogically fraught with different uses, different tones, different contextual nuances, and so on. In Volosinov's writing there is a more political view of such differences and how they are resolved (e.g., 'In the vicissitudes of the words are to be found the vicissitudes of word users' (Volosinov, 1987: 106)). While sharing this concern over ideologies, Bakhtin also saw an ethical dimension implied in how such differences of understanding were to be resolved. If the meanings of our words are what you make of them, and where you take them, then it would be ethically wrong (ideological, tyrannical) to insist that you understand and use our words our way. Creative understanding could therefore be seen as a call to step outside such conflicts over language, to find alternative genres and ways of developing shared understandings. It is also an antidote to the rigidities of meaning that can sometime dominate, as Shotter and Billig (1998: 27) suggest:

> Only if we are prepared to change our hierarchically ordered centripetal ways, and to balance them with ones of a more centrifugal and relational kind, can we ever hope to arrive at a psychology properly respectful of the 'little details' of people's 'inner lives', and to overcome some of the seemingly basic ideological motifs of our time.

Valentin Volosinov

> … what is important for the speaker about a linguistic form is not that it is a stable and always self-equivalent signal, but that it is always a changeable and adaptable sign.   (Volosinov, 1986: 68)

> Any human utterance is an ideological construct in the small … Of course, an ideology, once it has achieved formulation, exerts, in turn, a reverse influence on our verbal reactions.   (Volosinov, 1987: 88)

While there have been claims made that Bakhtin was author of all the important writings to come out of the Bakhtin Circle (these claims are rehashed in Morson and Emerson, 1990), two significant volumes purportedly authored by circle member Volosinov offer rich ideas. *Marxism and the Philosophy of Language* (1986) and *Freudianism: A Critical Sketch* (1987) take up the centripetal concerns we have discussed, how meanings and ways of communicating can take on systematized, ideological dimensions. It is the restrictive aspects of these dimensions in particular that concerned Volosinov. But alongside his critique runs a familiar exhortation: that established meanings and ways of communicating can be contested and modified to better serve the people who use them. Here is the revolutionary enthusiasm we spoke of in starting this chapter – but it is tied to a very sophisticated and daring view, for the time, of language and communications.

Much of what can be read in Volosinov has affinities with what is in Bakhtin's more widely known writing. But Volosinov spends more time with the notion that meanings and particular forms of discourse can become linguistic traps. Early in *Marxism and the Philosophy of Language* he sets out a contrast between two approaches to discourse, one that should be familiar by now. Discourse was anything but the 'dead' stuff linguists studied, that view of meaning where words or symbols determined meanings quite apart from the people involved in using them. Unsurprisingly for this Marxist, that somehow meanings or discourses could stabilize was a social matter, not something intrinsic to words and discourses. Further, for Volosinov, all words, symbols, utterances, and so on, come already ideologically packaged. In this sense, anything meaningful can be traced to prior speakers, and thus the value-based conversations the meanings took hold in. Remember the Marxist view, that people can become estranged from the processes and products that result from their efforts – this is what was squarely contested in Volosinov's writing. People's words and dialogues needed to be turned back to them, to do as they wanted with them, not left to the historical predeterminations of others.

For Volosinov, ideology does not stop at person-to-person discourse either: it is there in our inner dialogues as well – as influential extensions of our outer discourses. He wrote accordingly, 'The reality of the inner psyche is the same reality as the sign' (1986: 26). Consequently, part of his challenge to readers was to become better at identifying how discourses and meanings lose or have lost their meanings because they were not being creatively used in conversations and thinking. Language lives in how we use it, but it can be kept dead if we adopt a passive way of understanding and mindlessly using it with others. This extends to how speakers and writers make discourse alive with expressiveness, feeling tones and responsiveness to circumstance and recipient. Ideologies tend to fix meanings, assign appropriatenesses to how one is to communicate, and can bind adherents to tautologies of thought and action, or conflict with those espousing other ideologies. They are a case of extending a particular set of values and actions through thought, social interaction and person action in ways consistent with the ideology. The issue is not to escape ideology, for Volosinov sees this as impossible, but to interact socially in ways that do not bind people to what is already bound up in particular ideologies. Fortunately, dialogues require a kind of responsivity to each other and to our circumstances that can take us beyond the limits of particular ideologies. It is in this sense that Volosinov saw speaking words as a 'two-sided act', in that one uses words partly on the basis of how others have used them before, but also on the basis of reaching out or responding to others who may use or understand such words differently.

Associated with Volosinov's view of ideologies is a conception that they have contours that distinguish what is appropriate to speaking and acting from within them, and what would be inconsistent with those appropriatenesses beyond them (Shotter, 1998). In some respects, all conversations between people familiar with each other take on some of these contours that, in a sense, often guide them in ways that can help keep things familiar. But therein lies the linguistic and ideological trap: if these familiarities determine what can be said, and how things get said, speakers can drift back to Volosinov's concern, needing to wrest fresh potentials from their historical meanings and ways of conversing. This can apply as much to practitioners' dialogues with clients as it can with people who find their conversations and ways of relating growing stale and stodgy. But with these efforts comes introducing differences, unfamiliar ways of talking and meaning – sometimes it can seem easier just to stay familiar.

In *Freudianism: A Critical Sketch*, Volosinov (1987) saw another ideology. Bearing in mind that ideology does not end in dialogues between people but extends to their inner thoughts, he saw in 'Freudianism' another possibility for over-determined meaning and relating. It, as all ideologies and discourses require, has not only a way of understanding, but an implicit way of evaluating experiences as Volosinov pointed out: 'discourse does not at all reflect the extraverbal situation in the way a mirror reflects an object. Rather, *the discourse here resolves the situation*, bringing to it an *evaluative conclusion*, as it were' (Volosinov, 1987: 100; emphasis in the original). Even Freud stepped out of his own discourse to suggest that sometimes a cigar is just a cigar. But there is an important point we see Volosinov getting at, in the sense that discourses, if not 're-peopled' in his colleague Bakhtin's sense, can position people as mere ventriloquators of discourse, as people who extend the ideological means of discourse as they evaluate new experiences through the lens any discourse offers. As Shotter and Billig (1998) have pointed out, however, ideology tries to weave its way in between our words and utterances to give them a feeling tone that is 'its business', and not necessarily 'ours'. Our job, therefore, is to not feel swept along by the ideological content of discourse, but to notice the requirements it could make of us, and to replace these with meanings and ways of communicating more in line with our preferences.

Some 'final' words on Bakhtin

> The one who understands ... becomes *himself* a participant in the dialogue.
> (Bakhtin, as cited in Clark and Holquist, 1984: 1)

By now, it should be clear that Bakhtin and his circle were courageous and audacious thinkers of the first order. Perhaps it takes the kinds of cultural cataclysms and monologic tendencies they experienced, and were 'up against', to hone such rich ideas into the kind of dialogic idealism (dialogism, wrote Holquist, 1990) evident throughout their writing. Bakhtin was a man who paid for his writing and thinking dearly (obscurity in Siberia: he even ended up using a good portion of one of his manuscripts for cigarette papers). Yet, his vision of dialogue and its meaningful possibilities derived from studies of literature and linguistics yielded rich insights that are now very influential across many disciplines and artistic spheres.

It would be wrong to read Bakhtin as conveying a view of only the niceties of dialogue. His concern, whether with those who wanted to formalize language and authorship into singular meanings, or with political regimes that sought their own monologic control, was with the fundamental importance of seeing life in dialogic terms. Singular or orthodox meanings and ways of relating are Bakhtin's targets, and his resources in taking them on are authors, such as Rabelais or Dostoevsky, whose writings point to new social possibilities. This was what we meant when we started by describing Bakhtin's writing on dialogue as 'double-edged'. On one side, this translates to a way of thinking and communicating but, on the other, it refers to his 'dialogics of critique' (Gardiner, 1992). While not a foundationalist, or realist in the sense that there is a correct way of understanding and articulating experience, Bakhtin was no relativist either, as this passage from *Problems of Dostoevsky's Poetics* points out:

> It is hardly necessary to mention that the polyphonic approach has nothing in common with relativism (nor with dogmatism). It should be noted that

both relativism and dogmatism equally exclude all argumentation and all genuine dialog, either by making them unnecessary (relativism) or impossible (dogmatism).   (1984: 56)

What Bakhtin offered was a view of meaning as always having a 'loophole', where there is always more that can be said or written, in different words or genres, to understand and act within any 'hard and fast' reality. His poetic challenge should not, however, be confused with the use of words alone because such words must still fit our relationships and circumstances. Whether considering Bakhtin's notions of polyphony, carnival, heteroglossia, creative understanding, unfinalizability, speech genres or dialogue – there clearly are rich resources offered for considering meaning and how we construct it. Bakhtin was appealing to the creative and ethical author in each of us, to construct ways of relating that welcomed and worked with differences. In referring to Bakhtin's legacy, John Shotter wrote some appropriate words to close on:

> it is in our unique and novel uses of language, our own special ways of populating our words with our own accents, our own rhythms, our own ways of juxtaposing them, and so on, that we can offer or afford others the chance of a responsive understanding of our own unique inner lives.   (1998: 82)

6 Lev Vygotsky

> It is not the consciousness of men that determines their existence, but their social existence that determines their consciousness.   (Marx, 1859, Preface to his book *A Contribution to the Critique of Political Economy*)

> … the central fact about our psychology is the fact of mediation.   (Vygotsky, 1987: 166)

We doubt whether many of our readers have seen the English writer Tom Stoppard's play *Rosenkrantz and Guildenstern are Dead*. It is a rather weird play. Rosenkrantz and Guildenstern are minor characters in Shakespeare's tragedy *Hamlet*. As minor characters, they are not on stage much when *Hamlet* is being performed, and then only for a short time. Stoppard's plot happens 'backstage' of *Hamlet*. Every now and then, Rosenkrantz and Guildenstern have to leave the stage of his play to walk on to the set of *Hamlet* to play their part there, but we never see them performing in *Hamlet*. And having been part of the action there, they then 'exit, stage left', and walk back into their parts in Stoppard's play about them. And it all gets very clever, because Stoppard links what they do in his play as they come and go to what they were doing when they were offstage in *Hamlet*'s plot. Too clever by half for most people, including Rosenkrantz and Guildenstern – part of the plot being built around their attempts to understand what is happening to them – because you have to know *Hamlet* well enouugh to realize what they are involved in every time they get called away, and so get a handle on why they are like what they are like when they 'come back'.

But the play makes for an interesting analogy for understanding child development and even adult life. Infants 'pop into' a culture that is going on around them when they are born. Everybody but them seems to know what is going on, what the plot is, and their task is to start playing along with everybody else. How do infants cotton on to what is already going on, and find a way of playing along? Vygotsky has a lot to offer in helping us answer this question. With respect to adult life, then, while everyone walks around with their own concerns, they cannot help finding themselves walking into others' concerns, and needing to find ways of grasping what is going on. Part of a therapist's role is to assist in this process of renavigating their situation, if doing this becomes problematic and distressing for a person. Again, Vygotsky's work has a direct relevance here.

Lev Semenevich Vygotsky was born in the same year, 1896, as Piaget, but died prematurely at the age of 37 from tuberculosis. His active career as a psychologist was only around ten years long. During that time, his goals in the post-revolutionary climate of the emerging Soviet Union were to reconstruct psychology along Marxist lines, and to apply psychology to the massive problems confronting the emerging state, particularly in the field of educational psychology. He travelled extensively during this period, conducting research and assisting in teacher training, by teaching and helping in the establishment of new teacher-training institutions. He had no apartment of his own for several years, but lived, when in Moscow, in the basement of the Institute of Psychology. It is a testimony to his energy that he produced any writings at all under these circumstances. In 1936 his work was suppressed in the Soviet Union by a decree of the Central Committee of the Communist Party. This only changed after Stalin's death in 1953. His work became available in the west in 1962 with the publication of an abridged version of his 1934 book *Myshlenie i rech'* ('Thinking and speech') under the title *Thought and Language*, with a foreword by Jerome Bruner. Since then more translations and more titles have become available. Vygotsky is reported to have had a photographic memory, and his work is clearly influenced by his wide reading of contemporaries such as Wolfgang Kohler, Jean Piaget, Karl Buhler and William Stern. His early death means that he has not left us with any clearly articulated and formally elaborated theory, but rather a body of ideas to be mined for their riches.

There are a number of obstacles to an exact elucidation of exactly what Vygotsky was doing in writing about human psychology. First, the body of ideas he was both reacting to and building on were very different from those current today. The 'reflex', following Pavlov, played a major role in psychological theorizing, as did the 'stimulus' and 'response' notions of the American behaviourists. In 1924, in an address to the Second All-Union Congress of Psychoneurologists, held in Leningrad, Vygotsky claimed he was a bigger reflexologist than Pavlov (Vygotsky, 1982a: 58; 1994: 40), and the problem facing psychology was to combine the work done by the notion of reflexes with an understanding of subjectivity. A year later, he was clearly thinking somewhat differently: 'we should beware of any direct transportation of reflexological laws into psychology' (Vygotsky 1982b: 83). But, as Veresov points out:

> that change of Vygotsky's theoretical position is not reflected in the literature, and therefore, in the 'classical picture' of the development of Vygotsky's thought, these two articles are referred to as one period of that development (Minick, 1987), which is not correct historically nor methodologically. Even a brief textual comparative analysis shows that these articles represent two essentially different, but historically connected, periods of theoretical development of Vygotsky's views on the problem of human consciousness.
> (1999: 257)

That said, however, we would be hard pushed today to grasp the minutiae of Vygotsky's thinking, given our unfamiliarity with the conceptual milieu in which he was working. Similarly, different translations, as Veresov (1999) makes clear, provide different pictures: it is significant here that the first translation of Vygotsky into English (1962) is titled *Thought and Language*, whereas a later version (1987) is titled *Thinking and Speech* (1987), which has very different connotations.

The second problem follows from what we have just said. The majority of western scholars have taken from Vygotsky what they find useful to their particular frameworks of thought, and the dominant paradigm to which his work has been co-opted in the west following its 'rediscovery' is the cognitive paradigm. With respect to language, for example, the model here is that to speak a language a child needs to deduce from the utterances it hears what the rules are for generating those utterances, rules that are possessed by those who speak to them, and which enable the child's caregivers to produce those utterances. Because of the claim that the input the child receives is insufficient for it to decode the rules that generated that input, it has to be the case that the child's task is supplemented by innate knowledge as to the possible rules underlying this input, and these rules inform an internal Language Acquisition Device (LAD) (Chomsky, 1959), so as to enable the child to develop the necessary grammar via which to generate its own, acceptable, utterances. Bruner (1983) added to this idea, asking about

> how the linguistic community arranges speech encounters so that the young aspirant speaker can get a hold on how to make his own communicative intentions clear and how to penetrate the intentions of others. The principal vehicle of this assistance is the format, the patterned situations that enable adult and child to cooperate in the 'passing on' of a language.   (1983: 10)

He thus introduced the notion of the LASS, the Language Acquisition Support System, named in opposition to the LAD. It will be easy to appreciate how one of Vygotsky's central ideas – 'the zone of proximal development' (see below) – can be brought into this framework and thus elucidate how social practices can be made more readily available to the developing individual.

It is not clear, however, that this paradigm is the most sensible way of conceiving the 'transmission' of language (or culture, as well, because culture has also been (mis)conceived as the passing on of the rules that underwrite human activities), nor is it clear that this is how Vygotsky intended his ideas to be adopted. The situation in cognitive psychology is not dissimilar to that which Vygotsky was objecting about in his own time:

> The question of the psychological nature of consciousness is persistently and deliberately avoided in our scientific literature. Attempts are made even to take no notice of it, as if it does not exist for the new psychology. Without having a preliminary working hypothesis concerning the psychological nature of consciousness, it is impossible to undertake a critical revision of the accumulated scientific knowledge in this area, to select and screen it, to translate it into a new language, to develop new concepts, and to create new problems...
>
> Scientific psychology cannot ignore the facts of consciousness; it must materialise them, translate what objectively exists into an objective language, and once and for all unmask and bury the fictions, phantasmagoria, etc. Otherwise, no work is possible, neither teaching nor criticism nor research.
>
> It is easy to see that consciousness cannot be regarded as a phenomenon of a second line, neither biologically, physiologically, nor psychologically.

A place must be found for it, and it must be interpreted in the same line with all other reactions of the organism. This is the first requirement of our working hypothesis. Consciousness is a problem of the structure of behaviour.   (1925/1999: 252, 256)

Vygotsky, then, as a Marxist, starts his psychology within the Marxist identification of subjectivity as where world and actor meet, and in incorporating his ideas into the Cartesian-inspired framework contemporary psychology transforms them away from their original meaning, away from an understanding of how consciousness is structured by practice (see Newman and Holzman, 1997: 78–9).

The final problem we want to note here is linked to this second one. Reading Vygotsky inevitably means re-interpreting his writing but, at the same time, interpreting his writing means re-reading it. We say this from the practical problem of aiming to present his central ideas and themes in the next few sections. The problem is where to start, because all the themes, as Wertsch (1993: ix) has previously noted, are inter-related. We could begin with any one of them, but cannot do that one proper justice until we have dealt with the others. Thus it becomes necessary for anyone beginning Vygotsky to read, and then re-read from the beginning again, because whatever first theme we, or anyone, might begin with can only be appreciated for what it is in the light of the whole. It is rather like the apocryphal joke of the tourist asking the peasant how to get to the nearest city, only to be told 'If I were you, I wouldn't start from here.' With that proviso, we shall do our best.

Vygotsky's main themes

One of the leading lights in making Vygotsky's work available in the west is James Wertsch. The opening two paragraphs of his foreword to a translation of Vygotsky and Luria's joint monograph *Studies on the History of Behavior: Ape, Primitive, and Child* (1993: ix) set the scene here:

The theoretical perspective outlined by Lev Semenovich Vygotsky can be understood in terms of three general themes that run throughout his writings:

(a) the use of a genetic, or developmental method;
(b) the claim that higher mental functioning in the individual emerges out of social processes; and
(c) the claim that human social and psychological processes are fundamentally shaped by cultural tools, or mediational means.

… all three themes were interdefined in Vygotsky's thinking. Therefore, an account of each depends on advances in our understanding of the others. This interconnectedness should not be underestimated … in the end, the meaning of each can be understood only by understanding its relationship to the others. It is worth noting that Vygotsky himself never outlined his approach by laying out these three themes.

Quite so, and not all present-day commentators would place the same nuance on some of these themes. We offer our grasp of Vygotsky, and his principal ideas.

Higher vs elementary/natural psychological functions

Imagine you had grown up in total social isolation. Vygotsky's notion of 'elementary psychological functions' would then describe what your psychological abilities would be like in that situation. You have no language, you cannot read or write, but you have an intact nervous system that can do many things as well as, and many things beyond, what a primate can do. Have you ever played 'Kim's Game', in which you are presented with a tray full of disparate objects, and told you will be asked to remember what was there once you have looked for a short while before they are covered up or removed? Children under about 7 years of age approach this task differently from adults in literate cultures. They use eidetic imagery to keep track of things. They take a kind of 'mental snapshot' of the collection of items. When asked to recall the objects they have looked at, they will often close their eyes, and their eyes can be seen to be moving behind their eyelids, as though they are looking at the image they have retained to see what objects are in which position. (Literate) adults use a different strategy: they try and create a verbal list of the objects, and rehearse this to remember what was there. The children are using their 'elementary/natural mental functions', the adults are not. Vygotsky used eidetic imagery as an example himself to distinguish these two levels of functioning:

> A comparative investigation of human memory reveals that, even at the earliest stages of social development, there are two, principally different, types of memory. One, dominating in the behaviour of nonliterate people, is characterised by the non-mediated impression of materials, by the retention of actual experiences as the basis of mnemonic (memory) traces. We call this natural memory, and it is clearly illustrated in E. R. Jaensch's studies of eidetic imagery. This kind of memory is very close to perception, because it arises out of the direct influence of external stimuli upon human beings. From the point of view of structure, the entire process is characterized by a quality of immediacy.
> Natural memory is not the only kind, however, even in the case of nonliterate men and women. On the contrary, other types of memory belonging to a completely different developmental line coexist with natural memory. The use of notched sticks and knots, the beginnings of writing and simple memory aids all demonstrate that even at early stages of historical development humans went beyond the limits of the psychological functions given to them by nature and proceeded to a new culturally elaborated organization of their behaviour. Comparative analysis shows that such activity is absent even in the highest species of animals; we believe that these sign operations are the product of specific conditions of social development.   (1978: 38–9)

Thus, Vygotsky conceives unaided natural abilities – the elementary psychological functions – as distinct from those that use the resources of cultural items to augment them. He considers the 'augmented abilities' as not just what are naturally given to us plus a bit extra, but as abilities being transformed into something quite different altogether. Natural abilities allow us to do new things – like read – but in the same way as there are major differences between the ways novice readers and proficient readers 'read', so too do the kinds of abilities that arise through 'augmentation' – the higher psychological functions – differ from natural abilities. Think of paper money: with your natural abilities you see it as a patterned surface; with your augmented ones you see it as 'money'.

Wertsch (1985: 25) comments that in the above quotation Vygotsky has indicated the four major criteria that distinguish between the elementary and the higher mental functions:

1. the shift of control from the environment to the individual, that is, the emergence of voluntary regulation;
2. the emergence of conscious realisation of mental process;
3. the social origins and social nature of higher mental functions; and
4. the use of signs to mediate higher mental functions.

Intermental vs intramental abilities

Novel terms: 'intermental' means 'between people'; 'intramental' means 'within people'. How does Vygotsky apply these to human activity? Young infants give very little indication that they are trying to communicate when they yell. It seems likely they are just distressed, and that their crying is part of what it is to be distressed. But we adults-as-parents worry about what it is they are crying about, and do something in an effort to help them. We treat their yells as a cry for help; we treat them as if they were communicating with us, which they are, but by default. This is an example of what Vygotsky means by an *intermental ability*: the ability the infant has to communicate cannot be located within the infant, but only in the relationship between the infant and the other person who acts so as to constitute yelling as a means of communication. When the infant has figured out that this is the functional status of yelling, and can use it *in order to* get someone to do something, then we are talking about an *intramental ability*.

When the infant is somewhat older, a similar shift of an ability from between people to within the infant can be seen to occur, and this one is very important. Vygotsky's colleague Luria puts it like this:

> When he acquires a word, which isolates a particular thing and serves as a signal to a particular action, the child, as he carries out an adult's verbal instruction, is subordinated to this word... By subordinating himself to the adult's verbal orders the child acquires a system of these verbal instructions and gradually begins to utilize them for the regulation of his own behaviour.   (Luria and Yudovich, 1971: 13–14)

Derek Edwards has provided some concrete examples of this in his observations of an infant called Alice (1978: 462–3), aged around 19 months, who is learning how to stop herself from doing things by taking over elements of her mother's speech as her own. For example, when she is talking with her caretaker, she looks at her mother's watch which is out of reach and says 'Don't … mommy's watch', to which her caretaker replies 'Mummy's. No touch', and Alice says 'Don't touch.'

Alice is saying exactly what her mother would have said to her repeatedly in the past few months. She is using her emerging language ability to take over her mother's controlling function of her behaviour, and, via the *mediation* of these words, is coming to control her own actions. In Luria's way of putting it, her behaviour is subordinated to the word, but it is now her word, not her mother's. The control of her actions has shifted from the intermental to the intramental.

Vygotsky makes a bold claim in this context:

> Every function in the child's cultural development appears twice: first,
> on the social level, and later on the individual level; first, between
> people (interpsychological [= 'intermental']), and then inside the child
> (intrapsychological [= 'intramental']). This applies equally to voluntary attention,
> to logical memory, and to the formation of concepts. All the higher functions
> originate as actual relations between human individuals.   (1978: 57)

Development, then, in Vygotsky's sense, is not learning to do something new, but taking over the control of something you can already do in concert with somebody else. This same point has been stated independently by the Scottish philosopher and theologian John Macmurray (1961: 50):

> [The human infant] cannot, even theoretically, live an isolated existence ...
> he is not an independent individual. He lives a common life as one term in
> a personal relationship. Only in the process of development does he learn to
> achieve a relative independence, and that only by appropriating the techniques
> of a rational social tradition.

These techniques are 'appropriated' in the course of social interactions in which the developing child is 'subjected' to them, sometimes deliberately, and sometimes merely by default, because the tradition is one that structures the activities of the adults they interact with – their 'walking into a play that is already in progress' that we noted earlier.

The Zone of Proximal Development

The 'Zone of Proximal Development' is often shortened to the acronym 'zoped' or 'ZPD' for obvious reasons. The zone of proximal development is

> the distance between the actual developmental level as determined by
> independent problem solving and the level of potential development as
> determined through problem solving under adult guidance or in collaboration
> with more capable peers.   (Vygotsky, 1978: 86)

Note the implication in this formulation that to establish a zoped in interaction is a skill that requires the 'teacher' to be able to pitch their 'tuition' at a point determined by the learner's level of skill. Go above or below this level, and no new learning will be enabled, either because pitching it too low obviously cannot pull the learner's skills beyond where they already are, and pitching it too high fails to allow a connection to be grasped.

Note also that working with another in their zoped can accomplish two different outcomes: establishing goals and refining means to attaining them. A 'form-board' is a fairly standard toy for infants in the west: it is like a jigsaw puzzle, but the pieces have to be slotted into holes that correspond to them on the board, and not fitted together like jigsaw pieces. They generally have small knobs attached to them for ease of picking up. Young infants are quite clumsy at picking such objects up, and this is a skill they develop through practice. But young infants generally pick up these pieces and suck them: the very idea that these might be fitted into their holes doesn't appear to enter their thoughts. Adults, though, can set the pieces up so that clumsy babies knock the pieces into their holes, and then make 'a fuss', thus making it a spectacle that has been achieved; or they demonstrate how to do it; or they actually take the infants hand and 'make it' get the pieces into their holes. Over time, often quite quickly, infants 'get it': putting pieces in holes is a goal they can aim at. As Wertsch (1985: 166) puts it:

> They first participate in the execution of the goal-directed task on the interpsychological plane, and only subsequently do they recognise and master the strategic significance of their behaviours. Rather than understanding the task and then doing it, the children seem to have done the task (as a participant in interpsychological functioning) and then understood it.

Another way of putting this is that when an activity has come under intramental control, we mean that we have an idea of the implications of the actions we are engaged in, and we perceive 'what comes next' in our interactions with another or the world of objects. To begin with, only one participant in the interaction can 'see' the action-implications of the other's activity, and in acting on this perception, they act to create a zoped, so that the child can come to appreciate the 'meaning' that is constituted by her own contribution to the interaction.

There are also a number of other ways of putting it that have been independently formulated in the literature of development:

> Long before the child learns to speak he is able to communicate, meaningfully and intentionally, with his mother. In learning language, he is acquiring a more effective and more elaborate means of doing something which he can already do in a crude and primitive fashion.   (Macmurray, 1961: 60)

> Meaning can be described, accounted for, or stated in terms of symbols or language at its highest and most complex stage of development (the stage it reaches in human experience), but language simply lifts out of the social process a situation which is logically or implicitly there already. The language symbol is simply a significant or conscious gesture.   (Mead, 1934: 79)

> In order to subject a function to intellectual and volitional control, we must first possess it.   (Vygotsky, 1962: 90; cf. Bakhtin's phrase 'peopling things with our intentions' – see Chapter 5)

Hence, at first, our abilities lie 'outside' our control, in the perceptions of others (and thus they are intermental), and become apparent to us if that other can make them available to us. And the best way to make them available is to adjust one's actions back to the other so that they are 'just' apparent to them – make them 'appropriate' to the other's abilities by working in the zoped created by their current abilities. Children learn and develop by 'performing a head taller than they are' (Vygotsky, 1978: 102) in social interactions which 'scaffold' their abilities.

Psychological tools and mediation

> What is the key to the puzzle of the evolution of psychology from animal to human being, from primitive to cultural man?
>
> We believe that the answer is to be found in the evolution of those conditions of existence, in which we all live, as well as in the evolution of those forms of behavior that are determined by these external conditions. Modern man does not have to adapt to the external environment in the way that an animal or primitive man does. Modern man has conquered nature and what primitive man did with his legs or hands, his eyes or ears, the modern man does with his tools. Cultural man does not have to strain his vision to see a distant object – he can do it with the help of eyeglasses, binoculars, or a telescope; he does not have to lend an attentive ear to a distant source, run for his life to bring news, – he performs all these functions with the help of those tools and means of communication and transportation that fulfil his will. All the artificial tools, the entire cultural environment, serve to 'expand our senses' (Viner, 1909). Modern cultural man can allow himself the luxury of having the worst natural abilities, which he amplifies with artificial devices thus coping with the external world better than the primitive man who used his natural abilities directly. The latter broke a tree by beating it on a stone, modern man takes an ax or a frame-saw and does this work quicker, better, and with less energy wasted.   (Vygotsky and Luria, 1993: 169–70)

Vygotsky distinguishes between *technical tools* and *psychological tools*, but sees both of them as *mediators* of human actions. But tools are not just means-to-ends in a utilitarian way, they are simultaneously agents in the transformation and reorganization of human actions (see below) from impulsive behaviour aimed directly at a desired object into an 'instrumental' activity *mediated* by the tool. Tools serve to shift our abilities from a reliance on the *elementary functions* to the *higher psychological functions*, from a direct to an indirect, or mediated, relationship to the environment:

> The central characteristic of elementary functions is that they are totally and directly determined by stimulation from the environment. For higher functions, the central feature is self-generated stimulation, that is, the creation and use of artificial stimuli which become the immediate causes of behavior.   (Vygotsky, 1978: 39)

And, at the same time, we come to perceive the functional meanings of these creations as primary: we see 'money', not 'funny paper'. These 'psychological tools' come to mediate our lives and ways of thinking.

> Instead of an immediate interaction with problems posed by the environment, the human mind becomes involved in the indirect relationships mediated by more and more sophisticated systems of symbolic tools. Let us examine this transition using as an example the changing system of the measurement of time. The early forms of time measurement were characterized by using

> natural processes to immediately and perceptually mark equal intervals. In such measurements the comprehension of time duration was not yet detached from the natural processes involved, be it the movement of sand in a sand glass or running water in a clepsydra. No symbolic signifiers were interposed between the process of measurement and its representation to the individual. This original immediacy disappeared with the invention of the mechanical clock in which the actual process of measuring intervals of time is separated from the symbolic representation of the process on the dial. The actual movement of the hands of the clock remained the only link between the 'natural time' of the mechanism and the 'symbolic time' of the dial. The natural aspect disappeared completely and the chronometer became a purely symbolic tool when electronic digital technology replaced the clockwork mechanism. The process of perceiving time has become highly mediated. In order for an individual to read a watch, the whole system of symbols such as digits, language abbreviations, positions on the screen, etc., have to be learned.   (Kozulin, 1990: 134–5)

But in addition, the meaning of the time we read from a clock, our experience of its passing, is deeply reflective of the social relations between us. Bloch notes (1961a: 74) a dispute in medieval times as to whether the time for a contestant to appear for a duel has been reached. The court has to deliberate, and appeals to the clerics present, who are used to ringing bells to structure their daily prayers, and who thus have a better feel for the rhythms of time passing. Eventually, after much discussion, the court is able to decide that 'time is up'. In the same period, Bloch notes (ibid.: 84–5), there was a great deal of argument as to when the millennium and the anticipated coming of the Antichrist would occur. Indeed, for the majority of western men this expression, 'the year 1000, which we have been led to believe was charged with anguish, could not be identified with any precise moment in the sequence of days'.

It is unlikely that the modern quantitative measures of time that we are so familiar with had any common existence before the last decades of the sixteenth century (Nef, 1958: 7). And it is significant that then it was changes in the structure of social relations between people, in terms of the economic relations that came to structure 'work', that brought about this change, fitting in with Vygotsky's view that our higher, mediated psychological abilities have their origins in the social relations between people.

Semiotic potential and the decontextualization of mediational means

> The inclusion of a sign in one or other behavioral process … reforms the whole structure of the psychological operation as the inclusion of a tool reforms the whole structure of a labour operation.   (Vygotsky, 1928: 64; 1930/1982c: 103; cited by van der Veer and Valsiner, 1991: 222)

> The origin of all, specifically human, higher psychological processes, therefore, cannot be found in the mind or brain of an individual person but rather should be sought in the social 'extracerebral' sign systems a culture provides.   (van der Veer and Valsiner, 1991: 220)

With the development of agriculture and pastoralism, humans, for the first time, really faced the problem of keeping track of their 'stuff'. If you build a walled pen to keep your goats safe in overnight, and let them out to graze in the morning, how do you know if you have herded them all back in to safety the next night? The historical solution to this appears to have been by using 'tally sticks': make a mark or notch on a stick as each goat goes out of the pen in the morning, and 'cross it off' when the animal goes back into the pen that night. The beauty of this system is that one can use it solely on the basis of understanding one-to-one corre-spondence: each mark represents one animal; each crossed mark represents each animal safely home. And this system works without the user having any concept of number, nor any mathematical skills. Yet the system of marks contains a great deal of what Vygotsky terms 'semiotic potential'. The marks have the potential to constitute a number system; they have the potential to lead one to understand the meaning of 'equal'; and eventually, and after a long time, to elucidate the idea of 'zero'; to notice that odd and even numbers have different properties; that there are prime numbers, that adding and subtraction are possible.

To accomplish these things, to realize the semiotic possibilities of tallying and thereby 'reform the whole structure of … psychological operations', requires that the original technique be lifted out of its original context of practice and applied in others: to move from a concrete skill used in particular practices to a more abstract set of principles that can be reapplied in other practices. A similar idea has been put forward by Sir Karl Popper. Popper asks how animal paths might arise through a jungle:

> They are not planned or intended, and there was perhaps no need for them before they came into existence. But they may create a new need, or a set of new aims: the aim-structure of animals or men is not 'given', but it develops … out of earlier aims, and out of results which were or were not aimed at. In this way, a whole new universe of possibilities or potentialities may arise: a world which is to a large extent autonomous.   (1972: 118–19)

As an example of this autonomy Popper discusses the properties of mathematics. His discussion provides a view on the meaning of 'semiotic potential'. He main-tains that the sequence of natural numbers is a human construction, but

> although we create this sequence, it creates its own autonomous problems in its turn. The distinction between odd and even numbers is not created by us: it is an unintended and unavoidable consequence of our creation. Prime numbers, of course, are similarly unintended.   (ibid.)

Thus, the numbers have a potential for further applications, things that we can come to discover. And, in this context, different number systems have different potentials with respect to the structuring and practice of cultural abilities. It is easier to do maths with the Arabic system than with the Roman system, for example, even with a lot of practice. Thus, we can decontextualize mathematics from the act of counting, yet use the same set of symbols for each activity, while noting that some symbol systems have a greater facilitative (semiotic) potential to enable this than others (as though something gave symbols a more-or-less compatible zoped of their own with respect to our solving the autonomous problems they set us).

That said, we must not overlook the social ecology within which symbols are used, and the social practices they are used for. Both of these can give us a 'set' that allows the exploitation of semiotic potentials, and a subsequent decontextualization and generalization of the ways we use these symbols. For example, consider the formulation of what we now term 'Archimedes' Principle'. It may be mythical, but Archimedes is reputed to have 'discovered' this in his bath, shouted 'Eureka', and then run naked through the streets in his excitement. A certain amount of social organization underwrote the possibility of a naked primate being able to think about such arcane issues while wallowing in water, rather than keeping an eye out for the wild animals likely to eat him. And a hydraulic technology was needed in order to get the water to him, rather than his having to go to it. Another technology was needed to heat as large a quantity of water as one needs to wallow in and reflect on how the water level changes. And more hydraulics were needed to get rid of the dirty water afterwards, if only to prevent increasing the possibilities of diseases that would adversely affect the very urban environment that enabled all this thinking to be done where it was in the first place. It is such things that 'mediate' our psychological abilities, in Vygotsky's scheme of things, which is at one and the same time an inherently Marxist perspective

Thought and Language /Thinking and Speech/ 'Thinking and speaking'/ 'Meaning-making – language-making'

The first of Vygotsky's works translated into English (1962) was given the title *Thought and Language*. Calling these 'things' by means of nouns conveys a quite different slant on Vygotsky's ideas than its subsequent re-translation as *Thinking and Speech* (1987). Given Rieber's (2004: 2) 'imagined' statement by Vygotsky that 'What you need to keep in mind is that you should not look for entities. Your objective is to pay attention to the interaction process', then 'Thinking and speaking' might be a better title. Newman and Holzman (1993: 113) suggest from their reading of Vygotsky that a more accurate translation would be 'meaning-making/language-making', in that this would better reflect Vygotsky's main claims. Traditionally, Vygotsky's views on whatever we might call this issue have been stated in contrast to those put forward by Piaget (1926) in *The Language and Thought of the Child*, and thus the 'thought and language' characterization of his ideas has been the most widely adopted. Piaget's views may be thought of as 'inside out', Vygotsky's as 'outside in':

> our schema of development – first social, then egocentric, then inner speech – contrasts both with the traditional behaviorist schema – vocal speech, whisper, inner speech – and with Piaget's sequence – from nonverbal autistic thought through egocentric thought and speech to socialized speech and

> logical thinking. In our conception, the true direction of the development of thinking is not from the individual to the socialized, but from the social to the individual.   (Vygotsky, 1962: 19–20)

For Piaget, children act upon the world, and deduce the underlying concepts for thinking about space, causality, etc., from the results of these actions. They subsequently develop language and exploit the logic enshrined in it by virtue of this detached, contemplative ratiocination as their intelligence matures through various stages of 'internal operations'. To begin with, the symbols current in the speech of their culture are first tied to these individually deduced concepts for the child's own operational purposes – egocentrically – and are only finally liberated for social use with the advent of formal operations around 12 years of age. Vygotsky turns this on its head: thinking is situated in action; speaking is situated in interaction; and gradually the resources available in the symbols of interactive communication become fused with thinking-in-activity, first as so-called 'egocentric speech', which acts as a guide to planning and completing actions-in-progress, and eventually (though not inevitably) as a tool that enhances planning and action by providing it with a way of logically considering possible courses of actions in a coherent framework. Vygotsky is very clear on this:

> The relationship of thought to word is not a thing but a process, a movement from thought to word and from word to thought … Thought is not expressed but completed in the word. We can, therefore, speak of the establishment (i.e., the unity of being and nonbeing) of thought in the word. Any thought strives to unify, to establish a relationship between one thing and another. Any thought has movement. It unfolds … The structure of speech is not simply the mirror image of the structure of thought. It cannot, therefore, be placed on thought like clothes off a rack. Speech does not merely serve as the expression of developed thought. Thought is restructured as it is transformed into speech. It is not expressed but completed in the word. Therefore, precisely because of the contrasting directions of movement, the development of the internal and external aspects of speech form a true identity.   (Vygotsky, 1987: 250–51)

In addition:

> You might consider this concept of thinking to be something like the contemplation of an action, but it comes out of interaction processes within me, by which I was stimulating an action in you. Consider for a moment the possibility that, in the communicative act, I'm not really sure exactly what I think until I've heard myself say it. In other words, my thinking or my interactive dialogue with myself, which is not yet expression-ripe, obtains meaning from the feedback I get as I am listening to myself.   (Rieber, 2004: 2)

Shades of Bakhtin (Chapter 5) are clear here. There is a rich looping in this process such that growth, development, learning and action become fused with the processes and products of historical resources structured into cultures: action is not an ability to use what one already knows, to apply a tool as a means to an end, but action reorganizes what is there as something available to do something new, to produce new tools and results simultaneously.

It is from this analysis that we find ourselves choosing Newman and Holzman's preferred title for Vygotsky's book – 'Meaning-making/language-making' – over its earlier alternatives. Change occurs as actions make meanings with others and are, in the act of doing, incorporated back to reorganize the ways that doing can be done: it is 'where the action is' – in real-time conduct. This, again, is a departure from the Cartesian (and Kantian) subject who acts ... and then somehow reflects, and subsequently refers back to the results of this reflection to essay future actions: 'the historical child, unencumbered by any egocentric oak in her or his Kantian-Piagetian acorn, is busy making meaning, changing the determining totality, letting her/his revolutionary activity create more revolutionary activity' (Newman and Holzman, 1993: 116–17).

Applying Vygotsky

While Vygotsky's ideas have deservedly enjoyed widespread acceptance among western educators, they are only now coming to the attention of therapists and counsellors (e.g., Newman and Holzman, 1997; White, 2007). But, in fact, Vygotsky's practical relevance is quite profound. For Vygotsky, our potentials develop as we collaborate with others in ways that help us to acquire personally relevant understandings and actions derived from within those interactions. Consider his notion that what we 'know' develops first within social relationships (intermentally), before we draw on it later as a form of cognition (or what he termed intramental). Once, as a young commercial salmon-fishing deckhand, I (Tom) noticed the ocean starting to 'boil' and develop a ridge that seemed to indicate that the waters were about to part. As this was an unfamiliar experience, I had little to go on in making sense of it. One seemingly related prior social experience was that of Charlton Heston parting the Red Sea, in his movie role as Moses. This construction was somewhat anxiety-provoking until my skipper noted my concerned interest in what was happening and said, 'Oh, that's just a tide rip.' Later encounters with similar experiences had then been made recognizable and all right. In both meaning-making efforts, however, I was not developing understandings on my own. I acquired a language and way of evaluating an experience – socially first, but in ways that later served me as a cognitive resource. This resource, however, was semiotic or symbolic; I'd developed it with others as a relevant cognitive tool for making my way about. Now consider the origins of the understandings, problematic or otherwise, that clients bring to therapy. How are these acquired and sustained? Also ponder the therapeutic or helping relationship's potential to be a source of new understandings, useful to clients beyond therapy.

Vygotsky's view of how we make use of language and symbols is another rich aspect of his work worth careful attention. How we learn to problem-solve is by making or acquiring symbols for what is in our environment (or field of concern), and then using these as one might use tools to create differences in our physical environment. Our relations with others, immediately, or through what our cultural experiences make possible, generally afford the language and symbols we require for such problem-solving. It is how we combine and put these symbolic tools or resources to cognitive and other forms of work that marks human creativity. Our transition from beings able to quantify our experiences, to becoming creative users of mathematics for engineering problems, is but one example of our abilities to use symbols and tools, to create even greater tools. But, these tools and symbols are *our* creations; the world was not already named and quantified in ways for us to discover and manipulate. Vico was on to this sort of thing when he suggested humans turn their attention to their own constructions, like geometry, instead of focusing on nature, which is God's construction.

You may remember the Coke bottle in the film *The Gods Must be Crazy*. This 'piece of litter' became a fortuitous discovery for the Kalahari Bushmen who came across it. How they came to understand the Coke bottle and its constructive possibilities went far beyond the intended use for such bottles in the cultural circumstances in which they originated. Such differences in understandings, and the culturally diverse ways of building on them, exemplify Vygotsky's notion of 'culturally mediated tools'. The Kalahari Bushmen saw a multi-purpose tool in what those of other cultures saw as a container. In this respect, cultures and other forms of relationship develop ways of shaping not only our thinking but also what we do as an outgrowth of that thinking.

Vygotsky reminds us how important it is to recognize the extent to which the language and actions clients bring to therapy are culturally shaped or 'freighted'. Word usage, especially, highlights what we have been discussing. Misunderstanding is a good sign that words carry different cultural or relational meanings for the people involved. This is a point Garfinkel (Chapter 10) elaborates on in his notion of 'indexicality', that we usually reference somewhat different meanings when we use a word (Heritage, 1984). For Vygotsky, these differences are usually cultural. An example of this occurred in a village close to where I (Tom) formerly lived. For years in this village, girls and women complained to the local police that they were being 'bothered' by men around them. When an officer finally had the presence of mind to ask what 'bothered' meant he learned that it referred to sexually assaultive behaviour. The flip side to the concern being expressed here about language is that any meaning developed in therapy has to 'fly' back in the relational circumstances where it will be put to use. Narrative therapists, for example, frequently speak of how our words need to be 'experience-near' for clients. That 'experience', as we have been regarding it here, is rooted in the relationships and cultures where meanings have their own language – language that may be quite different from our own.

Modernity, in linguistic terms, saw many speakers communicate as if they all spoke from the meanings spelled out in the *Oxford English Dictionary* (*OED*). Such *OED* entries named and mapped phenomena with authoritative terms. But, for Vygotsky, as for Wittgenstein (Chapter 8), the meanings of words are found in the uses they acquire in particular relationships. The cultural freight of words becomes evident as speakers who habitually use the same word in different ways – in their different relational circumstances – try speaking the word to each other as if they were in their 'home' circumstance. In this regard, therapists can benefit from listening to words salient to clients and therapy (e.g., those words which describe problems, personal resources and values), learning about such words by inquiring about their meanings in the contexts where their use most matters. This involves adopting an ethnographic stance to listening to clients, given that clients usually use words in deceptively familiar ways, when too often that is not the case. As multicultural counsellors such as Paul Pederson (1999) suggest, much can be gained from responding to each encounter with clients as a cross-cultural one. We are not all on the same page of the *OED*, and thinking this way can cost us much as we listen to clients, and miss their meaning.

A recurring theme in our studies, and prominent in Vygotsky's thought, is the notion that meanings need to be understood within some relational context. He went a step further with this way of thinking: this is how new meanings are acquired as well. Remember: what we think derives from what we have learned from our interactions with others first. Vygotsky's zone of proximal development (zoped) can be regarded in many ways, but at its conceptual heart is a learner gaining greater cultural competence with the help of more culturally competent others. But zopeds require a particular kind of helpful relationship, one quite unlike that of the conventional teacher–student or therapist–client relationship. Within the zoped there is a high degree of relational attunement and coordination resulting in a mutually engaging form of collaboration. Part of the widespread fascination for the therapeutic work of Milton Erickson (Haley, 1973) arises from the creative ways he followed his dictum: each person needs their own custom-made therapy. There is collaboration within the zoped that develops in ways that cannot be predetermined. This can seem at odds with the detached scientist-practitioner stance advocated for psychologists, for example, especially in the recent push for their use of manualized diagnostic and treatment protocols. No, the learning Vygotsky envisioned in the zoped develops in non-instrumental ways particular to the people involved, in collaborations arising from within their resourceful attunement to each other.

There is another important piece here, however. The zoped is a means by which the learner acquires greater competence to participate in the culture of which she or he is a part. In this regard, the zoped affords an opportunity to practise forms of culture (its meanings and cultural practices) not yet (but becoming) within the competence of the learner. The primary role of the more culturally competent other(s) in this context is to develop the kind of customized learning we associated with Milton Erickson above. Here we see the scaffolding of activities that this person improvises from within the relationship, ways s/he contributes to the learner's development of greater cultural competence. If your thinking here is that such scaffolds are prefabricated and can be simply imported in a general fashion to the learning relationship, this misses the point being made. Scaffolds, like the zoped relationships they are developed within, are collaboratively developed means for promoting development. Therapeutic conversations based on such ideas are generative and engage both client and therapist in developing processes neither could anticipate or create on their own. While we do not want to mystify these relationships as having Ouija board-like characteristics, their customized quality arises from the relational attunement or reciprocal responsiveness of their members, and carefully worked out negotiations between them as to how to proceed. The upshot, however, is that within these relationships the learner acquires new competencies relevant to his or her desired participation within the culture of which s/he is a part.

One approach to therapy that draws heavily from Vygotsky's ideas on development is social therapy, as developed at the Eastside Brief Therapy Institute in New York. For its developers (Fred Newman and Lois Holzman, 1993, 1997), social therapy is a group process, where the group acts as a collective zoped facing together the developmental challenges articulated by its members. For social therapists, growth or development is what we require any time our understandings or actions become 'fossilized or fetishized' in aspects of life where we feel stuck. One difference between their approach to development and Vygotsky's, is that they do not see participation in group zopeds as helping members become 'better' participants in their culture. Rather, they adopt a dialectic view that change is instrumental in keeping cultures dynamic, and the changes produced in group work contribute to this. Consistent, though, with how we have been discussing Vygotsky is their view that the methods for development must derive from the group's collective efforts. So, those turning to the social therapy literature will find the therapy remarkably short on technique. Instead, the aim of social therapy is to engage people in ongoing creative ways of 'growing a head taller' as they tackle problems. Much of the creativity arises in the ways group members learn to improvise within their zopeds for each other's growth.

In closing, Vygotsky's ideas are a rich pool to draw from. His approach is quintessentially social: people construct their development in relational and cultural contexts, and they best do so in collaborative relationships that draw on the resourcefulness of the involved parties. Vygotsky reminds us as well that meaning and action are always contextual in ways particular to our relationships, and these relationships furnish tools for our participation as well as continued development.

7   Meanings and perspectives
George Herbert Mead and Jakob von Uexküll

George Herbert Mead

> It is true, of course, that once mind has arisen in the social process it makes
> more possible the development of that process into much more complex forms
> of social interaction among the component individuals than was possible
> before it had arisen. But there is nothing odd about a product of a given process
> contributing to, or becoming an essential factor in, the further development of
> that process. The social process, then, does not depend for its origin or initial
> existence upon the existence and interactions of selves; though it does depend
> upon the latter for the higher stages of complexity and organization which it
> reaches after selves have arisen within it.   (Mead, 1934: 226)

As is common with thinkers of the first order, knowing quite where to start into
Mead's work is hard call. Mead did not concentrate on just one topic, but over
the course of his lifetime produced an almost entire philosophy of everything.
He deals with the self, the nature of society, the nature of history, the nature of
objectivity, and other topics ad infinitum. His four books – *The Philosophy of
the Present* (1932), *Mind, Self, and Society* (1934), *Movements of Thought in the
Nineteenth Century* (1936) and *The Philosophy of the Act* (1938) – were constructed from lecture notes made by his students during courses he taught, and all
post-date his death. In the subtitle of his second book he styles himself as a 'social
behaviourist', and in taking such a position he may appear an unlikely candidate
for our purposes, but his concerns with the social nature of the construction of
mind and meaning put him centre-stage.

Important to our considerations of Mead is his pragmatism. Where many thinkers depict life in big picture and somewhat idealistic ways, Mead looked at how
life 'is done' by the people living it. In this respect he is similar to many of our
thinkers who take a 'bottom-up' approach to social interaction and being human.
Mead's approach also brings us to some important links between social action
and meaning, links we will continue to explore throughout this book. For practitioners, important connections can be made between Mead's view of socially
developed understandings and how such understandings (including those about
one's self) feature in client/professional interactions.

Mead was born in Massachusetts in 1863, and died in Chicago in 1931. He
gained his first degree at the age of 20, briefly worked as a schoolteacher, and then
was a railroad surveyor with the Wisconsin Rail Road Company for four years.

In 1887 he enrolled as a philosophy major at Harvard, living in William James's house as a tutor to the James' children, though he did not formally attend any of James's courses. He completed his MA in 1888, and went to Leipzig, Germany, where he enrolled for a Ph.D. in philosophy and physiological psychology, studying under Wilhelm Wundt and G. Stanley Hall. He transferred his studies to the University of Berlin in 1889, adding economic theory to his studies.

He abandoned his Ph.D. in 1891 when he was offered an instructor's position in philosophy and psychology at the University of Michigan, where he worked alongside such luminaries as Charles Cooley and John Dewey (with whom he established a close relationship). The person he replaced at Michigan was James Tufts, who had left to complete his Ph.D. at the University of Freiburg. Tufts returned to the USA a year later to a position in the newly established University of Chicago, and recruited Dewey to the new Chair in Philosophy, an appointment Dewey accepted on the condition that Mead was appointed to an assistant professorship. He held this position until 1902, when he was promoted to an Associate Professorship before becoming a full Professor in 1907, a post he remained in until his death.

Mead regards mental life – 'the mind' – as an inherently social phenomenon that arises from acts of communication. He regards communication as being founded on gestures, which he distinguishes into two types, 'significant' and 'non-significant' gestures, both of which are integral to his conceptualization of the nature of meaning. He regards a 'self' as coming, through development, to comprise three components, which he terms the 'I', the 'me' and the 'generalized other'. We will find resonances in his ideas with the concerns of, at least, Vico, the phenomenologists, von Uexküll, Vygotsky, Harré and Shotter. In parallel with Vico's project, he asks how humans could construct themselves, by their own efforts which they could come to understand retrospectively, out of a state of nature. In Vygotsky's terms, part of his project is to describe how we transform the realm of our natural abilities into that of 'higher mental functioning'. Mead also links forward to many of the ideas we are surveying here. The sociological school of 'symbolic interactionism' is largely drawn from the bases Mead outlined. This school is a part of the intellectual foreground for later developments such as ethnomethodology, and thence conversation analysis, etc., that we come to later.

Communication, gesture and mind

> Our contention is that mind can never find expression, and could never have come into existence at all, except in terms of a social environment; that an organized set or pattern of social relations and interactions (especially those of communication by means of gestures functioning as significant symbols and thus creating a universe of discourse) is necessarily presupposed by it and involved in its nature.   (1934: 223)

Mead regards 'the mind' as a consequence of social interaction and communication, not a precursor of, or precondition for, these processes. Thus, communication in a social setting is where the action is firstly at. Our individual abilities are constructed as a consequence of our immersion in a social world (which is similar to Vygotsky's distinction, then, between the primacy of intermental abilities and their gradual reconstitution as intramental ones).

Mead makes his argument on the basis of a distinction he draws between 'significant' and 'non-significant' gestures. He illustrates his notion of 'non-significant gestures' with the example of a dog-fight:

> Dogs approaching each other in [a] hostile attitude carry on such a language of gestures. They walk around each other, growling and snapping, and waiting for the opportunity to attack ... The act of each dog becomes the stimulus to the other dog for his response. There is then a relationship between these two; and as the act is responded to by the other dog, it, in turn, undergoes change. The very fact that the dog is ready to attack another becomes a stimulus to the other dog to change his own position or his own attitude. He has no sooner done this than the change of attitude in the second dog in turn causes the first dog to change his attitude. We have here a conversation of gestures. They are not, however, gestures in the sense that they are significant. We do not assume that the dog says to himself, 'If the animal comes from this direction he is going to spring at my throat and I will turn in such a way.' What does take place is an actual change in his own position due to the direction of the approach of the other dog.   (1934: 14, 42–3)

Non-significant gestures are responded to in reciprocal ways. The top dog doesn't 'frighten' itself when it growls, it frightens the other dog, and then reacts itself to what the other dog does. Dogs, and other animals, lack the ability to comprehend the viewpoint of another organism, and thus act from their own perspectives only, in what we might take as a 'mindless' or 'unconscious' fashion. This becomes clear when we consider the response many birds have to the sight of themselves in a mirror. Their actions become disrupted because the reciprocity of action and response is broken down: the bird in the mirror responds inappropriately, and the bird lacks the neurological substrate to map the actions of the image as corresponding to those of itself.

In contrast to these unconscious gestures are what he terms 'significant gestures' (and sometimes 'significant symbols'):

> significant symbols carried back to their origins prove to be gestures, i.e., parts of social acts through which individuals adjust their conduct to that of others. They become symbols when the act which they preface is aroused as an attitude in the other individual. They become significant symbols when the individual that uses the gesture which calls out such an attitude in another calls out the same attitude in himself.   (Mead, 1938: 221–2)

Note that the distinguishing characteristic of the significant symbol is that it has the *same* meaning for both participants in an act.

Language is a system of significant symbols, though Mead sees language as emerging out of these earlier 'conversations of gestures':

> Meaning can be described, accounted for, or stated in terms of symbols or language at its highest and most complex stage of development (the stage

> it reaches in human experience), but language simply lifts out of the social
> process a situation which is logically or implicitly there already. The language
> symbol is simply a significant or conscious gesture.   (1934: 79)

(Note that it is important to take the 'simply' here as meaning 'this is what language does, or is': the process whereby language is developmentally elaborated from earlier communicative abilities present in infants is by no means 'simple'.) This notion of 'calling out the same response' can perhaps be more easily grasped with respect to a concrete example from human development (see below). The example also points to something quite remarkable about language symbols – that, in their mature uses, they gain their meaning from a position 'outside' of the consciousness of their users (and this will give us a handle on Mead's notions of the 'generalized other', common sense, and his unique take on 'objectivity' below).

The point Mead strives for in his distinguishing of 'significant' (self-conscious) from 'non-significant' (non-self-conscious) gestures is that for significant gestures, their meaning is in relation to a perspective or stance located *outside* that given 'naturally' to the organisms that use them. This perspective is not that of the first-person (the 'gesturer'), nor second-person (the 'gesturee') participants in the symbolically communicative act, but that of the *third* person (either an objective observer, or one intersubjectively constituted as 'both of them' (first- and second-person interactants: i.e., the 'we' who agree).

For example, consider an act such as 'giving'. If A gives something to B, the object goes away from A towards B. Similarly, if B gives something to A, the object goes from B to A. But if a third person, C, triangulates on this act, the transferred object need have no motion towards or away from him or her. As a neutral observer, C has in addition no attitude vis-à-vis possession or loss: C can conceive of 'give', and not count the cost. Now, an infant can only do this once she has developed a deal of detachment, via symbolic forms that mediate her development. As a significant symbol, 'giving' has been denuded of its 'reciprocal meaning' with respect to A's and B's different perspectives on the activity, and become a symbol which has the 'same meaning' for both of them. Another way to think of it is that when I say 'I want you to do …', I somehow grasp that while you hear me say those words, you understand what I said to mean 'You want me to do …'

This 'outsidedness' of meaning is alluded to by Mead with his view of 'meaning as being objectively present' in social interaction. Somewhat technically, he puts it thus:

> Meaning arises and lies within the field of the relation between the gesture
> of a given human organism and the subsequent behavior of this organism as
> indicated to another human organism by that gesture. If that gesture does so
> indicate to another organism the subsequent (or resultant) behavior of the given
> organism, then it has meaning. In other words, the relationship between a
> given stimulus – as a gesture – and the later phases of the social act of which it
> is an early (if not the initial) phase constitutes the field within which meaning

originates and exists. Meaning is thus a development of something objectively there as a relation between certain phases of the social act; it is not a psychical addition to that act and it is not an "idea" as traditionally conceived. A gesture by one organism, the resultant of the social act in which the gesture is an early phase, and the response of another organism to the gesture, are the relata in a triple or threefold relationship of gesture to first organism, of gesture to second organism, and of gesture to subsequent phases of the given social act; and this threefold relationship constitutes the matrix within which meaning arises, or which develops into the field of meaning.   (1934: 76)

More briefly, we have the view that 'the basis of meaning is thus objectively there in social conduct' (1934: 80). Note that, used in this way, Mead's claims about objectivity are not to do with the status of objects in the world, and the particular stance someone might take towards them; nor are they claims that differentiate 'objectivity' from 'subjectivity'. Rather, meanings exist, or are constituted (a) *in* the coordinated social relationship between interactants, and subsequently (b) *in* the relation between the user of these symbols and the world these symbols make 'meaningful' to them.

Now, consider another long quote from Mead in which he further develops this view:

> Symbolization constitutes objects not constituted before, objects which would not exist except for the context of social relationships wherein symbolization occurs. Language does not simply symbolize a situation or object which is already there in advance; it makes possible the existence or the appearance of that situation or object, for it is a part of the mechanism whereby that situation or object is created. The social process relates the responses of one individual to the gestures of another, as the meanings of the latter, and is thus responsible for the rise and existence of new objects in the social situation, objects dependent upon or constituted by these meanings. Meaning is thus not to be conceived, fundamentally, as a state of consciousness, or as a set of organized relations existing or subsisting mentally outside the field of experience into which they enter; on the contrary, it should be conceived objectively, as having its existence entirely within this field itself. The response of one organism to the gesture of another in any given social act is the meaning of that gesture, and also is in a sense responsible for the appearance or coming into being of the new object – or new content of an old object – to which that gesture refers through the outcome of the given social act in which it is an early phase. For, to repeat, objects are in a genuine sense constituted within the social process of experience, by the communication and mutual adjustment of behavior among the individual organisms which are involved in that process and which carry it on. Just as in fencing the parry is an interpretation of the thrust, so, in the social act, the adjustive response of one organism to the gesture of another is the interpretation of that gesture by that organism – it is the meaning of that gesture.   (1934: 78)

Thus, while it is social interaction that *constructs* objects that otherwise would not exist, it is still possible to view these objects as having an objective existence, but an objective existence only *within* the social relationship that has acted to create them.

For example, I (Andy) am writing these words in Canada. It is quite clear to me that while I cannot physically see any geographical separation between that bit of land called 'Canada' and that bit of land over there called the 'USA', and while neither I nor the immigration officer I am dealing with can see my place of citizenship, New Zealand, our interaction at the border can only make sense on the basis of there really being such places. Yet they are places that only have their existence in the social relations we are immersed in, in this modern world. Hence:

> the social process, through the communication which it makes possible among the individuals implicated in it, is responsible for the appearance of a whole set of new objects in nature, which exist in relation to it (objects, namely, of 'common sense').   (1934: 79)

What we have to deal with is the fact that there are social processes and *social* processes. I may interact purely locally with an individual within the context bounded solely by that relationship – as, for example, an infant does with her mother, and create a common sense, common orientation to what something constituted in our interactive world means for us: that doing such and such constructs a greeting, for example. On the other hand, my local interaction may be in the context of some almost global social process – as it is between me and the immigration officer. We need to look further at this process of the expansion of our social horizons, and this requires us to go on to explore, first, Mead's view of the *developmental* process through which each of us is inducted through childhood into adulthood, and, second, the wider context within which each trajectory of development occurs, its *historical* context.

The implications of Mead's view of meaningful social interaction can be important when one turns to the 'objects' created in helping interactions. There is something very immediate in what Mead was saying about people relating and creating shared 'objects' both can recognize from their significant gestures and words. Helping interactions involve professionals and clients trying to create shared meaning and action through such words, gestures and other forms of expression. But meanings worked up in other interactions do not necessarily transport well to developments being worked out in the helping encounter. In a sense, clients and helpers work out, through their significant gestures and words, a developmental trajectory between them.

Self, other, I and me

The self and the other

> The self, as that which can be an object to itself, is essentially a social structure, and it arises in social experience. After a self has arisen, it in a certain sense provides for itself its social experiences, and so we can conceive of an absolutely solitary self. But it is impossible to conceive of a self arising outside of social experience.   (1934: 140)

Self-consciousness, for Mead, is an emergent from the social process. It comes from taking on the attitude of others towards oneself. We have encountered an example of this in Derek Edwards' (see also Chapter 13) observation of an infant, Alice, who begins to control her own behaviour by using the word 'Don't' that she has taken over from her mother's speech – when we considered Vygotsky (Chapter 6).

> The self is something which has a development; it is not initially there, at birth, but arises in the process of social experience and activity, that is, develops in the given individual as a result of his relations to that process as a whole and to other individuals within that process.   (1934: 135)

In taking over the attitude of the other towards 'ourselves', the self becomes, reflexively, an object unto itself: the 'individual enters as such into his own experience … as an object' (ibid.: 225). His point here is that, as experiential agents, humans are not, initially, able to reflect on their experience from a standpoint outside, so to speak, that immediately given experience. Other people and 'things' are out there in our experienced world in an immediate way from the point at which that experience is located, but that point cannot, in the beginning, take itself into account. The experiencer is blind to his or herself, and is only able to become (meta)aware of their otherwise taken-for-granted experience through the consequence of using significant symbols. Mead's account of the development of the self rests on three aspects of social activity: language, play and the game. All of these have a shared symbolic component, such as words, roles, rules, and so on. Language is the first mode that takes us toward having a self, because 'I know of no other form of behavior than the linguistic in which the individual is an object to himself' (ibid.: 142). That is, all languages provide names and pronouns that enable the grounds for grasping that one exists in the eyes, ears, emotions of others, in the same way that they are the objects of one's own experiences.

Close on the heels of language comes socially motivated play (as opposed to manipulative play with objects). Play, to begin with, is not truly social, as Piaget has documented in his classical observations. Children cannot, to begin with, readily coordinate their activities with their peers. But while play is thus essentially an individual activity, some of it, nonetheless, has a major social component. This is role-play, where the child pretends to be another, and so, in play, gains a limited experience of taking over the role of another into her own conduct. However, what the child is doing in this kind of role-play is limited to taking on just one role at a time. But to play *a game* is, in Mead's analysis, an altogether more important activity than mere play.

It takes quite a lot of time before children can really play a game such as soccer. It is not just a question of physical skill, but something much more demanding. Recalling my (Andy) own children joining a soccer team around the age of 6, what struck me about their games was the fact that even though the pitch was somewhat reduced in size for them, it was always too big for the way they played it. Check out any 6-year-olds' organized soccer game, and two things will strike you. All the action is crowded around the ball, and the coach is always yelling 'Spread out!' Soccer at this age is a game of 'chase the ball', to try and kick it in the right direction, whatever the skills of kicking the children actively possess. But it is not, in Mead's terms, the lack of physical skill that is only holding them back from really being able to play soccer. To play soccer requires a fundamental social skill, which children of this age lack, and which they are only starting on the path of getting to grips with.

On top of good physical skills, a good soccer player has to be able to hold a lot of social coordinates together. Assume you have the ball and your team is on the attack. How long do you hold it before you pass it, and where/who do you pass it to? You need to weigh up your options. Have you, now, at this point, got the chance of kicking a quick ball into a particular space that one of your own players can anticipate running into, to maintain your advantage, or is it better to draw a few defenders towards you so as to create the space you need for that telling through-pass that your striker can see thus opening up? And is your defence properly organized behind you in case things go wrong? Or are your opponents wise to what you are trying to do, and the better option would be to push it up the wing, where you know your own defender is rapidly making a run down, outside you, past your left shoulder? Resolving these questions is a very social skill.

You need, in Mead's way of framing things, the ability to somehow coordinate a set of rules that organize every participant's roles in the game, a kind of on-the-fly symbolic unity, a 'generalized other' (ibid.: 154) as an interpretive point, one that comprises 'an organized and generalized attitude' (1934: 195) that specifies the options available to you at any given moment, and makes those options appear to be 'obvious', since you do not need to think about them.

And so, you kick the ball, and within a fleeting moment you feel exhilarated by your success at putting your striker in for a goal, and you share in that success in a conscious exultation to the crowd whose applause celebrates the pride you feel. Or you curse and retreat, having screwed up, not only having given the ball away to the opposition with your poor choice of option and physical execution, but, with your outside defender now out of position because he was making forward ground in anticipation of your successfully making that pass that would outflank the defence, the opposition are making a break up the flank you have just exposed to them. Exult or curse, your self-consciousness is there because, through so much practice, you can identify your position reflexively from the standpoint of the generalized other, meaning that you are self-conscious, an object in your own perception.

> When a self does appear it always involves an experience of another; there could not be any experience of a self simply by itself ... When the response of the other becomes an essential part in the experience or conduct of the individual; when taking the attitude of the other becomes an essential part in his behaviour – then the individual appears in his own experience as a self; and until this happens he does not appear as a self.   (1934: 195)

Games and rituals are thus the activities within which the development of the self is fostered. Linguistic symbols become imbued with the attitude of 'common sense', that which 'everyone takes for granted', and which gives the emergent self a grasp of its position in the world – symbolic interactions enable the individual perceiver to 'take on the role of the other' and become thus an object in his or her own perception. Recall:

> Only in terms of gestures as significant symbols [i.e., linguistic symbols] is the existence of mind or intelligence possible; for only in terms of gestures which are significant symbols can thinking – which is simply an internalized or implicit conversation of the individual with himself by means of such gestures – take place.   (1934: 47)

It may not be too much of a stretch to suggest that professional helping has game-like or ritual-like qualities that clients and professionals enact between them. Tom recalls a client coming to see him who asked 'where's your couch?', as if anticipating a psychoanalytic ritual. The symbols that guide the rituals of helping can be imports (i.e., the 'couch', the professional's helping model and ethics, etc.) from other life contexts. But they still face constructive challenges in constructing how *their* relationship will proceed, including the symbolic resources they will use as they go. This gets worked out in their responses to each other that translate and negotiate such symbols from 'mine' and 'yours' to 'ours'. Enacting that sense of 'ours', using the familiar and anticipatable symbols and gestures developed as 'ours' over time, can develop into something that has the look and feel of a ritual or game. Whether this occurs in helping or other relationships, the point is that such rituals or games are anchored in socially developed meanings and actions that can be modified. For discourse analysts (see Chapter 13), this is how things get 'worked up' socially, in consequential interactions, that come to inform subsequent interactions.

The 'I' and the 'me'

The constructed self, however, does not mindlessly take over the attitudes of the generalized others of its community, as a passive reflection of them. A 'self', a person, is active, deciding what she will do in the light of what she knows of the given views she has distilled from her wider community, but her actions are not determined by these attitudes. It is for this reason that Mead conceives of the self as divided in two, comprising an 'I' and a 'me':

> The 'I' is the response of the organism [person] to the attitudes of the others; the 'me' is the organised set of attitudes which one himself assumes.   (1934: 175)

The 'me' is that socialized set of ways of seeing the world that every competent member of a social world has. By contrast, the 'I' is the specific set of interests that the individual has towards those views, her take on them. We can detect these two phases of the self quite easily, using Mead's terminology, far better than we can in everyday English usage. Mead views the 'I' as the cutting edge of action, the active subject that is essaying its actions out of the nexus of its unique 'irritability': its own unique stance or attitude to what it has been given to work with in making sense of the world.

We have a word for 'I', but we can only grasp that 'I' in retrospect, after the act of acting (also see here Schutz, Chapter 3, for an allied approach),[1] at which point the 'I' has, in fact, become part of the 'me', our self as we grasp it in its past form. The 'I' is thus not an object of immediate experience. However, because the 'I' is always moving into the past and, in doing so, restructuring the 'me', the 'I' of any present moment is also reformulating itself in responding to the 'me'. There is a continual dialectic in the relation of the 'I' and 'me'. These points will take us into Mead's view of time and perspective below.

Similarly, there is a constitutive dialectic between the self and society. Selves arise as we internalize the attitudes (Mead's term that we can take to include practices as well as stances) of the generalized other, and thereby constitute a component of the 'me', through our coming to use significant symbols, and to take part in the activities of play and games. This phase of the self, therefore, can be thought of as a means of social control, because 'society' is effectively re-creating its new members as psychologically active individuals in its own forms. At the same time, however, the 'I' cannot be expected to be completely subservient, as a fundamental aspect of its character is its reactivity to the socially constructed 'me'. In addition, and this is particularly true of modern, industrial cultures, a self can exist in relation to a number of 'generalized others', since no society is homogeneous.

Mead distinguishes two general classes of 'others' from whom a person can obtain her components of self. First there are immediate, concrete groups with whom an individual can directly interact, and whose differing attitudes may be taken on. Partaking in such groups can obviously lead to tensions within the self. One such tension could be what we subsume under the notion of 'confidentiality' in practice: where does one draw the line between respecting a client's right to confidentiality and society's right to protection from potentially 'dangerous' individuals of whom the therapist has privileged knowledge. Again, for academics, they have particular responsibilities to their subject, their profession, their students and their University, and these different responsibilities do not always match up as having or serving complementary interests.

Second, there are 'abstract social classes or subgroups' where

> individual members are related to one another only more or less indirectly, and which more or less indirectly function as social units, but which afford unlimited possibilities for the widening and ramifying and enriching of the

[1] For example:

> It appears that all possible communication presupposes a mutual tuning-in relationship between the communicator and the addressee of the communication. This relationship is established by the reciprocal sharing of the other's flux of experiences in inner time, by living through a vivid present together, by experiencing this togetherness as a "We".   (Schutz, 1970: 216)

> social relations among all the individual members of the given society as an
> organized and unified whole.   (1934: 157)

These differing levels of organization are clearly reflected within the structure of contemporary New Zealand Maori society, for example. An individual is a member of their close family, their *'whanau'*; which is itself a part of their extended family, the *'hapu'*; all of whom go to make up the larger, regional social group, the *'iwi'*; and nowadays, all the separate *'iwi'* make up what western culture has constructed as the generic 'Maori'; who are at the same time part of that western political organization of the state, 'New Zealand'; which is itself a part of the 'Commonwealth', whose members share a head of state: 'Her Majesty the Queen'. Not all these sources of attitudes that can be internalized as 'generalized others' need be in alignment, and thus the forces of social harmony are balanced by the sources of social conflict that are similarly engendered in any particular 'me'.

Further, these sources of conflict can lead to new resolutions, new forms of consensus. Enemies can become allies. And because the self is a social product, a reconstruction of society will lead to a reconstruction of the self – or in Vygotsky's terms, since the intramental (the 'self') arises from the intermental (the relations between people), then different possibilities for selves emerge out of different social organizations. However, these are not determinative situations where a self fully defines 'itself', or where social circumstance does, either.

> In short, social reconstruction and self or personality reconstruction are two
> sides of a single process – the process of human social evolution.   (1934: 309)

A view of self in terms of 'I's and 'me's, in inverted commas, can be disorienting or off-putting. Mead's self is a product of its responsive engagement within varying social circumstances. However, this is at odds with a typical modern conception of self which is expected to maintain some consistency ('integrity') across time and social circumstances. A colleague of Tom is interested in experiences of 'coming out' as gay or lesbian. There it is clear that a kind of symbolic negotiation of self plays out that encompasses the 'I' and 'me' distinctions we have been discussing. The meanings have real consequences for the people involved, for how they may understand and relate to each other. So, a change in self, by necessity, has social implications beyond the helping relationship.

So far, so good. But these notions of Mead now start to take us into some of the more difficult areas of his thinking. Difficult though they may be, they are nonetheless important for our present purposes. The two most important areas for us are Mead's frameworks for dealing with 'time' and 'perspective'.

Time and perspective

Time

> Instead of saying, as heretofore, that without time, there can be no living subject,
> we shall now have to say that without living subject, there can be no time.
>   (von Uexküll, 1957: 13)

> The now is contrasted with a then and implies that a background which is
> irrelevant to the difference between them has been secured within which the
> now and the then may appear.   (Mead, 1938: 161)

We did say this was going to be difficult. Time is, in fact, an incredibly difficult notion to say anything about, not only from an objective point of view as in science, but also from an experiential view. The difficulty, at root, stems from the fact that our perception of the other dimensions we can sense and experience presuppose that time exists, but we have no direct perceptual sensors that register time, nor present it to us directly as a part of the perceptions and experiences generated by our senses. It is more the case that our experience is so much wrapped up inside time that we cannot 'see' it, since it is the medium that makes experience possible. *Time*, then, *has to be constructed*, both as something we can 'grasp' as an experience, and as something we can conceive and talk about.

Time is an important element of Mead's philosophy, in that human experience has a temporal dimension, but our experience of time is a constructed one, not, in his view, a given. Further, this temporal dimension has a structurally dependent, dialectical nature, similar to the relation between the self and society that we outlined in the previous sections. The first dialectic that gives us our experience of time is when something occurs that presents us with a problem that prevents us from seamlessly continuing on.

Consider a world in which everything is going along smoothly. Our actions are structured by our internalized symbolic grasp of our society's generalized attitudes – our unreflective common sense of how to deal with the world. This gives us the basis for an unproblematic, unreflective life, provided the world does not chuck any surprises at us. Things make direct sense; we have untroubled certainties (in Vico's term), and intuitively grasp 'how to go on'. It is when an *emergent*, unanticipated spanner is thrown into our lives that, in Mead's approach, the temporal nature of our experience is brought into being (see also Heidegger, Chapter 4, for a similar view). Emergent, novel situations or crises establish a boundary in our experience between the instant and the future. Our actions are going forward smoothly into a predictable, intended future, and the transition from the present to that future is unproblematic, as long as we can rely on the perspective of 'who we unreflectively are' that has been constructed on the basis of our past. Without these disruptions, there would be no experience of experience at all: 'there would merely be the passage of events' (1938: 346) – the timeless world of mystic experience.

Perhaps some of the most dramatic examples of Mead's point in recent times are peoples' reactions to their experience of 11 September 2001. In one instant, a breach both with the past and with the future was created, that had not only immediate consequences – 'what does one do next, because this doesn't make sense?' – but also more distant ones that are still undecided. Human action occurs in time, but its temporal structure only becomes apparent when action is blocked. Yet no change is completely disruptive; there is always an element of continuity with the past. That continuity is the sense of the 'me' that is brought to awareness as the emergent event is experienced as change. That is, without a past that leads into a seamless future, disruption would not be noticed, and the present would not present itself as noticeable, since it meshes entirely with our expectations as part of the untroubled 'passage' from one instant to the next.

Another dialectic arises at this point in Mead's account, between the past and this unanticipated, emergent discontinuity with the future. The past has to be *reconstructed* to resolve and make sense of the emergent discontinuity. That is, there are aspects of the past that we had never noticed before, aspects that enable a new continuity with the present to be constructed. And in doing this, the past itself is reconstructed. The unexpected becomes determined, or understandable, when seen from this reconstructed past. Yet, at the same time, the character of the emergent itself determines the way in which the past is reconstructed, in the way in which previously unnoticed aspects of the past become 'seen'. Herbert Dreyfus makes this same point in his notion of 'retrospective needs determination':

> When we experience a need we do not at first know what it is we need. We must search to discover what allays our discomfort. This is not found by comparing various objects and activities with some objective, determinate criterion, but through … our sense of gratification. This gratification is experienced as the discovery of what we needed all along, but it is a retrospective understanding and covers up the fact that we were unable to make our need determinate without first receiving that gratification. The original fulfilment of any need is, therefore, … a creative discovery.   (Dreyfus, 1967: 25–6)

Or, as Wittgenstein notes it: 'now I can go on' (Chapter 8). We can now relate this creative discovery to our attitude to objects in the future, for at the instant of this discovery we rewrite our perspective on objects we previously had understood in a 'different' past. Infants, for example, appear to cry in the early months of their lives because they are uncomfortable. And during those early months, they will also have many encounters with the breast. But their experience of discomfort and their perception of where a breast fits into their lives changes as they come to fit the removal of discomfort into their valuing of the breast. Thus Piaget, for example, observes that around the beginning of the third month of age:

> Laurent only tries to nurse when he is in his mother's arms and no longer when on the dressing table…
> Lucienne at [age 3 months, 12 days] stops crying when she sees her mother unfastening her dress for the meal.   (Piaget, 1951: 58–60)

Here, both his children give evidence of having 'retrospectively discovered' the implied conditions of their needs, and their actions are now informed by these discoveries. As a result, infants come to live in a 'new' perceptual world in which objects and events have a familiar and anticipatable significance, an appreciation of which they previously lacked.

Dialectically, then, an emergent, disruptive event contains within itself characteristics that indicate continuities with the past such that it may be made sense of as having some continuity with a past that is reconstructed out of those emergent indications. The past thus becomes something that is 'both irrevocable and revocable' (1932: 2). It is 'irrevocable' in the sense that it 'really' happened, but what it is that happened is always open to being reinterpreted, since there are facets of the past that link it to the present or future that were not noticeable, or even potentially important, until something new happens. Mead wants to go even further and claim that, in fact, our very sense that something has happened has its roots in emerging novelty, for it is only then that we are pushed to look for a narrative that connects the present to a past. Thus:

> We find that each generation has a different history ... That is, as we look back over the past, it is a different past. The experience is something like that of a person climbing a mountain. As he looks back over the terrain he has covered, it presents a continually different picture. So the past is continually changing as we look at it from a point of view of different authors, different generations. It is not simply the future [and the present] which is novel, then; the past is also novel.   (1936: 116–17)

In addition to this ongoing structuring (and re-structuring) of our personal sense of time there runs a parallel process whereby our social lives and technology provide a rhythm that also structures our trajectories and actions, and the way we relate to them. Heidegger's language for this was attunement (see Chapter 4).

Perspective and 'reality'

Yet another dialectic. A perspective is

> the world in its relationship to the individual and the individual in his relationship to the world.   (1938: 115)

Individuals may have different perspectives; societies may have different perspectives; species may have different perspectives. Perspectives are not, for Mead, variously better or worse approximations of any absolute reality. On the contrary, reality is itself something that has been constructed in the dialectic that nature has brought into being over historical time between the organism and the environment. That which is created by an organism's perspective, which arises from the possibilities the environment extends to the potentialities of nature, *is* reality. For Mead, 'the organism ... is in a sense responsible for its environment' (1934: 130).

Mead distinguishes two kinds of perspective. The first is the *perceptual perspective*, and the second is the *reflective perspective*. The perceptual perspective is the immediately perceived world, the 'world that is there' (1938: 14). Objects appear as they are in relation to the perceiver. An object in my 'world that is there' – such as a table, for example – might be a different object in the world that is there for another species: something to sit or jump on in the 'world that is there' for a chimpanzee, or something to eat in 'the world that is there' for a termite. We act on perceptual objects, so defined. The reflective perspective is one that effectively stands back from the perceptual perspective and, well, reflects on it and the relations between separable perceptual perspectives. We consider and coordinate different perceptual experiences within reflective acts. We can do this because of and through the medium of significant symbols.

It is through adopting a reflective perspective that we are able to analyse perceptual objects and, in the end, constitute scientific objects.

> The whole tendency of the natural sciences, as especially exhibited in physics and chemistry, is to replace objects of immediate experience by hypothetical objects which lie beyond the range of possible experience.   (1938: 291)

This is all well and good, provided that a dangerous tendency inherent in the reflective mode is recognized: that is, reifying scientifically constructed objects as over and above, more *real*, than perceptual objects. 'The world that is there' is, in Mead's formulation, *the* real world. Science provides a reflection on this world, but the reification of scientifically constructed objects as somehow more real than perceptual objects is the result of adopting an 'uncritical scientific imagination' (ibid.: 21). Remember, 'the organism is part of the physical world we are explaining' (ibid.): the physical world only exists as 'the world as it is' because we are 'there', in it, bringing it into being and defining its form. Science does not, then, define an independent reality, but deals with aspects of the prior, perceptually constituted reality from which problems have emerged that can be solved by constructing hypothetical scientific objects. The map and the territory must not be confused. A quite similar approach to perspective and meaning, but from a different set of concerns, is also taken up in the work of Jacob von Uexküll.

Jakob von Uexküll

> It would be foolish if we attempted to impute or ascribe philosophical inadequacy to Uexküll's interpretations, instead of recognizing the engagement with concrete investigations like this is one of the most fruitful things that philosophy can learn from contemporary biology.   (Heidegger, 1995: 263)

> Uexküll, one of the main founders of ethology, is a Spinozist when first he defines the melodic lines or contrapuntal relations that correspond to each thing, and then he describes a symphony as an immanent higher unity that takes on a breadth and fullness ('natural composition').   (Deleuze, 1988: 126)

> we can understand a living being's organism as a unity of its body and Umwelt. But Umwelt is not passive and inert to the body; it is a result of an organism's activity.   (Chebonov, 2001: 171)

> the mind is an organ created by nature to perceive nature.   (von Uexküll, 1992: 281)

Jakob von Uexküll was born into an aristocratic family in Keblas, Estonia, in 1864. He became a student of zoology in Dorpat (now Tartu) in 1884, graduating with the academic degree 'Kandidat der Zoologie'. He went on to study physiology at the University of Heidelberg in 1890. He specialized in the field of muscle- and neuro-physiology of marine invertebrates, for which he received an honorary doctorate from the University of Heidelberg in 1907. He formulated a law of neuro-motor activity (1904a, 1904b, 1905) known as *Uexküll's law*: that nervous excitation always flows towards the stretched muscles, which is one of the first statements of the idea of 'negative feedback'. He was appointed to his first academic position at the age of 60, founding the Institut für Umweltforschung in the former aquarium at the University of Hamburg. Konrad Lorenz's (1935) famous study of imprinting in young ducklings and goslings was dedicated to him. Von Uexküll remained in Hamburg until 1940, and died in exile in Capri in 1944. With this background, it would be difficult to imagine a more unlikely figure appearing in this book. However, as the quotes above indicate, his work has attracted attention in seemingly unlikely places.

Jakob von Uexküll has a number of claims to fame: he has been recognized, along with F. de Saussure and C. S. Peirce, as a founding father of semiotics (the study of signs) (e.g. Sebeok, 1977); an early pioneer in the field that has come to be known as cybernetics – through being the first to develop the notion of negative feedback within the controlling systems of the nervous system (above); and as a pioneer in the establishment of ethology as a science. It is one aspect of his ethological work that we will concentrate on here: his formulation of the *Umwelt* as a lynchpin in the understanding of animal, and human, activity. The important point that he developed through this perspective provides a grounding for meaning as an inherent property of life-forms in their relation to their worlds. There is, here, a clear symbiosis with our concerns as to the construction of meanings within relationships, and, in a revisionist interpretation of his ideas, a new clearing within which to think about the question of relativism versus realism, that can be so troubling in some articulations of the social constructionist position.

The *Umwelt* is the world in which an organism lives, as constructed by its sensory and perceptual capabilities: 'Every animal is surrounded with different things, the dog is surrounded by dog things and the dragonfly is surrounded by dragonfly things' (von Uexküll, 2001/1937: 117). Dogs and dragonflies come equipped with different sensory capabilities, and hence register different aspects of 'the world'. These different aspects constitute a part of 'the world they live in' – the world as registered by them. Bats register higher-frequency sounds than humans; bees register ultraviolet and polarized light, where we cannot; moths detect odours at far lower concentrations than we do, for example. But, von Uexküll argues, there is more to an experienced world than this, because an organism brings to its perception a set of interests, such that what it senses is perceived as being meaningful to it.

> No one, who has the least experience of the Umwelten of animals, will ever harbour the idea that objects have an autonomous existence that makes them independent of the subjects. The variability of objects is the norm here.
> Every object becomes something completely different on entering a different Umwelt. A flower stem that in our Umwelt is a support for the flower, becomes a pipe full of liquid for the meadow spittlebug (Philaenus spumarius) who

sucks out the liquid to build its foamy nest. The same flower stem becomes an upward path for the ant, connecting its nest with its hunting ground in the flower. For the grazing cow the flower stem becomes part of a tasty morsel of food for her to chew in her big mouth.   (von Uexküll, 2001/1936: 108)

Further, von Uexküll argues that it is not the purely physical properties of these 'things-in-the-world' that organisms are responding to, but the meaning of the object in relation to its needs: 'what we are dealing with is not with an exchange of forces between two objects, but the relations between a living subject and its object' (von Uexküll, 1957: 11). Living things do not, in this view, respond to causal forces, but to perceptual signs (*Merkzeichen*) or 'meaning' (*Bedeutung*). Thus, for an animal, 'a thing is never separable from its relations with the world' (Deleuze, 1988: 125), because

> Every action ... that consists of perception and operation imprints its meaning on the meaningless object and thereby makes it into a subject-related meaning-carrier in the respective Umwelt (subjective universe).   (von Uexküll, 1982/1940: 31)

Note here that 'action' is comprised of both 'perception and operation': perception is not passive, but organized so that the organism's body can perform the appropriate operations upon the world as perceived. Perception is 'for' something; it is never neutral. What is perceived relates to what can be done to it, and what can be done to it is set up by the organism's needs, which biology has built into its '*Bauplan*' (plan of construction): evolution acts to establish informed perception and action, and in the case of organisms that can learn, provides an additional capability enabling previously uninteresting objects to be imprinted with a meaning – and thus becoming 'worth' acting on – that is, constructed during the course of that organism's lifetime. It is here that it is possible to appreciate the interest that certain mid-twentieth-century philosophers such as Heidegger and Merleau-Ponty took in von Uexküll's work: it is a phenomenological and embodied world that is being portrayed as 'where the action is at'. How experience is understood and related to is a human phenomenological endeavour – the 'objects' of experience do not convey inherent meanings or values humans are to correctly register.

More central to our concerns is the focus in von Uexküll's work on the constructed nature of this phenomenal world and its 'relational nature':

> Uexküll uniquely saw that the difference between objects of experience and elements of sensation is determined primarily not by anything in the physical environment as such but by the relation or, rather, network and set of relations that obtains between whatever may be 'in fact' present physically in the surroundings and the cognitive constitution of the biological organism interacting with those surroundings here and now.   (Deely, 2001: 127)

Any organism's *Umwelt* is shaped by its evolutionary and developmental histories: their experiences of the world have been constructed *as experiences* over time as a product of these histories of sensing. Vibrations, for example, are not just sensed: they are experienced, as colours or sounds for at least the more recently evolved animals. But even among much more simply designed organisms, which may just sense as opposed to experience 'the world', it is clear that their worlds already constitute organized *Umwelts*.

One example of this can be observed at the New Zealand Marine Studies Institute in Portobello on the Otago Peninsula: a demonstration of an indigenous Maori fishing technique. Paua, or abalone, have a shell about the size of a human hand, which contains a very large, snail-like foot about the size of one's palm. This is both a locomotory and adhesive organ, working by naturally generated suction to attach the animal to a rock, from which, because of its size, it is very difficult to dislodge. And why might anyone want to remove it from its rock? Because it makes for good eating. The easiest way to remove it is to have a large, seven-pointed starfish handy. Place this on top of a paua and, within about thirty seconds, the paua will release its suction grip, quite likely twist its shell a few times, and then start sliding off away from the starfish – and it can slide faster than a starfish can wiggle after it. In this locomotory phase, then, a paua is easy to lift off rocks. Seven-pointed starfish are the main predators of paua. Paua can detect the taste of a starfish (underwater creatures do not have a sense of smell). This input is related to the output of escape activity, and through this innate cycle the taste can be said to have its meaning within the *Umwelt* of the paua, despite the fact that a paua is highly unlikely to have any knowledge of starfish, danger, escape, and so on. Von Uexküll describes the situation thus:

> Meaning turns out to be a 'drama' … These dramas consist principally of two acts: In the first act a neutral object from the environment is 'harpooned' as a meaning-carrier by a perceiving organ or a perceiving cell, in the second act it is modifed by the effector organ (as meaning-utilizer) in such a way that it disappears again from the surrounding-world.   (von Uexküll, 1992: 304, 305)[2]

To deal with this meaningful character of the *Umwelt*, von Uexküll turns from a dramatic to a musical metaphor:

> It is … musical and not mechanical laws that we need to study if we want to find out about the laws of Life … the building of the form is bound to strict rules, that we can compare to tunes … The tones of a piece of music are pure perceptual cues, without any material effects. Under this assumption, musical theory has established the rules for tonal harmony and melody. In the same way we now regard the properties of things as pure perceptual cues and ask ourselves if they obey rules similar to those of music. This is in fact the case: all properties of living creatures we find connected to units according to a plan, and these units are contrapuntally matched to the properties of other units.

[2] Deely (1992: 309) expands this point: 'The being proper to experience is not the being of objects, still less the being of things. It is the being proper to the network of interpretive relations according to which the cognitive organism is inserted in the environment not merely as one physical thing among others (one substance with its accidents among other substances with their accidents), but as a being whose objective world is shot through and constituted by cares and interests species-specifically proper to it according to its biological constitution.'

> In this way we get the impression of a comprehensive harmonic totality, because the properties of lifeless things also intervene contrapuntally in the design of living things.   (2001: 117, 121, 122)

We will later re-encounter this general point in Wittgenstein's concept of 'language games' (Chapter 8), particularly in Harré's formulation of the concept, that 'ontologies are in effect grammars' (Chapter 15); in Shotter's realization that 'the future is open to further specification, but only specification of an already specified kind' (Chapter 16); and Vygotsky's claim that 'a word is a microcosm of human consciousness' (1962: 153). The point is actually quite revolutionary. Rather than there being a divide between the life-sciences and the humanities, both are brought back to a common ground, in that the principles underlying the elaboration of form and function in biology and discourse are shown to have a similar character.

Equating underlying principles of biology and discourse may sound heretical: is it not the case that the broad social constructionist account of human activity is inherently at odds with the reductionist, Cartesian paradigm so familiar in the contemporary landscape of psychology and its allied social sciences? Are we not providing another abstract metanarrative in making this claim? This is an issue we will return to. Here we want to draw attention to one 'update' from recent work that refines some of von Uexküll's pioneering ideas: studies of infancy and its biological components that contribute to the development of cultural practices. We need to look at these so as to dispel a possible interpretation that could be taken from both Mead and von Uexküll: that meaning is 'out there', in social interaction or in the directly perceived value an object has to an organism within its *Umwelt*, and hence we are back in the ballpark of individualistic determinism. Our point is, rather, that for humans there are certainly some relations with their environment that have a given significance that does not have to be learned: that, for example, 'other people are interesting; worth paying attention to'. But, given this, there is then a massive amount of negotiation that has to be worked through in real time with these 'interesting people' so as to become attuned to the social and cultural world that is one's life.

With respect to biology, we are intending here the idea that evolution equips organisms with an *Umwelt* that is tuned to their interests. A cat, for example, does not have to learn that mice are of interest to it, nor a herring gull chick that red spots on beaks are worth pecking at. Evolution has built them an *Umwelt* that is already organized so as to take these things into account in the directedness of their activities. What research with human infants has made clear over the past thirty years or so is that, almost from the outset, the human *Umwelt* is unique. It provides a 'felt immediacy' (Bråten, 2003) of others' actions; a participatory consciousness (Fogel, 2004); what Macmurray (1961) argued as a necessary, pre-given and tacit understanding that other people exist, which is a necessary requirement for human development (see also Buber, 1923/1971; Bateson, 1975; Trevarthen and Hubley, 1978; Trevarthen, 1979, 1992, 1993; Stern, 1985; Damasio, 1996, for related views).

'Minds', then, are socially oriented from the outset, and even though we may assume that minds and *Umwelts* involve brain activity, it is more the case that 'rather than being the seat of epistemologically private representations, the brain functions to regulate the body's interactions with its ecosocial environment' (Thibaut, 2005: 152).

To begin with, infant–adult interactions are characterized by their affective qualities, and it is out of these that later, symbolically mediated forms of communication are constructed. But, importantly, 'neither parent nor infant seem ... to have to *learn* how to get started with affective interaction' (Spurrett and Cowley, 2004: 454): that is, there is an already given backdrop to the culturally mediated social construction of human activity.

Where we need to be wary of von Uexküll's framework is his use of the terms 'law' and 'rule'. Both imply a degree of determinism that is a characteristic of neither evolution nor human action. These are creative processes that are rich in possibilities, though both are clearly circumscribed by the histories and horizons that constrain the set of possibilities available to them at any moment in their unfolding: it is in this sense that von Uexküll's musical analogy is apt.

From von Uexküll one gets a sense that meaning and experience are not easily uncoupled. Changing one's mind or 'story' is sometimes portrayed as a facile change of vocabulary or plotline. As with Wittgenstein's 'grammars', habits of meaning that extend already established customs for keeping meaning and interaction predictably familiar, human meaning, for von Uexküll, is biologically and ecologically grounded. While not prey to starfish, like paua, humans can be similarly tenacious in holding on to some meanings as if their very survival depended on doing so.

8   Ludwig Wittgenstein
'Shewing the fly out of the bottle'

> Philosophy is a battle against the bewitchment of our intelligence by means of language.   (Wittgenstein, 1953: aphorism 109)

> The myth of the given in modern philosophy of language involves as profound an alienation from the human world as that of classical empiricism from the natural world.   (Hacker, 2000: 48)

It is surprising that Wittgenstein has not featured more prominently in social constructionist writings about practice. His intellectual journey paralleled those of practitioners who began their careers bent on universal truths and practices, but ended up more humbly basing their practice on contextualized meanings used in language. If that journey seems familiar, Wittgenstein also brought exacting analytic rigour to his journey and we are the richer for his efforts. But, reading Wittgenstein ... well, that is perhaps why more constructionist practitioners don't cite his influence.

Ludwig Wittgenstein championed two nearly opposing approaches to philosophy: an analytic and an idealized view that language could correctly represent experience; and a focus on people's use of everyday forms of language. Both ways, Wittgenstein took us further into the reality–language connection. His efforts began with an attempt on the ultimate word for what Hacker above described as the 'myth of the given', only to abandon this project to consider how all forms of language can bewitch or optimally serve human understanding and interaction.

Wittgenstein's aims were practical and therapeutic. For him, philosophy was a challenge of 'shewing the fly out of the bottle' – the bottle being limitations in how we use language. He responded to philosophical problems, in his words, as one would respond to illness. Publishing only one book in his lifetime, entering philosophy with an engineering and mathematical orientation, Wittgenstein later felt philosophy could better be pursued as a poetic activity. His Cambridge lectures were legendary – these and his notebooks became a series of highly influential books (especially *Philosophical Investigations*) after his death in 1951. A figure of great controversy, a 'spoiled brat' from one of Vienna's richest families (whose wealth he later renounced), he was characterized by his biographer Ray Monk (1990) as a 'tormented genius'.

Wittgenstein taunted us with a wealth of ideas and questions that continue to inspire and provoke philosophers and scholars from diverse disciplines long after his death. In considering Wittgenstein we will start with a biography to help contextualize his thinking, and then move through his early analytic philosophy phase to the publication of the *Tractatus Logico-Philosophicus* (*TLP*) and its considerable influence on analytic philosophy. From there, we will consider his abandonment of *TLP*'s philosophical project to focus on some key aspects of his later, linguistically based philosophy. In particular, we will examine the following concepts: meaning, verification and criteria, language games, the private language argument, and language as grammatically governed relational activity. Finally, we will review these ideas as they relate to therapy, remembering that Wittgenstein himself saw philosophy as helping others 'dissolve problems'. As we go forward, keep in mind Daniel Dennett's description of Wittgenstein as one of *Time* magazine's 100 most influential people of the twentieth century, for his two, near-opposing, literary accomplishments:

> The fact remains that one's first exposure to either the *Tractatus* or *Philosophical Investigations* is a liberating and exhilarating experience. Here is a model of thinking so intense, so pure, so self-critical that even its mistakes are gifts.   (Dennett, 2000: no page number)

Biography

> When you are philosophizing you have to descend into primeval chaos and feel at home there.   (Wittgenstein, 1980a: 65)

Ludwig Wittgenstein was the last of eight children born to a rich Austrian industrialist family supportive of the artistic and intellectual community of Vienna. He was home-schooled until the age of 14, when he was enrolled in the Realschule at Linz, which Adolf Hitler also attended. Legend has it that Wittgenstein (a Jew who in later life converted to Christianity) had corrected Hitler for the pitch of his whistling, leading some to infer grounds for Hitler's later 'final solution'. Wittgenstein developed a penchant for engineering and later attended the University of Manchester, where he studied aeronautical engineering, and grew increasingly fascinated with mathematics. It was this fascination that drew him to the writing of Gottlob Frege and his soon-to-be Cambridge mentor, Bertrand Russell. For the young Wittgenstein, the foundations of mathematics held pristine possibilities for representing the factual and orderly nature of experience. No one had advanced the potentials of mathematical thinking further than Russell in his *Principles of Mathematics*, published in 1903. At Cambridge, Wittgenstein quickly became Russell's star pupil, only to bolt for the seclusion of the fjords of Norway two short years after they began their work together. The speculated reason for this abrupt departure was the death of Wittgenstein's father, and the deep depression this brought about (he had four brothers who committed suicide and thought this way at times himself). He continued to work on the problems of foundational mathematics during this time, through his stint with the Austrian army (including time as a prisoner of the Italians), concurrently producing the first of his landmark books (the only one in his lifetime): *Tractatus Logico-Philosophicus* (*TLP*). He managed to have *TLP* smuggled out of an Italian prisoner of war camp to Bertrand Russell, who helped to get it published finally in 1921.

TLP reads like a series of striking soundbites. Starting from an opening pair of aphorisms: '1. The world is all that is the case. 1.1. The world is the totality of facts, not of things', Wittgenstein closed with number 7: 'Whereof one cannot speak, thereof one must be silent.' For 'early' Wittgenstein, factual discourse, the focus of *TLP*, represented the world as it is, except where it could not – for mystical, moral and other more subjective dimensions of experience. For a man bent on mathematical and engineering solutions to everyday problems, *TLP* was a colossal effort to have the final word on factual discourse. Getting clear about language, as he attempted in *TLP*, remained a lifelong focus, but this first, classic stab at it was based on the idea that one could correctly map experience at its most fundamental level. *TLP* was eagerly welcomed by empirical thinkers, in particular those of the famous Vienna Circle, who sought to place philosophy squarely within the logical positivist thinking central to the natural and applied sciences of the day.

Between his discharge from an Italian prisoner of war camp in 1919, and his 'summons' to join the Vienna Circle in 1927, Wittgenstein again retreated into obscurity, mainly teaching in small village schools until he quit in 1926 after striking a student. During this period, he developed a spelling book for the local schools, helped design and build a home for one of his sisters, and had his only heterosexual relationship. Also, it was during this interim period that *TLP* began to make waves, and it was a surprise to the Vienna Circle to hear that the man to whom they turned for intellectual leadership was a village schoolteacher. Thus began Wittgenstein's slow resumption of academic life, marked by a return to England in January 1929, and the awarding of his Ph.D. by Cambridge University for *TLP*. It was during this initial period of return that Wittgenstein began to doubt the analytic and empirical philosophy he had championed.

Wittgenstein had arrived at Cambridge, already somewhat of a heroic figure because of *TLP*. He made his brilliant but tormented life evident to Bertrand Russell and others in doubts central to his lectures, grappling with them in the presence of his students, in quite mesmerizing ways. Imagine, openly doubting the accomplishments that brought him renown and a teaching position at one of the world's most prestigious universities – at the start of his teaching career – and you have some sense of his intellectual honesty and daring. His initial doubts focused on what it meant to verify the foundations he had articulated in *TLP*, and here began his concern with language, the stuff beyond words, in *TLP*'s last aphorism. This concern eventually brought him to question that language could, like pictures, accurately represent experience 'as it is'. His early questioning, and movement away from *TLP* and analytic philosophy, is evident in the notes he used in developing his later magnum opus: *Philosophical Investigations*. These notes were published posthumously as *The Blue and Brown Books* (so named after the colours of the notebooks he used in preparing his 1933–4, 1934–5 lectures), but one can find most of the general ideas (e.g., language games, private language, problems with certainty) associated with 'later Wittgenstein' gaining early articulation there. As an example, on page 69 of the *Blue Book*, he wrote: 'The use of the word *in practice* is its meaning' (1958; Wittgenstein's emphasis). *The Blue and Brown Books*, like many of the books published after Wittgenstein's death, were derived from his notes or lectures, by former students such as Rush Rhees, G. E. Anscombe and G. H. von Wright, during his intermittent periods at Cambridge.

In 1935, Wittgenstein completed his initial fellowship at Cambridge and, again, headed for the fjords of Norway. After a few nomadic years, he returned to Cambridge with a professorship, and a renewed vigour for tackling his former foundationalist ideas, particularly as they related to mathematics. By this point he was already well under way with the notes that would form the basis for *Philosophical Investigations* (*PI*), and a number of his other posthumous publications. During the war he also worked as a porter in a hospital, living a predominantly solitary life, save for some homosexual relationships he developed with younger men. In academic circles, Wittgenstein had some famous and combative encounters with scholars such as Alan Turing and Karl Popper. The latter exchange has been immortalized in *Wittgenstein's Poker* (Edmonds and Eidinow, 2001). The 'poker' referred to was allegedly waved by Wittgenstein at Popper as their ten-minute encounter over 'philosophical problems' escalated into a celebrated Wittgenstein temper outburst. The basic issue was over whether such 'problems' actually existed – for Wittgenstein the problem rested with the word 'actually'.

During these years at Cambridge, Wittgenstein's linguistic philosophy found its articulation, but, like *TLP* and most of his other, later, published works, it is expressed in staccato-like utterances, as if from a man with a stammer. These, however, remained Wittgenstein's private notes which he refused to see published because he was chronically dissatisfied with his work. His aphorisms hardly read like a narrative or conversation (Example from *PI*: 432–1: 'Every sign by itself seems dead. What gives it life? – In use it is alive. Is life breathed into it there? – Or is the use its life?'). And, this, from a man who advanced a very conversational view of meaning and influence.

In the postwar period Wittgenstein travelled to the US and continued to lecture on the issues that preoccupied him. Upon returning from the US in 1949, he was diagnosed with cancer, and in 1951 he died. By this point, some features of Wittgenstein's life, those which help us understand his unique contributions to philosophy, are becoming clear. Coming from a life of affluence, he grew up in very cultured circumstances and consistently held himself to the highest of standards as he tackled the huge questions that perplexed him. Brilliant, it was clear to his teachers and students that he possessed a near maniacal intensity that seemed on the verge of overtaking him as he pondered, then erupted, with audacious insights, and near misses. He would pursue an intellectual trajectory to its fullest, writing the seminal analytic and empirical philosophy book *TLP*, and later accept its limitations, only to build from it a view that infuriated those who had initially accepted *TLP*. For an authoritative understanding of Wittgenstein's life readers are recommended to consult Ray Monk's (1990) *The Duty of Genius*. In pursuing meaning and language to the extent realized in *PI* (another towering landmark of philosophical thought in the 20th century), he pushed thinking to limits that are still being explored for their implications. In our case, we will now more closely examine the development of these ideas, from the empirical aspirations he had for language in *TLP* to the conclusions later shared in the posthumously published *PI*.

'Early' Wittgenstein

> We expect the next big step in philosophy to be taken by your brother.
> (Bertrand Russell to Hermione Wittgenstein, 1912)

By the time Wittgenstein first showed up at Cambridge his interest in aeronautical engineering had metamorphosed into a personal mission to lay bare the foundations of mathematics and factual discourse. Despite Russell's obvious admiration for Wittgenstein's capabilities, his student was unable to meet the requirements and failed to finish his thesis, prior to his self-exile to the Norwegian fjords in 1913. Nevertheless, Wittgenstein devoted his considerable intellectual talents to the problem that 'imperfect language' created for philosophy, and these efforts persisted through his time as a World War I soldier and prisoner of war. If philosophy was to have the clarity one associated with mathematics, it required precise language, and the Wittgenstein of this period was convinced that one could equate words with their real-life referents. To that end, he committed himself to studying and 'cleaning up' the logical form that language can have to the world it represents. In this way he was attempting to put philosophy on a footing equal with the empirical sciences. *Tractatus Logico-Philosophicus* was written, painstakingly (there didn't seem any other way for Wittgenstein), into a seventy-page gem. Here is part of Wittgenstein's preface to *TLP*, his pinnacle achievement in his early career:

> If this work has a value it consists in two things. First that in it thoughts are expressed, and this value will be the greater the better the thoughts are expressed. The more the nail has been hit on the head. – Here I am conscious that I have fallen far short of the possible. Simply because my powers are insufficient to cope with the task. – May others come and do it better. On the other hand the truth of the thoughts communicated here seem to me unassailable and definitive. I am, therefore, of the opinion that the problems have in essentials been finally solved. And if I am not mistaken in this, then the value of this work secondly consists in the fact that it shows how little has been done when these problems have been solved.   (Wittgenstein, 1961: 3; originally published 1921)

TLP, in the context of its times, took a paradigm of thought (logical positivism) to what seemed an optimal articulation. Wittgenstein dissected the world into what could be known (and not known), and then formulated the logical and analytic bases on which that knowing seemingly could take place. In this manner, Wittgenstein's early philosophy squared with the continuing modern scientific efforts to describe, predict, and control – offering hope to those who saw the natural world as within the technical stewardship of humankind. To do this, however, he had also to distinguish fact from non-sense, the latter comprising such human domains as ethics, spirituality and values. These, thought Wittgenstein, stood in the way of the non-ambiguous language required for empirical and analytic philosophy. *TLP* systematically mapped out what he felt was required for such a language, especially the properties and propositional nature of the word–reality 'hook-up' as he then saw it.

In reading *TLP* one is confronted with a view of words that made eminent sense in its day. Words, in this view, spoke to us, revealing what they were about (if this kind of anthropomorphization concerns you, you are on to part of why Wittgenstein later abandoned this line of thinking). The aphorisms – bullet-like statements akin to the examples that follow – tautly put across Wittgenstein's thinking:

> 4.022 A proposition *shows* its sense.
>   A proposition *shows* how things stand if it is true. And it *says that* they do so stand.
> 4.124 The existence of an internal property of a possible situation is not expressed by means of a proposition: rather, it expresses itself in the proposition representing the situation, by means of an internal property of that proposition. It would be just as nonsensical to assert that a proposition had a formal property as to deny it.   (Wittgenstein, 1961; emphasis in the original)

Wittgenstein's prose modelled that which he sought for philosophy and, not surprisingly, reads like what you would expect from a mathematician – brief, relatively free of ambiguity, and systematic. The world, for him, could be reduced to atomistic facts and from them, in mathematical ways, relationships could be explained, as in this *TLP* (aphorism 6.5) comment: 'If a question can be put at all, then it can also be answered.'

The effect of *TLP* on the thinking of between-wars Europe was profound. Here is Rudolf Carnap, of the famous Vienna Circle (the pre-eminent group of logical positivist scholars at the time): 'In the Vienna Circle, a large part of Ludwig Wittgenstein's book *Tractatus Logico-Philosophicus* was read aloud and discussed sentence by sentence … Wittgenstein's book exerted a strong influence upon our Circle' (A. Rorty, 2003: 442). At Cambridge, when he returned in 1929, the book helped him secure a fellowship and the devotion of more than a few young scholars eager to see an acknowledged genius perform. But bear in mind Wittgenstein's last aphorism ('Whereof one cannot speak, thereof one must be silent'). *TLP* brought him to reflect deeply on this and a number of the other inadequacies he saw with analytic philosophy. Thus he began the intellectual journey that would eventually bring him to develop the notes we now know as his second masterpiece: *Philosophical Investigations*.

Segue

> Philosophers constantly see the method of science before their eyes and are irresistibly tempted to ask and answer questions the ways science does. This tendency is the real source of metaphysics and leads the philosopher into complete darkness.   (Wittgenstein, *Blue Book*, 1958: 18)

Premised, as *TLP* was, on the notion that language could philosophically and accurately map reality, the above quote shows the Wittgenstein of 1933 clearly looking beyond science alone for answers to his questions on meaning. This departure marks a significant development in Wittgenstein's movement toward a contextualized view of meaning as it relates to language use, in particular to 'language games'. This is no mere shift. Consider a view of meaning where experience could be represented accurately, and the only things standing between us and such an accuracy were perceptual difficulties or incorrect language use, and you have the gist of *TLP*'s meaning. Now, consider alternative views of meaning in which scientific understanding and methods were not fundamental or considered superior, as if those other views were deviations or distortions from a correct objectivity science could deliver. What Wittgenstein was readying himself and his students for was a shift to seeing meaning as not only developed within particular contexts, but scrutinizable on the bases of criteria people developed and used within those contexts as well. Thus, while scientists may have particular conventions for adjudicating the methods and findings of science, so too would people of different cultural groupings, from racial through interest and family groupings. Claiming an exclusive set of criteria and meanings for all groupings denies the meanings and ways of understanding them developed within such groupings. This is but one of the themes central to Wittgenstein's later career. Here is another passage from the *Blue Book*, notes written for his Cambridge lectures in 1933–4:

> I want you to remember that words have those meanings which we have given them; and we give them meanings by explanations … words in this sense then don't have a strict meaning. But this is not a defect. To think it is would be like saying that the light of my reading lamp is no real light at all because it has no sharp boundary.   (1958: 27)

Here we are confronted with Wittgenstein veering away from precise, predetermined language towards his growing preoccupation with language as it is used to accomplish meaning. The passage above suggests a very social view of language, one that requires some looseness of fit for different social circumstances. But, as we will examine in some detail later, what makes a word fit for those who use it are the criteria they bring to bear on it, in their relational circumstances – not criteria that can universally be applied, or are derived only from science. Science is but one human enterprise or domain of meaning, ill-fitting to many other meaningful human activities (love, arts, etc.) decided on quite different bases. Defaulting all understanding and human activity to a particular scientific 'language game', as Wittgenstein began referring to these ways of human interaction and understanding, obscured and subordinated many other, equally compelling aspects of being human. Here is Wittgenstein in the *Brown Book*:

> The picture we have of the language of the grown-up is that of a nebulous mass of language, his mother tongue, surrounded by discrete and more or less clear-cut language games, the technical languages.   (1958: 81)

The shift Wittgenstein is making in these notes is of Copernican significance. To move from a position on meaning where nature expresses itself and our job is to capture 'it' precisely in a scientific language that should subordinate all others, to a view where meaning relies on how people use words with each other, takes meaning from being out 'there' in the world, and anchors it in contexts of human communication and evaluation. Building on this, Wittgenstein was suggesting that there is more than one correct way to understand and communicate, that understanding could not be pre-mapped in a one-size-fits-all manner from which we could assess the accuracies of our communication and understanding. What passes for common sense owes more to our participation in particular 'language games' or contexts of word use than it does to getting things right with nature, and that includes the scientific language game. Here Wittgenstein is again, in the *Blue Book*:

> We seem to have made a discovery – which I could describe by saying that the ground on which we stood and which appeared to be firm and reliable was found to be boggy and unsafe. – That is, this happens when we philosophize; for as soon as we revert to the standpoint of common sense this general uncertainty disappears.   (Wittgenstein, 1958: 45)

At this point, Wittgenstein is foreshadowing a revolutionary view of understanding and common sense – that both are contextualized in the ways that people relate to each other, and to which they make reference. The 'boggy ground' Wittgenstein refers to above occurs when one discerns that there might be other equally valid ways to understand and relate – multiple realities where our ways of talking and understanding formerly were only capable of seeing one. We know this from cross-cultural experience and yet the full significance usually does not strike us. In the *Blue and Brown Books* Wittgenstein is blazing a dizzying trail (remember – these are notes from his lectures), one that gives a very different basis for some of the most taken-for-granted aspects of human existence: understanding and communication in context. From trying to nail down understanding and communication universally in *TLP*, to get at the kind of objectivity science idealizes, here he inverts his original quest for meaning: meaning is not immanent in how things are, it is immanent in how we talk about how things are. And there is more than one way to do that talking, to arrive at understanding. As a taste of the 'psychological' implications of his early forays into this way of understanding, here is Wittgenstein, one last time, before we move on to key aspects of his later thinking:

> Our ordinary language, which of all possible notations is the one which pervades all our life, holds our mind rigidly in one position, as it were, and in

this position sometimes it feels cramped, having a desire for other positions as well. Thus we sometimes wish for a notation which stresses a difference more strongly, makes it more obvious than ordinary language does, or one which in a particular case uses more closely similar forms of expression than our ordinary language. Our mental cramp is loosened when we are shown the notations which fulfill these needs. These needs can be of the greatest variety.   (Wittgenstein, 1958: 59)

Verification and Criteria

We just do not see how very specialized the use of 'I know' is.   (Wittgenstein, 1969: aphorism 11)

What is the proof that I know something? Most certainly not my saying I know it.   (Wittgenstein, 1969: aphorism 487)

Where *TLP* sought to put philosophy within the same methodological framework as empiricist science, anchoring its foundations, so to speak, by cleaning up the linkage between experience and the words correlated with it, Wittgenstein's later work had no such legislative agenda. Instead, Wittgenstein sought to understand the bases upon which people understood each other, and then derived his meta-commentary from such considerations. For him, knowing was a phenomenon particular to the people involved or, from the notes we now know as *On Certainty*, 'The truth of certain empirical propositions belongs to our frame of reference' (1969: aphorism 83). Where *TLP* explicitly pursued one 'correct' frame of reference, Wittgenstein now saw many in the particular ways people shared, and held each other to, various frames of reference. Where the criteria for such 'correctness' had been purportedly universal, and tied to the empiricist methods of science, he came to see humanly diverse and arbitrary criteria as central to what distinguished such frames of reference from each other. We will later examine the social contexts of such frames of reference under Wittgenstein's notion of 'language games', but for now it will help to consider such frames of reference as culturally distinct ways of relating to experience, for how they can be shared with other people.

It is also important to see that, in making his shift to 'language games', Wittgenstein was trying to get closer to the understandings people lived by. *TLP*, in seeking an ultimate philosophical language, looked right past how people successfully used language in their everyday interactions. McGinn (1997: 44; emphasis added) underscores a concern that Wittgenstein spent his last twenty years addressing:

> The tendency to isolate language, or abstract it from the context in which it ordinarily lives, is connected with our adopting a theoretical attitude towards it, and with our urge to explain *how* these mere signs (mere marks) can acquire their extraordinary power to represent something. Wittgenstein's aim is to show us that in this act of abstraction we turn our backs on everything that is essential to the actual functioning of language; it is our act of abstracting from

its employment within our ordinary lives that turns it into something whose ability to represent now cries out for explanation.

How people got by in different circumstances using the words and ways of communicating they did was clearly a different focus from Wittgenstein's former *TLP* stance on how language should be used properly, irrespective of context. But, with this shift came a host of new implications and questions about what successful or optimal language use would entail.

In *TLP*, and for the logical positivists, verification was the means by which the truth of any claim could be judged. For a claim to be judged correct, the means by which it should be judged so should be evident in how the claim is put. Thus, for example, for one to claim that the moon is made of green cheese should be highlighted in how this claim is supported. The support for the claim can then be seen as verifiable by those in a position to judge it. This is a cornerstone of most forms of knowing and rhetoric. But behind any process of verification lie criteria one turns to in order to judge the soundness of the claims proposed. The criteria used by astronomers in judging the moon's constitution would likely be different from those of poets. The crunch comes when we say which truth should claim authority. For Wittgenstein, the issue did not default immediately to science: truth was something established through the interactions of people upholding different versions of, and reasons for, it. Ironically, from Wittgenstein's point of view, while science claims decontextualized truths – those free of human subjectivity – it was in their conventions and criteria one finds their subjectivity, as worked out between scientists. These conventions and criteria are tied to particular endeavours (to describe, predict and control experience) that are value-based and thus subjective.

When Wittgenstein asks 'How then can the sense and truth (or the truth and sense) of sentences collapse (stand or fall) together' (1967: 131), we are invited to consider that famous phrase, 'it all depends'. What it depends on are the historically rooted and usually unquestioned criteria people bring to bear on any claim that purports to be truthworthy.

There is a scene in science fiction writer Frank Herbert's (1990) *Dune* in which the leader of an expedition encounters a leader from the host planet. The planet, extremely desolate and dry, has few inhabitants. When the two leaders meet for the first time, the host planet's leader spits on the expedition leader. This, for the expedition leader, was near grounds for warfare, but through the developments that followed the justification (or truth) of the action of host planet's leader became clearer: in a planet with virtually no moisture, no higher order of respect could be bestowed than to offer one's moisture to another, as in the spitting gesture. This is what some describe as frames of reference, evident in the particular ways people understand or judge the truth or goodness of actions or utterances. 'It all depends' suggests a common sense that arises in particular contextual judgements that give any meaningful utterance or action its meaningfulness. Here is Wittgenstein on this in *Zettel*: 'The "uncertainty" relates not to the particular case, but to the method, to the rules of evidence' (1967: aphorism 555). Wittgenstein was suggesting that evidence is judged using particular methods and criteria (rules of evidence) unique to those abiding by them. But in the spitting incident above, two very different ways of understanding and judging are reflected. They owe their differences to differences within what Wittgenstein referred to as 'language games', or their related 'forms of life'. Within each form of life or language game are already worked-out and agreed meanings and ways of relating – the kind that seem self-evident until new encounters point out otherwise. But the spitting encounter points out where differences in language games can be either a problem, or something to work out in new agreements on meaning. Without such agreements between them people lack familiar ways to 'go on together'; misunderstandings and conflicts can develop. The post-*TLP* Wittgenstein had turned away from philosophic ideals and abstractions to judge the truth or goodness of such actions or utterances, turning instead to how people work out, then uphold through their language games, what is true and false. In his words:

> 'So you are saying that human agreement decides what is true and what is false?' It is what human beings say that is true and false; and they agree in the language they use. That is not agreement in opinion but in form of life.   (Wittgenstein, 1958: aphorism 241–1)

Meaning: from pictures to use

> For Wittgenstein, at the bottom of life is *trust*, a particular mode of action.
>   (J. Edwards, 1983: 182; emphasis added)

> For words only have meaning in the stream of life.   (Wittgenstein, 1980b: aphorism 687)

Meaning preoccupied Wittgenstein throughout his adult life. First, he committed himself to cleaning up and adding precision to meaning – to better render the world as it could be explained rationally. But he grew dissatisfied with this idealized view of meaning, and how it failed to account for people quite successfully using language in different spheres of everyday life. For some critics, this is where Wittgenstein went off the rails, but for Wittgenstein – and for our discursive view – this is precisely where he takes on a challenging yet rewarding approach to meaning. To understand meaning, for Wittgenstein, is to understand how utterances and actions are used and appraised in social interactions and circumstances. It was important to Wittgenstein that we see our historical and creative role in developing and using meanings as we do, and not to see them as determined by experience 'as it is'. That didn't make sense to him; experiences didn't express their meanings to us. Rather, somewhere in our communicative histories, we gave such experiences their meanings, only to lose sight later of 'our' role in making such meanings. This extends to how we hold ourselves and each other to using such meanings. Being born into word- and gesture-using cultures and relationships, we come to adopt the words and gestures used by those around us. But to appreciate these words and gestures is not to see them atomized into distinct meaning-bits, but rather it is to see them for the functions they perform in our relationships and other dimensions of our experience.

This increasing emphasis on 'we', 'us', and 'our' accompanied Wittgenstein's shift on meaning. For meaning to be shared requires some measure of agreement, and subsequent solidarity – even if blindly given – to keep meanings socially familiar. For feminist scholar Alessandra Tanesini, this points to a fundamentally relational aspect of life

> Acts of saying 'we' which function as acknowledgments help us to test and realize the depth and breadth of our attunement in words, emotions and reactions. These are trivial things perhaps, but without them we could not agree or disagree with one another. Also, by means of projective imagination, acts of saying 'we' help us to expand and change the nature of such attunements.   (2004: 137)

Where before Wittgenstein saw meaning in terms of word-pictures (a word, symbol or gesture correctly representing some aspect of experience), he came to see this as a source of major confusion. Our principal point of reference for 'what things mean' is not private experience or a dictionary, but each other. Language, being a human creation, acquires its meaning through shared use, whether taught from a dictionary or textbook, or in parent–child (and adult–adult) interactions. Close examination of the *Oxford English Dictionary* (*OED*), even its abridged versions, suggests that meaning is all laid out for us, words can be traced back to particular guidelines for their use, and to use them otherwise is to 'mean incorrectly'. Seemingly, goes this line of thinking, experience 'calls out' certain meanings to us, and our job is to honour them with correct referents. But even looking at definitions within the *OED* forces us to confront significant ambiguities of word use (e.g., love can mean at least two things on the tennis court). Further, this does not explain how different groups develop meanings particular to them, as might a street gang using the word 'bad' in ways different from its conventional use (must one tell the street gang they are using the word incorrectly?). For these and other reasons, Wittgenstein shifted from an idealized position of nailing down a correct one-size-should-fit-all language, to recognizing the diverse ways in which meanings are given, used and assented to in different human contexts. He also abandoned word-pictures to look at how meaning is developed and sustained through social interactions. In *Zettel*, he offers a glimmer of this perspective on meaning, as it relates to understanding:

> But don't think of understanding as a 'mental process' at all. For that is the way of speaking that is confusing you. Rather, ask yourself: in what kind of case, in what circumstances do we say, 'Now I can go on', if the formula occurs to us.   (Wittgenstein, 1967: aphorism 446)

In attempting to better grasp Wittgenstein's approach to meaning it helps to see him considering his starting place in *TLP* as one frame of reference (or what we shall later refer to as a particular language game) – one of many. Building on this, one is forced to confront the issue of meaning as one might consider differences in meaning within different cultures: if we try to understand things only on the terms of our own frame of reference, we can lose the meaning as it is understood within another frame of reference. In anthropology we would be talking about emic (culture-specific) versus etic (cross-cultural) meaning. We have all had experiences of this, when we have attempted to grapple with the meanings and ways of communicating particular to a group of people we are new to. Certain utterances, stories, gestures, and so on, have acquired familiarity and acceptability to those sharing them, and so we must orient to what makes them familiar and acceptable, otherwise we can not share in their meaning. As we acquire a sense of a speaking group's jargon, its lore and its ways of using words, we gain a fluency not only in their meaning, but in their means of sharing meaning, the 'connexions' they make. For Wittgenstein, this linkage is crucial. Speaking involves more than transmitting information to each other; it is how we coordinate our interactions with each other; how we create unique 'forms of life' in and from such interactions.

Let us explore some implications of this line of thinking about meaning. Consider Wittgenstein's famous duck–rabbit drawing from *Philosophical Investigations* (1953).

Some may find parallels here with diagrams used by Gestalt psychologists, such as the old woman/young woman, or the wine goblet/face-to-face drawings. But there is a striking difference between how Wittgenstein and the Gestalt psychologists regarded differences in how these figures were interpreted. Specifically, Gestalt psychologists usually put the differences down to the psychologies of the individuals involved; whereas Wittgenstein saw these differences (seeing a duck or seeing a rabbit) as evidence of participation in different forms of life, different streams of meaning. In other words, we come to interpret our experience consistently with the ways we have learned to share our experience in our relationships, in the ways of communicating and understanding particular to those relationships. As with his concern about correct interpretation (back to *TLP*'s one-size-should-fit-all language and way of understanding), diagrams like the duck–rabbit help

Figure 8.1 *Wittgenstein's famous duck–rabbit drawing*

us to consider how and why there can be differences in meaning that cannot be attributable to such things as 'distortions or deviations' from correct understanding. This is particularly the case when one traces such differences in meaning to the different forms of life in which people are engaged.

In *On Certainty* (1969) Wittgenstein noted that 'Our talk gets its meaning from the rest of our proceedings' (aphorism 229). An issue in understanding meaning, for Wittgenstein, is to understand better those 'proceedings', in how they contribute to meaning. In the Wittgenstein of *TLP* this was simple; the 'rest of our proceedings' was presumably shared and articulable in a precise and rationally correct language. Temporally, the view of meaning in *TLP* was of timeless word-pictures that existed apart from humans. These word-pictures, in turn, could be transmitted between people; as meanings residing in these word-pictures unless human deficiencies are involved in their transmission or reception. Typically, for people who see meaning in *TLP* terms as self-evident in 'how things are', meaning is in what we mean as we say things. If someone else does not understand me, and I 'know' I have transmitted my meaning correctly, then they must be defective. This view of meaning is commonplace, and it presumes a shared context of understanding and agreement. But, bearing in mind that language is far from precise, that people develop particular understandings and uses of it in different social contexts, that they bring to any communicative exchange different social purposes they are trying to accomplish, and that these are all parts of the 'proceedings' as Wittgenstein described – this makes the transmission metaphor of communication ripe for relational difficulties.

Where things get particularly challenging – in a duck–rabbit kind of way – is when people bring different meanings to their social interactions. They might talk right past each other, but arguments and misunderstandings thrive on such differences, particularly if either party insists their meaning must be correct for the other. One person's irritation could be another's grievance. In *TLP* such differences would require expert adjudication to determine whose meaning is correct. Or, to use the duck–rabbit issue, pistols at dawn might be needed to decide whose criteria should be used to 'correctly' adjudicate such differences in understanding. We are now at one of those intellectual forks in the road that so perplexed Wittgenstein. To continue down *TLP*'s road would require coming up with final criteria for correctly deciding differences in understanding in places he warned about in *TLP*'s final aphorism ('Whereof one cannot speak …'). People speak all the time about the very things Wittgenstein wanted to banish from *TLP*'s considerations. Oops. Thus, if there are no final criteria to decide which meaning was correct, a challenge arises as to how differences in meaning should be regarded.

Wittgenstein's answer to this challenge in *PI* was to look at how such differences could be seen as meanings anchored in human interactions (proceedings) over time; with past meaningful interactions shaping (but not determining) present interactions. For Luntley (2003), this approach to meaning is 'animatory', in that humans bring to life the words, gestures and other symbols they use when interacting with each other. This view resonates with Bakhtin's (1981) phrase about words being 'naked corpses until used in dialogue'. Thus, the 'proceedings' Wittgenstein referred to above are complex. They are historical and largely based on how our use of words and other communications fare in our contextually based interactions with others over time. These proceedings do not decide the meanings, however: humans engaged in enacting the proceedings (blindly or more discerningly) do. For there to be shared meaning, there must be agreement on how conversations and other forms of human interaction proceed. Inside familiar conversations we can afford to use taken-for-granted words and ways of talking. With others conversationally unfamiliar with 'where we are coming from', this could be a recipe for misunderstanding or conflict. It is a good thing we do not have to mind each utterance in familiar conversations, but the very things that make these conversations easy to take for granted can make for difficult communications with others not sharing our familiarities. Arguably, *TLP*'s mistake was that such familiarities were to be regarded as universal when, in practice – and what else is there? – interacting and understanding are proceedings that almost always take on particular 'local' nuances, depending on the people and purposes involved. They become recognizable 'forms of life', ways of understanding and conducting social life one is expected to keep familiar. We will examine this latter point in greater detail when we consider 'language games' and their 'grammars'.

Wittgenstein's shift from word-pictures to meanings used by people in varied proceedings shatters an often held idealization that there is a correct and thus universally shareable way of communicating and understanding. His *TLP* sought to advance this idealization, bringing precision to the vocabulary people could interact from. Had he and others succeeded with this project we would not need phrases like 'it depends on the context'. We would be able to turn to the abstracted word-pictures of language and know their meanings in some ultimately decidable (abstract) way. This prevailing western view sees minds as information processors and communications as involving transmissions and receptions of information. This led Wittgenstein to once write something similar in what was later published as *Zettel* (1967: aphorism 606): 'The idea of thinking as a process inside the head, in a completely enclosed space, gives him something occult.'

This brings us back, then, to a very different basis for meaning from the kind of absolute view promised us by *TLP* and centuries of western thought. Meaning is social; it is there in how we come to use words, gestures and symbols in ways that are intelligible to us. Dictionaries do not legislate meanings, though we can, through our politics or business dealings, create legally binding meanings. If meaning is not 'out there' in some absolute sense, but 'between us' in ways we agree upon and then uphold through particular ways of interacting, then this is a very different approach to understanding, or what many like to speak of when talking about 'mind' or 'cognition'. Where realists like to describe our understandings of phenomena in word-pictures corresponding with their essences, Wittgenstein takes us a dizzying step away from essences as being self-evident via our word-pictures for them. Instead he suggests we look inside the rule-like familiarities of our 'language games', our varied ways of talking and understanding, for how meaning is to be understood. Some of this is alluded to by this challenging comment from *PI* (1953: 351), foreshadowing our next section: 'Essence is expressed by grammar.'

Language games

'So the proper question is not: how does he learn the use of the word?' but rather 'How does it come out that he uses it as we do?'   (Wittgenstein, 1980b: aphorism 376)

The harmony between thought and reality is to be found in the grammar of the language.   (Wittgenstein, 1974: 162)

In his discussion of 'language games' Wittgenstein takes us into a remarkably nuanced, yet general, consideration of the contexts of human meaning. In this regard, Wittgenstein's philosophy is incredibly social, especially for a man who seemed so antisocial. Abandoning *TLP*'s pursuit of uniform meaning, Wittgenstein 'went native', looking for how people made sense of each other. To that end, he saw some measure of orderliness in how people developed ways of communicating and understanding, ways he described as 'language games'. This concept is central to *PI* and to his later linguistic philosophy. For our purposes, it will help to see communications in the 'game-like' manner he alludes to, seeing it as somewhat of a rule-governed activity with the rules developed and upheld by those 'playing' the game. Do not let the word 'game' throw you; science would offer an example of a language game, in that forms of it have particular definitions, procedures and criteria to what participants hold each other, in how they 'play the game'.

Language games, for Wittgenstein, have their own contextualized 'grammars', above and beyond basic rules. Thus, speaking about how people 'correctly' talk and make sense of each other is something particular to expectations established in their communications over time. While we will later examine 'private' thought and feeling as Wittgenstein saw it, for now it helps to see any understandings and ways of relating them as developed in particular contexts, according to particular language games. Another way of seeing these 'language games' is offered by this quote: 'So we are talking about patterns in the weave of life' (Wittgenstein, 1992: 42).

Perhaps the most important distinction Wittgenstein drew in coming to think in terms of 'language games' relates to the idea that people interact with each other using language. This focus on use departs from the idea that things have their meaning independent of our ways of using or relating to them. But it also directs our attention to the activities involved when people communicate with each other. However, what should we make of this point from Wittgenstein?

27–1 We name things and then we can talk about them: can refer to them in talk. As if what we did next were given with the mere act of naming. As if there were only one thing called 'talking about a thing'. Whereas in fact we do the most various things with our sentences. Think of exclamations alone, with their completely different functions.

27–2 Water!
27–3 Away!
27–4 Ow!
27–5 Help!
27–6 Fine!
27–7 No!
27–8 Are you inclined still to call these words 'names of objects'?
(From Wittgenstein, 1953)

Clearly, Wittgenstein is pointing to how words more than simply represent experience or things. Elsewhere, he wrote 'Words are deeds' (Wittgenstein, 1984: aphorism 546–1). Of course, words alone do nothing, but when put to work in our relationships they help in accomplishing things that could only occur as a result of interactions between people. In the examples above he suggests some ways words get used, and to appreciate his point fully we need to look at what the use of such words accomplishes. This is where Wittgenstein's shift from a world where meaning was 'out there' and correctly nameable, to a relational view of meaning – what some term 'meaning in context' – acquires even greater significance. For Wittgenstein, the object or pictorial view of words, and what they mean, did not work – more happens in the use of words than an exchange of objects or mere information. People communicate with relational purposes in mind. In this regard, how words are used has something to do with those purposes, purposes that take form in the language games that shape their communication. Communicating from within a language game was like making chess moves for Wittgenstein; the rules or grammars of the language games placed constraints on what constitutes a 'legitimate' move. With Wittgenstein's shift to language games came his recognition that the criteria used to judge a word's meaning were contingent on the grammars of the language game 'played'.

The implications of what we do with each other's words relates to what we want our conversations with them to accomplish. But that raises another aspect of words; that their use is accompanied by non-verbal, yet still meaningfully communicative, aspects. People are involved in coordinating a feeling-tinged communicative choreography between them, beyond merely exchanging words. Such choreographies are part of what we have been calling 'language games', and the 'moves' within them are their 'grammars'. 'Mis-steps', so to speak, occur when people break from the established grammars and understandings of language games. Wittgenstein saw the rules or grammars of such language games as fairly negotiable and fairly indeterminate; we would know only when we had violated them by the responses of our (conversational) partners. More on this in a bit …

Wittgenstein's focus on language use as consequential activity defies those who try to objectify and systematize the use of words (or gestures, tones of voice, etc.) beyond the relational circumstances in which they are used. This can set up a tension between those who see merit in classification systems or dictionaries, and those faced with adapting the terms of those systems and dictionaries in actual conversations. By now, however, we hope it is clear that Wittgenstein was not advocating linguistic anarchy in his later career. Instead, what emerges from his exacting thoughts is a more nuanced view of how people communicate and understand, one that factors in differences given the purposes for and contexts in which conversations occur. Our ways of talking and the meanings of our words shift according to these purposes and contexts. But key to Wittgenstein's analyses is the notion that each kind of conversation can develop into recognizable patterned forms of life, holding particular familiar meanings and grammars, the language games to which we become accustomed. Problems, for Wittgenstein, occur when people overlook the requirements of understanding and communicating that particular language games have for us. He was suggesting that people become more linguistically adept at recognizing the language games in which they experienced problems of understanding or relating to others, so they could use language in more precise and rewarding ways together.

For those struggling with what has been said so far, consider a disagreement over how an experience might be named. There clearly is more than an exercise in description going on, for example, when someone tells another that they are deranged. There is an expectation that the description, so characterized, is the way that person should be seen, within a particular language game. What that person does with that description shapes where the conversation will go. If there is agreement, a language game related to the derangement of one of the conversational partners has been given a go-ahead. If there is disagreement, things might escalate as each side turns to other means to go forward (the originator of the deranged comment perhaps citing grounds for his/her use of the word, as in some objective discourse that sanctions the use of such a word). How does the use of such words get adjudicated? For Wittgenstein, it comes down to the grammars and related meanings of different language games, since no language game trumps another. Jean-Francois Lyotard (1988) took up this notion in considering problems as sometimes arising from 'differends' in language games, places where speakers use different language games, with their highly contextualized meanings and grammars. Imagine pro-life and pro-choice speakers talking about abortion and you have a classic example of differends.

Wittgenstein wrote as if the grammars of language games were like banks of rivers channelling communications via certain familiar ways of relating and understanding. The grammars are, in a sense, the 'rules' of language games, and they fascinated Wittgenstein because they seemed to set parameters on what could be discussed, and how. But these are not mental parameters (like John Donne's 'mind forg'd manacles'); they are social and participatory, developed in how we learn to respond to each other 'appropriately'. The grammars of language games are what sustain particular human interactions as unique 'forms of life'. And, like most conventional rules, there is no absolute requirement that these be respected or adhered to in specific ways. People under certain circumstances may need to ignore a red light at a traffic intersection, just as they might not stick by a habit or custom within their ways of relating as a family. But these grammars tend to function like taken-for-granted habits or customs, so when encountering others relating to an experience or issue from different language games, problems of understanding or communicating can arise. Still, people engage in many language games, or patterns of unique communication, within the same relationships, or in other ones. The family language game from doing dinner together can be quite different from the language games around discussing joys and sorrows, though there can be overlaps. In this regard, one issue that 'language games' raises relates to the particular grammars at work in any communicative activity. Learning the grammars required to relate within a military command structure will probably not carry over well into romantic or family life. And so 'language games' can help us to see how certain communication patterns serve certain purposes through particular ways of talking and meaning. These patterns also help to anchor our sense of what is real, as evidenced in this aphorism from *On Certainty* (Wittgenstein, 1969):

> 457. Do I want to say, then, that certainty resides in the nature of the language-game?

What anchors our sense of reality is our ability to interact with it and fellow humans (according to our understanding of it) in unquestioned ways. We want an understanding of experience that both works for us and the others we are to share it with. Language games are the means by which we do this sharing, the means by which we keep things acceptably familiar. But language games also possess grammars that constrain the possibilities for talk to suit certain purposes, despite differences among purposes and languages being ubiquitous. In this regard, it is helpful to see language games as binding us to particular ways of talking and relating to each other; and when those are not serving us, we have other language games we can turn to, to serve our purposes. Harmony, for the Wittgenstein of our initial quote for this section, comes when there is a good alignment between our purposes and the language we use for understanding and acting on them.

What relationship, then, does meaning have to grammar, given that the grammars of our language games are arbitrary and related to the attitudes and purposes we bring to experience (Hacker, 2000; Luntley, 2003)? How could Wittgenstein go so far as to claim that these grammars provide the essences of our meaning? Some, like Schatzki (1996), take up a comparable point that Heidegger raised about routinized social practices being used to 'carve up reality' in the ways we come to know and relate to it. Such social practices, in other words, are how humans meaningfully and familiarly coordinate their interactions around shared experiences. Since grammars can be a very challenging way of connecting meaning to socially coordinated action, then an example might help.

Remember, Wittgenstein saw meaning as related to history and 'the rest of our proceedings'. In this light, then, consider the phenomenon of people being able to anticipate the next words a conversational partner will say. How is this possible? Grammars are somewhat patterned ways of making sense, built up through interaction in particular language games. Thus, over time, conversational partners can come to recognize how each other talks – even to the point of recognizing how and where particular words or actions should fit within familiar patterns of talking. Conversation analysts (see Chapter 13) take this line of thinking to an extreme, speaking of familiar 'slots' into which people know what is appropriate to say or do next. To get even more specific, imagine a conversation between colleagues that occurs every Friday afternoon, just as work is ending for the week. It is a conversation that typically has two outcomes: either going out for a beer together, or not. It is also a conversation that begins with one or the other colleague poking his head in the other's cubicle or office in such a way that the entering colleague comes to be understood as the one who will pop the question. Suppose you are in the hallway at 4:30 p.m. on Friday and you come across this interaction:

> Bert starts to enter Bart's cubicle, only to hear 'sorry' from Bart, then Bert leaves.

Had you not known the history of this patterned encounter, how could you (or Bert for that matter) have made sense of Bart's single word? In the way we have been suggesting, a pattern (or language game grammar) has developed over time between Bert and Bart that makes such a word fit the 'slot' implied by Bert's entry. Had Bart said 'breakfast' or 'telemarketing' the pattern likely would be derailed (much like Harold Garfinkel's breaching experiments – see Chapter 10). A particular range of responses could make sense in such a slot, but any old response will not do. Context is thus cued up over time in temporal and geographical ways that Bert and Bart enact in a familiar Friday afternoon ritual. Things had become so 'grammatically' familiar that neither had to ask the 'do you want to go for beer?' question any more.

Let us now take this notion into a different realm. How do meanings get established between people unfamiliar with each other? Here Wittgenstein suggested that a kind of ostensive pointing and naming occurs in responding to a 'what do you mean by X?' kind of question. A version of this occurred when I (Andy) was in Adelaide for the birth of my first child. I was able to indulge myself, on the way home from the office that I was kindly allowed to use in the University, by stopping at Adelaide Market – one of the great fresh food emporia in the world – to buy the ingredients for dinner. The seafood stall was unbelievable, but I spoke a different sort of English from the proprietor and most customers. Everyone appeared to be on first-name terms, and you appeared to need to be so in order to get good service: my transactions with the proprietor were never routine. It was quite clear to me she was called 'Emma Chissett', but being a pom I was not confident in using people's real names in such situations, and more used to generics, such as 'Luv', or 'Me duck'. I recall commenting on this with my new colleagues at the University one day, and they all fell about. Subsequent to their explanations, I found buying seafood much easier, as I was, through their ostensive definition, able to handle my transactions like a native. 'Emma Chissett' was not her name at all, but the Adelaide way of pronouncing 'How much is it?' after you had pointed to the specimen you were considering buying. Having discovered this, I and the proprietor were able to establish a shared reference point, and I could accordingly take my part in the local language game.

Grammars, in the ways we have been describing, show people using actions and words to procedurally and contextually anchor their meanings as shared. It is in this sense that they develop, and then sustain, 'insider knowledge' between them via their actions and words in context. It is the kind of grammar that enables Bert to poke his head into Bart's cubicle with Bart needing only to say 'sorry' in response. Contrast this with a view that meanings are anchored in words according to their dictionary usage, and that all the things that go with context or specifics in how words are uttered just do not matter.

It is in this sense that practitioners working with clients are often not only presented with meanings that are unfamiliar to them, but with unfamiliar ways of interacting consistent with those meanings as well – the grammars implicit in clients' presentations. Wittgenstein saw such grammars as inseparable from the meanings anchored by them. Seen this way, conversations about problems are 'choreographed' in a performance of words, gestures and other communicative features. Practitioners are therefore faced with a decision as to how to welcome such a choreography – whether they should join clients in their problem language game, or expect clients to join the more familiar, professional language game.

Thought, private language and 'double description'

> The laws of thought are not instrumental for, but constitutive of, thinking and reasoning; as the rules of chess can be said to be constitutive of playing chess.   (Baker and Hacker, 1980a: 317)

It is important to now bring in Wittgenstein's view of where thinking fits in all this. For him, thought is a form of communication bound to the grammars of particular language games. In *PI*, he says in aphorism 330–1: 'Is thinking a kind of speaking? One would like to say it is what distinguishes speech with thought from talking without thinking. And so it seems an accompaniment of speech. A process which may accompany something else, or go on by itself.' Where this ties into language games is in how our thought can be seen as internalized speech in imagined or anticipated discussions with others. In this respect, the grammars of our language games, Wittgenstein would argue, apply. When we think, staying with Wittgenstein, we do so in a form of talk addressed to another person (or persons) and our thoughts can conform to the conventions, or grammar, of the talk we have established with them (for a related take on this, see Billig, 1996). Thinking is another means of sustaining unfinished or anticipated conversations with those persons. From another angle, remember that Wittgenstein felt we reverted to our most primitive language games when we were stuck, such as times when we are emotional. In this respect, the thinking that we do is bound to the grammars of the language games we learned earliest. We bring with us the constraints of those grammars in how we relate to such times, and it can be hard to speak or think beyond those grammars. For Wittgenstein, thinking, like speaking, is not merely a cognitive exercise: we can get as 'wound up' in thinking as we can in talking. What matters are the language games and their grammars, by which we do such thinking and talking. When we say any thought or concept has arisen out of a context we are not far from Wittgenstein's view that such thinking or conceptualizing occurs in the terms and grammars consistent with particular language games – as if any 'private thought' owed its existence to a particular language game.

Thought is often seen as something one does privately, if not idiosyncratically. While the idea that our thinking and talking are linked in some way did not begin with Wittgenstein, the notion that our thoughts are shaped by how we communicate with others showed him breaking rich conceptual ground. The grammars of language games, as we have been discussing, are the familiar means by which people talking and interacting come to share their meanings for experience. But surely our private realm of thought is not bound to the public ways we interact with others? We can entertain thoughts different from those others present to us, and we can consider many ways to understand and act.

Wittgenstein's view was that our thoughts come 'grammatically packaged' in ways derived from our prior interactions with others (and this would extend to our interactions with texts and other media). It is in this regard that our thinking is channelled by prior communicative interactions with others, but it is also limited to the words and symbols we acquired through those interactions. This is a very different view from suggesting that meaning and understanding manifests in us privately and is thus manipulable in ways independent of our experiences and interactions with others. Where Wittgenstein gets particularly challenging is in considering our seemingly sacrosanct 'private' experiences, such as those we associate with our feelings or opinions.

Private language

> An inner experience stands in need of outer criteria.   (Wittgenstein, 1953: aphorism 580)

> The point here is not that our sense-impressions can lie, but that we understand their language. (And this language like any other is founded on convention.) (Wittgenstein, 1953: aphorism 355–1)

The private language argument shows the later Wittgenstein taking on an aspect of philosophizing that has been continuously problematic. From one angle, Wittgenstein's private language argument is an answer to the problem of solipsism, wherein one never escapes tautologies in one's own thinking. People interacting (and this can extend to 'interacting' with others' texts, much like engaging with an author's meaning) can add to or change their understandings and intentions. From another angle, he throws into doubt that which we have come to see as subjectivity, or our private 'inner experience': our thoughts and feelings. The private language argument has kept philosophers arguing since it was introduced, and no review of Wittgenstein's thought would be complete without it. Let us start from these somewhat cryptic aphorisms from *PI*:

> I can know what someone else is thinking, not what I am thinking. It is correct to say 'I know what you are thinking', and wrong to say 'I know what I am thinking.' (A whole cloud of philosophy condensed into a drop of grammar.) (Wittgenstein, 1953: aphorisms xi-276–8)

It is important to see Wittgenstein's private language argument as built on how people acquire and use language in ways appropriate to their relationships – their language games. A naïve view of subjectivity suggests – much in the way Wittgenstein viewed language in *TLP* – that experience names itself, our job being to accurately hear 'its' call. In the case of thoughts, feelings or other versions of subjectivity, then, the truth of our subjective experience can be made personally evident to us. But here Wittgenstein remains empirical, asking how the correctness of any subjective experience could be established other than through social agreement, or via the grammars of particular language games. If our experiences are so knowably private, then what enables us to share them with others in ways they can also understand? Wittgenstein suggests we cannot be solipsistic and that we acquire our means for 'self-intelligibility' through social experience. The means by which we learn to name, judge and share our 'inner' experiences are, for Wittgenstein, all shaped by the social interactions through which we come to understand and communicate them.

The crux of Wittgenstein's argument rests with how we come to be able to recognize and report on our 'private' experience. Could a mythical, parentless and solitary Robinson Crusoe, for example, develop words or some other means to name and verify an internal experience, and then be able to reliably and correctly identify that experience in subsequent private experiences? Where would such an ability to identify and verify private experience come from (are we born with an innate and personal language, that becomes immanent in us, for describing our experience)? How is it that we collectively know what the experience of grief is, if not for having a shared language and means for verifying grief's presence? Using these kinds of questions Wittgenstein opposes the idea that somehow we have subjectively unique ways of understanding or making sense of our experiences. Instead, he proposes that by the same means that we recognize others as 'having' inner experiences we recognize them in ourselves. Try this aphorism from *PI*:

> 'You learned the concept "pain" when you learned language.'   (Wittgenstein, 1953: aphorism 384–1)

For most people this line of thought is deeply disturbing. Pain, like anger, is about as real (the phenomenologists would call this 'pre-predicative') an experience as anyone can point to; surely such experiences speak directly to us, unmediated by any prior or present social experiences. Here Wittgenstein suggests that the grammars of our language games structure what we come to understand, and speak of, as our 'private experience'. It is important not to see this merely in terms of words, however; infants get their initial 'grammars' through close-up interactions with parents. These are interactions where children learn to infer the subjectivities of their caregivers from the gestures and vocal tones shown them. In turn, they use these external cues as internal referents – that is what Wittgenstein meant above when he spoke of 'A whole cloud of philosophy condensed into a drop of grammar.' Said differently, correctly recognizing and understanding the truth of our private experience is something that begins externally, and relies on externally derived criteria for its later recognition and 'true' sharing.

This flies in the face of centuries of understanding. In the romantic tradition, feelings and thoughts were our most private and purest (i.e., untainted) aspects of experience that we could keep to ourselves. Suggesting that we learn how to make sense of pain or feelings defies conventional logic, especially when we extend this to how we communicate. For Wittgenstein, the issue lies in the language games in which we make our experiences shareable. If there is no shared basis for recognizing and articulating experience, how can we know if we are having a particular private experience, like a feeling, value or other subjective experience? The grammars of our language games provide ways to make our subjective experiences intelligible and communicable while furnishing the vocabularies to do so. Here is Wittgenstein's (1980a: 87) final comment, in *Culture and Value*, on what we have been saying: 'You cannot assess yourself properly if you are not well versed in the categories.' Wittgenstein's categories – recognizable, repeatable and communicable words, gestures and other features of communication – articulate an experience in social and personal ways. They do a reciprocal kind of double duty: those categories used for making personal sense of experience are the same as those used for communicating that sense to others in familiar ways. But, as in Vygotsky's view (1978; the 'intramental' starting 'intermentally' – see Chapter 6), we first learn our ways of making sense through social interactions.

Harré and Tissaw (2005) emphasized a related point of Wittgenstein, about how any new conceptual distinction required a lot of prior social or cultural 'stage-setting'. New meaning, to be understood by others, needs to fit as an extension of a shared context. Talking about the internet to pre-telephone or pre-computer era people would be unintelligible for them. Yet, when *Time* magazine featured a cover story on the frontiers of cyberspace and the internet in 1994, most people were ready for such new additions to their vocabularies and thinking. Grammars similarly provide a context in which new conceptual distinctions can make sense, offering already established ways for such new developments to be discussed. The same goes for people making sense of their 'private' experiences. By the time such experiences can be identified, there are already established ways to talk about them, with shareable vocabularies for their articulation.

The notion that we have inner processes that typically and unproblematically contribute to objective private experience, as much of psychology purports, was problematic for Wittgenstein. Naming those processes and their contents is more than a private exercise: the grammars in which we learned to name and share them are those we use to make sense of them. Of course, there are places where we can choose not to reveal our hurts or other feelings, but how we recognize them, and could make them shareable, clearly indicates that 'private' is the wrong term to use in a blanket fashion. Wittgenstein is, throughout his private language argument, also challenging Cartesian notions of mind–body dualism. For him, our faces and bodies said as much about our internal experiences as the words our minds purportedly gave us, and we attend to them as part of how we verify others' 'subjective' experiences. For babies, who do not possess language, gestures and tones of voice provide the 'categories' of our most primitive language games – those we sometimes default to when language does not serve us well. Wittgenstein frequently wrote of the face as being one of our most important means of communicating our 'private' experience, much like when Seal (2007) recently sang: 'If it's in my mind, it's on my face.' Thus, from early experience onwards, people use each other's facial and associated non-verbal gestures to make sense of each other, and how they are being received: that is, in direct inter-action, I do not just see you, I also see your reaction to me; and I do not just 'see' it, either, but flow with it.

Such attending to the nuances of body language and vocal performance is important to human relations. As Wittgenstein said in *PI*, 'our attitude to what is alive and to what is dead, is not the same. All our reactions are different' (aphorism 284). By extension, we also seldom simply report on our experience to each other; we communicate in ways particular to those we are responsive to in our language games. This shaping of our talk – for each other – is part of what we turn to in shaping our understanding of experience. For example, learning a particular way of relating (and relating to) grief can furnish us with a sense of what grief is, how grief affects us, what it means to experience and share it appropriately, and so on. Harré (1986a; see also Chapter 15) has gone so far as to suggest that our social and cultural interactions around emotions recognizably take shape in 'emotionologies' similar to what we have been describing as grammars. This is why people of different cultures, or even different families, for example, display grief in recognizably different ways.

If you see much of psychology being taken to task here, then you are correct: that was part of Wittgenstein's attempt to restore clarity to the language we use. For him, these purportedly internal and private experiences made no sense, and so he empirically tackled this romanticizing and psychologizing of 'subjectivity'. The argument is profound and suggests a very different basis for understanding what feelings, opinions, values and thinking is about. For most of psychology these are attributes or properties of people. For Wittgenstein, these are ways of recognizing and sharing experience, bound to the grammars of particular language games in which they find their sense and articulation. Psychology, as a discipline, is stuck having to infer 'subjectivity' in the same manner the rest of us are, from externally reportable or observable details, as Wittgenstein wrote in *PI*:

> Seeing, hearing, thinking, feeling, willing, are not the subject of psychology in the same sense as that in which the movements of bodies, the phenomena of electricity etc., are the subject of physics. You can see this from the fact that the physicist sees, hears, thinks about, and informs us of these phenomena,

and the psychologist observes the external reactions (the behaviour) of the
subject.   (1953: aphorism 571–2)

It is important to see, in the private language argument, the notion that what
passes for our 'feelings and other subjective states' owes much to the grammars
of language games we learned and share with others. It is through them that we
articulate and verify our subjectivity, which seldom occurs in social isolation.
Psychology, including the folk variety that has persisted for centuries, largely saw
subjective experience as something apart from social experience that could be
studied for 'inner' properties, as a physicist might. Cartesian views of selfhood
added to this; our minds could master (i.e., know, then control) the rest of our
experience. Subjectivity, and all its articulations, is hard to see in the same way
after encountering the private language argument.

Related to Wittgenstein's assault on mainstream psychological thinking are his
writings on what could be called 'double description'. Particularly since the time
of Kant, many point to a two-phase, logical process whereby people test their
theories of (or language for) experience with how things really are or develop.
This is the idea that we must go through an internal cognitive testing process to
check correspondences between words and experiences, or a 'two component
theory of knowledge' (Williams, 1999). But Wittgenstein consistently makes
the point that we undoubtedly participate in language games. A language game
offers more than a conceptual and processual stand-in for our engagements with
reality: for Wittgenstein it is the immediate reality in which we are engaged.
This is possibly why the notion of simply reframing an experience, giving it a
purported new meaning (i.e., without embedding it in the grammars of a new
language game), falls short for many people. But Wittgenstein was (long before
the first PC or Mac) persistently countering the view that our descriptions and
ways of engaging with reality are best explained by an information-processing
or computer metaphor.

Psychology has put a lot of stock into this metaphor of descriptions (or constructs) and the processes by which they are manipulated into outcomes, typically focusing on the purported perceptual or reasoning abilities of individuals.
For Wittgenstein, this would fail to account for the immediacies of our experience and for how they are grammatically packaged in socially shared ways,
not by individual cognitions and cognitive processes (remember, Wittgenstein
saw these as occult). A number of scholars (e.g., Baker and Hacker, 1980a;
Schatzki, 1996) support Wittgenstein in regarding these grammars as lived
social practices that animate a social conception of meaning and action – even
a social conception of mind (Williams, 1999). Luntley (2003: 67) puts the point
thus:

> Meaning is something that we do and something that resides in our actions.
> Ourselves and our actions are the loci of interest, not language as such. The
> patterns of correct use of language are such only because they are strings of
> actions of agents with a capacity for judgement. It is not the pattern that
> matters, it is what it is a pattern of.

Wittgenstein's philosophies and what they offer to relational practice

> The existence of the experimental method makes us think we have the means of solving the problems which trouble us; though problem and method pass one another by.   (Wittgenstein, 1953: aphorism xiv–2)

In some ways, Wittgenstein's career spanned an all-out attempt to forward empirical science and philosophy (in *TLP*) and a later, staggeringly complex, effort to give meaning and communication an entirely different basis from that of his original starting place. The link between these two radically different phases of his career as a philosopher lies in his view of language. To the Wittgenstein of *TLP* we owe credit for trying to link problems in logic with inadequacies in language. That he would shut out much of human experience (values, spirituality, feelings) as the stuff of which we could not factually speak, and should therefore be silent (as his last aphorism in *TLP* suggests), was clearly problematic. And so, not surprisingly, Wittgenstein grew dissatisfied with holding his philosophizing to the grammars of the scientific language game, as his quote above suggests. All along, however, Wittgenstein's view was that unreflectively using language was the bane of our existence: it impedes our abilities to go forward.

In some respects, the later Wittgenstein was quite psychological, favouring a more behavioural view of psychology for what its empiricism could tell us about humans in interaction. His views of meaning and 'private language', however, were a radical departure from conventional views of meaning and communication as universally systematizable and knowable. Indeed, in such efforts, Wittgenstein saw further linguistic traps. For our purposes, Wittgenstein, for his views on language games and their grammars, helps us nuance what is meant by understanding meanings and communications in context. Typically, 'context' is a word that seldom shows the activities of human actors as central; yet, with language games, we find a view of meaning and word use anchored in particular patterns of human conversation, patterns that go beyond a geographical and historical sense of how 'context' is usually understood. Meaning, in other words, gains its sense by how it is performed in patterned interactions. To see clients using terms in ways we sense are unfamiliar is commonplace in therapy. To see them as bound to relational conventions (the grammars of language games) is quite a different matter. In this respect, meanings develop their 'common sense' within particular language games, and there is no 'meta-language game' that can better judge that common sense. Wittgenstein felt that being able to recognize meanings and communications as particular to language games offered a way for us to alter our language games so as to find 'perspicuous' meanings, meanings and ways of talking that would better serve us.

In a striking reversal, it came to concern Wittgenstein that all human problems must be submitted to empirical or logical analysis (as in *PI*, aphorism 133–4): 'There is not a philosophical method, though there are indeed methods, like different therapies.' This line of thought has significant implications for different approaches to relational practice. To what extent are practitioners bound to particular language games, their particular ways of listening and intervening that restrict their abilities to understand clients, and helpfully move forward with them? Indeed, most approaches to helping are just that, approaches, or what we have been calling particular language games. Consistent with our analyses of the later Wittgenstein, one's use of words as a professional helper is consequential for how things develop with the people one helps. Do we bind them to our words and face the problem of incommensurable language games, or what many term 'resistance'? Or, do we see our use of language as an effort to coordinate a language game with clients, an effort which requires hearing and reconciling the contextual and 'grammar'-bound meanings clients bring to therapy with the particularities of our own? These are very complex questions, and not surprisingly many long for one, correct, language view (where the meaning of language was correctly represented in the words).

Many, after reading the later Wittgenstein, are never able to look at meaning and communication in the same way again. And, that was his point. He felt that his later writing was to establish 'roadposts' to help us recognize where we bump up against the limits of our understanding, so that we could make alternative choices in how we used language to give us such understandings. This equates to a cosmological shift: from humans living in a received world they could correctly interpret, to humans living in a world they understand through how they interpret and engage with it, and with each other. Efforts to incorporate Wittgenstein's views into therapies and pedagogies have taken off in this past decade, especially by communications theorists such as John Shotter (see bibliography, and Chapter 16) or therapists such as Lois Shawver (2001). It is not surprising that, as people catch up with Wittgenstein's later views (understandable to very few during his life and the first decades thereafter), they see in them implications clearly consistent with later social constructionism, post-structuralism and post-modernism. The projects of ethnomethodologists (e.g. Harold Garfinkel), conversation analysts (e.g. Harvey Sacks), postmodern theorists (e.g. J.-F. Lyotard) and discourse analysts (e.g. Jonathan Potter) all owe some debt to Wittgenstein's philosophizing. In fact, the 'discursive turn' is a commonly used phrase referring to the cosmological shift we partly credit Wittgenstein with originating.

It is difficult to separate Wittgenstein, the man, from his considerable contributions to philosophy, in particular linguistic philosophy. A brooding isolate, Wittgenstein spent much of his life labouring under grandiose and perfectionistic expectations for himself. In releasing *TLP*, he felt he had spoken the last word on what could be said about the truth of human experience – his final aphorism ('Whereof one cannot speak, thereof one must be silent') says as much. But for Wittgenstein, his intellectual honesty could not stop there, as he wrote in the notes that later became *Zettel* (1967: aphorism 687): 'Contradiction is to be regarded, not as a catastrophe, but as a wall indicating that we can't go on here.' In this regard, here is where man and method come together, where Wittgenstein invited us to think beyond some tautologies in how we regard language, and what it does and represents. Leaving analytical and empirical philosophy as the sole means for verifying understanding and scientifically building on it meant depicting that approach as *an approach*, as a language game among others. These other language games serve different purposes, and do not answer back to the analytical and empirical language game: they have their own rules and criteria for the understandings and actions taken within them. By the time Wittgenstein died, he had left behind lectures and notes that he may (had he lived on) have forbidden others to have published. We are fortunate that this was not the case, and that a considerable job in seeing these notes edited, translated and published was undertaken by his students.

What Wittgenstein has left behind is a very different way of linking language and reality. While earlier efforts, including his own in *TLP*, focused on getting nature right, in correct language, a requirement for an empirical view of life, Wittgenstein later saw this as a 'wall', like that described above. From there, he strained conventional thinking to a place where few could understand him, and where others are only now beginning to understand him. Seeing language as a relational accomplishment, as 'forms of life', or 'patterns in the weave of life', put him at odds with the modern project of describing experience in universals. Instead, he proposed understandings, and ways of articulating experience, that can now be seen as contextualized in people's ways of talking.

9 Gregory Bateson

A Cybernetic View of Communication and Human Interaction

> Rigor alone is paralytic death, but imagination alone is insanity.
> (Bateson, as cited in Keeney, 1983: 94)

How is it that people interacting over time come to create understandings and actions so familiar to them that they seem 'patterned'? To what extent can people be seen as apart from, or as a part of, patterns they share with others? Where might a patterned view of interaction fit with problems and solutions in therapy, the ecological movement and elsewhere? These kinds of questions fit our consideration of Gregory Bateson.

Gregory Bateson, resident sage at California's Esalen Institute in the 1970s, had a huge influence on family therapists and environmentalists. For Stephen Toulmin (1982), Bateson was that classic frontier figure: the scout. His research and writing spanned more than five decades, encompassing everything from anthropological treatises, genetic research, philosophy, psychology, linguistics, biology, psychiatry, ecology and family therapy. His studies of human communications and relationships will be our primary focus here; otherwise, he could seem an odd addition to a book on social constructionism. He approached communication in both macro and micro ways, bringing together his anthropologist's background to inform rigorous studies of micro-interactions in family therapy. Bateson's chief contribution was to relate *patterns* to human problems and practices associated with human change, importing biological systems and cybernetic views of relationship. One of his chief concerns was our 'epistemologizing', how we 'punctuate' reality with limited views of causal relationships. Bateson skewers simple stimulus–response behavioural accounts of interpersonal behaviour: 'Let's not pretend that mental phenomena can be mapped on to the characteristics of billiard balls' (Bateson and Bateson, 1988: 99). But in adapting his communications thinking and research to problems of 'psychopathology' and psychotherapy, family therapists found a generative source of clinical insights. His was a process view of life and relating, seeing connections between life-forms where scientific minds had been atomizing our ways of recognizing and studying them.

Gregory Bateson, son of the famous British geneticist William Bateson, was born in 1904 into the upper crust of Britain's academic intelligentsia (think names like Huxley and Darwin at the dinner table). After secondary school, he attended Cambridge University, initially specializing in Natural History but later turning to complete a Masters degree in Anthropology. In 1930 he headed off to New Guinea beginning studies of the Iatmul people, and meeting his future wife, Margaret Mead, while developing his initial process-oriented views on human relationships. This early phase of his career was capped in 1936 by the publication of *Naven*, a far-reaching book that looked, anthropologically, at patterns of interaction between cultures. Thinking in terms of patterns of relationships was to remain with Bateson throughout his career.

Bateson's second career phase involved a move from his former 'macro' analyses of human interaction, to a 'micro' focus on communications in psychiatry (see his 1951 *Communication: The Social Matrix of Psychiatry* – with Jeurgen Reusch). Moving in this direction, in part, came as he applied his anthropological thinking to the behavioural stimulus–response thinking gaining momentum in psychology. But Bateson was also an early participant in the cybernetic movement (more on this later), especially following the initial Macy Foundation conference in 1942 where his anthropological ideas were welcomed. It was Bateson's ideas in *Naven* that helped him receive his first psychiatric research grant (to examine paradoxes of abstraction in communication). This grant enabled him to bring some of family therapy's most famous names (Don Jackson, Jay Haley, John Weakland – and, later, Virginia Satir, Paul Watzlawick, among others) together under what later became known as the Mental Research Institute in Palo Alto, California. The creative talents of these researchers resulted in their developing a radically different view of psychiatric concerns (especially schizophrenia), based on pathologies of communication.

Never one to root himself in any particular research endeavour, Bateson in the 1960s moved on to study dolphins, and their patterns of interaction. There he looked at questions relating to the transformations different interactions contributed to the evolutionary developments in mammals. By the late 1960s, he began to bring these different phases of his research and writing together to consider their implications for problems of epistemology (how we know what we know) and ecology. In 1972, he published selected papers from his varied career in *Steps to an Ecology of Mind*, an enormously influential book for family therapists and ecological thinkers. It was also this book that put Bateson at the centre of the human potential movement of the early 1970s.

Recognizing in the late 1970s that he was dying from cancer, Bateson began writing his final full book, *Mind and Nature: A Necessary Unity*. This book offered an overview of his thinking: patterns in relationship, pathogenic communication, epistemologies, evolution and biology, and his concerns regarding our global ecology. In 1983, one of his students, family therapist Bradford Keeney, wrote a very accessible integration of Bateson's ideas as they relate to the practice of therapy: *Aesthetics of Change*. And, a few years later, Bateson's daughter, Mary Catherine Bateson, posthumously published some of her father's essays, including her own commentaries (in the metalogue style Bateson made famous in *Steps*) in *Angels Fear*.

Patterns and processes of relationship

> We are very impatient, you see, of the idea that there are patterns, that the patterns have rigidities and rigors which have to be respected. The nature of pattern is not something you can fool around with.   (Gregory Bateson, 1982: 353 – at a conference honouring his contributions shortly before his death)

Throughout his life Gregory Bateson insisted we break with the modern scientific view that the living world could be seen on the same terms as the inanimate world. Sentient beings do not move about like billiard balls. To relate to others, and the world at large, requires making sense of these circumstances, as we act within (and often transform) them somehow. But this sense-making, for Bateson, occurs at different levels of abstraction – the data of our immediate experience, and how we classify or string versions of it together. He goes one step further with this, however. Where the human knower is typically seen apart from the known, Bateson sees what most consider 'mind' as actualized in interaction. An example he often used was that of a person chopping a tree: as blows are made with the axe, the tree changes, necessitating chopping in different ways, and so on. Similarly, he asks of the blind man: where, when he is using a cane to make his way about, does the man end and the environment begin? It concerned Bateson that behavioural psychologists would break such patterns into discrete stimulus–response chunks (e.g., the blind man tapping the cane, without seeing it as one part within an assemblage of actions) without seeing those chunks in larger perspective. Central to Bateson's views were notions of how patterns were discerned and how they facilitated or impeded relationships.

It helps to go back to Bateson's *Naven* (1936) to understand his on-going fascination with pattern and meaning. For him, it was clear that the Iatmul people he studied used different categories of meaning from those of social scientists trying to explain the Iatmul's understanding of each other. The meanings they attributed to their interactions were used to discern relational patterns based on similarities or differences. Bateson was fascinated by the relational patterns that he felt led to 'schismogenesis': escalating symmetrical or complementary actions between groups that led to a breakdown of relations. Such symmetrical (like-for-like) group interaction over the cold war's 'arms race' almost brought 'mutually assured destruction'. Complementary interactions leading to schismogenesis might occur if one person talked increasingly loudly while another responded increasingly softly. It is the escalation of these ways of relating (more bombs, more/less volume in speaking) that can lead to relationship breakdown. Bateson saw these as pathologies of communication, or relating, which could be remedied by a more abstract level of understanding than that used by participants in the immediacies of their escalating interactions. Seeing patterns where, for example, more bombs on one side prompts the other to stock more bombs, can help one or both parties to exit from the pathological pattern.

Bateson's concern was with the *level* at which one sees patterns, such as with distinctions he made between *proto-learning* and *deutero-learning*. Where proto-learning might refer to developing a particular skill or understanding, deutero-learning referred to a more abstract level of learning: learning to learn. In *Mind and Nature* (Bateson, 1980) he described some observations regarding the ways that dolphins learned, noting that, over time, they developed performance skills in a discrete and sequential fashion. But, after a certain period, they suddenly developed and performed many untaught skills; a development Bateson felt exemplified the dolphins' abilities to learn how to learn. This notion of 'higher-level' meaning, meaningful abstractions we use to see patterns in relationships, is based on Bertrand Russell's 'theory of logical types', a classification system wherein one class of phenomena (for example blood vessels, skin, hair) might serve as a subset to another class (bodies), that in turn might be subsumable by another class (societies or cultures). For our purposes, it can help to think how some phenomena could be seen as part of a class of higher-order phenomena. This practice of connecting phenomena in such classes or orders, however, is a linguistic accomplishment, one that depends on human descriptions that satisfactorily account for the phenomena, or class (or order) of phenomena, described. As is sometimes said in qualitative research, data don't speak for or organize themselves, but researchers who identify, then translate, data distinctions into patterns and corresponding narratives most certainly do.

Patterns and process were a lifelong concern for Bateson. He was especially concerned in his final years that failing to see the processes and patterned connectedness of the life-world (he used Jung's word for this: 'creatura', with 'pleroma' referring to the non-living world) created an illusion that humans could take instrumental short-cuts that would, in fact, lead to ecological catastrophes. Seeing patterns, describing them, and intervening from understandings about them served as foundational thoughts to Bateson and bring us to another phase and essential piece of his research and writing: cybernetics. His focus on patterned reality is where he might get too non-constructionist for some readers.

Cybernetic epistemologies

> What circumstances determine that a given scientist will punctuate the stream of events so as to conclude that all is predetermined, while another will see the stream of events as so regular to be susceptible of control? ... What circumstances promote the specific habitual phrasing of the universe which we call 'free will' and those others which we call 'responsibility', 'constructiveness', 'energy', 'passivity', 'dominance', and the rest? For all these abstract qualities...can be seen as various habits of punctuating the stream of experience so that it takes on one or another sense of coherence and sense.   (Bateson, 1972: 163)

Seeing life in patterned processes, in cycles, raises questions like those Bateson raised above. Humans don't just describe the world they live in; they intervene in that world based on the understanding their descriptions provide. If we see nature as merely there for our use, and not something we live in patterned relationships with, we can irreparably alter those relationships. Drawing from Bateson, family therapist Bradford Keeney (1983) wrote that we use our language to 'carve up reality', to punctuate it in ways particular to our purposes. 'Punctuating reality' partly gets at what Bateson meant by 'epistemology'. But, as another family therapist, Paul Dell (1985), pointed out, Bateson used the term 'epistemology' in several ways: (i) epistemology as a theory of knowledge, (ii) paradigmatic epistemology, (iii) epistemology as biological cosmology, (iv) epistemology as science, and (v) epistemology as 'character structure'. Here we shall examine his views on epistemology, particularly as they relate to 'knowing' and the cybernetic systems view that played a role in inspiring family therapy.

Typically, 'epistemology' refers to theories of knowledge, how people purport to know anything. Bateson saw it as attempts to specify 'how particular organisms or aggregates of organisms *know*, *think* and *decide*' (Keeney, 1983: 13). A related concept, 'ontology', refers to 'how reality is'. For Bateson, these were inseparable concepts: *how* we know and *what* we know go hand in hand. We suggest you look upon the words epistemology and ontology as having multiple meanings or senses, and also consider different versions of *what* people know resulting from the *how*s of their different approaches to knowing. In this sense, it puts us back in the familiar hermeneutic territory Heidegger pointed to in *Being and Time*. We should not be surprised to see, from an anthropologist, this notion of plural realities, tied to cultural differences in how people make sense of their experience of reality. Back to Dell's observations of Bateson's use of the term 'epistemology', we can now further consider this relationship of knowing to known. To what extent can we consider each person as having a personal epistemology? To what extent can epistemology be seen culturally or paradigmatically (as in the differences between behavioural and analytic psychology at the time Bateson was writing on these topics)? Is there a correct epistemology, as Bateson often implied, to be equated with a biological systems view? Are science and epistemology synonymous? These kinds of questions can help us move forward. Here is Bateson, on what we have been considering:

> In the natural living history of the living human being, ontology and epistemology cannot be separated. *His* (commonly unconscious) beliefs about what sort of world it is will determine how *he* sees it and acts within it, and *his* ways of perceiving and acting will determine his beliefs about its nature. The living *man* is thus bound within a net of epistemological and ontological premises which – regardless of ultimate truth or falsity – become partially self-validating for *him*.   (Bateson, 1972: 34 – emphasis added to highlight the gender-blindness common to the era in which Bateson was writing)

Epistemology is sometimes equated with science, for being the human endeavour most devoted to knowing. The scientific method, with its logical-deductive procedures, has therefore been seen as primary when judging not only efforts at knowing, but also what is known. The many other forms of knowing found in human life are often seen as quaint, for lacking the rigour and critical scrutiny expected of scientists. By cultural default, therefore, the scientific method has served as our primary epistemology, especially for its purported ability to deliver objective truths, even certainties. In responding to religious forms of knowing – given some of the corrupt religious practices of pre-Enlightenment Europe – placing the methods of knowing back in the community and tied to peer-review processes was, for many, a step forward. But, culturally and anthropologically, there have always been diverse ways of knowing (the *hows*) and of *what* is known – we would not use the scientific method to choose our spouses, for example. We will not get into questions of which epistemology is superior, though it is probably safe to say that each form of epistemology fits the values, traditions and purposes of the people who practise it. Keeping in mind this diversity, epistemology can refer to the differing ways people make sense of their experience, personally and socially.

At this point, we need to return to the punctuating activities of epistemologizing, the ways we carve up reality with our descriptions and classifications. For Bateson, what mattered was that we consider the order or level of abstraction we use to describe any activity, because if we missed a pattern-/process-level description we may be acting inappropriately for our context. Here is a clinical example

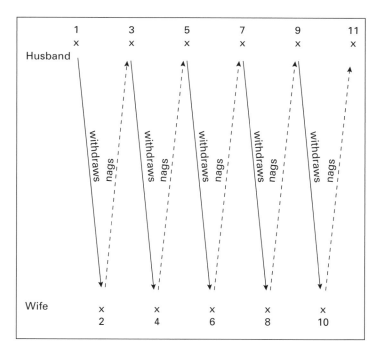

Figure 9.1 *Sample pattern/process description of husband and wife interaction. Redrawn from* Pragmatics of Human Communication: A Study of Interactional Patterns, Pathologies, and Paradoxes *by Paul Watzlawick, Janet Beavin Bavelas, and Don D. Jackson. Copyright © 1967 by W. W. Norton & Company, Inc. Used by permission of W. W. Norton & Company, Inc.*

of what we are referring to, taken from the *Pragmatics of Human Communication* by the research team that carried on Bateson's work, after he left the Mental Research Institute.

Consider yourself a spouse in the interactions depicted above. Clinically, a husband in this situation would describe his wife as nagging, necessitating his 'withdrawing' from the nagging. His wife, as you can see, would have a complementary (remember our discussion of schismogenesis earlier) description of her husband's behaviour, a description that would necessitate, in her view, a need to get beyond her husband's withdrawing behaviour. Taking a position that one or the other is correct in their views or behaviour would miss the obvious (to us) pattern as shown in the diagram above. The pattern makes evident the recursiveness, or cyclically repetitive nature, of these interactions. When the husband withdraws, the wife acts to try to alter this by commenting; when the wife comments, the husband withdraws. But, at the level (or order of interaction) each is describing, their individual perspective and corresponding behaviour make perfect sense. What is needed is a description that can abstractly capture the complementary nature of this interaction, as it plays out in its predictability.

Cybernetics fits into this way of considering patterned interaction, as Bateson saw things. Cybernetics, as a word, comes from the ancient Greek concept of 'self-steering' oarsmen, who kept their boats 'on course'. Central to the cybernetic view is the notion of feedback, or in Bateson's commonly used phrase: 'news of a difference'. But, such news does not simply announce its presence – an interpretive effort is required, one to be considered in terms of levels of description. This informationally based, interpretive dimension to Bateson's understanding stands apart from much of the physics-derived approach prominent during his time:

> All metaphors derived from a physical world of impacts, forces, energy, etc., are unacceptable in explanations of events and processes in the biological world of information, purpose, context, organization and meaning.   (Bateson, as cited in Keeney, 1983: 62)

One of his favourite analogies for what we are talking about was the thermostat. Thermostats are 'self-corrective', set to recognize a range of hot and cold temperatures, that, when exceeded, trigger the thermostat to go on (if too cold) or off (if too hot). In other words, information that indicates news of a difference (i.e., above or below the set temperature) activates the 'corrective' mechanisms required to maintain the desired temperature. Returning to our withdrawing and nagging couple, their 'corrective' behaviours are activated when one sees 'too much' nagging or withdrawing behaviour from the other; and de-activated when s/he has the response sought from his/her partner. This matches the diagram's points of oscillation, where the depicted behaviour undergoes reversals and moves in the opposite direction. These oscillations are what we earlier referred to as *recursiveness*, the recognizable repetition of parts (or all) of a pattern. And, it is through these oscillations that the stability of the relationship is maintained, through activities required to stabilize it as is.

Cybernetics mattered to the World War II allies because self-steering mechanisms were helpful in developing technologies such as the automatic pilots of aircraft or rockets. For Bateson, cybernetics epistemologically offered a patterned and process-oriented way to regard human relations. The oscillations, or stability-producing behaviours we earlier considered, offer a way for us to reconsider Bateson's conclusions about 'schismogenesis'. Remember, he was concerned about patterns that led to relational breakdown, ones that occurred in complementary (as in our nag/withdraw couple) or symmetrical (as in the nuclear arms race) fashion. Just as our couple 'knew' or 'calibrated' when to reverse their behaviours so that relational breakdown did not occur, so we find thermostats calibrating when to activate or de-activate. The knowing here is epistemological in the sense that descriptions, or information, that guide the behaviours in either example govern the range and nature of response. The husband senses when to stop withdrawing; the thermostat goes on when the room temperature is too cold. Complementary or symmetrical escalations (of withdrawing/nagging, or temperatures too hot/cold) leading to breakdown are thus prevented by *calibrating* the feedback and responding in ways consistent with what that calibration has come to mean to the interactants. But all this is based on particular information, ways of calibrating that information as corrective feedback, accompanied by patterned responses to such feedback.

Linking epistemology and cybernetics this way enables us to consider how people, individually and collectively, use particular forms of information as feedback to guide how they coordinate their behaviours so as to avoid schismogenetic kinds of breakdowns. Cybernetics offers a mechanical way to consider how patterns play out, of course, but much human behaviour can become patterned and almost predictable in the ways we associate with machines. The significance of this way of thinking comes in when we consider what passes for the 'self-regulating', or 'corrective' feedback – and what it is that can, metaphorically, reset the thermostat. Consider this diagram from Keeney (1983: 41).

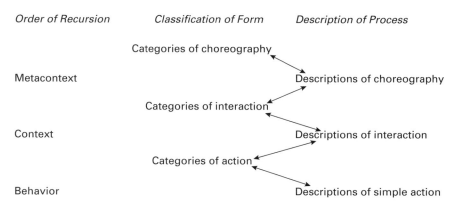

Figure 9.2 *Orders of epistemological analysis. Redrawn from* Aesthetics of Change *by Bradford P. Keeney. Copyright © 1983 by Guilford Press. Used by permission of Guilford Press.*

Bateson felt that interaction could be classified or described in terms of levels of abstraction, like those above; operating from a description that insufficiently reflected the patterned nature of certain forms of interaction led to pathologies of interaction. Most relevant to this way of conceptualizing human interaction are the descriptions that provide the 'feedback' people use in responding to each other. At the level of behaviour, as indicated above, we can enact a particular action in response to particular information or feedback, but if this information fails to address the situation for which the feedback was relevant one can find oneself in a situation of the 'same damn thing over and over again' (Watzlawick, Weakland and Fisch, 1974). At such a time, it can be helpful to look for patterns, and for a way of alternatively describing the circumstance in more contextual and less behavioural terms. In short, different kinds of feedback are required, *as is* a different kind of behaviour, behaviour that fits the contextual level of description or feedback, thus affording a more complete understanding for action.

Comparing human interactions to machine-like sequences can fall short for many. A cybernetic epistemology offers a way of considering alternative and more comprehensive forms of feedback to influence how levels of interaction persist or could be altered. It is a way of seeing the role that our descriptions, and calibrations derived from them (e.g., 'he really means business so I better stop'), play in perpetuating the often-patterned behaviour of human co-existence. Most systems are conservative in nature, drawing on the same information and patterned behaviour in their stabilizing (self-corrective) interactions. What is needed, when these conserving interactions are heading for a survival-threatening 'ecological cul de sac', is news of a difference, of interactions – be they through dialogue or some other form of interaction – that are read and responded to differently from prior feedback and corrective behaviours. This leads some to consider 'resetting the thermostat' as involving diagnostic thinking and tinkering associated with systems engineers (but humans aren't 'trivial machines' as cybernetician Heinz von Foerster used to say). This is a dissatisfaction some critics have had of the cybernetically based approaches to therapy and other forms of social change. But it can be helpful to think how our descriptions influence our behaviour in patterned relations where we are dissatisfied. What are such ways of knowing and acting helping to conserve? What information or feedback do we turn to, to justify our own behaviour in those patterns? How might alternative contextual descriptions or feedback justify new behaviours that could disrupt the recursiveness that may have developed? By what means do people keep even bad relationships from becoming schismogenetic? These kinds of questions point to where language fits into the 'feedback loops' that perpetuate unpreferred patterns of relating. Cybernetics was a way Bateson brought together the patterned ways of life he saw in creatura into ways that pointed to bigger-picture possibilities for intervention. It afforded a way of considering the patterned behaviour and feedback actively used to produce orders of stability and change. For human relations, as we will now examine more closely, this was a fruitful metaphor for research and intervention.

Pathologies of communication

> … the mental characteristics of the system are immanent, not in some part, but in the system as a whole.   (Bateson, 1972: 316)

By the late 1940s Gregory Bateson was enticed into psychiatric research. For someone used to seeing social reality in patterns, it made little sense for him to punctuate psychiatry's concerns as it had been traditionally – by focusing on individuals. So began the studies and writing that made him central to the development of a systemic view of human problems and solutions – bringing with him notions of pattern, epistemology and cybernetics. After writing theoretically about the fit of communications with psychiatry (with Jeurgen Reusch, 1951), Bateson received a sizeable research grant enabling him to bring together the creative team of researchers and mental health practitioners who later formed the nucleus of the Mental Research Institute in Palo Alto. And with the arrival of Don Jackson, a psychiatrist trained by the relationally focused analyst Harry Stack Sullivan, Bateson's studies of pathological communication gathered full momentum.

The Bateson team worked together from 1953 to 1962, and applied his hierarchical notions of description to studying the communicative interactions among family members, and between therapists and clients. Among the classic papers that came from the team during this time were 'Toward a theory of schizophrenia' (Bateson et al.: 1956 – reprinted in *Steps to an Ecology of Mind*), and Jackson's (1957) 'The question of family homeostasis'. The book best summarizing the research of this period was *Pragmatics of Human Communication* (Watzlawick et al., 1967), and therapeutic applications derived from this research can be found in two central books: Virigina Satir's (1964) *Conjoint Family Therapy* and *Change* (Watzlawick et al., 1974). Jay Haley, a key figure in this research, later developed the strategic model of family therapy (especially as described in *Problem-solving Therapy*). This was a very creative group who many consider essential to the development of family therapy as it is practised today. Team member John Weakland, at a conference shortly before Bateson's death, alluded to the groundbreaking research they were about to undertake:

> Normality was an implicit ideal in the minds of psychiatrists and psychologists. Nobody paid enough attention to what people actually *do* to create what might be normal in the sense of everyday behavior. Normality was an ideal of relational speech. If you tape anybody's speech, it doesn't come out anything like that ideal of normal rationality, even if they've never been in a hospital or fallen into the clutches of a therapist.   (1982: 46; emphasis in original)

Studying actual conversations, and relating them to the kinds of psychopathology endemic to the professional mindset of the times, made for challenging research and ideas. 'Toward a theory of schizophrenia' developed out of painstaking observations of, and intense discussions about, the micro-dynamics and content of conversations in therapeutic settings. Keeping in mind Bateson's notions of levels of communication, and schismogenesis, these researchers were particularly interested in communications that led to breakdowns. They also focused on, and contrasted the effects of, messages at a content or immediate behavioural level (what they later called digital language) with those that spoke to the relational or contextual level (how the message should be understood with respect to the relationship in which it is shared – later referred to as analogic language). In Weakland's words: 'communication is not just a process of conveying information, but also of influencing others' behaviour' (1982: 52). Foundational to the view of pathological communications they formulated (i.e., as they associated it with schizophrenia) was their conclusion that patients were people having to respond to incongruent messages – between the content and relational meanings of messages. This is what they termed the 'double bind', which theoretically required the following:

1. Two or more persons in communicative interaction.
2. Repeated experiences together (what we have been describing as recursiveness).
3. A primary negative injunction of two possible forms – a) 'Do not do X, or I will punish you' or b) 'If you don't do X, I will punish you.'
4. A secondary injunction conflicting with the first at a more abstract level, and like the first enforced by punishments or signals which threaten 'survival.'
5. A tertiary negative injunction prohibiting the victim from escaping the field (namely the relationship).
6. The victim has learned to perceive his universe in double bind patterns ... The pattern of conflicting injunctions may even be taken over by hallucinatory voices.   (From Watzlawick, 1963)

A classic situation of this kind involves a son or daughter who, in response to a parent, feels encouraged to grow up, but simultaneously needs to remain dependent on the parent. The message 'grow up' is qualified by a message (usually non-verbal) of greater relational significance: 'But I need you to need me as you have.' The 'damned if you do, damned if you don't' qualities of the double-bind experience are now the stuff of cultural cliché. It is important to see the recursiveness of such interactions as playing a role in shaping the normality of such ways of relating. And it is very important to see the feedback attended to by the parties involved in such a bind (for all the parties involved, it would be extremely rare for the double bind to be seen as the sole accomplishment of one figure in a relationship) required for the continuation of the pathological communications. In short, the meaning of the interaction has developed for the parties involved such that they are stuck in a pattern, a pattern that involves apparently conflicting (usually unconscious) messages.

Jackson's (1957) paper on 'homeostasis' extends the line of thought encountered in our cybernetic consideration of thermostats. In both cases, what provides homeostasis – or stability – is a lot of activity: furnaces clicking on and off, or family members engaged in specific feedback loops of interaction that keep things stable. By the mid-1950s pockets of family-oriented practitioners had noticed such things as mental patients having their symptomatology stabilize in hospital, only to become symptomatic again on returning to the patterns of interaction endemic to their family system. Jackson's paper examined scenarios where relationships developed interactive patterns that supported symptomatic concerns in one person in ways that stabilized the relationship. The successful treatment of a 'frigid' wife, for example, might lead to the subsequent development of impotence in the husband. For Jackson, family communications in such situations were analogous to closed cybernetic systems that relied on consistent feedback loops for their perpetuation.

It is important to consider carefully the distinction the Bateson team was making between the digital (behavioural level) and analogic meanings of messages. In another classic paper ('A theory of play and fantasy' – in *Steps to an Ecology of Mind*), Bateson asked, for example, how dogs distinguish play-fighting from serious fighting with each other. In human relations, how do we know when people are serious and when they aren't? Here we are talking about the analogic, or relationship, level of communications. I can say 'I'm happy' at the content level, but if I say it with a discouraged sounding voice, a frown, and a posture of defeat, I am clearly communicating something else. It is in interactions, such as between the dogs mentioned above, that analogic messages *frame* the relational significance of any digital communication (e.g., 'are we fighting or not?'). Bateson equated this with an algebraic equation where the content message could be bracketed and then altered qualitatively, as in the difference between 6+7 and 3(6+7) – the 3 here serving an analogic function to the 6+7 content. Back in human relationships, Watzlawick et al., (1967) wrote of analogic communications as 'invocations of relationship'. Staying with these authors, here is their observation that points toward some therapeutic implications we will explore later:

> What we can observe in virtually all these cases of pathological communication is that they are vicious circles that cannot be broken unless and until communication itself becomes the subject about which they are able to metacommunicate. But, to do this they have to step outside the circle.   (Watzlawick et al., 1967: 95–6)

Another Bateson team member, Jay Haley (1976), regarded crazy-making situations as those where we cannot comment on the nature and interactions of our relationships.

Pathologies of communication, the focus of the Bateson team's research, brought them to paradoxes – developments that occur when one tries to resolve problems with an inappropriate level of description. In the language of Watzlawick et al., paradoxes are a 'contradiction that follows correct deduction from consistent premises' (1967: 188). For example, a common paradox might go like this:

> Everything you read on this page is a lie.

People attempting to interpret a message like this at one level of communication (or with 'consistent premises') can become confused. Consistent with the double-bind research the Bateson team found paradoxical communication contributing to the dilemmas of pathological communication. Yet it would be wrong to assume that paradoxes always have negative effects. Family therapist Carl Whittaker told a story of a police officer who attempted to stop a suicidal man from jumping from a tall building. What brought the jumper down was the officer's exasperated demand: 'If you don't come down from there I'll have to shoot you!' In some respects, paradox resembles the problems Zen practitioners see as 'koans', problems of limited thinking that, when broken through (and not always logically), enable a new, deeper understanding to emerge. Of particular fascination to the Bateson team in this regard was the hypnotherapist Milton Erickson (see Haley, 1973), for the way he used therapeutic paradox and double binds in the famous hypnotherapeutic and other unusual therapeutic interventions he was famous for. Communications between Erickson and Bateson, and between Erickson and team members Jay Haley and John Weakland, played a significant role not only in formulating the double-bind theory of schizophrenia, but in developing the therapeutic implications of this interactional, communications-focused view.

The notion that patterns of communication can bog down in problematic understandings and interactions should now seem a familiar theme to readers. Bateson and his colleagues took this to a microscopic extreme, focusing on the recursive and repetitive nature of communications. For a while there was immense excitement within systemic approaches to therapy and change. The cybernetic metaphor offered practitioners a diagnostic way of conceptualizing limiting or conflictual interactions. Therapy and other forms of social practice offer contexts where presumably one could step outside vicious circles of relating, to recognize what may be crazy-making or limiting to those inside them. This implied that parties could set aside their participation in these vicious circles and open themselves to a more encompassing frame for explicating what could otherwise seem very personal and hurtful experience and understanding inside the vicious circle. But practitioners, in effect, become part of the relationship that Watzlawick and his colleagues suggested they step beyond. It was this insight that spawned a phase in family therapy known as 'second-order cybernetics' (e.g., Hoffman, 1985), where the emphasis shifted away from the presumed objectivity of the therapist in discerning patterns, and toward a more collaborative and focused co-constructing of such patterns together with clients.

Is it still useful for practitioners to consider problems of patterning in the way Bateson suggested? In answering this question, it can be helpful to return to the Greek oarsmen steering by feedback. Specifically, if one sees feedback as being in the eyes of the beholder, participants in problematic communication patterns can be tracking particular kinds of feedback that sustain them, but problematically – as in the nag/withdraw example earlier. Bateson was of the view that such problems could be pointed out logically to people, enabling them to correct themselves because the relationally more encompassing therapeutic frame proffered would make sense. Commentators using this logic on the cold war fared about as well as therapists offering therapeutic frames to counter the illogic (seen cybernetically) of couples arguing. Pointing out such paradoxes or pathologies of communication and prescribing alternatives did not necessarily translate to social change. Arguably, it can be useful to note patterns in word-use and how speakers respond to each other, their conversational 'dance' analogically. But introducing new conversational 'dances' involves more than receiving pointers on how each party steps on the toes of their partner, and what they can do differently.

Bateson's focus on pathological communication – as it related to psychiatric concerns – was a logical extension of his views about pattern and process, and about the utility of a cybernetic metaphor in understanding the recursiveness of human interaction. The Mental Research Institute remains a Mecca for family therapists all over the world, and continues to extend ideas developed during the Bateson research team's era. In the postmodern age many have taken exception to the mechanistic way this team and subsequent generations of practitioners adapted the cybernetic model to understanding clients' concerns and addressing them. However, MRI (particularly Paul Watzlawick, 1978) has been central to developing a constructivist approach to therapeutic communication. If the meanings that serve as 'feedback' for clients stuck in vicious circles were developed in particular communicative contexts, why not in others? By studying pathological patterns and processes of communication, the Bateson team furthered consideration of what might stand as therapeutic communication.

An ecological/interactional view of mind

> If you ask me concerning a particular cell what its function is, you've asked a question like what is the function of the second letter of every word in the English language.   (Warren McCulloch, as cited in Keeney, 1983: 114)

The tendency for psychology to locate intelligence in the mind was an example of faulty 'punctuating' for Bateson. This was a human equivalent of putting the earth at the centre of the cosmos and claiming that the rest of the universe related to it. Seeing life in patterns, it made no sense to Bateson to absent ourselves conceptually from them, as if our observations and actions within them were not influences on how they developed. In the later phases of his career, he grew fond of the term co-evolution (indeed, Stewart Brand developed a journal focused on ecological issues entitled the *Co-evolution Quarterly*, using this term). Systemic practitioners of therapy who felt they could discern cybernetic patterns and intervene in a detached way increasingly concerned Bateson. Relatedly, he saw profound difficulties with the concept that humans could use their perceived power to control their patterned circumstances:

> It was not so much 'power' that corrupts as the myth of 'power'... 'power', like 'energy', 'tension' and the rest of the quasi-physical metaphors are to be distrusted and, among them, 'power' is one of the most dangerous. He who covets a mythical abstraction must always be insatiable.   (Bateson, 1980: 248)

This position puts Bateson clearly at odds with the many postmodern critics (Foucault, for example) who see relationships in terms of dominance and of who holds power over others. For Bateson, the pursuit of power threatens the ecology of patterned relationships, in ways that can lead to schismogenesis. The instrumental nature of many humans, coupled with a view that they could somehow be apart from the contexts in which they participate was, in his view, an 'epistemological blunder'. Whether or not humans try to control their human or other contexts, for him this produced costly errors resulting from a misguided commitment to contextually insensitive expedience. Here he is getting at the same thing another way: 'People speak of the power of "mind over matter", but surely this relationship between "mind and matter" can obtain only if either mind has material characteristics or matter is endowed with mental characteristics such as "obedience"' (Bateson and Bateson, 1988: 51).

The atomized and predominantly material view of world phenomena, so dominant in social scientific conceptions of agents with 'free will', was at the heart of Bateson's concern. He wrote of a tendency by scientists to ascribe 'dormitive principles', his tongue-in-cheek term for the causal properties they gave to atomized entities, to different phenomena. This phrase arose from a description Bateson took from reading Molière, where, when a student being examined was asked by an examining committee as to why dogs should go to sleep after ingesting opium, he triumphantly responded that opium had 'dormitive principles'. Present efforts to locate genes, or any causal factor (social or otherwise), isolated from the patterns of interaction such phenomena might have with others, remains commonplace. This is another application of those quasi-physical metaphors Bateson saw as problematic. For him, creatura, the life-world, proceeds on the basis of the information derived from interaction with other sentient life forms; and for changes to occur,

> [t]o produce news of difference, i.e., information, there must be two entities (real or imagined) such that the difference between them can be immanent between them in their mutual relationship; and the whole affair must be such that news of their difference can be represented as a difference inside some information-processing entity, such as a brain.   (1980: 76)

Extending this to interacting with an inanimate world, Mary Catherine Bateson (his daughter with Margaret Mead), sharing her father's view that mind needed to be seen as relational activity, wrote, 'The rock sculpts the sculptor, as much as the sculptor sculpts the rock' (cited in Keeney, 1983: 91). We are beings contributing and responding to developments in our relational and other environments, and so we constantly adjust our reactions to what takes place before us. Having to respond to developments in our life contexts that we have contributed to – whether about diminishing forests, or an argument where we think the other 'just doesn't get it' – reminds us of our connections to the world we experience and act in. Failing to recognize this results in an epistemological error humans are capable of overcoming by bearing in mind the level of abstract description they bring to recognize patterns of which they are a part.

Bateson says all this another way in *Mind and Nature: A Necessary Unity* (note the subtitle):

> Even if we think of some larger circuit systems extending beyond the limits of the skin and call these systems mind, including within the mind, the man, the ax, the tree that he is felling, and the cut in the side of the tree; even if all this can be seen as a single system of circuits … there is no tree, no mind, no ax in the mind. All these 'objects' are only represented in the larger mind in the form of images and news of themselves. We may say that they propose themselves or propose their own characteristics.   (1980: 210)

Bateson and relational practice

> Psychologists commonly speak of the abstractions of relationship ('dependency', 'hostility', 'love', etc.) as real things which are to be described or 'expressed' by messages. This is epistemology backwards: in truth, the messages constitute the relationship, and words like 'dependency' are verbally coded descriptions of patterns immanent in the combination of exchanged messages.   (Bateson, 1972: 275)

> It is in dealing with the universe, message plus environment, that the evolution of verbal language has made the greatest strides.   (ibid.: 423)

As a person devoted to seeing patterns, as well as interactions and meanings that sustain them, Bateson brought a profoundly different view to the understandings and practices of practitioners concerned with human change. He contributed directly to one of the most important innovations in psychotherapy in the twentieth century: a systemic approach to practice that continues to serve as the primary foundation for family therapy. His concern with meaning and patterned behaviour was derived from studies that spanned several scientific disciplines. By the time he became a mainstay at Esalen in the 1970s he deservedly had come to be seen as a sage, a raconteur of endlessly fascinating stories devoted to his ecological (i.e., interactive) view of life.

The Bateson research team of the 1950s morphed into the Mental Research Institute, home to some of family therapy's most important pioneers. Central to their approach to practice was the cybernetic view, a way of seeing human interaction as recursively organized into patterns that relied on particular feedback and behaviours for their maintenance. Families (it was these who were primarily seen) were often ensnared in limiting communication patterns – double binds or paradoxes of communication – that kept them in feedback loops that conserved their understandings and interactions in limiting or injurious ways. This research also led to developing the practice of 'reframing'. The premises people in relationship use to determine 'correct' responses to the feedback can be seen as tied to a particular *frame* of reference. Such frames serve as interpretive lenses through which meanings for actions are understood. A weird example arose in a conflictual relationship between siblings. One sibling had cursed the other for having been given what was a wonderful gift. This gesture was oddly seen by the gift-receiving sibling as his brother's way of continuing an argumentative sibling rivalry. Bateson was concerned about the tautological nature of such framings; they are self- and other-fulfilling prophecies that furnish a modus operandi for how people interact with each other. Reframing requires a 'double description', one which offers a new framing of the pattern, in ways that fit the 'facts' of the situation (for family members) at least as well as the prior framing, offering new premises for their ways of relating. It would be pointless to think of reframing outside of the relational contexts in which it is attempted. But many important changes occur for people as the meaning – the premises according to which they have primarily acted towards each other in a circumstance – shifts, whether that is because these premises have grown to feel pointless or because a more fitting understanding for what had been bothering them has come about. Seeing a higher-order connection in (or framing of) patterned interaction can be therapeutic in and of itself.

Cybernetics, for our purposes, is evident discursively as much as the behaviours which sustain patterns. What we have been discussing as feedback, calibrations, frames or orders of description are all accomplishments in socially constructed meaning. Bateson reminds us that meanings can occur at, at least, two levels: the informational and the relational. People tend to forget the latter. Stephen Toulmin (1982), in reviewing *Mind and Nature*, felt that Bateson not only did much to help people think systemically, but he was also a 'prophet of postmodern science', one who articulately countered the ahistorical and disconnected view of humans to their circumstances that was the legacy of Descartes. Bateson asked us to think about how we co-evolve with those with whom we interact, and this extends to therapists and the parts they play in developing meanings and actions with clients. Patterns influence them and us at many levels, and to act otherwise is to commit, for Bateson, an 'epistemological blunder'.

10 Sociologies – Micro and Macro
Garfinkel, Goffman and Giddens

Sociology is a natural discipline for us to pass through in considering the many important contributions to contemporary social constructionism that took form there. If you accept that sociality is our primary reality in being human, then accounting for social life is critical to knowing who we are and why we think and act the ways we do. The diversity of social life points out how differently we can be human, even within our own lives for differences expected in how we are to think and act in different social arenas. Do these various social contexts determine what we think and do? No, but it is hard to suggest that they (or, rather, the people in them) do not influence our thoughts and actions. While we will deal with constructionist conceptions of the self in greater detail elsewhere, here we will consider some conceptions of social life where social and individual life are reconciled, without making either recede into the background.

Sociology has been home to a macro/micro debate that continues to cleave constructionists into distinctive camps, particularly when it comes to practice. At the heart of this debate are conceptions of people shaping or being shaped by their social surroundings or their embeddedness in others' lives. The debate itself reflects the binary thinking over whether humans shape or are shaped by their social circumstances. Sartre, for example, once wrote 'Hell is other people' while members of the labour movement speak of 'solidarity forever'. But when we turn to a term like 'social constructionism' a conjoining of individual and social life can seem implied, and questions like the following can become central:

> To what extent can people shape their own destinies given the immediate and broader social relationships in which such destiny-shaping usually occurs? Where do social influences end and individual capacities to transcend them begin?
> Can we even talk about individuality, given our interdependence with others?

For readers of a psychological bent the individual can too often seem to disappear, or become subordinated, in sociological theories of cognition, action and transformation. Treating people as if their membership in groups fully decided their personal experience, judgement, and so on, is associated with this line of thought. Add to this the notion that what enables people to succeed socially and individually is competence in using social constructions (e.g., language and norms of interpersonal behaviour), then distinctions between the social and the individual seem to blur somewhat. Competent individuals do not act irrespective of these social features of life. But they aren't at the mercy of them either – as sociological studies of deviance, social transformation, and the aleatory nature of individual life trajectories clearly point out.

We will examine three important sociologists whose ideas are consonant with many aspects of contemporary social constructionism. None would be comfortable with the label 'postmodern' and each brought a micro perspective to account for social life. It is in this sense that each of our thinkers offers interesting ways of considering how social and individual life cannot be uncoupled, in how they account for social actions and understandings shaping individual life – and vice versa. We begin with the audacious thinker Harold Garfinkel, who railed against the common sociological notion that individuals amounted only to cultural dopes. His is a sophisticated account of how individuals, through coming to share 'ethnomethods', shape and are shaped by their social interactions. From there we turn to Erving Goffman, who presented a dramaturgical view of humans interacting resourcefully using the social frames and conventions accessible to them. Finally, we turn to Anthony Giddens, who has tried to keep grand theorizing in sociology alive by incorporating insights from many thinkers, including Garfinkel and Wittgenstein. Our hope is that in reading this chapter you are left with a greater and more nuanced appreciation for the 'social' in social constructionism.

Harold Garfinkel and Ethnomethodology

How do you account for the apparent orderliness of human conduct? By extension, how does this orderliness help us understand and communicate? Two widely divergent and influential responses to such questions can be traced back to Harvard's sociology department in the mid-twentieth century. The dominant view at the time was that of Talcott Parsons, chair of this department. His structural approach exemplified the big-scale theorizing of its day: the world and our social interactions within it could be correctly understood, much like the laws of physics. For Parsons, the mechanisms that structure social life are largely given, implicit in how we reproduce culture through *its* values and ways of interacting. Garfinkel felt such a view made us out to be 'cultural dopes'.

Looking back, Parsons 'big-picture' theorizing was consistent with the social sciences of his day. Psychology, anthropology, economics and political science – emulating the natural sciences – sought foundational knowledge akin to that which the natural sciences provided for engineering and medicine. For Parsons, human beings were 'rule (norm) followers' of varying *accuracy*. Parsons' theory stretched a 'received world' (i.e., experience as given and immutable) view about as far as it could go. People's understandings and social interactions were in tune with an objectively knowable real world unless distorted and driven by human foibles. This social world caused them to perceive, act and communicate in the ways they do. With Parsons as his Ph.D. supervisor, Garfinkel put his supervisor's views to empirical test, from near opposite assumptions.

For Garfinkel, variations on social order and intelligibility are human accomplishments observable as *works in progress*. Ethnomethodology, the research programme Garfinkel primarily launched, asks: *What unique understandings and social practices do people require to participate competently in different social orders?* Garfinkel chose audacious research topics: delineating social rituals of degradation, identifying the personal and social requirements in managing a change in sexual status (i.e., after surgery and hormonal treatment), understanding why bad clinical records were good for the institutions requiring them, and understanding how clients made sense of meaningless counselling advice. Such research dramatically highlighted how social understandings and orders were situated accomplishments in which the people's activities and understandings were *context shaped and context renewing*. In other words, the social contexts we inhabit are our constructions as much as they shape who we become.

Garfinkel the iconoclast

Harold Garfinkel (born 1917) is Professor Emeritus at the University of California (Los Angeles). Still publishing in 2002 (*Ethnomethodology's Program*, with Anne Rawls), his breakthrough came in 1967 with the publication of his classic book: *Studies in Ethnomethodology*. But we need to go back to 1946 to see the questions and concerns that still preoccupy him. Unlike Parsons, he was committed to empirical answers and wary of his mentor's 'premature theorizing', particularly given how those theories seemingly 'legislated' what should be found. To Parsons' credit, Garfinkel persisted and successfully defended his dissertation – a series of empirical studies that effectively disproved most of Parsons' theory – under his supervision. Garfinkel can be seen as re-inserting humans back into the creation of *their* orderliness, partly via Alfred Schutz's view of the phenomenology of intersubjective experience. In so doing, he repositioned humans as competent beings relating resourcefully to each other, and as anything but the cultural dopes of Parsons' view.

To read Garfinkel's *Studies in Ethnomethodology* (1967), in the context of its times, is to see a creative mind bent on subverting a view of humans (as cultural dopes) that remains fairly entrenched right up to the present. To conventional thinkers of his day his research-derived conclusions seemed almost dangerous: multiple realities, humans shaping the contexts of their lives, indigenous understandings logical to those holding them, and a view of meaning based on behaviour and use – not on pre-established and objectively knowable certainties. For our purposes, it will help to examine Garfinkel's contributions in different areas, on the road to pulling them together into his strikingly original attitude towards human interaction. We will begin by exploring his (and some of his fellow ethnomethodologists') enduring commitment to empirical study, and some of his more striking conclusions. From there we will examine some core concepts behind his method: indexicality of meaning and action, reflexivity and documentary methods. Morality in human interaction takes on a very different connotation in Garfinkel's view, as we shall see. Finally, we will consider ethnomethodology as a kind of meta-theory of human understanding and interaction and relate it to relational practice.

Garfinkel's radical empiricism

> The term 'ethnomethdology' thus refers to the study of a particular subject matter: the body of common-sense knowledge and the range of procedures and considerations by means of which the ordinary members of society make sense of, find their way about in, act on circumstances in which they find themselves.   (Heritage, 1984: 4)

Most people look upon social order as a given. Garfinkel approached social orders curious about how people accomplished and sustained them. Such orders for social theorists were explainable in terms of processes and thinking beyond the influence of those living in such orders. Parsons (1949), for example, saw social order as socialized *inside* the people, who then enacted such orders in particular processes and ways of thinking. This is like saying society determines our thoughts and actions; we merely do 'its' bidding; or, in Heritage's (1984) phrase, society functions – 'as if behind our backs'. A variation on this theme featured in Adam Smith's 'invisible hand' guiding the economy. The running theme through such accounts was that social order came before people's interactions or individuality, and that forces beyond their perception or influence made them think and do what they did in ways that sustained social order. Garfinkel had little time for such unempirical explanations of social interaction and social influence.

Garfinkel's ethnomethodology (literally, the study of cultural methods) saw social activity as the means by which people understood and coordinated their interactions with each other – the researcher's job was to make evident these coordinated interactions. His microanalyses showed people as competent in understanding and influencing each other, via *their* methods of interaction. To ethnomethodologists it is important to see social orders as humanly sustained contexts that support understandings and actions particular to those contexts. Thus, they aim to reveal an 'insider's' logic and competence for the contextually different ways humans work out coexistence. What, for example, is unique to how halfway-house residents (i.e., for prisoners making the transition to everyday life) and staff relate? What particular understandings and actions are required to uphold any social order people have developed together? Answers to such questions are empirical in that the ethnomethodology (EM) researcher needs to show *how* social group members sustain their insiders' logic within these orders – through their communicative interactions. These are the 'ethno' methods they use with each other.

Before proceeding much further, an important distinction is necessary, one that inverts normal psychological thinking. In EM, the focus is on actions or practice, for it is these that ground our understandings and interpretations, not the other way round as commonly portrayed in cognitive psychology. It takes others' repeated-until-anticipatable acknowledgements in shared social practices (Schatzki, 2002) to sustain familiar understandings with others. What gives any social reality its mundane familiarity is that we and others practise it in ways that, once reliably established, we can afford to let slip under our conscious radar. What is novel requires our attention differently from what is familiar. EM's attention to the mundane, the stuff people take for granted as they interact, is focal (Pollner, 1987). The flipside (not holding to these reliably used and expected social practices) threatens the social realities we uphold in mundane ways.

Garfinkel explored such questions about social reality in reverse, by examining what happened when people's mundane social practices were 'breached'. For example, he instructed student confederates to respond to people's everyday greetings with answers like 'What do you mean?' By breaching the orderliness of such greeting–response sequences he could then show how people attempted to re-establish their normal sense of social order in such sequences. Studying violations of social orderliness provided Garfinkel with a means to understand social orders in terms of the human practices used to sustain them, including how people held each other to such orderliness.

Garfinkel is particularly interested in how people sustain social orderliness through interactions they come to share as familiar and anticipatable. One could see EM as being concerned with how individuals interact (their 'ethnomethods') so as to keep things socially acceptable and familiar to each other.

Garfinkel's focus was on these ways of keeping things socially familiar and acceptable, to acquire a member's taken-for-granted sense of what that entailed. The required methods would be largely context-shaped (replicating acceptable familiarities for those involved) and context-renewing (ways of holding each other to what they deem sufficiently acceptable and familiar). EM, in other words, is a research method that tries to identify how this context-shaping and context-renewing is upheld and worked out between members of different social orders.

In a classic study of astronomers, Garfinkel and his colleagues (Garfinkel, Lynch and Livingston, 1981) examined the particular methods and ways of talking they used to 'discover' a new pulsar, observing how they used language and other conceptual resources, observational techniques and the conventions of astronomy to make this 'discovery'. Without these already worked out methods and resources, how could such a 'discovery', intelligible and defensible to others, be made? Important to EM's radical empiricism is how meanings and forms of relatedness are developed and sustained in practices particular to people in context. Relational practitioners, we contend, greatly benefit from adopting EM's radical empiricism, becoming attuned to how thoughts and actions are sustained in mundane social practices and their accompanying understandings. In a sense, this can heuristically guide practitioners to observe and listen for how clients, and those sharing their social realities, methodically sustain those realities, the problem realities included. In the language of EM, what is needed is that practitioners acquire and use familiar methods to pass as a member of the social order they are trying to understand.

Indexicality

> The appropriate image of a common understanding is ... an operation rather than a common intersection of overlapping sets.   (Garfinkel, 1967: 30)

Indexicality holds that the meaning of any utterance or action is bound to the social interactions and context in which it is used. Most pay lip service to this notion, while proceeding from an opposite assumption: our world is objectively evident in a shareable language all can master. To EM researchers, the orderliness of our social reality through our talking may be illusory; when we converse we use words we *index to* particular social interactions we may yet not share with others. For example, a Native American woman repeatedly told police in her village that her cousin and uncle 'bothered' her. When someone finally asked her what she meant by her use of this word, she described being regularly sexually abused. To those who see such an example as a misuse of the English language, an important point is missed.

Indexicality can be related to Bakhtin's (1984) notion of 'heteroglossia' (see Chapter 5), as meanings developed and in ways particular to time, place and difference between the people involved. Hence a word like 'suffering' can mean different things to people using them in medical, spiritual or S&M sexual contexts (contexts here being likened to language games). For Wittgenstein (1953), our words and actions usually bear sufficient 'family resemblances' to serve us when trying to understand and influence others – they *seem* the same. However, this can lull us into a problematic complacency should we equate our meanings with those used by others, as in the 'bothered' example. It is important for Garfinkel not to see this as a problem a perfect language could overcome. Instead, the imprecision and ambiguity of indexical meaning enables people to work out what they mean as they use utterances and actions. Much of this work is, in EM terms, 'glossed', because people typically believe they have resolved what their indexed meanings are with each other: a certain glance can come to mean something shared to a couple, or a jargon term can develop familiarity for members of a particular social context. These are ways in which people can eventually take for granted ('gloss') the experiences they have indexed together in the course of their interaction. They use and respond to what becomes meaningful to them in reliably familiar ways; thus, Garfinkel's reference to these understandings as 'operations' in the earlier quote. To an 'outsider' these glossed meanings, and the social interactions supporting them, can hardly be considered shared.

There is another sense to indexicality that conversation analysis (or CA, a branch of EM research) points to: meanings contingent on developments within a sequence of talk. Thus far we have been describing indexicality in primarily geographical and historical terms, as if the meanings of an utterance were indexable to particular social contexts. But there is another way of seeing indexicality. Witness this Tom and Andy exchange:

TOM: Andy you seem angry.
ANDY: I'm not really. (in a calm tone)
TOM: But Andy, that isn't how you are coming across.
ANDY: I'm not.
TOM: Oh come off it, Andy, you're really pissed at me.
ANDY: I'm NOT!!!
TOM: See, I told you, you were angry.

This little exchange highlights a performative dimension of language, where the meaning of what transpires is literally 'worked up' in the course of the talk. Such meanings cannot be determined by one speaker, but are *accomplished* in how speakers show each other that they make sense of each other in conversation's back and forth. Again, it is important to look beyond the words and tones of voice, to how interactions become interpreted in ways that can ground (or index) meanings for the people involved.

Important to our consideration of indexicality is the inherently flimsy portrayal of everyday understanding that is revealed by Garfinkel and EM research. That people socially accomplish what they do, from this perspective, relates to how they are able to *use* actions and utterances in recognizable and anticipatable ways. Elsewhere, Wittgenstein (1974) referred to such recognizable and anticipatable social interactions as 'grammars'. Making things recognizable through language is a social accomplishment and not something reflective of speakers' correct use of language so as to optimally align experience and words. Most importantly, Garfinkel insists that any effort to use language to get to bedrock, universal meaning, or 'brute facts' is impossible. At best we get indexical descriptions to describe other indexical descriptions of experience. Surely, the world's many languages highlight this, but turning further to variations of meaning within the English language we get in serious trouble when we consider our words and our experience as one and the same. As mentioned earlier, love on the tennis court can index at least two meanings: try confusing them.

Indexicality can be juxtaposed with a view of meaning that, in EM terms, must be seen as idealized. That speakers could use words or make gestures that could be gauged for their accuracy was a bleak and bureaucratic view where the meaning of experience must be seen as separate from the people having such experiences. By implication, such an idealization suggests a world where knowing can take place correctly, where there are knowers and less-knowing others requiring their correction, and where a one-size-fits-all language can represent all variations of human experience irrespective of context. Modern Euro-American culture is steeped in such an idealization. Garfinkel and EM take a radically different stance: indexicality implies that our efforts to understand are meaningfully tied to words and actions socially developed in times and places that at best resemble each other. That we coordinate our social ways of being together through words and gestures developed in different contexts can show how illusory meaning can be. But this shows another dimension critical to Garfinkel's view: we 'work up' our understandings and actions – and then sustain them – through *how* we interact. An important extension of this work-up now faces us as we turn to reflexivity as another important EM construct.

EM can at times seem counter-intuitive so an illustration might help. Imagine five people speaking different languages and having very different customs being shipwrecked for an extended time on a desert island. They would immediately face a challenge of how to be understood and communicate, for no person could legitimately claim their language or customs must supersede others on the island. To coexist successfully they would need to 'work up' ways of communicating and being understood that worked for them, then use those ways of communicating and understanding repeatedly. Over time, these 'worked-up' ways of communicating and understanding would require less and less effort provided that their social use evolved into unquestioned effectiveness. Problems in understanding and communicating occur when new understandings are called for, or when there is a breakdown of some kind in assumed ways of understanding or communicating. The actual ways of communicating and understanding are quite arbitrary; what matters is how they serve the people making use of them. To continue with our desert island dwellers: let's say they come to agree on, and then repeatedly use with each other, the utterance 'freg' to denote food. After a while it is no longer necessary to recall that 'freg' was worked up and agreed to; as an utterance it comes to 'stand in' for food in ways that require no further thought or explanation. Understanding is, in this manner, socially 'worked up' in expected and eventually taken-for-granted ways of communicating. The meanings for phenomena, like 'freg', rely on social agreement and repeated use; but otherwise, such selections or articulations are quite arbitrary. This should not be surprising given the many languages used to socially (and successfully) articulate similar phenomena in the world.

A common perception of humans is that they are mere rule-followers and this extends to their use of language. Such perceptions can seem to imbue language with rules of its own, when, from an EM sense, such rules are 'worked up' then upheld in people's interactions with each other. The important, yet subtle, EM distinction here rests with where the force of such rules resides – in the people who expect them to be obeyed and who react, often strongly to each other, when a rule (i.e., 'their' rule) is not obeyed. Such rules gain their 'force' in how people hold each other accountable to them. As this relates to indexicality, specific expected utterances are worked up, then thereafter used expectantly, to index an experience as socially shared, as in 'freg'. The rule for using 'freg' belongs to those who index this term as meaningful to them; they hold each other to using it as the agreed-upon way of mutually referring to food.

The practical implications of indexicality suggest that we see language use and social behaviour as having meanings (often implicit) particular to people's interactions in social contexts. Thus, trying to understand clients' meanings and actions according to the practitioner's understandings can leave client and practitioner in parallel and unshared universes of meaning. Client–professional interactions exemplify a context in which new meanings and norms of social conduct are 'worked up' (i.e., through the course of their turns in talking) into a specific, shared social reality. At a minimum, indexicality asks practitioners to be mindful of important differences in meaning attributable to words and actions – theirs included.

Reflexivity

Reflexivity implies that we do more than merely receive experience via our sense organs; we participate in its creation. If this notion seems challenging, then ponder how we might have come to think otherwise. Our scientific traditions idealized this separation of ourselves from our experience as 'objectivity'. The scientific quest for objectivity has permeated western thinking to the point where, in Hilary Putnam's (1981) characterization, we purportedly relate to our experience as if from a 'brain-in-a-vat'. This sort of Cartesian detachment, and the objective or pristine qualities of experience it purportedly should yield, fits well with a 'received world' view where the presumption is that we need to learn to explain and fit into the world as it is. But this didn't wash for Garfinkel, who saw people constituting their experience through how they share it. Reflexivity refers to how people co-construct their realities through their interactions.

It helps to bear in mind that EM sees what we are discussing as follows: people's interactions (and the meanings derived from those interactions) are context-shaped and context-renewing. Instead of people passively receiving their experience, Garfinkel saw them as active in 'its' constitution, even if that meant renewing understandings through interactions that kept the sense of things the same. EM research focuses on this participatory dimension of experience. Such efforts, at the most mundane level, support social orders and their corresponding understandings – this is why flouting social conventions can evoke outrage. For Garfinkel, not seeing our part in supporting our social realities was 'much like complaining that if the walls of a building were only gotten out of the way one could see better what was keeping the roof up' (1967: 22). Indexing any understanding are the social activities we use to support 'it'. Take those 'supportive' activities away and one no longer has the social grounds for a shared understanding, as Garfinkel's breaching experiments showed. It was also in this sense that Wittgenstein (1969) suggested that, for there to be knowledge, there must be acknowledgement.

Our spoken words can be seen as being actions about something, *and* part of that something at the same time. You saw that in the Tom-getting-Andy-angry sequence earlier. Minimally, reflexivity asks us to examine how we shape our experience through what we bring to it, especially in what this brings out when interacting with others. For example, therapists can clearly see this when they engage clients in symptom-focused versus resource-focused clinical conversations. Each conversation constructs understandings consistent with the focus adopted. This kind of involvement with our experience, through how we language and relate to it, shows how our involvement is consequential to that experience.

Reflexivity also suggests that all analysis (scientists' included) is a constitutive process (Pollner, 1991). In other words, we change what we study through how we study it. What passes for 'fact', in any scientific discipline, must pass through a defensible process of production and peer scrutiny (a version of what Wittgenstein called 'acknowledgement'). In this way, the conventions of the discipline (its methods, evaluative criteria, constructs and reporting procedures) specify how the findings are to be made and reported. 'New' knowledge must therefore be generated using familiar methods, against a backdrop of familiar understandings from which it can be judged.

If you are seeing circularity here, in which how one purportedly knows relates to what one can know, you are seeing an important aspect we will revisit in our next section on 'documentary methods'. For now, consider how we are actively involved in what passes for 'real' in our life, through our active endorsement or use of particular methods and understandings we bring to our interactions. Some might read reflexivity as suggesting we can create our own realities, but Garfinkel reminds us that any effort to do so does not take place in social isolation. Instead of Parsons' cultural dope who responds to the dictates of a received world, Garfinkel sees competent actors accountably producing and holding each other to realities they constitute through their highly contextualized interactions. Parsons' dope obeys reality 'as it is'; Garfinkel's social member holds to a version of reality that s/he has played in working up, sustaining and extending it from within a particular social order. Social interactions thus offer us a 'reality check' should we stray too far from what passes for 'real' or 'good' in any social order. This should make more sense as we now turn to 'documentary methods' of interpretation.

Documentary methods

> What members of an order bump up against and know as 'reality' is available to sociology as the empirical activity that provides for the possibility of perceived social order.   (Hilbert, 1992: 72)

Documentary methods are the means by which people in social orders support their versions of reality. This is what Garfinkel saw as 'fact production in flight': members bringing their background expectations, understandings and methods to bear (in a near seamless manner) on new experiences and social interactions, to render these recognizable and acceptable to each other. 'Understanding' can come up a bit short as a way of capturing what we mean, and, given the embodied and interactive sense we want to highlight, a more apt word would be 'grasp'. In another of Garfinkel's experiments student subjects were asked to relate a concern and request for advice to an unseen counsellor ('whose' responses were actually a tape-recorded message) 'who' arbitrarily responded with 'yes' or 'no' to the advice requests. In following up with the students, researchers found that students constructed the advice given as fitting to their normative expectations. In short, they made what they heard recognizable and acceptable to them, even if the advice seemed 'off the mark'.

EM aims at revealing these ethnomethods or documentary methods of interpretation – how members make sense of each other and hold each other to their established, yet often highly contextualized, ways of sense-making. How, for example, do spelunkers (cave-explorers) hold each other to 'their' shared words and ways of spelunking? While Garfinkel's breaching experiments were designed to reveal such local methods in reverse, it can be much simpler and more respectful to attend to how members of any group make evident (i.e., to each other) its understandings, expectations and particular ways of relating to and understanding experience. Reflexivity reminds us, however, that documentary methods are tied to our memberships in particular social orders. It is in our social interactions in such orders that we actively put our understandings to a social test. Documentary methods reveal how social realities are upheld; they are the conventions (like greeting/response sequences) which members hold each other to.

It is useful to bring up Garfinkel's foil, Parsons, at this point. Remember, Parsons saw humans as rule-followers who, to varying degrees, obey reality on 'its' terms. Instead, EM sees local variations of 'reality' worked out between members in what we have been calling documentary methods of interpretation, *how* they accomplish their social realities with each other. But, once accomplished, they hold each other to interactions consistent with those social realities. Culturally, we know this; within cultures people develop particular takes on reality – try violating those takes with practices and understandings foreign to them. Many aspects of experience we might treat as 'universal' can falter here. For example, Rom Harré (1986a) similarly sees emotions as culturally embedded in 'emotionologies', where cultures such as the Ifaluk express emotions unfamiliar to Euro-Americans. But in EM it is important to see such differences as *methodical*, as features of how people locally and reliably work out their ways of understanding and influencing each other. Try raising a discussion of the unconscious with behavioural therapists: because the unconscious cannot be revealed with a behaviourist's documentary methods of interpretation, then the conversation will likely be brief, if not acrimonious. Documentary methods are how we, through social interactions, share the meanings of our experiences – showing how we know what we know to each other, while expecting the same in return. This is not a case of comparing our experiences with reality so much as it is to be in step with how those around us expectantly understand and act on reality. Understanding what Garfinkel means by this sense of 'expectantly' will now become the focus of our attention. For Garfinkel, a different view on morality becomes evident.

Morality

> [people]… are themselves entitled and entitle others to claim that they know what they are talking about and that what they say is understandable and

> ought to be understood. In short, their seen but unnoticed presence is used
> to entitle persons to conduct their common conversational affairs without
> interference.   (Garfinkel, 1967: 41–2)

What is it that holds different social orders to their particular documentary methods of interpretation? Here, Garfinkel sees a world where people's interactions are based on trust developed through forms of accountability (their reliably shared use of particular documentary methods of interpretation). Think of the often angry reactions to the breaching experiments; people reacted as if the 'breachers' had morally wronged them, and attempted to bring them back to the established orderliness of their lives. Morality, in this sense, refers to normative expectations of common sense or social interaction being upheld. This very different view of morality, from, say, Christian morality, speaks to people interacting according to what has become normal or commonsensical for them. And it is here where words like 'common sense' take on a decidedly local flavour, in that what becomes expected or shared as common sense in one social context often does not transfer over to other contexts. One example is that institutional common sense in the military often does not translate well in one's intimate or parenting relations.

Morality, for Garfinkel, is about peoples' 'local' ways of acting and grasping sense being sustained through how they interact with each other. For the most part this local morality is assumed and practised without reflection – a variant of social normality people expect and practise. This morality, or expected sameness of social normality, is based on a fundamental trust between people to *interact* consistently. 'Moral problems' arise when this trust-won and expected consistency is violated with actions that do not fit what has come to be expected. For example, when people stray from an established version of common sense they are typically required to provide 'error accounts', to demonstrate that they are not threatening the established understandings and orders to which they belong. Garfinkel, in his inimitable way, spoke of these error accounts, these ways of restoring trust, as 'devices for burying monsters'. The morality of social orders requires members to use documentary methods and indexed meanings – the stuff for which we are held to account as a member of a social order – or face sanctions for not doing so.

If this feels a stretch, consider departures from normalcy as breaches of trust, or deviations from 'how things should be' – and you are closer to Garfinkel's meaning of morality. The important dimension in this view of morality rests with how it is consistently practised in local interactions between people. This dimension has two complementary aspects: people are *expected* to sustain established ways of making sense and interacting together AND they *hold each other to* performing these established ways of making sense and interacting together.

In this regard, we can see social orders as morally (and collectively) governed contexts of possibility. This 'moral governance' is made possible by people interacting in trustworthy and expected ways that are familiar and already accepted by them. Deviations from what is already established must be carefully negotiated (or become grounds for moral correction) because the connectedness of people's histories together can seem at stake. For helpers, change for one person in a moral order can threaten that moral order itself, or create problems for that person back in her or his moral order. This insight has guided family therapists and organizational specialists and community development workers who prefer to include members of local moral orders in such negotiations of change.

Let us reiterate some key features of morality in EM terms. Morality in EM is different from the kinds of morality one associates with adhering to particular virtues, such as those one might find in religious texts or codes of moral conduct. Instead, EM morality refers to the trusted interactions people expect from each other, including their own social behaviour in those interactions. These expected interactions are how they keep things mutually familiar. But, in this sense, morality is expectantly *practised* in and through such interactions, though usually the practices have been routinized to the point of being beyond conscious awareness. However, should someone in a local moral order act in unexpected ways, the 'error' is quite recognizable (as in the breaching experiments) in ways that invite correction or needed negotiations for some new development in the local moral order. Essential to these moral interactions is trust, familiarity and agreement – and efforts to keep things that way. Those efforts are the ongoing (i.e., they do not stop – lapses are 'moral' problems to be locally worked out) *ethnomethods* people use to sustain local moral orders in and through their interactions with each other.

These ethnomethods can confuse newcomers to EM, so let us say a bit more. Ethnomethods are social practices involving many 'doings and sayings', to use a phrase from Schatzki (2002). Where things can get particularly confusing is when, for example, an expected word or gesture is seen as a social practice, or ethnomethod. For example, normally when people are negotiating an outcome there is an expectation that an affirmative word or gesture is required to conclude such a negotiation successfully. Failure to arrive at such a word or gesture from either party can effectively derail the negotiation. Similarly, when Garfinkel's confederates responded with 'what do you mean?' to another's rhetorical 'how's it going?' this breached normal social relations. Our point is that very subtle and assumed 'doings and sayings' are the ethnomethods that give local moral worlds their 'common' sense and keep them socially intact. But these 'doings and sayings' vary according to the social contexts in which they have been worked up into familiar and expected ways of being social together. We will now get more specific about this, looking at particular orders EM researchers call 'institutional realities', or others refer to as 'contexts'. But, before we do that, here is Hilbert again on what we have been discussing:

> Ethnomethods are social practices whereby members orient to a pre-supposed social-structural order, reifying and reproducing it in the course of their activity and *imposing its reality on each other as they go.*   (1992: 194; italics in original)

Contexts or 'institutional realities'

> ... to imagine a language means to imagine a form of life.   (Wittgenstein,
> 1953, aphorism 19–1)

What are we referring to when we speak of 'context'? For EM researchers, social orders – contexts of understanding and action – are accomplishments people create, sustain and extend through their communicative interactions with each other. But such orderliness can seem illusory, built on trust and moral accountability developed through, and as a result of, their interactions. Intuitively, most of us recognize the indexicality implied when we speak of understanding things 'in context', but specifying what we mean by 'context' is where things can get fuzzy. Some get historical or geographical when considering context, pointing to factors they consider non-indexical. Context, for them, has the kind of structurally deterministic effects Garfinkel objected to; this is where 'context' can get controversial as a topic.

There is a longstanding debate in conversational research circles about whether researchers must include demographic detail such as gender, race or socioeconomic status in their analyses (see, for example: Psathas, 1995; Billig and Schegloff, 1999; Arminen, 2000; Hester and Francis, 2000). For most EM and conversation analysis (CA) researchers these features are relevant to peoples' lives and their social orders to the extent that they demonstrate their relevance to each other. These are the doings and sayings (ethnomethods) people tacitly expect of, and reproduce for, each other. Close-up analyses of people's social interactions should show how these 'demographic' features are oriented to or made use of (how gender is shown to be relevant to the interaction). In other words, people reproduce their socially shared contexts through how they consistently use such doings and sayings. Thus, we are not cultural or contextual dopes determined by, or doing the bidding of, contexts or cultures. Our ethnomethods are the means by which we keep our interactions and our social contexts acceptably familiar to each other.

Both EM and CA treat contexts or 'institutional realities' as an empirical issue, one that should be evident in the language and ethnomethods members of any social order use in influencing and making sense of each other. These researchers take a stance of 'ethnomethodological indifference' (cf. Husserl's 'epoché', Chapter 3 above), seeing it as their job to show how their formulations of what takes place between people in any social order are *consistent with the understandings and orientations of the people involved*. Thinking otherwise can lead to a 'bucket theory of context', where interaction is seen as 'contained' by some social structure that determines its occurrence. This critique comes up short for those who feel issues of power are very much part of 'contexts', as in the influence of culture or gender (see Billig in the rollicking good debate: Billig and Schegloff, 1999). For them, EM and CA have a misplaced faith when seeing social order as merely what its members reveal to each other through their interactions. They see EM and CA committing to a socially uncritical stance. It can help to strip this issue down to some basics. Behind the EM and CA stance is a persistent concern about researchers' premature theorizing: if one goes on looking for cultural determinism in any way, one can expect to find it. Conversely, those troubled by EM's 'indifference' see a naïve epistemology claiming that analysis must proceed only on the basis of how the people in interaction being studied ostensibly make sense of each other. Both sides of this debate make points worth bearing in mind as we delve further into 'context' and social interaction.

EM researchers have long tried to learn what it means to interact competently and *mundanely* within any social order. This preoccupation with the mundane, for the EM analyst, shows up where members take for granted, or 'gloss', the documentary methods they use in sustaining any social order, or (in sociological lingo) 'institution' (e.g., the family, professions, work settings, etc.). EM research has focused on such institutions, examining the taken-for-granted methods used in doctor–patient, judge–jury, astronomer–astronomer interactions. There they found – at a very mundane level – that a doctor asks questions/a patient answers them, that judges use different reference points and arguments for their judgements than jurors, or that astronomers use a discipline-determined language to help them make sense of what they look at through their telescopes. Why should the mundane matter, you might wonder?

The mundane behaviours of any context, or institutional reality, require symmetry in their production and recognition – to be understood requires using a language understandable to speaker and listener, for example. This relates to our opening quote from Wittgenstein for this section: implicit to any unique context is a language that gives it its 'form of life'. Accordingly, you will recognize feeling like an 'outsider' when people use words and interact in ways that seem somewhat foreign to you. Getting specific about what that 'foreign-ness' is about – especially when analysis shows how 'insiders' gloss or take for granted their words and interactions – fits with how EM research tries to 'crack' the assumptive reality of any social order. Where an outsider sees foreign-ness, or what Garfinkel termed 'what anyone knows', there usually is a contextualized 'common sense'. Here is Garfinkel again, on the ubiquity of what we have been discussing,

> the objective reality of social facts as an ongoing accomplishment of the concerted activities of daily life, with the ordinary, artful ways of that accomplishment being by members known, used, and taken for granted is … a fundamental phenomenon.   (1967: vii)

In EM, contexts or institutional realities display understandings and ways of interacting that people index to those contexts. They also configure what it can mean to participate in those contexts, why some institutions constrain normal conversation or dialogues in ways particular to what they aim to accomplish. Thus, for example, when police–citizen interactions are studied they usually show a skew to the conversation as primarily managed by the police – though not always. The 'artfulness' Garfinkel refers to above can be shown in, for example, how citizens and police take up their roles in responding to each other. But an institutional feel to such interactions is recognizable in what the institution of police–citizen interaction won't countenance, what is 'in bounds' or 'out of bounds'. Notice, that 'in/out of bounds' is context-shaped and context-renewed in the course of police–citizen interaction; participants make the context relevant in how they orient to and relate to each other. How each participant acts is not fully predetermined, and they stop being cultural dopes in how they *improvisationally* relate to each other within the constraints of the institution or context. This was why Garfinkel's good clinics needed 'bad' clinical records; or, as Hilbert elaborated, 'practical bureaucratic life depends for its utility upon the subordination of bureaucratic idealizations to immediate here-and-now concerns making that action "nevertheless" in accord with these very idealizations' (1992: 154). Thus, a tension between such an idealization (i.e., a good clinic) and the practical means needed to achieve it can show people artfully improvising ways to sustain the idealization.

This is far from an 'anything goes' view of such improvisations, which are worked out within the moral and institutional contexts where they are used. Part of the 'good clinic' idealization is that people simply implement policy (e.g., in record keeping) in right or wrong ways. But close examination shows much more, as people make ad hoc judgements as to what is acceptable to record keeping, and sometimes this means record keeping at the boundaries of what is in and out of bounds. A prior sense of what is institutionally 'in or out of bounds' serves as a basis for evaluating members' improvisational judgements and actions – in this case on what are acceptable records. What we hope is emerging is a negotiated sense of what can fit being in and out of bounds in the light of idealized behaviour. A further example can be seen in the survey research examined by Maynard and Schaeffer (1996). In their research they examined phone surveys, surveys meant to be (i.e., idealized) conducted in standardized ways. Such a standardized survey 'should' be a simple matter of posing questions and having respondents answer them. However, this research showed a highly improvised process in the varied ways surveyors elicited adequate responses to their questions. What, for example, is acceptable in getting an adequate response: a restatement or rewording of the question, a check-in on the respondent's answer to see if it was properly understood, a bit of further coaching to get the answer? Our point in raising this notion of improvisation in light of idealizations is that close examinations show people interact in highly improvised ways where practical judgements and actions as to what is acceptable are in effect negotiated in the moment. This is a very different view of 'rule-following' (or policy adherence) than is commonly portrayed where people are seen as simply enacting the rule. This is where, for Garfinkel, people 'ad hoc' their ways through to accepted methods and outcomes.

To take another example: suppose a citizen orders a police officer around, or an officer exceeds 'appropriate' conduct – each may try to influence the other to keep things 'in bounds'. Institutional realities or 'contexts' reflect all we have been saying so far: they are sites of indexically understood and produced actions, these actions reflexively constituting both the context and what is recognized within them. Such actions can be understood as the documentary methods used within the context. What maintains these realities are members' interactions which hold each other to those methods and understandings. In this respect, people within social contexts together 'work up', and then sustain, particular ways of communicating that *typify* (in Schutz's, 1970, sense; see Chapter 3) how they are expected to interact with each other. These ways include the indexed words, gestures and other communications that keep things acceptably familiar.

It is easy to feel overwhelmed by Garfinkel and EM. But the emphasis here is on how social orders take on their unique understandings and social ways of being via what their members do to keep things acceptably familiar between them. For practitioners, a simple version of this is that one needs to keep in mind how differences relate to context. There's a conceptual trap lying in wait, however, if one sees people as cultural dopes of their circumstances. Garfinkel's research brings people back as active constitutors and maintainers of their social contexts – their reliably practised interactions keep things familiarly contextual. In a sense, practitioners joining social contexts from this perspective are joining a moral choreography that they may be breaching with their accustomed understandings and ways of practice.

Erving Goffman

> What nature divides, talk frivolously embeds, insets and intermingles. As dramatists can put any world on their stage, so we can enact any participation framework and production format in our conversation.   (Goffman, 1979: 24)

Think of relational life as being conducted on a morally charged stage, by actors who never quite fully play the roles others expect of them. See these actors' responses to each other as mostly scripted forms of social interaction worked out in face-to-face situations where they attempt to 'manage the impressions' others have of them. No, Erving Goffman was not a cynical Machiavelli. His concern was to help us get beyond the confines of socially prescribed being. He sought evidence of this resistance, even in social situations where such resistance was not countenanced. For Goffman, social reality went far beyond the words of our conversations; we participated in frameworks of understanding together, enacting our roles, so to speak, within them.

Erving Goffman is one of the twentieth century's most influential sociologists. He focused on individual behaviour at a micro-social level, while embedding it in society's ritualistic ways of behaving and understanding. He has been credited as being 'pre-postmodern' for considering how multiple social realities are performed – but he would not fully extend his ideas to the notions of indexicality and reflexivity common to most post-structuralists, social constructionists and ethnomethodologists. The son of Canadian prairie farmers, Goffman completed his Ph.D. at the University of Chicago with a study that would later form the basis of his initial book: *The Presentation of Self in Everyday Life* (1959). Using his central dramaturgical metaphor he devoted his life to understanding how people worked out the immediacies of their social lives, how they 'stage-managed' their ways of being with each other. Increasingly, his research focused on communication and conversation where he made huge contributions to the field of socio-linguistics. This curiosity led him to become an important consultant on mental health issues (he saw psychotherapists as 'absentee landlords of clients' domains of intimacy'), with stints at the University of California (Berkeley), and the University of Pennsylvania, where he died an early death at age 60 in 1982. In his final year of life, he was elected President of the American Sociological Association.

Goffman was a keen observer of social life, an 'ethnographer of the self' who wrote in a captivating style described by conversation analyst, Emmanuel Schegloff (1988), as 'sociology by epitome'. He found evidence (or exposés) for his dramaturgical perspective in such places as the behaviours of mental patients, the talk of 'con' men, conversations between talk radio hosts and phone-in guests, Richard Nixon's admonitions to a female journalist, and people 'managing' stigma in different relationships. In this manner he promoted a view of 'self' as finding dignity and value in responding to, and resisting, social pressures in ways that were resourceful. As we look more closely at Goffman, we will consider three inter-related themes in his writing: performing social relations, 'frames' and talk.

'Performing' our social lives

> There is a relation between persons and role. But the relationship answers to the interactive system – to the frame – in which the role is performed and the self of the performer is glimpsed. Self, then, is not an entity half-concealed behind events, but a changeable formula for managing oneself during them. Just as the current situation prescribes the official guise behind which we will conceal ourselves, so it provides for where and how we will show through, the culture itself prescribing what sort of entity we must believe ourselves to be in order to have something show through in this manner.   (Goffman, 1974: 573–4)

> whenever worlds are laid on, underlives develop.   (Goffman, 1961a: 305)

It is hard not to consider Goffman a cynic. After all, if we perform for each other in ways that don't reflect our 'moral character' – if we only stage-manage impressions socially – what does this say about the sincerity of social conduct? But we can read Goffman an entirely different way if we accept his point that different social circumstances require us to *perform* different selves. In this sense he could be read as postmodern; no essential self comes across in consistent ways irrespective of social context. We are a different person as a parent than as a friend or work colleague. Goffman, however, doesn't fully relinquish the essentialist self either; for him it partly emerges in our resistance to others' social prescriptions for who we are 'supposed to be'. Arguably, his was a 'bucket-like' social context, in which the cognitively understood context, not the people sustaining it, prescribes (or circumscribes) our possible thoughts and social actions.

Seeing us as beings who must do 'face-work' with each other, Goffman was particularly curious about these activities as the bases for individual *and* social behaviour. He saw human behaviour as role-defined, with the roles being connected to how interactive contexts were socially defined, something we will explore in greater detail when examining his notion of 'frame'. For him, these roles are 'situated' in 'a bundle of activities visibly performed before a set of others and visibly meshed into the activity these others perform' (Goffman, 1961b: 96). How we perform our roles is a measure of our adaptability to a setting, evident in the way we resourcefully draw on conventional (or at least acceptable) ways of interacting with others. Our performances, in other words, must fit 'local moral worlds' where we act within parameters of 'acceptable behaviour and understanding' consistent with these 'worlds', and our readings of each other. This is a far cry from the view of many psychologists and sociologists of Goffman's day: that we are mere rule-followers. He saw, instead of predefined rules to govern our social behaviours, individuals who drew on social 'scripts' and conventions as they worked out their relationships with each other. And, lest this sound like a prescription for self-interested anarchy, Goffman also believed that what kept things from going this way was our ability to attune to each other, and thereby coordinate our social interactions, via what he called 'participation frameworks'. If you think of improvised comedy – how one person tries to engage another in a shared topical activity with neither knowing where their process might take them – you are getting a sense of what it means to pull off such combined activities of understanding and action. Goffman saw us relying on culturally developed roles, ritualized behaviours and understandings ('resources') in doing this performing.

Goffman's dramaturgical metaphor was his attempt to portray the individual as an actor working with and within specific societal constraints and resources. While his focus was on what some term 'micro-sociology', Goffman did not subscribe to the common (Parsonian) sociological view that social factors determined individual behaviour. In this way, seeing life as a stage on which our unfolding dramas are enacted was key to how he saw individuals reconcile their sociality with their individuality. From this perspective, Goffman chose settings in which he could observe individuals responding to extreme social circumstances: mental patients in asylums, individuals socially stigmatized, and callers to talk radio. In this way, he could see these individuals participate in and resist social situations in which their roles seemed fully defined. From this angle, Goffman could see 'impression-management' at work, in the *fronts* such people put up to get by, while not letting themselves be totally defined by their social circumstances. He spoke, for example, of the 'moral career' of asylum patients whose socially defined roles could be interpreted as efforts to meet the requirements of a job description. Goffman asks us to be sure that we conceptually separate the *regular performance* of a role from the *regular performer* of a role. We aren't our job descriptions, or the sum total of the roles we take up socially – but it is from within our different roles that we show a multiplicity of selves able to meet the challenges of different social expectations. In addition, it is important to not see these roles as always imposed, as the early Goffman wrote:

> When an actor takes on an established social role, usually he finds that a particular front has already been established for it. Whether his acquisition of the role was primarily motivated by a desire to perform the given task or by a desire to maintain the corresponding front, the actor will find that he must do both.   (Goffman, 1959: 28)

A fair reading of Goffman shows him finding dignity in how we acquit ourselves in these roles and still are more than them. It takes more than a chameleon to meet social expectations adequately, and to do this in ways that leave a trace of our individuality. In fact Goffman felt that we got our sense of self by going beyond what seems expected of us socially. In that sense, part of our humanity comes through in our resistance to being defined by others and our circumstances, as he wrote:

> it is …against something that the self can emerge. Without something to belong to, we have no stable self, and yet total commitment and attachment to any social unit implies a kind of selflessness. Our sense of being a person can come from being drawn into a wider social unit; our sense of selfhood can arise through the little ways in which we resist the pull. Our status is backed by the solid buildings of the world; while our personality often resides in the cracks.   (Goffman, 1961a: 320)

Performing our selves is a way of seeing how people develop meaningful actions to relate effectively with each other. Metaphors that portray humans as 'impression-managers' who put up fronts seem crass, but at the same time they were Goffman's clunky way of asking us to consider humans in their different social contexts – to see the differences as understandable and artful ways of fitting into those contexts. In this respect, he saw people as amateur sociologists, participant observers in social circumstances they make sense of, and interact within. You can probably feel a moral dimension hovering here: performances sometimes do not work because people don't uphold the expectations others have of them. To meet these expectations, and not be confined to them, they intelligently respond to established social orders, and when confronted with ambiguity about those orders they turn to culturally developed resources (prior understandings, ritualized behaviours and ways of communicating) to co-develop their sociality. In this respect, Goffman builds on the writings of Schutz and Mead in a way that highlights human resourcefulness in the course of social interaction. The stage metaphor points to a way of seeing humans as individually active in adapting to and transcending their circumstances. Goffman was also clear about its limitations:

> 'The language and mask of the stage' is a mere intellectual scaffold, and 'scaffolds, after all, are to build other things with, and should be erected with an eye to taking them down'.   (Freidson (citing Goffman), 1983: 362)

'Frames'

> Activity framed in a particular way – especially collectively organized social activity – is often marked off from the ongoing flow of surrounding events by a special set of boundary markers or brackets of a conventionalized kind. These occur before and after the activity in time and may be circumscriptive in space; in brief, there are temporal and spatial brackets. These markers, like the wooden frame of a picture, are presumably neither part of the content of activity proper nor part of the world outside the activity but rather both inside and outside … One may speak, then, of opening and closing temporal brackets and bounding spatial brackets. The standard example is the set of devices that has come to be employed in Western dramaturgy: at the beginning, the lights dim, the bell rings, and the curtain rises; at the other end, the curtain falls and the lights go on.   (Goffman, 1974: 252)

The language of frames and 'reframing' has become commonplace, weaving its way into everyday discourse as people talk of how any circumstance has been 'framed', in perspectives on any circumstance. While 'frames' are often interpreted as perspectives or construals, that would insufficiently reflect the social view that Goffman meant the term to have – frames could be seen too solipsistically. Goffman, borrowing from Gregory Bateson, keeps things social and here his dramaturgical metaphor fits: we bring our interpretations to any social circumstance, and, with them, our sense of what our part should be in that circumstance. But things don't stop there; we also need to be working within a shared frame, to not be at cross-purposes. Here is an early Goffman addressing this issue: 'A teammate is someone whose dramaturgical co-operation one is dependent upon in fostering a given definition of the situation …' (1959: 81).

Frames, as Goffman saw them, require a combination of shared definition and purpose: a premise or understanding from which people could take up actions together. He also spoke of 'participation frameworks' as if individuals acted from different roles from the same script, and to some extent these reflect culturally recognized rituals participants can enact. They also have a 'production framework', in that results within them are generally produced in accordance with the frame, or, in Goffman's words:

> Frame, however, organises more than meaning; it also organises involvement. During any spate of activity, participants will ordinarily not only obtain a sense of what is going on but will also (in some degree) become spontaneously engrossed, caught up, enthralled.   (1974: 345)

In this respect, we take to a circumstance, like a doctor's visit, a repertoire of understandings and actions consistent with the role we expect to enact during that visit. Within such a shared frame (i.e., doctor–patient), the doctor generally asks us the questions and conducts the investigations, while our role includes such socially 'understood' activities as answering symptom-oriented questions, removing clothing for investigations, and presenting an initial concern. In this respect, a frame is recognizable, and performable on the basis of its social recognizability. The frame, in other words, has a shared conceptual life of its own (i.e., irrespective of others upholding it or holding us to it), and directs social interactions accordingly.

Within a frame is a range of activities and understandings; and its 'boundary' (as the above quote implies) is something we recognize the moment that behaviours inconsistent with the frame are introduced by any party. If, for example, the doctor begins a political discussion with the patient, or if the patient requests a loan from the doctor, actions within the normally, socially recognizable, doctor–patient frame no longer are 'in bounds'. Many social circumstances lend themselves well to this notion of framing; social conventions implicit to frames almost prescribe particular social interactions: we know what our parts should be at a wedding, what is appropriate when asking for a date, or even what our behaviour 'should' be in classroom learning. This is not the same as rule-like behaviour because there is an indeterminate range of behaviours we can perform in these situations while staying within a recognizable frame, by staying 'in bounds'. Indeed, where most sociologists saw norm-guided social behaviours Goffman saw 'frame space', the latitude participants afford each other to improvise within a frame – with this often being further constrained by conventional (and acceptable) expectations for behaviours within a recognizable frame.

Where frames get particularly interesting, however, is when we enter into ambiguous circumstances with others; or, when others defy our sense of a circumstance's social framing with 'out of bounds' actions. Here Goffman reminds us of our social challenge:

> whenever we come into contact with another through the mails, over the telephone, in face-to-face talk, or even merely through immediate co-presence, we find ourselves with one central obligation: to render our behavior understandably relevant to whatever the other can come to perceive is going on. Whatever else, our activity must be addressed to the other's mind, that is to the other's capacity to read our words and actions for evidence of our thoughts, feelings and intent. This confines what we say and do, but it also allows us to bring to bear all of the world to which the other can catch allusions.   (Goffman, 1983: 51)

In short, Goffman was saying here that we must still find ways to make our actions understandable and worth joining as shared activity. Seen this way, frames are not definitions that social conventions impose on us, especially when we do not have a frame to serve as a map for social appropriateness in an ill-defined or undefined circumstance. This was exactly the kind of determinism Goffman tried hard to steer sociology away from. Many who take a structural view see context or circumstance defining individuals and their experience in ways that miss the individual performances central to his view of individual–social interaction. Here he is again on this theme:

> when one nominates the 'context' to account for the differences between what is said and what is meant, one may forget that in real social life persons come equipped with bits of egocentric evidence as to what they are about and, thus equipped, can themselves constitute the context.   (Goffman, 1983: 15)

Framing can also be seen, therefore, as a constitutive act people accomplish through their interaction. If they are to be attuned in understanding and purpose they cannot let the egocentricities Goffman referred to get the better of them, or they will be unable to coordinate their social interaction. This coordination is how people work out the various framings of their coexistence – a social challenge we face as individuals. Back at the individual level, here is how Goffman sized up the challenge:

> But what is presented by the individual concerning himself and his world is so much an abstraction, a self-defensive argument, a careful selection from a multitude of acts, that the best that can be done with this sort of thing is to say that it is a lay dramatists's scenario employing himself as a character and a somewhat supportable reading of the past.   (Goffman, 1974: 558)

In the end, Goffman's frames can be seen as products of prior social interactions, conventional ways of recognizing situations defined in ways that enable us to know what our participation with others 'should' entail. They are human answers to the problem of meaning, ways of resolving the social problems that arise where there is ambiguity. And frames can be nested within larger frames, such as when the doctor–patient frame can be nested within the broader professional–client frame. This hints at what Goffman termed 'laminations', the multiple definitions possible for any circumstance. To some extent we use them as moral/social maps to act in acceptable ways with each other. But framings can also be what we need to work out with each other in order to have shared understandings and purposes. Frames are, inescapably, human constructions, definitions and premises already (somewhat) developed for shared social activities; or definitions and premises we need to work out with each other using our stock of prior understandings. To get a researchers' view of what it means to incorporate Goffman's perspective on framing to examine interactions within psychotherapy, you may wish to consult Chenail's (1995) paper on 'Recursive frame analysis'. Competently interacting within any recognizable social frame involves understanding and acting in ways others share as familiar (i.e., the familiarities are implicit in the social frame).

A range of practical implications follows from Goffman's notions of 'frames' and performances. At worst, clients and professionals can join in extending their prior stereotypes or culturally derived expectations for what 'framed' encounters between them 'should' be like. In this sense, they could find themselves bound to cultural roles and scripts ill-fitting to their purposes. Unpacking such stereotypes and expectations, to enable other kinds of interactions, can be a useful starting place. This can also be a double-edged kind of invitation: to see client–professional interactions as somewhat improvised, but also to see social interaction in general as more than simple adherence to already learned roles and scripts. While Goffman saw frames as facts of social life, his invitation was to recognize them, then resourcefully perform within and beyond them. His most striking writing was about people living dignified lives through partially resisting the performance 'obligations' of the frames most prominent in their lives.

'Talk'

> One clearly finds, then, that coordinated task activity – not conversation –
> is what lots of words are part of. Presumed common interest in effective
> pursuance of the activity at hand in accordance with some sort of overall
> plan for doing so is the contextual matrix which renders many utterances,
> especially brief ones, meaningful. And these are not unimportant words; it
> takes a linguist to overlook them.   (Goffman, 1979: 16)

> In the matter of presuppositions, then, that which language allows us to study
> takes us beyond language arrangements that are essentially nonlinguistic.
> (Goffman, 1983: 24)

Goffman's views on talk were central to his micro-sociology focused on
face-to-face-interaction. Most sociologists (e.g., Talcott Parsons) avoided this
analytic focus, preferring instead to see larger, structural forces at work in individual and social behaviour. For Goffman, however, people fashion their social
circumstances somewhat by 'reading' the conduct of others and performing
appropriately, meaning that their conduct meets moral strictures upheld by the
parties in such circumstances. Talk is part of an interaction order we work out
with each other (what he terms above, 'coordinated task activity'). Where many
sociologists saw 'rules' (social conventions) for how we interact, Goffman saw
resourceful individuals creatively making use of these rules: con men knowing how to 'cool out their mark' (Goffman, 1952), or mental patients preserv-
ing their dignity in interactions with asylum staff (1961a). Goffman wanted us
to look beyond the normative expectations we have of each other in conversation, so that we could see the specifically artful ways people 'meet' those
expectations.

It is through our interactions with each other that we develop and sustain a joint
focus (what we've been calling a 'frame'), analysable in what Goffman termed
'civil inattention'. This is our means of 'editorially' assenting to each other's
actions (a way of agreeing by not disagreeing). But there are also many micro-
agreements evident in how people coordinate their social interactions – ways they
indicate to each other they are 'on the same page'. Where much conversational
research focuses dyadically, on speaker and listener, Goffman was more broadly
interested in the 'focused encounter', the means by which people engage each
other in conversation. For him, agreement to talk was largely worked out prior to
conversation by non-verbal means, often paired with references to context. For
example, a doctor's patient might be directed to a chair while the doctor signalled
an interest in what the patient was about to say. Such orienting gestures can be seen
as part of what we earlier described as attuning to a shared frame, with the frame
already partly 'furnished' by normative social conventions (e.g., being directed to
sit in the chair) pertinent to that context. Attunement comes through participants
meeting 'system requirements' (demonstrations that they are capable of participating within the frame) and 'ritual requirements' (normative/moral expectations
for how interaction will take place). Talk is thus a part of how we coordinate our
social coexistence with others; we also rely on prior conventions and our readings

of each other to work out the participation and production formats that will frame our focused endeavours.

Goffman did not see humans constituting new ways and meanings for talk, an extension of Mead's reasoning where humans interact using established understandings and ways of talk – like prefabricated parts for buildings. But he felt we were endlessly creative in how we talked within the constraints of these conventions:

> The box that conversation stuffs us into is Pandora's. But worse still. By selecting occasions when participants have tacitly agreed to orient themselves to stereotypes about conversation, we can, of course, find that tight constraints obtain … But there are other arrangements to draw on … In these circumstances the whole framework of conversational constraints – both system and ritual – can become something to honor, to invert, or to disregard, depending as the mood strikes. On these occasions it's not merely that the lid can't be closed; there is no box.   (Goffman, 1981: 73–4)

It is this focus on the individual acting artfully from scripts that riled conversation analysts, like Schegloff (1988). But true to CA's heavy empiricist bent, Schegloff felt that Goffman's notions of frame and script were mystifyingly psychological in ways that could not be made evident through analysing conversation. It would be wrong to say that Goffman did not bring increased empiricism to his studies of conversation (particularly his 1981 book *Forms of Talk*), but look again at the last sentence of the first quote for this section. Goffman found his students Sacks and Schegloff too narrow and rigid in their micro-empiricist focus on talk's consequentiality. He would not pass Sacks's dissertation, and stepped down as his supervisor. Sacks and Schegloff, for their part, found him insufficiently dialogic in the ways people's utterances – beyond the rituals and social conventions Goffman pointed to – shaped the course of their talk and meaning with each other. But CA is only one sphere of research in the broader study of communication where Goffman's work is seen as highly influential, especially in furthering the field known as socio-linguistics.

Goffman, late in his career, introduced the notion of 'footing' in conversation. It was his answer to the following question:

> Given that you have something that you want to utter to a particular other, how do you go about getting into the circumstances that will allow you to appropriately do so? (The opposite question is of interest, too; namely How do you go about avoiding the circumstances in which you would be obliged to disclose something you would rather not?)   (Goffman, 1983: 32)

Footing was Goffman's way of showing how people shifted the 'ground' of their conversation. But it also speaks to their activity in grounding utterances to particular meanings, including the meaning of the frame in which this meaning-making is taking place. Conversation is a resource we need to serve us in different contexts, whether those contexts are physical or social. That means we require our talk to fit different contexts and ways of interacting within them – and we need to get from Frame A to Frame B sometimes with each other. How, for example, do people change topics or the moral context of their talk with each other? Goffman's classic article on 'footing' (1979) begins with a transcript of Richard Nixon at a press conference being asked what must have seemed like an impertinent question by a female reporter. Noting that the reporter was dressed in slacks, Nixon shifted the topic of discussion to why the woman was not wearing 'proper clothing'. Goffman, was interested in how these shifts reflected more than mere talk, involving a reconfiguring of the participation framework in which people interact.

Footing, like frames, is what enables us to point to some aspect of our shared experience and have a shared language and context for understanding it. In communications terms we create the phenomenon of *deixis* – ways in which utterances become semantically and socially anchored (or reified) to a particular frame or footing. When people get to a place where they can turn to an aspect of shared experience and know the other regards it the same way as they do, they have accomplished deixis. A teacher who has reached a place with a class such that they know what his/her cold, steely glare 'means' has socially accomplished deictic meaning that no longer requires explanation – it can be taken for granted. This aspect of footing indicates what happens when interactants get beyond an attunement phase with each other. In some respects well-established footings for conversation have many deictic dimensions to them – we know how we are to proceed, what the words mean, etc. This is the very stuff other communications analysts want to deconstruct or unpack. How does meaning go from finding some footing to being taken for granted in that footing?

Footing, like participation/production frameworks and Goffman's stage metaphor, is useful in that it contextualizes meaningful interaction in ways that are tied to the people involved. By focusing on face-to-face interaction Goffman furthered conversation as a research topic. But he still retained psychological and sociological notions, hard to support empirically, that remain a heuristic inspiration for many conversational researchers. Specifically, Goffman's view of conversation was that it was embedded in improvisable (to a degree) social conventions and constructs that served people as script-like resources in their different circumstances. It was how talk was part of people's means of influencing each other in conventional ways that interested him, yet he still yoked his views to society's existing accomplishments – its words and ways of talking.

Goffman and practice

> we must start with the idea that a particular definition is in charge of the situation, and that as long as this control is not overtly threatened or blatantly rejected, much counter-activity will be possible ... face-to-face interaction provides an admirable context for executing a double stance – the individual's task actions unrebelliously adhere to the official definition of the situation, while gestural activity that can be sustained simultaneously and yet noninterferingly shows that he has not agreed to having all of himself defined by what is officially in progress.   (Goffman, 1961b: 133)

Goffman's individual seemed always to keep up a front, responding artfully and with dignity to situations with definitions s/he might not want to embrace, but in which s/he could get by. In this respect he saw people resourcefully using what society has constructed to meet the demands of particular contexts, especially in face-to-face social encounters. Psychology and sociology, in Goffman's day, typically saw humans as determined by their environments, or by psychological responses to them in ways that we commonly associate with the endurables of personality, irrespective of context. He instead saw humans as contextually and relationally adaptive, but that adaptability was to be honoured, and seen as only part of the picture of who anyone was. Behind any front people use to get by in situations is a much richer understanding that spoke to how they kept from being totally defined or submissive in those situations. Beyond the seeming zombie-like 'resignation' of asylum patients, for example, he found ample evidence of people adapting to that context while revealing glimpses of their character that had not been overtaken by the expectations of that context. From Goffman we get a view of humans as unrelentingly acting on their own behalf, where much sociological and psychological thinking sees the same humans as determined by, or passive in the face of, their experiences – especially 'psychogenic' ones.

Clients, à la Goffman, would stage-manage their relations with practitioners, especially in the attunement phase of any therapy – being ready to take up the 'role' of client as it 'should be played'. It can thus be important to invite clients into discussions about stereotypes ('frames') brought to the practice context that could constrain the possibilities of interaction and change. In some respects, Goffman's work can be seen as honouring the resourcefulness and utility of resisting what seems culturally given (Wade, 1997) – client–professional contexts being a sometime focus of his work. Goffman's emphasis on the individual in a ready-made world, who creatively used its resources to get by, did much to push social scientific thinking toward post-structural thinking, as evidenced in his influence on writers such as Jean-Francois Lyotard and Michel Foucault. In short, his influence was to move thinking further along to what we now know as contextualizing human thought and interaction. He saw humans as shapers of those contexts but not to the extent the post-structuralists would. Here is one final word from Goffman on his view of what it means to 'perform' our lives.

> In performing a role, then, the individual is likely to take minor liberties, ducking out for a moment to stretch or apologize. These fleeting derelictions are but shadows of acts, very easily unseen; certainly sociology has managed for long to ignore them. That a stage performer must disavail himself of these lapses when presenting a character (except when they are scripted) should quicken our interest in them and lead one to appreciate more clearly that although the social world is built up out of roles sustained by persons, these persons have, and are seen to have a right to have, a wider being than any current role allows. These very small acts celebrate very large issues.   (Goffman, 1974: 544)

Anthony Giddens

> All social systems, no matter how grand or far-flung, both express and are
> expressed in the routines of daily social life, mediating the physical and
> sensory properties of the human body.   (Giddens, 1984: 36)

It might seem, after reading about Garfinkel and Goffman, that the grand days of
theorizing social life in big-picture systematic ways had come and gone. Not so.
The influential writings of Anthony Giddens show that social theorizing is still
alive but without the kind of structural determinism one would associate with
sociologists like Parsons. What Giddens has tried to square with his theory is how
the micro-activities of everyday life line up with the macro-exigencies of social
existence. These, for Giddens, are complementary in nature: the micro is shaped
by the macro, and the macro is shaped by the micro. Giddens' theorizing about
'structuration' serves as counterpoint to the view that social life is worked out
solely in the immediacies of social interactions. Drawing heavily from Garfinkel
and Wittgenstein in seeing the contextual specificities and mutability of particular
social orders as reflexively performed, he turned to others like Foucault, Bourdieu
and Habermas in asserting that people are influenced by those orders. Some see
a waffler in Giddens for wanting things both ways (Bryant and Jary, 1991), or, at
best, an incomplete theorist for inadequately accounting for how the micro and
macro dimensions of social life are reciprocally influencing (Urry, 1991). Still
others dismiss Giddens as a philosophical sociologist for not grounding his ideas
in empirical research (Loyal, 2003). Giddens has influenced not only sociology;
his 'third-way politics' (1994, 1999) served as an ideological foundation for the
policies of Tony Blair's Labour Party. The gist of his 'third-way' reads like another
integrative compromise (making him a neo-liberal apologist to many): that there
can be a middle way between left and right politics. Our look at Giddens offers an
opportunity to revisit a classic debate: the extent to which a comprehensive theory
can or must ground practice.

Giddens was a product of late 1950s to early 1960s English university life,
and completed his Masters thesis at the London School of Economics in 1961.
Thereafter, he went on to lecture at Leicester University, where he taught alongside Norbert Elias (see Chapter 11). It was Elias who, Giddens claimed, partly
inspired his pursuit of grand-scale sociological theorizing. Further stints (1966–8)
as a lecturer followed, first at the new Canadian Simon Fraser University, and then
at UCLA. These experiences helped Giddens distance himself conceptually from
European structural sociologies, while bringing him in contact with the dramatically different sociological thinking of Garfinkel and Goffman. After returning
from North America, he took up a lectureship at Cambridge in 1969, acquired
his doctorate there in 1974, and in 1985 assumed the Chair in Sociology. In 2004
Giddens became Baron Giddens and sits in the House of Lords for the Labour
Party. He remains active as a writer and socio-political commentator.

Giddens is a prolific writer who has published thirty-four books (as of October,
2007) and over 200 articles. He cut his teeth by critiquing the big thinkers in

sociology (Weber, Durkheim, Parsons, Marx) while building up his own view of how sociology should be understood and practised. His writing can be seen as a theoretical hybrid derived from selectively synthesizing the ideas of others. In 1976, he published his first major book, *New Rules of Sociological Method*, his attempt to bridge the micro/macro dualism that seemed to divide sociology at that time. Like Garfinkel and Goffman, he rejected the notion that people were pawns in some larger social game, arguing instead that humans as interpretive actors can resourcefully alter their social circumstances, despite acting and thinking in ways shaped by those circumstances. In this respect, he borrowed from the hermeneutic thinking of Gadamer, Heidegger and others and the critical emancipatory theory of Habermas. His theory of structuration was largely underpinned by the central idea that human beings, though immersed in the traditions of particular social orders, could agentively alter those orders.

Structuration

'Structuration' is the central focus of Giddens' writing after 1976. The central notion associated with 'structuration' follows Garfinkel's view of moral order. Specifically, people, through their interactions, create the larger social structures that govern their lives. Our core theme here will be familiar: how humans are shaped by their circumstances, yet through resourceful action they can shape such circumstances. In other words, there is a relationship between what humans do in interacting with each other, and how they sustain or alter the context for their interactions. Giddens' synthesis in articulating 'structuration' pulls together a wide range of understandings from diverse academic fields. His starting place, like Garfinkel's, was to rail against the monolithic views of structural determinists (e.g., Parsons) who saw people's sense-making and interactions determined by social contexts. Giddens posited a rational human actor able to interpret and act resourcefully within such contexts, when interacting with other humans. But interpreting and acting within these contexts takes on the qualities of *being* or acting one associates with Heidegger. Herein lies Giddens' tension, compromise or creative synthesis, depending on how you regard 'structuration'.

Giddens sees structuration as accounting for the dualism of human agency within the constraints of culture, how we reproduce culture *and* transform it, through social interactions. We continually create, through our social interactions, the social realities that open us to some possibilities for understanding and action, while constraining alternative understandings and actions that fall outside of these possibilities. This is a short version of what is meant by structuration. Thus, human thought and action are both contextually shaped and shaping (*pace* Garfinkel) in routines or normative forms ('structures') that rational and resourceful actors can influence. Thought and action adapt to 'codes of signification', a term one could see as analogous to the 'rules' or grammars of Wittgenstein's language games. These conceptually and practically organize what is in and out of bounds, so to speak, as thoughts and actions consistent with the 'structure' – much like Goffman's participation frameworks. Seen this way, humans are more than rule or routine followers. Giddens sees a rational actor able to influence, if not transform, social structures. Each structure affords two contextually related kinds of resources to this rational actor: 'authoritative resources, which derive from the coordination of the activity of human agents, and allocative resources, which stem from control of material products or of material aspects of the world' (Giddens, 1984: xxxvi). It is in this regard that Giddens sees humans able to differently shape the social structures in which they participate.

Giddens wrote of the stratification of social structures, something which occurs as much through actors' intended actions as it does through the unintended consequences of their actions, that in turn ground the unacknowledged conditions of their actions. Since humans practically interpret and judge each other, their intended actions, as they interact, sometimes do not play out in causally certain responses; they might elicit unintended reactions. With Garfinkel we saw people using ethnomethods to keep things familiar between them, but we also saw that such familiarity was itself negotiable. We experience this every day when people respond to us in unanticipated ways, and we then need to find some way to work things out. Our intentions, in other words, are not always met in how others respond to us and that translates to some follow-up relational or conversational work. Out of that work can come unintended consequences, however, and these consequences, when routinized, can serve as the (taken-for-granted) conditions for later action – our way of creating social circumstances we have yet to learn to transcend.

We might, for example, engage a friend in ways that elicit acrimony and then conclude that actions with this friend (i.e., conditions for future action) will inevitably lead to further acrimony. But it is here that Giddens' rational human actor's potential really comes to the fore. We can learn from these unacknowledged conditions and factor them into subsequent actions. Thus, Giddens proposed a final stage he sees as helping humans rise above their social circumstances. The diagram below summarizes what we have been discussing, showing how, with increased awareness of what we produce through our interactions, we can become more reflexive agents in transforming our circumstances.

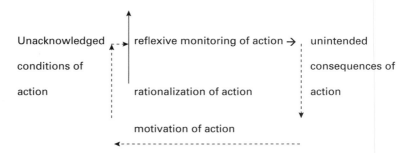

Figure 10.1 *Reflexive processes of structuration, adapted from Giddens, 1984: 5*

Giddens' concern is that we increase our awareness of how social behaviour and thinking can stabilize or innovate. Hermeneutically, such behaviour and thinking derives its sense from a social backdrop of intelligibility (the 'conditions' mentioned earlier), in habits of thought and action that either extend established traditions, or in new actions that depart from them. Looking at the figure above, the left side dotted line points to a progression of actions taken from unconscious motives in unfamiliar circumstances to increasingly more purposeful and relationally responsive actions as circumstances become familiar. At the highest level actors are capable of acting from their responsiveness to others, which can shift in moment-to-moment, unanticipatable interactions. Such knowledge of context (rationalization of action) translates to know-how, how to act socially in ways that meet social conventions, or transcend them in carefully worked-out ways with others. Post-structuralists should feel at home here, for, as Giddens put it, 'Structure has no existence independent of the knowledge that agents have about what they do in their day-to-day activity' (1984: 26). This is a reciprocal view of interacting tied to what Heritage (1984) described as the 'morality of cognition'. We act from understandings and social conventions we expect of others, and that they expect of us, but these typically are outside our awareness. This morality (as in EM) is based on upholding normative expectations. Successful efforts to get beyond such stable understandings and actions require mindfully reflexive interactions with others, to keep others' social reality from feeling unacceptably 'breached'. It is in this sense that some social constructionists consider that such changes in thought and social actions require careful negotiation (e.g., Gergen, 1999).

Giddens takes structuration from actor-focused interactions through to their institutional implications, tracing how routinized interactions come to anchor shared cognitions ('codes of signification'). In turn, he relates how some routinized interactions and their accompanying understandings ('symbolic orders') come to dominate and be legitimated as the means by which participants in any structure think and act. In the end Giddens offers a reciprocally dynamic 'bottom-up' (i.e., actor-enabled) and top-down (structure affording and constraining) account of how individuals 'structure' social life, and vice versa. In this manner he accounts for 'sequestered' differences occurring across time in a process-oriented manner. By sequestered, he refers to how interactive contexts structure differences in the ways thought and action play out. He bumps things up a further cultural notch (Giddens, 1999) when translating how structuration features in a national politics in tune with both individual action and globalizing tendencies. Giddens (1991) sees humans as both socially accountable and capable of being socially transformative.

This is big-picture theorizing indeed, but an oxymoron of sorts: a post-structuralist theory of how social life is 'actually' structured. Giddens has pulled together a hybrid of many ideas we have already encountered, but he adds a thrust that some find odious for endorsing 'neo-liberal' views of individual actors influencing and overcoming their social circumstance by dint of their reflexively aware social actions (Loyal, 2003). But Giddens is also clear that he is no postmodernist.

He sees a risk of society continually reorganizing social time and space at the same time as it 'disembeds' people from social contexts where they have shared traditions with others. This makes self-identity a 'reflexive autobiographical project' requiring individuals to re-author their understandings of self in adapting to and transforming new social contexts (Giddens, 1991). Here, for example, is where Giddens sees therapists of help:

> Therapy is not just an adjustment device. As an expression of generalized reflexivity, it exhibits in full the dislocations and uncertainties to which modernity gives rise. At the same time it participates in that mixture of opportunity and risk characteristic of the late modern order. It can promote dependence and passivity; yet it can also promote engagement and reappropriation ... [therapies tend to] interpret the reflexive project of the self in terms of self-determination alone, thus confirming, even accentuating, the separation of the lifespan from extrinsic moral considerations.   (Giddens, 1991: 180)

There is a recurring theme around reflexive self-determination and social influence in Giddens' theorizing. It is a touchy topic for those committed to exposing and overcoming social injustices. Giddens offers a view of being social tied to our social participation, with such participation being addressable through increasing awareness and alternative forms of social participation. His politics conspicuously omit any sense that injustices, or emancipatory concerns, require efforts to contest. Instead one reads about emancipatory structures made possible through collective actions that flow from 'life politics' grounded in shared concerns about freedoms, morality and ethics. If one can recruit others to social change and, collectively, such changes are won through political actions, both individual and society purportedly benefit.

Are we further ahead for having Giddens' structuration theory? Arguably, his synthesis brings together some of the innovative elements from many of our theorists. We are offered a view of individual and social action that sounds plausible: human life is understood and performed differently in differently sequestered social 'structures', and there is a situated dynamism associated with what it means to be an actor supporting and transforming those 'structures'. To critics, Baron Giddens' modern individual (1991) has been imbued with agentive powers to shape social life that sound nostalgically Ayn Rand-like. Such thinking can be seen to justify neo-liberal policies that result in economic winners and losers; the same goes for enterprising participants in the global economy.

For Giddens, theorizing has an aim of showing people as actors in the social circumstances in which they can otherwise feel victims. He accords a lot to the rational actors able to deduce their reflexive contributions to their social realities and transcend them (potentially, this is where practitioners can be of help, too). But, there are many therapies that now take up this line of thought (narrative and cognitive therapy partly do this). Extending this thinking to practice, it can be quite useful and respectful to become more mindful of practitioners' reflexive contributions to the institutional or professional realities they co-construct with clients. This point is strongly emphasized in the later writing of Donald Schön (1983) on what he called 'reflective practice'.

Coda

We can now shift back to the thinking we introduced at the start of this chapter, about how the social and the individual can be seen as coming together in ways useful to informing practice. Of course, client–professional practice itself involves social interaction, but psychological conceptions of clients and of practice have tended to focus on individuals. Our look at Garfinkel, Goffman and Giddens highlights a very different sense of selves as social actors, actors whose thought and actions take form in responsive relations they have to one another. In each of the three thinkers we have examined, the individual is shown quite intricately interwoven into the social thinking and interactions that shape their lives. People's micro-interactions, between each other, are shaped by, while still shaping, their macro-social circumstances. It is in this sense that one can speak of Garfinkel and Goffman as 'micro-sociologists'. While people are not determined by their social contexts, social life, according to each of our thinkers, relies on their (usually unaware) participation to uphold particular shared ways of thinking and acting. These thinkers suggest that we may be complicit in the social orders we take part in. But that oversimplifies what causes such participation or what that participation entails.

Each also suggests that the different contexts we uphold through our interactions have different requirements of us, requirements we normally hold others to as well. Garfinkel refers to this as a kind of local morality, but this is a morality based on the normative expectations we learn to have of others, and that they learn to have of us. Small wonder, then, that when people get unconventional in ways that are uncomfortable for others, conflicts in generational and other differences arise. The social point is that, while there may be 'wiggle room' to negotiate ways of being, breaches can occur if changes take place without respect for others. There is a sense that our trusted ways of interacting can be violated and that generally we act so as to stay morally 'in bounds'. But it is easy from here to take a kind of 'reality-adjusting' view as a practitioner, helping others learn what it means to work within, or at the margins of, social acceptability. Goffman's stance was particularly instructive in this regard, though it was hardly revolutionary. Giddens can seem a sentimental individualist for seeing people's ability to know the social rules of particular contexts well enough to transform them. But sociologists tend to focus on social organization, and unsurprisingly the sociologists reviewed here offer nuanced accounts of social life and where individuals fit into it. Garfinkel, Goffman and Giddens advanced a view that we construct and then sustain – through our interactions – the varying contextual and cultural features of social reality. Contexts do not exist independently of us – that we enact them together with others is one of their messages. In this sense our social and cultural lives rely on the ways we interact so as to keep them acceptably familiar to each other. This connects us to our part in the social realities we live by and points to the fundamental trust that underlies and shapes our efforts to be familiar and influential with each other.

11 Sources of the self

> If it were possible to lay bare and unfold all the presuppositions in what I call my reason or my ideas at each moment, we should always find experiences which have not been made explicit, large-scale contributions from past and present, a whole 'sedimentary history' which is not only relevant to the genesis of my thought, but which determines its *significance*. (Merleau-Ponty, 1962: 395)

> … only members of the in-group, having a definite status in the hierarchy and also being aware of it, can use its cultural pattern as a natural and trustworthy scheme of orientation. (Schutz, 1944: 504)

Arriving at an airport in a foreign land makes us aware of two things. The first is an immediate awareness of how much of this 'new' everyday life one doesn't understand. Taking a bus trip from the airport into town requires a ticket: where does one get one? Is it at an office or on the bus? If on the bus, from the driver or a conductor? Do you need the correct money, or do they give change? What are these coins, anyway; which is worth what? How do you get the bus to stop where you want to get off? Secondly, and less immediately, these experiences reveal how much 'we didn't know we knew' about how these things are done at home: that at home, these things are not a problem at all, but part of our natural and unreflective grasp of our circumstances. The differences between our grasp of the familiar and unfamiliar run deeper than just interacting with these minutiae of everyday life, and go beyond what we might think of as a survival kit of local knowledge. All the facets of our cultures have a history; and we – who we think we are, how we might study ourselves (and why we do), what we take to be correct ways of acting, of accounting for our actions, the ways we feel about things – are among those facets. It is not the case that human beings all have one, universal stance in a plethora of different cultures that have been variously elaborated around them: human being is likewise differently constituted in its different life ways.

What we have just said is a central plank in any social constructionist perspective. It is there in different guises in every previous chapter: Vico, Marx, Vygotsky, Mead, Schutz, all provide varying 'grand statements' of the socio-historical foundations of consciousness, action and self; others, such as Wittgenstein, the ethnomethodologists, the discourse analysts, work to articulate at a much finer grain how the end products of past life ways are handled, essayed and negotiated in the here-and-now of real-time living. Our intention in this chapter is to look at the middle territory between these two poles, and inquire as to what, in the past, has contributed to constructing the way of life we – as middle-aged, twenty-first-century, white, western males – live in and through: how did we become us? Our account is selective and biased: how could it be anything else? It is selective because the topic is huge. But we need to beware of lulling you into a false security here: it is not the case that there is, out there in the literature from which we are selecting, a definitive account of how we came to be who we are. Similarly, our selection is biased not just because we come to the literature with a necessarily parochial grasp of it, but also because a different, equally accidental history of reading could have produced a different account. As should be clear by now, there is, in our view, no essential, once-and-for-all-times, true account that can be provided. In addition, our account is necessarily self-reflexive: in trying to account for who we are and how we became like that, we necessarily transform ourselves and become different from who we were when we set out. There are no essential selves that remain constant throughout our encounters with either the worlds of everyday life or the worlds of ideas that we bring to bear on understanding them.

The issues we consider here are not independent of each other. Many of the ways in which we think have been influenced by our particular pathways into 'knowledge'. We have been educated in a rational tradition in which science has been an influential component – not something anyone of our generation could escape in obtaining a university qualification. We have been educated, too, in a particular realm of etiquette, so as to know how to be polite in company. We have been educated to believe that there are certain goals that we should strive towards, so as to be good citizens. But these different educations are not independent. Rather, they interpenetrate each other at a number of levels, particularly through the discursive resources that cut across and inform our possibilities of knowing and judging and the standards of civility.

On the practical, everyday side of things, talk of 'selves' can come across as a form of linguistic irresponsibility – right up there with talk of 'realities'. In a society that prizes individuality, responsibility for 'self'-development, culpability for wrongdoing, and so on, constructionist talk of 'selves' is almost heretical. Where social scientists have often focused on getting a 'correct reading' of the self, social constructionists see such efforts as leading to a kind of ideological or cultural entrapment. Add to this the enduring humanist notion about getting in touch with and acting from one's 'core self', and social constructionists can sound a bit out there. Popeye could say 'I am what I am' two generations ago, and everyone seemed to know what he meant. Outside of academia and literary culture, most clients do not know what to make of talk of selves, or how to 'construct alternative selves', so this presents a challenge for the constructionist practitioner who considers 'selves' a conversational focus.

For our purposes, where things get interesting is in considering how a sense of self has been a moving target as history and culture cycle through new metaphors and discourses for talking about and regarding self. This is part of the point of constructionist practice with respect to self: by what means, resources and criteria is our sense of self constructed personally, socially and culturally? What do we turn to as evidence for our sense of self and how contestable or modifiable is that evidence? Where do our genes and biology stop and discursive and relational influences take over in accounting for self? How do we transcend our own autobiographies in ways that permit significant change, and are not mere extensions of existing narrative plotlines? These are just a few questions that can be considered in reflecting on a socially constructed self.

The roles of technology and urbanization in establishing our discourses

The present occidental world has recently been shaped by the spectacular success (and now unintended consequences) of western science and the technology it has made possible. This situation has occurred very rapidly. The symbol systems that underpin it, such as alphabetic writing and many mathematical notations and procedures, are all relatively recent – a few thousand years – in the larger scheme of things. The methods that have enabled us to use these symbols to build modern technology have an even shorter history – a few hundred years. The very pace of change is staggering – my (Andy's) father was born in the year the Wright brothers got off the ground, and he died just after Neil Armstrong stood on the moon (and returned to tell the tale). There can be no denying the power and effectiveness of science. Along with – even because of – its power, science has had a dominating effect on how ideas have been formulated in pursuit of a coherent view of nature, and, by analogy, with how humans are to be conceived and studied among the social sciences. How did this come about?

In retrospect, the social sciences, as a body of theoretical knowledge aiming to explain human activity, have been dominated by two questions throughout history. First, what is it that humans are 'about': that is, what is it that is in need of explanation? Second, what terms should that explanation be couched in? The ways of deciding on these questions have been very much determined by the problems people have been variously confronted with in their daily lives of living together practically, and the technologies they have developed to deal with these practical issues. Marshall (1977) quotes Farrington's (1947) view that a decisive move in western thought was first taken in the sixth century BC near Miletus in Asia Minor, by such men as Thales, Anaximander and Anaximenes, men 'obsessed by tinkering around with gadgets':

> The central illumination of the Milesians was the notion that the whole of the universe works in the same way as the little bits of it that are under man's control … The vast phenomena of nature, so awe-inspiring in their regularity or their capriciousness, in their beneficence or their destructiveness, had been the domain of myth. Now they were seen to be not essentially different from the familiar processes engaged in by the cook, the farmer, the potter, and the smith.   (1977: 476)

And, as Marshall goes on to note (ibid.: 476), once the trick of interpreting the natural world through the framework of human technology was made, 'the next move was to interpret man himself in the same fashion', as a part of nature so conceived, with that move being made by Hippocrates (460–375 BC), cementing a similarity between engineers and physicians in the repair of different systems that have broken down. At this point, the 'mind' is ripe for a similar explanation. From here, western understandings have 'been dominated by metaphors drawn from the high technology of the day' (ibid.: 476).

The high technology contemporaneous with these early Greek conceptual moves was hydraulic, a consequence of the major practical problem created by urbanization. The issue here was how to distribute clean water to the inhabitants of a city, and then get dirty water out of a city (a problem that has never really gone away). Water needs to be stored, distributed and discharged, and what better metaphor for understanding the working of the psyche than the techniques of mastering this vital fluid, and regarding them as appropriate descriptions of the reservoirs of imagination, memory and reason, which are transferred via the nerves (conceived as hollow pipes) that link the sensing of the world to the muscular work required. Even today, vestiges of this model are still preserved in the conceptualization of the sodium-potassium *pump* theory by which nerve impulses are transmitted (by electricity, conceived as a *current*). Similarly, memory can be appropriated to the allied problem created by taxation and trading: that of storing goods or coins in warehouses and vaults, and being able to keep track of them. Again, the various technologies for record keeping and organization have been pressed into service as explanations of human abilities. Both Plato and Aristotle propose that sensory images are retained just as impressions are preserved on wax tablets, and Cicero describes memory as 'the treasure house of all things'.

Urbanization also played a role in specifying what it is that humans are 'about'. Sir Isaiah Berlin proposes that a major shift in the way the early Greek philosophers approached this question followed shortly after the death of Aristotle in 322 BC: 'it is as if political philosophy had suddenly vanished away. There is nothing about the city, the education of citizens to perform their tasks within it … the notion of fulfilment as necessarily social and public disappears without trace' (2002: 302). Berlin argues that humans were conceived in the classical Greek period in largely social terms as Aristotle paradigmatically states in his *Politics*: 'One should say not that a citizen belongs to himself, but that all belong to the *polis*: for the individual is part of the *polis*' (ibid.: 294). By contrast, twenty years after Aristotle's death Epicurus is on a different tack: 'Man is not by nature adapted for living in civic communities' (ibid.: 304). For humans, there is nothing above and beyond individual happiness.[1]

---

[1] A conception still current as 'obvious' 2000 years later: 'We hold these truths to be self-evident, that all men are created equal, that they are endowed by their Creator with certain unalienable Rights, that among these are Life, Liberty and the pursuit of Happiness. That to secure these rights, Governments are instituted among Men, deriving their just powers from the consent of the governed' (American Declaration of Independence, 1776).

Berlin's view is that this shift marks a revolutionary point in western cultural history: it marks the birth of individuality. 'For the first time the idea gains ground that politics is a squalid occupation, not worthy of the wise and good. The division of ethics and politics is made absolute' (ibid.: 310). Civil issues – justice, taxation, voting – have no value in themselves, only a utilitarian, pragmatic value in how much happiness they can secure for the individual. Berlin sees this divorce between ethics and politics as the first of five characteristics of this revolution. The second is that inner life becomes valued over the outer. Third, while ethics are those of the individual, individuality itself – with notions such as a need for privacy and a recognition of individual rights – is only nascent, taking centuries to emerge. Fourth, the idea of the 'goodness' of the state, and the worth of acting so as to secure it, becomes a poor second to the pursuit of individual goals: politics was degraded by an ever increasing division between the public and private spheres. Finally, in demarcating the individual from the public, a comparison between the two became possible, enabling individuals to experience disenchantment and alienation for the first time.

'For the first time' prompts the realization that there is a relation between the social world, the problems it generates, and the resources that it makes available for the construction of the lives of the people who comprise it. Prior to the flourishing of classical Greek life was a world described in the writings of Homer, a world of warriors not dissimilar to an entire form of heroic culture that spread from India in the east, through to Ireland in the west, and Scandinavia in the north. Julian Jaynes (1976) has offered a (controversial) interpretation of selfhood in these times – which lasted longest in their western and northern instantiations. Men (of women little is even speculated) were dominated by almost uncontrollable passions, and there was little sense of a self most in the west now take for granted as the controlling centre that resists emotive impulses. And if we take Jaynes's observation of this as having a ring of truth, we can appreciate how the stirrings of urbanization in Greece created conditions that set the problem of how such people were going to be able to 'respond' in ways that would enable them to actually live together (we will return to this topic more fully later in this chapter, through the lens provided by the work of Norbert Elias).

Greek urbanization thus required the institution of new forms of psychic life, such that spontaneous outbursts of dangerous emotion could be restrained. At the same time, it enabled an ideology that placed the common good as the ideal, so as to maintain a more secure way of urban life. 'Rationality' emerges out of urbanization more easily than it can from a nomadic, tribal life among warriors, because it cushions its members from the dangers of nature and the unrestrained actions of one's fellows. And in doing this, urbanization slowly, of its own dynamic, creates inhabitants of its way of life who are more 'self-aware', and more reflective. With that, there necessarily emerge the words – the discursive resources – that structure the individual psyche, and the ideologies that position that individual in a relationship to nature. Individuality, post-Aristotle, only became possible because the constraints of the *polis* – which were paramount – disciplined people, restructured their sense of 'self', and provided – as if miraculously – the resources of ideas and 'thought-techniques' (e.g. a grasp of syllogistic reasoning) that contained the seeds for the passing of the valuations required by the *polis*.

This is the prime facie argument for the narrative of 'social constructionism' we are putting forward here: that there is an intimate link between the social world, the resources for 'being' that it provides, and the ways of thinking it makes possible by the situational possibilities it provides for ways of life, for common sense, and for unreflective apperceptions of 'how things are'. Volosinov puts it thus:

> Every sign, as we know, is a construct between socially organized persons in the process of their interaction. *Therefore, the forms of signs are conditioned above all by the social organization of the participants involved and also by the immediate conditions of their interaction* ... This is the order that the actual generative process of language follows: *social intercourse is generated; ... in it verbal communication and interaction are generated; and in the latter, forms of speech performances are generated; finally, this generative process is reflected in the change of language forms.* (1986: 21, 96; italics in original)

These links between technological metaphors as resources for thinking and social life are apparent in the origins of Enlightenment science. Science relies on the initial formulation of nature, and human nature, as intelligible through the high technologies of the day – the understanding of the world as a 'mechanism' – and the consolidation of this objective stance to nature leads to our background sense of what the world is like for us today: something to be used and controlled through 'knowledge'. The roots of this go back to Descartes in his sixth discourse (1968: 78): 'knowing the power and the effects of fire, water, air, the stars, the heavens ... we might put them all ... to all the uses for which they are appropriate, and thereby make ourselves, as it were, masters and possessors of nature'. And the consequence of this formulation?

> By excluding values and reducing everything tangible to matter in motion according to mathematically expressible laws, Descartes, among others, helped destroy [an] older notion of the cosmos. His practical philosophy had the effect of displacing people, from a position of immersion and interplay within it, ... and of transporting them to a place beyond it, thus making what then became their 'external world' (Russell, 1914) available to them (or at least to some of them) for their appropriation and use. (Shotter, 1984: 33)

The social world in which Descartes wrote was a world in crisis (Toulmin, 1990). The pragmatic scepticism of the pre-seventeenth-century humanists, such as Erasmus, Montaigne, Rabelais and Bacon, was reflected in their appreciation of the diversity of human lives and societies, which led to tolerance and living with differences. But in the seventeenth century tolerance failed, and people of different beliefs, particularly about religion, took up arms against each other across Europe, prompted by various economic crises. Any sense of certainty one might have unreflectively have had that 'all was well in the world' was being shaken by Christians using force to defend their particular interpretations of God's will. With a plethora of interpretations, how might one decide what was 'true'?

Descartes effectively heralded the modern period, and put in place many of the beliefs that underwrite 'theories of knowledge'. His aim was to provide rational proofs that could underpin beliefs by providing them with a certainty that was neutral among all religious positions (Toulmin, 1990: 81). Descartes' approach enabled a spectacular science, an objective and rational framework in which to investigate and codify nature, to bring it under technological control. According to Toulmin, the modern era fuses the idea of cosmos (the order of nature) with the polis (the order of society) to create a harmonic world – the cosmopolis. The philosophical idea generated from this view is that 'the structure of nature reinforces a rational social order' (ibid.: 68). In a cosmopolis, which is the ideal rational city, the focus is on certainty, objectivity and universal, unified systems of knowledge, and in which education enables all people to become enlightened individuals themselves, amenable to scientific explanation. Being human, then, means we have an individualistic nature, and are an object that can be studied. Thus most people nowadays, in our English-speaking societies, assume, with little need for reflection, that they are unique individuals, with minds located in their heads and containing their powers of reasoning and memory, and certainly have an inner, private self, which can act on the world and exercise its will-power.

It comes, then, as a shock to read in Godfrey Lienhardt's seminal anthropological study of the Dinka people of the southern Sudan that:

> The Dinka have no conception which at all closely corresponds to our popular modern conception of the 'mind' as mediating and, as it were, storing up the experiences of the self. There is for them no such interior entity to appear, on reflection, to stand between the experiencing self at any given moment and what is or has been an exterior influence on the self.   (1961: 149)

With no notion of 'minds', the Dinka have little foundation for thinking of themselves as having 'selves'. Thus, where we might say, 'I recall (to mind) when …; I remember that …; My memory is failing me …; It's somewhere in the back of my mind …', the Dinka conceive of memory in terms of the agency of external sources. Lienhardt notes of a man who called his child 'Khartoum' – a place in which he had been imprisoned – that it is not he who names his child, but that 'it is Khartoum which is regarded as an agent, the subject which acts, and not as with us the remembering mind which recalls the place. The man is the object acted on' (1961: 150). The anthropological literature is replete with examples of the different ways in which humans make sense of themselves and their relation to the world they live in.

There is a postcolonial thread that runs through social constructionist thinking that can be traced through thinkers such as Clifford Geertz, Edward Said and Homi Babha. The gist of this thread is critical and relates to a cultural presumption by western explorers, religious figures and settlers of 'new' lands that highbrow European culture was the standard for individuality against which all other individuals and cultures should be judged. This has particularly been the case in how 'man' (*sic*) has been constructed by philosophers and social scientists. Said (1978) took up this theme when he examined academic and cultural constructions of 'orientals', how people of the Middle East had been 'othered' by occidentals. If there is to be one 'self', where do people from outside 'normal' cultural and academic specifications of 'man' fit? To what extent do such idealized, non-inclusive conceptions of 'self' become norms against which we and others judge ourselves? What personal and social tensions arise from such judgements? This line of questioning and critique has been central to what many have termed the 'culture wars' of the last few decades and points to a whole political dimension of 'self-hood' that can be quite relevant to professional helping. This is also where helpers can become 'reality adjusters', by reinforcing the societal status quo on such matters as where 'selves' fit with respect to social inequities.

One of the great achievements of scholarship and research over the past fifty or so years has been the realization that our occidental way of making sense of 'ourselves' is just one among a myriad of different ways. A hundred years ago, our way was the gold standard. But this privileging of one view over all others cannot be justified. If selves or whatever else humans think they are, for example, are constructed out of cultural resources, then they are quite different from the kinds of objects that are found in nature: the whole exercise of investigating and classifying human nature through the methods of science becomes futile. This conclusion is also reached from a different perspective, a moral one, by the Canadian philosopher Charles Taylor.

Charles Taylor: the construction of moral selves

> The moral world of moderns is significantly different from that of previous civilizations.   (Charles Taylor, 1989: 11)

Taylor has published widely during the past forty years or so, during which time he has been Chichele Professor of Moral Philosophy at Oxford and Professor of Political Science and Philosophy at McGill University. He is currently Professor of Law and Philosophy at Northwestern University. Here we provide a partial sketch of the line of thinking he develops in his book *Sources of the Self: The Making of the Modern Identity* (1989). Taylor's aim is to elucidate the historical changes in philosophical thinking in the west that have led to the set of ideas and discursive resources we now find in our western culture that give us our sense of 'who we are': a sense that is neither inevitable nor universal, but historically constructed. As Taylor points out, his concern is with the history of philosophical ideas and arguments, and thus leaves out of the picture the concomitant changes going on in other spheres. The 'full picture' is much more complex and elusive than anyone can sketch. We will turn to some of these other influences in the remainder of this chapter.

Taylor puts the view that our ways of understanding and articulating our sense of self constitute our 'moral take' on the social worlds we act in. There are three dimensions in what can be termed, in the most general sense, 'moral thought': respect for others; our understanding of what makes a 'good life'; and our notions of 'dignity'. However, these dimensions are not separate orders of thought, but intertwined with each other in complex ways, particularly as ideas pertinent to one dimension change over time and thus reorient ideas in another dimension.

Respect

Taylor identifies three main differences along three 'dimensions' that comprise 'respect'. The first is in terms of 'respect for others'. It is not just that the 'boundary of respect' that we draw has expanded, such that whereas in earlier cultures respect would be parochially circumscribed, in western civilizations we now take all human life to be worthy of respect. Rather, Taylor points out, there has also been a shift, occurring in western traditions in the seventeenth century, from rights as a legal privilege under natural law to rights as 'natural rights' which one possesses 'as of right'. What this does is to reposition the subject from being under the law to a position of having obligations that the subject 'can and ought to act on to put [their rights] into effect' (1989: 11).

> To talk of universal, natural, or human rights is to connect respect for human life with the notion of autonomy. It is to conceive people as active cooperators in establishing and ensuring the respect which is due them.   (ibid.: 12)

'Liberty' is thus constructed as a universal, natural right. Of course, this transition is not complete, and we find conflicts between still being 'under the law' versus having 'natural rights' to exercise our freedom – such as in the case of 'voluntary euthanasia' or abortion, for example. But these tensions only serve to highlight the fundamental change that has occurred. This is, as well, not the only reason why we feel 'autonomous', but a component in a more general cultural sea-change (of which more later).

Second, there has been an increasing importance placed on the avoidance of suffering. Punishment and torture still certainly occur, but not in public, and not without considerable condemnation. The public spectacles of execution, flogging, disembowelling, and burning at the stake, to which parents would bring children for 'entertainment', are mercifully a thing of the past, and we consider those who find such things appealing as perverted. The notion that we should minimize suffering 'is an integral part of what respect means to us today' (ibid.: 13), and so strong that we extend it through codes of humane treatment to animals. We no longer 'see any point in ritually undoing the terrible crime in an equally terrible punishment [because] the whole notion of a cosmic moral order, which gave this restoral its sense, has faded for us' (ibid.: 13). (And, as we will come to in looking at Elias' work below, there has been a concomitant restructuring of our emotional reactions as well.)

The third component Taylor identifies he terms 'the affirmation of ordinary life ... meant roughly to designate the life of production and the family' (ibid.).

While this is a component of our notions of what we should respect, it is also a field of conceptual change that can be considered in its own right.

The meaning of 'the good life'

What Taylor wants to point us to here is a sea-change in western civilization as to what we unreflectively take as our structuring values, what we should be aiming at, what we evaluate our actions against in establishing whether we are being 'good people'. For example, his reading of Aristotle is that 'ordinary life' was a necessary background to the pursuit of the higher goals of 'a good life', a life of contemplation and civic action. Prior to that notion of 'the good life' emerging, we see in the Homeric portrayal of Greek warrior life a different valuation: to be a warrior commanding respect was to strive for a different goal beyond the mundane activities of everyday life, that is, for 'glory' – it is often better to die in the pursuit of glory than live a life of 'shame' at having failed. After Aristotle (and Plato) we find the 'good life' in the Christian west structured around piety and monastic seclusion, a world away from the everyday.

Emerging in the Reformation, however, 'we find a modern, Christian-inspired sense that ordinary life was on the contrary the very centre of the good life. The crucial issue was how it was led, whether worshipfully and in the fear of God or not. But the life of the God-fearing was lived out in marriage and their calling. The previous "higher" forms of life were dethroned, as it were' (ibid.: 13), and replaced by a revaluing of production and the family.

> This sense of the importance of the everyday in human life, along with its corollary about the importance of suffering, colours our whole understanding of what it is truly to respect human life and integrity. Along with the central place given to autonomy, it defines a version of this demand which is peculiar to our civilization, the modern West.   (ibid.: 14)

Dignity

Our dignity is 'our sense of ourselves as commanding [attitudinal] respect' (Taylor, 1989: 15). Dignity is yet another example of the intersubjective foundations of our being.

> The very way we walk, move, gesture, speak is shaped from the earliest moments by our awareness that we appear before others, that we stand in public space, and that this space is potentially one of respect or contempt, of pride or shame. Our style of movement expresses how we see ourselves as enjoying respect or lacking it, as commanding it or failing to do so.   (ibid.: 15)

Our dignity can be

> our power, our sense of dominating public space; or our invulnerability to power, or our self-sufficiency, our life having its own centre; or our being liked and looked to by others, a centre of attention. [Or it may be grounded among one of the other dimensions above, as in the affirmation of everyday life.] For

> example, my sense of myself as a householder, father of a family, holding down
> a job, providing for my dependants ...   (ibid.)

In other cultures and times, dignity might subsume the dimension of 'the meaning of life', as it would appear to in archaic Greek times, where the meaning of one's life was to be a warrior of power and dignity. Doubt as to one's life's meaning is, in such cases, defined by an unquestioned framework, which, while allowing one to question or doubt whether 'I am a good warrior', does not allow the possibility of casting doubt on whether to be a warrior is a worthy, meaningful pursuit. Today, 'frameworks are problematic ... no framework is shared by everyone, can be taken for granted as *the* framework tout court, can sink to the phenomenological status of unquestioned fact' (p. 17), while, at the same time, the possibility is still there for individuals to live within a felt certainty that they are 'right'. For many, however, the quest for meaning might end, as it always could have done, in failure through personal inadequacy, or the twists of fortune. Previously, though, the possibility that there might not be any sensible framework, making the quest for meaning inherently futile, was not a serious matter.

And how is that sense found?

> We find the sense of life through articulating it. And moderns have become
> acutely aware of how much sense being there for us depends on our powers
> of expression. Discovering here depends on, is interwoven with, inventing.
> Finding a sense to life depends on framing meaningful expressions which
> are adequate.   (ibid.: 18)

This is again different from how it was in the past. Luther did not suffer a crisis of meaning. The meaning of his life was clear, and it was from this meaning, prior to his insights about how 'salvation through faith' was possible, that his fear of condemnation arose. His existential predicament was 'quite different from the one where one fears, above all, meaninglessness', which is, Taylor considers, the defining fear of our age (ibid.: 18).

These aspects of 'moral thinking' constitute for us what Taylor terms *frameworks of qualitative distinctions*, 'which provide the background, explicit or implicit, for our moral judgements, intuitions ... To articulate a framework is to explicate what makes sense of our moral responses ... To think, feel, judge within such a framework is to function with the sense that some action, or mode of life, or mode of feeling is incomparably higher than the others which are more readily available to us' (ibid.: 26, 19). It is within these frameworks that our identities are constructed and judged. We take it as basic that 'the human agent exists in a space of questions. And these are the questions to which our framework-definitions are answers' (ibid.: 29).

> The question Who? is asked to place someone as a potential interlocutor in
> a society of interlocutors ... But to be able to answer for oneself is to know
> where one stands, what one wants to answer. And that is why we naturally
> tend to talk of our fundamental orientation in terms of who we are ... And
> this orientation, once attained, defines where you answer from, hence your
> identity.   (ibid.: 29)

Our 'selves', then, are constituted in these orientations to 'the good', so that essentially we define ourselves by where we stand on these matters. Consequently, selves are quite different from the objects which science studies. In the canons of science:

First: *'The object of study is to be taken "absolutely", that is, not in its meaning for us or any other subject, but as it is on its own ("objectively")'* (ibid.: 33). However, we cannot do this for selves, since these are defined in the way that things have significance for us, and 'these things have significance for me, and the issue of my identity is worked out, only through a language of interpretation which I have come to accept as a valid articulation of these issues. To ask what a person is, in abstraction from his or her self interpretations, is to ask a fundamentally misguided question, one to which there couldn't in principle be an answer' (ibid.: 34).

Second: *'The object is what it is independent of any descriptions or interpretations offered of it by any subjects'* (ibid.). But we are not selves in the way we are organisms, in that we don't have selves in the same way as we have organs. 'We are living beings with these organs quite independently of our self-understandings or interpretations … But we are only selves insofar as we move in a certain space of questions, as we seek and find an orientation to the good' (ibid.).

Third: *'The object can in principle be captured in explicit description'* (ibid.). However, a self's interpretations can never be fully explicit: 'we clarify one language with another, which in turn can be further unpacked, and so on' (p. 34), which is Wittgenstein's point. But the essential difference here with respect to scientific objects is that, for selves, 'the language which can never be made fully explicit is part of, internal to, or constitutive of the "object" studied. To study persons is to study beings who only exist in, or are partly constituted by, a certain language' (ibid.: 34–5).

Fourth: *'The object can in principle be described without reference to its surroundings'* (ibid.: 34). But here 'a language only exists and is maintained within a language community … One is a self only among other selves. A self can never be described without reference to those who surround it' (ibid.: 35).

In addition, all these facets of the self, of our identity, have to be

> woven into [our] understanding of [our] live[s] as an unfolding story. But this is to state another basic condition of making sense of ourselves, that we grasp ourselves as a *narrative*. … making sense of one's life as a story is also, like orientation to the good, not an optional extra … our lives exist in this space of questions, which only a coherent narrative can answer.   (ibid.: 47)

Taylor draws heavily from a hermeneutic conception of what it means to be human. It is in this sense that each cultural moment affords a kind of horizon of possibilities for being human. But tied to these possibilities is a very situated sense of what it means to be properly 'oneself' – a set of cultural specifications for how one is to conduct oneself and judge others. Recently, Taylor (2007) returned to some of the themes just discussed to articulate a convergence of cultural and historical developments that have made possible the increasing secularity of western society. Among these developments is the increasing cultural diversity of western society and what this has entailed when it comes to the increased possibilities for self-hood. Ken Gergen (see Chapter 14) has also taken up these themes, writing of a 'saturated self' (1991) in the face of such possibilities.

For helping professionals, what can arise here are questions of what it means to conduct oneself when the cultural possibilities and evaluations are so varied. There are of course cultural limits on 'being oneself' that can, when exceeded, translate to incarceration, hospitalization, or worse (such as in murder and torture). So, too, are there 'rules' of sorts within families as to how far one can go in 'being oneself'. What Taylor's research shows is how the possibilities and evaluations for self are negotiated over time and circumstance. We don't have to look far to see those negotiations continuing in areas of human rights. And, closer to home, families, like that of the former US vice-president Dick Cheney, have had to face discussions about members 'coming out', for example. In helping conversations people can explore the seeming cultural and familial specifications for personhood that inform their sense of who they can be. They of course still would need to negotiate that sense with others.

Civility: Norbert Elias's account of the 'civilizing process'

> The nature of the human mind has to be investigated in the history of the successive forms of its social expression.   (Stuart Hampshire, 1959: 234)

Norbert Elias was born in Breslau in 1897, and died in Amsterdam in 1990. He was an 'academic' from the beginning of his student days at the University of Breslau in 1918, following armed service in the Great War. He began studying medicine and philosophy (under Honigswald), and took some of his philosophy papers in Freiberg and Heidelberg under Jaspers and Husserl. He decided to concentrate on philosophy rather than medicine, and from here on his academic career and publication history was unusual. He completed his D.Phil. in Breslau in 1924. He moved to Heidelberg in 1925, hoping to begin his *Habilitation* under Max Weber's brother, Alfred. Weber agreed, though his commitments were such that he would not commence supervision for 'four to five years'. Elias met and became friendly with Karl Mannheim, and assisted him in his teaching in an unpaid and unofficial capacity.

Mannheim moved to a Chair in Frankfurt in 1929. He offered Elias an assistant's position in exchange for supervision, and Elias moved there in 1930. Because of the political situation Mannheim left Germany in 1933 for a Chair at the London School of Economics. Elias took a trip to Switzerland in an unsuccessful attempt to find an academic position, and then moved to Paris, where, again, he could find no position. In 1935, though speaking little English, he went to London, where he spent the next three years working on a book, *Uber den Prozefs der Zivilization (The Civilizing Process)*. This proved difficult to publish because of the situation in Germany. It was eventually published by Karger in two volumes in 1939. However, when, after the war, Elias was able to meet with the publisher, he found that more copies of the work had been sent out for review than had been sold.

In spite of this, his luck appeared to have turned with the publication of his book, and he was offered a Senior Research Fellowship at LSE. The LSE was evacuated to Cambridge, but Elias was soon interned in Liverpool and on the Isle of Man as an enemy alien, for a period of eight months. After his release he was effectively unemployed until 1954 when he was offered, at the age of 57, a Lectureship in Sociology at Leicester University, where he stayed until he 'retired' in 1962. He then took up a Chair in the University of Ghana, returning to Leicester in 1964, where he maintained an annual teaching contract until 1974. During this period he began writing more steadily again. *The Civilizing Process* was republished in German in 1969, and translated into French in 1973.

He received many offers of guest positions in Holland, beginning in 1969, and was spending so much time there that he left his house in Leicester in 1978 (when the first volume of *The Civilizing Process* was finally published in English) and moved to Bielefeld, where he worked at the Zentrum fur Interdiszipliare Forschung (ZiF), until his return to Amsterdam in 1985. He completed two further books – *Time* and *The Symbol Theory* – and lectured at the Collège de France at the invitation of Pierre Bourdieu, finally dying in his chair at his desk in 1990.

Becoming polite

Norbert Elias's study (1978) of European etiquette manuals dating back over the last 700 years provides the material for his brand of sociological theorizing. His work can be read as revealing that the processes of social interaction have unintended consequences; that they 'create' new ways of being that are only subsequently capable of description (or discoverable); and that the ways of being human that emerge from this unintended process of 'social construction' have an intrinsic ordering to them, which thus acts consequently as a constraint on the order in which we come to 'apprehend' them. It is this temporal aspect of his theorizing that has sometimes led to his views being dismissed as a form of social Darwinism. While his interpretation of the historical process can, at a stretch, be read as a narrative of 'progress', to do so would be to miss his main thrust.

Elias's rationale for interpreting the material he presents rests on two points. First, if a manual explicitly proscribes a form of behaviour, then we may assume that those people to whom the advice is targeted would otherwise unreflectively do the opposite. Second, if over the course of centuries particular advice drops out of these manuals, this does not reflect a mere change in fashion, but that people no longer need to be told about such niceties of behaviour, for they have been 'socialized' not to perform in these ways.

Among other things, Elias establishes the historical course of elaborating western practices for dealing with the assorted accumulations of the material that periodically inhabits the human nasal passages (1978: 143–52). Thirteenth-century advice is basic, and, remember, stating it indicates what 'normal' behaviour was:

> Precept for Gentlemen: When you blow your nose or cough, turn round so nothing falls on the table.

In the early sixteenth century a much more 'refined' mode of clearing your snot was being railed against, and knowledge of a much more modern mode being pre-supposed. From *De civilitate morum puerilium*, by Erasmus, Chapter 1 above:

> To blow your nose on your hat or clothing is rustic, and to do so with the arm or elbow befits a tradesman; nor is it much more polite to use the hand, if you immediately smear the snot on your garment. It is proper to wipe the nostrils with a handkerchief, and to do this while turning away if more honourable people are present.
>
> If anything falls to the ground when blowing the nose with two fingers, it should immediately be trodden away.

If you had attained the level of possessing a handkerchief, you needed to know how and how not to use it. From *Galateo*, by Della Casa (1558):

> Nor is it seemly, after wiping your nose, to spread out your handkerchief and peer into it as if pearls and rubies might have fallen out of your head.

Seventeenth-century advice reveals politeness taken a stage further. Now, the act of blowing your nose with a handkerchief, not just the blowing of it, needs to be controlled. From Courtin, *Nouveau traité de civilité* (1680):

> [At table] to blow your nose openly into your handkerchief, without concealing yourself with your serviette, and to wipe away your sweat with it … one filthy habit fit to make everyone's gorge rise.

In addition, it is apparent that what your audience finds distasteful has changed. Two hundred years earlier, openly blowing your nose into a handkerchief would have been the height of refinement.

At the root of the changes Elias documents in what is considered polite is a hierarchy of actions: blowing the nose; hiding the blowing of it by using a handkerchief; hiding the blowing of it into a handkerchief; and so on. But most importantly, in his view, it is in among these changes that a new subjective state, embarrassment, is being invented. Embarrassment is a self-reflexive emotional state created concomitantly with this developing hierarchy of concealment and prohibition in everyday life: for embarrassment to be realized, a self-censorious ability has to be established. People have to become able to reflect on their own behaviour – that is, on how they act in company – where previously they had not done so. Establishing self-restraint produces a different order of control over one's ways of behaving, as compared to being ordered by an external authority not to act in such a way. There is a shift from pre-reflective to reflective activity, to an exercise of control that foregrounded that there must be something there that was in control: a self, and the discursive resources for framing it, begins to emerge as a part of each person, and as a perspective to be reckoned with in everyday life and in theory.

Over all the activities he considers, there emerges from Elias's study the strong implication that this self-regulating ability was not just lacking in the area of nose-blowing, but that it was unavailable for any activity: people generally did not reflect on what they were doing. Hence, they did not provide the necessary conditions that would enable them to feel embarrassed. In Elias's view, the kind of change in interpersonal behaviour that such advice reflects is not one of fashion; further,

> it does not involve solely changes of 'knowledge' or transformations of 'ideologies', in short, alterations of the content of consciousness, but changes in the whole human make-up, within which ideas and habits of thought are only a single sector.   (Elias, 1982: 284)

These changes reflect a reorganization and transformation of

> the whole personality throughout all its zones, from the steering of the individual by himself at the more flexible level of consciousness and reflection to that at the more automatic and rigid level of drives and affects.   (ibid.: 284)

Elias predicates these changes in personality structure on structural changes in society brought about by the expansion of trade; the diffusion of money; the monopolization of power and physical force by a central 'state'; and the growing stabilization of the central organs of society. In sum, 'as the social fabric grows more intricate, the sociogenic apparatus of individual self-control also becomes more differentiated, more all round and more stable' (ibid.: 234). He offers the following explanation as to why there is this relationship:

> From the earliest period of the history of the Occident to the present, social functions have become more and more differentiated under the pressure of competition. The more differentiated they become, the larger grows the number of functions and thus of people on whom the individual constantly depends in all his actions, from the simplest and most commonplace to the more complex and uncommon. As more and more people must attune their conduct to that of others, the web of actions must be organized more and more strictly and accurately, if each individual action is to fulfil its social function. The individual is compelled to regulate his conduct in an increasingly differentiated, more even and more stable manner.   (ibid.: 232)

Elias considers that it is the relationship between the psychological functions controlling an individual's actions that changes during historical time; that it is

> these relationships within man between the drives and affects controlled and the built-in controlling agencies, whose structure changes in the course of a civilizing process, in accordance with the changing structure of the relationships between individual human beings, in society at large.   (ibid.: 286)

(Note that this formulation is very 'Russian', and could be put in Vygotskian terminology with minimal difficulty: cf. Vygotsky's distinction between the inter- and intra- psychological planes, and his claim that every element in the child's development appears twice, first between people and second within the child. There are again clear resonances with Foucault's conceptualization of 'the gaze'; with Taylor's transition from being under the law to a position of having obligations; with… The links go on in this alternative tradition we are constructing here.)

At the same time there is an increasing modesty being cultured in the mode of dealing with the body in all its facets. For example, the late seventeenth and eighteenth centuries saw the arrival of the two-pronged fork, to be used on one's own plate rather than fingers dipped in the communal bowl; the wearing of night clothes; and the sale of commodes, washbasins, baths and soap. Aries cites many examples from French etiquette books; for instance:

> One should not dress or undress in public when performing one's natural functions, nor wash ostentatiously immediately afterwards, nor draw attention to excrement on the roads, nor get people to smell stinking things.
>   One should avoid offending other people's senses by grinding one's teeth, whistling, gurgling, yawning, keeping one's mouth open or looking in one's handkerchief.   (1973: 371–2)

Such behaviours were all symptomatic of an increased individual restraint, sensitivity to others, and intimacy in personal activities. The nightdress, for example, symbolizes the individual's increasing sensitivity towards the body. Shame, embarrassment and modesty became attached to behaviours that had previously been free of such feelings. The emergence of manners, defined by a set of clearly differentiated patterns of external behaviour, mark a development in the growth of the psychological processes of individuality.

One point that should be coming through from our examination of Elias's view of social history is that humans construct moral contexts that shape not only their moral conduct, but their thinking and values as well. We know this in looking at political constitutions, institutional life (e.g., the military) and legal systems, but Elias's research points to something more implicit and less codified. A simple codeword for what we are talking about is 'appropriateness', but tracing its origins, manifestations and influences – as they relate to any thought or action – can be hard. Such appropriatenesses are expectations of self and others to which we become 'accustomed'. As a therapist, I (Tom) repeatedly hear people recounting accustomed thoughts and actions as if these were as self-evident as gravity. So I can feel like a Martian anthropologist when I ask about them, but often very interesting conversations ensue about how things came to be thought about or acted on 'just so'.

Interaction, discourse and cognition

How do we relate these changes in western psychological structure to discourse? Elias's argument is subtle. His essential point is that our personalities, our conceptions of ourselves and others, our emotional experiences and our views of the world are explicated from phenomena whose existence is created beyond us in our social worlds. Human beings and their conceptual systems are explicit renderings into particular forms of individuals with subjectivities, identities and minds – choose your framework – fabricated from the implications of their social discourses. This is the social constructionist's credo.

First: we need to remember that the changes in conduct that Elias charts are occurring against a background of a diversifying society. Travel was becoming easier, leading to more and different people meeting each other. Cities were emerging in a contrastive role to the countryside, resulting in trade and trade specialization, the establishment of a merchant class, and so on. In general, people were becoming less socially homogeneous, roles were becoming specialized, and so people were sharing less common knowledge among themselves; they had fewer common presuppositions. This had obvious repercussions on the process of communication between fellows. Essentially, it became much harder to make oneself understood.

Second: we need to think about the consequences of these changes with respect to the 'knowledges' a person would need in order to act effectively in such a changing world. Because it was much more difficult to get a message across to another, communication failure could occur much more frequently, making the individual actually aware of the communication process itself. Further, the diversity of interaction would provide the individual with many more perspectives on the presentation of his or her self.

Third: in response to the increasing meetings of strangers, languages necessarily began to code new concepts and to be used more explicitly. On the one hand, the loss of presuppositionality in everyday discourse will force an increasingly elaborated and explicit linguistic coding of communication: people would have been required to make explicit to strangers information they had previously left implicit in their discussions within their circumscribed milieu of peers. On the other hand, an increasingly complex society can create all sorts of new situations and experiences among the people whose actions bring it into being: these may come to be expressed in language. Hence, information concerning the presentation of the self would have been available directly to an individual. A society with differentiated roles might well force an awareness upon an individual of the aspects of individuality that those roles are simultaneously constructing. It may eventually provide linguistic concepts for rendering these explicitly. The main point here is that the socially constructed facets of personality will increase, through the explicit realization in discourse, of the number of different perspectives an individual can formulate of his or her self, while at the same time increasing the individual's ability to transcend his or her presupposed, unreflective, non-meta-awareness of his or her self through a richer fabric of communication and conceptual resource.

Fourth: Luria and Yudovich have noted that words have a profound effect on individual psychological functioning:

> When he acquires a word, which isolates a particular thing and serves as a signal to a particular action, the child, as he carries out an adult's verbal instruction, is subordinated to this word ... By subordinating himself to the adult's verbal orders the child acquires a system of these verbal instructions and gradually begins to utilize them for the regulation of his own behaviour.   (Luria and Yudovich, 1971: 13–14)

In this view, through the medium of language, one of the major transitions noted by Elias – from external control of behaviour by threat of punishment to internal control via the self-reflexive censors of shame and guilt – can be effected; and through these particularly social forms of emotional cognition 'people become ... sensitive to distinctions which previously scarcely entered consciousness' (Elias, 1982: 298).

Post-Wittgenstein, we have come to realize that selves are embedded in 'forms of life', and that we use the resources of our discourse communities – the 'language games' of our communities – in a double-edged way. These resources give us the words to give a form to these feelings, to describe our experience, at the same time as they construct that which we are describing. There is, in this view, no one timeless, true and essential self waiting to be discovered behind our multifarious ways of doing and acting and talking. Selves are not there, waiting to be found, but are made out of a set of practices, which simultaneously serve to supply the words that we consequently use to flesh out what has been made. Selves are contingent on such resources, not universally prior to them. And, as Taylor has shown, our selves are very much tied up with what we feel to be 'good': the goals that structure our conduct.

Much of our thrust in looking at thinkers such as Taylor and Elias has been to consider thought, action, propriety, etc., as knowledges and practices situated in history and culture. This thrust runs counter to the modern narrative (Toulmin, 1990) about there being an increasing convergence on what should pass as knowledge and civilized behaviour. Situated knowledges and social practices suggest something quite different. There is diversity to deal with as well as the sense that our thinking and action owes something to 'where one is coming from'. But, as I (Tom) type in the word 'knowledges' to denote where Taylor, Elias and many of our thinkers are coming from, my spellchecker urges me, with a squiggly red line, to drop the 's'. This is a small example of how we reflexively create social realities that can open or constrain our possibilities for thought and action. The different implications following from these words can be huge: the singular 'knowledge' reflecting the idea that there is one overall body of knowledge versus the idea that there are discrete 'knowledges' particular to people in different cultures and eras. Keep these implications in mind as we consider further other aspects of constructing the human world that have gone on to be profoundly influential in western society. Then, bearing in mind our earlier postcolonial concerns, we might usefully ponder on how and why these may not be globally shared.

Other indicators

Representing individuality

The reflexive self that was emerging during the time period studied by Elias is evident across a number of separate indices, and demonstrates an increased valuing of individuality in western European cultures. English coinage, for example, had a tradition of picturing the king on one side. But prior to the mid-1100s that image was more a stock portrayal than a recognizable likeness. The same is true of English funerary monuments: they move from stock effigies in the early 1500s that portray, through heraldic symbols, the status of the dead person and their family, to recognizable portrayals of the deceased in the 1600s, indicating it is the individual that is now more important (see Stone, 1979). The same occurs in art around this time. Nicholas Hilliard is credited with producing the first English self-portrait in 1577, and Thomas Whythorne with writing the first English autobiography a year earlier, in 1576. Over two hundred English autobiographies have survived from before 1700, with only twelve of these dating from before 1640. It was only late in the seventeenth century that these shift from the religious reflections and agonies of various Puritan non-conformists to the secular and romantic concerns of the writer. Diaries, too, begin to appear around this time, again firstly concerned with inner Puritan struggles and only slowly with secular personal experience. Examples taken from Pollock (1983: 74–7) include:

> I did write down these mercies of God.   (Nehemiah Wallington, 1598–1658)

Self-analysis and improvement seem to be the reasons for the later texts:

> [This diary] is to be in some sort a register of my life, studies and opinions.   (Benjamin Newton, 1762–1830)

> To have some account of my thoughts, manners, acquaintences and actions … is the reason that induces me to keep a Journal – a Journal in which I must confess my every thought – must open my whole heart.   (Fanny Burney, 1752–1840)

Eighteenth century diaries appear more intimate, introspective and analytic than the earlier texts. The bawdy diaries of Samuel Pepys and later of James Boswell reveal not only their behaviour, but also their emotions and morals. Diaries show a growing trend towards introspection and self-privatization:

> My diary is of such a nature that I should not like to trust it to anyone but my other self.   (William Steadman, 1764–1837)

Changes in address between husband and wife provide some evidence for the emergence of new, interpersonal sentimentality in marital relations. The seventeenth-century mode of address, Sir or Madam, was slowly replaced by the use of Christian names, nicknames and 'pet' names. In 1707, for example, Richard Steele, after his marriage, addressed his wife as Madam, but soon slid into 'Dear Creature', 'My Loved Creature', and later was writing to her as 'Dear Prue'. In 1732, while Catherine Banks closed her letters to her husband with 'I am dear Mr Banks your most affectionate C. Banks', in 1735 her husband was writing to her six days a week as 'Dear Kitty' (Stone, 1979: 220). By the eighteenth century, much of the formality had been abandoned, and a kind of hermetic language was used to stress the solidarity and intimacy of family members as a unit apart from other people. Thomas Gisbourne in 1797 noted: 'the stiffness, the proud and artificial reserves which in former ages infected even the intercourse of private lives are happily discarded.' (Stone, 1979: 221). Not just 'pet' names, but pets too. Lapdogs appear on the scene in the early 1700s, indicating the beginnings of a non-economic but sentimental relationship between, in this case, English women and dogs.

Privacy

One of the most significant changes during this period was a movement from an open and public form of life to a more private and personal mode of living, both in terms of attitude to individual bodily functions and to family privacy (Sennett, 1977). The density of social life in the fifteenth and sixteenth centuries made privacy impossible (Laslett, 1972). Families lived in suites of rooms. Members of the household and servants often had to walk through each other's rooms to get to their own. The use of the corridor in house architecture, in the seventeenth century, was a major contribution to physical privacy. That this development took so long is surprising, the idea of the corridor being present in monasteries, Roman times and outside in the 'street'.

Corridors led to a reorganization of the house. It became more subdivided and more specialized in function. Sleeping accommodation was moved upstairs to the 'bedroom' and the ground floor became the living quarters where the family would eat, cook, receive visitors, etc. Interestingly, similar sub-compartmentalization was emerging in the design of furniture. Chests of drawers replaced the simple chest for clothes and linen, dressing tables with mirrors and wardrobes were developed (Cowie, 1973). It may be stretching a point, but this architectural subdivision and specialization neatly parallels changes that were occurring in the structure of the family: a decrease in kin ties and growth in the role and function of the immediate family members. Architectural changes had, albeit indirectly, important consequences for the freedom of servants, who were either moved out of the house, or offered wages instead of bed and board. This enabled a more private family life 'with some escape from the prying eyes and ears of the ubiquitous domestic servants who were a necessary evil in every middle- and upper-class household' (Stone 1979: 169).

Music, gardening and leisure

Changes in music and gardening in the time period we have been discussing are also instructive. The cultivation of plants has a long history. But gardening in England and France is more recent, beginning around 1600. By 'gardening' we mean the non-economic cultivation of plants for the purposes of 'sensual delight'. Garden designs began with a formal structure, culminating in that of the Palace of Versailles. Gardens thus index the imposition of reason upon Nature in a very clear way. But by the mid-eighteenth century another tactic has crept in. Nature is still subject to reason, but rather than strive to make nature visibly conform to the will, the aim now, with gardeners such as Capability Brown, was to make nature conform better to Nature, to make it more pleasing on the eye in the informal, natural and romantic senses. The indication is that the relation between 'the self' and its environment is changing.

Within the same time frame, similar changes are apparent in the move from the formally constructed music of J. S. Bach to the more fluid forms that move through Haydn to Mozart and Beethoven. Bach imposes mathematical structure on sound, while Beethoven's Pastoral Symphony is only pastoral in the sense that gardening had produced a more 'pastoral-than-pastoral' landscape for it to be evocative of, and enable us to relate emotionally with, such a 'super'-natural, yet sanitized of danger, landscape. With both gardening and music we can detect a shift that reflects a way of being a self. We begin with an imposition of reason on nature and sound; we move to an exploration of the properties of those formalisms to realize a new imposition, one that strives to be 'natural' by another high exercise of constraint. In the first cases, it is the imposition of an imagination that is just creating and becoming susceptible to reason; in the second, the imposition of an imagination fostered on the products of rationality. It is not, we now understand, that the self remained constant throughout these changes in human activity, that some constant motivation and vision was just 'playing new games'. Rather, our ideas of 'how we are' were changing too, and these ideas were more articulated – they presented us with more diverse resources for self-making.

Again, yet more resources became available for such ends with the invention of tourism. Here, as with gardening and having pets, we see a de-economization of yet another activity: travel. People have travelled for aeons, for reasons ranging from our origins as hunter-gatherers to some becoming empire-builders. However, it was not until the early 1700s that we find the institution of tourism with the start of the Grand Tour. Tourism is purely for the delight of the self. But while it may have trivial motivations, it can have serious consequences: one meets 'others' for purposes no longer those of actively exploiting them, and thus has to begin to find ways of dealing with them and the reflections of difference they make apparent to the tourist. This is Elias's point above, but played out in an epoch motivated by new sensibilities.

We could continue the above narrative into the present: the consequences of industrialization; empire-building; the impact of the Great War; the rise of nationalism; the economic effects of the Depression; racism; drugs, sex and rock and roll; monetarism; consumerism; globalization, etc. Historical change always provides those shifts of social organization that allow new social ecologies to emerge in which identities can be constructed and reconstructed. The dynamics of these new sensibilities, however, have an added dimension that is embedded in the characteristics of the discourses that enable and constrain the elaboration of social life as new 'spaces' for the structuring of subjectivities become available. It is this dimension that we turn to in the next chapter: the nexus of power and knowledge as conceptualized by the French philosopher Michel Foucault.

12 Michel Foucault and his challenges

Unlike Vico – with whom we started our narrative, and whose work is almost unheard of by contemporary social scientists – everyone has heard of Foucault. One of Foucault's earlier works, *Les Mots et les choses: Une archéologie des sciences humaines* (1966; English translation by Alan Sheridan, as *The Order of Things*, 1970) was an instant best-seller in France, which might be thought odd given it makes no concessions to a lay readership. However, as his translator Sheridan points out, Lacan's work, *Écrits* (also 1966, also translated by Sheridan, 1977), which is perhaps one of the most impenetrable of books on the human condition, similarly attained best-seller status. Both books are most likely children of their time – in much the same way as Stephen Hawking's *A Brief History of Time* was to the late 1980s: a book as a commodity that one, or one's coffee table, needed to be seen with. That Foucault's work was attacked by France's premier intellectual, Jean-Paul Sartre, also made for good advertising copy.

Foucault's work has been enormously influential in recent social science and humanities scholarship. Foucault is, undoubtedly, a difficult though evocative read, and consequently there has been a massive literature of commentary and introduction aimed at making his work more accessible. While a great deal of this literature is itself also difficult to penetrate, its existence narrows our task here more to Foucault's impact on the general project of social constructionism than to a summary of his work (not that such a summary would be possible: his work is in many ways a moving target).

There are two main formative strands to Foucault's work: personal and academic. He was born in Poitiers in 1926 and had a varied school history of brilliance and failure. At the end of World War II he qualified in fourth place in the national competition for entry into the École Normale Supérieure, where he gained degrees in both psychology and philosophy. However, he also suffered from acute depression during this time, requiring psychiatric treatment, and also dealt with the difficulties of recognizing and accepting his homosexuality. Consequently, two main strands of Foucault's work, on the 'history of psychiatric practice' in its broad sense, and the historical manifestations and transformations of sexuality, can be seen to have a clear personal motivation. His first book *Maladie mentale et personnalité* (Paris: PUF, 1954) was reissued as *Maladie mentale et psychologie* in 1962; his last works are the uncompleted series of volumes on *The History of Sexuality* (1976–84). In addition, during his formative academic years, Foucault voluntarily subjected himself to periods of exile from France – in

Sweden, Poland and Germany – and subsequently in Tunisia between 1965 and 1968. These exiles were linked to the comings and goings of his partners, and where one initial reason for moving to Sweden was a desire to find a more tolerant and liberal atmosphere, 'the main lesson he drew from his experience was that a certain degree of freedom could have as many repressive effects as a directly repressive society' (Macey, 1993: 50).

Academically, a component of Foucault's work can be taken as a reaction to three dominant strands of the French intellectual landscape of the 1950s: Marxism, phenomenology and structuralism. One of Foucault's intentions is to contextualize and historicize different kinds of truth, knowledge, rationality and reason as they are embedded within the cultural fabric in which they have their existence. He is not concerned with elucidating fundamental, timeless truths. This, then, marks his departure from Marxism, and an opposition to the view that the course of history has an inevitability to it. Similarly, he breaks with a great deal of phenomenology, given the emphasis there on the ability of its methodology to reveal absolute and essential truths that provide the bedrock of experience. Heidegger, however, is somewhat redeemed for Foucault through his emphasis on the social and cultural contexts in which truth and meaning are produced.

His retreat from structuralism is less clear-cut. The notion from de Saussure (see Chapter 13) that words and events get their meaning in relation to other words and events and are not meaningful 'in themselves' has a key role in Foucault's work (leading some to have identified Foucault as a structuralist). In addition, this point ties in with the Heideggerian insight that people are less free than they might imagine in their thinking and acting, because both are produced by the social, political and cultural structures in which, and through which, people live. But while a structuralist approach may explain what the rules of these systems are, it offers no account of peoples' activities – why the rules are used in one way rather than another.

An important influence, in a more positive than reactive sense, was his discovery of the work of Nietzsche (during his time in Sweden). The attraction was to Nietzsche's view of history not as a process that unfolds in a rational, progressive way, developing ever higher forms of reason, but through the exercise of power. Such power was seen to be exercised as the will of one group is imposed over that of another group: this exercise of 'the will' being the major factor determining – somewhat arbitrarily – historical change. Yet this important anti-Enlightenment sentiment does not mean Foucault regarded his work as being in opposition to many facets of the Enlightenment project. His view was that the Enlightenment project should not be identified with taking

> a theory, a doctrine, nor even a permanent body of knowledge that is accumulating; it must be conceived as an attitude, an ethos … in which the critique of what we are is at one and the same time the historical analysis of the limits imposed on us and an experiment with the possibility of going beyond them.   (Foucault, 1997: 319)

There are four main ways in which we see Foucault's thought as important. The first is in his analyses of the history of human practices in the west, whereby distinctions are made and legitimized, and so gain the values of 'right' and 'wrong', 'normal' and 'abnormal', for example, within their particular cultural eras. The second is in the ways in which he glimpsed how these distinctions go further than just grounding norms for changing etiquettes and norms within society, but actually enter into the construction of what we take it to be human, and how we handle our 'selves' in differently structured everyday ways of life. The third is an extension of this that Foucault undertakes in his later work on sexuality and ethics, concerning the means by which we adopt particular cultural ideas and practices to govern ourselves 'appropriately'. The fourth is in the dialectical nature of many of his arguments and the way these illuminate the 'fixing' of words so that, without thinking much about it, people use them in the way that does not in fact label 'pre-existing social facts' that have been laboriously discovered, but simultaneously 'creates those facts' and locates them (by sleight of mind) as if they were discoveries of the 'way things really are'.

Distinctions and their consequences

A central notion in Foucault's work is that of 'discourse', which we may loosely translate as the worldview of a culture as it is established in practice at a particular time and place. Discourses tend to have an internal consistency, and even where certain ideas are not expressed in them, these principles of consistency provide 'spaces' as to what might 'legitimately' be subsequently expressed, and, by implication, what might not be expressed. 'Not expressing' something has two facets. First, the set of ideas cohering in a discourse make some stances toward the world much harder to formulate. Second, the way of formulating the world in a particular discourse acts to make some things appear to be 'the natural way that things are', because there is a consistency among them that intuitively makes (unreflective) sense to those who speak through it. In addition, deviations from what is thus constituted as acceptable lead to conflict between those who have positions of power within the culture and those that do not: to disagree with the requirements of being loyal to a dictator likely has unfortunate consequences. This is one aspect of Foucault's well-known conflation of knowledge with power, which we will return to further below.

Foucault's purpose in *The Order of Things* is to show how arbitrary are many of the classifications people use, as opposed to their implicit, unreflective belief that their systems of classifying the world in order to talk about it are both 'true' and 'natural' (that discourses have this property is another aspect of his equation of knowledge/power: discourses have the power to have us think what they state are true and natural characterizations of the 'way things are'). Foucault makes his point (along with another two that easily fall out of this) very succinctly in beginning the book with an example taken from a Chinese encyclopaedia as to how the animal kingdom should be categorized:

> (a) belonging to the Emperor, (b) embalmed, (c) tame, (d) suckling pigs, (e) sirens, (f) fabulous, (g) stray dogs, (h) included in the present classification, (i) frenzied, (j) innumerable, (k) drawn with a very fine camelhair brush, (l) *et cetera*, (m) having just broken the water pitcher, (n) that from a long way off look like flies. (Foucault, 1970: xv)

To us, this system is absurd, in that it does not reflect the given, biological system that we use, following Linnaeus: invertebrates/vertebrates; warm-blooded/cold-blooded; etc. But, and here is his second point, this Chinese system only looks absurd to us from our point of view within a different discursive regime. That is, how we analyse one discourse can only be performed from a standpoint within another discourse, and the discourse of objectivity is just that: another discourse. From here, then, we do not have any guarantees that can reveal any transcendent truths about the world: truth has its existence within discourses and the practices and understandings produced by and through them. Truth, in human affairs, is historically and culturally situated in practical activities, not abstractly transcendental and existing outside these practices.

The third point that falls out here is that, in classifying animals as the Chinese did, each animal becomes subjected to the classification system: it becomes an object specified under it. Ergo, the same is the case for people: they become objects within any discursive system of classification, objects of a certain kind. This is a point at which Foucault often seems difficult to newcomers, because he refers to this process of objectification as one of 'subjectification' – the process whereby a person becomes the subject of the power of the discursive system they are defined by. This power does more than dominate or coerce people into acting in certain ways: it also has a constructive side, in that in being *subjected* to a discourse one is simultaneously *created* as a person of a certain sort, a subject within the modern state, for example. Foucault's main area of interest, then, is to reveal the history of the different ways in which western cultures have acted to make people into 'fit' subjects as well as subjects who fit (Foucault, 1978). Foucault identifies three 'modes of objectification', or social-discursive principles, to account for how individuals become subjects: dividing practices; scientific classification; and subjectification itself.

Dividing practices

Dividing practices are introduced in Foucault's early work (e.g., *Madness and Civilization*, 1965) and more fully developed later in *Discipline and Punish* (1977). A dividing practice is at once both social and spatial: certain members of a society are judged as having undesirable characteristics; and are then often physically excluded from mainstream society. A contemporary example is one that I (Andy) became aware of on the first occasion I lived outside Britain for an extended period of time, in Spain in the early 1980s. It had been common where and when I grew up to see men, practically on every street, who were amputees, former soldiers who were injured during their service in the First World War. As I grew older, there were fewer of them, as they died from natural causes. Living in Spain brought this change into focus, since here were these men again, victims of the Spanish Civil War. In addition, there was another group of people on the streets whom I hadn't experienced in my childhood: people who were variously mentally handicapped and even insane. With my ingrained colonial superiority I assumed that this was something to do with genetics, this being a quite isolated, rural community. There was a deal of embarrassment when I discovered how wrong I was: there were neither more nor less people like this where I grew up, but in Britain they were excluded from everyday life, and shut away from view in special institutions. British people treated this group of its population very differently from the Spanish: Britain had a 'dividing practice' that perceived such people as a threat to the community, and so 'put them away' – for care and treatment, of course. Britain had not always had such a practice: the 'village idiot' having an accepted role within earlier British society, and an important one when played out by a court jester.

Concomitant with the changes brought about by what Elias (see Chapter 11) termed 'the civilizing process', the consequences as to what western societies did after dividing off certain groups changed over time. Groups were first ignored, the prime case being lepers, and later the mad. Second, they could be punished, generally bodily through torture. Third, they could be treated or reformed, with the emphasis moving away from torture to rearranging the 'soft fibres of the brain' (Foucault, 1977: 130). Alongside the development of the state, crime moved away from being an act that affected an individual or group to one where the criminal was legally defined as being against the entire social realm, an act that created the expectations as to how one should behave. As a result, in Foucault's view, around the start of the seventeenth century the social apparatus became such that prevention became better than cure. Discipline shifted to an unconscious form of training, in which the role of an external agency in controlling the body became internalized as a subject able to discipline the activities of his/her own body, though still with the social assistance of the 'gaze' of others, which normalizes or sanctions some activities rather than others: 'each gaze would form a part of the overall functioning of power' (Foucault, 1977: 171). In an important passage, Foucault crystallizes a number of his insights:

> Thus discipline produces subjected and practised bodies, 'docile' bodies. Discipline increases the forces of the body (in economic terms of utility) and diminishes these same forces (in political terms of obedience). In short, it dissociates power from the body; on the one hand, it turns it into an 'aptitude', a 'capacity', which it seeks to increase; on the other hand, it reverses the course of the energy, the power that might result from it, and turns it into a relation of strict subjection.   (Foucault, 1977: 138)

The important point here is the general one: that consequences follow from particular dividing practices (there is dispute as to whether the specific historical data drawn on by Foucault in reaching his conclusions are particularly accurate; see, for example, Scull, 2007).

Scientific classification

Foucault's claim is that many of the technologies emerging during the Enlightenment became recruited to the justificatory practices of classification. What was previously regarded as 'normal' by either intuition or an appeal to religious dogma could now be rested on 'reason': the person becomes subjected to a scientific documentation that defines them as normal, or not. People can now be rigorously examined, and their status documented, transformed into 'file selves' (Harré, Chapter 15). It is not just natural science that is a standard here: 'clocking on' to work constitutes part of being the 'normal employee', or, as Foucault writes, the 'subject who labours', and is another example of a socially produced specification (Foucault, 1978). It is these consequences of the scientific approach when applied to people that has led to Foucault's reputation as being anti-Enlightenment: reason is a double-edged sword.

How helping professionals apply the social science of their day was a concern of Foucault (2006), a concern taken up with a particular critical interest in the 'psy complex' research of health sociologist Nikolas Rose (1985, 1989, 1996). Seen one way, Rose's research joins with concerns of radical psychiatrists such as Szasz and Laing to highlight the role that mental health workers play in 'helping' clients adapt to 'reality', however unjust such a reality might be. Rose points out, in particular, that psychologists, through their normative approach to evaluating and 'helping' individuals, become de facto arbiters and promulgators of the societal status quo. They articulate a conception of psychological normality, develop corresponding evaluative tools and helping practices consistent with that conception, and offer the lay public expert forms of knowledge they can appropriate for self-governance – to guide their efforts to be psychologically normal. Many find this a heavy-handed critique, but Foucault and Rose have been concerned with how psychiatric and psychological knowledge and practice becomes intertwined with broader notions of governance. As human problems become translated into expert diagnoses and conceptions of normalcy, which different therapeutic practices can address, an extension of this approach is taken up as individuals use these ideas and practices on themselves. In a related fashion, critical psychologist and discourse analyst Ian Parker has taken a deconstructive approach to mainstream psychological knowledge and practice, publishing or contributing to a series of edited volumes (Parker and Shotter, 1990; Parker et al., 1996; Parker, 1999). The gist of Parker's scholarship on these themes has been to deconstruct the mainstream knowledge and discourses of psychology, to historicize them, and to make evident how particular knowledges and practices crowded out others.

Cumulatively, what emerge from Foucault's writing and lectures on psychiatry, and are extended by Rose and Parker, are important observations and concerns about the generally unquestioned origins and applications of psychiatric and psychological knowledge. One of Foucault's fascinations was with how particular cultural concerns or virtues came to be articulated into apparatuses of power, where 'experts' developed and used knowledge in ways that specified and produced certain social ways of being. Understandably, the lay public does not want to be shut out of such expert power, so they take up such knowledges and practices to use on themselves, as in the case of clients in therapy, self-identifying according to DSM diagnoses, and using self-management strategies found in the self-help literature. The 'psy complex' refers to dominant psychological knowledge, with its associated cultural and self-applications.

Subjectification

Foucault's third 'mode of objectification' is one in which the self itself acts to turn itself into a subject, rather than suffering passively at the behest of external impositions. We come to 'police' ourselves and our bodies, as Elias (see Chapter 11) also points out. We become subject to a new form of discipline, one which works through us because of our necessary buy-in to the social-discursive resources that constitute our identities. 'Identities', in this sense, refers to how we use such resources to 'self'-identify. A mild version of this can come with feeling obliged to meet the seeming exigencies of cultural trends or peer pressures. Subjectification, as an exercise of power, is always, in theory, open to resistance, but not always in practice. Two things are required for effective resistance: to be able to formulate an alternative – to essay a counter-culture – and to have the courage to act.

The first – essaying a counter-culture – can be illustrated in the context of the work of narrative therapists (particularly Michael White and David Epston, 1990) with anorexics, through the process they describe as 'externalizing conversations' (e.g. White and Epston, 1990). In some senses, anorexia can be regarded as an act of policing the body to reach rather over-inflated, but culturally supported, ideals of what it is to be good. How might the effects of anorexia be resisted? This is a very difficult task when the discursive regime in which anorexia is manifested identifies and conceptually imprisons the person who has it as inherently ill, the defective source of their own condition: people 'are' anorexic; they 'have' anorexia; there is something wrong with them. Externalization seeks to drive a wedge between the person and the problem, so that the person can begin to mobilize their own counter-cultural discursive resources against the ways in which societal discourses have positioned them, and led to their overly disciplining their bodies into 'docility'. It takes a great deal of courage to resist a subjugating discourse (see below), but it also takes a great deal of courage to starve oneself, often to the point of death. What is needed is for that courage to be recruited to the task of resistance, but this is nigh impossible when the problem is identified with the person. If, though, a wedge is driven between the person and the problem, then this becomes possible. 'Externalizing' is one way of achieving this.

White and Epston (1990: 38) write:

> Externalizing is an approach to therapy that encourages persons to objectify and, at times, to personify the problem that they experience as oppressive. In this process, the problem becomes a separate entity and is external to the person or relationship that was ascribed as the problem. Those problems that are considered to be inherent, as well as those relatively fixed qualities that are attributed to persons and to relationships, are rendered less fixed and less restricting.

The intent in externalizing a person's way of understanding their situation, the 'problem discourse' they are subjected to, is to separate the person from the problem and/or the constraints that work to maintain for them the dominant discourse or stories about their problem. The problem is located outside the person or relationship that has been objectified, identified and constructed as the source of the problem by the prevailing discursive regimes that specify it as possible to 'be that way': the problem itself is objectified and given a name (White and Epston, 1990). In seeking to formulate a new relation with the problem, the practice of externalization can act to free people from the subjugation of subjugating and totalizing descriptions. In addition, emphasizing the political dimension of the problem helps weaken the hold of the dominant scientific story being used to categorize who the person is, and how this person should conduct his or her life. Change becomes possible through the construction and deployment of a new discursive field.

There are less lethal ways in which some people can survive total subjugation to the gaze of dominant normative practices. One of these has been captured by Garfinkel (see Chapter 10) in his formulation of the practice of 'passing' (1967: 116–85) in his case study of Agnes, a 19-year-old woman who had been born and raised as a male. Agnes at 19 looked like a woman, lived her life as a woman, but also possessed fully developed male genitalia. Because, as Garfinkel points out, our society 'prohibits wilful or random movement from one sex status to another' (ibid.: 125), Agnes, to live as a woman, had to employ a range of strategies so as to be able to 'pass' scrutiny: to not get 'caught out'. The details of these need not concern us here: Garfinkel's conclusion is that 'normally sexed persons are cultural events' (ibid.: 181).

This is a conclusion also reached by Foucault in his studies of *The History of Sexuality* (1978–86), in which he traces where our recent 'restrained, mute, and hypocritical sexuality' (1986: 3) has come from. 'Normal' sex is defined in discursive regimes, and legislated by society's legal system. Why, today, is sexual intercourse regarded as the highest expression of intimacy between two people of different sexes? Why is orgasm via penetration 'right', but via masturbation, cunnilingus or fellatio 'wrong', while if achieved through sodomy illegal and depraved? Why must you be 16, or 18, or whatever, for intercourse to be legal? As with Garfinkel's case study of Alice, Foucault's investigation is inherently illuminating. We will not dwell on its details here, but will rather use this work to touch on the second requirement for possibly resisting normative discursive regimes: courage. We will explore 'courage' in the context of Foucault's conclusions about the 'normalization' of sexual relations, which are independently summarized in Garfinkel's already noted conclusion that 'normally sexed persons are cultural events', that is, a discursive category that brings with it all the constitutive and subjugative aspects of dividing practices.

A central component of the twentieth-century discursive regime framing homosexuality was 'the closet'. Being 'in the closet' would be a tough place to be, let alone 'come out' from. To be homosexual was to be defined as 'abnormal' (and worse, under early versions of the DSM scales one would also be psychiatrically disturbed). Being in the closet demanded two things of people. The first was to be able to deal with feelings of guilt and self-loathing, even in private, if one suspected, even for a moment, that one might be homosexual: being abnormal, having 'sinful thoughts', is a tough place to be. The second was to be very careful not to be found out, requiring the development of good skills at what Garfinkel termed 'passing', so as to escape detection and explicit, sanctioned opprobrium and possibly prosecution. To have the courage to come out of the closet would be almost as bad in its consequences as declaring oneself a paid-up spy for the KGB if one worked in America (or just admitting to having communist sympathies in the era of McCarthyism): a 'stupid' move, but one that some nevertheless made. As the social climate changed after the 1960s, the discourse about being abnormal was provided with an alternative, making 'coming out' still a courageous act, but involving a different sort of courage, one now open to an increasing restructuring within a newly available discursive realm. Again, 'the closet' is no longer 'a closet': one 'comes out' in a different sense. The major point here, then, is that discursive practices construct associated norms of practice, including language use, that their 'users' are under an obligation to hold themselves and each other to: 'holding to' implies recrimination should one step discursively 'out of bounds'. A secondary point, one picked up and elaborated subsequently by Harré (see Chapter 15), is that even so-called 'biological propensities' such as emotional feelings are given different modes of expression in different 'language games'.

This realization leads to the third Foucauldian point we want to highlight here: that individual subjectivity becomes the site at which the power/ knowledge couplet is realized and made active; it produces that site and is embodied at that site, and so, in a sense, produces itself. This insight adds a twist to the way we might nowadays conceptualize what Vico termed the 'providence' active in human affairs (see Chapter 2). People create new possibilities and at the same time become victims of their creations: they are active in creating the cultural and discursive parameters of their self-subjugation. What Foucault accomplishes here is conceptually important. Power and knowledge are not reified abstractly in his account, as in other sociological accounts of a more modernist flavour: power/ knowledge is made real, at the nexus of human living as realized through the available discursive resources through which subjectivity is individually constructed as a social activity. Selves are manufactured, sedimented through with the words that enable them to reproduce themselves: there is not an essential self to discover, but a site of living subjectivity to be socially realized, or constructed.

Foucault's discursive self

> The task of testing oneself, examining oneself, monitoring oneself in a series of clearly defined exercises, makes the question of truth – the truth concerning what one is, what one does, and what one is capable of doing central to the formation of the ethical subject.   (Foucault, 1986: 58)

> The care of myself must therefore be such that it also provides me with the art ... which will enable me to govern others well.   (Foucault, 2005: 51)

It took a trip to Berkeley, California, in the mid-1970s for Foucault to see that his concerns about cultural discourses and power were playing out in the so-called sexual revolution of the times. His historically oriented elucidation of the ways of dealing with madness had a personal component to them, and now his work was again to become more personal in another context. Foucault was a gay man, Berkeley offered a much different sexual context from the repressive environment he associated with France, and sexuality offered a window on how *selves* were culturally constructed. In his words, 'How does a man enjoy his pleasure "as one ought"?' (1985: 53).

For humanists and lovers of the notion of a 'true' and autonomous self, Foucault's conclusions are bleak, even counter-intuitive. Sure, people have freedom to express themselves – but within discursive constraints. They can even pass for being frank and sincere – provided that they do so in ways that fit culturally expected ways for doing so. Bringing readers' considerations to historically reviewing sexuality, cultural notions of appropriateness become more than just ideas; these notions are *practised* in ways that limit what is sexually acceptable. Further, Foucault looked beyond sexuality to how people came to discipline their bodies and socially relate to each other according to historically varying virtues and the expert knowledge of the day. His interests about the self relate to some of the terms he came to use: biopolitics, technologies of the self, psychagogies, and governmentality.

We can begin to appreciate Foucault's historical research on sexuality and the self by considering our most primary way of being, as unreflecting beings who simply act in response to our needs and what is before us in our immediate surroundings. Man (*sic*) had not, as Foucault pointed out (2005), begun to establish 'a new and strange relation to himself' (1985: 16). What makes a relation with oneself possible are the discursive ways of conceptualizing that relationship, along with conceptions of how it might be understood and 'governed'. We are in somewhat familiar territory if we think back to Wittgenstein's private language argument (see Chapter 8). To articulate an understandable self involves drawing from the cultural discourses available for the task. But Foucault took things one important extra step by linking such discourses to how people adopt these as not only understandings but as 'technologies of the self'. Changing discourses on sexual virtues or appropriateness serve as his most striking example. 'Biopolitics' inherently follow in the positions one takes with respect to the discursive options available; our biology and modes of self-'governance' (e.g., Rose, 1989) are tied to where we place or find ourselves with respect to these discursive options.

To live 'as one ought' means to be living in harmony with what is explicitly and implicitly acknowledged as culturally appropriate. To understand and relate to oneself as chaste, for example, implies living in accordance with particular moral precepts, and 'disciplining' one's body accordingly. It is partly in this sense that Foucault speaks of freedom. Yes, we can choose to embrace dominant cultural virtues – by making them ours in ways that we personalize – enough to do so in congruent ways that show their 'truth' for us. The challenge comes in 'bucking the system', so to speak. Elsewhere we have talked about how such virtues can play out in cultural ideals of thinness that invite people into disciplining their bodies to meet those ideals. A cultural virtue can turn into a 'personal' and often unquestioned vice. This is why for many women and men to be other than thin is unthinkable and comes with perceived recriminations.

To read Foucault's three-volume *History of Sexuality* (1978, 1985, 1986) is to be immersed in his analyses of what the historical record (typically in the writings of early philosophers but also in historical texts) says about what the 'proper' practice and regard for sexuality was in different days. Just as one could survey the sexual mores of the past century and find cultural pendulum swings on things like hemlines or body image, or recent developments like homosexual marriage, one finds in Foucault's *History* changing cultural values on everything from masturbation, sex with slaves, how to regard sexual dreams, and so on. What is valorized and held up as appropriate by authors of the texts in any era Foucault reviewed is considered as supplying the cultural understandings and sexual ways of being that people normatively would take up as 'theirs'. Similar arguments are presented about the role that the media and cultural celebrities play today in 'advancing' the contours and possibilities of what is 'in bounds' sexually. The difference, however, between today and antiquity is that arguably there were not the same degrees of cultural diversity (and possibilities) as there are presently.

It is in Foucault's 1981–2 lectures at the Collège de France, *The Hermeneutics of the Subject* (2005), that his scope widens to consider the broader array of historico-cultural appropriatenesses that have come to be 'self'-expected. And it is in this book that he traces key developments in conceptualizing the self as a kind of cultural project dressed up as a personal endeavour. For example, he links first mention (as he was able to determine) of turning one's gaze from others to oneself ('applying your mind to the self', 2005: 213) as a critical step in learning to be able to recognize and hold oneself to cultural expectations. Much of Foucault's historical review focused on classical Greek and Roman writers, and, later, on writers of the early Christian era. What he took from these writers were their prescriptions for virtuous or correct living. Foucault saw in these prescriptions, not just customs for interpersonal conduct, but 'psychagogies', instructions for how to self-monitor and discipline one's mind and body appropriately ('we can, I think, call "psychagogical" the transmission of a truth whose function ... is to modify the mode of being of the subject to whom we address ourselves' (2005: 407)).

If part of the way selves are to be accomplished is to invite people into adopting a relationship with respect to one's 'self', the ideas and means for that relationship get to the heart of what Foucault was raising as concerns about 'psychagogies' or 'technologies of the self'. These ideas and means are not immanent in people – like the acorn developing into a full-grown oak; the ideas and means are developed in and taken from particular cultural discourses. Writers such as Seneca, Marcus Aurelius and Galen were central figures in advancing such historical discourses, and with their writings came many instructions for being 'oneself'.

Foucault is particularly interesting in his discussion of 'parrhesia', one's ability to speak and act with frankness, candor and congruence. These are normally signs that one is acting from one's core or true self. But Foucault locates what is true in the specifications of cultural discourses, specifications that can be enacted and monitored in ways that are culturally sanctioned and recognizable. This may seem at odds with some views of self-authenticity wherein some individuals act like outsiders or mavericks. For Foucault, however, personal truth cannot be separated from the cultural truths which provide the specifications (a kind of cultural mirror, so to speak) as to what living truthfully 'ought' to look like. The crux of Foucault's argument here comes down to his thoughts on 'governmentality' – how to act in ways consistent with how we would expect others to act towards us. We act on ourselves so as to produce ways of being we similarly expect of others. But, as the term governmentality implies, the value-laden principles for such governing (i.e., of self and others) uphold and promote some ways of being over others. As with political governance, self-governance invariably occurs according to the dominant ideas and practices of the day or cultural context (Rose, 1989).

Where things get particularly insidious, however, comes with how people hold themselves to meeting tests of 'correct' subjectivity. This is where Foucault's limited view of freedom gets too cynical for some, and too revolutionary for others. Remember, for Foucault technologies of the self are defined as

> the procedures, which no doubt exist in every civilization, offered or prescribed to individuals in order to determine their identity, maintain it, or transform it in terms of a certain number of ends, through relations of self-mastery or self-knowledge.   (Foucault, 1997: 87)

'Meeting the test' of correct subjectivity, therefore, is about being able to pass acceptably (in Garfinkel's sense – see Chapter 10) as a member of a culture. To not pass the test is to be socially shunned, jailed or worse. Therefore, people exercise their 'freedom', so to speak, in ways that enable them to stay sufficiently culturally 'in bounds', so as to avoid these social outcomes. There is no despot or Wizard of Oz enforcing such rules, or pulling these cultural strings; there are just people holding themselves and each other to particular cultural expectations. In this sense, people are free, or at least accomplices in social orders they may find oppressive or constraining. In upholding these social orders through their expectations of self and others they are unwittingly complicit.

It is in our cultural discourses that we find particular prescriptions and practices for being 'oneself', but it is through our participation and extension of such discourses that these prescriptions and practices become 'truly ours'. The abiding virtues or expert knowledge that come to inform such discourses are taken up by people not as explicit acts of self-subjugation but as culturally valorized ways of being. It is in this sense that people talk about the 'tyranny of fashion' or peer pressure. Foucault never says, however, that there is a bottom-line authentic self that could make personally 'true' choices. He instead suggested that our sense of 'self' will invariably find its articulation and performance inside the dominant discourses we knowingly (or, more likely, unknowingly) take up. The more 'at home' we feel in them, and interact in ways congruent (or consistent) with a cultural discourse, the more parrhesia (frankness, eloquence) is evident. To some extent, hermeneutic scholars (see Chapter 4) look upon authenticity in similar ways, as a kind of attunement to the ways of being in one's cultural context (e.g., Guignon, 2004). A cultural context or cultural discourse, in this regard, provides the contours for what is acceptably familiar in terms of action, understanding and communication. Inside those contours are culturally valorized or dominant ways of understanding and being 'oneself' – Foucault's 'technologies of self', or ways one 'ought to be'.

Foucault and helping practice

The possibilities opened up by Foucault's historical analyses and conclusions have been a central feature in what is now considered a 'critical' approach to the social sciences. An academic version of the 'culture wars' (Cussert, 2008) followed from Foucauldian questions such as: how is it that certain terms, practices and discourses acquire and maintain taken-for-granted 'T' truth status – that, with critical reflection, might become contestable? A spate of books (e.g., Henriques et al., 1984; Rose, 1989; Prilleltensky, 1994; Danziger, 1997a; Parker, 1999) turned a Foucauldian critical gaze on psychological discourse and practice itself, seeking to contest such taken-for-granted ways in which that discipline has been understood and practised. Feminists (e.g., Weedon, 1987) saw in Foucault's analyses the critical means to expose inadequate or unjust textual representations (and the cultural practices which follow from them) of women's lives. Postcolonial theorists, such as Edward Said (1978) or Homi Babha (1994), borrow from the same analyses to address the role of discourse in 'othering' people from non-dominant cultures. A new research paradigm, critical discourse analysis (see Chapter 13), emerged, in large part out of Foucault's scholarship, to challenge dominant discourses and representations of any kind. Narrative therapy (e.g., White and Epston, 1990) took as one of its most important principles Foucault's critical post-structuralism. The impetus behind all of these efforts boils down to a recurring theme in Foucault's scholarship: to unmask and make contestable the ways dominance is perpetuated through the discursive practices and language used to sustain such dominance.

A heuristic from narrative therapy can feature in all forms of Foucauldian-inspired helping: why this discourse, story or way of naming and relating to an experience over others? As we have seen throughout this chapter, what passes for virtuous ways of being or expert knowledge varies with time and context. It is when these ways are confused with 'how things are or must be' that one might beneficially turn to the kinds of critical analyses Foucault described and inspired. This is particularly the case with 'self'-knowledge, as we earlier related. How does any assumed understanding of oneself begin and move on to be sustained through social interaction? Foucault was particularly interested in how ideas or practices fit in the truth games (in Wittgenstein's sense of language game) that make such ideas and practices seem the only way of understanding or doing things. But the helping challenge isn't as simple as exposing dominance, or changing the names we give experiences and each other. Foucault's analyses encompass the power relations which sustain dominance. It is one thing to point out textual dominance (the use of a particular language over others) but another matter to negotiate alternatives. And, as with the examples of feminism and cultural diversity, strides can be made toward more inclusive discourse and relations through exposing where understandings and interactions have been otherwise.

In the conversations of helping practice, Foucault's work points to ways of engaging clients in reflecting upon the 'oughts' and assumed ways of understanding and acting that they use in 'governing' their lives. In a sense normally associated with Derrida (1976), such understandings and actions can be *deconstructed*, by locating them in the particular cultural discourses in which they acquire their 'truth' status. Where, for example, do ideas about being a 'proper man' come from? Where does it say that people's problems must be understood as evidence of their psychopathology? With respect to any given problem, how does a person come to accept one particular description as more true than others – and what follows from that description? These kinds of questions help to locate the origins of particular understandings and ways of acting, while 'unmasking' any sense that such understandings and acting are the sole means by which one needs to proceed. Clients, in this sense, are invited into editorship roles in their lives to judge more reflectively the languages and actions they might use in going forward.

Many see a pessimistic or nihilistic relativism in Foucault's work, a point he conceded in his final years as a somewhat valid criticism (1997). Unlike many philosophers, he did not assert a particular positive vision for how things 'ought' to be, but turned his critical attention more generally toward how 'oughts' featured in cultural and personal life in limiting ways – often in ways that escaped our notice. We joked in our introductory chapter about a 'dark side' to constructionism. Foucault was its chief proponent, and his influence on the humanities and social sciences has been huge. It could be argued that one half of socially constructing preferred ways of living comes with taking up the kinds of enhanced critical awareness that Foucault's studies of discursive dominance promoted. To construct such preferred ways of living often requires an awareness of how much the assumed understandings and practices by which we have lived need not be the only way we could live.

Relativism

Arbitrary classification, discursive regimes that warrant 'knowledge' as 'true' and 'naturally taken for granted', closets disappearing: these and other aspects of Foucault's work have a central role in an issue that has been a bugbear of constructionist thought – relativism. It is one that has divided the three contemporary champions of the constructionist movement we look at in the final chapters (see also contributors to Parker, 1998a). It is not an issue that is unique to constructionist thought, but can be found in the work of many others. The point is effectively there in Mead and von Uexküll's positions on perspectives (see Chapter 7): that organisms effectively live in different worlds, worlds that are relative to their interests. Similarly, the ecological views of Gibson (e.g., 1979) fit in here. Gibson's claim was that we directly perceive the 'values and meanings of things' (ibid.: 127). He characterized these values and meanings with the term 'affordances': 'what [the environment] offers the animal, what it provides or furnishes, either for good or ill' (ibid.). Clearly, affordances are relative to the animal's interests, what it brings to the situation: a ledge on a cliff, for example, provides a climber with somewhere to rest; and a bird somewhere to launch from.

Again, the pioneering anthropological linguist Sapir (1929: 209) was of the view that

> The fact of the matter is that the 'real world' is to a large extent unconsciously built up on the language habits of the group. No two languages are ever sufficiently similar to be considered as representing the same social reality. The worlds in which different societies live are distinct worlds, not merely the same worlds with different labels attached.

His name was later united with that of Benjamin Whorf to result in the Sapir-Whorf hypothesis: that people who use different languages think differently because they live in differently conceived worlds. Numerous philosophers have taken up a similar position; for example:

> the formulation in terms of 'comparison', in speaking of 'facts' or 'realities', easily tempts one into the absolutistic view according to which we are said to search for an absolute reality whose nature is assumed as fixed independently of the language chosen for its description. The answer to a question concerning reality however depends not only upon that 'reality' or upon the facts, but also upon the structure (and the set of concepts) of the language used for the description.   (Carnap, 1949: 126)

> 'Objects' do not exist independently of conceptual schemes. We cut up the world into objects when we introduce one or another scheme of description. (Putnam, 1981: 52)

The same point has been made with respect to the historical changes in scientific views: that there are different paradigms within science, and a new paradigm 'produces disciples forming a school, the members of which are separated for the time being by a logical gap from those outside it. They think differently, speak a different language, live in a different world ...' (Polanyi, 1958: 151). Kuhn also puts this view:

> In a sense that I am unable to explicate further, the proponents of competing paradigms practice their trades in different worlds ... Practicing in different worlds, the two groups of scientists see different things when they look from the same direction.   (1970: 150)

Here, Kuhn takes us closer to our particular interests, through introducing the term 'practice': that is, that social realities are rooted in coordinated actions among people that effectively define their common worlds. Such views are clearly at odds with the often unarticulated presuppositions of empirical science, which seeks to establish the facts of the nature of the real world and the objects, including people, within it. This leads to the charge that social constructionist claims are often deluded, since they could be seen as legitimating an 'anything goes' approach to understanding humans, who, after all, should instead be naively assumed to have universal thought processes internally located in their universal cognitive apparatus. A similar line of argument can also follow from the brief examples we considered in the previous chapter as to the changes in interpersonal relations, and relations with nature, during the past few hundred years of western history. These all index a reconstruction of how people can be, a different structuring of that pre-reflective mode of being that we find coming to the fore in the analyses of the human 'life world' by the phenomenologists and the later Wittgenstein. How one 'is' is thus, again, relative to when and where one is.

In our view, having made a shift from the objective stance – in Taylor's sense (see Chapter 11) – to the meaning-making paradigm of social constructionism in its general sense, it actually becomes possible to pursue, once again, questions as to how selves can be constructed, and the parameters within which selves can be structured. In chasing such questions, we need to be aware that we can be charged with a contradiction: that we are moving away from all we have been saying about the importance of local knowledges as opposed to 'grand narratives' in human affairs, and thus are seemingly engaging in a new form of totalizing 'knowledge and truth' as universals. But rather than being the victims of contradiction, we see here the possibility of signalling a rich, new phase for constructionist work. We need to recall that the Enlightenment project of science is founded, for the natural world, on the conceptual creativity of Newton. In a strong sense, Newton invented the notions of 'matter', 'energy', 'force', 'gravity', and so on: he did not discover them. Similarly, the laws Newton arrived at have a non-empirical character, in the same way that the mathematical statement '2 + 2 = 4' cannot be subjected to empirical test. Thus, it is not possible to devise an experiment to determine whether a 'force' is 'any influence that causes a body to be accelerated', any more than to devise an experiment to determine whether all children have mothers (or vice versa). What Newton accomplished was a *pre-empirical framework* within which empirical science became possible. Psychology has effectively omitted this phase in its history, and regarded itself as a purely empirical project. There have been efforts made to set out such a framework within psychology, notably in the descriptive psychology of Peter Ossorio (e.g., 1995) and the psycho-logic of Jan Smedslund (e.g., 1988, 1994a, 1994b). But as impressive as these efforts are, they are very much predicated on the assumption of a rational, Cartesian individual set over against the world, rather than the engaged, embodied and inherently social forms of being we have been considering in this book. An engagement between these developments and our concerns here is likely long overdue, but that would be another project.

Here, we restrict ourselves to a much lesser aim. We want to suggest that a more useful way of looking at the realism–relativism issue is from a consideration of possibilities and constraints. We will expand this suggestion through a consideration of the work of the American social anthropologist A. Irving Hallowell. Hallowell provides a framework for considering the parameters of human life from a very basic claim, that it is impossible to live as a human without some grasp of what it is to be a human. This grasp is reproduced and made available to people through the cultural practices they engage in. These practices orient people to who, where and when they are, and there are certain dimensions to acting as a person that must be constructed in practice such that people can function as people (a point that is also there in the work of ethnomethodologists, particularly Garfinkel (Chapter 10) and also Wittgenstein (Chapter 8)). However, while people can only be people within these necessary, culturally provided orientations (constraints), there is a variety of possible ways these orientations can be elaborated.

A. Irving Hallowell

Hallowell, in our view, is quite 'out there' when he got to thinking about 'what it is to be human', such that many social constructionists would fail to see his relevance. We see him as important because his view is, at bottom, that humans construct their cultures; that they could not be human without these constructions (so far so good); that 'selves' are mutually co-constituted out of the resources provided in these constructed cultures (okay); that the 'selves' that people thereby create consequently vary across cultures in time and space – that there is, therefore, no one, essential 'self' to be discovered (hooray). But, at the same time, among this co-constitutive relativity of self and culture there are some fundamental universals that can be charted as *the* dimensions that all selves may vary along, which are intrinsic, necessary and therefore 'essential parameters' for anyone to have any possible variety of 'a self' at all. Selves may be very variable, but they are all variations on underlying, universal 'themes'. It is this analysis that makes Hallowell look like an unabashed positivist, not a constructionist, and thereby, we think, mistakenly ignored. He is a pre-empirical constructionist, delineating the parameters of what can be constructed.

We want to introduce his work as a possible 'tool for thought'. We want you to approach him along the following lines. If you think of a narrative therapist looking to find ways to help a client re-story a particular problem situation in ways that help them move forward, then, if the interchange provides some hope of moving on, of becoming 'unstuck', we might say that a new story has begun to be constructed to replace the old story. But both the old and the new are versions of possible 'stories': and not things of different categories. Similarly, a collaborative therapist will become involved in different forms of collaboration with different clients, but they are all versions of ways to collaborate: there is an interactive construction of the next move, not an imposition of one will on another, an exercise of coercion. Collaborations can come about in various ways, but there is something about them that gives them a family resemblance – that makes them variations on the same theme rather than categorically different exercises.

This is Hallowell's point with respect to selves: that there are only so many dimensions – and all of them are required – on which they can vary and still be 'things' that can be counted as 'selves'. Thus, for example, the chimpanzees we note below demonstrate some of the bases for having a self – 'the integration of attention, perceiving, thinking, purposiveness and the postponement of action in a rudimentary form' (Hallowell, 1960: 351) – but they lack an orientation to what it would be to be a 'good' versus a 'bad' chimpanzee. And if you lack that ability, you do not, by definition, have a 'self'. This is not to say that a chimpanzee needs to have 'our' set of values as to what is good or bad – or a Christian's, a Muslim's, a Zoroastrian's, a Fascist's, or anyone else's, for that matter. Any old criteria by which to decide 'Hey, I did good/bad there' will suffice to let them in the 'self' club. But with no evaluative criteria, you cannot join. Lacking an ability or the criteria to judge whether one has done well or poorly, successfully or unsuccessfully, you would lack self-awareness: you would not have a self.

Hallowell's main field of research as a cultural anthropologist was with the Ojibwa people in North America. His approach was to try and become a native, to get 'inside their heads' and so see the world from the perspective of another culture. Whether he 'got it right', or even whether it is possible to do so, is neither here nor there for our present purpose. What he encountered in his fieldwork research made him aware that there were clearly very different ways of 'seeing' the world from the way he had been brought up to see it. The Ojibwa not only appeared, to him, to 'see' the world differently from the way he did, but, perhaps as a consequence, also thought of themselves in quite different ways from the way he, as a white American, had come to think of himself, and what it was to 'be human'. And yet, both he and they were so obviously 'human' in their relation to each other, that he and they could interact with each other as 'brothers'. It was quite clear that there was something very different in being an Ojibwa person from being a white, twentieth-century American academic. Part of the project Hallowell pursued was to get at the similarities that underpinned the differences.

What held these immense differences together? How could people think about who they were in such different ways and yet still get along?

Hallowell wrote a great deal about 'the self', taking into account cross-cultural data, and thinking about the topic phylogenetically. Were he writing today, he might well have framed things differently. But his central point would remain: the view that everyone has an account to offer of 'who they are', even if these accounts are framed very differently. What 'counts' as 'an account' of who anyone is? What characteristics does something have to have in order to be judged an account? Could there be any commonalities in these accounts? Given, in his experience, that there could be very different ways of 'being human', and thus talking about what it was to have a 'self', could these differences be shown to be just variations in some greater scheme of things? In other words, are there limits within which an account could be given of 'what it was to be human'? Or is it the case that the differences between the ways in which different cultures give one resources to think about 'who one is' are just so outlandishly different that they are not comparable? Hallowell's aim was to establish the parameters that made any form of selfhood possible. We summarize his views below. Note that, as elsewhere, we have aimed to stay close to the original source.

Hallowell takes the concepts of *self* and *culture* as interdependent: one cannot exist without the other. Thus, while it has become commonplace to regard the self as a cultural product, and in traditional psychology to inquire as to the 'environmental' (cultural) factors that lead to the expression or inhibition of this or that aspect of the self, the reverse perspective should not be forgotten; that culture itself is a product of the self. Selves are constituted within culture, and culture is maintained by the community of selves. For Hallowell, selves are nurtured within a culture, and cultures vary in the self-constituting concepts they provide (thus the conventional). But culture has itself arisen from the protoself of preconceptual humans (thus the universal). In this context, he notes Hebb and Thompson's report (1954) on chimpanzees at Orange Park zoo. On seeing visitors arrive they ran quickly to a drinking fountain, and after filling their mouths with water waited quietly for the visitors to approach before discharging it at them. Such an ability exemplifies 'the integration of attention, perceiving, thinking, purposiveness and the postponement of action in a rudimentary form' (Hallowell, 1960: 351) which is basic to the elaboration of culture from protoculture, a foundation for the more complex inner world of human experiences. Cultures provide external symbols that have emanated from inner experiences – experiences of time, place, goal, purpose, etc. The way in which such experiences are conceptualized will vary from place to place (the conventional); but that it is *such* experiences that are conceptualized will be constant (the universal).

Hallowell: the necessity of selves in human life

Humans are not only *social* animals but also *cultural* ones, and that means that we are also moral animals: thus our society exhibits both a social order and a *moral order.* This moral order comprises norms of conduct and effective social sanctions, implicit or explicit, to back them up. Hence, the members of such an order are required to recognize some locus of responsibility for their actions in society. This, in turn, implies a

> self-awareness of one's own conduct, self-appraisal of one's conduct with reference to socially recognised standards of value, some volitional control of one's own behaviour, a possible choice of alternative lines of conduct, etc. … without the development of self-awareness as an intrinsic part of the socialisation process, without a concept of self that permits attitudes directed towards the self as an object to emerge and crystallize, we would not have some of the essential conditions necessary for the functioning of a human society.   (Hallowell, 1971: 83)

As Hallowell goes on to note, self-awareness is necessary and basic to the successful performance of the many different roles which the individual has to adopt within society. In order for a culture to maintain itself its individual members must have some awareness of their social standing with respect to age, sex, hierarchies of social precedent, etc. 'If [they] were not aware of [their] roles they would not be in a position to appraise their own conduct in terms of traditional values and social sanctions' (ibid.: 83). Thus, self-awareness is at once both a distinctive and necessary component of human life: 'we must assume that the functioning of any human society is inconceivable without self-awareness, reinforced and constituted by traditional beliefs about the nature of the self' (ibid.: 83).

Three things may be said about self-awareness:

(i) *Self-awareness is a socio-cultural product.* To be self-aware is, by definition, to be able to conceive of one's individual existence in an objective, as opposed to subjective, manner. In Mead's (1934) terms (see Chapter 7), one must view oneself from '*the perspective of the other*'. This level of psychological functioning is only made possible by the attainment of a symbolic mode of representing the world. Again, this mode of mental life is generally agreed to be dependent upon the existence of a cultural level of social organization. We thus come to a fundamental, though apparently tautologous point: that the existence of culture is predicated upon that of self-awareness; and that the existence of self-awareness is predicated upon that of culture.

(ii) *Culture defines and constitutes the boundaries of the self: the subjective–objective distinction.* It is an evident consequence of being self-aware that if one has some conception of one's own nature, then one must also have some conception of the nature of things other than oneself, i.e., of the world. Further, this distinction must be encapsulated explicitly in the symbols one uses to mark this polarity. Consequently, a symbolic representation of this divide will have become 'an intrinsic part of the cultural heritage of all human societies' (Hallowell, 1971: 75). Thus, the very existence of a moral order and self-awareness, and therefore human being, depends on the making of *some* distinction between 'objective' (things which *are not* an intrinsic part of the self) and 'subjective' (things which *are* an intrinsic part of the self).

> This categorical distinction, and the polarity it implies, becomes one of the fundamental axes along which the psychological field of the human individual is structured for action in every culture … Since the self is also partly a cultural product, the field of behaviour that is appropriate for the activities of *particular* selves in *their* world of culturally defined objects is not by any means precisely coordinate with any absolute polarity of subjectivity – objectivity that is definable.   (ibid.: 84)

Similarly, Cassirer in the context of kinship terminology writes:

> language does not look upon objective reality as a single homogeneous mass, simply juxtaposed to the world of the I, but sees different strata of this reality: the relationship between object and subject is not universal and abstract; on the contrary, we can distinguish different degrees of objectivity, varying according to relative distance from the I.   (1953: 262)

In other words, there are many facets of reality which are not distinctly classifiable in terms of a polarity between self and non-self, subjective or objective: for example, what *exactly* is the status of this page – is it an objective entity or part of its authors' selves; an objective entity that would exist as a page, rather than marks on a screen, without a self to *read* it? Again, are we responsible for all the passions we experience, or are we as much spectators of some of them as our audience is? While a polarity necessarily exists between the two – subjective and objective/ self and non-self – the line between the two is not precise, and may be constituted at different places in different contexts by different cultures. The boundaries of the self and the concomitant boundaries of the world, while drawn of necessity, are both constituted by cultural symbolism, and may be constituted upon differing assumptions.

(iii) *The behavioural environment of individual selves is constituted by, and encompasses, different objects.* Humans, in contrast to other animals, can be afraid of, for example, the dark because they are able to populate it with symbolically constituted objects: ghosts, bogeymen, and various other spirit beings. As MacLeod (1947: 205) also pointed out, 'purely fictitious objects, events and relationships can be just as truly determinants of our behaviour as are those which are anchored in physical reality'.

In Hallowell's view:

> such objects, in some way experienced, conceptualised and reified, may occupy a high rank in the behavioural environment although from a sophisticated Western point of view they are sharply distinguishable from the natural objects of the physical environment. However, *the nature of such objects is no more fictitious, in a psychological sense, than the concept of the self.*   (Hallowell, 1971: 87; our emphasis)

To the sophisticated mind, such objects are not naturally but only symbolically constituted; but in the psychological sense of their affecting a self which draws a boundary between the objective and subjective at a different point, such objects are necessarily as real as the self they are defined in opposition to, and 'must thus be considered as relevant variables because they can be shown to affect actual behaviour'. The environment in which humans live may best be described then as a 'culturally constituted behavioural environment' (ibid.: 87).

In their book, *Objectivity,* historians of science Lorraine Daston and Peter Galison (2007) have recently described the history of objectivity in terms of 'epistemic virtues' that coalesce in particular methods and criteria for judging phenomena 'objectively'. This underscores a point about how notions of what is objectively real for people sharing a culture is tied to their historical and cultural ways of deciding and talking about what is real. This extends to what is involved in being a 'real' scientist, but history shows how much conceptions of, and conventions for, what is objectively real can change.

Hallowell: orientations of the self

Culture not only constitutes our behavioural environment, but also provides us with basic orientations that enable us to act in an intelligible manner in a world so constituted: all these are orientations for the self, and serve to give it its particular structure.

1. Self-orientation

Culture provides a self-concept through the linguistic marking of self from non-self. All languages must provide deictic marking if they are to be humanly serviceable. Personal pronouns, kinship terms and personal names all function to this end. But, as Hallowell notes:

> while one of the constant functions of all cultures … is to provide a concept of self along with other means that promote self-orientation, the individuals of a given society are self-oriented in terms of a provincial content of the self-image.   (1971: 90)

Thus, while all cultures will provide a basic vocabulary for self-orientation, none of those lexical or conceptual items need be directly translatable into those of another culture. In using the word 'self' here as a universal marker, it does not follow that *our* provincial concept of self, indicated, unfortunately, by the same word, has any universality in human conception.

2. Object-orientation

If the self is recognized and delineated, then so necessarily is the non-self, in that it is

> a diversified world of objects … discriminated, classified, and conceptualised with respect to attributes which are culturally constituted and symbolically mediated through language … Object-orientation … provides the ground for an intelligible interpretation of events in the behavioral environment on the basis of traditional assumptions regarding the nature and attributes of the objects involved, and implicit or explicit dogmas regarding the 'causes' of events.
>   (Hallowell, 1971: 91)

Such orientating cosmologies supply the conceptual framework that makes human action possible.

3. Spatio-temporal orientation

Place-names appear to be among the universally occurring categories of deictic markers, for a culturally constituted orientation to a world of objects other than the self *must* be integrated with a spatial orientation of the self that provides a frame of reference for action. Time and place are intertwined for a self-aware being: 'for self-awareness implies that the individual not only knows where he *is*, but where he *was* at some previous moment in time, or where he expects to be in the *future*' (ibid.: 93; italics in original). This further implies the existence not only of a self-identity component of self-awareness, but a self-continuity one as well. And this brings us full circle to the concept of culture as a moral order in which a temporal dimension for the self is necessary, for in order to maintain roles and assume moral responsibility, 'I not only have to be aware of who I am today, but be able to relate my past actions to both past and future behavior' (ibid.: 95). There is a further important relation between this temporal orientation of the self and self-continuity: the time-span of recalled experiences that are related to the self. Thus we find, for example, in the Hindu doctrine of rebirth that events 'recalled from previous lives' may be regarded as having happened to the self. Hallowell notes that in many cultures '[s]elf-related experiences are given a retrospective temporal span that far transcends the limits beyond which we know reliable accounts of personal experience can be recalled' (ibid.: 95).

4. Motivational orientation

A motivational orientation is as necessary for the continuance of a moral order as it is for the orientation of a self within that order, since motivational factors – needs, desires, goals, and attitudes – underpin the functioning of human social orders. The world of objects which the self inhabits is not only discriminated but classified as possessing attributes, positive or negative, that are culturally constituted as relevant to the self. Needs necessitate actions and actions require direction: this is why the self requires motivational orientation to be able to discriminate the relevant objects towards which it must act.

5. Normative orientation

> Since the human social order is also a moral order, there is always the presumption that an individual is not only aware of his own personal identity and conduct in a spatio-temporal frame of reference, but that he is capable of judging his own conduct by the standards of his culture. Thus normative orientation is a necessary corollary of self-orientation.   (ibid.: 106)

From this it follows that an individual possesses volitional control over his or her own acts. But this does not necessarily imply that acts for which the individual is morally responsible will be attributed by him or her to his self or her self. For as Hallowell goes on to note:

> Just as, in terms of a given self-image, naturalistic time and space may be transcended in self-related experience and the self may interact socially with other-than-human selves, so in the moral world of the self the acts for which the self may feel morally responsible may not all be attributed to waking life, nor to a single mundane existence, nor to interpersonal relations with human beings alone   (ibid.: 101).

Hallowell and therapy

Hallowell's research stresses themes we have visited in a number of ways in the course of our studies: people construct and uphold understandings and actions in culturally consistent ways. It is Hallowell's focus on the self that mostly interests us here. While neither Hallowell, nor our other theorists, saw culture as determining our selves, he saw culture as the responsive backdrop out of which selves develop. In particular, cultures use their symbols, language and practices to help individuals acquire the 'self-awareness' required of them to participate competently as members. Further, such participation delimits that 'self-awareness' in ways consistent with a culture's norms and preferred actions and understandings over time. In a similar manner we develop culture-specific ways of understanding other non-human aspects of our experience. In short, our cultural experiences (via their symbols, languages and practices) furnish us with ways to regard ourselves and our experience.

For therapists and counsellors, Hallowell's views are evident in the differences clients show in their understandings and actions. Their cultural traditions, in a sense, map out the coordinates relevant to most aspects of their lives. Particularly when clients and therapists/counsellors use the same language, this can obscure the different orientations to the self that Hallowell raised as culturally developed *universals*. His five orientations can thus serve as useful domains of inquiry and potential action in therapy. For example, reflecting upon the orientation one has to 'her/his' culturally derived norms or motivations for thought and action can make evident their cultural specificity while prompting consideration of those constructed differently elsewhere. In terms of one's sense of self, or of phenomena beyond the self, we can consider these as being interpreted and related to within the parameters set by culturally specific horizons of understanding.

Depending on your view of helping there can be culprits in what we have been saying; that our social experiences are what put blinkers on our senses of possibility. That, as Gregory Bateson (see Chapter 9) might say, would be an odd way to punctuate things. The notion of a pristine and unfettered individuality – like a pre-Friday Robinson Crusoe, let's say – has been an odd kind of ideal upon which many modern assumptions of self have been hung. Other people, because of our interactions in a social world we share, inescapably feature in how we understand our selves and our possibilities. Indeed, by using the languages and evaluative practices we acquire by learning to interact with them, our individuality is inseparable from our sociality.

In a postmodern, culturally diverse world where the kind of cultural boundedness Hallowell was talking about is hard to imagine, a different set of issues emerges. In particular, as Deborah Battaglia (1995) pointed out, there arise more 'rhetorics of self-making'. At the same time, the social cohesion one could formerly turn to for one's confident sense of self has become more diffuse, or loosely bound. Some might see panoramic possibilities for identity in this, but at the same time – if our sense of self grows out of a sense of communal interaction with others – self-making becomes more challenging. Alienation can be as much a problem as a socially stifled sense of self. Perhaps unsurprisingly, some forms of social constructionist therapy (e.g., social therapy, and the community work of narrative therapists) have moved to more communal forms of helping. The notion of an individual therapist and client talking identity projects away from the social contexts in which those projects must play out can seem suspect. But surrendering one's individuality to the social collective can cost both the individual and the collective. There are many rich conversations to be had about how one negotiates selves in the different social arenas where they are differently called for.

Foucault provides a meta-analysis of discursive practices. In contrast to his approach, there is a large field of inquiry into actual discursive productions at the micro-level. It is this work that we turn to in the following chapter. How do conversations actually work in practice?

13 Discourse analysis

It can be easy to look past the primary activity of professional helping, discourse, to account for what 'really goes on' in bringing about human change. Some of this is because the dominant view of human discourse (including conversation) has been based on a 'conduit metaphor' of information transmission and reception (Lakoff and Johnson, 1980). Things can get even more confusing when considering discourse in its noun and verb forms. As a noun, scholars and practitioners point to systematized differences in the meanings people use for making sense of and communicating their experiences. Others favour a pragmatic, verb-like sense of discourse, as things people do in and with their developing communications with each other (Levinson, 1981). For most discourse analysts, looking at language alone (the noun stuff) is not enough; one needs to see also how language is used, and what results from that use. At the heart of our considerations of professional helping is how discourse used for understanding (noun-like language) can at the same time be used for social influence (in verb-like dialogues).

Discourse is what we use to understand and influence each other. As anyone travelling to a foreign country finds out, without a shared means of understanding and communicating social life becomes a huge challenge. Discourse is 'already there' for us most of the time, we grow up with it being used around us, and one of our most important challenges is to learn to use it effectively with each other. But, as Ferdinand de Saussure (1983) pointed out early in the field of linguistics, there is a big difference between the already said and what we are about to say in the immediacies of our speaking with others. Students of discourse tend to give a different emphasis to this dichotomy, studying aspects of different languages as one might study species of butterfly, or studying language-use as speakers pursue different endeavours. Very different implications follow from how one considers language and its use.

Our concern here is not with an exhaustive review of linguistics and discourse analysis, of which there are many forms and antecedents. Instead, we trace particular developments related to our social constructionist narrative, retaining the tensions between de Saussure's *langue* (already spoken) and *parole* (speaking) distinctions. While we have the capacity to use language creatively with each other, we also typically speak from and hold each other to what Paul Ricoeur (see Chapter 4) once called the 'well-rutted road' of prior discourse. We cannot say whatever we want – toasting the bride in Klingon, or addressing her father in ways he might find insulting. But the language and ways of speaking that enable speakers to stay familiar and 'appropriate' with each other can also bind them to static ways of relating to their changing circumstances. We continuously straddle de Saussure's linguistic modalities, seeking competence in language as it is already developed, while also seeking effectiveness in using language (and new linguistic constructions) to address the discursive challenges before us.

Perhaps some of the confusion around discourse comes from the Bible where, in John 1:1, one finds the sentence: 'In the beginning was the Word.' The seeming innateness of language can feel God-given until one considers terms that weren't around at the time of John, such as internet, laptop or punk rock. Things get more complicated when cross-cultural experience shows people getting by with terms and ways of speaking quite different from English. Take a further step inside English, or any language, and more cultural distinctions become evident. Psychologists use a different language for some experiences than do spiritual leaders; and, as we have noted before, 'bad' can mean 'good' on the street. Peek inside a good dictionary and the complexity of nailing down common meanings gets clearer, and this is before considering that a sizeable portion of the first complete *Oxford English Dictionary* was developed by a certified madman (Winchester, 2005). The closer one looks, the less language seems a one-size-fits-all-for-any-purpose feature of life. Indeed, critical discourse analysts often see differences in language-use as a kind of contest for the dominance of meaning. This is a far cry from seeing language as something one should learn to use neutrally or correctly in some absolute sense.

Our foray into the broad field of discourse analysis begins with William Labov's contributions to socio-linguistics, a sub-discipline that tends to see social differences in language in de Saussure's '*langue*' sense. Labov's contributions can partly be related to linguistic anthropology, particularly the work of Edward Sapir (1949) and Benjamin Whorf (1956), who saw linguistic differences between cultures as shaping culturally shared realities. Labov's project has been more specific, validating changing cultural variations in the English spoken and understood within North America.

William Labov

What do searching for variations in how 'r' is pronounced in New York City, explaining the intellectual integrity of African American Vernacular English, mapping North American dialects, finding out what occurs when people share stories, analysing therapeutic discourse and accounting for linguistic change have in common? Through such inquiries William Labov helped launch the field of socio-linguistics. For Labov, still active today, there has always been a central question: 'How do people manage to understand each other if the language keeps changing under their feet?' 'The language' is far from uniform, as his studies of English speech, meaning and dialect variations show.

Labov left an unsatisfying career as a trade journalist to study language as it is used in social contexts. His dissertation, published (1967) as *The Social Stratification of English in New York City*, extended an earlier study he made of sound changes in the spoken English of citizens of Martha's Vineyard, Massachusetts. Labov was interested not only in variations of spoken English, but in how these variations took place – how people change the language they use. Their differences in pronunciation – particularly across age, cultural and socio-economic groups – showed how communities of speakers 'pressure' language to conform to shared versions of it. Particularly interesting was his conclusion that lower-class speakers 'hypercorrected' their English to meet the norms of pronunciation, norms he considered 'targets' these speakers 'exceeded'. This, for example, was why he was interested in how 'r' would be spoken. To his studies Labov brought rigorous and primarily quantitative methods to systematically highlight linguistic variation. In a Labov book or article you will likely find odd charts and graphs capturing some nuance of communication you might, at first consideration, dismiss.

How many ways, for example, can the 'r' be measured for how it is pronounced, and why should this be important?

Labov has devoted his career to accounting for language-use and its role in sustaining distinctive societies and activities. Problematic for him is the view that there is a unitary English from which speakers deviate in ways that suggest inferiority or a need for correction. So, for example, here is Labov in a classic article, 'The logic of non-standard English', at his controversial best:

> Our work in the speech community makes it painfully obvious that in many ways working-class speakers are more effective narrators, reasoners, and debaters than many middle-class speakers who temporize, qualify, and lose their argument in a mass of irrelevant detail.   (1969: republished online, 1995)

Here, Labov is taking a swipe at the conclusions of Basil Bernstein and others who felt lower-class speakers had (and came from cultural circumstances of) impoverished linguistic capabilities. Harvard's Arthur Jensen advocated even more pessimistic conclusions: that the alleged inferiority of Black Americans was genetic and racially bound. Regardless of its causes, this view served as the rationale for American educational initiatives, such as Head Start, in the 1960s.

Labov, speaking from his linguistic analyses of actual speaking interactions, countered this and other notions of 'the myth of verbal deprivation'. By contrasting the speech interactions between black children and researchers with those of black children and other black speakers, Labov was able to show how differently the children performed in each context. As with his comment above, Labov felt that the black children he studied spoke with a rhetorical competence and effectiveness that surpassed the speaking competence he found in other speakers. Here he is again writing in *Atlantic Monthly* back in 1972:

> inner-city children [do not] necessarily have inferior mothers, language, or experience, but ... the language, family style, and ways of living of inner-city

> children are significantly different from the standard culture of the classroom, and ... this difference is not always properly understood by teachers and psychologists. Linguists believe that we must begin to adapt our school system to the language and learning styles of the majority in the inner-city schools.

This controversy persisted for some time, until, in the 1990s, a decision was made by the Oakland school board to honour 'Ebonics' (Black English Vernacular or BEV) in its curriculum. Labov's research provided key support for this frowned-upon and ridiculed decision. To those bemoaning the 'abuse' of standard English, wanting to hold others to its meanings and pronunciations, Labov's research charts quite different territory. Specifically, his studies show how dialect variations must be understood on their own terms, as evidence of speech communities competently transacting their social business differently (i.e., not in inferior ways) from those using 'proper' English.

Let us digress for a moment. Particularly impressive about Labov's work is the rigour he brought to understanding what transpires in communicative interaction. In a classic article with Joshua Waletsky, Labov examined how people shared personal narratives (Labov and Waletsky, 1967). Thirty years later, a full issue of the *Journal of Narrative and Life History* (1997, Volume 7) revisited this ground-breaking research and its implications. For Labov, story-telling involved using the present to narrate and analyse the past in ways that are socially reportable and credible. His language and metaphors for narrative processes ('transfers of objective and causally linked experiences'), and narratives understood in objective structural terms ('there' to be narrated), don't wash with constructionist thinkers in the journal issue previously mentioned. Still, most feel Labov's more important contribution was to move analysis – in this case of narratives – from theoretical to more empirically supported accounts of what transpires in actual conversations.

Extending this empirical work in another direction, we have Labov to thank for conducting one of the first comprehensive examinations of therapeutic conversation (Labov and Fanshel, 1977 – *Therapeutic Discourse: Psychotherapy as Conversation*). For Labov, analysing therapeutic conversation, particularly because of its (psychoanalytically) interpretive focus, offered a chance to see how therapist and client did psychotherapy. His concern was with the tendency of therapists to give their theories primacy in accounting for what occurred in therapy – he wanted to bypass this theorizing for an empirically supported version of what occurs. But he did not want to stop at the words exchanged alone. Thus, he looked at the pitch and intensity of the presentation of those words, seeing them as part of performances both therapist and clients were making to be understood and influential. These he considered speech actions they jointly used to conduct the interpersonal business of therapy. By highlighting these actions, thereby magnifying them for examination, he started trying to identify 'what did s/he mean by that?', later replacing such efforts at attributing meaning with an analysis of the function these actions performed in the therapeutic conversation. Such a shift should make sense: how could he determine what intentions speakers had as they spoke? So, he took a turn we will increasingly see in the later work of conversation analysts: 'The major aim of formal linguistic analysis is to discover the sets of options available to speakers at any given point in the development of the linguistic structure' (Labov and Fanshel, 1977: 358).

The 'linguistic structure' to which Labov and Fanshel refer is therapy's social activity in which speakers choose and perform what they see as classifiable speech acts consequential to how therapeutic conversation develops. It is critical to bear in mind that Labov sees conversation as involving more than words. There is always some element of ambiguity involved as speakers try to accomplish things with their speech acts, and some of this ambiguity is necessary because 'Speakers *need* a form of communication which is deniable' (1977: 46; emphasis in the original).

If this performative view of language is starting to resemble a particular linguistic dance to which speakers bring recognizable steps and preferences, then you are getting Labov's analytic drift. But the analysis of therapeutic discourse was not meant to stop at therapy, as this next passage indicates: 'conversation is not a chain of utterances, but rather a matrix of utterances and actions bound together by a web of understandings and reactions' (Labov and Fanshel, 1977: 30). Thinking of conversation in this fashion brings us back to Labov's earlier conclusions about linguistic variation (examples: the 'r' of New Yorkers' talk, or the integrity of Black English Vernacular). It is important to step back from Labov's rigour and conclusions, to see what implications we can draw from his view of conversation as having locally determined meanings and ways of talk.

Why would Labov conclude that speakers of Black English Vernacular accomplish their social business with each other with greater rhetorical skill than other speakers? Or why should it matter if some speakers clip their 'r's', or that stories tend to be told in particular ways? Labov has played a pivotal role in showing what close-up and bigger-picture examinations of conversation make evident. For him, people are constantly shaping language to make it fit their purposes and circumstances. But people also develop normative understandings and ways of talking to which they hold themselves, and each other. So, what we get out of this is something conversationally akin to what Wittgenstein referred to as 'forms of life', conversations with distinctive purposes, norms and possibilities. To those who see language as something that can be used correctly across contexts, Labov's conclusions are deeply unsettling.

Labov's socio-linguistic approach to variations in language helps us segue into discourse analysis, a family of approaches for researching differences in language and its use. We begin from a contrast of two language-focused research approaches. Consider the case of 'content analysis' (Holsti, 1969), where the focus is on the quantitative use of particular words in spoken or written discourse. Suppose, for example, you were reading our words electronically and had the option of doing a 'find' search for, let's say, the word 'understand'. And say you discover its use 120 times in this book. What might this tell you about our meaning? Suppose instead that you wanted to get a read on how and why Andy and

Tom use 'understand' in this book. You might look at 'understand' as a codeword for implying certain shared constructions of reality over others, to see how we might be pulling the wool over your eyes. Seeing words as having unchanging meanings to be counted and generalized, versus examining how they are used for particular rhetorical purposes, highlights one difference between linguistic and discourse analyses. But, as Labov's research showed, cultural variations in language-use can be studied as phenomena in themselves. These different ways of representing and talking about reality are matters to be worked out conversationally in what John Shotter (1993b) referred to as the 'cultural politics of everyday life'. Translated to people in dialogue, what is involved in people understanding and influencing each other requires more than neutrally using words according to pre-specified meanings from a presumably shared dictionary.

Our look at discourse analysis, as a family of research methods with related theories, will now focus on three very different projects: critical discourse analysis (CDA), conversation analysis (CA) and the discursive psychology (DP) project at Loughborough University. While there are many approaches to discourse analysis (each with different theoretical constructs, methods and aims), here we will examine these prominent approaches, each offering useful ideas to discursively oriented practice. Practitioners of CDA see their primary role as identifying and subverting discourses that dominate and contribute to negative power differentials and outcomes in relationships. CA focuses on the micro-practices speakers use to be understood and influence the course of their conversations and relationships. DP, among other things, aims to show how the cornerstone constructs of psychology (attitudes, emotions, thought, 'facts', memory, diagnoses, etc.) can be seen as discursively constructed and sustained in interaction. In that sense, they can be seen as extending the research developed out of Wittgenstein's concern for the over-psychologizing of our understandings of individual and social behaviour. We will encounter important controversies between CDA , CA and DP, while considering how far language and 'reality' can be equated or differentiated.

Critical Discourse Analysis

> What is so perilous, then, in the fact that people speak, and that their speech proliferates? Where is the danger in that?   (Foucault, 1972: 216)

> In our practical engagement with the world, we are brought up against its nature and are forced to recognize which constructions it will and will not bear.   (Parker, 1998a: 18)

In our lead quote above, Foucault (see also Chapter 12) is about to launch fully into his famous 'Discourse on language'. He starts from an unusual place for his primarily western audience: the perils of free speech. But Foucault saw speech in much broader terms than most of us do. For him, discourse related to how people organized their ways of talking in order to pursue particular aims; and in so doing they limited how they could talk about things, so as to stay consistent with those aims. Here is Foucault, again, on such limits:

> We must conceive of discourse as a violence that we do to things, or, at all events, as a practice we impose upon them; it is in this practice that the events of discourse find the principle of their regularity.   (1972: 229)

Thus, in Foucault's view of discourses we find familiarity and regularity in how we talk and think, but in using them we accept or impose particular views and language on our experience. The 'peril' Foucault warned us about above relates to what happens should we talk beyond these familiarities and regularities.

Discourse usually refers to language as it is patterned or systematized beyond mere words or sentences. To some extent this systematization occurs in how we 'package' our thinking and talking in particular ways, in ideological or philosophical terms. For example, a forest industry representative and a conservationist would probably talk differently about a stand of trees. Systematically, their words, sentences and other means of communication will most likely be distinct, reflecting differences in values and outlooks. Reflect on conceptions of women before and after the women's movement and you have a further example of differences in discourse. And it should be clear that discourse could extend, in such examples, beyond words: to media images used in 'packaging' a particular way of regarding experience. While it would be incorrect to see discourses as discrete ways of talking and thinking, their differences become evident when their dominance is contested, as in the example of the women's movement.

Critical discourse analysts are concerned with 'who uses language, how, why and when' (van Dijk, 1997). To that end, they examine communication in many different settings (face-to-face dialogue, professional–client consultations, interactions in public and private settings, etc.), and via different media (telephone conversations, online communication, newspaper articles, advertising images, political speeches). While some focus primarily on aspects of verbal communication (words, metaphors, choice of active and passive voicing, value-laden terms, etc.), others might analyse non-verbal aspects of communications, such as gestures or features of vocal presentation. These, in other language, are all forms of semiotic practices. Still other analysts, such as Norman Fairclough (1995), focus on the use of a wider range of semiotic resources to pursue particular ideological aims. Most critical discourse analysts prefer to study communicative interaction as it is used to accomplish social purposes in particular contexts. To this end, they analyse these different dimensions of discursive interaction to offer interpretations that differ from those of the people and interactions studied. Critical discourse analysis sees a link between what we communicate and what we experience, and that we generally regard things the way we do because that is how they are predominantly talked about. Such talking and thinking usually becomes taken for granted, so part of the value of discourse analysis is in how it can help us become aware of the link between our taken-for-granted ways of talking and how they shape our thinking.

> Critical discourse analysis can only make a significant and specific contribution to critical or political analyses if it is able to provide an account of the role of language, language use, discourse or communicative events in the (re)production of dominance and inequality.   (van Dijk, 1993: 28)

Critical discourse analysis (CDA) is a relatively new field of research, which has mostly developed since the early 1990s. Sometimes the term 'critical linguistics' is used interchangeably with CDA, and at the heart of CDA is a view that what matters is how language is used in context. Most of us seldom consider the extent to which discourses dominate our ways of thinking and talking, but for most CDA practitioners, everyday language-use is hardly a neutral activity. Borrowing from critical theorists such as Habermas, Gramsci or Althusser, CDA examines how particular ideologies are pursued through people's communicative interactions. To that end CDA can be seen as a tool in examining and subverting how language serves power relations. How, for example, has the western conception of female beauty become so dominated by particular ways of representing it?

CDA often sees communicative interaction as a contest for discursive dominance. A good example of this can be seen in the work of Norman Fairclough and his colleagues who study, for example, how the discourse of the 'new global economy' features in different communicative contexts. This 'neo-liberal' discourse, for them, is pursued in ways that diminish democratic rights and encourage governments to abandon costly social services, all as part of 'freeing-up' the marketplace. Whether examining political speeches, advertisements, everyday talk, the ubiquity of corporate logos, or changes in government and corporate policies, this group of critical discourse analysts aims to show how the language of the 'new economy' plays out in terms of human interaction, and impacts on people's shared ways of living.

For Fairclough, language figures in such interactions and effects in three broad ways: as part of the action – acting and interacting is partly using language in particular ways; in representing the world and social life in particular ways – differences in wording are different ways of representing things; and as part of the constitution of ways of being – identities (Chouliaraki and Fairclough, 1999). Let us unpack these points further. First, the discourses we turn to in order to understand and communicate with each other are those most accessible to us. These discourses provide us with particular meanings and ways to use them. Second, any discourse contains buzzwords or other symbolic markers that distinguish it from other discourses. To that end, the use of 'new economy' discourse should be quite identifiable. For analysts the issue is to find examples of the discourse as it is used, to see how it is used and what effects arise from its use. As western governments have embraced the economic discourse of the 'new economy' they have used its language in conveying to people 'how things are and should be'. Where CDA plays a role is in highlighting how this language gets used and contested. How do the media portray the use of such a discourse, how does the person on the street make use of it? What consequences can be discerned from the use of this discourse and its effects on people as it plays out (examples: cuts to social services coinciding with cuts in corporate taxes)? Third, to the extent that people 'inhabit' any discourse, they show how its words and understandings are 'theirs' in how they see themselves and their affairs. In this regard, any discourse seeking dominance succeeds in so far as it becomes the primary one people use to make sense of their experience for themselves and each other.

Of critical interest to CDA researchers are communicative interactions where discourses can be contested. That might seem odd because, for the most part, our conversations seldom have the feel of a 'contest'. To some extent that could be seen as a reflection of how our talk with others takes place in discourses where we share values and familiar ways of understanding. Talk nevertheless has its contests, and these are often over what 'should' be valued or familiar. What means do users of particular discourses employ to assert their discourse's dominance, or contest the dominance of another discourse? Recently, the premier of the province of Alberta (in Canada), in debating the Kyoto agreement on greenhouse gases, spoke of earlier climate changes as 'probably related to dinosaur farts', in order to discredit the science and discourse of 'global warming'. Users of discourses sometimes turn to particular 'rhetorical practices' to assert the dominance of their discourse while subverting those of others. Teun van Dijk (1993, 1997) has, for example, long been concerned with showing how racist discourses are used to counter immigration policies, or see funding withdrawn from school second-language programmes.

CDA sees its efforts as focused on the 'losers' in such social interactions. To that end their analytic efforts are 'emancipatory' and focused on advocacy. Good analytic work should show how discursive contests (or potential contests) play out, making evident the discourses and rhetorical practices used, along with the 'winners and losers'. Of particular interest to CDA are the ways in which users of dominant discourses try to prohibit such discursive contests, to further the dominance of their familiar and value-based ways of communicating.

Fairclough (1995) proposes the following as an analytic framework for doing CDA, adapted from the work of critical theorist Roy Bhaskar (1989):

*Focus upon a social problem which has a semiotic aspect.
*Identify the obstacles to tackling the social problem, through an analysis of the network of discursive practices the problem is located within, relating the semiotic resources (e.g. language, symbols used) to other elements within that network of discursive practices and resources.
  *structural analysis: the order of the discourse
  *interactional analysis
  *interdiscursive analysis
  *linguistic and semiotic analysis
*Consider whether the social order (network of practices) in a sense 'needs' the problem.
*Identify possible ways past the obstacles.
*Reflect critically on the analysis.

Let us do a walk-through of Fairclough's framework. Suppose we focus on 'the youth problem'. First, we need to consider how this 'problem' is reflected in different forms of communication. To that end, we could examine these different forms in different contexts where features of 'the problem' are communicated. Hence, we might want to look at portrayals of young people in different media, considering such things as which pictures predominate, or how newspaper articles represent youth, or how the topic of youth is discussed in venues such as political forums, parent online listservs, or school policies, or in the everyday conversations of young people as they interact. Analysis would focus on how these portrayals are made and countered (or not countered), the 'practices' used in communications relevant to the construction of 'the problem'. In particular, we could focus on interactions where dominant views are asserted in ways that present obstacles to other views. How is this attempted or achieved through the use of particular words, symbols and rhetorical practices? Being able to answer this question is critical in showing how discursive dominance occurs, and can support the analysts' recommendations as they pertain to getting beyond the obstacles involved where dominance occurs. In the case of our youth example, if analysis showed that 'the youth problem' required certain dominant constructions (for example, that young people are non-communicative) with related discursive practices that sustained those constructions (such as through shutting down the means by which young people could communicate), then recommendations could focus on alternative practices (e.g., youth forums) that could enable other constructions.

CDA can be seen as a tool to view how dominant constructions of people and social phenomena are developed through the use of particular rhetorical practices, symbols, words, and so on. Such developments are not causal, though they play a role in shaping what Teun van Dijk (1993, 1997) sees as 'social cognition', for most discourse analysts do not make significant distinctions between thought and talk. For van Dijk, social cognition is where macro-levels of dominant cultural talk play out at the micro-level. When someone uses a negatively connoted description to describe him or herself (e.g., 'I'm a loser'), we have an insidious example of this at work. It is the value-laden basis of discourse that CDA wants to make explicit and available for contest. Describing oneself as 'fat' or 'disabled' can reflect less than neutral uses of language. Any time words convey how things are, or are not, 'supposed to be' we are looking at an aspect of discourse that can be seen as political. Arguing over what it means to be of a certain nationality can show who wins and loses in that nationality's construction. Similarly, we can look at constructions of gender, morality, aesthetics, governance, and so on, to find discourses dominating and up for contest. At the root of this perspective, there is no bottom-line description of how things are or should be. Instead, CDA highlights critical concerns for how our cultural understandings and practices are put together, seeing their norms as products of social interactions that inescapably favour some people, constructs, and practices over others.

CDA offers tools for us to reflect on how any understanding or practice comes to dominate our thinking and interactions with others. Foucault, in particular, helped us to see that when such thought and interaction comes packaged in particular, value-based discourses, we can miss its effects, much like a fish would hardly see itself as existing in water. CDA reminds us that anything that passes for real or good probably owes its status as such to a discourse we use in which that is how it is regarded. Thinness hasn't always been how beauty has been socially constructed. For it to have been regarded this way, other constructions of beauty had to be subordinated. For the DSM-IVR to have ascended to the language of psychiatry, other languages and constructs had to be subordinated. The point here, for CDA, is that, if all understandings and practices are contestable, how do some come to dominate? In some cases, discursive dominance will not be an issue. Upon critical reflection people will see such understandings and practices as best in serving their purposes. But in other cases, CDA can help unmask discursive constructions and practices that are harmful to those living with and by its effects.

Within psychology, CDA, particularly when combined with historical analyses, has been useful in 'deconstructing' dominant or taken-for-granted psychological knowledge and practices (e.g., Burman, 1994; Danziger, 1997a; Parker, 1998a). How, for example, has the computer metaphor become such a prevalent way of seeing humans as mere information processors, while other competing (e.g., psychodynamic or narrative) accounts of being human have been subordinated? How do some versions of pedagogy, therapeutic practice or other sanctioned professional endeavours come to be justified as exclusive or best? How competing versions of science come to dominate has become a focus for those sharing this general view (e.g., Kuhn, 1962). The point to be taken here is that when competing versions of 'what's right' play out in any sphere of human activity, the means by which some versions gained prominence should be evident both historically and in empirically analysable interactions that show how that prominence is sustained. Depending on your view of professional practice, the dominance of any meaning, either in society or a client's thinking, is grist for a CDA kind of conversation. Tracing such meanings back to the cultural discourses in which they acquire their sense of correctness, so that these meanings and discourses can be contested for alternatives, has become a common practice in narrative therapy (White and Epston, 1990).

In a sense, CDA presents a primarily macroscopic view of the workings of cultural discourse – how it shapes social interaction and understanding in dominant ways. This can seem to be the case of people merely doing the bidding of aggregate ways of talking and understanding, as if they were ventriloquizing cultural discourses that determine their thoughts and interactions. At worst, this view comes close to portraying people as Garfinkel's (1967) (see Chapter 10) 'cultural dopes', but a more nuanced consideration shows discourses as circumscribed cultural fields of possibility. Said another way, there are infinite and creative ways one could advocate for the new economy, but one would likely be considered 'out of bounds' if favourably mentioning government-administered health care. Cultural discourses are seen to shape the micro-dynamics of social interaction in this 'in and out of bounds' way. But there is another approach to discourse analysis that looks at communicative interaction even more microscopically, as our means of reconciling being social with the personal: conversation analysis.

Conversational Analysis

> The search for good problems by reference to known big issues will have large-scale, massive institutions as the apparatus by which order is generated and by a study of which order will be found. If, on the other hand, we figure or guess or decide that whatever humans do, they are just another animal after all, maybe more complicated than others but perhaps not noticeably so, then whatever humans do can be examined to discover some way they do it ...That is, we may alternatively take it that there is order at all points.   (Sacks, 1984: 22)

Conversation Analysis (CA) takes Harold Garfinkel's (1967) study of situated orders in a particular scientific direction that flourishes today. Initially the brain-child of Harvey Sacks (1995), CA follows Sacks's attempt to 'reverse engineer' what he referred to as an 'architecture or technology of intersubjectivity'. Such reverse engineering aims to show conversation as the means by which people sustain their relationships through how they handle particular shared problems in living. Sacks liked to show the particular conversational means people used to resolve such things as their membership in particular social groups, or how they brought a conversational topic to a close, or how they produced and handled lying. For him, these were ways of doing talk, and he referred to these ways in some-times off-putting mechanistic and technological language, as 'devices' for human communicative accomplishments. Where sociologists had typically turned to big-picture explanations for human interaction, he went microscopically inter-subjective, focusing on mostly unrecognized aspects of conversation he sought to classify and understand for their effects.

Sacks, a Yale-trained lawyer who studied sociology at Berkeley under the supervision of Erving Goffman (who refused to pass Sacks's dissertation but later arguably came to draw on his ideas), came into contact with Garfinkel in 1959, then forged a collaborative working relationship with Emmanuel Schegloff and Gail Jefferson, the chief proponents of CA today. Here is Sacks, with Garfinkel, in 1967 (the paper actually came out as a book chapter in 1970):

> We ask what it is about natural language that permits speakers and auditors to hear, and in other ways to witness, the objective production and objective display of commonsense knowledge, and of practical circumstances, practical actions, and practical sociological reasoning as well. What is it about natural language that makes these phenomena observable-reportable, that is, account-able phenomena?   (Garfinkel and Sacks, 1970: 342; emphasis in original)

Sacks took Garfinkel's ethnomethodological indifference and empiricism to an extreme, seeking to find in conversation equivalents to the classifiable phenomena

identified in forms of biological life. In 1963, he fortuitously acquired record-
ings and transcriptions of phone calls to the Los Angeles Suicide Prevention
Centre, and these sparked his curiosity in the orderliness of conversation. He
was wedded to the idea that there could be a natural science of conversation
much like other natural sciences (Lynch and Bogen, 1994). Sacks approached
this task by seeking conversational activities 'adequate' in accounting for how
people handled (at the most mundane level) particular everyday conversational
challenges. On this task, here he is again: 'What one ought to seek to build is
an apparatus which will provide for how it is that any activities, which members do in such a way as to be recognizable to members, are done, and done
recognizably' (Sacks, cited in Lynch and Bogen, 1994: 72). The apparatus to
which Sacks refers is what he and subsequent CA researchers have attempted to
'reverse engineer' from their detailed observations and classifications of everyday and other forms of conversation. Regrettably, Sacks died in a car accident
in 1975, but many since then have continued his work, Schegloff being the most
notable.

Particular to CA is its focus on the consequentiality of talk – how developments
can be observed to play out in actual sequences of talk. Sacks got very basic
about this, beginning with the most fundamental aspect of talk, that it hinges on
what takes place as people exchange turns in talk, in what CA researchers refer
to as 'adjacency pairs'. Here are Sacks, Schegloff and Jefferson's (1974) conclusions about the nature of an adjacency pair: (1) it is a sequence of two utterances,
which are (2) adjacent, (3) produced by different speakers, (4) ordered as a first
and second part, and (5) types, so that a first part requires a particular second
part (or range of second parts). Consider how adjacency pairs are performed in
greeting–response sequences and note that up to point five things look pretty
basic; after these comes a range of what the second speaker does with the first
speaker's greeting. Studying such a range of responses is typical to CA research;
what classifiable responses can be discerned from them in completing such a
conversational interaction? In answering such a question CA shows the different
ways a greeting–response adjacency pair is accomplished.

For Sacks and CA researchers conversation is where people do two important
things: they talk about something, and they talk so as to further certain ways of
relating. It is this second aspect of talk that normally goes unrecognized, but it is
central to how conversation contributes to social order. Sacks was very curious
about how people managed their relationships through how they talked, something he only wanted to do in the presence of data, of 'talk-in-interaction'. Here is
Emmanuel Schegloff, on this point:

> (intersubjective) activities and their organization can be, and should be, studied
> locally (that is, in the environments of their natural occurrence) and through
> the detailed examination of the indigenous practices through which it is (or
> they are) composed. And, further, that much more of what composes the social
> world than has been imagined by most sociologists may be investigated in
> terms of activities and their procedural infrastructure.   (1992: 1341)

If you are reacting to the language (e.g., 'procedural infrastructure') here, bear in mind the 'reverse-engineering' project CA researchers are pursuing. Their project, however, goes beyond trying to understand conversation in situ; they want to account for the 'machinery' of conversation generally – across contexts. This is partly where ethnomethodologists and CA researchers part company: Garfinkel saw situated orders with their own methods, Sacks and crew saw some of these methods as universal. But here is Sacks et al., in a classic CA article on turn-taking:

> Conversation can accommodate a wide range of situations, interactions in which persons in varieties (or varieties of groups) of identities are operating; it can be sensitive to the various combinations; and it can be capable of dealing with a change of situation within a situation. Hence there must be some formal apparatus which is itself context-free, in such ways that it can, in local instances of its operation, be sensitive to and exhibit its sensitivity to various parameters of social reality in a local context.   (1974: 699–700)

Generally, then, CA researchers seek universals in talk, ways people converse to manage particular common junctures in talk so as to stay mutually intelligible and in relationship. Thinking like Sacks, you might ask a question such as, 'how do people deal with differences of opinion?' and CA offers you a particular path to answering this question.

CA has become a well-defined method of research, evident in the following conventions:

1. a topic of relevance to communication and human relationships is suggested (e.g., sharing bad news);
2. gather samples of naturally occurring conversation that address the topic by taping and transcribing them (including important performative dimensions of talking and listening, such as pauses, gestures, intonations);
3. select sequences of talk that highlight the topic;
4. orient to these recorded/transcribed sequences with 'ethnomethodological indifference' (i.e., without theoretical or other assumptions);
5. consider how the speakers' packaging of actions, including their selection of reference terms, provides certain understandings of the actions performed and the matter talked about; consider the options for the recipient that are set up by that packaging;
6. consider how the timing and taking of turns provide for certain understandings of the actions and the matters talked about;
7. consider how the ways the actions were accomplished implicate certain identities, roles and relationships for interactants (see also Pomerantz and Fehr, 1997).

There are many features of talk one could focus on in this way of regarding the components of conversations: transition relevance places (places where turns in talk could but don't necessarily take place), adjacency pairs, places where the talk of participants overlaps, error accounts, formulations (where people offer the gist of what they've understood another to say) and conversational repairs – to name a few. CA can be a useful method for examining how speakers conversationally work out (or not) certain social challenges, such as forging agreements, repairing misunderstandings, and so on.

For example, in his dissertation, Jerry Gale, a research therapist and CA researcher, considered particular conversational strategies that solution-focused therapist Bill O'Hanlon used in a marital therapy session (Gale and Newfield, 1992). Among the strategies he observed O'Hanlon using was 'modifying his assertion until he receives the response he is seeking'. Gale named this 'modifying' strategy from close observation and analysis of occasions of phenomena that roughly matched this description, using what we have termed steps 5 to 7 above. Recognizing such a conversational phenomenon once is a start. But for it to be recognized as a 'conversational device' requires finding other comparable samples and then coming up with an apt description that captures what these occurrences demonstrate (in this case, 'modifying his assertion until he receives the response he is seeking'). The broader the range of ways such a device is performed, and responded to, the better for analytic purposes.

Any article of CA research (see the comprehensive CA bibliography at Paul ten Have's website (n.d.), for example) usually consists of the conversational data (in micro-detailed transcriptions according to conventions developed by Gail Jefferson) and analyses made directly from them. The onus is on the researcher to show how the inferences they have made from the transcribed conversations fit the parties involved in those conversations. In particular, it should be clear how the sequential order developed in conversation between parties relates to how those parties speak to each other, and what results from that speaking. In this way, those talking orient to prior conversations as a context they renew, either through replicating the context (its prior 'rules', understandings, etc.) or (sometimes) by modifying that context in new meanings and ways of talking. CA researchers see everyday conversation as the baseline from which more exclusive forms of talk, such as institutional talk, occurs. Normal talk is where conversation is not 'distorted' by conversational rules and roles particular to institutional talk. But CA can show, through how people make such rules and roles evident, institutional talk at work.

This pragmatic view of human communication holds that conversation involves speakers practically interpreting and responding to each other using accessible communicative resources (e.g., words and ways of communicating them). This view can seem at odds with that taken up in CDA for according people personal agency in what their conversations 'talk into being' on the one hand, while making general claims about conversational actions irrespective of speakers' cultural discourses on the other. One place where CA and CDA do converge is on the notion that speakers hold each other to normative conventions in how they listen and speak. That is, there is some expectation that speakers communicate in ways that meet shared norms of talking and understanding between them. Departures from these norms can lead to confusion, conflict and breaks in relatedness. But CA does not make the extra step of locating talk to cultural discourses, attributing any accomplishments in talk to what is already circumscribed as possible within these discourses. Where both differ from common everyday understandings of discourse is over the role of pragmatics in communicative interaction.

CA affords a microscopic look at what people do with their talk, how they use it to accomplish different purposes with each other. As a qualitative form of research, it operates from a rigour that owes much to the attention to detail one finds in reading Harvey Sacks. Fortunately, Sacks tape-recorded many of his lectures, which have been masterfully transcribed and edited, complete with introductory chapters by Emmanuel Schegloff, by Gail Jefferson (Sacks, 1995). In these lectures one can see the genesis of Sacks's science of conversation, a science that has been carried forward by Schegloff, Jefferson, Pomerantz and others (the latter two being former students of Sacks) since the mid-1970s. CA has affinities to Garfinkel and ethnomethodology, but is clearly a project that takes a stance that is more modern in its scientific tone than the post-structural-like views one would find through most EM research (see Lynch and Bogen, 1994, and Bogen, 1999). CA has become an interdisciplinary research approach, and examples of its research can be found in social psychology, sociology, anthropology and other journals where conversation is studied. Two texts (Hutchby and Woffitt, 1998; and ten Have, 1999) offer good entry points, and the ambitious can check out the reading possibilities in ten Have's (n.d.) huge bibliography at his website.

Harvey Sacks took exploring the taken-for-granted in conversation to a microscopic and fine art. CA reminds us that big things can happen at conversational turns, but usually they escape our notice. It also reminds us that, within conversation, we are influencing how we are relating to each other, as much as what we are talking about. Some might find it useful to delve into CA's conceptual repertoire, a growing body of conversational devices 'discovered' in the course of microscopic analyses, a repertoire that has relevance for such basics in conversation as how bad news gets discussed, how people 'repair' misunderstandings between them, and so on. More important, in our view, is the heuristic value of attending to the effects of talk, to see what practitioners contribute to developments within their conversations and what those conversations uphold unchanged or alter in accordance with the goals clients bring to therapy.

Straddling the macro-view and perspectives of CDA and the micro-view and perspectives of CA is a particular project which has drawn from both. The Discursive Psychology Project is pursued by members of the Discourse and Rhetoric Group at Loughborough University in Britain and has a particular critical and analytic focus – on psychological discourse.

The Discursive Psychology Project

We are concerned with the nature of knowledge, cognition and reality: with how events are described and explained, how factual reports are constructed, how cognitive states are attributed. These are defined as discursive topics, things people topicalize or orientate themselves to, or imply, in their discourse. And rather than seeing such discursive constructions as expressions of speakers' underlying cognitive states, they are examined in the context of their occurrence as situated and occasioned constructions whose precise nature makes sense, to participants and analysts alike, in terms of the social actions those descriptions accomplish.   (Edwards and Potter, 1992: 2)

A statement's meaning does not merely depend on the internal meanings of the words that compose it, but it also depends on the counter-statements, which are being opposed. The implication is that the same statement can have different meanings if it is opposing different counter-statements. Should the same statement be used to do very different argumentative jobs, then its meaning will alter.   (Billig, 1996: 275)

What passes for fact, particularly in psychology? This question serves as a heuristic for a group of Loughborough University scholars and researchers. But their efforts are not about trying to get in the final word on psychological facts – they are more interested in psychology's scientific and conversational process and its shifting outcomes. The Discourse and Rhetoric Group at Loughborough is home to Jonathan Potter, Derek Edwards, Michael Billig, Charles Antaki, and Malcolm Ashmore, among others. They are critical of the premise that foundational psychological knowledge can be 'discovered', so where mainstream psychology presents its knowledge in such a manner, their research aims to show the constructed nature of that knowledge. To that end, the Discursive Psychology Project (hereafter DP) has tackled such constructs as attitudes, memory, emotions, Freudian 'repression' or 'disability' – showing how they depend on particular research conventions and conversational practices for their centrality to mainstream psychological knowledge. Using methods largely borrowed from ethnomethodology, conversation analysis, and critical discourse analysis, DP sees in psychology, and everyday conversations where psychological constructs are used, a laboratory to observe how its constructs are developed, sustained, contested and altered.

The origins of DP can be traced back to its most prominent members. In the 1970s social psychologist Michael Billig took on orthodox social psychology for its methods and conclusions, shifting his research increasingly in that decade to the roles that rhetoric and ideology played in social life. He came to Loughborough in the mid-1980s, and by 1987 the Discourse and Rhetoric Group was formed, and included present members Derek Edwards and Jonathan Potter. While there are other members of this group who have also made considerable contributions (Charles Antaki, Dave Middleton, John Cromby and Malcolm Ashmore for example), for brevity's sake we will restrict our primary focus to the work of Potter, Edwards and Billig. What members of this Loughborough group shared were interests in discourse, rhetoric, activity and conversation – all of which remain central to their prolific writing and research. Central to their research is an aim to represent psychology in discursive terms. Where much of psychology has traditionally adopted methods from the naturalistic sciences to 'discover' its foundational knowledge, DP challenges such discovery science, countering with its discursive view. Here is Potter getting to the heart of the matter in his 1996 book *Representing Reality*:

> Reality enters into human practices by way of the categories and descriptions that are part of those practices. The world is not ready categorized by God or nature in ways that we are all forced to accept. It is *constituted* in one way or another as people talk about it, write it, and argue it.   (1996: 98; emphasis in the original).

Psychology's categories (examples: emotions, memories, understandings, attitudes, attributions), seen this way, are not found. Rather, they are the product of practices and conversations particular to psychologists. The constructs which DP tackles are especially those which psychology tends to locate inside people. So, for example, memory is often treated by psychology as the material property of our minds, something inside our heads. Extending their Wittgensteinian view (see his 'private language argument', Chapter 8), DP sees memory as the relational activity of remembering (Middleton and Edwards, 1990; Edwards and Potter, 1992; Edwards, 1997). In this regard, remembering is an activity that emanates from a relational request (that we offer a memory) that must be satisfied in honouring that request. Whether this occurs in examinations, everyday or imagined conversation with others, courtroom testimony, or psychotherapy interviews, remembering is an activity that, for DP, is performed, and thus observable, in relationships. It is mainstream and 'common-sense' conceptions of memory that have had us 'look inside' for memory. Ironically, as Wittgenstein (1953) long ago pointed out, to 'find' what is inside we require a language to name our memories and do that finding, and a language to report on and verify what we find, all done as part of relational activities that occur between people. This is a strikingly different view that defies our initial 'common sense', so let's look at some other examples of 'common-sense' psychological and 'internal' constructs that DP examines in conversational ways.

We turn now to examine 'social knowing', what many social psychologists refer to as 'attribution'. Typically, knowing refers to a retrievable aspect of our mental or inner lives. In this regard, efforts to retrieve knowing are seen as the projects of individuals who, according to the ubiquitous computer metaphor, search 'their files' for what has been registered as knowing. This knowing is then rendered, or applied, as circumstances require. Here are Edwards and Potter (1992: 84) on what we have been discussing: 'The discursive approach to attributions urges that these be studied as social acts performed in discourse, and not merely as cognitions about social acts, which happen to be expressed within conversation.'

Discursively, knowing is not merely about neutral information, but typically also relays evaluations regarding that information. Further, this information can be seen as a particular formulation of the topic under discussion. In this way, what is shared, as a 'fact', is thus a formulation and valuation that is potentially contestable (i.e., things don't have inherent value – humans assign value to things). Translated to the conversational activities where 'knowing', 'remembering', or even emoting, are relationally displayed – what takes place is more than a display of inner experience. Many conversational practices are involved in the articulation, countering and verification of these 'inner' experiences – and these shape what we see externally as reflections of these 'inner' experiences. People seldom passively respond to others' reports of experience, but play a role in articulating those reports. It may be through listening to another person telling them a story (even if only by using head nods to indicate one is following the story as told), arriving at some disputable 'truth' on a matter, or a disclosure that holds implications for the relationship in which that disclosure takes place. How such reports on our inner experiences are accomplished, in other words, is anything but an individual project – they are shaped in the back and forth of conversational activity.

If this seems challenging, consider that much psychological 'sampling' of 'inner experience' requires communication between any study's participants and the researcher, via interviews, paper and pencil tests, or behavioural assessments. Each of these activities usually requires words or other communicative gestures, from which the researcher infers 'inner experiences' on the basis of theories that account for how these reports relate to 'inner experiences'. This is precisely the psychological research practice that DP takes exception to, preferring instead to examine what is observable for how those reports influence the actions of those involved in their sharing. As would conversation analysts and ethnomethodologists, DP is interested in how people (including psychologists and their subjects) demonstrate they understand and make use of these commonplace psychological terms as they interact. How, for example, are our emotions to be understood? Are they inner energies that have named themselves to us and others? Or are they understood via conversations and other non-verbal behaviours that give them their names, and subsequently shape the way they are shared between people – as Wittgenstein (1953) suggested in his 'private language argument'? From another angle, does my experience and display of sorrow emanate from me, uninfluenced by prior experiences or the people before me as I display them? Such questions about psychological constructs (normally seen as 'internal' to people) can be profoundly disorienting. But, for DP, all such constructs need to be examined in the light of their relational performance and relevance.

Recently, Michael Billig (1999) re-examined Freudian notions of 'repression' in ways consistent with DP's critical focus on rendering what psychology has portrayed as 'internal' in conversationally performable and observable ways. For Billig (and many other discursive thinkers), our ways of communicating structure the way we think: what is understood as repression can be seen in terms of conversational practices used in emphasizing certain aspects of talk over others. Repression, seen this way, can be a useful conversational strategy to avoid talking about things of negative consequence to our relationships. We should consider Billig's long-term interests in rhetoric, ideology and argument here, for his focus has not always been on the kinds of topics we have been discussing so far. In his classic book, *Arguing and Thinking*, Billig contends that our thinking is shaped by how we anticipate it will perform for us in the conversational interactions with others where we might put such thinking to use. In his words,

> Any reasoned argument seeks to exclude, or persuade against, counter-arguments. In this way, affirmation and negation are intertwined, as the logoi of discourse are also anti-logoi, to be understood in relation to the context of controversy.   (1996: 2)

Put another way, our 'private thoughts' are shaped by how we conceptualize making them public – we take the anticipated arguments and responses of others into how we think. This is yet another way of saying that what mainstream and lay psychology has considered private and internal experience can be seen in conversational terms – especially as it is reported. Billig (1996) theorizes here, but take a moment to consider how your private thoughts are shaped by how you feel others would receive them.

At this point it makes sense to bring up arguments that others, particularly Ian Parker (Parker and Burman, 1993; Parker, 1998a; Parker, 1998b), have made in response to the DP ideas and research. DP sees reality as largely a conversational accomplishment, and any claim to fact or objectivity itself relies on particular conventions and conversational practices (Edwards, Ashmore and Potter, 1995; Potter, 1996). Some critics of this view, such as Parker, see an untenable moral relativism in DP (and other forms of postmodern thinking, for that matter), that it is too ready to see the material realities (as perceived by those CDA aims to help) as one of a range of other plausible constructions of those realities. For Parker, not all constructions are equal, and this raises important cultural considerations as to why. For CDA, those who benefit from things remaining uncontested do things to keep contestable meanings from being contested. To that end, they use particular conversational practices to dominate conversation. The 'realities' DP describes, to critics like Parker, tends to overlook such aspects of discourse. One nub of the argument here relates to a point DP proponents won't concede to Parker and others: that some realities are more real than others. In this line of thought they see a slippery slope back to an incontestable reality.

> Though realism is excellent rhetoric, maybe the best in a purely technical or instrumental sense, such rhetoric cannot be an adequate reason to accept it as a serious intellectual position. In its tropes of Death and Furniture we see a rhetoric that refuses to acknowledge its own existence; a politics that can claim a critical-radical credibility only by the selective use of its opponents' analytical tools; and a theology that is deeply conservative and seeks nothing less than the death of disruptive, disturbing inquiry. While tedium, good taste, political and moral sensibility will properly determine what sorts of given realities are thought worthy of inquiry, those considerations are no grounds for promoting a realist ontology for science, nor any other science, nor for rejecting relativism. On the contrary, relativism is social science par excellence.   (Edwards et al., 1995: 42)

Parker saw this as a 'quintessentially academic position', and not reflective of the inequitably lived realities of many. Another critique of the DP position is levelled at its seeming 'neutral' stance, tantamount to accusing DP of claiming the very kind of objective detachment it takes to task in its different discursive analyses. Ironically, it was Billig who took up the CDA perspective when directing this very argument to the chief spokesperson of conversation analysis, Emmanuel Schegloff (Billig and Schegloff, 1999).

The Discursive Psychology Project has turned the analytical tools of discourse analysis on psychology itself, contesting foundational psychological knowledge most would have thought uncontestable. Their constructionist view, in this regard, is reflected in the methods they use to show how 'facts' are constructed and used in different conversational arenas (you might recall Garfinkel's 1967 comment about 'fact construction in flight'). By casting psychology's many 'inner constructs' in performable, observable and (therefore) analysable interpersonal behaviours, they have made its dominant constructions accessible to contest as the following quote suggests.

> What we are left here is not a world devoid of meaning and value (or a world of absolute amorality where 'everything is permitted', as in the Nietzschean-Dostoevskian conclusion) but precisely the reverse. It is a foregrounding of meanings and values, to be argued, altered, defended and invented; including even the metavalue that some of these meanings and values may profitably be declared universal and even self-evident ('We hold these truths to be self-evident …'). Self-evidence here is the outcome rather than the denial of argumentation.   (Edwards, Ashmore and Potter, 1995: 36)

Their research on thought, attitudes (like racism), memory and emotions extends Wittgenstein's (1953) insight that the 'private language' typically used to conceptualize 'inner life' is one that originates and is verified in social interaction.

Socio-linguistics, CDA, CA and DP – what do they offer a discursive approach to relational practice?

> The alphabetized intellect stakes its claim to the earth by *staking it down*.   (Abram, 1996: 267; emphasis in the original)

By now it should be clear that we see language and how it is used as anything but a neutral human activity of swapping information correctly put into words. For starters, 'correctly', for us, suggests a particular discursive location with criteria adopted by speakers within that location. As speakers and listeners we are born into and grow up in conversations in progress, conversations that use particular understandings and ways of communicating that do not necessarily carry over to other conversations. There is a kind of anthropological dimension to all of this; one that we contend can inform a respect for and sensitivity to variations in meaning and conversing. This is quite a different notion of meaning and conversing from the view that our words can correctly represent and transmit reality. Therapy, from the latter view, could be seen as a case of aligning one's words with how things really are, using expertise in the nuances of the word–reality hook-up to correct and direct clients based on what is already known. But, socio-linguistically, this takes us back to Labov's concern about 'correct' ways of talking and understanding over others, and what that means for these other ways that flourish and by which those using them generally do fine. Wittgenstein, as you will recall, went down the linguistic correctness path, only to later turn to how people did forms of life in their varied language games.

Accepting a discursive view that things can be talked about and understood differently, in viable ways for those doing these different kinds of talking and understanding, is an uncommon stance to take on relational practice. It raises issues of how to communicate so as to bridge differences in understanding and ways of talking. It also raises issues as to which ways of understanding and talking should inform practice: those of the practitioner or those clients will continue to use (albeit often in modified form) back in the everyday conversations they share with others. In therapy these issues have received a lot of attention, since the primary activity of therapy is conversation. Therapists who have taken a discursive turn in their practice are mindful of differences in meaning, of what might be problematically taken for granted as uncontestable understandings, and of how even the languages they were trained in might be suspect for furthering some forms of cultural dominance. This is before one considers the actual back and forth of what gets said and heard as client and therapist talk their way through their time together.

There are several ways to consider what a discursive perspective offers to relational practice. Drawing from socio-linguistics, one way is to see conversation as a means of orienting to the discursive uniqueness of clients' ways of talking about and understanding experience. Seen this way, one challenge for the practitioner is to listen 'ethnographically', to hear differences in how language is used to represent experience, and how clients perform conversation itself. But it is one thing to be discerning of and sensitive to such discursive differences and another to engage with clients talking from such differences. This can put the onus (rightly, we think) on the practitioner to be the discursively flexible party in professional conversations (Strong, 2002). Such flexibility encompasses both the listening and speaking domains and involves finding ways to bridge discursive differences with ways of communicating that suit both parties. Without such flexibility practitioners and clients may be talking right past each other.

From critical discourse analysts comes an appreciation for how any presenting problem discourse may initially preclude other discursive articulations of problems and their solutions. To extend a point made by Gramsci (1971), problem descriptions can slip from being one of many possible descriptions to a seeming sole description in the absence of critical reflection and consideration of alternatives. The dominance of any problem discourse partly relies not only on its unquestioned use, but sometimes in the expectation others have of our holding to such a discourse. Witness the political consequences for those 'soft on terrorism' for any questioning of US troop deployment in Iraq. Using the change-oriented resources of CDA to subvert dominant constructions of experience sustained in particular discourses can feel like a daunting exercise. Sometimes this can seem like inviting others to join in deconstructing Santa Claus, while other times it can feel like going after bullies (try countering a bully's language). One route into these kinds of conversations is to invite reflection on how things came to be understood and talked about as they have been – and then to ask about the alternatives passed over in so doing. But this takes a relationship wherein one feels comfortable in being asked to (publicly in a sense) question often 'hard-won' understandings.

Family therapist Tom Andersen (1996) once wrote that 'language is not innocent'. Its availability to us owes something to the purposes it has already been put to, purposes that might not fit a circumstance to which it may be imported. Primary school classrooms can be talked about using the new economy discourse, but that would present the students, teachers, curriculum and so on in a very different light from, say, a discourse about things growing from nurturing actions and resources. Taken another step, such discourses present dramatically different ways to relate to people and what they get up to. Questions can arise here about the exclusivity of any discourse. Can people talk about bereavement, for example, in both medical and spiritual discourses, talking about one's wellbeing and one's relationships in the same breath? In CDA, the chief concern is with dominance of meaning and dominance of the discourses which people use in relating to problems. It can often be the case that people are not well served by the hand-me-down languages they unquestioningly use for relating to their concerns. Questioning the dominance of any linguistic construction or discourse can be a way of creating the thinking and conversational space for alternative constructions and discourses to be considered.

Pondering the utility of CA for relational practice reminds us of the joke about asking the centipede how she moves all those legs. The answer can paralyse, given the complexities involved. For ethnomethodologist Harold Garfinkel the micro-interactions that sustain particular social versions of reality are like walls that hold up buildings. His colleague Harvey Sacks questioned how people 'do' the basic things that sustain their relatedness. One can apply his reverse engineering attitude to considering how people do some problems in ways that sustain the problems. If you see the therapist Bill O'Hanlon (1992), he'll tell you how he has 'done his depression' en route to asking you how you do yours. A similar inquiry could profitably be considered for relational concerns. Problem interactions can be understood in terms of their requisite actions and understandings.

Most people involved in relational practices rely heavily on their communications with clients to accomplish what they can in working with them. In this sense, they are hopefully mindful of what clients do with their talk at each critical juncture in their conversations, since evidence of how they are received is available after each turn at talking – in how clients respond (Strong, Busch and Couture, 2008). Harlene Anderson (1997) speaks of 'coordinating intentionalities' through helping conversation. For her this refers to a careful process of co-constructing a shared language of intentions that is continually revisited and revised to promote a collaborative and generative relationship. When the meaning of our communications can be understood in terms of the responses we get to them, our challenge is in creating conversations where, as with a good dance partner, we can find a synchrony in how initiatives are taken and responses made – all within shared understanding and aims. It is in this respect that linguist Herbert Clark (1996) described people using their talk to arrive at 'common ground' in their understandings and conversational practices. Without it each party can listen and talk from different, discursive, 'reality tunnels'.

Related to the previous point, CA offers practitioners who videotape their work a resource for analysing critical interactions. Much, for example, can be learned from the micro-interactions involved in arriving (or not arriving) at shared goals, working through misunderstandings, or 'teachable moments'. What are the taken for granted things that we do or say in our conversational turn-taking when things go well, or not so well? What can we learn from going micro- in how we regard our relational practices?

Finally, DP often shows how steeped most of us are in psychologized views of relational practice. One point Wittgenstein was firm about was that we relate to each other on the basis of what is socially observable for us – nothing of what matters to social interaction is hidden. DP challenges psychological discourse for turning our attention inward, away from the interactions that animate our so-called private experience and make it at least somewhat discernible to others. Others' cognitions are made evident to us through talking, writing and through non-verbal inferences we make from their responses to us. But many psychologists claim to be able to assess our 'inner' being, sampling a host of 'inner things' that DP sees in discursive terms: emotions, attitudes, defence mechanisms, cognition, and so on. To describe these 'things' as at least somewhat socially constructed seems to challenge some fundamentals of how we know ourselves personally. The same goes for how we think we have inferred our senses of each other – to know someone is purportedly to know what is in their hearts and minds. DP, along with many discourse analysts, suggests we look instead at what our interactions with others 'occasion' in terms of the stuff we elicit and then make inferences from.

If the stuff of our inner being (i.e., the stuff we consider psychological) is bound up in discursive processes (in actual, imagined and anticipated 'inner' interactions), what are we to make of the discursive interactions we have with clients? Clients, too, often come to understand and present their concerns in psychological discourse because it is so available to them via different media (Cushman, 1995; Starker, 2002). Emotions, thoughts, attitudes and so on do not emanate from within us, irrespective of the culturally available languages and social interactions in which we come to understand and talk about them, goes DP thinking. Psychology's focus on these 'private properties of our being', the privileges accorded to practitioners using psychological discourse to better name and direct us to manage them, can turn people away from reflecting on and shaping such discourses. Kenneth Gergen (1999) once described some psychological discourses as 'progressively enfeebling' for how they turned those depicted by them away from altering their engagements with others and life. While, in some cases, labelling a problem as PTSD can validate a concern and enable particular means of treatment, a downside can occur when, for example, a family problem gets translated into the language of symptoms articulated in psychological discourse. Practitioners play a major role in how experiences get named, and whether the people they help look inwardly or outwardly to make sought-after changes in their lives. They also can invite clients to step back from particular constructions and practices and engage in discursive processes that might modify them.

Coda

Thinking about the role language and discourse might play in making evident some understandings and actions, while constraining others, is a fairly recent endeavour. But to understand experience and be able to communicate it to others involves using language. Different research projects have helped us to understand better how humans use language in ways that we take for granted. With these understandings come new ways to think about how we communicate with each other. Not just any language will do. As the creators of the linguistic resources we use, it is our job to make these resources serve us, rather than be limited by them.

Discourse analysis, in the broad sense, is a classic case of turning rigorous, scientific attention to what is often taken for granted in human affairs. From past thinkers – ethnomethodologists such as Garfinkel (Chapter 10), for example – and from Wittgenstein (in his language games, Chapter 8), we have learned that language-use involves social practices (or interactions) that can maintain social order, or that might negotiate or depart from the normative conventions that maintain such order, in all its local and cultural variations. Seen one way, discourse analysis involves research approaches that study how social life is accomplished – studying the discursive means by which people interact so as to keep things acceptably familiar between them. In Harvey Sacks's language, what matters here is how people normatively 'do' aspects of social life through their communications. Greetings, introducing new topics in conversations, handling disagreements, and so on, are all examples to which some discourse analysts turn their attention. There is another aspect of discourse analysis, very much in vogue these days, that is used to expose and contest how social orders are accomplished. Critical discourse analysts, in this sense, borrow from other discourse analysts to turn conversation or social interaction reflexively 'on to itself'. The assumption here is that social norms are an often taken-for-granted consequence of people's social interactions. By turning attention to how things are discursively maintained, people are in a better position to question such normative, discursive practices should they desire. So, taken together, discourse analysis points to how social meaning and order is constructed, but critical discourse analysis suggests the means by which such meanings and order can be deconstructed as well. When one further adds the thinking of later-day hermeneutic scholars (Gadamer, Ricoeur, Habermas and Levinas – see Chapter 4) on discursive ethics, then reflection on and modification of language-use as it relates to others becomes possible. This said, the key to discourse analysis is to see language-use as a meaningful activity for how it accomplishes social and cultural relations – preferred or otherwise.

As we move to our contemporary theorists – Ken and Mary Gergen, Rom Harré, and John Shotter – we will find their unique syntheses of the insights of discourse analysis (and the ideas of many of the thinkers we have been covering) into both critical (i.e., deconstructive) and generative approaches to social practice. What emerges from these contemporary theorists are ways to reflect on dominant practices and understandings in the social sciences, alongside very practical ways of looking at human interaction. Big-picture ideas are refracted through their writing and combined with the discourse analyst's focus on how social life is 'done' in human interaction. The results point to some very useful ways of considering the collaborative and generative possibilities of professional dialogue.

14   Ken and Mary Gergen

> Traditions of cultural life furnish numerous avenues to suffering; the challenge is to develop resources for moving through cultural life effectively as opposed to sedating ourselves for the journey.   (K. J. Gergen, 2006: 159)

> Our words constitute forms of action that invite others into certain forms of relationship as opposed to others.   (M. M. Gergen and K. J. Gergen, 2001: 13)

Psychology has been the source of many ideas and interventions when it comes to professional practice. A major fork in the road occurred early in the discipline's history when most psychologists decided on a natural science over human science direction. This shift saw most psychologists aiming to explain human experience using methods and ideas one associates with the 'hard sciences': statistical prediction, 'objectivity' and knowledge readily adaptable to technological purposes. While psychologists tend not to wear labcoats these days, culturally many view psychology as the enterprise best positioned to deliver the foundational truths needed to guide such social practices as education, management strategies and policies, psychotherapy, even advertising. At the time of writing this book the American Psychological Association implicitly condones the participation of its members in ensuring scientifically warranted practices of torture.

Not every psychologist took the same direction at the fork in the road, of course, nor has the discipline ever abandoned the notion that its science and practices could be closer to those Vico or Dilthey might have envisioned. Such a human science, and the practices that might follow from it, start from very different premises about humans as practical interpreters and agents within their circumstances. To paraphrase cybernetician Heinz von Foerster (1984a), many object to seeing humans as trivial machines. So, the other fork in the road has had its followers, while waxing and waning in cultural influence (e.g., the human potential movement of the late 1960s). For the most part, however, many taking this road less travelled had at the centre of their psychological thinking the autonomous, humanist individual of the romantic era, as Ken Gergen has pointed out (1991).

Outside of psychology, the 1970s saw remarkable developments: feminist and postcolonial critiques; strikingly different linguistic philosophies; imported social conceptions of psychology from Vygotsky; and a general Zeitgeist of change following the conservatism of the Second World War. Psychology, an enterprise focused on improving human life, suddenly was criticized for exclusionary knowledge and practices, for promoting bandwagons in education and other social practices that had not cashed out well, while its lab rats were caricatured by cartoonists as having conditioned the psychologists studying them. Making sense of these developments, integrating them into useful conceptions of social practice, while critiquing mainstream psychology from understandings derived from these new developments, have been the focus of Ken and Mary Gergen's articulation of social constructionist thought and practice. Thus, their approach has been both critical and generative; advancing collaborative and resourceful relational practices while challenging psychological understandings, methods and practices they see as lacking such collaboration and resourcefulness. From Ken's early concerns about psychology's ahistorical approach to knowledge (K. J. Gergen, 1973) and insufficiently social conceptions of self (K. J. Gergen, 1971), through Mary's suggestions to reconstruct psychology on more feminist terms (M. M. Gergen, 2001), and through many collaborations (e.g., Gergen and Gergen, 2004), their efforts have been central in articulating a social constructionist view of people and relational practice. In recent years, they have been instrumental in founding the Taos Institute through which they and others advance social constructionist ideas and practices in fields as varied as business and organizational development, psychotherapy and community relations.

We shall approach the Gergens' social constructionism by considering several strands in their writing. First, we will examine Ken's critiques of psychology as a human science, especially as these relate to his integrative efforts to fashion a social constructionist counter-narrative to psychology's dominant understandings and practices. We shall then more specifically consider his social constructionist and 'postmodern' views of self. Mary's contributions will be reviewed in terms of her efforts to expand the research focus and qualitative methods of psychology. Finally, we shall turn our attention to the shared efforts of Ken and Mary in furthering relational and cultural practices that are socially just, collaborative and generative.

Psychological knowledge and practice

> In generating knowledge about social interaction, we also communicate our personal values. The recipient of knowledge is thus provided with dual messages: Messages that dispassionately *describe* what appears to be, and those which subtly *prescribe* what is desirable.   (K. J. Gergen, 1973: 311)

A social psychologist by training, Ken Gergen approached his subject matter in ways that extended beyond the usual scope of his colleagues. His early scholarship, in his first faculty role at Harvard in the 1960s, was wide-ranging and took up issues as varied as ageing, race and role relations, conformity or lack thereof, and the self in social interaction. But social psychology was a sub-discipline posing conceptual and other challenges to scholars aiming to reconcile individual with social life. A focus on the 'psyche' of individuals often translates to downplaying the fundamental relatedness and historical rootedness of human life, as a beginning (K. J. Gergen, 1997). It is perhaps unsurprising that Ken turned to thinking from outside his discipline to help make better sense of what it meant to be 'socially psychological'. By the early 1970s one increasingly finds sociologists, historians, philosophers and novelists referenced alongside psychologists in his writing (e.g., K. J. Gergen, 1971). But, it was with his seminal 1973 article, 'Social psychology as history', that Gergen took on his discipline for the knowledge claims it was making and the use made of those claims.

To a field striving for scientific status, the primary challenge raised by Ken – that psychology could at best offer knowledge contemporaneous with its cultural circumstances, methods and concerns – was an audacious criticism. For physicists this was nothing new; Einstein had encouraged this realization more than a half century earlier. But for many psychologists bent on determining causal laws and transcendent descriptions of human psychological functioning, Gergen's argument seemed seditious. For others, it was a welcome acknowledgement of psychology catching up with developments in science and linguistic philosophy. 'Social psychology as history' is a hermeneutic account of psychology's methods and developing knowledge base. Whether seen as a wake-up call to a profession needing to acknowledge its historical and cultural rootedness, or an insult to those engaged in efforts to get the final word on human behaviour, the article serves as a landmark in psychology's development as a science and profession. Let's look more closely at why this is the case.

In a sense, Ken Gergen was speaking to an emerging crisis in social psychology. Already the sub-discipline was having to grapple with developments such as Mischel's (1968) situational view of self and Gergen (1971) himself had described the self in terms of the varied social processes and concepts relevant to 'its' development. His 1973 article tackled some important themes still current in his writing today. He began with distinctions between knowledge claims from the human sciences and those of the natural sciences. Psychology's purportedly timeless knowledge base was historical and cultural. Social psychology's knowledge, once accessible to the lay reader, influences those it studies, in effect putting the discipline and society in a transformational dialogue with each other. Giddens (1976) would elsewhere refer to this as a 'double hermeneutic'. That people are now able to self-identify using psychopathological terms further underscores Gergen's (1990) point. The dominant view at the time was that social science knowledge, for revealing the enduring truth of human experience, could serve the same functions as physical truths did for engineering. Presumably, correct social prescriptions could be made from such knowledge. By suggesting that social psychology be seen as a mode of history-making, Gergen challenged psychologists' social use of their knowledge as 'scientifically warranted'. Psychologists' social knowledge was insufficiently stable to serve as a foundation from which to engage in social engineering. In 'Social psychology as history' Gergen called for a more humble, historically grounded psychology:

> In essence, the study of social psychology is primarily an historical
> undertaking. We are essentially engaged in a systematic account of

> contemporary affairs. We utilize scientific methodology, but the results are not scientific principles in the traditional sense. In the future, historians may look back to such accounts to achieve a better understanding of life in the present era. However, the psychologists of the future are likely to find little of value in contemporary knowledge.   (K. J. Gergen, 1973: 317)

Such comments earned Ken Gergen lightning-rod status for waves of criticism he endures to the present day. Critics read such comments as broadsides against their aims, methods and outcomes, while decrying what they saw as implicit historical and cultural relativism. These attacks have been vociferous (Schlenker, 1974) and personal (Ratner, 2005). Where most social scientists critically refute what they see as inadequate methods and problematic research outcomes, Gergen responded to his critics as if engaged in a historico-cultural dialogue where knowledge claims and the methods from which they were derived could be rigorously contested and supplemented. In a social science bent on getting the final word, many of his colleagues refused to join the dialogue. The decade which followed saw him articulate an integrative yet critical view of psychology that culminated in his *Toward Transformation in Social Knowledge* (1994b; first edition, 1982). There he squarely took on his critics, displaying considerable erudition and coherence in articulating his social constructionist approach to practice.

Toward Transformation in Social Knowledge shows Ken Gergen advancing arguments he saw as needed. His concerns were as fraught with implications for psychology as Copernicus's arguments were for medieval astronomy. Though 'Social psychology as history' brought him many critics, it also led to fruitful exchanges on parallel developments occurring outside psychology – a 'revolution' was occurring in the social sciences. *Toward a Transformation in Social Knowledge* (hereafter *TTSK*) ambitiously challenged modern psychology on many fronts: that social science could yield foundational knowledge; that language could unproblematically represent and communicate knowledge; that there could be 'correct' psychological theorizing; that there were inevitable shortcomings in authoritative and predictive accounts of psychological development; and that psychology fails to recognize itself as a history-making endeavour.

Gergen prefaced *TTSK* with his hope for a 'reawakened' discussion about psychology developing as a human (instead of natural) science. Turning back the clock, despite very involved discussions at the start of the twentieth century, mainstream psychology elected to adopt the methods and thinking of natural science as it was then being conducted. Such an approach to the variability and diversity of human life reduced our knowledge of human conduct and understanding to presumed universal 'laws'. In this respect, psychological science could be seen as handmaiden to a global, psychological monoculture where cultural and idiopathic differences are treated as statistically irrelevant noise. The 'aleatory' experience of life as consequential encounters with the unpredictable was shunted out of psychology's research focus, for a presumed universal pathway of human development. How language fits in representing and in communicating psychological knowledge and practice (i.e., how psychological descriptions can, in effect, become prescriptions) is also a focal concern in *TTSK*. More radical was Ken's view that theory can be more than predictive – it can be useful and generative. But his chief concern was with psychologists' quest for the one correct or certain theory. No doubt he stirred the ire of more than a few psychologists with quotes like the following: 'The search for certainty is a child's romance, and like most, one holds on to the most fragile shard attesting to continued life. The question that now must be confronted is how to pass successfully into the second century' (1994b: 209).

TTSK's sweeping critique of the premises, practices and uses of psychological research remains relevant today given that its arguments were unfortunately dismissed, ignored or scarcely heeded by a majority of psychological researchers. For those bent on discovering ultimate truth, Gergen's advocacy that psychologists aim for more modest and generative understandings useful to society at large was not well received. But *TTSK* helped to place Gergen at the forefront of developments he would later (K. J. Gergen, 1985) summarize in a 'programmatic statement' in *American Psychologist*: 'The social constructionist movement in modern psychology'.

Gergen's 1985 article reads like a manifesto, in a positive way. It offers a concise description of his concerns regarding psychological science while articulating benefits he felt a social constructionist approach could offer psychology. Here was his definition of social constructionist inquiry in that article:

> Social constructionist inquiry is principally concerned with explicating the processes by which people come to describe, explain, or otherwise account for the world (including themselves) in which they live. It attempts to articulate common forms of understanding as they now exist, as they have existed in prior historical periods, and as they might exist should creative attention be so directed.   (K. J. Gergen, 1985: 267)

Gergen, in other words, was asking psychologists to look at their research and its dissemination as socially constructive processes for the shared understandings they yielded, instead of looking past people's everyday languages for psychological explanations of 'what was really going on'. In this regard, he was asking psychologists to consider the wide-ranging implications of the 'linguistic turn' seen in later Wittgenstein, and in hermeneutic scholars such as Gadamer and Ricoeur. This 'turn' suggests that meaning cannot be given to experience in any absolute sense, but must instead be seen as contributions to an ongoing human and cultural endeavour. An examination of *American Psychologist* in the mid-1980s shows Gergen was not alone in bringing this perspective to the fore. Articles from colleagues such as Edward Sampson (1981) and Martin Packer (1985) show related ideas in circulation. In Britain, critics of psychology sharing a similarly discursive perspective had also been challenging the field's premises, methods, applications and potentials (e.g., Shotter, 1975, 1984; Henriques et al., 1984; Rose, 1985). While a forceful critique (like *TTSK* or 'Social psychology as history'), the 1985 article eloquently served as a kind of clarion call for the potentials of 'social constructionism' in psychology, and in so doing invited another round of scathing critiques as foretold in this comment:

> constructionism will inevitably confront strong resistance within psychology ... It forms a potential challenge to traditional knowledge claims; psychological research itself is placed in the uncomfortable position of a research object.   (K. J. Gergen, 1985: 272)

Ken Gergen's apparent aim was to make way for a view of generative knowledge creation, to optimize the benefits for users and constructors of such knowledge (K. J. Gergen, 1995). This extends to his view of therapeutic processes (e.g., McNamee and Gergen, 1992; Gergen, 2006) as targets of criticism: for insufficient considerations of language-use in therapeutic practice, and in interpreting and articulating research and clinical phenomena; for the view that psychological knowledge could be unproblematically applied to humans much like natural science knowledge could be applied in biomedicine; and for considering the proper units of investigation as psychological phenomena and processes *inside* individuals. Gergen's critiques were exhaustive and wide-ranging efforts that drew from diverse strands of philosophical, historical and literary thought. The upshot, for sympathetic readers, is a sound overview of diverse ideas cohering in a psychologist's account of the linguistic turn and its implications. Gergen was harshly criticized in academic psychology's arena, but was not beyond being provocative himself, such as when suggesting that a vindication of social constructionism could lead to psychology's obsolescence as a discipline (K. J. Gergen, 1997: 724). Still, he continues constructively engaging his critics as recent exchanges in *Theory and Psychology* and *American Psychologist* show (K. J. Gergen, 2001a, 2001b). Behind his critiques of psychology one finds an enduring concern for what pragmatically follows from psychological research, knowledge and its human applications. Here is one summation of his hopes for psychology as a generative social science in light of the implications, as he saw them, of social constructionism:

> If our descriptions and explanations of the world are not demanded by the nature of the world itself, then we are released from the shackles of the taken for granted. Most importantly, we are invited into a posture of theoretical creativity. As scientists we are liberated from our task as mere mirror holders to the 'world as it is,' and challenged to articulate new and potentially transformative conceptions. Our task is not simply that of describing what currently exists, but of creating intelligibilities that may foster worlds to come.   (K. J. Gergen, 2001b: 810)

The socially constructed and saturated self

> The languages of self are malleable indeed, and as they change so does social life.   (K. J. Gergen, 1991: 15)

By this point, it will be no surprise to learn that Ken Gergen has had longstanding concerns about how the self has been depicted and researched by psychologists.

The very idea that selves can be defined apart from the social interactions in which they take form can be shown to be an ideological view (MacPherson, 1962) recast as a psychological verity. Inside mid-twentieth-century psychology, the self seemed promisingly knowable. Already psychology had public advocates for a better society made possible through the technocratic knowledge and skills of psychologists (e.g., Skinner, 1961). But this was also an era in which humanist psychology was on the rise, with exhortations that people connect with, and more authentically live by, their *real* or core selves (e.g., Rogers, 1961; Jourard 1971). The 1970s even came to be known as the 'me decade'. So it might seem out of cultural step (but consistently so) to find Ken Gergen writing in the early 1970s: 'Rather than speaking of *the* self or self-concept, it is much more fruitful to speak of multiple conceptions' (1971: 20; italics in the original).

While most psychologists start from a view of self as given and knowable, Gergen has challenged this view on many fronts. The impetus for and scope of his challenges becomes evident in reading the broad range of conceptual resources his writing brings from outside psychology. What heed, for example, should psychologists pay to the micro-sociological views of Erving Goffman (1959), the pragmatic views of George Herbert Mead (1970), the linguistic philosophies of Gadamer (1988) or Wittgenstein (1953), philosophy of science views of Kuhn (1962), or historical notions of self (e.g., Aries, 1962)? A lot, if you are Ken Gergen. Possibly, this is where Gergen violates, in the views of many of his colleagues, the 'language game of psychology'. But to read Gergen's (1991) popular volume, *The Saturated Self*, is to encounter a wide-ranging account of 'self' that goes beyond the treatment found in most psychology textbooks.

From the outset, Ken Gergen's concern is with the concept of 'self' as it has become so central to everyday life. As he wrote early on, the 'self' can be understood as both a process and a structural definition consistent with 'the system of concepts available to the person [or others] in attempting to define himself' (1971: 23). Even then, he was concerned about psychology's apparent fixation on the consistency (read: personality) of the self. Nevertheless, in the preface to *The Saturated Self* he set the stage for concerns he would address about why the self is so important: 'Beliefs about self seem pivotal to all our undertakings. We believe that as normal human beings we possess reasoning powers, emotions, conscience, intentions; these beliefs are critical to the ways we relate to others' (1991: x). This foreshadowed his later comments, that features we readily associate with our private sense of self may be more appropriately seen as extensions of social life. For readers committed to a view that the self is the source or animating force for such things as cognition, emotion, even self-understanding, *The Saturated Self* is frustrating. For more sympathetic readers it can be an exhilarating and vertigo-inducing read.

When the languages and interactions that articulate our sense of self are social, why does society give such primacy to the individual? Can individual human experience be mapped out on to a clinical language of normalcy and pathology (K. J. Gergen, 1990)? Doesn't preoccupation with individual rights and psychological well-being position people to conflict or look past each other for solutions to life problems? And what about the 'core self'? Isn't this a constraining fiction when one sees how varied our ways of acting, feeling and thinking can be in different human contexts? These kinds of questions and concerns serve as grist for *The Saturated Self,* a book in which the often reviled term 'postmodernism' is used to denote a convergence of cultural developments (media, cultural diversity, feminism, the 'linguistic turn' and so on) that, Gergen suggested, called for a changed view of 'self'. Postmodernism as it relates to self, for Gergen, is summarized as follows:

> Under postmodern conditions, persons exist in a state of continuous construction and reconstruction; it is a world where anything goes that can be negotiated. Each reality of the self gives way to reflexive questioning, irony, and ultimately the playful probing of yet another reality. The center fails to hold.   (1991: 7)

Such a depiction of self and self-development sounds ungrounded in biology and a century's worth of psychological science – even threatening – to those who read into it the loss of their most personal touchstone, a self (their 'centre') from which they organize and conduct life. Is it not the case that our lives are consequentially worked out in more social arenas than was the case for our predecessors? Doesn't essentializing our 'self' into an immutable and knowable core translate to inflexibilities or insincerities in those arenas, when so often our immediate experience in those arenas suggests otherwise? *The Saturated Self* was a book aimed at a public readership, and Ken was raising such troubling questions about the extent one could 'know' and socially conduct oneself.

Much of his concern relates to the social and relational difficulties that follow from an individualistic conception of self. How we primarily understand the self is through the vocabularies available for 'its' articulation: the words, discourses and stories we use to make sense of who we are. Therefore, such a focus on the individual self comes with associated vocabularies that can supplant others we might turn to, to enhance relational connection and interaction. Said another way, given a dearth of relational language we can literally find ourselves at a loss for words when we need them in relational circumstances. In spheres of relational practice, such as family therapy, *The Saturated Self* was well received, particularly for practitioners open to comments like, 'As belief in essential selves erodes, awareness expands of the ways in which personal identity can be created and re-created in relationships' (K. J. Gergen, 1991: 146). Gergen saw an ethical dimension to the languages we use for identifying ourselves and each other, suggesting we be mindful of the reflexive (i.e., constructive) power of language when characterizing others. The powerful discourse of psychopathology which locates problems inside people offers a case in point, as an authoritative language for depicting 'what is really going on' for people. Contesting the idea that there can be a unitary, correct language to characterize the self is one of the book's major themes.

Another theme relates to the possibilities that postmodern life and social constructionist ideas and practices afford. Our various (and potential) relationships offer opportunities for 'ersatz being', a 'capacity for entering into identities or relationships of widely varying forms' (K. J. Gergen, 1991: 183). Throughout the book Ken challenges us to leave behind the romantic notion that there is a true self one must keep in touch with and reveal to others. Like it or not, the internet presents novel opportunities to 'self-identify', and in the absence of shared relational history we are able to enact possibilities for relating not afforded us elsewhere. What's 'saturated' about the 'saturated self' is that peoples' identities can vary across increasingly diverse social contexts, yet our vocabularies for self seem stuck in limiting humanistic and essentializing discourses. People can experience themselves as 'contradictions', or worse (losing 'integrity'?), should a previously enduring story or description of self encounter a social circumstance requiring actions or understandings inconsistent with that story. Meanwhile, most psychologists continue with the essentializing project of 'discovering' a knowable self. Soon after *The Saturated Self*, Ken Gergen wrote in *Realities and Relationships* of his dismay with his discipline: 'to take account of the peregrinations of psychological science in the present century is to peer into the inner sanctum of cultural justification. It is to enter the Fort Knox of individualism and assay our condition of wealth' (K. J. Gergen, 1994a: 5).

A few key points can be taken from Ken Gergen's writing on the self. First, being an individual is a culturally complex matter where one often takes part in multiple social contexts, each of which influences particular performances and understandings of self – in what Gubrium and Holstein (1999) once referred to as 'geographies of self-making'. Anchoring ourselves to particular stories or descriptions of self can constrain our resourceful and collaborative ways of interacting with others. Second, if the self we know is the self we narrate, language clearly plays a role in articulating an 'identity', but such language can help in supplementing or revising 'it' as well. Self-narration is a way of using language to link particular valorized events and attributes into a story of self. Such stories neither write themselves, nor have self-evident plotlines that informed others can discern better than we can. This also points to a third dimension or concern about self that Ken takes up. Our 'self' understandings are articulations derived from relational interactions that see us use language that already has the moral and cultural freight of prior speakers. How we and others use a language of self is thus an ongoing rhetorical and ethical challenge. And if it is clear that one party in a relationship cannot insist on how the other party is to understand them, then it is to our actions and words within relationships that we turn for understandings of self that work for us in our relationships.

Mary Gergen's feminist social constructionism

> Psychology has had little to say about middle age generally, and even less about women in adulthood.   (M. M. Gergen, 2001: 92)

While Ken Gergen is perhaps the name most seen as synonymous with social constructionist psychology, Mary Gergen has also been influentially pushing boundaries within psychology for over three decades. A feminist scholar (e.g., 1988, 1999, 2001; Goldschmidt et al.,1974) and innovator of qualitative research methods (1992, 2007), Mary is author or co-author of many books on topics related to feminist psychology, social constructionism and research. She has co-authored numerous publications with Ken, who cites her as one of his most important influences. Here, we shall primarily consider Mary Gergen's contributions as a feminist social constructionist and qualitative researcher.

Mary first got to know Ken Gergen while working as his undergraduate research assistant at Harvard. They married in 1969, and Mary later completed a Ph.D. at Temple University, and then went on to teach at Pennsylvania State University, from which she recently retired. From early on, Mary's focus was with advancing the status, well-being and life possibilities of women (e.g., Goldschmidt et al., 1974; M. M. Gergen, 2001). Being a feminist scholar, particularly in late twentieth-century psychology, meant engaging in many struggles: to gain recognition for women within psychology, to shift contemporary thinking and cultural practices regarding women, and to sort out the kinds of scholarship best able to advance women in general. Early feminist scholarship in psychology had understandably been used to identify discriminatory practices and address a deficit in research about women (cf. Enns, 1993). But with this latter research, as it moved into the 1970s and 1980s, came epistemological concerns of the kind Ken had been raising (1973, 1994b). Thus, at the very time feminist psychologists were using contemporary methods to address inequities, psychologists who had taken a linguistic or social constructionist turn were calling these methods into question. In particular, if there was no 'essential' woman to psychologically study and argue for, when a large stock of such essentialist knowledge had been accruing for men, where might this leave feminist scholarship and the women's movement it served?

Both in her writing with Ken, and in her own scholarship, Mary Gergen found in social constructionism ideas critically helpful for calling into question the societal status quo. In three feminist psychology books (1988, 2001; M. M. Gergen and S. Davis, 1997), and many articles and chapters, Mary has addressed a range of feminist concerns: the gendered body, ageing and menopause in patriarchal society, feminist metatheory and women's relationships. Where some feminist scholars have focused on explicating and resolving gender differences, Mary described her postmodern, constructionist approach as 'to question – but not to deny – all linguistic categories, and especially to resist the reification of universal, atemporal ones, including gender' (2001: 10). This should not be surprising for someone who has advocated for, and suggested innovations to, narrative understandings of self since the early 1980s (e.g., K. J. Gergen and M. M. Gergen, 1983; M.M. Gergen and K. J. Gergen, 2006).

Mary Gergen's most recent volume (2001) features topics and ways of writing that are boundary-pushing for academics. For example, here one finds 'performance' chapters in which the aim is to move readers with poetically evocative and unusually presented prose in ways normal psychological writing could not. A particularly interesting chapter relates to our connections with 'social ghosts', the imagined or recalled people we consequentially engage with in our inner dialogues. Mary has also played an important role as an explicator and innovator of research methods, both quantitative (M. M. Gergen and Iversen, 1997) and qualitative (2007). Associated with this role is her concern for 'a feminist psychology based on the notion of relational science: that is, one that would emphasize the collaborative nature of knowledge making and be more inclusive' (2001: 194).

It is hard to assess the extent to which Ken and Mary have influenced each other, but together they have frequently published and presented since the 1970s. The Gergens' prolific writing spans critical efforts to call modern psychological knowledge and practice into question, together with generative attempts to advance collaborative and resourceful practices with the people psychology has intended to serve. While we will delve further into their writing on relational practices below, two other writings merit attention: the fun, performative autobiography Mary shared in *Forum: Qualitative Social Research* (Jones, 2004; a similar autobiography can be found there on Ken: Mattes and Schraube, 2004), and the article she wrote with Ken on their marriage for the journal *Feminism & Psychology* (M. M. Gergen and K. J. Gergen, 2003). In the latter article, a public dialogue of sorts about marriage with Ken, she wrote, 'every day it is a priority to nurture the relational core of this emotional bond. If the fire is not fed, it will die. And then the glory of the relational bond can become a cold, dark, devastating outer-space' (ibid.: 473). It is to their writing on collaborative research, therapeutic and organizational practices which we will now turn.

Social constructionism and relational practice

> the achievement of generative theorizing will ultimately depend on whether the scientist is willing to withdraw from the comfort of convention and play dangerous games with accepted truths.   (K. J. Gergen, 1994b: 145)

While both Ken and Mary Gergen have used social constructionist theory to become highly visible critics of mainstream psychology, they have also been important articulators of relational practices that are generative, socially just and collaborative. To this end, they have, with others, founded the Taos Institute, a private foundation devoted to the articulation, research and instruction of social constructionist ideas, and collaborative and generative practices, in areas as diverse as organizational development, social research, education and psychotherapy. Their view of relational practice follows from the notion that judgements about collaboration and utility are not the prerogative of the practitioner; these are relationally constructed in relational interactions. This calls for kinds of relationships between professionals and clients different from those for which roles and corresponding actions are considered culturally or professionally pre-configured – thus the comment about 'generative theorizing' above.

While Ken has published most frequently on collaborative therapeutic relationships (e.g., McNamee and K. J. Gergen, 1992; K. J. Gergen, 2006), and Mary on collaborative research relationships (e.g., M. M. Gergen, 2007), together both have explored the potentials of social constructionism for organizational and cultural change (e.g., M. M. Gergen, K. J. Gergen, and F. Barrett, 2004). The emphasis throughout this writing is on relational practices that balance concern with what is taken for granted in people's understandings and actions with what is preferred and possible for them with respect to their concerns and aspirations. Thus such relationships are seen as negotiated in ways that do not privilege the practitioners' language or ideas. Instead, reflective and resourceful dialogues are seen as the central negotiated feature, calling upon practitioners to act in flexible and ethical ways that cannot be prescribed beforehand. While this might seem an invitation to anarchy with clients, a new relational responsibility is called for, though it too is not pre-specified (McNamee and Gergen, 1999). Instead, the Gergens promote relational practices where 'clients' are invited into taking on active roles in shaping and sustaining dialogues they deem as resourceful and collaborative. Two examples feature in the work of other Taos Institute partners: Harlene Anderson (1997) for her collaborative approach to psychotherapy, and David Cooperrider for his contributions to Appreciative Inquiry (e.g., Cooperrider, Whitney and Stavros, 2008).

The primary thrust of the Gergens' focus on relational practice is on how procedural and linguistic decisions are talked through collaboratively so that shared efforts and resources can be brought to bear on what clients want. No specific methods are advised, though at times both have showcased methods such as solution-focused therapy (in McNamee and K. J. Gergen, 1992) or narrative research (in M. M. Gergen, 1988). Instead, theirs is a more general focus on resourceful dialogue, as suggested by the following quote:

> … let us move toward conversational processes in which multiple discourses of relatedness are employed … it is within conversational processes that explore the dimensions of relatedness that transformation of the participants' relationship occurs.   (McNamee and K. J. Gergen, 1999: 11)

Such transformations, of course, apply to the professional as well as the client. But the Gergens have consistently looked beyond the consulting room and the boardroom for broader changes as well. While new ideas and actions might take root in the helping dialogue, there remains the challenge of how these ideas and actions will fare where they are needed. It is in this regard that their view of relational practice is acutely and contextually sensitive, without the kinds of decontextualized general prescriptions or methods one associates with many forms of professional helping. The bigger cultural concerns are what they tackle in their academic and popular writing.

Coda

> For the constructionist words are themselves a form of social practice and
> it is imperative that these practices not remain closeted in the house of
> privilege.   (K. J. Gergen, 1999: 142)

Ken and Mary Gergen are two of contemporary social constructionism's most
central figures. Together both have done much to question mainstream psychology, as they articulated their 'postmodern' view of knowledge construction and
relational practice. It has been a bumpy journey at times, requiring both to endure
scathing and often off-target criticisms (e.g., that they are cynical moral relativists) from colleagues. But social constructionism is now an unignorable feature
of contemporary psychology. For practitioners, much can be taken from their
integrative and generative writing. Their critical stance on contesting ways of
research and practice that promote social injustices and fall short of collaboration with the people psychology aims to help is complemented by their generative approach to advancing relational practices that are resourceful, engaging and
imaginative for these same people. Both Ken and Mary remain very active on the
conference circuit, and in publishing ideas that continue to extend the possibilities
of social constructionist thought and practice.

15 Rom Harré

> Despite the fact that questionnaires and check-lists and so on are called 'instruments', and the answers that are given to them are called 'data', and the results of analyzing these discourses are called 'measurements', they are nothing of the sort, if these words mean what they mean in physics. If they do not mean what they mean in physics it would be well for the researchers who use them to enlighten us as to what they do mean … While these psychologists think they are doing mainstream psychology and conforming to the scientistic paradigm, they are actually doing something different but quite respectable, namely some small scale discourse analysis. What they present as causal laws are none other than discourse conventions. They are narratologists, despite themselves.   (Harré draft of 2002: 175)

A common criticism of social constructionism is that it is anti-scientific. For the Oxford philosopher of science and social psychologist Rom Harré, that concern can represent a narrow understanding of science. This has particularly been the case given that much social science, particularly psychology, has tried to account for what it is to be human without acknowledging the central human characteristics of reasoning, agency and social interaction. Harré's discursive view of being human is a powerful critique of, and antidote to, prevailing psychological perspectives.

In his classic text that put the original first generation of cognitive psychology on the map, Ulrich Neisser noted that 'the basic reason for studying cognitive processes has become as clear as the reason for studying anything else: because they are there … Cognitive processes surely exist, so it can hardly be unscientific to study them' (1967: 5). But Harré, along with most social constructionists, takes Wittgenstein's criticisms of 'double process metaphysics' on board with respect to mentalistic versions of cognitivism – the notion that there is some unobservable mental activity going on in the head behind people's activities. Thus:

> If the abstract cognitive processing mechanism cannot be found behind much that we do, then Ockham's razor had better be wielded and the thing amputated. But if we do that, aren't we in danger of slipping back into behaviorism again? Not if we have understood Wittgenstein correctly. Of course, there are cognitive processes, but they are immanent in the discursive practices that are right in front of our noses, so to speak … What, then, should psychologists do if the second cognitive revolution is on the right track? Why, study cognition where it lives, in discourse, considered in a broad sense to include all sorts of symbolic manipulations according to rules.   (Harré, 1992: 6–7)

Horace Romano (Rom) Harré was born in the small, rural township of Apiti in the lower North Island of New Zealand, where his father was the headmaster of the local school. He gained his first degrees from the then University of New Zealand in mathematics, which he subsequently taught, along with physics, at King's College, Auckland, and later at the University of the Punjab. He then became a student in Oxford under J. L. Austin (a pupil of Wittgenstein's), the founder of Speech Act philosophy. After teaching the philosophy of science at the Universities of Birmingham and Leicester, he was appointed a fellow of Linacre College, and the University Lecturer in the Philosophy of Science at Oxford. He later held this post concurrently with his present position of Professor of Social Psychology at Georgetown University, Washington DC.

As with most of the other figures we are discussing here, Harré's work is based very much on a dissatisfaction with the Cartesian picture of the world that has so largely influenced contemporary psychology and social science. This is the view that lies behind the way psychology is still presented to undergraduates, and which they need to 'buy into' in order to get good marks and eventually come out the other end accredited in that much lauded role of the 'scientist-practitioner'. The underlying presuppositions of this view are these. There is a reality that exists independently of humans. Knowledge of that reality can be gained through empirical investigations. From these investigations we can refine the fit between our language and the independent objects that it describes. Hence we become more enlightened about the real state of things. And thus, for example, with a bit more work, we will be able to make better diagnoses of such currently difficult-to-be-sure-of afflictions as 'border-line personality disorder'. It will no longer be a matter of interpretation: the descriptive criteria will better fit the pre-existent reality. Harré's work begins with his thoroughly questioning the viability of building a science of human activity from this base.

He has written, co-written, edited and co-edited over forty books on the philosophy of science and the foundations of social psychology in the past forty years. His 1972 book, co-authored with P. F. Secord, *The Explanation of Social Behaviour*, became a 'Citation Classic', and is the foundation source of much modern social psychology. In it, Harré and Secord initiated the turn away from the dominant empiricist position in social psychology, towards a more hermeneutic one. Their basic claim is now uncontroversial: that people have an understanding of the meaning of their actions, and that, consequently, the accounts they give of their actions must constitute the main data of social psychology. But at the time, their claim that, for the purpose of a scientific understanding of human behaviour, one should adopt an *anthropomorphic* model that treated people '*as if they were human beings*' (1972: 6) was radical. While this book has been one of the most influential publications on how to do psychology in the past thirty years, we are not going to spend much time on it here. Our reason for this is that, while that work established the base-camp from which Harré's work has subsequently developed, the route from there to his present views has been massively supplemented by new insights he has gained along the way. For example, the most cited authors in the index of his recent book *Cognitive Science: A Philosophical Introduction* (2002) are Wittgenstein (12) and Vygotsky (5) (though these numbers hardly reflect their pervasive influence throughout its 300 or so pages). By contrast, the 1972 book indexes Wittgenstein twice (and in the text the references are in passing) and Vygotsky not at all. Let us begin by looking at Harré's view of postmodernism.

Harré and postmodernism

Consider the view of Edward Wilson, the founder of socio-biology:

> philosophical postmodernists, a rebel crew milling beneath the black flag of anarchy, challenge the very foundations of science and traditional philosophy. Reality, they propose, is a state constructed by the mind, not perceived by it. In the most extravagant version of this constructivism, there is no 'real' reality, no objective truth external to mental activity, only prevailing versions disseminated by ruling social groups. Nor can ethics be firmly grounded, given that each society creates its own codes for the benefit of the same oppressive forces.   (Wilson, 1997: 43)

Harré is a major contributor to the social constructionist paradigm in psychology, and constructionism has a sympathy with postmodern ideas, as does Harré. It might be thought odd, then, to find him writing in a similar vein to Wilson:

> Of all the genres of stories and instructions of our era surely that of the sciences is pre-eminent in many aspects of our lives. Yet in the last decade there has been an outpouring of 'anti-science'. The most insidious attack has come from within the academic world – the loose cluster of doctrines we call 'postmodernism'. Disconcertingly, it has its origin in some of the same insights that have powered the attempts to develop a truly scientific cognitive psychology, particularly those that have called attention to the dominant role of symbolic interactions, discourse, in our lives. It is of the utmost importance to distance ourselves from the irrationalism and relativism of Post-modernism.   (Harré, 2001: unpublished draft, no page numbers)

However, this is not odd in the least, and it takes us to the centre of Harré's views. Much of his philosophical position is worked out in *Varieties of Realism* (1986b) and jointly with Michael Krausz in *Varieties of Relativism* (1996). Here we are necessarily brief in outlining the development of his ideas with respect to psychology.

In our reading of Harré's work, there are a number of legacies in the intellectual landscapes allied to postmodernist writings that he would see as central to the transformation of our views as to 'what it is to be human' in the past decades. Put simplistically, the postmodern contribution and conundrum is this. *If our knowledges and ways of being human are socially constructed on the bases of discursive practices made up of symbols; and those symbols gain their meanings through their relations to other symbols and the contexts in which they are produced (rather than being solidly grounded in their relation to some objective* reality from which they gain their referential meaning); *and* these relations between symbols are open to multiple, local interpretations; *and* these interpretations are themselves contestable by interacting members of the cultural traditions so constituted; *then* there is no absolute reality against which we can judge the discourses of the human sciences.

This conclusion opens the door to a radical relativism in which the project of science is doomed, and we are left with ever-changing realities that vary locally and historically. There is also, then, no universal human nature: it can be made anew, time and time again, because any account of human nature is itself a reading, and open to a discursive analysis as to how it has been produced – that is, these accounts are contestable. In our reading of Harré we do not find much here that he would disagree with, *until* one gets to the '*then* …' part of our caricature. He would, we think, agree that there are genuine and important insights here that psychology must take serious note of. But, that conceded, he wants to address the question as to whether a radical relativism follows from them: whether there are no 'human universals' whatsoever; no stable moral principles, semantic rules, or explanatory accounts of human action that the social sciences can establish. In addressing this issue of relativism, he manages at the same time to take a distinctive step away from an essentialist account of 'what it is to be human'.

To accomplish this balancing act, Harré first asks: 'What are the conditions that are necessary for anyone to use language in social life?' His answers 'draw' on Holiday's (1988) arguments as to the universal moral bases that are universal to human forms of life (the inverted commas around 'draw' are because Holiday's account is based on the Ph.D. thesis he submitted under Harré's supervision).

> Holiday (1988) suggested that there were three conditions for the possibility of linguistic communication which were also moral. If this could be demonstrated then the attempt to argue for a radical moral relativism, that all moral judgements are only locally valid, by the use of language is self-defeating. In my version of Holiday's scheme these were:
>
> 1. **Trust**: that we must assume that on most occasions people do mean what they seem to mean, that is we must be able to trust some of our interlocutors at least some of the time.
> 2. **Justice**: that we must concede to all of whom we demand that they listen to us the complementary right to be listened to.
> 3. **Ritual**: that conventions of language use cannot be established by force, but must be accomplished by our joint reverence for social procedures.
>
> In so far as the trusting relation induces a moral obligation on the one who is trusted, and justice is based on reciprocal rights, these two conditions are clearly moral. It might be argued that establishing coordinated behaviour by ritual is pragmatic rather than moral, but even if that were conceded it remains a requirement on the possibility of any arrangement which purports to be a human form of life and is therefore universal.
>
> The upshot of Holiday's argument then is the demonstration that those who use language must concede that there are at least some moral universals, and perhaps some pragmatic universals as well.   (Harré, 1997)

We can pull in at least two further strands of argument here, from Wittgenstein (see Chapter 8) and Hallowell (see Chapter 12). The Wittgensteinian argument is that, because there cannot be any form of a private language – since private states are not public, and hence not amenable to being pointed at, words cannot be learned by referring to them, but must be developed by substituting a symbol for an expression of a private experience that is intersubjectively shared – then language symbols are originally grounded in an affective ethology. This provides for the possibility for and natural regulation of any form of communal life: 'unless there were certain sorts of natural regularities then a vast stretch of our most characteristically human vocabularies could never be established' (Harré, 1997). By grounding eventual language games in expression, we simultaneously find a way of elucidating the moral basis of ritual – in that while language, particularly semantics, cannot be imposed, the natural semantic expressions of infants must be *accepted* at face value by their caretakers, and in this acceptance a joint reverence – or certainty – is grounded. Hallowell's arguments provide an additional set of universal constraints on the subsequent elaboration of symbolic systems that are grounded in this way: there may be arbitrary, and hence relativistic, ways in which time and space, for example, can be symbolically constructed, but any language game constituting a viable human 'form of life' *must* contain spatial and temporal distinctions. Similarly,

> If there were no natural expressions of feeling then there could be no verbal expressions of feeling either. So, in so far as there is a common human ethology, and commonsense and biological science supports the idea that there is, then there is something universal upon which all the varieties of human vocabularies and all the variations of the psychologies of feeling, emotion and so on are erected. Varieties of emotions and variations in vocabularies for feelings are very great, but they are bounded by the constraints that are immanent in what Wittgenstein called 'the human form of life'. And that is itself bounded by human biology. There could be no 'patriarchal' nor 'feminist' discourses if there had not been at least two sexes.   (Harré, 1997)

This said, however, there is no slide into biological universalism in Harré's view of the emotions. The wide variation, cross-culturally and historically, of the range of human emotions points otherwise: there are specific 'emotionologies' (Stearns and Stearns, 1985; cf. Harré and Gillett, 1994: 148–61) that apply in different places and times. Emotions must have a socially constructed component. Why, for example, are the bodily feelings associated with being tired, or wanting to go to the loo, not regarded as emotions? Because, unlike emotions, they are not embodied expressions of judgements about one's social situation, or ways of accomplishing certain social acts, and thus are not tied up with the moral order of a society where, while 'emotion feelings and displays as expressions of judgements lack premises' (ibid.: 147), they still have normative force.

Harré is one of the few thinkers who take up Wittgenstein's linguistic insights and extend their applications to mainstream psychology (see, for example, Harré and Tissaw, 2005). Perhaps the most important extension, just discussed, is the idea that understandings and actions acquire their situated meaning through the interactions of the people who developed and sustain them. One could call these language-games and then point to how people come to share them – their words, the non-verbal communications accompanying them, and the regularities in how all these feature in social interaction. There are many ways in which this is a radical departure from normal psychological understandings of humans in interaction with each other. As we build on Harré's adaptation of these insights, a quite different view of cognition and social behaviour emerges from the conception found in most psychology textbooks. The 'mental' in Harré's writing takes on social and discursive dimensions rich in practical implications.

Positioning, sedimentation, social obligations and language

A pivotal study in Harré's developing framework is his work with Peter Mühlhäusler, *Pronouns and People* (1990). It is pivotal because it is a detailed, evidence-based survey that in retrospect marks a transitional point in Harré's opus. It provides a take-off point for his ideas as they have subsequently been developed into a discursive (e.g., Harré and Gillett, 1994), and subsequently 'hybrid' approach (e.g., Harré, 2002) to formulating a scientific psychology. It is a cross-cultural study of the use of language as people talk to, with, and about each other and the world in which they are located: a study of pronouns – in English, the words 'I', 'me', 'mine' 'you', 'he/she', 'we', 'us', 'ours', 'they', 'them', 'theirs', 'this', 'that', etc. It is a rich study. Here we will consider just one aspect of it: pronoun use and the concept of self among speakers of English.

Mühlhäusler and Harré's claim is that the word 'I' is not a label for an entity that owns and exercises our mental and moral attributes. Rather, they argue that the way selves are experienced has an underlying duality of location: 'a person is an embodied being located in a spatio-temporal structure of things and events, so having a point of view; and is also an active being located in a structure of the rights and obligations, so having a sense of moral responsibility' (Mühlhäusler and Harré, 1990: 88). A sense of identity emerges, then, from a junction between these two ways of locating oneself, physically and morally:

> Each distinct social group has a concept of a 'person' determined by the local variations and the degree of interaction of these structures. One such structure, that given in perception, is in a sense natural. It emerges from the organic characteristics of the human organism. The other is an artefact. It is acquired in mastering certain social practices, particularly those involved in the taking and assigning of responsibility. In consequence we hold that persons, like language, are not wholly natural objects. They come to exist in their fullness as individual human beings learn the locally valid theory of personhood.   (ibid.: 88)

(Note here the similarity with Harré's position regarding the emotions, above.)

What one finds cross-culturally is a plethora of distinctions of status and the like that need to be marked linguistically in talking so as to perform relationships with the correct levels of respect, deference, etc. Doing things 'properly' is obviously not just a case of getting the words right, but their tone, their accompanying gestures, eye contact, bowing, giving or exchanging gifts, and so on.

From this distinction, they move on to what they term the 'thesis of double indexicality'. This thesis follows from a distinction between two ways of using language to refer to the external world. 'Denoting' occurs when an object is named so as to identify it as a real world object for both speaker and hearer: 'for instance, in the sentence "Mapes is closed", "Mapes" is a denoting expression since it helps all concerned to pick out one among the many casinos on Virginia Street so that something can be said about it' (Mühlhäusler and Harré, 1990: 91). 'Indexing' works differently: 'in the sentence "That is Mapes" the word "that" indexes whatever "Mapes" denotes with a spatial location some distance from the position of the speaker' (ibid.). From here, the thesis of double indexicality is that:

> *I* and other first-person expressions are not used to denote anything, but as indices of location.
>   (a) *I* indexes whatever is denoted by the speaker's utterance with its spatio-temporal location in relation to the location of the speaker and the moment of his or her utterance.
>   (b) But *I* also indexes the utterance with the person who is to be held morally responsible for its illocutionary force and its perlocutionary effects – namely, in English, the speaker …

In 'I demand to see my lawyer' the indexing goes as follows:

> *Spatio-temporal indexing*
> The 'requiring' is located at the speaker.
> The act of requesting is contemporaneous with the speaking.
>
> *Responsibility indexing*
> The effectiveness of the demand is relative to S's [speaker's] right to issue one.
> Responsibility of the outcome is taken by S.   (ibid.: 92)

There is, then, a physical and moral geography of speaking, with the latter showing a wide variety across cultures. Within this space, 'positioning' refers to where a speaker is placed in the moral geography, with varying rights, duties and obligations pertaining (see further below). Let us pick up two related issues.

First, if, as Mühlhäusler and Harré argue, *I* and other first-person pronouns are used indexically, rather than referentially as with third-person pronouns, names and descriptive words, then here is another nail in the coffin of the Cartesian position. The Cartesian *I* names a substance, and qualities and properties – such as thoughts, beliefs, feelings – are predicatively attributed to it. 'But if the uses of *I* can be exhaustively accounted for as indices of locations in physical and moral space, then a substantialist metaphysics which accounts for personhood by the doubling up of substances is gratuitous' (ibid.: 96). There is, then, in this view, an echo of Wittgenstein's point about the perils of mistaking the grammatical status of a word, one which the Cartesian legacy appears founded on, within which the mind or self is erroneously treated grammatically as an object. When this grammar is abolished for one that conforms to the indexical way that selves are handled in spatio-temporal and moral spaces, the chimera is blown away. There has thus been a 'sedimentation' of denotation into English where it is not necessary.

Our second example is of a sedimentation of social relations into language, one that is reflective of a (re)structuring of moral obligations over time, and one which compounds the above accident of self as substance: ways of expressing possession. There are many different possessive relationships that people can enter into that in English are all lumped together and not marked in speaking that are so marked in other languages. One distinction is between inalienable and alienable possession: between those things that are very close to one by birth or physical embodiment, such as '*my mother*' and '*my leg*', as against those possessions that are more temporary or not a result of birth or manufacture, '*my wife*', '*my car*' or '*my breakfast*'. In English these are all spoken of in the same form. In many other languages, particularly those of pre-political, small-scale traditional societies, these distinctions are made explicitly. Lévy-Bruhl (1928: 73ff.) notes that this distinction recurs in a very large number of languages; hence an individual is in relation to direct kin in the same way as they are to their own bodies, but differently positioned with respect to indirect kin. For example, in the Melanesian language Mekeo, the possessive marker '*gu*' is placed after the noun for inalienable possession, but before it for alienable possession. Thus

a manua-*gu*	my wound
hahin i-*gu*	my sister
anu-*gu* hahin	my wife
anu-*gu* tunan	my man/husband

In addition, many languages and, importantly, those that are ancestral to English, lack a possessive verb for *have*, and 'they may express the meaning through the use of a locative, comparable to the use of the dative in Latin, as in *mihi est liber* = I have a book' (Lehman, 1992: 108). English now uses *have* to code all manner of relationships between experience and the world, and the metaphor of ownership has been adopted for many purposes: to express the past '*I have eaten*'; the future '*I have an essay to write*'; necessity '*I have to do it*'; states of existence '*I have a hangover*'; control of events '*We have lift-off*'; and so on. Many past tenses have become archaic: *I rode/I had a ride*; *I bathed/I had a bath*. Halliday (1985: 327) terms this change as 'metaphor turned grammar' leading to a 'grammatical conspiracy' that unwittingly provides a contour for how we position ourselves in relation to our world, and structure our moral sense of responsibility. It provides a framework for considering the self as an object that owns its possessions, and continues to blind us to how things might be under a different grammar.

The grammars of 'domains'

> Words and chess pieces are analogous; knowing how to use a word is like knowing how to move a chess piece. Now how do the rules enter into playing the game? What is the difference between playing the game and aimlessly moving the pieces? I do not deny there is a difference, but I want to say that knowing how a piece is to be used is not a particular state of mind which goes on while the game goes on. The meaning of a word is to be defined by the rules for its use, not by the feeling that attaches to the words.
>
> 'How is the word used?' and 'What is the grammar of the word?' I shall take as being the same question.   (Wittgenstein, 1979: 2)

> Ontologies are, in effect, grammars.   (Harré, 1998: 47)

Wittgenstein introduced a new meaning to the term 'grammar' that takes us out of the usual realm we might have encountered in school or in linguistics. We can, in traditional grammar, take nouns to be 'the names of things', but to do this can obscure for us what we use names for, and can thus mislead us as to what their grammar is, in Wittgenstein's sense of grammar. For example, the word 'clock' is a noun, the name of a thing, and we can ask 'where is the clock?'. 'Mind' is also a noun, but is it likewise the name of a thing? Can we ask 'where is the mind?' In a sense we can, because we often use nouns to refer to invisible things. In fact, though, a lot of our language can confuse us into believing that lots of activities are 'things': 'The wind blows', does it not? Or is 'wind' just a way of talking about a process of movement, rather than the action of a 'thing'? Similarly, is it the case that a 'mind' thinks, or contains cognitive representations of the world?

> Our investigation is … a grammatical one. Such an investigation sheds light on our problem by clearing misunderstandings away. Misunderstandings concerning the use of words, caused, among other things, by certain analogies between the forms of expression in different regions of language.
> (Wittgenstein, 1953: aphorism 90)

One level of analogy that can be misleading to us is our ability in English to turn actions (verbs) into things (nouns) – a technical part of linguistic grammar called 'entification'. Thus we have the option of saying 'Yesterday, interest rates rose', or 'Yesterday, there was a rise in interest rates.' Actions result in changes in the state of affairs, and English gives us ways of focusing on either. Similarly, we 'invent' things to talk about. 'Nations' are an example here. There is no physical differentiation between a land-locked country such as Switzerland and the countries surrounding it, yet walking across a mountain range can place a person under different jurisdictions, and lead those who live in the different places to construct their identities very differently – as Swiss, or French, or Italian, for example.

What Wittgenstein wants to point out by his term 'grammar' is, in one sense, to say that when you begin to establish a language game – a particular way of using words, distinguishing one thing from another in a particular way – then lots of other things follow from the original distinction. We are often unconscious of these 'things that follow', but there is a kind of blind, tacit intuition that some things follow while other things do not. Small-scale examples regularly crop up in cross-cultural comparisons. Dorothy Lee provides an example in her study of Trobriand Island speech (1950). In English, we might describe someone as either a good or bad gardener. But a Trobriand Islander cannot see the sense of this, because a 'bad gardener' to them is a contradiction in terms: a 'gardener' is, by definition of use, a term applied to someone who grows things, which distinguishes them categorically from someone who cannot do this. They are not in 'the same sort of category – gardener – but with different qualities': they are different sorts of things entirely, and thus the concepts of 'gardener' have different entailments in the two languages: different grammars. But different grammars also occur in all languages. For example, in the kinds of grammar we would have learned in school, the sentences 'The pain is in my shoulder' and 'The knife is in my shoulder' would assign the same grammatical status to 'pain' and 'knife', but they are very different kinds of things from Wittgenstein's perspective on grammar. While pain is difficult to verify in another person, it would not make sense, for example, for a person to say, 'Oh, I made a mistake; actually the pain is in my leg.' Similarly, different feeling words have different grammars: I cannot wonder if I am in pain, but I can wonder if I am in love.

Using words skilfully can also lead to stating something without actually saying it. In the grammar of British protocol, one cannot sit down in the presence of the monarch without being invited to. This 'rule of use' can be used to express Royal displeasure, as happened to Margaret Thatcher in one of her weekly briefings to the Queen as her Prime Minister. Something that Her Majesty's Government was pursuing as policy got up the Royal nose, and the Queen is reported to have greeted her PM for the weekly briefing at Buckingham Palace, sat down to receive it, and then left Mrs Thatcher to stand in front of her for an hour to discuss affairs until dismissing her. She never invited her to sit down. And so, by the rules, unspoken, the grammar of the situation was played out, and the Royal displeasure conveyed. It would have been nice to have been there.

It is this sense of 'grammar' that has come increasingly to the fore in Harré's work, firstly in the way words in discourse act to position the interactants, and secondly in the way that words have implications. Hence, certain things follow when one buys into particular foundational assumptions as to what can be counted as real (i.e., particular ontologies), and what the 'norms' are by which one can act correctly.

> Grammar tells us what kind of object anything is.   (Wittgenstein, 1953: aphorism 373)

> Grammar is not accountable to any reality. It is grammatical rules that determine meaning (constitute it) and so they are not answerable to any meaning and to that extent are arbitrary.   (Wittgenstein, 1978: aphorism 133)

For Harré, 'contemporary Anglo-American patterns of thinking, feeling and acting seem to be shaped by four main grammars' (2002: 148).

A Person or P-grammar is used as a framework for talking about people, defined as embodied beings who have a responsibility for their actions. We applaud the shot of a brilliant snooker player, not the motion of the balls involved. The player accepts the applause, and basks in our recognition of his skill; the balls are inert, and their activities are describable through a *Molecular or M-grammar*. Their properties arise through natural necessity, and snooker balls are in no way responsible for their performance, and thus cannot make mistakes. Current western discourse makes use of a third grammar, an *Organism or O-grammar*, which applies, by and large, to the organic world of behaving, as opposed to intentionally acting, life-forms. We would not prosecute a lion for killing a zebra; the lion acts out of natural necessity, and is not responsible for its actions in the way a murderer is. People can act like animals, and pets can be 'a good boy or girl', but these are metaphorical uses of this grammar. The fourth current grammar is the *Spiritual or S-grammar*. Foundational here is some higher being to whom the judgements of right and wrong are ascribed, and whose judgements relate to the disembodied soul of a person. While predominantly religious rather than secular in its use, this grammar enables a powerful political rhetoric of various fundamental shades, justifying an action because God's on our side.

The S and P grammars express semantic and logical necessities. The O and M grammars express natural necessities. The former apply to agents, the second to causal mechanisms. This distinction leads Harré to a crucial point about how psychology needs to be conducted, because, in his view, psychology is rarely an empirical science. In an empirical science, investigators seek to explain the relationships discovered between independently defined events through hypothesizing a causal-mechanistic account of this relationship, to explain why it occurs. Harré (2001: 161) illustrates this with the example of identifying coffee-drinking by one set of criteria, and Parkinson's disease by a completely different set of criteria. This guarantees that the relationship that has been established between drinking coffee and a low incidence of Parkinson's disease is an empirically discovered one, since the two sets of criteria brought into relationship have nothing to do with each other. But in many psychological investigations, the independence of the variables cannot be guaranteed: 'if we use a PET scan to pick out the parts of the brain that are activated when someone is reading, the criteria for identifying those parts include the criteria for knowing whether someone is reading' (ibid.: 161). The established relationship here is thus conceptual rather than empirical. And this, in Harré's view, is the case in many areas of psychology, because, as the study of moral agents, the person grammar/ontology necessarily takes precedence. This takes us full circle, in that for the purpose of building a scientific psychology it is necessary to treat people 'as if they were human beings' (Harré and Secord, 1972: 6).

Harré makes the point that for most human activities the different grammars become intertwined when we talk about the world. The primary distinction is between the 'person grammars', which deal with agents who have intentions, and the 'organic and molecular grammars', which treat events as objects that do not have intentions, but which are blind in their functioning. Sports' reporting is a good example of where the different grammars applied to a game produce a hybrid discourse. Sports are played by people who are striving to do their best and win, and the person grammar applies. But the conditions also affect the game. There are advantages to winning the toss so as to play under certain conditions, and this can lead to a great deal of discussion in the case of cricket as to what to do if one wins it. Southern hemisphere rugby is played with a different brand of ball from that of northern hemisphere rugby and this affects the performance of star kickers. Moreover, the game can be played at sea-level in New Zealand versus at high altitude in South Africa – both the ball and the altitude affect the game; a player may be carrying an injury or have taken drugs. The different genres of grammar become interwoven here.

Such interweaving occurs most pertinently in bureaucracies that operate with 'file selves' (Harré, 1983: 69–74). People apply for jobs by submitting a CV – employers, banks, lawyers, government agencies and all kinds of organizations hold files containing selected information on people.

> Unlike a real-self a person can be present as a file-self at many different locations and in many different situations simultaneously, most of which will be unknown to the real-self. In these circumstances the real-self or person can exert very little influence on how his or her file-self is interpreted by the relevant functionaries. Unlike a real-self a file-self cannot refuse to answer. A file-self is never mute. A file-self cannot produce a tactical lie or a clever evasion or a significant elaboration. File-selves are neither conscious nor have they autonomous agency.   (Harré, 2003).

Except in the case of the CV, the file self is not constructed by the real self it relates to, and rarely is it constructed at the instigation of the real self, particularly in the broad field of 'mental illness' – families or other social agencies, including the police, prompt the opening of a file self because a person is making a nuisance of themselves. And typically, file selves are closed by other people, who judge that the real self is no longer a nuisance. A file self is also typically composed in the O- or M-grammar of objectification. The person is interviewed in the vernacular, but the file self is coded in diagnostic terms, and referred to a specialist who has more specialist knowledge of how to refine the diagnosis and treat it. This treatment will, most likely, require the actual person to be present, and a translation of the different discourses of the vernacular and the diagnostic to be variously translated to and fro to delineate more precisely the intervention that is appropriate. In his study of file selves in psychiatric treatment, Harré (2003) notes that this 'cycle of translations not only resulted in massive loss of data, but also created an eventual file-self that deviated in important ways from the real-self from which it was ultimately derived'.

Positioning

'Role' has been a central concept in social psychology since the 1950s and 1960s. But given that the fabric of society is woven from a moral base, and we recognize that there are similarly moral components to acting in a role – such as authenticity, integrity, sincerity, and so on – then the explanatory limits of roles are quickly circumscribed. Harré and his colleagues have been outlining a different way of treating social interactions over the past two decades, reformulating the concept of role into that of 'position(ing)' (Davies, 1989; Davies and Harré, 1990; Harré and Van Langenhove, 1992; Harré, 1993; Harré and Van Langenhove,1998; Harré and Moghaddam, 2003; Moghaddam, Harré, and Lee, 2007).

In a social constructionist framework, the main questions concern how joint meanings are created, interpreted and negotiated by participants in the course of their ongoing, unfolding interactions. Harré places these activities within the moral framework triangulated by an actor's rights, duties and obligations, and these vary (unlike roles, that are often quite permanent) with respect to features of the discursively constructed situations within which interactions are conducted, and the ways in which etiquette – from formal to informal – is handled. Different rights, duties and obligations accrue to being a 'host' at a family party as opposed to a diplomatic gathering; to the right to determine the flow of conversation in a board room as opposed to an informal discussion. People 'position' themselves differently in these situations. Thus, unlike roles, positions are more context-specific than permanent; positions can be challenged, accepted and defended; and positions can be taken up and left behind within the moment-to-moment conduct of interaction.

It is important to add here that 'moral', in the way Harré use the term, reflects normative expectations tied to the grammars of particular language games. In this sense, morality is not one set of expectations (as in Judaeo-Christian morality) so much as understandings and actions expected in particular kinds of human interaction. For example, the moral expectations in the language games of shopping are different from those of borrowing from others. Such thinking extends to social proprieties involved when socially expressing emotion (what Harré and Gillett (1994) have referred to above as emotionologies) to capture the different grammars or morals that can be operative. There are affinities here with what Goffman (1974) referred to as social frames for behaviour, but frames lack the grammatical sense Harré adapts from Wittgenstein.

Positioning theory can be thought of as a way of unpacking the interplay between rights, duties and obligations. It also has a much more micro-focus than Foucault's use of 'power' (see Chapter 12). Within democracies with the right of free speech, for example, one could do or say anything at any particular time, but in reality there are only a number of things one might do or say at any moment that could be considered appropriate. Hence there is a tension between what one could say or do and what one may say or do. Some of what one might say or do are duties that follow from the position one is in. However, there is a degree of free play involved in the way these duties might be carried out: should, for example, a patriot view it as their duty to enlist in the armed forces in a time of war, or campaign against the conduct of that war? How people interpret and take up their duties is variable. In addition, among what one might be able to do, there are

courses of action that one can do, and ones that one cannot, either for tempera-
mental or other contextual reasons. Can these constraints be specified? Do I voice
my opposition to my vice-chancellor in public debate on principle, or do I take a
more pragmatic view, understanding that letting the cat out of the bag in this context might well prove counter-productive to my concerns in the long run? When
might I become a whistle-blower; and if I do not, what holds me back? There are
multiple storylines in all cases that we might relate to, or position ourselves with
respect to. So, my best friend is cheating on his wife: do I tell her? If I don't like
her, maybe I won't, she deserves it, he'll be happier without her; if I am in love
with her and want to prise her away from him, maybe I will; but heck, he's
married to my *sister*!

Rights, duties and obligations, being moral categories, likewise necessarily
have a political character. The consequence of this is that social reality, and the
judgements we make of it, always have a relativistic aspect, because the events
in social reality are open to numerous interpretations (and it is because of this
that processes of negotiation as to what is to be counted as reality are so important). Social events have such a multiplicity of alternative, possible, ongoing
consequences that it is very often only through the resolution of the contests
between alternative discursive repertoires that a 'party-line' consensus can be
established, a line that one needs to position oneself with respect to. Historical
events happen, but what their significance is, is not so easy to establish, nor,
even once established, is that significance certain for all time. Positions, social
restructurings and stories intertwine and co-constitute each other. Change can
be made possible through these intertwinings, as the new juxtapositions of
each create new possibilities, new duties, rights and obligations. The historical
transformations of social life from egalitarian hunter-gathering, through chiefs,
kings, empires and the like, open up new positions, and all that then follows,
from these changes in power relations between people. A king, for example, can
impose duties on those who become his subjects but, having done so, he reciprocally creates obligations for himself that they have a right to expect him to carry
out, unless he is to remain just a tyrant or despot, at risk of being overthrown by
the next, more powerful, and unrestrained rival (and thus Harré's formulation of
positioning accounts for the operation of what Vico (Chapter 2) ascribed to the
hand of providence).

Implicit in the above is the understanding that there are regularities to be found
in human life, and that these are, to some extent, predictable. This predictability
may mislead us into thinking that it is possible to uncover the laws that determine
human activities. Presuming this may be possible is one of the major mistakes to
which psychology has been blind during most of its history. Human interactions
rely on the interpretation of meanings and are, as such, not amenable to a causal
analysis that could establish laws. There is, though, a similarity, and a beguiling
one at that, between the logic of establishing laws and testing them, and that of
specifying the expectations as to how human events will (or 'should') unfold, and
why they do not necessarily do so as predicted.

For example, consider Newton's laws. They apply to idealized (imagined) bodies: if an object is perfectly spherical (a conceptual idealization, as there are likely to be no perfect spheres out there in reality), and it collides (interacts) with another perfectly spherical object, then the subsequent motion of the object it collides with is perfectly predictable. If the object it collides with behaves contrary to the prediction, then a good physicist does not take that departure from expectation as grounds that disprove the law. Rather, a good physicist will look for the additional factors that must have intervened in the situation that can account for why a departure from what may have been expected actually occurred. This is similar to what we often do in social investigations. If, for example, somebody wants to do something, has the ability to do it, and is put in a situation where it is possible for them to do it, then we may expect that they will do what we have thus predicted: and if they do not, we will assume that there most be other factors involved that intervened, and we will go in search of them. Thus, the logic behind the activities of physicists and psychologists appears to be the same: therefore, it is assumed, they are doing the same thing; and therefore, since physicists are doing science, so must psychologists be doing science.

Herein lies an error that we have been emphasising throughout this book: the presumption that the logic of a method applies irrespective of the phenomena it is applied to, and so acts as a guarantor of the status of the 'truth' that is established through its application. We began our highlighting of this error with the ideas of Vico; we have pursued it through the works of subsequent thinkers. Harré's recent work brings another perspective to bear on this topic: his development of points first raised by Wittgenstein. In a nutshell, Harré would point out that while there are similarities in the logic of the physicist and the psychologist in a structural sense, we are making a major mistake if we see them as similar in any other sense: he terms this mistake, following Wittgenstein, a 'grammatical' one. We turn here to looking at his take on this. At root, it is quite simple: the consequences of 'collisions' are very different from the consequences of 'wanting to do something', because these are very different events: to think that because what follows from 'collisions' and what follows from 'wants' has a similar logical structure somehow equates these two situations as being of the same nature is fundamentally incorrect. It is a problem that comes from the inappropriate equation of different grammars.

Positioning is a generative concept when extended to helping practice. To begin with it implies a kind of discursive situatedness. Narrative therapists (e.g., Winslade, 2005), for example, sometimes locate problems in cultural discourses; that is, in ways of thinking, speaking and social interaction governed by particular discourses. But positioning can also be considered in less 'macro' terms, for language games recognizably develop out of the recurring regularities in people's communications. It is in this sense that one can know what is 'in and out of bounds' when talking with a relative. Positioning can constrain thought and action to the seeming exigencies of a particular language game. Such constraints act like tunnel vision; hence an insight into the discursive or rhetorical moves that can help people think, talk and act beyond such discursive constraints is important.

Since most helping occurs as a discursive activity, positioning is an inescapable feature of client–professional communications. This recognition can be used to promote a mindful reflection on how positioning may feature in constraining clients' seeming possibilities for understanding and action with respect to their concerns and aspirations. It can also point to how helping conversations can themselves become constrained by the positions taken up in them. What is important to remember here is how much human understanding and communication rely on our abilities to develop and sustain familiarities. These familiarities are at the heart of positioning, whether they are imported to helping conversations, or created between speakers (their own language game, so to speak). But their downside comes with how conversations can become constrained by positions taken – in already established understandings, actions, and ways of talking. What is needed are ways of talking beyond such constraints.

Fortunately, when professionals talk to clients they have many ways of inviting discussion beyond problematically established positions. For example, questions are a rhetorical means of inviting clients to speak from alternative positions, a point long ago made by Karl Tomm (1988). Conflict for a couple often has developed into a language game involving very familiar understandings, ways of interacting, and so on. Asking such clients to speak from a different position – say, from times when they feel closest and most at ease with each other – is one example of engaging them in a very different language game, with different understandings and ways of interacting. What is important to bear in mind here is that positions speak to familiar understandings and ways of interacting that are anchored in recurring patterns of interaction. As we saw with Gregory Bateson (see Chapter 9), pointing out such patterns, or positioned ways of understanding and interacting, is often insufficient as a means of promoting change. Put differently, merely recognizing a pattern or position is insufficient for change: talking and acting in ways inconsistent with, or beyond, the pattern or position can be more helpful. Inviting clients to take up new positions via questions or enactments that require thinking, speaking and interacting in ways beyond their default position can help establish more preferred patterns, more satisfying positions. Wittgenstein saw language games, and their associated grammars, as 'forms of life'. Being able to act and think in ways associated with preferred positions can be like trying on preferred forms of life.

16   John Shotter

> It's like I was playing some kind of game, but the rules don't make any sense to me. They're being made up by all the wrong people. I mean no one makes them up. They seem to make themselves up.   (Benjamin, in *The Graduate*, 1967)

> When will John Shotter stop playing with his self?   (Graffiti, Department of Psychology, Nottingham University, 1976)

The answer to this question turns out to be 'never'. John Shotter's work has a continuously developing character in which themes and sources are revisited as each little reworking of them enables him to discover a richer set of insights and syntheses around the central question: 'what is it to be human?' He has been, along with his frequent collaborator Ken Gergen (see Chapter 14), a central figure in the elaboration and legitimation of the approach in contemporary psychology termed 'social construction'. His work draws from the sources and stirrings that we have been outlining during this book, and casts a penetrating light that brings out their relevance for understanding what humans are about, and what the character of our lives is. We predict you will experience an 'Aha!' feeling time and again as you begin to read of his work here: 'Aha! so that's what all this stuff is about.' This is one of the reasons why his work has become of increasing interest to contemporary discursive therapists.

For helping professionals, Shotter can be a daunting and rewarding writer: daunting because his writing is packed with challenging ideas, and rewarding because these ideas point to collaborative and resourceful possibilities for conversational practice. In Shotter's writing one finds rich contemplation of what is entailed in negotiating developments with others in ethical ways that are illuminated by constructionist insights. Like Gergen, he saw much to criticize in mainstream psychology's approach to understanding humans as social beings. But Shotter brings big-picture ideas to the immediacies of dialogue and in this manner he has an important role in translating thinkers such as Wittgenstein, Bakhtin, Garfinkel and Vygotsky into terms relevant to frontline practice. These ideas come across more as provocations than prescriptions for practice.

Shotter originally left school at 16 to be an apprentice in an aircraft factory, as he recalls in the preface of his (1993b) book *Cultural Politics of Everyday Life*. He subsequently enrolled in the mid-1950s as an undergraduate student in mathematics in Bristol, a city that was at the forefront of the revitalization of post-war British 'culture' until it was eclipsed by the Liverpool of the 'fab four'. Peter O'Toole's performance in *Waiting for Godot* at the Bristol Old Vic at this time, for example, is one of the turning points of British theatre in the twentieth century. The distractions of this vibrant life perhaps contributed to his exam performance not proving sufficient to enable him continue his student-exempt status from conscription into the armed forces for a two-year period of National Service, when he was whisked away into the Royal Air Force and trained as a radar technician. He whiled away the time until 1960 dismantling and reassembling radar equipment on the shores of the Baltic, and enrolled, on his discharge, as a part-time student in psychology in Birkbeck College, London, while supporting himself as an electronics technician in the Phonetics Department at University College London – working on speech analysis and synthesis machines.

On completing his degree he became an electronic 'research assistant', split between the Department of Electrical Engineering (headed by Raymond Beurle, who was both the inventor of night-vision binoculars and the first person to simulate a nerve network on a computer), and the Department of Psychology at Nottingham University. His first abandoned Ph.D. there was to do with a statistical decision-theory analysis of the performance of night-vision binoculars – looking at the interplay between amplification and resolution. Next, he began (but also never finished) a Ph.D. thesis that aimed to build an electronic device that operationalized transformational grammar so it could speak. The thesis was abandoned not through laziness (see, for example, Shotter, 1966), but because of a nagging and growing doubt – even if one could construct a machine that passed the famous 'Turing test'* – as to whether such a simulation told one anything interesting about what speaking was 'really about'.

These doubts have to be seen against a background of an almost total empiricist domination of British academic psychology and psychological politics at that time, with the main proponents of empiricism being Donald Broadbent and Hans Eysenck. Reading Broadbent's essay 'In defence of empirical psychology' in the in-house journal of the British Psychological Society (1970) can capture a flavour of the times. Here Broadbent cited an informal survey of British psychologists, showing that while about 50 per cent of senior psychologists called themselves 'behaviourists', none of the junior ones did. He then proceeded to give a vigorous defence of empirical psychology, both as a theory and a method, firmly identifying himself as 'on the behaviourist side of the fence'. Shotter and his colleague Alan Gauld wrote a critique, published in *American Psychologist*, in which they argued that 'Broadbent's "empirical" theory is logically incoherent', concluding that

> the inability of 'empirical' theory and of traditional empirical methods to cope adequately with our linguistic abilities and performances thus emerges as only

---

* If a machine can be built so that it answers a human interrogator in ways such that the interrogator could not decide if he or she were communicating with a machine or another human being, then it passes the test.

a part (but a central part) of their general inability to cope with human rule-following actions – an inability which … stems from a failure to distinguish the different relations which we have to the material world and to each other. The choice which lies before psychology at present would appear to be either, on the one hand, continuing with the established theoretical presuppositions and methods of investigation and dealing only with those problems which happen to be amenable to them, or, on the other hand, taking up the fascinating and vitally important problems of human conceptual thought and rule-regulated behaviour, and siding with those who, however haltingly, and with whatever difficulty, are endeavouring to find new theoretical concepts and practical methods with which the problems can be effectively tackled.
        (Shotter and Gauld, 1971: 465)

He added that 'our own sympathies in these matters will be abundantly clear' (ibid.). It was a fair, though not necessarily politically astute, statement to publish with respect to the only psychologist to have then been elected a Fellow of the Royal Society, the high bastion of high science. Broadbent replied to these accusations in his fuller, book-length treatment of his position *In Defence of Empirical Psychology*, labelling Shotter and Gauld 'the last kicks of an outdated culture' (1973: 8–9). It was not a great testimonial for the epitome of the establishment to hang on the head of a then junior lecturer in a provincial British university, and one whose personal effects might be ironically discerned in the title of one of Shotter's later books, *The Cultural Politics of Everyday Life* (1993b), for certainly, within the intervening years, Shotter became a prophet unhonoured in his native land, eventually taking a chair in Holland before moving to the United States.

Many of the themes that continue to occupy Shotter's thinking and explorations up to the present time were set out at this point. This can be seen in the following quotation from unpublished seminar notes from 1972 – to their eventual fuller development in a critique edited by Nigel Armistead, *Reconstructing Social Psychology* (1974) – which begins with Descartes' claim as to how we might 'render ourselves masters and possessors of nature', and harks back to the concerns outlined about empiricism by Shotter and Gauld (above):

While classical science demands that we study everything as if it were matter in motion according to natural (or an absent God's established) laws, occasionally *people* seem able to act from a belief, a mere conception of a law, thus exempting themselves from this demand. In attempting to live according to laws, people may fail; they may act inappropriately, rightly or wrongly, legitimately or illegitimately, etc. And in acting thus, according to laws, they have a responsibility to others in their actions; they must make their actions intelligible to themselves in others' terms; and the laws structuring their reality must be open to negotiation and re-negotiation.

If we are to have the *power* to determine the world (and in it we include ourselves), then the world itself must be essentially *indeterminate*. And if alternative determinations are to be possible then *unrealised potentialities* must in one way or another exist. Thus it would be possible for human beings to act responsibly if they possessed *powers of determination* in an essentially *indeterministic* world of real *potential* … [I will] suggest a form of psychological inquiry not directed towards discovering how the mind (or the

> brain) 'works' leading indirectly to the domination of men by men, but directed towards increasing the mastery of all over their own way of life.   (1972)

We see here a number of threads that have come to preoccupy psychological and social theorists:

- the distinction between action and behaviour – which lies at the heart of *Images of Man in Psychological Research* (1975), and which led, in collaboration with Alan Gauld, to a study of hermeneutics – *Human Action and its Psychological Investigation* (1977);
- the realization, subsequent to this distinction, that there was a sphere of activity that was neither the province of individual action or behaviour (nor both), but a zone of uncertainty (what Vygotsky pointed to in his concept of the zoped – to others, the ZPD) in which natural propensities and cultural influences are interwoven: the sphere of 'joint action', to which Shotter has been returning to refine and elaborate ever since;
- the notion of responsibility that humans have to others for their actions – culminating in *Social Accountability and Selfhood* (1984);
- the claim that human realities are negotiated – leading to an ongoing interest in Vygotskyean themes, brought together in *Cultural Politics of Everyday Life* (1993b) and *Conversational Realities: Constructing Life Through Language* (1993a);
- a concern with the moral nature of human activity, continual through the above;
- a 'worrying about' the place of language and 'theory' in relation to action, bringing in a trawling through the works of Vico, Wittgenstein and Bakhtin from 1980 onwards;
- a similarly central, though not always explicit, wondering about the nature of experience, and hence an interest in, and appeal to, phenomenological work, particularly the social and corporeal versions of Schutz and Merleau-Ponty.
- finally, as a culmination of the above, an outlining of a 'knowing of a third kind', not a 'knowing that', nor a 'knowing how', but a 'knowing from within', refined from one of those initial insights first put forward by Vico (see Chapter 2).

When we look at the citations in the finished piece in Armistead's (1974) collection, we see an indication of these traditions to which Shotter was already turning: Berger and Luckmann, Garfinkel, Harre, Mead, Schutz, Vico, and Vygotsky, among others.

This continuing worrying away at central themes makes Shotter's early work quite remarkable in retrospect. In a sense, it is 'all there' to begin with. The chapter in Armistead's book (1974) is thus a premonition of what follows. He sets out his main points thus:

> There are four central issues:
>
> 1. That which seems to anchor me as a person in reality is the sense of responsibility that I can have for my own actions;

2. That treating *time* realistically as the medium through which people develop leads to the idea of an indeterministic contingent world in which, to a degree, what happens is up to us;
3. That [humans] construct for themselves a human world from out of the natural world, and, in using it to express new forms of humanity, transform themselves;
4. That the source of responsibility for people's actions may not always be located *in* individuals: sometimes it is shared *between* them. Thus at first parents share with their babies responsibility for what their babies do, only later do babies become responsible for themselves. Shared responsibilities can become located solely in the individual, thus increasing their powers of self-determination.

It is only in an indeterminate world that men can have the power to determine themselves, to construct laws and choose to act in accordance with them.
    (1974: 54–5)

Implicit in these four concerns are a number of themes that are worked out in more explicit detail over the next decades. In addition, there emerged in the early 1980s a fifth insight that establishes Shotter's views as distinctively his, an insight that led in the early 1990s to an exploration of 'knowing of the third kind'. This fifth insight is that despite a person's sense of their own responsibility for their actions, and their capacity to discriminate between events for which they *are* responsible and those which occur *independently* of their agency to control, it is necessary to recognize a *third* realm of events: outcomes of human interaction which cannot be traced back to the actions of any specific individual. He called this realm that of 'joint action', and first set out some of its properties in a chapter 'Action, joint action, and intentionality' published in a volume edited by Brenner (1980).

Is this how Shotter himself sees his trajectory? We thought we would ask him, in an e-mail interview:

ANDY: John, what do you see as the main themes of your work?
JOHN: I think there are, basically, two of them. One is a negative theme. I have been trying to express, not just the technical inadequacy of the Cartesian mechanistic paradigm in the human and behavioural sciences, but its pernicious moral effects – the undermining of our intrinsic human relatedness. The second is positive. Beginning around 1980, in relation to the concept of 'joint action', I have been exploring the philosophical, empirical and methodological consequences of the – essentially Viconian and Vygotskian – assumption that, as living embodied beings, we cannot help but be spontaneously responsive to both the others and othernesses in our surroundings. In this work, I have focused most intensely on the writings of (initially) Vygotsky and Vico, especially on Wittgenstein, but also (more recently) on Voloshinov and Bakhtin, as well as on Gadamer and Merleau-Ponty.
TOM: How would you describe your approach?
JOHN: In general, my stance toward all these problems can be described as *social constructionist* (in the sense introduced by Rom Harré [1983] and Ken Gergen (1985, 1994b), although in my 1984 book

[Shotter, 1984], I called my approach *social ecology*, and I am now returning to that designation. What strikes me as wrong with current social constructionist approaches is their still Cartesian, (post) structuralist, dualistic approach to language – as if we are only in an *external* relationship to it, rather than having our very being *within* it. They thus still take its referential-representational function as central, whereas I have taken its central function to be of a relationally responsive kind. In my two 1993 books, I explored what I called then a *rhetorical-responsive* version of this approach, concerned with studying that dimension of everyday, spontaneous but contested interpersonal language use, that works to 'construct' or 'constitute' the style of our social relations, the grammars of our forms of life. And how these, in turn, are formative of our different experiences of both ourselves as individuals, and of the supposed 'realities' surrounding us.

ANDY: How did you get into this line of work? I mean, it seems an unexpected turn for someone who has a degree in electronics, and who can still build a computer from a box of parts.

JOHN: Very originally, back in 1964–65, my research was on the computer simulation of language learning – with a computer model in which a 'mother' who already knew a set of 'linguistic' rules transmitted them to a 'child', and my first published paper is in *Nature* upon this topic [1966]. However, through difficulties arising from within this project, I came to realize that it was *not the following of rules* that made linguistic meaning possible for people, but *being able to mean* – due to people's spontaneous bodily responsivity – that made it possible for people to follow rules. And I switched to the videotape study of the interactive activities between actual mothers and children. At that time, in 1975, I outlined my research project as that of attempting to understand the question 'What is it in the everyday interaction with the others around one, that makes it possible to develop into a morally autonomous person?' And in the studies I did in the 1970s, I began to map out arguments for ways of interpreting observations made in the videotape studies, as relevant to that question.

TOM: But that question changed?

JOHN: Yes, it grew. In my 1975 book, I had talked vaguely of people being 'positioned' in social life in some way, and of them as transmitting their culture in their social actions. In articles between 1978 and 1980, I introduced the term 'joint action' to account for that special form of social activity that cannot be attributed to any of the individuals involved in it, but which is itself productive of the 'situation' that they are in and, as such, provides them with resources for their continued action within it. While the notion of 'joint action' remains central to my whole research programme, my conception of social life at large grew more complex. And in my 1984 book, I began to talk of everyday social life as possessing a 'moral ecology' – as if people acted from within a landscape of ethically defined but still contestable rights and duties. That landscape contained a 'political economy of developmental opportunities', with certain regions of it containing more such opportunities than others, with different people having a differential access to such opportunities. In that book, I also explored further the whole social ontology of a world in which it was possible for human actions to make a real difference to its future – a world of becoming rather than being.

The main influences upon my thought at that time were drawn from Wittgenstein, Vico, Vygotsky, Mead, Bakhtin, Billig and MacIntyre; my main then interest was in what could be called 'traditions of argumentation', and in how viewing social life as constituting such a living tradition – rather than a static structure – opens up a whole new range of phenomena for study. In particular, it brought into focus that aspect of cultural politics to do with those activities in which people are able to play a part in the constructing of their own way of life: being able to voice (or not, as the case may be) the character of one's concerns, and have them taken seriously by the others around them, is an essential part of being a citizen and having a sense of belonging in one's society.

ANDY: So, the 1984 *Social Accountability* was a kind of summing up to date and the springboard to further work?

JOHN: Yes, this is where 'cultural politics' came to the fore. What then became of interest to me, was why it was so difficult to introduce the study of 'joint action' and other 'developmental' processes into psychology as a discipline: processes within the discipline itself seem to render them 'rationally invisible', few were prepared to treat these issues as important. In developing the theme of joint action further, I began to use it not only to provide a critique of the (one-way, monological) methodology in experimental psychology, but also to provide a positive account of people's social development – with the eventual aim of giving a comprehensive account of human personhood, i.e., what it is to have a *voice* in influencing the conditions of one's life. Indeed, then, my work was focused on the nature of disciplinary writing and research, and the way in which it worked to silence important marginal 'voices'.

ANDY: And there was a personal angle in this as well? Your own 'cultural politics' and marginalization?

JOHN: Well, yes. Thatcherism was changing British life to make the kind of social situation of my first job as an apprentice with British Aerospace endemic and pervasive across the entirety of British life. Universities were coming under the sway of managerialism. Psychology was becoming professionalized and more 'scientific', so I was certainly feeling myself as being a marginalized voice, and being deliberately held in the lower levels of the profession. But the work I was doing led to an opportunity which resulted in my appointment in 1987, as a full professor, to one of the three directorships of a new General Social Sciences programme, with special reference to 'Language, Thinking, Perception and Culture', in the Rijksuniversiteit Utrecht, The Netherlands. The overall theme of the Utrecht program was 'Citizenship and Development', and it was thought, and I agreed, that that was indeed the main thrust of my work there. And it has continued to be my main focus ever since. But it was at this point that I began to reorient away from psychology and toward the communication discipline.

TOM: The move was important?

JOHN: Yes, because influenced both by events within the interdisciplinary program in which I was involved, and on the continent of Europe itself, my work began to take a more practice-situated turn. I became convinced that my original way of formulating the problems to do with self-determination and moral autonomy was still far too general and abstract, insufficiently political or historical, and far too centred in ahistorical, individualistic, systematic Enlightenment notions centred around 'the nature of Man'. Further, theoretical work both on the nature of deconstruction and rhetoric in literary theory, upon historical traditions of argumentation in moral philosophy, and upon Bakhtin's notion of utterance, voice and speech genres, have led to a whole new, rich and active field of problems to do – not just with personhood – but with identity and belonging, with issues of citizenship, and that aspect of politics present in interpersonal relations to do with 'whose' way of life is the one that is developed in an interaction. Further, it has led me also to a concern with a special form of knowledge – which is neither theoretical nor technical – but is a third kind of knowledge *from within* a way of life to do with knowing how to conduct oneself prudently within it. And it is to the nature of this third kind of (cultural-participatory) knowledge that I have given much attention in recent years.

TOM: So another deepening of similar themes?

JOHN: Yes. Most of what appeared in my two 1993 books had been written after the '84 *Social Accountability* book and before I moved to the University of New Hampshire in 1991. The original enticement was an offer to help begin a Graduate Program in the Department of Communication at UNH. That, unfortunately, was overtaken by the concern with financial stringency that struck the university about that time. Thus my supervision of Ph.D. research, instead of continuing here at UNH, was cut short. But it provided more space to read, write and pursue some practical research activities.

There are two realms of activity that have occupied practically everyone's attention in the social sciences, in social theory, and in philosophy: the realms of action and behaviour. Action can be studied and explained in terms of an individual's (culturally conditioned) reasons for his or her actions, while in the study of behaviour we seek the (natural) causes of an individual's movements. But between these two great realms, containing a mixture of both cultural and natural influences, is another great realm, *sui generis*. In Vygotskian developmental psychology, it is called the zoped (zone of proximal development), but this is not to give it its full importance as the 'inexpressible' background flow of everyday practices 'against which whatever [we] could express has its meaning' [Wittgenstein, 1980a: 16]. Its complex, mixed, *chiasmic* character arises out of the fact that, as soon as a second living human being spontaneously responds to the activities of a first, what the second does cannot be accounted as wholly their own – for they act in a way partly 'shaped' by the first's actions (while the first's actions, in being addressed to the second person, were also responsive to their very presence). Thus what happens between people, between you and me, is neither wholly yours nor mine, but ours – but neither wholly ours either, for we must be responsive to those over there too. In other words, the results of joint action are public property, so to speak. But more than that, such activity is always intrinsically creative, for people's activities are not only uniquely responsive to each other's, but also to particular events occurring in the rest of their surroundings. Such *chiasmically* structured activity is thus full of unique, 'first-time' forms of interaction which, if those involved in them continue to be responsive to them, can be developed into, to use a Wittgensteinian term, new 'forms of life'.

It is our embedding in this unbroken stream of spontaneously responsive, bodily activity, it can be argued, that makes everything else we do as the self-conscious, culturally conditioned, individuals we grow up to become, possible. This third realm of activity is currently being explored by a number of contemporary philosophers (e.g., Dreyfus, Searle and Taylor) in terms of the concept of 'the background'. Its very strange character is only just becoming apparent. Rather than upon the theories and mental processes supposedly hidden inside people's heads, it focuses on our social practices, their beginnings, their sustaining, and upon their further refinement, elaboration and development. It is in this sphere of social practices that my work has its application, for rather than theories of their nature, I have focused on methods for their development.

Indeed, from the time of my appointment to Utrecht onwards, with further scholarly work on Vico, as well as on Wittgenstein, Vygotsky, Bakhtin, Voloshinov, and recently on Goethe (who was influential on all except, of course, Vico), I have begun to develop a comprehensive account of developmental practices all the way from the individual's growth to personal autonomy, to the Swedish 'Learning Regions' project, and medical interviewing.

ANDY: And where are things presently?

JOHN: My present work is on the implications of our embedding in an unbroken background stream of spontaneously responsive bodily activity. I finished a long paper – entitled: 'Spontaneous responsiveness, chiasmic relations, and consciousness: the realm of living expression' – just before my retirement, in which I explore the relevance of chiasmically intertwined activity for an understanding of consciousness. In the paper I suggest that our ways of talking are not just simply a matter of representing, or picturing a state of affairs, so that how others act in relation to what we say is a matter, always, of *interpretation*, a matter of inference or hypothesis formation. Rather, an important aspect of people's verbal communication is their possession of the *right*, as first-person agents, to *express* themselves, to make certain expressive bodily movements. Such expressions are living movements which, as elaborations of our natural, spontaneously expressed responses to events occurring around us, work in a *gestural* fashion to communicate *our own unique* orientation, our own unique relations to our surroundings. Further, in not being simply changes in the position of our bodies in space, but *physiognomic* changes within our bodies themselves, such gestures 'point' for others to aspects of what we call our 'inner lives'. As parents, we make use of such expressions, and of our children's spontaneous responses to them, in teaching them the practices instituted in our society, so that they become trained into spontaneously responding to the expressions of those around them in a *con*(withness)-*scientia*(knowing) manner, a manner shared in by, or sharable with, others. Such bodily expressions are connected with bodily feelings in such a way that all 'feelings' (unless one has learned to suppress them) have their *characteristic* expressions.

This account draws heavily on Wittgenstein's later work. Two themes are central to it. One is that *rules are a result*, not the prior cause, of our being able to mean things to each other in our living bodily expressions – enabling us to move from communication in which we *develop* meanings over time, to one-pass, skilful communication. The other is that consciousness – *con*(withness)-*scientia*(knowing), i.e., knowing along with others – is a *social* phenomenon from the start; and 'the world of consciousness' is not to be found hidden away, privately, inside the heads of individuals, but is 'out there' between us, emerging each time afresh in our meetings.

Grasping Shotter

We cannot do justice here to the ever-expanding and deepening set of themes that have been continuously explored in Shotter's oeuvre for more than forty years. Many of the ideas we have already grappled with in this book go some way towards setting the scene for his work, for his writing is immensely scholarly in its style. Most of his points and arguments are developed as symphonies that elaborate and echo themes from different melodies in an orchestra of others' voices. These themes emerge through the quotations that liberally pepper his writing, and which work to both anchor and carry his plot: Mead, Vygotsky, Bakhtin, Volosinov, Wittgenstein, Garfinkel, Goffman, among others, are juxtaposed verbatim to create his onward flow. Here we take two quotations that, we think, bring into focus where his project is currently at:

> Perhaps what is inexpressible (what I find mysterious and am not able to express) is the background against which whatever I could express has its meaning.
>   (Wittgenstein, 1980a: 16)

> People know what they do; they frequently know why they do what they do; but what they don't know is what what they do does.   (Michel Foucault, pers. comm., quoted in Dreyfus and Rabinow, 1982: 187)

Perhaps the most important words here are 'the background'. Something pre-exists our ability to ever be rational: in this sense, there is a 'background' that grounds our rationality and the historical tradition that has enabled us to become people who unreflectively take it as normal that we are now seemingly rational, and individual, selves. There is something that has made this construction possible (but not inevitable). In addition, as this historically mediated construction, through appropriating the symbolic resources available in our nascent cultures, developmentally progresses, it is transformed from a background we are endowed with from birth, and elaborate during out interactions with others during infancy, into a cultural 'backdrop' within which we act. One of Shotter's struggles is to articulate these 'backgrounds and backdrops', these 'somethings' that make going on possible.

Shotter himself does not use these terms of 'background' and 'backdrop', but we bring them in here to highlight what we see as an important thrust in his work. He draws from a number of sources we have already explored, and which enable a grasp of a central point: there is, ineffably, something unique about being human that is provided to our infants, an ability to partake in an intersubjective, dialogical life right from the start, a life that is further constructed – developed, so to speak – in the dialogic crucible of zones of proximal activities. This is the 'background'. From this crucible there emerges an enculturated being who conducts his or her activities in ways that are little different from their initial starting points – they are responsively vital – but that are overlaid by the cultural resources available to them to structure symbolically how they conceptualize these activities. These resources provide the interpretive 'backdrop' that makes their being and their grasp of it possible, something that can be talked about and investigated.

Part of Shotter's thrust is that these interpretive backdrops work to blind us to the fact that the background is still, mysteriously, preserved. In a perverse way, western culture's historically dominant systems of symbols create 'backdrops' that blind us to the ever-present 'background' that both makes it possible for us to have become cultural participants, and enables us to sustain our roles as cultural participants: this is 'knowledge of the third kind' in Shotter's terminology. We are tempted to say 'Q.E.D.' at this point: if the general thrust of what we have been arguing in this book were readily apparent, then it would not have taken us so long to uncover it: or, combining a Shotterian point with our own words, a 'rational backdrop' renders the necessary 'background conditions' that enable its existence to be 'rationally invisible'. Thus, we are 'bewitched', to use Wittgenstein's formulation, by the Cartesian inheritance we have assumed as our interpretive backdrop, bewitched into trying to formulate the background of our everyday lives as though it were the mysterious product of the collision of monads, the culturally relative 'I's that Descartes framed his conceptual system within, and which now tinges everything that makes us 'us'.

There are a number of tensions here. The first is the peculiar character of Shotter's project, which stems from one of the points of departure for his work: 'treating *time* realistically as the medium through which people develop' (1974: see above). In treating time 'realistically', he adopts the view that our grasp of the world is, in its very character, an indeterministic, unspecified one, but at the same time, one in which particular characteristics of how, at any particular time, that future is constrained: 'an action in progress can, while having so far produced a certain degree of specification into its content, leave that content open to yet further specification – but only specification of an already specified kind' (Shotter, 1981: 276). There are two consequences that follow from this view.

On the one hand, if we take a system that has been humanly constructed, such as the phonemic system that structures the way we make distinctions between the sounds that carry our meanings when we speak, then it is quite clear that different cultural traditions make these distinctions in different ways. Thus, the distinctions used in any linguistic system have an *arbitrary* character, and one that is established as a result of the first distinctions that are made, and which consequently specify what further distinctions are possible. Similarly, this will be the case with any humanly constructed human system: a set of concepts are interrelated in a systematic way that is relative to the starting distinctions that are made, and are, then, basically arbitrary: *they could have been differently drawn*. From here follows one of the tenets of post-structuralism and social constructionist dogma: *relativism*: the rational self is a historical construct, and the ideas we have about truth and necessity could well be otherwise. On the other hand, however, there is a *foundational* aspect to this construction: distinctions are made, and made *between* people, not by the imposition of the will of one person upon another, but in the social process of negotiating coordinations of agreement – an intersubjectivity whose structure is not planned – that ground the whole process of making meanings possible. Importantly, this process is, Shotter claims, something that has been rendered invisible to us – rationally invisible – by the construction of the rational lens through which we now peer out on to the world. Consequently:

> Descartes' view of us as a 'thing that thinks' not only represents us to ourselves as monological, disembodied creatures, it also leaves out our spontaneously responsive and expressive, living, continuously changing, bodily relations to all the others and othernesses around us – it is only through our *Reason* that we get to know that we are surrounded by others like ourselves. Indeed, it leaves out of rational consideration the whole uninterrupted realm of ceaselessly flowing, spontaneously occurring, always interplaying, activities – material activities as well as those of a psychosocial and sociocultural kind – within which we are willy-nilly embedded and to which we ineradicably owe our identities as the kind of people we are (Shotter, 1984). It is from out of this unremitting flow of *background* activity that the more deliberate aspects of our own activities emerge, and back into which they must be directed and related if they are to make sense.
>
> As soon as we turn ourselves around from a focus on the kind of world confronting the inquirer as an individual thinker to a focus on the world inhabited by two or more inquirers in dialogically structured, communicative relations to each other, then, like someone emerging out of Plato's cave into the sunlight of day, we find ourselves situated within an entirely new realm of phenomena. While Descartes sought that embodied sense of an 'it' in which to 'ground' or 'root' his inquiries solely within himself, it is within the practicalities of our meetings with others, rather than in our own individual reflections, that I think the new starting points for our inquiries can be found.   (Shotter, 2006: 2, emphasis added)

Here it will be apparent that the term 'background' is actually inappropriate, because what is being pointed to here is something within which we are immersed – or 'embedded'. It is a 'knowingness' of 'being there', a 'knowledge not detached from our being but determinative of what we are' (Bernstein, 1992: 25): 'a kind of knowledge one has only from within relationships with others, whether the relationship is actual or imagined' (Shotter, 1994: 2).

> I shall call it a knowing of the third kind. For: i) It is not theoretical knowledge (a *'knowing-that'* in Ryle's 1949, terminology) – for it is knowledge that is

only present to us in our everyday social practices; however, ii) it is not simply a technical knowledge of a skill or craft (a *'knowing-how'*) either – for it is a joint kind of knowledge, a knowledge-held-in-common with others, and *judged* by them in the process of its use. iii) It is its own kind of knowledge, *sui generis*, that cannot be reduced to either of the other two.   (1994: 1)

It cannot be reduced to knowing-that, because it is the source from which ways of knowing anything as a 'that' (which is a relative 'that' – specified by its arbitrary history of specification) are elaborated. Neither is it quite a knowing-how, because it is not really something we *know how* to do; it is more something we are *able to do*, not on our own to the world, but with others in our interactions with them and the intersubjective world we are both simultaneously in. And: 'I cannot emphasise enough the strange nature of this kind of knowledge, the difficulties involved in focusing upon its workings, or the elusiveness of its existence' (Shotter, 1994: 1). How have we missed it? Because, as Wittgenstein put it, we have been 'bewitched by language', and language is not our primary reality:

> The origin and primitive form of the language game is a reaction; only from this can more complicated forms develop. Language – I want to say – is a refinement, 'in the beginning was the deed' [Goethe]   (Wittgenstein, 1980a: 31)

> But what is the word 'primitive' meant to say here? Presumably that this sort of behaviour is *pre-linguistic*: that a language-game is based *on it*, that it is the prototype of a way of thinking and not the result of thought.   (Wittgenstein, 1981, aphorism 541)

What, at this point, can be said about this strange form of knowledge? Quite early in his writing, Shotter picked up on Giddens' (1979; see Chapter 10 above) notion of 'duality of structure', making the point that the character of joint action is not structured either by reference to internal representational models, nor by executing scripts or rules, but in a different way, via a network of possibilities that open up in the course of activity. Shotter's adoption of 'duality of structure' suggests that 'the moment of control of my action can be informed – not by my consulting an "inner representation" or "plan", ... but by what I have just specified in my action remaining "on hand" so to speak, as a structured context into which I can act further' (1983: 33). Structure is thus an emergent out of the process of real-time interaction, as Giddens claims, both the medium and the outcome of social action. Shotter terms this process the 'social ecology' of action. It is not an ecology in which fixed niches pre-exist and, in that sense, predetermine the direction in which an action can unfold. Rather, it is one that constructs the possibilities for its future continuation from its own momentum, so to speak, and specifies these as it comes up against the responsiveness or otherwise of what it engenders at any moment with its conversational partner: maybe I can now go on, in the flow with the other; or change direction; or even come to a stop against an unanticipated reaction. This is the conversational reality of human interaction: the structures we might find in it are a joint production (much like the form a tree attains in interaction with the environment as it meets that environment during the course of its growth (see Chapter 7), not a predetermined unfolding, nor a form for which the responsibility for its appearance can be allocated to either participant. 'Knowledge of the third kind' is not so much a background against which we reflectively act, but a medium in which we spontaneously act.

This formulation of social action leads us to a conundrum, and one that Shotter has been working to resolve in his work since the early 1980s: to further specify and convey what he takes a self to be. The issue is that, traditionally, to count as an authentic, autonomous self, it is necessary for one to be able to distinguish between that which just happens to one and that which one is responsible for making happen (cf. Hallowell, Chapter 12). This distinction is difficult to sustain in the light of recognizing the key role that joint action has in the character of human affairs, where many outcomes in real time have a character that was unanticipated by both parties, and where the responsibility lies 'between' them, in their interaction, and not in anything inherent in either individual. There are three complementary strands to his efforts. The first is his realization that selves are embodied. The second is to convey a sense of what it is like to be an embodied self. The third has been to worry out an appropriate account of what it is that is going on when an 'I' does something in which it, as a bodily-centred source of action, essays activities into the world, actions that are (i) simultaneously structured by the prior flow of 'self'-generated activity, and are (ii) instantaneously restructured in the course of their activity through a lived-in, spontaneous reactivity.

Just getting a handle on all of this is incredibly difficult. We have tried to convey in previous chapters a sense of how different thinkers have realized that being a human being – a self – was quite different in the earlier histories of the cultures we live in today. It is often difficult to imagine a world in which what we describe of people seems so alien. It is equally difficult to imagine what it might be like to be in such an alien world: to empathize with people who delight in the spectacle of human sacrifice; burning at the stake; or someone being publicly hanged, let alone hung, drawn and quartered. It is difficult to entertain the idea that we could have been there, and enjoyed it. It is difficult, but not impossible, as Vico (Chapter 2) was the first to signal in our narrative. And yet, to what extent can this 'impossible' be really accomplished? If, as Elias (see Chapter 11) argued, there has been an historical reconfiguration of our very personalities; if, as Hallowell (see Chapter 12) analyses the dimensions of self-hood, there are many ways to be a self; then can we ever do anything more than create an ersatz empathy other than through our particular ways of structuring our experience? How can we relate to such 'other' ways of being? This problem, in our reading, is central to understanding a major thrust in Shotter's work, particularly as he developed it in his book *Social Accountability and Selfhood* (1984): partaking in social activities is different from accounting for one's participation, even though the discourses of accountability anyone has at any particular historical moment clearly feed back into the style of one's partaking.

What Shotter works to do is to have us step out of our language, our academic discourses and arguments, to encompass the realization that we are embodied centres of a combined 'being-and-doing', who are actually restructured moment by moment through our conduct with the world and those with whom we interact. For this is central to what Shotter is exploring: that, in everyday life, we are not, moment-to-moment, reflective participants in our lives, but are spontaneously reactive to the flow of events as they happen, and spontaneously restructure our participation 'on the fly', without thinking. To capture this way of 'knowledging' requires, first, that we study 'the actual processes of behavioural encounter from out of which 'knowledging' activities grow, emerge or develop. And to do this, we need to focus on events occurring *between* people – on meetings, encounters, etc. – not on events occurring *within* them' (Shotter, 2007: 76). There is a sense in which this thrust links up with that of Garfinkel (see Chapter 10). Unbeknownst to themselves, people are engaged in sustaining their interactions in ways that are an assumed and ingrained patterning of their being that handles their present way of life. It is only in the breaching of these ways of going on that we ever gain a glimpse of this unreflective aspect of 'being social together', the 'glue' that keeps social life on track. And when a breach occurs, then we only have the discursive resources of our everyday cultures available to us to offer an account of that breaching experience: resources that do not take account of this assumed ground within which they occur. How could they?

To even approach this question requires our realizing that

> while we can study an already completed, dead structure from a distance, seeking to understand the pattern of past events that caused it to come into existence, we can enter into a relationship with a living form and, in making ourselves open to its movements, find ourselves spontaneously responding to it. Thus, instead of seeking to understand a dead form in terms of an objective, explanatory theory, we can come to understand a living form in quite a different way, to understand it in terms of its meaning for us. It is only from within our involvements, our engaged meetings with other living things, that this kind of meaningful, responsive understanding becomes available to us.   (Shotter, 2007: 76–7)

This responsive, conversational understanding is thus very different from the form of understanding traditionally constituted as 'knowledge' – a knowledge that is gained from an objective stance and formulated in linguistic symbols. It is, rather, a form of understanding that we 'live through', while at the same time not noticing it, unless the relational interactions somehow go awry for one or more of the people involved. It is in many ways hidden from us, in the same way that Mead's notion of 'I' is: we can grasp a 'me' from the position in time and space he term's 'I', but 'I', being the grasper, is always elusive. But it is this elusive activity and reactivity of living in the world in specific ways that keep things unproblematically familiar that is the necessary foundation for understanding how human life is conducted. It is in these ways that knowledge of 'the third kind' is such a difficult realm to get a handle on. It is not something that can be translated into words; it is a grounding that makes words possible, an unwritten script that enables a connecting to others.

In revealing the outlines of this form of understanding, we find Shotter reconceptualizing another line of his earlier thinking. An important influence in his 1970s work were two points drawn from Vygotsky: that symbolic functions all begin between people, intermentally in their interactions, before they become something an individual can use for their own purposes; and that an ability must be in our spontaneous repertoire before we can bring it under voluntary control. Putting these two points together, we can appreciate that from the beginning infants are spontaneously capable of acting in an intermental fashion, in sustaining joint action; and that these joint actions are formative of themselves and their symbolic abilities as they come to take these over into their own realm of (thereby reconstituted) spontaneity. In this sense, an infant's becoming self-aware is distilled out of joint action through the resources joint action provides for them. Similarly, then, adults who engage in joint action with each other can provide the conditions to reveal to themselves the character of the joint activities they are constructing in the course of their joint actions. And what are the characteristics of this form of understanding? This is one issue that Shotter's recent work begins to make explicit.

First, action in real life is never wholly someone's sole possession. That it is not is shown both by the way in which we act if we think we are in private, and how we react when we find we were in fact being observed; but also by how we do act when in private, for such acts are always oriented towards an other: in Bakhtin's approach (see Chapter 5), social action is always anticipatory, though not necessarily in a reflected-upon way. As Garfinkel (see Chapter 10) showed, it sometimes takes a disruption of such anticipated social acts in order to point out how much they were taken for granted.

Second, 'as a result of entering into interaction with each other, when they separate, they can no longer be described as before – they are "infected", so to speak, with the "otherness" of the other' (Shotter 2005: 137). As an example, one of the bedroom scenes in Mike Nichols' film *The Graduate* (1967) begins with Benjamin trying to get a reluctant Mrs Robinson to have a conversation: 'Now – do you think we could say a few words to each other first this time?' It takes a while, but a 'conversation' eventually gains some momentum:

BENJAMIN:	We're talking, Mrs Robinson. We're talking.
MRS ROBINSON:	Calm down, Benjamin.
BENJAMIN:	Now let's keep going here.

In a short while, Benjamin is happy how the conversational topic is turning out – 'Man, is this interesting' – but it manages to go sour very quickly, and take an excursion into 'Who's afraid of Virginia Woolf?' territory. Both characters become very angry with, and rude to, each other, and then work out a resolution that Benjamin submits to, the scene ending with a very dejected Benjamin:

MRS ROBINSON:	Thank you. (pause) Benjamin –
BENJAMIN:	Let's not talk about it. Let's not talk at all.

Benjamin's initial desire to have a conversation, because previously they did not have any, turns sourly into a recognition that they cannot sustain his intention, not just to the point of no longer wanting to sustain 'it' so as to conclude a reflective resolution of their points of contention, but without a desire to 'talk at all'. He has been 'infected' with the 'otherness' of the 'other', and is no longer who he was. Al Stewart also captures this in the ending of his song 'Love Chronicles' (1969):

> Of all the girls I ever knew some loved and some denied me
> And all the words I ever said have been no use to hide me
> And all the songs I ever sung each one of them untied me
> And all the girls I ever loved have left themselves inside me.

Third:

> all such meetings, i.e., entanglements, intertwinings, or chiasmically
> structured events, are not only uniquely related to the context of their
> occurrence, but they also have the quality of passing or transitory events;
> they are not stable, recurrent states, but only 'once-occurrent events of Being'
> (Bakhtin, 1993) or events occurring for yet 'another first time' (Garfinkel,
> 1967) – thus, they cannot be described in terms of an already existing
> vocabulary depicting 'finished' events'.   (Shotter, 2005: 137)

The point here is that we need to focus on the ongoing unfolding of an interaction so as to properly describe it, and understand the character of what is going on. Interaction is not generated by a rule-following, stable, quasi-automaton, but is accomplished creatively and openly. It is only 'after the fact' that we have 'closed' Benjamin's and Mrs Robinson's conversation above that it is delimited as an 'episode' of interaction. In fact, the interaction goes on, constructing and reconstructing its participants. It is, for ethnomethodologists, context-shaped and context-shaping.

Fourth:

> to the extent that all the outcomes of such spontaneous, inter-activity cannot
> be traced back to the specific actions of any of the individuals involved, they
> are experienced by participants in such meetings as due to the presence of
> an invisible third agency, an 'it' with its own requirements – invisible 'real
> presences' (Steiner, 1989; Shotter, 2003) with a life of 'their own' can emerge
> in such meetings and we can find ourselves feeling compelled to answer to the
> 'calls' they exert upon us.   (Shotter 2005: 137)

Again, a glimpse of an invisible real presence is afforded in our previous example: 'MRS ROBINSON: Thank you. (pause) Benjamin –'. The pause, then his name, indicate a felt obligation on her part to resolve the unsatisfactory course of the recent conversation: she is under an obligation, experiencing an 'ought' that has emerged out of their 'spontaneous inter-activity' that she feels compelled to address. Rituals, in general, also work to manufacture a high dramatic effect, from which, through our bodily involvement in them, other 'real presences' are constructed. Similarly drama, which can conjure all kinds of anticipatory responses as to 'what might happen next', even though these responses are towards what is emerging from a spectator's role rather than through active participation. There is an affinity here with Harré's positioning account (see Chapter 15) where people find themselves exposed to shifting rights, duties and obligations as conversations unfold.

Fifth, then, as we have just outlined, 'due to the fact that there is always a kind of developmental continuity involved in the unfolding of all living activities, the earlier phases of the "it's" activity are indicative of at least the style of what is to come later – thus we respond to "it" in an anticipatory fashion' (Shotter, 2005: 138). Finally, 'this all necessarily occurs within living meetings – and can thus only be made sense of from within those meetings' (ibid.). This all points, then, to a much needed reorientation of social inquiry and practice.

For practitioners, the implications of what Shotter raises with 'knowing of the third kind' is where things can get quite complicated. Some of this is because of how helping interactions are portrayed in textbooks and other forms of instruction. For example, rapport with clients is commonly depicted as achievable through the practitioner's use of particular rhetorical skills, such as Carl Rogers' (1961) active listening skills. Elsewhere, interventions used by other professionals are often presented as if they were scripts to be administered to clients. In other words, the active professional is shown to operate almost conversationally on a presumably receptive (unless 'resistant') client. Some go so far as to say the professional 'manages' such conversations, as if clients were subordinates to be directed. This is where conversation can be idealized to serve the purposes of the professional who uses her or his model successfully. Microanalyses of such conversations (e.g., Strong, 2006a) show a much less tidy endeavour occurring.

As we saw in Goffman's (see Chapter 10) account of 'facework', a lot more is going on. First of all, both professional and client are simultaneously engaged in practically interpreting each other – showing each other how they are making sense as they move the dialogue and their relationship's course along through their responses to each other. This is a good case of where individual contributions often yield more than the sum of their parts – a unique relationship (yours/mine → *ours*) develops from their back and forth in dialogue. Bakhtin (see Chapter 5) saw something spiritual occurring in these back and forths; it is where words come alive in particular and often unpredictable ways, given how speakers respond to each other. There can be a Ouija-board-like quality to what we have been describing as the conversation takes on a life of its own that in turn influences its participants. Despite the instrumental aims of practitioners, unanticipated or unwanted conversational developments and client responsiveness in the immediacies of dialogue are not matters to override to get the conversational work of professional helping done. It is here that Shotter asks practitioners to be relationally responsive so as to include what clients show as relevant and preferred in shaping the conversation's unfolding developments. It is this responsive dimension to clients and to unanticipated conversational developments that is part of Shotter's dialogic challenge to practitioners: dialogue is a reciprocally influential practice easily thwarted by non-responsiveness. Of course, there are lots of ways that practitioners can become non-responsive, such as when they too strictly adhere to their models of and scripts for helping.

Shotter's current position is, then, distinctive, and, in his own words, marks a return to a position in which his focus is on 'social ecology' founded in relationships. His view is that other versions of primarily linguistic social constructionism and other post-structuralist approaches to interaction

> are not radical enough. They have left in place Descartes's account of our background reality as 'a chaos as disordered as the poets could ever imagine' (1968: 62), a vision of our spontaneously responsive social relations to each other as similar to those of dust particles in Brownian movement. And this of course gives us no shared guidance at all in our controversies with each other as to which of each other's claims to adopt for the best.   (Shotter, 2002)

Thus a relativist position, such as that stated by Rorty (1989: xiii), 'that there is nothing "beneath" socialization or prior to history which is definatory of the human being' is specious:

> to claim that there can be no shared background structure of feeling, no shared tendencies to respond to the other's expressions, no shared anticipations of the moves that they might make – even if the background in question is one without a long history, but is only created at that moment of meeting, when one living being acknowledges the presence of another – would be to claim that there is no shared basis at all in terms of which to form any agreements, nothing which is *constitutive* at all of shared, practical 'ways of going on'.   (Shotter, 2002)

17 Concluding remarks

> The greater part of reality-maintenance in conversation is implicit, not explicit.
> Most conversation does not in so many words define the nature of the world.
> Rather, it takes place against the background of a world that is silently taken
> for granted.   (Berger and Luckmann, 1991[1967]: 172)

We noted in our introduction that social constructionism is a broad church. The sources we have presented as stirring up the central tenets of constructionism – attempts to elucidate meaning-making, both how it is done and what it does – confirm that breadth, and make it clear that a definitive summing up here is a futile task. That said, we still see a great deal of value and rich possibility coming from the ideas we have trawled through. The nineteenth-century debates – the *Methodenstreich* – as to whether a human science compatible with physical science is possible are not just still unresolved, but perhaps unresolvable. But we do see a richer, almost hybrid, form of investigation and practice that has been signalled by the explorations since that debate.

From where we have been looking, we see some problems in the received academic paradigm of psychology. The first is its omission of the fact that people have (inter)subjective experiences, and that these experiences are central to human activity. Coupled with this subjectivity, people have a tacit grasp, from the inside, as to what it is like to be human. 'Scientific' psychology has developed as a body of theory that almost totally ignores this. This omission, we suggest, actually contradicts psychology's claim to be a science. Subjective experience is not something that can just be tacked on to cognitive explanations of how people do things by information processing. Rather, it is where the study of human activity needs to begin, and is central to how professional practice occurs.

We thus find a problem of how to go forward, for there is a very deep issue here. Something, surely, must be going on inside the skin (and brains) of people when they act. And, surely, we can get a handle on what this is, develop a true account of how this is done. Or so we think. But how can we reconcile this with Wittgenstein's claims that 'nothing is hidden?' Or that 'following a rule' is a practice, an activity that is different from processing information to generate a plan which the body can then execute, detect the results of that execution, process these results as to whether expectations have been met, re-adjust the next action, and so on? We are so very ingrained in these traditional ways of thinking that it is difficult to see possibilities outside of 'well, that's how it must be done' (see here Shotter, 1993a, Chapter 7, 'Conversational realities and academic discourses', for an account of how psychology students are inducted into seeing the world in these terms as the naturally obvious way 'things must be'). The cognitive perspective adds to this by characterizing these internal processes as having an organic substrate. Thus the blurb for Anderson and Lightfoot's (2002) book, *The Language Organ: Lingustics as Cognitive Science*, tells us that it 'treats human language as the manifestation of a faculty of the mind, a mental organ whose nature is determined by human biology and whose functional properties should be explored just as physiology explores the functional properties of physical organs'. They are not alone in this view, for many linguists, cognitive scientists and philosophers think that the ability to speak and understand language is biological in nature and that this biologically based capacity for language is a distinct mental organ and an underlying mechanism that embodies linguistic knowledge (Stein, 1997: 185).

There are a number of reasons for thinking this a rather odd way of proceeding. If we pursue the organ analogy, then are we happy to say that the kidney embodies 'excretion knowledge' or the heart embodies 'pumping knowledge?' Rather, it would seem that there are processes involved here whereby the organ's functions are spontaneously reactive to its changing situation, and it is not involved in referring that situation to a body of knowledge that tells it how to react. A number of the sources we have considered take a similar view of 'spontaneous reactivity' between people as a characteristic of their interactions, and it is through these that language and thought are socially constructed from this 'pre-linguistic grasp' (cf. Husserl, Schutz, Mead, Garfinkel and Goffman). Meaningful language originates between us, not issues from within us, and it thus provides 'the prototype of a way of thinking and not the result of thought' (Wittgenstein, 1981: aphorism 541). Language is appropriated and elaborated in spontaneous practices that develop between pre-linguistic infants and their caretakers, practices which are already embedded in the wider socio-cultural traditions those caretakers are enacting (and thereby sustaining). This elaboration is within the infant's 'zone of proximal development', where all enculturated mental skills that individuals come to control are first elaborated intermentally (see Vygotsky, Chapter 6).

Clearly, we can legitimately ask how it is possible that developing infants are able to bring the resources of these traditions that they are spontaneously reactive to under control, and further we have reasons to assume that there is something biologically unique about them that enables this, but that would be to miss the crucial point, well made by Shotter (1999: 130), that:

> It is only as we come to articulate and elaborate the structure of such responsive reactions from within the relations they establish, that a way of thinking as such emerges – along with a specific form of life with its associated language-game. Activities within such forms of life are meaningful, not because people are thinking anything in particular while performing them, but because they have their origins in, and occur as refinements of, already spontaneously meaningful activities: 'our language is merely an auxiliary to, and further extension of, this relation' (Wittgenstein, 1981, no. 545).   (Shotter 1999: 130)

In this same article, Shotter brings out Goffman's take on this crucial component of human activity, how it is that conducting conversations brings an almost
autonomous set of demands into people's intersubjective conduct:

> the individual's actions must happen to satisfy his involvement obligations,
> but in a certain sense he cannot act *in order* to satisfy those obligations, for
> such an effort would require him to shift his attention from the topic of the
> conversation to the problem of being spontaneously involved in it, [and this is]
> an important way in which the interactional order differs from other kinds of
> social order.   (Goffman, 1967: 115)

And we can all tell, immediately, when this spontaneous responsiveness of being
'in' an interaction is not occurring, through being sensitive to the ever-changing
direct experience of each other that is the product of our interaction, and not
something attributable to either individual involved.

> This is what makes joint actions special: it is not just me coordinating with you
> and you with me, but us each being sensitive to a continuously changing 'it'
> between us... What is involved in joint actions is a primitive kind of collective
> social behavior, *sui generis*, irreducible to any other ... It is ... this background
> of 'preintentional capacities that enable all meaning and understanding to take
> place' (Parret et al.,1992:145) that we must now study. But how?'   (Shotter,
> 1999: 132–3)

How do we deal with what Schutz calls 'the unquestioned but always questionable
background' (1982: 57)?

We want to indicate here that there are a number of possible ways of going
forward with these questions. These ways fall into the two categories that we get
by paraphrasing Marx (see Chapter 5): '[psychologists] have hitherto only interpreted the world in various ways; the point is to change it'. That is, there exist the
options of theory and explanation, and/or using new formulations to guide practice and conduct to recreate the worlds we construct and thus live in and through.
In both cases, we see the lines of thinking we have introduced and surveyed
here – what we are terming the 'sources and stirrings of social constructionism' –
as of central importance.

Theory and explanation

> Since our theories are constitutive of the known world but *not* of the *world*, we
> may always be wrong, but *not* anything goes.   (Harré, 1983: 401)

> [we] encounter [the everyday world] ... as already constituted, ... already-
> given; [we] are always conscious of its historicity [as it is] pregiven to both the
> man in the world of working and to the theorizing thinker.   (Schutz, 1982:
> 133, 247)

For us, one of the important, and perhaps surprising, factors that comes out of
this survey is that, despite having been allied with those aspects of postmodernism that give rise to metanarratives, social constructionism actually offers a

very compelling metanarrative of its own, an articulation of 'human nature' as everywhere elaborated within historical, cultural traditions through the concrete interactions that occur between people. These interactions have a powerful, transformative character that we are only slowly becoming aware of, but they are the site of that activity that Vico (Chapter 2) termed 'providence'. We have some insights into how providence does its stuff from Elias's analysis (Chapter 11) of the 'civilizing process', whereby restructurings of subjectivity are brought about through the changing demands made upon individuals as to how to conduct themselves when local presuppositions are challenged by the increasing distances that concrete interactions bring into the conduct of everyday life: a challenge met by an incorporation of unordinary otherness into individual conduct. Allied to this are the insights of Vygotsky (Chapter 6) as to the socially constituted nature of human development, and the role that different cultural symbolic tool kits can play in constituting the characteristics of thinking, speaking and acting.

Without even contemplating any further shift in the way psychology conceives its subject matter, these realizations provoke an important change of perspective. It is just not adequate to consider an individual as a bounded unit of analysis, and to then ask empirical questions as to how that individual is affected by the social and cultural factors that impinge upon them. There is not some kind of given, universal blueprint that would develop as a true human nature that is obscured because of these various influences on that course of development. Rather, concrete human development is made possible by a constructional process, such that development is the negotiation and elaboration of skills that are concrete outcomes of ever-changing possibilities, where what is brought biologically to the situation is interwoven with what is brought by the socio-cultural world into which that biology is thrown. Thus, a whole new landscape of empirical investigations is opened up.

The consensus in the material we have considered indicates a further shift is needed in psychology, a changed focus on what it is biology brings to this nexus that is the site of development. Biology brings an embodied, subjective experience into the world in which that subjectivity is structured by encounters with what is already being concretely acted out; that is, the socio-culturally embodied ways of being that each new locus of subjectivity meets and is submersed in, and which is recognized 'as such' from very early on. A psychology that leaves out subjectivity is necessarily a poor approximation of an adequate psychology, because 'not anything goes'. Once we make this shift, again, more new questions arise. How is this primary 'prepropositional awareness' that makes development possible itself made possible? (Here recent work on mirror neurons clearly beckons as important, e.g. Arbib, 2006, and contributors.) What shape might a psychological account of cognition take as to how embodied intersubjectivities do their stuff (and here developments in the theorization of embodied, situated cognition appear as relevant, e.g. Pfeifer and Bongard, 2007)? How is language elaborated from this base, and how, when we consider the interactive properties of language as pointed to by the members of the Bakhtin Circle (Chapter 5), do its characteristics interweave with the spontaneous relational reponsivity of its use to maintain an ongoing dialogical construction and reconstruction of ourselves in our 'forms of life'? These questions are clearly not exhaustive, but point us in new directions towards what have traditionally been central issues in psychology: what is there, inside our skin, so to speak, that makes these things possible?

There is more: what goes on outside our skin becomes a legitimate site for psychological investigation. There is a side of social constructionist thinking that legitimates and illuminates this territory. Ken Gergen (Chapter 14) puts the view that one can ask how discourse works to empower and disempower people. Rom Harré (Chapter 15) points to the moral nature of this discursive field – the conversational reality we live in – and seeks to uncover how the demands of interaction position us in particular ways, to create those obligations that John Shotter (Chapter 16) points to in his explorations of 'knowledge of the third kind'. The concrete ways in which language is used in everyday life is made available through the work of the discourse analysts (Chapter 13) from their varied perspectives, and extended to the conduct of everyday life in the trajectories explored by Garfinkel and Goffman (Chapter 10). Our view at this point is that the ideas we have surveyed, ideas which have developed in parallel to the narrative that academic psychology has actually pursued, now provide an essential resource for enabling the discipline to focus properly on the characteristics of human activity. And there is yet still more. This reformulation of psychology's conceptual base and focus of investigation keeps us within that traditional sphere that Marx pejoratively referred to as just 'interpreting human activity'. How, then, might one take this new perspective and apply it to his call to 'change the world'?

Practice

> [N]either the fact that the world ... is a world for all of us, nor the fact that my experience of the world refers a priori to others, requires explanation.
> (Schutz, 1975: 83)

> Language remains alive when it refuses to 'encapsulate' or 'capture' the events and lives it describes. But when it seeks to effect that capture, language not only loses its vitality, but acquires its own violent force. (Butler, 1997: 9)

If it is in the dialogues of our relationships that we elaborate the languages and ways of interacting from which understanding and social influence become possible, then it is reasonable to conclude that this premise should extend to what might transpire in professional practice. Throughout this book we have brought forward theorists whose ideas converge in ways that we think have very different implications for practice when compared to those that arise from the dominant psychological narrative. What makes things socially real is our ability to articulate and enact them in the language and social practices we share with others. An unshareable reality clearly is problematic, and so is a reality that is beyond human agency to transform.

Language in this sense can never provide ultimate understandings, but it can provide effective ways of relating to reality, depending on our purposes. It is in this sense that language takes on a central role in professional practice, but as all our writers point out, one cannot speak of language independently of its relational and cultural use. That language can be used in taken-for-granted ways is a cultural and social accomplishment, requiring trust and agreement.

How all this relates to practice can be a daunting issue for practitioners used to turning to the acquired wisdom of their professions so as to map out the understandings and prescriptions clients purportedly need from them. By contrast, constructionist practice, at first glance, can look positively anarchic. Where a single diagnostic language offers purported clarity, constructionist practitioners talk about discourses, positions and language games. With respect to professional intervention, dominant practice depicts practitioners as conversational surgeons, able to dissect and correct what clients say, or as profferers of directives or expert knowledge. Constructionist practitioners join clients in finding perspicuous language for their concerns and aspirations, and in developing solutions consistent with perspicuous language. Theirs is a much more negotiated helping process, not simply a circumstance of taking clients' goals and problem descriptions, and then professionally taking over the helping process from there. The probabilistic generalizations won by social science up to this point, in our view, offer no certainties or 'laws' that are translatable into all-purpose client descriptions and prescriptions. This is despite the increasing transformation of therapeutic practice into a single language for describing problems (as medical conditions *in* people) and 'corresponding', evidence-based, treatment protocols.

Some concrete examples are useful here. An issue that much exercises educational psychologists is 'under-achievement', particularly among children who are classified as gifted on the basis of their IQ scores. Grobman (2006: 200–1) lists the standard explanations in the psychological literature for gifted under-achievement as:

> a poor educational fit …; peers who rejected them; inadequate parents; environmental mismatches of various kinds; internal factors such as perfectionism, low self-esteem, self-regulatory problems, maladaptive strategies, social immaturity, or asynchronous development …; parents with serious psychopathology, or parents who neglected or misperceived their children's gifts and or parents who were controlling or domineering.

For the sample Grobman was working with, many of these 'standard explanations for their gifted under-achievement did not seem entirely adequate' (2006: 200). He thus pursued in-depth therapeutic interviews with the individuals in his sample. What he reports is that

> their most troublesome conflicts and anxieties arose not from fears of ostracism, fears of failure, or lost opportunities, but from fear that giftedness had distorted and twisted them as human beings. Would their developing power, grand ambitions, and charisma turn them into self-involved narcissistic destructive people?

> Because these deeper conflicts were largely out of their awareness, they could not grapple with them effectively. Instead, to escape from their anxieties, they resorted to primitive psychological methods of denial, avoidance, provocative behavior, and projection of blame onto others. The usual result was depression and anxiety, as well as self-destructive behavior and underachievement.   (ibid.: 209)

Note how this entire account roots the issues within a self-contained individual, and that the problems to be solved are ones that are tied up with the selves with which they are identified (specifically, note the possessive pronoun 'their' and the work it does in this account). Most psychologists, though, would see this as a quite standard and factual account of the issues.

Consider, in contrast, an alternative account, coming from the perspective of a narrative therapist. Narrative Therapy has its origins in the collaborative work of David Epston, who practises in Auckland, New Zealand, and Michael White, who practised in Adelaide, Australia (e.g., White and Epston, 1990). Its aim is to help people resolve problems by discovering new ways of storying their situation. Thus their approach is not based on an essentialist view of either human nature or its possible defects that can be diagnosed and then treated. Rather, it regards problems that clients present as stories they have about themselves and their situations that are drawn from the mainstream of a culture's discursive resources. These stories construct the person's understanding of who they are and frame their interpretations of what is troubling them. The role of the therapist is to help the client find an alternative and preferable story, one that enables them to repudiate and escape their problem-saturated situation.

This collaborative practice of therapy begins with settling on a mutually acceptable name for the problem. The problem then becomes the focus of the therapy, because it is the problem that is the problem; it is not the person who is the problem. The problem is often 'personified', and can be talked about as having its own intentions and a set of tactics whereby it achieves these. We might find, for example, that a person who has been having great difficulty overcoming an addiction uses a set of available cultural discourses to account for their difficulty in quitting: it is a failure of will, and, anyway, they are weak-willed. In this way, the problem and the person are somewhat compounded. But if the problem is separated from the person, it becomes possible to get a handle on how it works its influence. And the person who knows best how that happens is not the therapist, but the person (or family) who has direct experience of how the problem affects them. This focuses the investigation on how the problem has disrupted, dominated or discouraged the person and/or his or her family.

But there are always occasions on which, and ways in which, the client has not been dominated or discouraged by the problem, and when it has not disrupted their lives. The evidence can then be gathered that bolsters a view of the client as having been competent to have stood up to, contested or escaped from the dominance or oppression of the problem. This enables the therapist to evoke speculations from the person or family about what kind of future can be expected for the strong and competent version of the person that has emerged from the interview so far, and for them together to find or create an audience that can acknowledge and legitimate the new identity and story that is being co-constructed.

In exploring the knowledge the person has of their problem a rich window is opened on what we might otherwise call 'their thoughts'. Alice Morgan (2000: 26–7) provides this example, constructed from an ongoing discussion over a number of sessions with Madeline – an underachiever who is 8 years old – about 'Dumb Bug'.

ALICE:	So what does Dumb Bug tell you about yourself?
MADELINE:	It says I can't do anything and tries to stop me trying.
ALICE:	How does it stop you from trying?
MADELINE:	It says, 'You won't be able to do that. It's too hard. There's no point even starting, 'cos you won't be able to do it.'
ALICE:	How does it say that? Does it have a special sort of voice or way of speaking?
MADELINE:	Oh … it's sort of a loud voice.
ALICE:	A loud voice?
MADELINE:	It booms at me and yells at me and says it meanly.
ALICE:	Does it always speak meanly to you?
MADELINE:	Always. It never says anything nice, just things like 'You are dumb', 'You are stupid.'
ALICE:	When does it say these things? Is it all the time or only some of the time?
MADELINE:	Just some of the time but usually when I get my work from the teacher and also it says things to me at sport.
ALICE:	What does it say at sport?
MADELINE:	'Your dumb, you can't play in that team because the other kids won't want you.'
ALICE:	So it criticizes you? Is that right?
MADELINE:	Yes, it always criticizes me, in everything; even when I am at home it criticizes how I dry the dishes.
ALICE:	How does Dumb Bug work? Do you know it's coming? Does it give you any warnings?
MADELINE:	Sometimes I know it's there because it makes my stomach churn.
ALICE:	So it targets your stomach first? Is that right?
MADELINE:	No. Before that it is in my head saying things and then it goes to my stomach.
ALICE:	Then what happens?
MADELINE:	Well then it has got me because when my stomach churns, I can't do anything and I can't think.
ALICE:	So its tactic is to first grab your thoughts and then it works on your stomach.
MADELINE:	Yes.
ALICE:	How long would it take to do this? Does it work quickly or slowly?
MADELINE:	Once it puts its mind to it, the Dumb Bug moves fast.

Now that they have a fix on Dumb Bug, they are able to go forward to figure out ways of countering or thwarting it. Without having that fix, and a separation between the problem and Madeline, a way forward is more difficult. Without Dumb Bug they cannot disentangle Madeline from her problem. In fact, they would be limited to considering her as being responsible for the problem, because she shows an oversensitivity in her thinking. To assist Madeline in overcoming the situation when it is essayed in those terms is much more difficult because of the double-bind that conceptualization would create. Trying to turn things around might only serve to confirm her low level of self-esteem. But even when so conceived in an externalizing conversation with a skilled therapist, some problems are very clever. And duplicitous.

Within our culture's dominant discourses, 'psy' clinicians are able to assert that 'The child is an underachiever.' The child also has a grasp of this way of constructing their world: 'I am an underachiever', 'I am stupid', fall off the tongue easily. It makes far less sense, and may even seem nonsensical, to say, 'Underachievement has captured this person.' But if one shifts to this non-dominant construction, a way of contesting underachievement becomes possible. The 'patient' is no longer 'the problem': the problem is the problem. This shift of perspective constitutes one of the key points in the practice of narrative therapy.

The tactic of externalizing conversations, earlier known in the writings of narrative therapists as the 'externalization of the problem', drives a wedge between the person and the problem. If I am an underachiever, then there is little I can do about it. But if I am separate from this problem, then maybe I can do something. Similarly, if I am depressed, I am instituting myself as depression, and I have little recourse but to unreflexively live out and through that way of linguistically formulating depression as my way of being-in-or-against-the-world. I need to be treated. But if either depression or underachievement is linguistically separated from the self, then perhaps an alternative identity can be constructed that can counter the narrative of depression or underachievement that the dominant construction allows, and which entraps people.

We can take the above illustration a little further by noting that the question 'Which of these ways of categorizing the underachiever's situation is the correct one?' is not something that is resolvable by an empirical study. To assume it could be is exposed as incorrect if we ask an analogous question: 'Does water boil at 100 degrees Celsius or 212 degrees Fahrenheit?' Further, it is not possible to establish empirical grounds for adopting a particular methodology as canonical and appropriate in psychology. The adoption rests on pre-empirical decisions, and these decisions set up an ontological grammar from which certain consequences follow. And here, as Coulter (1997: 299) trenchantly notes, 'Grammar – the rules of concept-formation and conceptual deployment – provides for us the (logical) possibilities of phenomena, not the other way around.'

Constructionist helping is often a practice wherein past language-use is reflected upon, contested and negotiated in ways that clients feel they can take forward into their relationships. Helping dialogues offer ways to reflect on one's linguistic understandings outside the hurly-burly of the world in which they are employed, but as words like transference and countertransference point out, client and helper do not stop being relationally responsive to each other in doing this. They bring interpretive backgrounds of their own that, depending on the purposes for their dialogues, might factor into their ways of responding to each other. Ideally, the helper brings a kind of discursive flexibility (Strong, 2002) that welcomes clients' ways of articulating concerns and aspirations, such that the language of these concerns and aspirations can be eventually reflected upon. We say 'eventually' because a kind of negotiation into reflection is entailed, one that starts from each speaker's interpretive ways of being that likely have not yet been coordinated into shared ways of talking and understanding. Discursive flexibility is what can assist helpers from getting stuck on particular ways of understanding and responding to clients, en route to this kind of language coordination.

Along with coordinating language comes the challenge of coordinating intentions as expressed in language: language being both words and the ways of communicating that accompany them. For Wittgenstein's student and later editor Elizabeth Anscombe (2000), intentions are 'actions under descriptions'. Seen this way, part of sharing intentions comes with sharing mutual descriptions, particularly when it comes to intended meanings and actions. Thus, a shared (client and helper) search for perspicuous descriptions can be a way of coordinating intentions in the language that guides speakers in 'going on', to return to Wittgenstein. Family therapy chronicler Lynn Hoffman (2002) described narrative therapist Michael White as always trying to work within inches of a client's intended descriptions. This way of portraying helping dialogue suggests a descriptive ethic for helping (see Brinkman and Kvale, 2005): using a shared language of description that is acceptably familiar to clients.

Of course, helping is not just about describing things as they seem to be; it is also about describing things as one would like them to be. The same descriptive ethic applies to collaboratively articulating intentions for action – whether those intentions are about helpers inviting client reflection on the aptness of their language in light of their circumstances and preferences, or about finding ways of going forward. An implicit negotiation can be involved in arriving at acceptably familiar language that clients have co-edited into useful action. But questions can arise here for some practitioners about the extent to which such negotiations can ever become truly mutual between helper and client. How does one engage client editorship in the interview, to see their articulated intentions and preferences brought to bear on the conversational process, and to not drive them underground in the belief that the helper has the final say? For critical discourse analysts, like Fairclough (Chapter 13), we are now in places where the professional's discourse very likely dominates, but here is also where the professional can turn clients into Garfinkel's cultural dopes.

What can aid this kind of meaning negotiation when cultural expectations militate against it? Client resistance, or non-compliance with helper directives, is one way that clients show they want their say on how things develop in the 'helping' dialogue. But it is quite another thing for helpers actively to invite clients to contest their meanings, or accept uninvited interruptions, supplementation and even questions from clients. Clients, in the sense that they are the enactors of consultation meanings beyond the helping dialogue, are de facto editors-in-chief for what is taken forward from the dialogue. Finding ways to involve clients into the editing of where helping dialogue is going can become a kind of collaborative 'wordsmithing' activity (Strong, 2006b) as the direction of the dialogue is worked out around the words meant to carry it forward for both speakers. Questions can become interventions of sorts into the process of arriving at such useful language (Tomm, 1988). With respect to ideas and words that helpers might have, the issue is not with their presumed usefulness, but with what is done with them in the editing and talking process that carries both parties forward. Used with finality, a particular interpretation or directive can be easily dismissed. Seen and responded to as grist for the dialogic mill, such interpretations or directives can help helper and client to customize a language and solutions befitting the client's preferences, circumstances and capabilities.

There might appear something wholly unsatisfying about these constructionist approaches to helping when they are held up against clearly defined interventions tied to a particular conception of a client's concern – in a kind of use of solution X for problem Y kind of algorithm. There is a lot of untidy, unscripted, conversational work implied in collaboratively customizing a language of description and action together with clients. There has been plenty of discussion within social constructionist helping approaches (e.g., narrative, solution-focused and collaborative language therapies) about the extent to which the helping itself needs to be structured by the helper. Thus, one finds the use of particular practices (the miracle or externalizing questions) or aims (solution language, better stories) alongside conversational processes that involve this kind of unpredictable conversational work, as clients fashion particular questions into meanings and actions they find useful. How tightly scripted or methodological these approaches might be is thus one dimension of constructionist helping, one that relies in part on the discursive flexibility of the helper. But, each constructionist approach advocates a kind of client-directedness on what should be helpful, typically with particular questions or conversational structures open to clients shaping meanings and actions into what they will take forward. All of this requires a relationship in which such client editorship is possible.

The take-home message from the ideas we have surveyed is that there is a counter-tradition to the one that has sedimented itself into mainstream psychology. It is a loose tradition with many varying emphases and perspectives. But it appears to us that it provides a more adequate framework than the dominant tradition for conceptualizing and then exploring the meaning-saturated reality of being human. Our meaningful reality is much 'messier' than the Cartesian heritage has had us believe, and much more mysterious. Rommetveit puts it thus:

> What happens when a monistic outlook is replaced by a consistently pluralistic paradigm is … a radical reformulation of assumptions and focal issues of research on human intersubjectivity and verbal communication. The problem of *what is being meant by what is being said* cannot any

> longer be pursued in terms of stipulated unequivocal 'literal' meanings of expressions.   (1985: 186–7)

That is, meanings are not somehow stored in a mental dictionary that links them to the symbols that code them, so as to be transmitted to another individual who decodes them to get the meaning (as though a communicative channel were a pipe into which units of meaning are rolled from one individual to another). Rather, meanings are very dependent on contexts, and meaning is established by an active negotiation towards agreement in the course of communication. Sometimes, this can occur in highly routinized ways so as to *appear* to be an automatic process of sending units of meanings down the pipe from sender to receiver, but in fact most conversation occurs outside such routines, and requires an active joint effort to establish agreement. Making that effort has to be seen as the key to effective practice. What the social constructionist, or discursive, turn brings is a new-found attention to the ingenuity needed to transcend the shortcomings of prior human constructions in addressing human and natural problems.

Bibliography

Abram, D. (1996) *The Spell of the Sensuous: Perception and Language in a More-than-Human world*. New York: Pantheon Books.

Ackerman, D. (1999) *Deep Play*. New York: Random House.

Andersen, T. (1991) *The Reflecting Team: Dialogue and Dialogue about the Dialogues*. New York: Norton.

(1996) Language is not innocent. In F. Kaslow (ed.), *The Handbook of Relational Diagnosis* (pp. 119–25). New York: John Wiley & Sons.

Anderson, H. (1997) *Conversation, Language and Possibilities*. New York: Basic Books.

Anderson, S. R. and Lightfoot, D. W. (2002) *The Language Organ: Linguistics as Cognitive Science*. Cambridge University Press.

Anscombe, G. E. M. (2000) *Intention*. Cambridge, MA: Harvard University Press.

Arbib, M. A. (ed.) (2006) *Action to Language via the Mirror Neuron System*. Cambridge University Press.

Aries, P. (1962) *Centuries of Childhood*. New York: Random House.

(1973) *Centuries of Childhood* (trans. R. Baldick). Harmondsworth: Penguin.

Arminen, I. (2000) On the context sensitivity of institutional interaction, *Discourse and Society*, 11: 435–58.

Armistead, N. (ed.) (1974) *Reconstructing Social Psychology*. Harmondsworth: Penguin.

Armitage, L. K. (2001) Truth, falsity, and schemas of presentation: A textual analysis of Harold Garfinkel's story of Agnes, *Electronic Journal of Human Sexuality*, 4 (29 April).

Austin, J. L. (1962) *How to Do Things with Words*. Cambridge, MA: Harvard University Press.

Babha, H. K. (1994) *The Location of Culture*. New York: Routledge.

Baker, G. P. and Hacker, M. S. (1980a) *Wittgenstein: Rules, Grammar and Necessity*. Oxford: Basil Blackwell.

(1980b) *Wittgenstein: Understanding and Meaning. An Analytic Commentary on the Philosophical Investigations*, vol. 1. University of Chicago Press.

(1984) *Language, Sense and Nonsense*. Oxford: Basil Blackwell.

Bakhtin, M. M. (1981) *The Dialogic Imagination: Four Essays* (ed. M. Holquist, trans. C. Emerson and M. Holquist). Austin, TX: University of Texas Press. (Original written during the 1930s.)

(1984) *Problems of Dostoevsky's Poetics* (ed. and trans. C. Emerson). Minneapolis, MN: University of Michigan Press.

(1986) *Speech Genres and Other Late Essays* (trans. V. W. McGee). Austin, TX: University of Texas Press.

(1990) *Art and Answerability: Early Philosophical Essays by M. M. Bakhtin* (ed. M. Holquist and V. Liapunov; trans. V. Liapunov). Austin, TX: University of Texas Press.

(1993a) *Rabelais and his World* (trans. H. Iswolsky). Bloomington, IN: Indiana University Press. (Originally written in 1941 as Bakhtin's doctoral thesis.)

(1993b) *Toward a Philosophy of the Act* (ed. M. Holquist; trans. V. Lianpov). Austin, TX: University of Texas Press.

Bakhtin, M. M. and Medvedev, P. N. (1978) *The Formal Method in Literary Scholarship: A Critical Introduction to Sociological Poetics* (trans. A. J. Wehrle). Baltimore, MD: Johns Hopkins University Press.

Barnhart, A. (n. d.) Erving Goffman: The presentation of self in everyday life. Available online: http://employees.cfmc.com/adamb/writings/goffman.htm (retrieved 18 September 2009).

Bateson, G. (1936) *Naven: A Survey of the Problems Suggested by a Composite Picture of the Culture of a New Guinea Tribe from Three Points of View*. Cambridge University Press.

(1972) *Steps to an Ecology of Mind*. New York: Ballantyne.

(1980) *Mind and Nature: A Necessary Unity*. New York: Bantam.

(1982) Paradigmatic conservatism. In C. Wilder and J. Weakland (eds.), *Rigor and Imagination: Essays from the Legacy of Gregory Bateson* (pp. 347–55). New York: Praeger.

Bateson, G. and Bateson, M. C. (1988) *Angels Fear: Towards an Epistemology of the Sacred*. New York: Bantam.

Bateson, G. and Jackson, D. (1964) Some varieties of pathogenic organization, *Disorders of Communication*, 42: 270–83.

Bateson, G., Jackson, D., Haley, J. and Weakland, J. (1956) Toward a theory of schizophrenia, *Behavioral Science*, 1: 251–64.

Bateson, G. and Reusch, J. (1951) *Communication: The Social Matrix of Psychiatry*. New York: Norton.

Bateson, M. (1975) Mother–infant exchanges: The epigenesis of conversational interaction. In D. Aronson and R. V. Rieber (eds.), *Developmental Psycholinguistics and Communication Disorders* (pp. 101–13). New York: New York Academy of Sciences.

Battaglia, D. (1995) Problematizing the self: A 't'hematic introduction. In D. Battaglia (ed.), *Rhetorics of Self-making* (pp. 1–15). Berkeley: University of California Press.

Bauman, Z. (1978) *Hermeneutics and Social Science*. New York: Cambridge University Press.

Berger, P. and Luckmann, T. (1967) *The Social Construction of Reality: A Treatise on the Sociology of Knowledge*. London: Penguin.

Berlin, I. (1976) *Vico and Herder: Two Studies in the History of Ideas*. London: Hogarth Press.

(2002) *Liberty* (ed. H. Hardy). Oxford University Press.

Bernstein, R. J. (1992) *The New Constellation*. Cambridge, MA: MIT Press.

(1983) *Beyond Objectivism and Relativism: Science, Hermeneutics and Practice*. Philadelphia, PA: University of Pennsylvania Press.

Bhaskar, R. A. (1989) *Reclaiming Reality: A Critical Introduction to Contemporary Philosophy*. London: Verso.

Biemel, W. (2000) The decisive phases in the development of Husserl's Phenomenology. In R. O. Elveton (ed. and trans.), *The Phenomenology of Husserl: Selected Critical Readings* (2nd edn) (pp. 140–63). Edmunds, WA: Noesis Press.

Billig, M. (1996). *Arguing and Thinking: A Rhetorical Approach to Social Psychology* (2nd edn). New York: Cambridge University Press.

  (1999) Freud and Dora: Repressing an oppressed identity. Online paper available at: www.massey.ac.nz/~alock/virtual/dora4.htm.

Billig, M. and Schegloff, E. (1999) Critical discourse analysis and conversation analysis: An exchange between Michael Billig and Emmanuel A. Schegloff, *Discourse and Society*, 10: 543–82.

Bloch, M. (1961a) *Feudal Society. Vol. 1: The Growth of Ties of Dependence* (trans. L. A. Manyon). London: Routledge & Kegan Paul.

  (1961b) *Feudal society. Vol. 2: Social Classes and Political Organisation* (trans. L. A. Manyon). University of Chicago Press.

Bogen, D. (1999) *Order without Rules: Critical Theory and the Logic of Conversation.* Albany, NY: SUNY Press.

Bouma-Prediger, S. (1989) Rorty's pragmatism and Gadamer's hermeneutics, *Journal of the American Academy of Religion*, 57 (2): 313–24.

Bråten, S. (2003) Participant perception of others' acts: Virtual otherness in infants and adults, *Culture and Psychology*, 9: 261–76.

Brenner, P. (1981) *Social Method and Social Life.* New York: Academic Press.

Brentano, F. (1973/1874) *Psychology from an Empirical Standpoint* (trans. A. C. Rancurello, D. B. Terrell and L. McAlister). London: Routledge. (Originally published 1874 as *Psychologie vom empirischen Standpunkt*, Leipzig: Duncke & Humblot.)

Brinkmann, S. and Kvale, S. (2005) Confronting the *ethics* of qualitative research, *Journal of Constructivist Psychology*, 18: 157–81.

Broadbent, D. E. (1970) In defence of empirical psychology, *Bulletin of the British Psychological Society* 23: 87–96.

  (1973) *In Defence of Empirical Psychology.* London: Methuen.

Bruner, J. S. (1983) *Child's Talk: Learning to Use Language.* Oxford University Press.

Bryant, C. G. A. and Jary, D. (eds.) (1991) *Giddens' Theory of Structuration: A Critical Approach.* London: Routledge.

Buber, M. (1923/1958) *I and Thou* (trans. W. Kaufmann). Glencoe: Free Press.

Burke, P. (1985) *Vico.* Oxford University Press.

Burman, E. (1994) *Deconstructing Developmental Psychology.* London: Routledge.

Burr, V. (2003) *Social Constructionism.* London: Taylor & Francis.

Butler, J. (1997) *Excitable Speech: A Politics of the Performative.* New York: Routledge.

Carnap, Rudolf (1949) Truth and confirmation. In H. Feigl and W. Sellars (eds.), *Readings in Philosophical Analysis* (pp. 119–29). New York: Appleton-Century-Crofts.

Cassirer, E. (1953) *The Philosophy of Symbolic Forms. Vol. 1: Language.* New Haven, CT: Yale University Press.

Chebonov, S. V. (2001) Umwelt as life world of living being, *Semiotica,* 134: 169–84.

Chenail, R. (1995) Recursive frame analysis. *The Qualitative Report*, 2 (2). Online paper: www.nova.edu/ssss/QR/QR2–2/rfa.html.

Chomsky, N. (1959) Review of *Verbal Behavior* by B. F. Skinner, *Language*, 35: 26–58.

  (1965) *Aspects of the Theory of Syntax.* Cambridge, MA: MIT Press.

Chouliaraki, L. and Fairclough, N. (1999) *Discourse in Late Modernity: Rethinking Critical Discourse Analysis*. Edinburgh University Press.

Clark, H. H. (1996) *Using Language*. New York: Cambridge University Press.

Clark, K. and Holquist, M. (1984) *Mikhail Bakhtin*. Cambridge, MA: Harvard University Press.

Cole, M. (1985) The zone of proximal development: Where culture and cognition create each other. In J. V. Wertsch (ed.), *Culture, Communication, and Cognition: Vygotskyean Perspectives*. New York: Cambridge University Press.

(1990) Cultural psychology: A once and future discipline? In J. Berman (ed.), *Nebraska Symposium on Motivation: Cross-cultural Perspectives*, 37: 279–335.

Cooperrider, D. L., Whitney, D. and Stavros, J. M. (2008) *Appreciative Inquiry Handbook for Leaders of Change* (2nd edn). Brunswick, OH: Crown.

Coulter, J. (1997) Neural Cartesianism: Comments on the epistemology of the 'cognitive sciences'. In D. Johnson and C. E. Erneling (eds.), *The Future of the Cognitive Revolution* (pp. 293–301). Oxford University Press.

Courtin, Antoine de (1680) *Nouveau traité de la civilité qui se pratique en France parmi les honnestes gans*. Paris: Helie Josset.

Cowie, L. W. (1973) *A Dictionary of British Social History*. London: Bell.

Critchley, S. (1999) *Ethics, politics, subjectivity*. London: Verso.

Cushman, P. (1995) *Constructing the Self, Constructing America*. New York: Plenum.

Cussert, F. (2008) *French Theory: How Foucault, Derrida, Deleuze, & Co. Transformed the Intellectual Life of the United States* (trans. J. Fort). Minneapolis, MN: University of Minnesota Press.

Damasio, A. (1996) *Descartes' Error*. London: Macmillan.

Danziger, K. (1997a). *Naming the Mind: How Psychology Found its Language*. London: Sage.

(1997b) The varieties of social construction, *Theory and Psychology*, 7: 399–416.

Daston, L. and Galison, P. (2007). *Objectivity*. New York: Zed Press.

Davies, B. (1989) *Frogs and Snails and Feminist tales: Preschool Children and Gender*. Sydney: Allen & Unwin.

Davies, B. and Harré, R. (1990) Positioning: The discursive production of selves, *Journal for the Theory of Social Behavior*, 20 (1): 43–63.

Dawkins, R. (1995) *River out of Eden: A Darwinian View of Life*. London: Harper-Collins.

de Saussure, F. (1983) *Course in General Linguistics* (ed. C. Bally and A. Sechehaye; trans. R. Harris). La Salle, IL: Open Court. (Originally published in 1916.)

Deely, J. (1992) Philosophy and experience, *American Catholic Philosophical Quarterly*, 66: 299–319.

(2001) Umwelt, *Semiotica*, 134: 125–35.

Deleuze, G. (1988) *Spinoza: Practical Philosophy* (trans. Robert Hurley). San Francisco, CA: City Light Books.

Dell, P. (1985) Understanding Bateson and Maturana: Toward a biological foundation for the social sciences, *Journal of Marital and Family Therapy*, 11: 1–20.

Dennett, D. (2000). *Philosopher: Ludwig Wittgenstein, Time*, 100: Scientists and thinkers. Available online: www.time.com/time/time100/scientist/profile/wittgenstein03.html.

Denzin, N. K. and Lincoln, Y. S. (2005) *The SAGE Handbook of Qualitative Research*. London: Sage.

Derrida, J. (1976) *Of Grammatology* (trans. G. C. Spivak). Baltimore, MD: Johns Hopkins University Press.

— (1991) At this very moment in this work here I am (trans. R. Berezdivin). In R. Bernasconi and S. Critchley (eds.), *Re-reading Levinas* (pp. 11–48). Bloomington, IN: Indiana University Press.

Descartes, R. (1968) *Discourse on Method and Other Writings* (trans. and introd. F. E. Sutcliffe). Harmondsworth: Penguin.

— (1979) *La recherche de la vérité* (trans. I. Berlin). In *Against the Current: Essays in the History of Ideas*. London: Hogarth Press. (Originally published in *Oeuvres*, vol. 10 (ed. C. Adam and P. Tannery). Paris: Cerf, 1908.)

Dewey, J. (1922) *Human Nature and Conduct*. New York: Random House.

Diprose, R. (2002). *Corporeal Generosity: On Giving with Nietzsche, Merleau-Ponty, and Levinas*. Albany, NY: SUNY.

Dostal, R. L. (ed.) (2002) *The Cambridge Companion to Gadamer*. Cambridge University Press.

Drew, P. and Wootton, A. (eds.) (1988) *Erving Goffman: Exploring the Interaction Order*. Boston: Northeastern University Press.

Dreyfus, H. L. (1967) Why computers must have bodies in order to be intelligent, *Review of Metaphysics*, 21: 13–32.

Dreyfus, H. (1991) *Being-in-the-world: A Commentary on Heidegger's Being and Time, Division I*. Cambridge, MA: MIT Press.

Dreyfus, H. L. and Rabinow, P. (1982) *Michel Foucault: Beyond Structuralism and Hermeneutics*. Sussex: Harvester Press.

Edmonds, D. and Eidinow, J. (2001) *Wittgenstein's Poker: The Story of a Ten-minute Argument Between Two Great Philosophers*. New York: Harper Collins College.

Edwards, D. (1978) Social relations and early language. In A. J. Lock (ed.), *Action, Gesture and Symbol: The Emergence of Language* (pp. 449–70). London: Academic Press.

Edwards, D. (1997) *Discourse and Cognition*. Thousand Oaks, CA: Sage.

Edwards, D. and Potter, J. (1992) *Discursive Psychology*. Newbury Park, CA: Sage.

Edwards, D., Ashmore, M. and Potter, J. (1995) Death and furniture: The rhetoric, politics and theology of bottom line arguments against relativism, *History of the Human Sciences*, 8 (2): 25–49.

Edwards, J. C. (1983) *Ethics without Philosophy: Wittgenstein and the Moral Life*. Gainesville, FL: University Press of South Florida.

Elias, N. (1978) *The Civilizing Process. Vol. 1: The History of Manners*. Oxford: Blackwell.

— (1982) *The Civilizing Process. Vol. 2: Power and Civility*. Oxford: Blackwell.

Enns, C. Z. (1993) Twenty years of feminist counseling and psychotherapy: From naming biases to implementing multifaceted practice, *Counseling Psychologist*, 21: 3–87.

Fairclough, N. (1995). *Critical Discourse Analysis: The Critical Study of Language*. London: Longman.

Farber, M. (1967) The ideal of presuppositionless philosophy. In J. J. Kockelmans (ed.), *Phenomenology: The Philosophy of Edmund Husserl and its Interpretation* (pp. 37–58). Garden City, NY: Doubleday.

Farrington, B. (1947) *Head and Hand in Ancient Greece*. London: Watts.

Festinger, L. (1957) *A Theory of Cognitive Dissonance*. Stanford University Press.

Fogel, A. (2004) Remembering infancy: Accessing our earliest experiences. In G. Bremner and A. Slater (eds.), *Theories of Infant Development* (pp. 204–32). Oxford: Blackwell.

Foucault, M. (1965) *Madness and Civilization: A History of Insanity in the Age of Reason* (trans. R. Howard). New York: Random House.

(1970) *The Order of Things: An Archaeology of the Human Sciences.* London: Tavistock.

(1972) *The Archaeology of Knowledge & the Discourse on Language* (trans. A. M. Sheridan Smith). New York: Pantheon Books.

(1977) *Discipline and Punish: The Birth of the Prison* (trans. A. M. Sheridan). Middlesex: Peregrine Books.

(1978) *The History of Sexuality: An Introduction* (vol. 1) (trans. R. Hurley). New York: Pantheon.

(1985) *The History of Sexuality: The Uses of Pleasure* (vol. 2) (trans. R. Hurley). New York: Vintage.

(1986) *The History of Sexuality: The Care of the Self* (vol. 3) (trans. R. Hurley). New York: Vintage.

(1997). *Ethics, Subjectivity and Truth: Essential Works of Foucault* (vol. 1) (ed. P. Rabinow; trans. R. Hurley and others). New York: New Press.

(2005) *The Hermeneutics of the Subject: Lectures at the Collège de France 1981–1982* (ed. F. Gros; trans. G. Burchell). New York: Picador.

(2006) *Psychiatric Power: Lectures at the Collège de France 1973–1974* (ed. J. LaGrange; trans. G. Burchell). New York: Palgrave Macmillan.

Freidson, E. (1983) Celebrating Erving Goffman, *Contemporary Sociology*, 12: 359–62.

Friedman, S. (ed.) (1993) *The New Language of Change.* New York: Guilford.

Frye, N. (1964) *The Educated Imagination.* Bloomington, IN: Indiana University Press.

Gadamer, H.-G. (1976) *Philosophical Hermeneutics* (ed. and trans. D. E. Linge). Berkeley, CA: University of California Press.

(1988) *Truth and Method* (2nd rev. edn) (trans. J. Weinsheimer and D. G. Marshall). New York: Continuum.

Gale, J. and Newfield, N. (1992) A conversation analysis of a solution-focused marital therapy session, *Family Process*, 18: 153–65.

Gardiner, M. (1992) *The Dialogics of Critique: M. M. Bakhtin and the Theory of Ideology.* New York: Routledge.

Garfinkel, H. (1967) *Studies in Ethnomethodology.* Cambridge: Polity Press.

Garfinkel, H. and Rawls, A. (eds.) (2002) *Ethnomethodology's Program.* Lanham, MD: Rowman & Littlefield.

Garfinkel, H. and Sacks, H. (1970) On formal structures of practical action. In J. C. McKinney and E. Tiryakian (eds.), *Theoretical Sociology: Perspectives and Developments* (pp. 337–66). New York: Appleton-Century-Crofts.

Garfinkel, H., Lynch, M. and Livingston, E. (1981) The work of a discovering science construed with materials from the optically discovered pulsar, *Philosophy of Social Sciences*, 11: 131–58.

Gauld, A. and Shotter, J. (1977) *Human Action and its Psychological Investigation.* London: Routledge & Kegan Paul.

Gergen, K. J. (1971) *The Concept of Self*. New York: Holt, Rinehart & Winston.

(1973) Social psychology as history, *Journal of Personality and Social Psychology*, 26: 309–20.

(1985) The social constructionist movement in modern psychology, *American Psychologist*, 40: 266–75.

(1990) Therapeutic professions and the diffusion of deficit, *Journal of Mind and Behavior*, 11: 353–68.

(1991) *The Saturated Self: Dilemmas of Identity in Contemporary Life*. New York: Basic Books.

(1994a) *Realities and Relationships: Soundings in Social Construction*. Cambridge, MA: Harvard University Press.

(1994b) *Toward Transformation in Social Knowledge* (2nd edn). Thousand Oaks, CA: Sage. (1st edn 1982.)

(1995) Relational theory and the discourses of power. In D. Hosking, H. P. Dachler and K. J. Gergen (eds.), *Management and Organization: Relational Alternatives to Individualism* (pp. 29–49). Aldershot: Avebury.

(1997) The place of the psyche in a constructed world, *Theory and Psychology*, 7: 723–46.

(1999) *Invitation to Social Construction*. London: Sage.

(2001a) Constructionism in contention: Toward consequential resolutions, *Theory and Psychology*, 11: 419–31.

(2001b) Psychological science in a postmodern context, *American Psychologist*, 56: 803–13.

(2006) *Therapeutic Realities: Collaboration, Oppression and Relational Flow*. Chagrin Falls, OH: Taos Institute.

Gergen, K. J. and Gergen, M. M. (1983) Narrative of the self. In T. Sarbin and K. Schiebe (eds.), *Studies in Social Identity* (pp. 254–73). New York: Praeger.

(2004) *Social Constructionism: Entering the Dialogue*. Chagrin Falls, OH: Taos Institute Publications.

Gergen, M. M. (ed.) (1988) *Feminist Thought and the Structure of Knowledge*. New York University Press.

(1992) Life stories: Pieces of a dream. In G. Rosenwald and R. Ochberg (eds.), *Storied Lives* (pp. 127–44). New Haven, CT: Yale University Press.

(1999) Feminist psychology. Entry for the *Encyclopedia of Psychology* (ed. Alan E. Kazdin). Washington, DC: American Psychological Association.

Gergen, M. M (2001) *Feminist Reconstructions in Psychology: Narrative, Gender and Performance*. Thousand Oaks, CA: Sage.

(2007) Qualitative methods in feminist psychology. In W. Stainton-Rogers and C. Wittig (eds.), *Handbook of Qualitative Research in Psychology* (pp. 280–95). Thousand Oaks, CA: Sage.

Gergen, M. M. and Davis, S. N. (1997) *Toward a New Psychology of Gender*. New York: Routledge.

Gergen, M. M. and Gergen, K. J. (2001) Ethnographic representation as relationship. In C. Ellis and A. Bochner (eds.), *Ethnographically Speaking* (pp. 11–33). Lanham, MD: AltaMira Press.

(2003) Marriage as relational engagement, *Feminism and Psychology*, 13: 469–74.

(2006) Narratives in action, *Narrative Inquiry*, 16: 112–28.

Gergen, M. M., Gergen, K. J. and Barrett, F. (2004) Appreciative inquiry as dialogue: Generative and transformative. In D. Cooperrider and M. Avital (eds.), *Advances in Appreciative Inquiry* (vol. 1, pp. 3–27). Bristol: Elsevier Science Ltd.

Gergen, M. M. and Iversen, G. (1997) *Statistics: A Conceptual Approach*. New York: Springer-Verlag.

Gibson, J. J. (1979) *The Ecological Approach to Visual Perception*. Boston: Houghton Mifflin.

Giddens, A. (1976) *New Rules of Sociological Method: A Positive Critique of Interpretative Sociologies*. London: Hutchinson.

(1979) *Central Problems in Social Theory: Action, Structure and Contradiction in Social Analysis*. London: Macmillan.

(1984) *The Constitution of Society: Outline of the Theory of Structuration*. Cambridge: Polity Press.

(1991) *Modernity and Self-identity: Self and Society in the Late Modern Age*. Stanford University Press.

(1994) *Beyond Left and Right: The Future of Radical Politics*. Stanford University Press.

(1999) *The Third Way: The Renewal of Social Democracy*. Cambridge: Polity Press.

Goffman, E. (1952) On cooling the mark out, *Psychiatry: Journal of Interpersonal Relations*, 15 (4): 451–63.

(1959) *The Presentation of Self in Everyday Life*. New York: Doubleday Anchor.

(1961a) *Asylums: Essays on the Social Situation of Mental Patients and Other Inmates*. New York: Doubleday Anchor.

(1961b) *Encounters: Two Studies in the Sociology of Interaction*. Indianapolis, IN: Bobbs-Merrill.

(1964). *Stigma: Notes on the Management of Spoiled Identity*. Englewood Cliffs, NJ: Prentice-Hall.

(1967). *Interaction Ritual: Essays on Face-to-Face Behavior*. New York: Doubleday Anchor.

(1974). *Frame Analysis: An Essay on the Organization of Experience*. New York: Harper & Row.

(1979) Footing, *Semiotica*, 25: 1–29.

(1981). *Forms of Talk*. Oxford: Basil Blackwell.

(1983) Felicity's condition, *American Journal of Sociology*, 89: 1–53.

Goldschmidt, J., Gergen, M. M., Quigley, K. and Gergen, K. J. (1974) The women's liberation movement: Attitudes and action, *Journal of Personality*, 42: 601–17.

Goldstein, J. (1999) Emergence as a construct: History and issues, *Emergence: Complexity and Organization*, 1: 49–72.

Gramsci, A. (1971) *Selections from the Prison Notebooks*. London: Lawrence & Wishart.

Grobman, J. (2006) Underachievement in exceptionally gifted adolescents and young adults: A psychiatrist's view, *Journal of Secondary Gifted Education*, 17: 199–210.

Grondin, J. (2003) *Hans-Georg Gadamer: A Biography* (trans. J. Weinsheimer). London: Yale University Press.

Gubrium, J. and Holstein, J. (1999) *The Self we Live by: Narrative Identity in a Postmodern World*. New York: Oxford University Press.

Gubrium, J. and Holstein, J. (eds.) (2007) *The Handbook of Constructionist Research.* New York: Guilford.

Guignon, C. (ed.) (1993) *The Cambridge Companion to Heidegger.* New York: Cambridge University Press.

Guignon, C. (2004) *On Being Authentic.* New York: Routledge.

Habermas, J. (1975) *Legitimation Crisis* (trans. T. McCarthy). Boston: Beacon Press.

(1985) *Theory of Communicative Action* (vols. 1 and 2, trans. T. McCarthy). Boston: Beacon Press.

(2005). *Truth and Justification* (trans. B. Fultner). Cambridge, MA: MIT Press.

Hacker, P. M. S. (2000) *Wittgenstein: Mind and Will (Part I, Essays).* Oxford: Blackwell.

Haley, J. (1973) *Uncommon Therapy: The Psychiatric Techniques of Milton Erickson, M.D.* New York: Norton.

(1976) *Problem-solving Therapy.* San Francisco, CA: Jossey-Bass.

Halliday, M. (1985) *An Introduction to Functional Grammar.* London: Edward Arnold.

Hallowell, A. I. (1960) Self, society and culture in phylogenetic perspective. In S. Tax (ed.), *Evolution after Darwin. Vol. II: The Evolution of Man* (pp. 309–72). University of Chicago Press.

(1971) *Culture and Experience* (2nd edn; 1st edn 1955). Philadelphia, PA: University of Pennsylvania Press.

Hampshire, S. (1959) *Thought and Action.* London: Chatto & Windus.

Harré, R. (1983) *Personal Being: A Theory for Individual Psychology.* Oxford: Blackwell.

Harré, R. (1986a) The Social Construction of Emotions. Oxford: Blackwell.

Harré, R. (1986b) *Varieties of Realism.* Oxford: Blackwell.

(1992) Introduction: The second cognitive revolution, *American Behavioral Scientist*, 36: 5–7.

(1993) Positioning in scientific discourse. In R. Harré (ed.), *Reason and Rhetoric: Anglo-Ukrainian Studies in the Rationality of Scientific Discourse.* Lewiston, NY: Edwin Mellen Press.

(1997) Post-modernism in psychology: Insights and limits. Unpublished manuscript.

(1998) *The Singular Self: An Introduction to the Psychology of Personhood.* London: Sage.

(2001) Unpublished draft ms. Notes for Harré (2002).

(2002) *Cognitive Science: A Philosophical Introduction.* London: Sage.

(2003) The logical basis of psychiatric meta-narratives. Unpublished draft manuscript.

Harré, R. and Gillett, G. (1994) *The Discursive Mind.* London: Sage.

Harré, R. and Krausz, M. (1996) *Varieties of Relativism.* Oxford: Blackwell.

Harré, R. and Moghaddam, F. (2003) *The Self and Others: Positioning Individuals and Groups in Personal, Political, and Cultural Contexts.* Westport, CT: Praeger.

Harré, R. and Secord, P. F. (1972) *The Explanation of Social Behaviour.* Oxford: Blackwell.

Harré, R. and Tissaw, M. (2005) *Wittgenstein and Psychology: A Practical Guide.* Aldershot: Ashgate.

Harré, R. and Van Langenhove, L. (1992) Varieties of positioning, *Journal for the Theory of Social Behaviour*, 20: 393–407.

(1998) *Positioning Theory: Moral Contexts of Intentional Action.* Oxford: Blackwell.

Hebb, D. O. and Thompson, W. N. (1954) The social significance of animal studies. In G. Lindzey (ed.), *Handbook of Social Psychology,* Vol. 1. Cambridge, MA: Addison-Wesley.

Heidegger, M. (1969) *Being and Time* (rev. edn) (trans. J. Macquarrie and E. Robinson). Toronto: Harper Collins Canada. (Originally published 1927.)

(1971a) *On the Way to Language* (trans. P. Hertz). San Francisco, CA: Harper & Row.

(1971b) *Poetry, Language and Thought* (trans. A. Hofstadter). New York: Harper Colophon Books.

(1995) *The Fundamental Concepts of Metaphysics: World, Finitude, Solitude.* Bloomington, IN: Indiana University Press.

Henriques, J., Hollway, W., Urwin, C., Venn, C. and Walkerdine, V. (1984). *Changing the Subject: Psychology, Social Regulation and Subjectivity.* New York: Methuen & Co.

Hepworth, J. (1999) *The Social Construction of Anorexia Nervosa.* London: Sage.

Herbert, F. (1990) *Dune.* New York: Ace.

Heritage, J. (1984) *Garfinkel and Ethnomethodology.* New York: Polity.

Hester, S. and Francis, D. (2000) Ethnomethodology, conversation analysis, and 'institutional talk', *Text,* 20: 391–413.

Hilbert, R. (1992) *The Classical Roots of Ethnomethodology: Durkheim, Weber and Garfinkel.* Chapel Hill, NC: University of North Carolina Press.

Hoffman, L. (1985) Beyond power and control, *Family Systems Medicine,* 3: 381–96.

(2002) *Family Therapy: An Intimate History.* New York: W. W. Norton & Co.

Holiday, A. (1988) *Moral Powers: Normative Necessity in Language and History.* London: Routledge.

Holquist, M. (1990) *Dialogism: Bakhtin and his World.* New York: Routledge.

Holstein, J. and Gubrium, J. F. (eds.) (2008) *Handbook of Constructionist Research.* New York: Guilford.

Holsti, O. R. (1969) *Content Analysis for the Social Sciences and Humanities.* Reading, MA: Longman Higher Education.

Husserl, E. (1900) *The Logical Investigations* (trans. J. N. Findlay). London: Routledge.

(1913) *Ideas: General Introduction to Pure Phenomenology* (trans. W. R. Boyce Gibson). London: George Allen & Unwin Ltd.

(1927/1981) 'Phenomenology', Edmund Husserl's article for the *Encyclopaedia Britannica* (trans. R. Palmer). In P. McCormick and F. A. Elliston (eds.), *Husserl: Shorter Works* (pp. 21–35). University of Notre Dame Press.

(1931) *Cartesian Meditations* (trans. D. Cairns). Dordrecht: Kluwer.

(1970) *The Crisis of European Sciences and Transcendental Phenomenology: An Introduction to Phenomenological Philosophy* (trans. D. Carr). Evanston, IL: Northwestern University Press. (Originally published in 1936.)

Hutchby, I. and Woffitt, R. (1998) *Conversation Analysis.* Cambridge: Polity.

Jackson, D. (1957) The question of family homeostasis, *Psychiatric Quarterly Supplement,* 31, Part 1: 79–90.

Jacobitti. E. E. (1989) On the wisdom of the most recent Italians, or, how Italian is 'weak thought'? http://tell.fll.purdue.edu/RLA-Archive/1989/ItalianTamburri-html/Jacobitti-FF.htm (retrieved 18 December 2009).

Jaynes, J. (1976) *The Origin of Consciousness in the Breakdown of the Bicameral Mind.* Boston: Houghton Mifflin.

Jones, K. (2004). 'Thoroughly post-modern Mary': A biographic narrative interview with Mary Gergen by Kip Jones, *Forum: Qualitative Social Research*, 5 (3), Article 18. www.qualitative-research.net/index.php/fqs/article/view/554/1200.

Jourard, S. M. (1971) *The Transparent Self*. New York: Van Nostrand Reinhold. (Originally published in 1964.)

Kabat-Zinn, J. (1990) *Full Catastrophe Living: Using the Wisdom of your Body and Mind to Face Stress, Pain, and Illness*. New York: Delta.

Kearney, R. (2004) *On Paul Ricoeur: The Owl of Minerva*. Burlington, VT: Ashgate.

Keeney, B. (1983) *Aesthetics of Change*. New York: Guilford.

Keeney, B. and Thomas, F. (1986) Cybernetic foundations of family therapy. In F. Piercy and D. Sprenkle (eds.), *Family Therapy Sourcebook* (pp. 262–87). New York: Guilford.

Kelly, G. A. (1955) *The Psychology of Personal Constructs*, vols. I, II. New York: Norton.

Kogler, H. H. (1996) *The Power of Dialogue: Critical Hermeneutics after Gadamer and Foucault*. Cambridge, MA: MIT Press.

Kozulin, A. (1990) *Vygotsky's Psychology: A Biography of Ideas*. Hemel Hempstead: Harvester Wheatsheaf.

Kuhn, T. (1970/1962) *The Structure of Scientific Revolutions*. University of Chicago Press.

Labov, W. (1972). Academic ignorance and black intelligence, *Atlantic Monthly* (June). Available online: www.theatlantic.com/issues/95sep/ets/labo.htm.

(2006) *The Social Stratification of English in New York City*. New York: Cambridge University Press. (Originally published in 1967.)

Labov, W. and Fanshel, D. (1977) *Therapeutic Discourse: Psychotherapy as Conversation*. New York: Academic Press.

Labov, W. and Waletzky, J. (1967) Narrative analysis. In J. Helm (ed.), *Essays on the Verbal and Visual Arts* (pp. 12–44). Seattle, WA: University of Washington Press.

Lakoff, G. and Johnson, M. (1980) *Metaphors we Live by*. University of Chicago Press.

Laslett, P. (1972) *Household and Family in Past Time; Comparative Studies in the Size and Structure of the Domestic Group over the Last Three Centuries in England, France, Serbia, Japan and Colonial North America, with Further Materials from Western Europe*. (Edited, with an analytic introduction on the history of the family, by P. Laslett with the assistance of R. Wall). Cambridge University Press.

Latour, B. (1996) *Aramis, or the Love of Technology*. Cambridge, MA: Harvard: University Press.

(2005) *Reassembling the Social: An Introduction to Actor-network theory*. New York: Oxford University Press.

Lee, D. (1950) Lineal and nonlineal codifications of reality, *Psychosomatic Medicine*, 12: 89–97.

(1959) *Freedom and Culture*. Englewood Cliffs, NJ: Prentice-Hall.

Lehman, W. P. (1992) *Historical Linguistics*. London: Routledge.

Levinas, E. (1985) *Ethics and Infinity* (ed. and trans. P. Nemo). Pittsburg, PA: Duquesne University Press.

(1998) *Otherwise than Being* (trans. A. Linguis). Pittsburg, PA: Duquesne University Press.

Levinson, S. C. (1981) *Pragmatics*. New York: Cambridge University Press.

Lévy-Bruhl, L. (1928) *The 'Soul' of the Primitive* (trans. L. A. Clare). London: George Allen & Unwin (new edn with foreword by E. E. Evans-Pritchard, 1965).

Lienhardt, G. (1961) *Divinity and Experience*. Oxford: Clarendon Press.

Lorenz, K. (1935) Der Kumpan in der Umwelt des Vogels, *Journal für Ornithologie*, 83: 137–213.

Loyal, S. (2003) *The Sociology of Anthony Giddens*. London: Pluto Press.

Luft, S. R. (2003) *Vico's Uncanny Humanism: Reading the New Science between Modern and Postmodern*. Ithaca, NY: Cornell University Press.

Luntley, M. (2003) *Wittgenstein: Meaning and Judgment*. Oxford: Blackwell.

Luria. A. R. (1979) *The Making of Mind*. Cambridge, MA: Harvard University Press.

Luria, A. R. and Yudovich, F. A. (1971) *Speech and the Development of Mental Processes in the Child*. Harmondsworth: Penguin.

Lynch, M. (1997) 'Order', as background knowledge and assumption, *Text*, 17: 383–403.
(2000) The ethnomethodological foundations of conversation analysis, *Text*, 20: 517–32.

Lynch, M. and Bogen, D. (1994) Harvey Sacks's primitive natural science, *Theory Culture Society*, 11 (1): 65–104.

Lyotard, J.-F. (1988) *The Differend: Phrases in Dispute* (trans. G. van den Abbeele). Minneapolis, MN: University of Minnesota Press.

Macey, D. (1993) *The Lives of Michel Foucault*. New York: Vintage.

MacLeod, R. B. (1947) The phenomenological approach to social psychology, *Psychological Review*, 54: 193–210.

Macmurray, J. (1961) *Persons in Relation*. London: Faber & Faber.

MacPherson, C. B. (1962) *The Political Theory of Possessive Individualism: Hobbes to Locke*. New York: Oxford University Press.

Maranhão, T. (1986). *Therapeutic Discourse and Socratic Dialogue*. Madison, WI: University of Wisconsin Press.

Marshall, J. (1977) Minds, machines and metaphors, *Social Studies in Science*, 7: 475–88.

Martin, J. and Sugarman, J. (1999) *The Psychology of Human Possibility and Constraint*. Albany, NY: SUNY Press.

Marx, G. T. (1984) Role models and role distance, *Theory and Society*, 13: 649–62.

Marx, K. (1930/1867) *Capital* (trans. from the fourth German edition by Eden and Cedar Paul; introd. G. D. H. Cole). London: Dent.

Marx, K. (1845a) Theses on Feuerbach. Marxist Internet Archive: www.marxists.org/archive/marx/works/1845/theses/theses.htm (retrieved 22 August 2008).

Marx, K. and Engels, F. (1845b/1976) *The German Ideology*. Moscow: Progress Publishers.

Mattes, P. and Schraube, E. (2004) 'Old-stream' psychology will disappear with the dinosaurs! Kenneth Gergen in conversation with Peter Mattes and Ernst Schraube, *Forum: Qualitative Social Research*, 5 (3).

Maynard, D. W. and Clayman, S. E. (1991) The diversity of ethnomethodology, *Annual Review of Sociology*, 17: 385–418.

Maynard, D. W. and Schaeffer, N. C. (1996) Closing the gate: Routes to call termination when recipients decline a telephone survey interview, *Sociological Methods and Research*, 26: 34–79.

Mazzotta, G. (1998) *The New Map of the World: The Poetic Philosophy of Giambattista Vico*. Princeton University Press.

McGinn, M. (1997) *Wittgenstein and the Philosophical Investigations.* New York: Routledge.

McMullin, E. (1980) Vico's theory of science. In G. Tagliacozzo, M. Mooney and D. P. Verene (eds.), *Vico and Contemporary Thought* (pp. 60–93). London: Macmillan.

McNamee, S. and Gergen, K. J. (eds.) (1992) *Therapy as Social Construction.* Newbury Park, CA: Sage.

McNamee, S. and Gergen, K. J. (eds.) (1999) *Relational Responsibility: Resources for Sustainable Dialogue.* Thousand Oaks, CA: Sage.

Mead, G. H. (1932) *The Philosophy of the Present.* University of Chicago Press.

(1936) *Movements of Thought in the Nineteenth Century.* University of Chicago Press.

(1938) *The Philosophy of the Act.* University of Chicago Press.

(1970/1934) *Mind, Self, and Society: From the Standpoint of a Social Behaviorist* (ed. and introd. C. W. Morris). University of Chicago Press.

Mendez, C., Coddou, F. and Maturana, H. R. (1988) The bringing forth of pathology, *Irish Journal of Psychology,* 9: 144–72.

Mental Research Institute (n.d.) Official website: www.mri.org/.

Merleau-Ponty, M. (1954) in *L'Express,* Paris, 9 October.

(1962) *Phenomenology of Perception* (trans. C. Smith). London: Routledge & Kegan Paul.

(1963) *The Structure of Behavior* (trans. Alden Fisher). Boston: Beacon Press.

(1964a) *The Primacy of Perception and Other Essays* (trans. J. M. Edie). Evanston, IL: Northwestern University Press.

(1964b) *Signs* (trans. R. C. McCleary). Evanston, IL: Northwestern University Press.

(1968) *The Visible and the Invisible* (trans. A. Lingis). Evanston, IL: Northwestern University Press.

(1968) *The Visible and the Invisible* (ed. C. Lefort; trans. A. Lingis). Evanston, IL: Northwestern University Press.

Messer, S. B., Sass, L. A. and Woolfolk, R. L. (eds.) (1990) *Hermeneutics and Psychological Theory: Interpretive Perspectives on Personality, Psychotherapy, and Psychopathology.* London: Rutgers University Press.

Middleton, D. and Edwards, D. (eds.) *Collective Remembering.* London: Sage.

Miller, H. (1995) The presentation of self in electronic life: Goffman on the internet. A conference paper available online: www.ntu.ac.uk/soc/psych/miller/goffman. htm (retrieved 27 May 2008).

Milton H. Erickson Foundation (n.d.) Foundation website: www.erickson-foundation. org/.

Minick, N. (1987) The development of Vygotsky's thought: An introduction. In *The Collected Works of L. S. Vygotsky. Vol. 1: Problems of General Psychology* (pp. 17–36). New York: Plenum.

Mischel, W. (1968) *Personality and Assessment.* New York: Wiley.

Moghaddam, F., Harré, R. and Lee, N. (2007) *Global Conflict Resolution through Positioning Analysis.* New York: Springer.

Monk, R. (1990) *The Duty of Genius.* London: Jonathan Cape.

Morgan, A. (2000) *What is Narrative Therapy? An Easy-to-read Introduction.* Adelaide: Dulwich Centre Publications.

Morson, G. S. and Emerson, C. (1990) *Mikhail Bakhtin: Creation of a Prosaics.* Stanford University Press.

Mühlhäusler, P. and Harré, R. (1990) *Pronouns and People: The Linguistic Construction of Social and Personal Identity*. Oxford: Blackwell.

Nagel, T. (1974) What is it like to be a bat?, *Philosophical Review*, 83: 435–50.

Nef, J. U. (1958) *Cultural Foundations of Industrial Civilizations*. Cambridge University Press.

Neisser, U. (1967) *Cognitive Psychology*. New York: Appleton-Century-Crofts.

Newman, F. and Holzman, L. (1993) *Lev Vygotsky: Revolutionary Scientist*. New York: Routledge.

Newman, F., and Holzman, L. (1997) *The End of Knowing*. New York: Routledge.

O'Hanlon, W. H. (1992) History becomes her story. In S. McNamee and K. J. Gergen (eds.), *Therapy as Social Construction* (pp. 136–48). London: Sage.

Ossorio, P. (1995) *The Collected Works of Peter G. Ossorio, vols. 1–5*. Ann Arbor, MI: Descriptive Psychology Press.

Packer, M. J. (1985) Hermeneutic inquiry in the study of human conduct, *American Psychologist*, 40: 1081–93.

Parker, I. (ed.) (1998a) *Social Constructionism, Discourse and Realism*. London: Sage.

    (1998b) Against postmodernism: Psychology in cultural context, *Theory and Psychology*, 8: 601–27.

    (ed.) (1999) *Deconstructing Psychotherapy*. New York: Routledge.

Parker, I. and Burman, E. (1993) Against discursive imperialism, empiricism and constructionism: Thirty-two problems with discourse analysis. In E. Burman and I. Parker (eds.), *Discourse Analytic Research: Repertoires and Readings of Texts in Action* (pp. 155–72). New York: Routledge.

Parker, I., Georgaca, E., Harper, D., McLaughlin, T. and Stowell-Smith, M. (1996) *Deconstructing Psychopathology*. London: Sage.

Parker, I. and Shotter, J. (1990) *Deconstructing Social Psychology*. London: Routledge.

Parret, H., Verschueren, J., Searle, J., Boyd, J., Dasal, M., Holdcroft, D., Jucker, A. H., Roulet, E., Sbise, M., Schlegloff, E. A. and Streek, J. (1992) *(On) Searle on Conversation* (compiled and introd. by H. Parret and J. Verschueren). Amsterdam/Philadelphia: John Benjamins.

Parsons, T. (1949) *The Structure of Social Action*. New York: Free Press.

Pedersen, P. (1999) *Multicultralism as a Fourth Force*. Washington, DC: Taylor & Francis.

Pfeifer, R. and Bongard J. C. (2007) *How the Body Shapes the Way we Think: A New View of Intelligence*. Cambridge, MA: MIT Press.

Piaget, J. (1926) *The Language and Thought of the Child* (trans. M. Gabin). London: Routledge & Kegan Paul.

    (1951) *The Origins of Intelligence in Children*. London: Routledge & Kegan Paul.

Polanyi, M. (1958) *Personal Knowledge*. London: Routledge.

Pollner, M. (1975) The very coinage of your brain: The anatomy of reality disjunctures, *Philosophy of the Social Sciences*, 5: 411–30.

    (1987) *Mundane Reasoning*. New York: Cambridge University Press.

    (1991) Left of ethnomethodology: The rise and decline of radical reflexivity, *American Sociological Review*, 40: 417–27.

Pollock, L. A. (1983) *Forgotten Children: Parent–Child Relations from 1500 to 1900*. Cambridge University Press.

Pomerantz, A. and Fehr, B. J. (1997) Conversation analysis: An approach to the study of social action as sense making practices. In T. A. van Dijk (ed.), *Discourse as Social Interaction* (vol. 2, pp. 64–91). Thousand Oaks, CA: Sage.

Pompa, L. (1975) *Vico: A Study of the 'New Science'*. Cambridge University Press.

Popper, K. (1972) *Objective Knowledge: An Evolutionary Approach*. Oxford University Press.

Potter, J. (1996) *Representing Reality: Discourse, Rhetoric and Social Construction*. Thousand Oaks, CA: Sage.

Potter, J. and Wetherell, M. (1987) *Discourse and Social Psychology: Beyond Attitudes and Behaviour*. London: Sage.

Prilleltensky, I. (1994) *The Morals and Politics of Psychology: Psychological Discourse and the Status Quo*. Albany, NY: SUNY Press.

Psathas, G. (1995) 'Talk and social structure' and 'studies of work', *Human Studies*, 18: 139–55.

Putnam, H. (1981) *Reason, Truth and History*. Cambridge University Press.

Rabil, A. (1967) *Merleau-Ponty: Existentialist of the Social World*. New York: Columbia University Press.

Ratner, C. (2005) Social constructionism as cultism: Comments on 'old-stream' psychology will disappear with the dinosaurs! Kenneth Gergen in conversation with Peter Mattes and Ernst Schraube, *Forum: Qualitative Social Research*, 6 (1): Article 28.

Ricoeur, P. (1973) The model of the text: Meaningful action considered as text, *New Literary History*, 5 (1): 91–117.

(1975) *The Rule of Metaphor: Multidisciplinary Studies of the Creation of Meaning in Language* (trans. R. Czerny). Toronto: University of Toronto Press.

(1984) *Time and Narrative*, vols. 1 and 2 (trans. K. McLaughlin and D. Pellauer). University of Chicago Press.

(1985) *Time and Narrative*, vol. 3 (trans. K. Blamey and D. Pellauer). University of Chicago Press.

(1992) *Oneself as Another* (trans. K. Blamey). University of Chicago Press.

(1996) *The Hermeneutics of Action* (ed. R. Kearney). London: Sage.

Rieber, R. W. (2004) A dialogue with Vygotsky. In *The Essential Vygotsky* (Vienna Circle Collection) (ed. R. W. Rieber and D. K. Robinson) (pp. 1–8). New York: Springer.

Riggins, S. H. (ed.) (1990) *Beyond Goffman: Studies on Communication, Institution, and Social Interaction*. New York: Mouton de Gruyter.

Rilke, R. (1995) *Ahead of all Parting: The Selected Poetry and Prose of Rainer Maria Rilke* (trans. S. Mitchell). New York: The Modern Library. (Originally published 1934.)

Rogers, Carl (1961) *On Becoming a Person: A Therapist's View of Psychotherapy*. London: Constable.

Rogoff, B. (1990) *Apprenticeship in Thinking: Cognitive Development in Social Context*. New York: Oxford University Press.

Rogoff, B. and Wertsch, J. V. (1984) *Children's Learning in the 'Zone of Proximal Development'*. Monograph No. 23. In *New Directions for Child Development* (pp. 1–102). San Francisco, CA: Jossey-Bass.

Rojcewicz, R. and Schuwer, A. (1989) Translators' introduction to E. Husserl, *Ideas Pertaining to a Pure Phenomenology and to a Phenomenological Philosophy*, Second Book (trans. R. Rojcewicz and A. Schuwer). Dordrecht: Kluwer.

Rommetveit, R. (1985) Language acquisition as increasing linguistic structuring of experience and symbolic behaviour control. In J. V. Wertsch (ed.), *Culture, Communication and Cognition: Vygotskian Perspectives* (pp. 183–204). New York: Cambridge University Press.

Rorty, A. (2003) *The Many Faces of Philosophy: From Plato to Arendt*. New York: Oxford University Press.

Rorty, R. (1979) *Philosophy and the Mirror of Nature*. Princeton University Press.

(1989) *Contingency, Irony and Solidarity*. Cambridge University Press.

Rose, N. (1985) *The Psychological Complex: Psychology, Politics and Society in England, 1869–1939*. London: Routledge & Kegan Paul.

(1989) *Governing the Soul: The Shaping of the Private Self*. London: Routledge.

(1996) *Inventing our Selves: Psychology, Power and Personhood*. Oxford: Oxford University Press.

Russell, B. (1914) *Our Knowledge of the External World*. London: Allen & Unwin.

(1967) *The Autobiography of Bertrand Russell*. Toronto: McLelland and Stewart.

Ryle, G. (1949) *The Concept of Mind*. London: Methuen.

Sacks, H. (1984) Notes on methodology. In J. M. Atkinson and J. Heritage (eds.), *Structures of Social Action: Studies in Conversation Analysis* (pp. 413–29). Cambridge University Press.

(1995) *Lectures on Conversation*, vols. 1 and 2 (ed. G. Jefferson). Oxford: Basil Blackwell.

Sacks, H., Schegloff, E. and Jefferson, G. (1974) A simplest systematics for the organization of turn-taking in conversation, *Language*, 50: 696–735.

Said, E. W. (1978) *Orientalism*. New York: Vintage Books.

Sampson, E. E. (1981) Cognitive psychology as ideology, *American Psychologist*, 36: 730–43.

Sannicolas, N. (1997) Erving Goffman, dramaturgy and on-line relationships. *Cybersociology: Magazine for Social Scientific Researchers of Cyberspace*. Available online: www.cybersociology.com/files/1_2_sannicolas.html.

Sapir, Edward (1929) The status of linguistics as science, *Language*, 5: 207–14.

Sapir, E. (1949) *Selected Writings in Language, Culture and Personality* (ed. D. Mandelbaum). Berkeley, CA: University of California Press.

Satir, V. (1964) *Conjoint Family Therapy*. Palo Alto, CA: Science and Behavior Books.

de Saussure, F. (1966) *Course in General Linguistics*. New York: McGraw Hill. (Originally published 1916.)

Schatzki, T. (1996) *Social Practices: A Wittgensteinian Approach to Human Activity and the Social*. Cambridge University Press.

Schatzki, T. R. (2002) *The Site of the Social: A Philosophical Account of the Constitution of Social Life and Change*. University Park, PA: Pennsylvania State University Press.

Schegloff, E. (1988) Goffman and the analysis of conversation. In P. Drew and A. Wootton (eds.), *Erving Goffman: Exploring the Interaction Order* (pp. 89–135). Boston: Northeastern University Press.

(1992) Repair after next turn: The last structurally provided defense of intersubjectivity in conversation, *American Journal of Sociology*, 97: 1295–345.

Schegloff, E. and Sacks, H. (1973) Opening up closings, *Semiotica*, 8: 289–327.

Schlenker, G. (1974) Social psychology and science, *Journal of Personality and Social Psychology*, 27 (1): 1–15.

Schön, D. (1983) *The Reflective Practitioner: How Professionals Think in Action*. New York: Basic Books.

Schutz, A. (1942) Scheler's theory of intersubjectivity and the general thesis of the alter ego, *Philosophy and Phenomenological Research*, 2: 323–47. (*Collected Papers*, vol I: 150–79.)

(1944) The stranger: An essay in social psychology, *American Journal of Sociology*, 50: 499–507. (*Collected Papers*, vol. II: 91–105.)

(1945) On multiple realities, *Philosophy and Phenomenological Research*, 9: 533–76. (*Collected Papers*, vol. I: 207–59.)

(1950) Language, language disturbances, and the texture of consciousness, *Social Research*, 17: 365–94. (*Collected Papers*, vol. I: 180–203.)

(1953) Common sense and scientific interpretation of human action, *Philosophy and Phenomenological Research*, 13: 1–37. (*Collected Papers*, vol. I: 3–47.)

(1957) Das Problem der tranzendentalen Intersubjectivität by Husserl, *Philosphische Rundschau: Eine Vierteljahresschrift fur Philosophische Kritik*, 5: 81ff. (*Collected Papers*, vol. III: 51–84.)

(1959) Tiresias, or our knowledge of future events, *Social Research*, 26: 71–89. (*Collected Papers*, vol. II: 277–93.)

(1962) *Collected Papers I: The Problem of Social Reality* (ed. Maurice Natanson). The Hague: Martinus Nijhoff.

(1964) *Collected Papers II: Studies in Social Theory* (ed. Arvid Brodersen). The Hague: Martinus Nijhoff.

(1966a) *Collected Papers III: Studies in Phenomenological Philosophy* (ed. I. Schutz). The Hague: Martinus Nijhoff.

(1966b) Some structures of the life world. (*Collected Papers*, vol. III: 116–32.)

(1967) *The Phenomenology of the Social World*. Evanston, IL: Northwestern Universities Press.

(1970) *On Phenomenology and Social Relations* (ed. and trans. H.R. Wagner). University of Chicago Press.

Schutz, A. (ed.) (1975) *Collected Papers 3: Studies in Phenomenological Philosophy*. The Hague: Martinus Nijhoff.

Schutz, A. (1982/1962) *Collected Papers 1: The Problem of Social Reality* (ed. M. Natanson). The Hague: Martinus Nijhoff.

Schutz, A. and Luckman, T. (1973–89) *The Structures of the Life-world* (trans. Richard M. Zaner and H. Tristram Engelhardt, Jr). Evanston, IL: Northwestern University Press.

Scull, A. (2007) The fictions of Foucault's scholarship, *Times Literary Supplement*, 21 March 2007. http://tls.timesonline.co.uk/article/0,,25347–2626687,00.html.

Seal (2007) If it's in my mind, it's on my face. Song from the album *System*, Warner Brothers.

Sebeok, T.A. (1977) Neglected figures in the history of semiotic inquiry: Jakob von Uexküll. In *The Sign and its Masters* (pp. 187–207). Lanham, MD: University Press of America.

Sennett, R. (1977) *The Fall of Public Man*. New York: Cambridge University Press.

Shawver, L. (2001) If Wittgenstein and Lyotard could talk with Jack and Jill: Towards postmodern family therapy, *Journal of Family Therapy*, 23: 232–52.

Shields, C.M. (2007) *Bakhtin Primer*. New York: Peter Lang.

Shotter, J. (1966) The existence of the crossroads policemen, *Nature* (Lond.), 211: 343–5.

(1972) unpublished seminar notes, University of Nottingham.

(1974) What is it to be human? In N. Armistead (ed.), *Reconstructing Social Psychology* (pp. 53–71). Harmondsworth: Penguin.

(1975) *Images of Man in Psychological Research*. London: Routledge.

(1980) Action, joint action, and intentionality. In M. Brenner (ed.), *The Structure of Action* (pp. 28–65). Oxford: Blackwell.

(1981) Vico, moral worlds, accountability and personhood. In P. L. F. Heelas and A. J. Lock (eds.), *Indigenous Psychologies: The Anthropology of the Self* (pp. 265–84). London: Academic Press.

(1983) 'Duality of structure' and 'intentionality' in an ecological psychology, *Journal for the Theory of Social Behaviour*, 13: 19–43.

(1984) *Social Accountability and Selfhood.* Oxford: Blackwell.

(1993a) *Conversational Realities: Constructing Life through Language.* London: Sage.

(1993b) *Cultural Politics of Everyday Life: Social Constructionism. Rhetoric, and Knowing of the Third Kind.* University of Toronto Press.

(1994a) Conversational realities: from within persons to within relationships. Paper prepared for the Discursive Construction of Knowledge Conference, University of Adelaide, 21–25 Feb. 1994. http://pubpages.unh.edu/~jds/Adelaide94.htm.

(1994b). 'Now I can go on'. Wittgenstein and communication. Downloadable paper: www.massey.ac.nz/~alock/virtual/wittgoon.htm.

(1995a) In conversation: Joint action, shared intentionality, and ethics, *Theory and Psychology*, 5 (1): 49–73.

(1995b) Wittgenstein's world. Beyond the way of theory toward a social poetics. Downloadable paper: hwww.massey.ac.nz/~alock/virtual/poetics.htm.

(1996) Vico, Wittgenstein, and Bakhtin: 'Practical trust' in dialogical communities. Downloadable paper: www.massey.ac.nz/~alock/virtual/js.htm.

(1998) Life inside the dialogically structured mind. In M. Cooper and J. Rowan (eds.), *The Plural Self: Multiplicity in Everyday Life* (pp. 71–92). London: Sage.

(1999) Must we 'work out' how to act jointly?, *Theory and Psychology*, 9: 129–33.

(2002) 'Real presences': The creative power of dialogically-structured, living expression. First and probably final draft for KCC 123 Conference, Canterbury, 1–3 July. http://pubpages.unh.edu/~jds/KCCoutline.htm.

(2003) 'Real presences': Meaning as living movement in a participatory world, *Theory and Psychology*, 13: 435–68.

(2005) Goethe and the refiguring of intellectual inquiry: From 'aboutness'-thinking to 'withness'-thinking in everyday life, *Janus Head*, 8: 132–58.

(2006) Getting it: 'Withness'-thinking and the dialogical … in practice. http://pubpages.unh.edu/~jds/bookpage.htm.

(2007) Re-visiting George Kelly: Social constructionism, social ecology, and social justice – all unfinished projects, *Personal Construct Theory and Practice*, 4: 68–82.

(n.d.) Talk of saying, showing, gesturing, and feeling in Wittgenstein and Vygotsky. Downloadable paper: www.massey.ac.nz/~alock/virtual/wittvyg.htm.

Shotter, J. and Billig, M. (1998) A Bakhtinian psychology: From out of the heads of individuals and into the dialogues between them. In M. M. Bell and M. Gardiner (eds.), *Bakhtin and the Human Sciences: No Last Words* (pp. 13–29). London: Sage.

Shotter, J. and Gauld, A. (1971) The defense of empirical psychology, *American Psychologist*, 26: 460–66.

Skinner, B. F. (1961) *Walden Two.* Toronto: Macmillan. (Originally published 1948.)

Smedslund, J. (1988) *Psycho-logic.* Heidelberg/New York: Springer.

(1994a) Nonempirical and empirical components in the hypotheses of five social psychological experiments, *Scandinavian Journal of Psychology*, 35: 1–15.

(1994b) What kind of propositions are set forth in developmental research? Five case studies, *Human Development*, 37: 280–92.

Spinosa, C., Flores, F. and Dreyfus, H. L. (1997) *Disclosing New Worlds: Entrepreneurship, Democratic Action and the Cultivation of Solidarity*. Cambridge, MA: MIT Press.

Spurrett, D. and Cowley, S. J. (2004) How to do things without words: Infants, utterance-activity and distributed cognition, *Language Sciences*, 26: 443–66.

Starker, S. (2002) *Oracle at the Supermarket: The American Preoccupation with Self-help Books*. Vancouver: University of British Columbia Press.

Stein, E. (1997) *Without Good Reason: The Rationality Debate in Philosophy and Cognitive Science*. Oxford University Press.

Steiner, G. (1975) *After Babel: Aspects of Language and Translation*. New York: Oxford University Press.

(1989) *Real Presences*. University of Chicago Press.

Stearns, P. and Stearns, C (1985) Emotionology: Clarifying the history of emotions and emotional standards, *American Historical Review*, 90: 13–36.

Stern, D. (1985) *The Interpersonal World of the Infant*. New York: Basic Books.

Stone, L. (1979) *The Family, Sex and Marriage in England 1500–1800*. London: Weidenfeld & Nicolson.

Strong, T. (2002) Collaborative 'expertise' after the discursive turn, *Journal of Psychotherapy Integration*, 12: 218–32.

(2006a) Reflections on reflecting as a dialogic accomplishment in counselling, *Qualitative Health Research*, 16: 998–1013.

(2006b) Wordsmithing in counselling?, *European Journal of Psychotherapy and Counselling*, 8: 251–68.

Strong, T. and Paré, D. A. (eds.) (2004) *Furthering Talk: Advances in the Discursive Therapies*. New York: Kluwer Academic/Plenum.

Strong, T., Busch, R. S. and Couture, S. (2008) Conversational evidence in therapeutic dialogue. *Journal of Marital and Family Therapy*, 34: 288–305.

Tannesini, A. (2004) *Wittgenstein: A Feminist Interpretation*. Cambridge, MA: Polity.

Taylor, C. (1985) *Human Agency and Language: Philosophical Papers I*. New York: Cambridge University Press.

(1989) *Sources of the Self: The Making of the Modern Identity*. Cambridge, MA: Harvard University Press.

(1990) The moral topography of the self. In S. B. Messer, L. A. Sass and R. L. Woolfolk (eds.), *Hermeneutics and Psychological Theory: Interpretive Perspectives on Personality, Psychotherapy, and Psychopathology* (pp. 298–320). London: Rutgers University Press.

(2007) *A Secular Age*. Cambridge, MA: Harvard University/Belknap Press.

ten Have, P. (1999) *Doing Conversation Analysis*. Thousand Oaks, CA: Sage.

(n.d.) Ethnoca/CA News Resources, An online resource for ethnomethodologists and conversation analysts. Available at: www2.fmg.uva.nl/emca/.

Thibault, P. (2005) The interpersonal gateway to the meaning of mind: Unifying the inter- and intraorganism perspective on language. In R. Hasan, C. Matthiessen and J. Webster (eds.), *Continuing Discourse on Perspective in Language: A Functional Perspective* (pp. 117–56). London: Equinox.

Tomm, K. (1988) Interventive interviewing. Part III. Intending to ask lineal, circular, strategic or reflexive questions, *Family Process*, 27: 1–15.

Toulmin, S. (1982) The charm of the scout. In C. Wilder and J. Weakland (eds.), *Rigor and Imagination: Essays from the Legacy of Gregory Bateson* (pp. 357–68). New York: Praeger.

(1990) *Cosmopolis: The Hidden Agenda of Modernity.* New York : Free Press.

Trevarthen, C. (1979) Communication and co-operation in early infancy: A description of primary intersubjectivity. In M. Bullowa (ed.), *Before Speech* (pp. 15–46). Cambridge University Press.

(1992) An infant's motive for speaking and thinking in the culture. In A. H. Wold (ed.), *The Dialogical Alternative.* Oxford University Press.

(1993) The self born in intersubjectivity. In U. Neisser (ed.), *The Perceived Self.* Cambridge University Press.

Trevarthen, C. and Hubley, P. (1978) Secondary intersubjectivity. In A. J. Lock (ed.), *Action, Gesture, and Symbol: The Emergence of Language.* London: Academic Press.

Tugendhat, E. (1986) *Self-consciousness and Self-determination* (trans. P. Stern). London: MIT Press.

Urry, J. (1991) Time and space in Giddens' social theory. In C. G. A. Bryant and D. Jary (eds.), *Giddens' Theory of Structuration: A Critical Approach* (pp. 160–75). London: Routledge.

van der Veer, R. and Valsiner, J. (1991) *Understanding Vygotsky: A Quest for Synthesis.* Oxford: Basil Blackwell.

van Dijk, T. (1993) Principles of critical discourse analysis, *Discourse and Society,* 4 (2): 249–83.

(ed.) (1997) *Discourse as Social Interaction.* London: Sage.

van Langenhove, L. and Harré, R. (1998) *Positioning Theory: Moral Contexts of Intentional Action.* Oxford: Blackwell.

Verene, P. (1981) *Vico's Science of the Imagination.* Ithaca, NY: Cornell University Press.

Veresov, N. (1999) Undiscovered Vygotsky: Etudes on the pre-history of cultural-historical psychology, *European Studies in the History of Science and Ideas,* 8: 251–81.

Vico, G. (1948) *The New Science of Giambattista Vico,* revised translations of the third edition of 1744 (trans. T. G. Bergin and M. H. Fisch). Ithaca, NY: Cornell University Press.

(1965) *On the Study Methods of our Time* (trans. E. Gianturco). Ithaca, NY: Cornell University Press.

Viner, O. (1909) *Rasshireniie Nasikih Zhuvstv* [Extension of our senses]. St Petersburg.

Volosinov, V. (1926/1983) Discourse in life and discourse in poetry: Questions of socio-logical poetics. In A. Shukman (ed.), *Bakhtin School Papers* (pp. 5–30) (Russian Poetics in Translation, 10). Oxford: Oxon Publishing.

Voloshinov, V. N. (1973) *Marxism and the Philosophy of Language.* Cambridge, MA: Harvard University Press.

Volosinov, V. N. (1987) *Freudianism: A Critical Sketch* (ed. I. Titunik and N. H. Bruss; trans. I. Titunik). Bloomington, IN: Indiana University Press.

von Foerster, H. (1984a) *Observing Systems* (2nd edn). Salinas, CA: Intersystems Publications.

(1984b) On constructing a reality. In P. Watzlawick (ed.), *The Invented Reality* (pp. 41–62). New York: W. W. Norton.

(2003) *Understanding Understanding: Essays on Cybernetics and Cognition.* New York: Springer.

von Uexküll, J. (1904a) Studien über den Tonus II. Die Bewegungen der Schlangensterneb, *Zeitschrift für Biologie*, 46: 1–37.

(1904b) Die ersten Ursachen des Rhythmus in der Tierreihe, *Ergebnisse der Physiologie*, 3 (2. Abt.): 1–11.

(1905) Studien über den Tonus III. Die Blutegel, *Zeitschrift für Biologie*, 46: 372–402.

(1957) A stroll through the worlds of animals and men. In Claire Schiller (ed. and trans.), *Instinctive behavior: The Development of a Modern Concept* (pp. 5–80). New York: International Universities Press.

(1982/1940) The theory of meaning, *Semiotica*, 42: 25–82.

von Uexküll J. (1992) A stroll through the worlds of animals and men: A picture book of invisible worlds, *Semiotica*, 89: 319–91.

von Uexküll, J. (2001/1936) An introduction to Umwelt, *Semiotica*, 134: 107–10

(2001/1937) The new concept of Umwelt: A link between science and the humanities, *Semiotica*, 134: 111–23.

Vygotsky, L. S. (1925/1999) Consciousness as a problem in the psychology of behavior. In N. Veresov, Undiscovered Vygotsky: Etudes on the pre-history of cultural-historical psychology, *European Studies in the History of Science and Ideas*, 8: 251–81.

(1928) Problema kul'turnogo razvitija rebenka, *Pedogogia,* 1:58–77.

(1930/1982c) Ravzite vysshickh psikhich funkjii. In L. S. Vygotsky, *Sobranie sochinenji. Tom 1. Vporosy teorri i istorii psikhologii*. Moscow: Progress Publishers, 103–8.

(1962) *Thought and Language*. Cambridge, MA: MIT Press.

Vygotsky, L .S. (1978) *Mind in Society*. Cambridge, MA: Harvard University Press.

Vygotsky, L. S. (1982a) Metodika refleksologicheskogo i psihologicheskogo issledovaniya. In L. S. Vygotsky, *Sobraniye sochinenii* (vol. 1, pp. 43–62). Moscow: Pedagogica.

(1982b). Soznanie kak problema psihologii povedeniya. In L. S. Vygotsky, *Sobraniye sochinenii* (vol. 1, pp. 78–98). Moscow: Pedagogica.

(1987) *The Collected Works of L. S. Vygotsky. Vol. 1: Problems of General Psychology. Including the Volume 'Thinking and Speech'*. New York: Plenum.

(1993) *The Collected Works of L. S. Vygotsky. Vol. 2: The Fundamentals of Defectology*. New York: Plenum.

(1994) The methods of reflexological and psychological investigation. In R. van der Veer and J. Valsiner (eds.), *The Vygotsky Reader* (pp. 27–45). Oxford: Blackwell.

(1997a) *The Collected works of L. S. Vygotsky,* vol. 3: *Problems of the Theory and History of Psychology*. New York: Plenum.

(1997b) *The Collected Works of L. S. Vygotsky,* vol. 4: *The History of the Development of the Higher Mental Functions*. New York: Plenum.

Vygotsky, L. S. and Luria, A. R. (1993) *Studies on the History of Behavior: Ape, Primitive, and Child* (ed. and trans. V. I. Golod and J. E. Knox). Hillsdale, NJ: Erlbaum.

Wade, A. (1997) Small acts of living: Everyday resistance to violence and other forms of oppression, *Contemporary Family Therapy*, 19 (1): 23–39.

Warnke, G. (1987) *Gadamer: Hermeneutics, Tradition and Reason*. Stanford University Press.

Watzlawick, P. (1963) A review of the double bind theory, *Family Process*, 2: 132–53.

(1978) *The Language of Change: Elements of Therapeutic Communication*. New York: Basic Books.

Watzlawick, P., Bavelas, J. B. and Jackson, D. (1967) *Pragmatics of Human Communication: A Study of Interactional Patterns, Pathologies, and Paradoxes*. New York: Norton.

Watzlawick, P., Weakland, J. and Fisch, R. (1974) *Change: Principles of Problem Formation and Problem Resolution*. New York: Norton.

Weakland, J. (1982) One thing leads to another. In C. Wilder and J. Weakland (eds.), *Rigor and Imagination: Essays from the Legacy of Gregory Bateson* (pp. 43–64). New York: Praeger.

Weedon, C. (1987) *Feminist Practice and Poststructuralist Theory*. Oxford: Blackwell.

Wertsch, J. V. (1985) *Vygotsky and the Social Formation of Mind*. Cambridge, MA: Harvard University Press.

(1991) *Voices of the Mind: A Sociocultural Approach to Mediated Action*. Cambridge, MA: Harvard University Press.

Wertsch, J. (1993) Foreword. In L. S. Vygotsky and A. R. Luria, *Studies in the History of Behaviour: Ape, Primitive, and Child* (trans. V. I. Golod and J. E. Knox). Hillsdale, NJ: Erlbaum.

White, M. K. (2007) *Maps of Narrative Practice*. New York: W. W. Norton & Co.

White, M. and Epston, D. (1990) *Narrative Means to Therapeutic Ends*. New York: Norton.

Whittaker, C. A. and Bumberry, W. M. (1988) *Dancing with the Family: A Symbolic-Experiential Approach*. New York: Psychology Press.

Whorf, B. L. (1956) *Language, Thought, and Reality: Selected Writings of Benjamin Lee Whorf* (ed. J. B. Carroll). Cambridge, MA: MIT Press.

Williams, M. (1999) *Wittgenstein, Mind and Meaning: Towards a Social Conception of Mind*. New York: Routledge.

Wilson, E. O. (1997) *Consilience: The Unity of Knowledge*. New York: Knopf.

Winchester, S. (2005) *The Professor and the Mad Man: A Tale of Murder, Insanity, and the Making of the Oxford English Dictionary*. Toronto: Harper Collins Canada.

Winslade, J. M. (2005) Utilising discursive positioning in counselling, *British Journal of Guidance and Counselling*, 33 (3): 351–64.

Wittgenstein, L. (1953) *Philosophical Investigations*. Oxford: Blackwell.

(1958) *The Blue and Brown Books: Preliminary Studies for the 'Philosophical Investigations'*. New York: Harper Torchbooks.

(1961) *Tractatus Logico-Philosophicus* (trans. D. F. Pears and B. F. McGuinness, introd. B. Russell). London: Routledge & Kegan Paul. (Originally published in English 1922; original German edition 1921.)

Wittengenstein, L. (1967) *Zettel* (ed. G. E. M. Anscombe and G. H. von Wright; trans. G. E. M. Anscombe). Oxford: Blackwell.

Wittgenstein, L. (1969) *On Certainty* (ed. G. E. M. Anscombe and G. H. von Wright). Oxford: Blackwell.

(1974) *Philosophical Grammar* (ed. R. Rhees; trans. A. Kenny). Oxford: Blackwell.

(1979) *Wittgenstein's Lectures, 1932–35* (ed. A. Ambrose). Oxford: Blackwell.

(1980a) *Culture and Value* (trans. P. Winch). Oxford: Blackwell.

(1980b) *Remarks on the Philosophy of Psychology, Vol. I* (ed. H. Nyman and G. H. von Wright; trans. C. G. Luckhardt and M. A. E. Aue). Oxford: Blackwell.

(1980c) *Remarks on the Philosophy of Psychology, Vol. II* (ed. H. Nyman and G. H. von Wright; trans. C. G. Luckhardt). Oxford: Blackwell.

(1981) *Zettel* (2nd edn) (ed. G. E. M. Anscombe and G. H. von Wright). Oxford: Blackwell.

(1992) *Last writings on the Philosophy of Psychology. Vol. II: The Inner and the Outer 1949–1951* (ed. H. Nyman and G. H. von Wright; trans. C. G. Luckhardt and M. A. E. Aue). Oxford: Blackwell.

Wodak, R. and Meyer, M. (2001) *Methods of Critical Discourse Analysis.* Thousand Oaks, CA: Sage.

Zappen, J.P. (2004) *The Rebirth of Dialogue: Bakhtin, Socrates and the Rhetorical Tradition.* Albany, NY: SUNY Press.

Zimmerman, M. E. (1993) Heidegger, Buddhism, and deep ecology. In C. Guignon (ed.), *The Cambridge Companion to Heidegger* (pp. 240–69). New York: Cambridge University Press.

Index